W9-BFW-464

BOSTON ACCESS®

Orientation

Steeped in history, yet assiduously cutting-edge, Boston is one of those quirky, cosmopolitan cities that seduces with an ever-shifting array of moods and appearances. It may only be the 20th-largest city in the country, but its grandeur is genuinely impressive. And though the climate is trying at times (the seaborne weather can be quite capricious), it's certainly never boring. Summer's lush abandon cedes gradually to bracing autumns and bitter-cold Decembers, but greenery and sanity reemerge with the magnolias abloom along magnificent Commonwealth Avenue, and willows weeping around the Public Garden lagoon.

The students who flock here—some 100,000 a year—keep Boston young and constantly in flux. Many are tempted to stay on, and do. "It's so livable," they marvel, meaning walkable and packed with odd pleasures. The palimpsest of history (three-and-a-half-centuries' worth) will make you want to walk all over town, not that the shortest distance between two points is ever a straight line. The older parts of the city, particularly Beacon Hill, the North End, and Cambridge, were laid out helter-skelter along cow paths, Native American trails, and the ghosts of long-gone shorelines (from the very start, the city has pushed the envelope with massive infusions of landfill). Logic is useless in assailing the maze; even longtime residents have to haul out a map when planning to stray from their own well-worn paths. But getting "lost" is half the fun. You could spend a day wandering the narrow cobblestoned streets of "the Hill" and never run out of charming 18th- and 19th-century town houses with interior lives you can only guess at. Furnish your own dream abode out of the grab bag of Charles Street antique stores, or while away a lazy afternoon sampling the market wares in the North End—here a nibble of fresh mozzarella, there a briny olive, and virtually everywhere a cappuccino topped with lively conversation. Eventually you'll gravitate, as the natives do, to the banks of the Charles River, where runners, walkers, bicyclists, and skaters whip by on their invigorating rounds.

After a day on your feet, you'll be anxious to dive into a seafood feast (one of Boston's trademarks) or perhaps a gourmet meal. As recently as 10 years ago you might have had trouble coming up with more than a handful of interesting restaurants in Boston; now the problem is choosing among them. The past decade has seen a number of talented chefs spring forth in an atmosphere of camaraderie rather than competition. Literature likewise provides rich repasts. Harvard Square is said to boast the largest per-capita concentration of bookstores in the country, and readings often draw crowds in the hundreds. And finally there are the Boston sports teams. As frustrated as they may get with the players, Red Sox fans are inevitably caught up in the romance of tiny Fenway Park, a classic dating from the golden age of ballpark design. But this should come as no surprise to anyone who knows a born-and-bred Bostonian. They are a people who savor the intimacy, the authenticity, and, above all, the history of their lovely city—and rightly so.

Rowes Wharf

BOSTON ACCESS® is arranged by neighborhood so you can see at a glance where you are and what is around you. The numbers next to the entries in the following chapters correspond to the numbers on the maps. The type is color-coded according to the kind of place described:

Restaurants/Clubs: Red   **Hotels:** Blue

Shops/ ⬤Outdoors: Green   **Sights/Culture:** Black

 ♿ **Wheelchair accessible**

Rating the Restaurants and Hotels

The restaurant ratings take into account the quality, service, atmosphere, and uniqueness of the restaurant. An expensive restaurant doesn't necessarily ensure an enjoyable evening; however, a small, relatively unknown spot could have good food, professional service, and a lovely atmosphere. Therefore, on a purely subjective basis, stars are used to judge the overall dining value (see the star ratings at right). Keep in mind that chefs and owners often change, which sometimes drastically affects the quality of a restaurant. The ratings in this guidebook are based on information available at press time.

The price ratings, as categorized at right, apply to restaurants and hotels. These figures describe general price-range relationships between other restaurants and hotels in the area. The restaurant price ratings are based on the average cost of an entrée for one person, excluding tax and tip. Hotel price ratings reflect the base price of a standard room for two people for one night during the peak season.

Restaurants

★ Good

★★ Very Good

★★★ Excellent

★★★★ An Extraordinary Experience

$ The Price Is Right	(less than $10)
$$ Reasonable	($10-$15)
$$$ Expensive	($15-$20)
$$$$ Big Bucks	($20 and up)

Hotels

$ The Price Is Right	(less than $100)
$$ Reasonable	($100-$175)
$$$ Expensive	($175-$250)
$$$$ Big Bucks	($250 and up)

Map Key

1 Entry Number   **Freeway**

City/Town ⬤   Highway   [Tunnel

Ⓣ = subway stop

Point of ■   Tertiary Road
Interest

Logan International Airport (BOS)

Gate Locations for Major Airlines

A Colgan Airways
Continental Airlines
USAir Shuttle
(to LaGuardia
in NY only)

B American Airlines
American Eagle
America West
Cape Air
Delta Shuttle
Midwest Express
Mohawk Airlines
Quantas Airways
Sabena World Airlines
(departures only)
USAir/USAir Express
Virgin Atlantic Airways
(departures only)

C Delta Air Lines
Delta Connection
Skymaster
TWA (domestic)
TW Express
United Airlines
United Express

D **Charter Flights**
Alitalia Airlines
(departures only)

E **International Flights**
Northwest Airlines
(domestic)

Car-rental counters and baggage claim are located on the lower level.

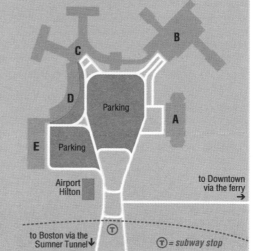

Area code 617 unless otherwise noted.

Getting to Boston

Logan International Airport (BOS)

Serving domestic and international flights, Logan is accessible via the **Callahan Tunnel** from Boston.

Though it's only three miles east of Downtown Boston, legendary traffic snarls can lengthen the trip to 30 minutes or more in a car. Driving from the airport, take the **Sumner Tunnel** (poor timing will find you inching along in either tunnel).

Airport Information 561.1806
Customs and Immigration 565.4658
Ground Transportation Hotline 800/235.6426
Medical Emergencies 569.8652
Parking Information 800/235.6426
Traveler's Aid 542.7286
Lost and Found 561.1714

Lost or damaged baggage: See the airline representative in the baggage-claim area.

ATMs: Cirrus, NYCE, Yankee 24

Orientation

Car Rentals

Take a shuttle from the baggage-claim area to the rental-car counters, which are open 24 hours.

American International 569.3550, 800/527.0202
Avis 561.3500, 800/331.1212
Budget 787.8200, 800/527.0700
Hertz 569.7272, 800/654.3131
National 569.6700, 800/227.7368
Thrifty 569.6500, 800/367.2277

To get to Logan by public transportation, take the **Massachusetts Bay Transportation Authority (MBTA)** subway to the **Airport** stop (Blue Line), where free **Massport** shuttle buses leave every few minutes for the airport terminals; check the sign outside the door of the shuttle bus for your airline. It's a 10-minute ride from the **Aquarium** or **Government Center** subway stops in Downtown Boston to the Airport Station.

The **Airport Water Shuttle** (439.3131) also carries travelers to and from Logan. Going into the city, a free shuttle bus takes you from your airline terminal to the **Logan Boat Dock,** and from there it's a seven-minute ferry ride (a fare is charged) across **Boston Harbor** to **Rowes Wharf** (at Atlantic Avenue) on the edge of Downtown Boston.

Taxi stands are located at all airport terminals; the common practice is to share a ride with others headed your way, since traffic congestion can easily run up the fare.

You can also take a limousine or minibus: **Airways Transportation** (267.2981) runs daily between Logan and mainly Back Bay hotels. **Hudson Bus Lines** (395.8080) goes between Logan and outlying areas of Greater Boston and beyond, including southern New Hampshire.

To sum up, the MBTA subway is the cheapest way to and from Logan and takes a reasonable amount of time; the Airport Water Shuttle charges a moderate fare, takes a scenic route, and avoids traffic entirely; and limos and taxis are the most expensive, with taxi fares fluctuating greatly during peak travel times. Plan your itinerary so you'll never arrive at or leave from Logan between 4PM and 6PM on a weekday—especially a Friday. Parking is available at the airport and nearby.

America's first postal route was established between Boston and New York City on 22 January 1673.

In Boston, a "regular" means coffee with cream, and some coffee shops automatically add sugar unless you specifically ask them not to.

Getting around Boston

Buses

Crosstown and local services are offered throughout Greater Boston and Cambridge. Tokens, exact fare, or MBTA passes are required. For information, call the MBTA at 722.3200 or 800/392.6100.

Driving

If you have a choice, don't drive. Boston is a pedestrian city, with confusing street patterns in many neighborhoods. Even if you have the derring-do to "compete" with Boston's notoriously brazen drivers, be forewarned that signage is generally poor and there are lots of one-way streets. Invest in a city street map.

On highways, the speed limit is 55 miles per hour. Right turns on a red light are permitted in Massachusetts except where prohibited by posted signs. Tolls are charged for using the Massachusetts Turnpike (I-90), tunnels, and various bridges.

Long-Distance and Commuter Buses

There are two bus terminals in Boston, about 10 blocks apart. The **Greyhound Terminal** is located at 10 St. James Avenue in the Back Bay. The **Peter Pan Terminal** is near South Station at 555 Atlantic Avenue on the Waterfront. Several lines use each terminal and some use both, depending on your destination. Assume nothing. Call; they're very helpful.

Bonanza .... 423.5810 (Northeast US)
Concord Trailways .... 426.7838 (New Hampshire)
Greyhound .... 423.5810 (Nationwide)
Peter Pan Bus Lines ... 426.7838 (Central MA, NY City)
Plymouth and Brockton .... 423.5810 (the Cape)

Parking

Street parking is limited and highly regulated, so read signs carefully. Many neighborhoods, such as **Beacon Hill,** have almost no parking for nonresidents. It's very common to be ticketed and/or towed away to Boston's hinterlands; if your car is towed, retrieving it will be costly and time-consuming.

There are numerous parking garages in town, and various open lots, some of which are listed below. Prices vary widely for hourly and day rates, with the most expensive in the Financial District/Downtown area.

In Boston:

Auditorium Garage ♦ 50 Dalton Street (near the Hynes Convention Center); 247.8006

Boston Harbor Garage ♦ 70 East India Row; 723.1731

Copley Place Parking ♦ 100 Huntington Avenue; 375.4488

Government Center Garage ♦ 50 New Sudbury Street; 227.0385

Prudential Center Garage ♦ 800 Boylston Street; 267.2965

In Cambridge:

Charles Square Garage ♦ 5 Bennett Street, Harvard Square; 491.6779

Harvard Square Parking Garage ♦ 65 JFK Street; 354.4168

Walt Whitman on the city's quirky topography:
"...Crush up a sheet of letter-paper in your hand, throw it down, and there is a map of old Boston."

Subway

The **Massachusetts Bay Transportation Authority (MBTA)** operates subways, streetcar lines, buses, commuter trains and boats, and vans for riders with special needs. The rapid-transit system, commonly referred to as "the **T**," is the nation's oldest subway system. Four lines—**Red, Blue, Orange, Green**—radiate from Downtown. The symbol (pictured above) indicates stops. Inbound refers to trains going to central Downtown stations: **Park Street, Downtown Crossing, State,** and **Government Center.** And outbound trains head away from these stations. Tokens, exact fare, or passes must be used; you may purchase tokens at the stations.

The T has minor eccentricities, best learned from experience. On the Green Line, many of the street-level stations do not have ticket booths, so you must have exact change ready (tokens are also accepted, supplemented by change). Drivers do not make change, although helpful passengers often will. Note: Certain inbound lines charge higher fares from outlying stations; always ask. And going outbound on the Green Line, no fare is charged if you board at an aboveground station. Smoking is not allowed in stations or on trains.

MBTA lines operate Monday through Saturday from 5AM to 12:45AM, and Sunday and holidays from 6AM to 12:45AM. Discount passes for elders are available at the **Downtown Crossing Concourse;** student passes are sold at schools (children five to 11 pay half fare, children under five ride free). The **Boston Passport,** a visitor pass good for three or seven days, is sold at the **Boston Common Visitor Information Center,** open daily from 9AM to 5PM, or at the **Airport Station,** open daily between 9AM and 4:30PM.

For more information, call 722.3200 or 800/392.6100. **Telecommunications Device for the Deaf (TDD)** can be reached at 722.5146. For daily recorded service conditions, call 722.5050. Those with special traveling needs should call 722.5123, 800/533.6282, TDD 722.5415. And monthly passes are available at various rates, with the option to combine subway and bus travel. Call 722.5219 for more information.

Taxis

There are usually plenty around town, except between 4PM and 7PM (especially on Friday) and in the worst weather. They're easiest to find near major hotels, on **Newbury Street,** and at **Downtown Crossing** and **Faneuil Hall Marketplace.** Available cruising taxis have a lighted sign on the roof. The standard tip is 15 percent. Some local companies are:

Boston:

Checker Taxi 536.7000
Red and White Cab 742.9090
Red Cab 734.5000
Town Taxi 536.5000

Cambridge:

Ambassador Brattle 492.1100
Cambridge Yellow Cab 547.3000
Checker Cab of Cambridge 497.9000

The name Boston is an elision of St. Botolph's Town, named for the patron saint of fishing, whose name was derived from *bot* (boat) and *ulph* (help).

Trains

North Station: MBTA commuter trains (the **Purple Lines**) for destinations north and west of the city leave from this station at 150 Causeway Street. This is where droves of Bostonians catch trains to the North Shore and its beaches.

The **Rockport Line Commuter Rail,** which is nicknamed **the beach train,** fills up fast on hot summer days. The MBTA **Green** and **Orange Lines** also stop here. For more information, call 722.3200 or 800/392.6099.

South Station: Amtrak trains depart from South Station, which is located on Atlantic Avenue at Summer Street, and stop at **Back Bay Station,** 145 Dartmouth Street, and 15 minutes west of Boston at **Route 128 Station** in Westwood. Call 402.3000 or 800/872.7245 for information.

MBTA commuter trains (the **Purple Lines**) leave from South Station for points south of the city; for schedules, call 227.5070 or 800/392.6099. The MBTA **Red Line** stops at South Station and the **Orange Line** stops at **Back Bay/South End Station** (which also serves as Amtrak's Back Bay Station).

FYI

Bed-and-Breakfasts

Many B&B-referral organizations serve a number of neighborhoods and towns. Some of these include:

AAA Accommodations; 491.6107

Bed & Breakfast Associates, Bay Colony; 449.5302

Bed and Breakfast Cambridge and Greater Boston; 576.1492, 800/888.0178

A Cambridge House Bed-and-Breakfast Inn; 491.6300, 800/232.9989

Host Homes of Boston; 244.1308

New England Bed & Breakfast Inc.; 244.2112

Drinking and Smoking

You must be 21 to purchase liquor. Blue Laws vary slightly in Cambridge and Boston, and also depending on the establishment's license. In general, no liquor is sold in bars after 1AM or before noon on Sunday. In stores, no liquor is sold after 11PM Monday through Saturday, and none on Sunday except near the New Hampshire border. And there's a strong antismoking sentiment in Boston and Cambridge (especially Cambridge), with some restaurants banning it entirely and most offering nonsmoking sections. Many public places forbid smoking.

Money

Boston banks do not commonly exchange foreign currency, so bring American dollars or exchange currency at **Logan International Airport** at **Bay Bank Foreign Money Exchange,** Terminal E, 567.2313. You can buy foreign currency at **Thomas Cook Foreign Exchange,** 426.0016; **Shawmut Bank of Boston,** 292.2000; and **Bank of Boston,** 434.2200. Banks, many stores, and restaurants accept traveler's checks, generally requiring a photo ID. You can purchase them at **American Express,** 723.8400; **Barclay's Bank,** 423.1775; **Thomas Cook,** 227.3121; and at most major banks.

Personal Safety

Always keep an eye on the traffic, since Boston drivers—and cyclists—are aggressive and often run red lights. Use common sense; be careful if you venture off well-worn paths in the city.

The subways are safe within Boston, Cambridge, and Brookline, but keep your wits about you. After dark, avoid the parks, Boston Common, the Combat Zone (the red-light district near Chinatown), alleys, and side streets.

Orientation

Publications

Local newspapers and periodicals for news and events information include: *The Boston Globe* (daily); *Boston Herald* (daily); *Christian Science Monitor* (Monday through Friday); *Boston Phoenix* (weekly); *Boston Magazine* (monthly); and *The Tab* (weekly, with different editions for specific neighborhoods). Especially helpful for events information are the *Globe's* "Calendar," published Thursday, and the *Boston Herald's* "Scene" section and the *Boston Phoenix,* both published on Friday.

Recreation

A sporting town like Boston naturally has plenty of municipal sports facilities. Most are available on a first-come, first-served basis; some require reservations or permits. Call the **Parks and Recreation Department** at 725.4505 if you're interested in baseball and Little League diamonds; softball fields; basketball, tennis, and street hockey courts; or ice-skating rinks (free public skating is also permitted on the **Public Garden** lagoon in winter, and ice skates are rented on the spot).

Call the **Metropolitan District Commission (MDC)** at 727.9547 or 727.5215 (recorded information) for information on baseball, football, tennis, swimming, fishing, skiing, and ice skating. (One of the most popular MDC rinks is the **Steriti Rink** on Commercial Street in the **North End,** where you can skate with a fine view of the **Bunker Hill Monument.**)

If you want to play golf, try the **William Devine Golf Course** (436.7586); the par-70 course is the country's second-oldest municipal golf course. For camping and hiking information, call or drop by the **Appalachian Mountain Club,** 5 Joy Street, 523.0636 (they can tell you about skiing, too); the **Sierra Club,** 3 Joy Street, 227.5339; or the **National Park Service Visitor's Center,** 15 State Street, 242.5642.

Numerous public beaches around Boston (including some on the **Boston Harbor Islands**) are under the supervision of the MDC. For information, call 727.7090. Many of the beaches—although not all—are on dirty Boston Harbor, which is undergoing a long-overdue cleanup. You're better off driving or taking a beach train from **North Station** to one of the popular North Shore swimming spots such as **Singing Beach** in **Manchester-by-the-Sea.** Other favorite beaches include the **Crane Memorial Reservation** in Ipswich; the **Parker River National Wildlife Refuge** on Plum Island near Newburyport; **Wingaersheek** and **Good Harbor Beaches** in Gloucester; **Nantasket Beach** in Hull; and **Duxbury Beach** in Duxbury.

Taxes

In Massachusetts, a five-percent tax is charged on all purchases except services, food bought in stores (not restaurants), and clothing under $175. A 9.7-percent hotel tax is also assessed.

Tickets

Here are a number of ticket sources for Boston-area events. Per-ticket service charges vary by outlet.

Bostix Half-price tickets for same-day events: sports, cultural, music, theater, and dance. Bostix sells full-price tickets, too, and is a Ticketmaster outlet. No credit cards. ♦ Faneuil Hall Marketplace. 723.5181

Charge-Tix Comedy clubs and other shows. Credit cards only. ♦ 542.8511

Concertcharge Sports, theater, concerts, special events. Credit cards only. ♦ 497.1118, 800/442.1854

Concertix Tickets for the Regattabar jazz performances and other events. ♦ 876.7777

Hub Ticket Agency Sports and theater tickets. ♦ 240 Tremont Street, Theater District. 426.8340

Out of Town Ticket Agency Sports, theater, concerts, special events. No credit cards. ♦ Harvard Square MBTA Station, Cambridge. 492.1900

Ticketmaster Cabarets, concerts, circuses, sports. A computerized ticket service. Credit cards only; ask for cash-only outlet locations. ♦ 931.2000

Ticketron Sports, theater, dance, music. Credit cards only. A computerized ticket service is also available; ask for cash-only outlet locations. ♦ 720.3434, 800/302.8080

Tipping

In restaurants and for personal services, tip 15 to 20 percent.

Tours

By Trolley, Bus, or Car:

Beantown Trolley	287.1900
Boston Trolley Tours (The Blue Trolley)	427.8687
Brush Hill Transportation	986.6100
Commonwealth Limousine Service	787.5575
Gray Line Sightseeing	426.8805
New England Sights	232.1130
Old Town Trolley Tour of Boston	269.7010
Uncommon Boston	731.5854

On Foot:

Boston by Foot/Boston by Little Feet	367.2345
Historic Neighborhoods Foundation	426.1885
Uncommon Boston	731.5854

By Boat:

Boston by Sail	742.3313

(Other boat tours are listed in the Waterfront chapter, which begins on page 56)

Visitor's Centers

Boston Common Visitor's Information Center ♦ Daily 9AM-5PM. 147 Tremont Street. 426.3115

Cambridge Discovery Information Kiosk ♦ M-Sa 9AM-6PM, Su 1-6PM June-Labor Day; M-Sa 9AM-5PM, S 1-6PM Labor Day-late June. ♦ Harvard Square. 497.1630

Charlestown Navy Yard Visitor's Center ♦ Daily 9AM-5PM. Charlestown Navy Yard. 242.5601

Greater Boston Convention and Visitor's Bureau ◆ M-F 9AM-5PM. Prudential Plaza, Back Bay. 536.4100

Massachusetts Tourism Office ◆ M-F 9AM-5PM. 100 Cambridge Street, Government Center. 727.3201, 800/447.6277

National Park Service Visitor's Center ◆ Daily 9AM-5PM. 15 State Street, Financial District. 242.5642

Weather

Since you're likely to be exploring on foot, be prepared for the changing climate. Summer can be very hot and humid, but is often cooled by the sea; winter is usually cold and damp with snow and ice, or brisk and sunny. The most comfortable times are spring and fall, but each season has its charms.

Months	Average Temperature (°F)
December through February	30
March through May	46
June through August	71
September through November	53

Phone Book

The Boston area code is 617 (outlying areas use 508; and the rest of the state uses 413; if you're not sure which area code applies to you, ask the information operator or check the telephone book). As of press time, New England Telephone (NET) and AT&T pay phones cost 10¢ for a local call, with no charge for information (dial 411 for local information). However, a number of other companies have installed pay telephones that cost 25¢. Have plenty of change; these amounts are for limited minutes and calls are disconnected without further payment.

Emergencies

Police/Fire/Ambulance	**911**
Coast Guard	565.9200
Dental	956.6828
FBI	742.5533
Medical	726.2000, 956.5566
Poison Control	232.2120
Rape Hotline	492.7273
24-hour drugstores (in Boston)	523.1028/4372
(in Cambridge)	876.5519

Important Numbers

American Youth Hostels (AYH)	731.5430
Amtrak	482.3660, 800/872.7245
Bay State Cruise Company (ferry service)	723.7800
Boston Public Library	536.5400
Greater Boston Convention and Visitors Bureau	536.4100
Handicapped-Visitor Information	727.5540
Mass Bay Lines (ferry service)	542.8000
Massport Ground Transportation	800/235.6426
Parking Violations (in Boston)	635.4410
(in Cambridge)	349.4705, 498.9036
Police (nonemergency)	247.4200
TDD (Boston Public Library Access Center)	536.7055
Traveler's Aid	542.7286/9875
24-hour convenience stores	227.9534, 424.6888
US Customs	565.6152
US Immigration and Naturalization	565.3879
US Passport Office	565.6998

Recorded Information

Marine Weather Forecast	569.3700
MBTA service (daily conditions)	722.5050
Time	637.1234
US Postal Service	451.9922
Weather	936.1234/1212

Sports and Recreation

Appalachian Mountain Club	523.0636
Bicycling	491.7433
Boston Bruins (hockey)	227.3200
Boston Celtics (basketball)	523.3030

Orientation

Boston Parks and Recreation	725.4505
	725.4006 (recording)
Boston Red Sox (baseball)	267.8661
Canoeing	965.5110
Ice skating	725.4006, 727.5215
Mayor's Office for Events	725.4500
National Park Service	242.5642
New England Patriots (football)	800/543.1776
Sierra Club	227.5339
Skiing conditions	207/773.7669 (ME)
	800/258.3608 (NH), 802/229.0531 (VT)
State Fisheries and Wildlife	727.3151
State Forests and Parks	727.3180

Boston by the Book

To learn more about the history, residents, architecture, and life in general in this popular East Coast city, here are a few pages worth flipping through before you tour the town.

About Boston: Sight, Sound, Flavor and Inflection
by David McCord

The Bell Jar
by Sylvia Plath

Boston: A Topographical History
by Walter Muir Whitehill

The Bostonians
by Henry James

The City Observed: Boston
by Donlyn Lyndon

Cityscapes
by Robert Campbell and Peter Vanderwarker

Frederick Law Olmsted and the Boston Park System
by Cynthia Zaitzevsky

Historic Walks in Boston
by John Harris

Historic Walks in Cambridge
by John Harris

Imaginary Boston
by Shaun O'Connell

Lost Boston
by Jane Holtz Kay

Make Way for Ducklings
by Robert McCloskey

The Proper Bostonians
by Cleveland Amory

Uncommon Boston
by Susan Berk with Jill Bloom

Beacon Hill

Stroll across **Boston Common,** an enormous grassy blanket that Bostonians have used since the city's birth, and then prepare yourself (with comfortable shoes) for poking about the nooks and crannies of historic Beacon Hill. You'll quickly find this neighborhood to be a walker's dream and a driver's nightmare. Beacon Hill is a redbrick quarter of handsome houses crowded along crazy-quilt streets. Boston is one of America's most European cities, and Beacon Hill looks ever-so-English. Its slopes are easiest to navigate in good weather, but well worth a bit of slipping and sliding to enjoy **"The Hill's"** serene winter stillness.

A fashionable enclave today, Beacon Hill in colonial times was infant Boston's undesirable outskirts—crisscrossed with cow paths and covered with brambles, berries, and scrub. The **Puritans** called it **Trimountain** because its three-peaked silhouette resembled a person's head and shoulders. Whittled away by early developers to create new lots and landfill, today only Beacon Hill remains. The completion in 1798 of the majestic **State House,** designed by **Charles Bulfinch,** spotlighted the Hill's potential and drew affluent **Brahmins** to settle here. Beacon Hill blossomed as the city's intellectual and artistic Renaissance unfolded in the first half of the 19th century, and a number of cultural luminaries gathered here.

Beacon Hill alone is divided approximately into three districts. **The flats,** the newer, more orderly section, runs down to the **Charles River** from **Charles Street.** Up from Charles Street is the Hill's sunny **south slope,** extending from **Beacon**

Street to **Pinckney Street**, and the shady **north slope**, descending from Pinckney to **Cambridge Street**. While the south slope's mansions and row houses exude Brahmin privilege, the north slope's smaller houses and former tenement walk-ups relay a history of ethnic diversity and the struggle of many groups—especially blacks—to make their way on the Hill. Coursing through the Hill, infusing it with vitality, is Charles Street, an eclectic, surprisingly friendly thoroughfare where most of Beacon Hill's shops, services, and businesses are located.

In older cities, the chicken-or-the-egg question is: Which came first, the streets or the dwellings? It's clear that the houses came first on the hodgepodge Hill and that the streets have simply made do. As you wend your way over bumpy brick sidewalks, you'll probably agree that Beacon Hill wouldn't be so appealing without the jigs and jogs of the streets, the surprise of **Louisburg Square**, and the glistening river glimpsed below. The Hill is an intimate, people-scaled place where idiosyncrasies reveal the layers of lives

that have enriched this large heap of brick and granite. Iron handrails fastened to buildings help you climb up the steeper blocks; gardens and gatherings enliven the rooflines; ornate doorknockers, bootscrapers, and wrought-iron embellishments dress up some of the most modest facades; and tunnels lead to concealed courtyards and hidden houses.

Most Beacon Hill homes are Greek Revival or Federal in style, but refreshing upstarts have sneaked in here and there. Master carpenters, called "housewrights," built most of the structures, since the trained American architect was a brand-new breed. Notice the many graceful bowfronts, a Beacon Hill innovation. In 1955 the Hill was officially declared a historic district; today the **Beacon Hill Civic Association** watchdogs its precious repository of buildings, even dictating exterior color choices. Come back in 30 years, and it will all look the same. True, as buildings change hands there's less single ownership, and more condos and luxury apartments belong to young professionals instead of "Proper Bostonians." Yet Beacon Hill lore continues to linger. Holding sway here for generations, Boston's famous "First Families"—the **Cabots, Lodges, Codmans,** and **Lowells,** to name a few—have passed their stories on, the facts fuzzied by the time and telling. Yes, the Hill clings to its elitist past, but Jewish and Italian immigrants, Depression-era bohemians, artists, and college students have also made their homes here.

If the Hill's tranquil charm and careful-when-you-touch air begin to grow tiresome, remember that just ahead there's a startling or delightful nuance to discover. Watch the world go by over a *caffè* at **Il Dolce Momento;** find that slip of a street called **Acorn;** then come down from the heights and take an afternoon promenade in the **Public Garden.**

The four subway stops most convenient to Boston Common, Beacon Hill, and the Public Garden are Park Street (Red and Green Lines), Charles (Red Line), and Boylston or Arlington (Green Line). The entire neighborhood can be toured by foot easily from any of these stations.

1 Boston Common Fifty sprawling acres, the Boston Common is the oldest public park in the country. Now the city's heart, the Common was once its hinterland. In the early 1600s it was part of the farm belonging to **Reverend William Blaxton,** the first English squatter on the Shawmut Peninsula. A reclusive bachelor in the style of Thoreau, Blaxton shattered his own blissful solitude by generously inviting the city's Puritan founders to settle on his peninsula and share its fresh water. His neighbors then too close for comfort, Blaxton sold them

the Common in 1634 and retreated to Beacon Hill. There the city's first—but not the last!—eccentric tended to his beloved orchard, reputedly riding about on his Brahma bull for recreation. But when the busybody Puritans then tried to convince Blaxton to join their church, he fled south to Rhode Island.

The Common has belonged to Bostonians ever since. Cattle grazed its grass until outlawed in 1830. Justice—of a sort—was meted out here with whipping posts, stocks, and pillories. Indians, pirates, and persecuted Quakers were hanged here; and so was **Rachell Whall** in the late 1700s for the crime of highway robbery (she stole a 75¢ bonnet). Until 6 July 1836 blacks couldn't pass freely on the Common. This is where Redcoats camped during the Revolution, and Civil War troops once mustered. **General Lafayette** returned to the US in

1824 and shot off a ceremonial cannon here, and the **Prince of Wales,** future **King Edward VII,** reviewed the troops on these very same grassy lawns in 1860.

Long the site of great public outdoor theater—sermons, duels, puppet shows, balloon ascensions, promenades, hopscotch championships, fire-engine and flying-machine demonstrations, horse races, antislavery meetings, fireworks, hoop rolling, and ox roasting—the Common still offers some of Boston's best people-watching. Arrive before nine on a sunny morning and relish your leisure while working folk push on to their jobs, leaving you to saunter among the magicians, musicians, mounted police, artists,

Beacon Hill

baby strollers, religious proselytizers, skateboarders, soapbox orators, pigeons, and pushcart vendors along the Common's walkways. Return some summer evening to watch a softball game in one corner of the Common, while in another corner an unofficial dog-walking group meets after work to chat while their quad-ripedal pals romp. One cautionary note: as is true of most urban parks, the Common isn't a safe place to be after dark.

1 Park Street Station Designed by **Wheelwright and Haven,** the first subway system in the US opened here to incredible fanfare on 1 September 1897. (The subway line originally ran only as far as today's Boylston Station, just one stop across the Common.) "First Car Off the Earth!" trumpeted *The Boston Globe.* Before you hurry aboveground to leave the dankness, popcorn and donut smells, and throngs on the subway platforms, look for the mosaic mural immediately inside the turnstiles. It depicts the first streetcar entering the subway, with a woman rider holding aloft that day's *Globe.* Aboveground, Park Street Station's two copper-roofed, granite-faced kiosks are **National Historic Landmarks.**

Head a short distance down the Common along Tremont Street to the blue-trimmed **Visitor's Information Center,** where you can find out about all the local goings on—from museum exhibitions to helicopter rides and whale watches—and where Boston's renowned **Freedom Trail** begins. On the way is *Brewer Fountain* (completed in 1868), a bronze replica of the lauded fountain of the 1855 Paris Exposition and a popular rendezvous. ◆ At Hamilton Pl

2 Boston Common Ranger Station Stop on the Tremont Street side of the Common for information on the walks led by **Park Rangers,** including historic tours of the Common and the **Granary Burying Ground,** and a "What's in Bloom?" walk or "Family Stroll" in the **Public Garden.** For kids, there's the "Make Way for Ducklings" tour, which includes reading the famous children's storybook and meets at the Public Garden's bronze ducklings; and the "Horse of Course" program about a day in the life of a Park Ranger horse. ◆ Daily 9AM-8PM. 522.2639

The Freedom Trail

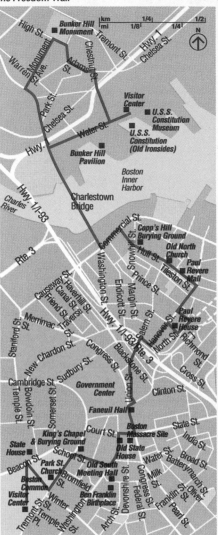

3 The Freedom Trail At the Visitor's Information Center begins the famous self-guided, 2.5-mile tourist pilgrimage on which you track an elusive red line connecting 13 historical sites from colonial and Revolutionary times, including **Paul Revere's House** and the **Old North Church** (see the map above). You'll end up in **Charlestown,** which means a trek or ride back, and you really could invent a more entertaining odyssey of your own. But if you're in the mood to follow in the footsteps of countless others, the tour takes about three hours. If you prefer a guided tour (which lasts about 90 minutes and visits five sites), call the **National Park Service** at 242.5642 to get the daily schedules, and at 242.5689 for group reservations. The guided tours begin at 15 State Street, across from the **Old State House.**

 3 Parkman Plaza Left of the Visitor's Information Center, facing the Boston Common, the plaza's bronze figures enshrine Puritan values.

Take the path just left of *Industry*—called **Railroad Mall** because it led to the terminal of one of Boston's first railroads in 1835—for a brief, lovely stroll to the neoclassical **Parkman Bandstand**. Mount this neglected but still-handsome structure, where you can watch the squirrels skitter while you imagine long-silent strains of music (try to ignore the graffiti). In the fall, surrounded by rustling leaves and frequented by Boston homeless people, this is one of the city's most evocative settings.

4 Central Burying Ground Once you're in a thoroughly contemplative mood, follow Railroad Mall to find history etched on 18th-century tombstones. Legend claims that here lie American soldiers who died at the **Battle of Bunker Hill** and British soldiers who succumbed to illness during the **Siege of Boston.** At least a dozen **Boston Tea Party** guests are here, as is portrait artist **Gilbert Stuart,** who painted **Martha** and **George Washington.** Stuart died in poverty, humiliated to be eclipsed by less-talented but more socially skilled painters. The inscriptions that mention "strangers" refer to Irish Catholic immigrants buried here. In early colonial graveyards like this one, headstones often face east—from where would come the Day of Judgment trumpet call—and are paired with footstones, creating a cozy bed for the occupant's eternal rest.

5 Flagstaff Hill Climb the Common's highest point, atop which the *Soldiers and Sailors Monument* commemorates Civil War combatants. Gunpowder was stored here long ago. In 1979 **Pope John Paul II** held an outdoor Mass on the northwest slope.

5 Frog Pond True, it's a frogless, sometimes-empty concrete hollow instead of the marshy amphibian abode it once was (**Edgar Allan Poe** derisively called Bostonians "Frogpondians"), but in steamy weather the pond is filled with children cavorting under its fountain. (Even the cynical Poe called the Common "no common thing.")

6 Beacon Street Mall In the shadow of the State House, this wide, dappled promenade along the Common's north side is where **Ralph Waldo Emerson** and **Walt Whitman** paced back and forth, arguing about taking the sex out of Whitman's *Leaves of Grass.* Emerson was utterly convincing, Whitman concluded: "I could never hear the points better put—and then I felt down in my soul the clear and unmistakable conviction to disobey all, and pursue my own way." Despite their disagreement, the friends went off together to partake of "a bully dinner."

7 William Hickling Prescott House Built in 1808, this graceful pair of brick bowfronts, now joined, is adorned with many of the delicate Greek architectural details favored by architect **Asher Benjamin.** The left-hand house, now a **National Historic Landmark** and headquarters for the **National Society of the Colonial Dames of America,** inspired the setting for *The Virginians* by British author **William Makepeace Thackery,** a houseguest of a former owner. On Wednesday you can peruse the colonial and Victorian artifacts collected and preserved by the Dames if you take the tour. ♦ Admission. W 10AM-4PM. 54-55 Beacon St (at Spruce St). 742.3190

8 Harrison Gray Otis House (circa 1805) This is the last and largest of the three imposing residences designed by **Charles Bulfinch** for the larger-than-life grandee **Harrison Gray Otis**—one of Boston's first big-time developers, a Boston mayor, and a US senator. Otis, a man who believed in living the good life, added a fourth repast to his regular meals, breakfasted daily on pâté de foie gras, and—surprise, surprise—was a gout victim for 40 years. Each afternoon the politicians and soci-

ety guests who were gathered in Otis' drawing room consumed 10 gallons of spiked punch from a punchbowl perched on the landing. Otis feted all of fashionable Boston in his magnificent rooms. Yet even Harry's house didn't have plumbing. (Bathwater was considered a health menace because it supposedly attracted cockroaches, so tubs weren't allowed until the 1840s.) The **American Meteorological Society** is now the fortunate resident of the house. ♦ 45 Beacon St (between Spruce and Walnut Sts)

8 Somerset Club Painter **John Singleton Copley** lived in a house that once stood on this site, until he went to England in 1744 and never returned. Now an ultra-exclusive private club, the Greek Revival granite bowfront that replaced Copley's house aggressively protrudes beyond its neighbors' facades. **Colonel David Sears** erected the right-hand half in 1819, adding the left half in 1831—doubling **Alexander Parris'** original design and spoiling it in the process. Look for the baronial iron-studded portal with its lions' head knockers—a very showy touch for Beacon Hill. ♦ 42 Beacon St (between Spruce and Walnut Sts)

9 Appleton-Parker Houses Built in the early 1800s by **Alexander Parris,** these two Greek Revival bowfronts were, respectively, the abodes of Boston's merchant prince **Nathan Appleton** of the textile-manufacturing family and his former partner, **Daniel Parker. Henry Wadsworth Longfellow** courted and married **Fanny Appleton** in her family's front parlor in 1843. And sardonic **Edgar Allan Poe,** characteristically misbehaving before the ladies at an Appleton soiree, was given the heave-ho. Both houses are **National Historic Landmarks.** ♦ 39-40 Beacon St (at Walnut St)

9 Purple Window Panes The famed "purple panes" of Beacon Hill are the lavender-hued windowpanes that are the proud possession of a handful of houses on the Hill. Actually, the treasured tint was a fluke—in shipments of glass sent from Hamburg to Boston between 1818 and 1824, manganese oxide reacted with the sun to create the color. Although numerous copies exist, very few authentic panes have survived. You can look for the originals at Nos. 39, 40, and 63 Beacon Street, and 29A Chestnut Street, among others.

10 Little, Brown and Company Imagine **Louisa May Alcott** dropping by to look over the galley proofs for *Little Women*. Established in 1837, this venerable Boston publishing house also

Beacon Hill

has on its backlist **John Bartlett** (of that household tome *Bartlett's Familiar Quotations*), **J.D. Salinger, Evelyn Waugh, Fanny Farmer** (of cookbook fame), **Margaret Atwood,** and **Berke Breathed,** creator of the retired *Bloom County* cartoon strip. The firm moved its headquarters here in 1909, and although the Adult Trade division decamped to New York a few years ago, certain imprints remain. ♦ 34 Beacon St (at Joy St)

10 George Parkman House In one of the most sensational murders of the century, **George Francis Parkman's** father, **Dr. George Parkman,** was murdered in 1849, allegedly by Harvard professor **John Webster,** a fellow Boston socialite who had borrowed money from the doctor. Webster finally was hanged for the crime; it so happened that the judge handling the case, **Lemuel Shaw,** was related to the victim. After the furor, Parkman's son retreated with his mother and sister from public scrutiny, remaining a recluse here until his death in 1908.

Built in 1825 by **Cornelius Coolidge,** the house overlooks the Common; Parkman must have found solace in this unchanging landscape because he left $5.5 million in his will for its maintenance. For generations, Boston mayors lived in this house, which belongs to the city but is now used only for civic functions. ♦ 33 Beacon St

11 The State House The 23-karat gilded dome of the Massachusetts State House (pictured on the opposite page) glitters above the soft, dull hues of Beacon Hill, luring the eye. In fact, it was the capitol building (always, always called the State House, never the Capitol) that first drew wealthy Bostonians away from the crowded Waterfront to settle on the more salubrious Hill, still considered "country" at the start of the 18th century.

Charles Bulfinch spun out his remarkable designs at a breathtaking rate, leaps and bounds ahead of city officials in his brilliant urban-planning maneuvers. Completed in 1798, the State House is his finest surviving gift to the city. When construction began, **Governor Samuel Adams,** the popular Revolutionary War patriot, laid the cornerstone with **Paul Revere's** help. Looking up from Beacon Street, imagine away

the two marble wings, added more than a century later by **Chapman, Sturgis, and Andrews.** Facing the Common, Bulfinch's imposing south facade is dominated by a commanding portico with 12 Corinthian columns, surmounting an arcade of brick arches. Topping the lantern above the dome is a gilded pinecone, a symbol of the vast timberlands of northern Massachusetts, which became the state of Maine in 1820.

This striking neoclassical edifice cut a much less flashy figure in Bulfinch's time: the dome was originally made of whitewashed wood shingles, replaced in 1802 with gray-painted copper sheeting, installed by **Paul Revere and Sons;** gilding wasn't applied until 1874. The dome was briefly blackened during World War II to hide from moonlight during blackouts, so it wouldn't offer a target to the Axis bombers who never came. In 1825 the redbrick walls were painted white (a common practice when granite or marble was too costly); in 1845 repainted yellow; then white again in 1917 to match the new marble wings. Not until 1928 was the redbrick exposed once more. Around the back is the monstrous yellow-brick heap of an extension, six times the size of the original building.

Statues of the spellbinding orator and US senator **Daniel Webster,** educator **Horace Mann,** and Civil War general **Thomas Hooker** on his charger stand beneath the central colonnade. On the lawns below are pensive images of **Anne Hutchinson** (below the left wing), who was banished from Boston in 1645 by the Puritan community for her freethinking religious views (not until 1945 did the **Great and General Court of Massachusetts** revoke the edict of banishment), and Quaker **Mary Dyer** (below the right wing), who was hanged on the Common for protesting Anne's banishment. There's also a statue of a serious, striding **John F. Kennedy.** Climb the steps and enter Bulfinch's **Doric Hall** (named for its 10 colossal columns) on the second floor under the dome. The hall's main doors only open when a US president visits or a Massachusetts governor leaves the State House for the very last time.

On the third floor is the resplendent **House of Representatives** gallery. Here hangs the *Sacred Cod* carved in pine, presented to the legislature in 1784 by Boston merchant **Jonathan Rowe** as a reminder of the fishing industry's importance to the state economy. This wooden fish effigy garnered such ridiculous reverence that in 1895 it was wrapped in an American flag and carried to the new State House by four messengers, escorted by a committee of 15 House members. And on 26 April 1933, when the fish was codnapped by *Harvard Lampoon* as a prank, all business in the House was suspended for several days, the members fuming over their missing fish. The thieves relented, and phoned to tell the House that their mascot was concealed in a closet beneath their chamber. In the barrel-vaulted **Senate Reception Room,** the original Senate Chamber, each of four original Ionic columns by Bulfinch was carved from a single pine tree. Directly beneath the gold dome is the

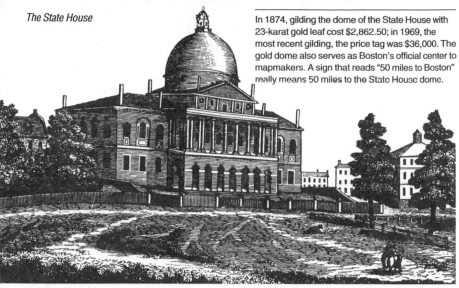

The State House

In 1874, gilding the dome of the State House with 23-karat gold leaf cost $2,862.50; in 1969, the most recent gilding, the price tag was $36,000. The gold dome also serves as Boston's official center to mapmakers. A sign that reads "50 miles to Boston" really means 50 miles to the State House dome.

sunburst-ceilinged **Senate Chamber,** where **Angelina Grimke** became the first woman to address a US legislative body when she gave an antislavery speech in 1838. ♦ Building M-F 9AM-5PM. Information and tours M-F 10AM-4PM, Doric Hall. Closed state holidays. Enter from Bowdoin St. 727.3676 &

12 Robert Gould Shaw Memorial Across from the main entrance to the State House, sculptor **Augustus Saint-Gaudens'** monument honors the **54th Massachusetts Regiment** volunteers of African descent, and the nation's first black regiment, which enlisted in Boston. The troops fought in the Civil War under the command of 26-year-old Shaw, son of a venerable Boston family. For two years, until a shamefaced Congress relented, members of the 54th refused their pay because they received only $10 a month instead of the $13 paid to whites. Shaw and half his men died in a valiant assault on Fort Wagner, SC, in 1863.

Saint-Gaudens took 13 years to complete this beautifully wrought bas-relief, which Shaw's abolitionist family insisted must honor the black infantrymen as well as their son. Erected in 1897, the monument today seems somewhat patronizing for its portrayal of the white Shaw as a heroic figure on horseback, towering above the black troops, but it was, in fact, remarkably democratic in its day. Draw near and study the portraitlike, ennobling treatment of the men's expressive faces. The angel of death hovers above. *Glory,* a Hollywood film about Shaw and his brave regiment, was released in 1989. **Charles McKim,** of the architectural firm **McKim, Mead & White,** designed the memorial's classical frame. It sits on a petite plaza whose granite balustrade overlooks the Boston Common.

The **Black Heritage Trail,** a guided walking tour that retraces the history of Boston's 19th-century black community, begins at the memorial. Call the **Boston African American National Historic Site** at 742.5415 for information.

13 Park Street Called **Sentry Lane** in the 17th century, this was the pathway the sentry took to the top of Beacon Hill, where a bucket of tar mounted on a post in 1634 was ever-ready for emergency lighting (until it blew down in 1789). An almshouse, a house of correction, an insane asylum, and a "bridewell"—a lovely name for a jail—populated this street when it was part of Boston's outskirts; now Park Street is home to a number of decidedly reputable institutions. In 1804 architect **Charles Bulfinch** straightened out the lane and designed nine residences facing the Common that became known as **Bulfinch Row.** Only the **Amory-Ticknor House** at the corner of Beacon Street survives—although it's disastrously altered.

13 The Union Club The flag bearing the Union Club's logo forever waves over No. 8, formerly separate 19th-century mansions (the right-hand one was demolished in 1896 and replaced) owned by two of Boston's most illustrious families. Members use the *Social Register* as their telephone book and chat over lunch about strictly nonbusiness topics. ♦ 8 Park St

The MBTA's Park Street Station—arguably the hub of the Hub—has 105,000 travelers passing through daily, about the same number of people who showed up on opening day in 1897, when the fare cost all of five cents. The subway was built—at a price of $4,404,958.25—to avert electric-trolley gridlock (in the 1890s tracks covered three of Tremont Street's four lanes). As the system was upgraded, the company was at pains to improve employee appearance, specifying the following warning in 1902: "Our conductors must be presentable, for the very appearance of some men gives offence quickly in a cultured community. These men must have all their fingers and thumbs, and nowadays must have all their toes...[and] a reasonable number of either real or artificial teeth."

Restaurants/Clubs: Red   **Hotels:** Blue
Shops/ ☙ Outdoors: Green   **Sights/Culture:** Black

13

14 Park Street Church When heading northeast on the Common, all eyes irresistibly rise to this majestic 1809 church looming at Park and Tremont streets, opposite the subway station. **Henry James** heaped praise on the elegant late-Georgian edifice, pronouncing it "perfectly felicitous" and "the most interesting mass of brick and mortar in America." Influenced by his much more illustrious English compatriot **Christopher Wren,** architect **Peter Banner** capped the crowning glory of his career with a stalwart 217-foot-tall telescoping steeple that points to the sky like an orator's emphatic forefinger. Locals have always relied on its easy-to-read clock for time and rendezvous. The illustri-

Beacon Hill

ous **Handel & Haydn Society** formed here in 1815, drawing many of its voices from the church choir. And here the anthem *America* was first sung on 4 July 1831; 24-year-old **Samuel Francis Smith** reputedly dashed off its lyrics a half-hour before schoolchildren sang it on the church steps. The church once stood next to a workhouse, the Puritan answer to homelessness and poverty. ♦ Daily 10AM-4PM, July-Aug; by appointment only Sept-June. Services Su 9AM, 10:45AM, 6PM. 1 Park St (at Tremont St). 523.3383 &

14 Brimstone Corner Where Tremont and Park streets meet was supposedly dubbed for the fire-and-brimstone oratory of the Park Street Church's Congregational preachers—including abolitionist **William Lloyd Garrison,** who gave his first antislavery address here in 1829. But a more banal explanation is that brimstone, used to make gunpowder, was stored in the church crypt during the **War of 1812.**

14 Granary Burying Ground Nestled to the right of the Park Street Church, this graveyard (pictured below, with sample epitaphs listed at right) was named for the 1738 granary that the church replaced. Created in 1660, it is the third-oldest graveyard in the city. In this shady haven lie many Revolutionary heroes—**Samuel**

Adams, John Hancock, James Otis, Robert Treat Paine, and **Paul Revere**—although the headstones have been moved so often you can't really be sure who's where. The five victims of the **Boston Massacre** (including black patriot **Crispus Attucks**), philanthropist **Peter Faneuil** (for whom **Faneuil Hall** is named), **Benjamin Franklin's** parents (he's in Philadelphia), and **"Mother" Goose** are also here. **Judge Samuel Sewell** likewise rests easy, having cleared his conscience as the only judge to ever admit publicly that he was wrong to condemn the **Salem Witches.** But the best reason to visit this free, two-acre museum *en plein air* is to examine the tombstones' extraordinary carvings—remember, rubbings are forbidden here—of astonishing skeletons, urns, winged skulls, and contemplative angels. In this haunting place, you will be transported back to the 17th century, from which the earliest tombstones date. The winged hourglasses carved into the Egyptian-style granite gateway, designed in 1830 by **Solomon Willard,** were added in the 19th century. ♦ Daily 8AM-4PM

15 The Boston Athenaeum Although **Edward Clark Cabot** modeled the 1849 building after **Palladio's** Palazzo da Porta Festa in Vicenza, Italy, the Athenaeum is a Boston institution to its bones. Enlarged and rebuilt in the early 1900s by **Henry Forbes Bigelow,** the structure is now a **National Historic Landmark.** Only 1,049 ownership shares exist to this independent research library, founded in 1807, and all can be traced to their original owners. You're

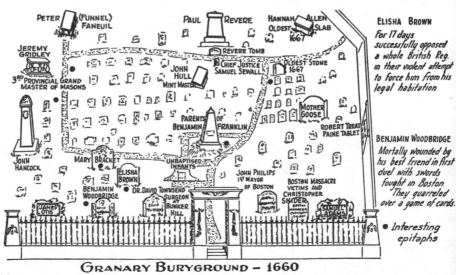

PETER (FUNNEL) FANEUIL · PAUL REVERE · HANNAH ALLEN OLDEST SLAB 1667 · ELISHA BROWN
For 17 days successfully opposed a whole British Reg. in their violent attempt to force him from his legal habitation

JEREMY GRIDLEY · REVERE TOMB · 3RD PROVINCIAL GRAND MASTER OF MASONS · JOHN HULL MINT MASTER · CHIEF JUSTICE SAMUEL SEWALL · OLDEST STONE 1667 · PARENTS OF BENJAMIN FRANKLIN · MOTHER GOOSE · ROBERT TREAT PAINE TABLET

JOHN HANCOCK · MARY BRACKET · UNBAPTISED INFANTS · JOHN PHILIPS 1ST MAYOR OF BOSTON

BENJAMIN WOODBRIDGE
Mortally wounded by his best friend in first duel with swords fought in Boston. They quarreled over a game of cards.

ELISHA BROWN · DR. DAVID TOWNSEND SURGEON · BUNKER HILL · BOSTON MASSACRE VICTIMS AND CHRISTOPHER SNYDER · JAMES OTIS · BENJAMIN WOODBRIDGE · SAMUEL ADAMS

● *Interesting epitaphs*

GRANARY BURYGROUND - 1660

invited to tour and look at—but not touch—books on the first and second floors, and to visit the **Athenaeum Gallery,** which offers on-going exhibitions. Two groups frowned upon in most public places—dogs and smokers—are welcome. Take a tour and visit Boston's most pleasant place for musing, the high-ceilinged, airy **Reading Room** on the fifth floor, with its sunny alcoves. As **David McCord** wrote, the room "combines the best elements of the Bodleian, Monticello, the frigate *Constitution,* a greenhouse, and an old New England sitting room." Make sure you step out onto the fifth-floor terrace, with its gorgeous plantings and view of the **Granary Burying Ground.**

The Athenaeum's superb collections include **George Washington's** private library and Con-federate imprints, as well as history, biography, and English, American, and Gypsy literature. There's a notable mystery collection, too. Mem-bers and visitors who've gained special dispen-sation can actually handle many of the books, but may receive a lesson in the proper way to remove a volume from its shelf (work your fin-gers "around" its sides, *don't* pull it out from the top!). Take a ride in the charmingly hand-painted elevator, a former employee's handi-work, with its framed bookplate display. Part of the library's appeal is the way Oriental carpets and art treasures are casually strewn about. Keep an eye out for the wonderful statue of *Little Nell* on the first floor next to the stairs. Special exhibits are mounted throughout the year (pub-lic welcome), and tours are offered Tuesday and Thursday (reservations required). You'll leave full of envy for the fortunate 1,049 members.
♦ M 9AM-8PM; Tu-F 9AM-5:30PM; Sa 9AM-4PM, Oct-May. 10½ Beacon St. 227.0270 ♿

16 Goodspeed's Book Shop Charles E. Good-speed began business nearby in 1898, and a branch of his distinguished firm has been in one place or another on the Hill since the 1930s, purveying old maps, prints, and books. "We'll always be right on Beacon Hill," **George T. Goodspeed,** son of the founder, has promised his patrons. ♦ M-F 9AM-5PM; Sa 10AM-3PM. Closed mid June-mid Sept. 7 Beacon St (at Somerset St). 523.5970. Also at: 310 Washing-ton St (in the basement of the Old South Meet-ing House). 523.5970

17 Black Goose ★★$ Crowds gather regularly for the Coliseum-size Caesar salads and luxuri-ant pesto served in the midst of majestic Corin-thian columns. In good weather, find a sun-warmed table out front for lunch, and watch scholars and book-browsers coming and going beneath the **Boston Athenaeum's** dignified sandstone facade across the way. ♦ Italian

♦ M-W 11:30AM-10PM; Th-F 11:30AM-11PM; Sa 5-11PM. 21 Beacon St. Reservations rec-ommended. 720.4500 ♿

17 Lodge's Pushcart $ A compact showcase of North End Italian treats, this grocery-store-cum deli-counter serves overstuffed calzone and deep-dish *pizza grande,* along with spe-cialty coffees and the waffle cookies called *pizzelle.* ♦ Italian/Deli ♦ M-F 6AM-7:30PM; Sa 7AM-3PM. 23 Beacon St. No credit cards. 723.5353

18 The Golden Dome ★$ The Hill's legislators hold court daily in this clubby little pub, which has been called "the State House Annex," and

it's a show worth catching. Whenever there's a roll call at the State House, someone phones over and a waitress yells to the house; watch how no one moves. Those fingers just keep hoisting their precious cargo, such as the Dome's delectable turkey clubs (the turkey's roasted on the premises) and toothsome fried-potato wedges. Daily specials keep the pols happy. ♦ American ♦ M-F 11AM-11PM (kitch-en 11:30AM-3PM). 150 Bowdoin St. No credit cards. 227.7100

18 The Fill-A-Buster $ Gracious **Vaios Grigas'** friendly crew serves their hearty fare with Greek highlights—egg-lemon soup, falafel, spinach-cheese pie, and kabobs—for a clientele of pols and media types. The breakfast specials are just as bountiful, plus you can smell Grigas' fa-mous homemade muffins a block away. Once you're a regular here, they'll have your coffee poured and waiting before you've crossed the threshold. Ah, the working life. ♦ Greek/Ameri-can/Takeout ♦ M-F 7AM-4PM. 142 Bowdoin St. 523.8164

19 Tangiers ★$ This tiny stepdown grotto moves at its own languorous tempo, a world apart from the hubbub of the nearby hospital, student, and government beehives. The Leba-nese dishes are so good and cheap, you'll sus-pect the restaurant of altruistic motives. (The owner's been known to concoct a special tea to soothe a customer's sore throat.) *Lamajune, munazali, kubbeh, mujadarra*—it's a heady se-lection, so come with friends who like to share. If you're in a talkative mood, linger over an ex-otic coffee or *mentha,* a cool concoction of soda water, milk, and mint extract. The hours can be erratic, since the owner often stays up with his last customers, then opens late the next day. He deserves his rest. Call ahead to check. ♦ Middle Eastern/Takeout ♦ M-Th 11AM-3PM, 5-10PM; F-Sa 11AM-3PM, 5-11PM. 37 Bowdoin St. 367.0273

20 Lyman Paine House This understated house's distinctive character comes from its intriguing asymmetrical windows and refined Greek Revival ornamentation. ♦ 6 Joy St (at Mt. Vernon St)

21 Appalachian Mountain Club Founded in Boston in 1876, the AMC can give you plenty of information on outdoor recreation around Boston and New England. ♦ M-F 8:30AM-5:30PM. 5 Joy St. 523.0636

22 32 Mount Vernon Street Julia Ward Howe and **Dr. Samuel Gridley Howe** took up housekeeping here in the 1870s. Anthem-author Dr. Samuel is best known for founding the **Perkins Institute for the Blind,** but he also organized

the **Committee of Vigilance** to protect runaway slaves, helping hundreds of fugitives and pulling off an occasional daring rescue when word arrived that slaves were aboard the ships pulling into **Boston Harbor. General Ulysses S. Grant** and writer **Bret Harte** were among the Howes' notable houseguests. ♦ Between Joy and Walnut Sts

23 Nichols House Museum Remarkable **Miss Rose Standish Nichols,** niece of sculptor **Augustus Saint-Gaudens,** spent most of her genteel life in this house, built in 1804 by **Charles Bulfinch.** A gardening author, world traveler, peace advocate, and pioneer woman landscape architect who earned her own living, Miss Rose also founded the **International Society of Pen Pals** in her front parlor. Stop in to see the furnishings, memorabilia, and ancestors' portraits—collected by Miss Rose and her family over centuries—which she bequeathed to the public along with her home. The museum curator will take you on a witty tour. Call for hours. ♦ Admission. 55 Mt. Vernon St. 227.6993, recorded information 720.0786 &

Within the Nichols House Museum:

The Beacon Hill Garden Club Their annual spring **Hidden Gardens Tour** is your one chance to roam through greenery that otherwise can only be glimpsed tantalizingly beyond brick walls. ♦ Tour information 227.4392

24 John Callender House One of the first houses on the street, Callender's small abode cost $2,155 for the lot and $5,000 to $7,000 for construction when it was built in 1802. A lavish garden blooms behind this bargain-basement structure. ♦ 14 Walnut St (at Mt. Vernon St)

25 13, 15, and 17 Chestnut Street Charles **Bulfinch** kept busy building for patrons' daughters, and, in fact, this most famous trio of row houses was dubbed the "Daughter Houses." In 1805, while her husband, **Colonel James Swan,** cooled his heels in a French debtors' prison, Boston heiress **Hepsibah Swan** built these houses as wedding gifts for her daughters. No. 13 is a **National Historic Landmark.** ♦ At Walnut St

26 29A Chestnut Street In 1865 tragedian **Edwin Booth** was enjoying a successful run in *The Iron Chest,* a drama about a murderer

haunted by his crime, and was staying here at the home of the theater manager. But on the eve of Edwin's last performance, brother **John Wilkes Booth** murdered **President Abraham Lincoln.** Edwin's last performance was canceled, and he left secretly for New York, not appearing before an audience again for nearly a year.

27 Acorn Street Stand at the crown of this, one of Boston's skinniest streets, and watch cars shimmy and shake as they torturously climb its cobbled length. On one side, look up at the trees waving from the hidden gardens backing Mount Vernon Street; opposite are the diminutive houses that belonged to coachmen serving families in mansions on Chestnut and Mount Vernon streets. Study the entrances to Nos. 1, 3, and 5 and notice the ornamental acorns that correspond in number with each address. The humble original homeowners would be pleased to know their houses now hobnob with the best on the real-estate market.

28 Harrison Gray Otis House (1802) Ever an onward-and-upward kind of fellow, Otis abandoned a spanking-new manse on **Cambridge Street,** also by **Charles Bulfinch,** to take up residence in this fashionable neighborhood of his own making. One of the only houses on the Hill with ample elbow room, towering No. 85 was intended to set a Joneses standard of freestanding mansions on generous landscaped grounds, but Boston's population boom soon made this impossible. The structure is now on the **National Register of Historic Places.** ♦ 85 Mt. Vernon St

Building Blocks: How Charles Bulfinch Shaped the City

For his enduring stamp on Boston buildings and topography, **Charles Bulfinch** (1763-1844) deserved to have many more places in the city named after him; after all, painter **John Singleton Copley's** name appears all over, and that Anglophile left America for good on the eve of the Revolution. No matter; this architectural genie didn't hanker after fame and fortune.

The first Bostonian to take up architecture as a profession, he was a creative dynamo who began life in a notable Boston family, then skirted poverty throughout his adulthood because he was a poor businessman and gave too much free architectural advice. A patriot through-and-through, Bulfinch nonetheless emulated English architecture, infusing his concern for harmony, hierarchy, public order, and propriety—he was Boston's police chief, after all, and head selectman for many years. Bulfinch didn't stop at buildings, either; he had grand visions for entire city segments. A pioneer urban designer, he was one of the **Mount Vernon Proprietors,** engineering the shaping of Beacon Hill. With entire streets and scores of houses, public buildings, banks, churches, hospitals, offices, and schools to his credit, it was Bulfinch who turned an 18th-century town into a 19th-century city. A happier chapter of Bulfinch's life was spent in Washington, DC, where he felt much more appreciated—well-paid at last—and contributed to the design of the United States Capitol.

29 Louisburg Square Suddenly, the houses of the Hill open wide and you're swung in a new direction at the edge of one of Boston's most serenely patrician places: Louisburg—be sure to pronounce that "s"; you'll horrify locals if you say "Louie-burg!"—Square. If Bulfinch had had his way, the square would be three times larger and three decades older, but the **Mount Vernon Proprietors** didn't act on his 1826 plan. The redbrick row houses and the oval park they overlook aren't extraordinary in themselves; it's the square's timeless aura that has always appealed to Bostonians. Deteriorating statues of *Aristides the Just* and *Columbus* coolly survey all comers.

Finally a literary success, **Louisa May Alcott** brought her perennially penniless family to No. 10, where mercury poisoning—she got it while a Civil War nurse—slowly crippled her. No. 20 is a happier address: here soprano **Jenny Lind** ("The Swedish Nightingale") skyrocketed to fame by **P.T. Barnum,** was married in 1852 to her accompanist. **Samuel Gray Ward,** a representative of Lind's London bankers, also lived here; among his banking coups was arranging America's purchase of Alaska from Russia for $7.5 million. ♦ Located between Pinckney and Mt. Vernon Sts

30 Pinckney Street Begin at its base, and with luck you'll time your arrival at the summit as the late afternoon sunlight turns molten, and the trees become sparkling lanterns stretching down toward the Charles River. Called by one author the "Cinderella street" of Beacon Hill, Pinckney was once the dividing line between those who were and those who were not. Pinckney's buildings—many handsome, many humble—are utterly delightful. ♦ Between Joy St and Embankment Rd

30 62 Pinckney Street Built in 1846 and owned by **George S. Hilliard,** this residence was a stop on the underground railroad that ran through Boston in the 1850s. Whether Hilliard knew fugitives were harbored in his home is debatable, but his staunchly abolitionist wife certainly did. Workmen discovered the secret attic chamber in the 1920s. ♦ At Anderson St

31 Boston English High School The first interracial public school in Boston, accepting boys only, opened in this austere cruciform edifice—now condos—in 1844. ♦ 65 Anderson St (at Pinckney St)

32 Pie-Shaped House The interior reveals what the exterior conceals: squeezed between its neighbors, this house comes to a point like a piece of pie. Look at the roofline for a clue. ♦ 56 Pinckney St

33 House of Odd Windows When **Ralph Waldo Emerson's** nephew renovated this former carriage house in 1884, he turned the facade into a montage of windows—each singular and superbly positioned—in an inexplicable burst of artistry. Notice the quirked eyebrow dormer at the top. ♦ 24 Pinckney St

33 20 Pinckney Street Bronson Alcott, mystic, educator, "other-worldly philosopher," and notoriously bad provider, brought his wife and four daughters to live here from 1852 to 1855. The close-knit family and their struggle with poverty inspired daughter **Louisa's** heartstring-tugger *Little Women.* ♦ Between Joy and Anderson Sts

34 9 1/2 Pinckney Street The Hill's hodgepodge evolution created labyrinthine patterns of streets and housing that led to hidden gardens, and even hidden houses (No. 74 1/2 is the famous "Hidden House," left to your imagination). The iron gate here at No. 9 1/2 opens onto a tunnel that passes through the house and into

Beacon Hill

a courtyard skirted by three hidden houses. Crouch down for a glimpse. ♦ At Joy St

34 Middleton-Glapion House George Middleton, a black jockey, horsebreaker, and Revolutionary War veteran, and hairdresser **Louis Glapion,** collaborated in the late 1700s on this minute clapboard house, so untouched by time that the pair might have strolled out the front door this morning. ♦ 5 Pinckney St

35 Myrtle Street When Brahmin elegance begins to stultify, seek out this narrow, down-to-earth street. Tenements and Greek Revival row houses commune along Myrtle's length with the laundries, markets, shoe-repair shops, playground, pizza parlor, and other unfashionable establishments that make this the most for-real neighborhood on the Hill. Look at the rooflines and spot the funky gardens that aren't found on any "Hidden Gardens of Beacon Hill" tour. Perched here in the heights, you can see the lazy **Charles River** and **Massachusetts Institute of Technology.**

36 African Meeting House Free black artisans built this meeting house (pictured above) in 1806, and **Asher Benjamin's** architecture influenced its town-house style. A **National Historic Landmark,** it's the oldest black church still standing in the US. Nicknamed "Black Faneuil Hall" during the abolitionist era, here is where **William Lloyd Garrison** founded the **New England Anti-Slavery Society** on 6 January 1832. Late last century, blacks began migrating to the South End and Roxbury; by the '20s, Irish and Jewish immigrants had moved in. The Meeting House was sold to an Orthodox Jewish congregation and remained a synagogue until purchased by the **Museum of Afro American History** in the 1970s. ♦ 8 Smith Ct

Restaurants/Clubs: Red	**Hotels:** Blue
Shops/ 🌿 Outdoors: Green	**Sights/Culture:** Black

36 Museum of Afro American History The first grammar and primary school for black children in Boston opened in 1834, replacing the school that had met in the Meeting House basement. It was named for **Abiel Smith,** the white businessman who bequeathed the funds for its construction. The school closed 20 years later when the state upheld the demand for integrated schools, ending the practice of taxing blacks to support schools that excluded their children. Now you can explore African-American history in New England in the former school building. ♦ Free. M-F 10AM-4PM. 46 Joy St (at Smith Ct). 742.1854

Beacon Hill

36 William C. Nell House America's first published black historian and a member of **William Lloyd Garrison's** circle, Nell boarded in this 18th-century wooden farmhouse from 1851 to 1856. He led the crusade for integrated public schools in the city, and his **Equal School Association** organized the boycott of the neighboring **Abiel Smith School** until the state legislature finally abolished restrictions on black children's access to public schools. Black clothing-dealer **James Scott,** who purchased Nell's house and ran it as a rooming house starting in 1865, sheltered fugitive slaves here. The structure is now a **National Historic Landmark.** ♦ 3 Smith Ct

37 Venice Ristorante ★$ This is the kind of place you can walk by a hundred times without noticing, but stop in once and try the food and you're sure to become a regular. Crisp-crusted pizzas topped with ultrafresh ingredients even come in a "personal" size for one. Or choose from an enormous selection of salads, pastas, subs, and daily specials. If the weather's lousy, there's free delivery. ♦ Pizza/Takeout ♦ M-Th 11AM-1AM; F-Sa 11AM-2AM; Su noon-1AM. 204 Cambridge St (at S. Russell St). No credit cards. 227.2094 ⚹

38 Rollins Place Countless passersby have glanced down Rollins Place and been charmed by this little white house tucked snugly at its end. But the inviting Southern-style facade is really a false front. The architectural trompe l'oeil masks an old cliff running between Revere and lower Phillips streets. Continue down the same side of the street and slip into **Goodwin Place** (No. 73), **Sentry Hill Place,** and **Bellingham Court,** all charming cul-de-sacs along Revere Street that also disguise the cliff, but without such fanciful deceit. ♦ 27 Revere St

The American Revolution was a turning point for African-Americans in Massachusetts; at its end, there were more free blacks than slaves.

Boston's land mass today covers more than four times the area of the original Shawmut Peninsula. The city's original 785 acres or so have expanded to more than 4,000 acres, owing to landfill projects that began in 1803 and continue today.

39 Lewis Hayden House A fugitive slave himself, Hayden (pictured above) became one of the most famous abolitionists, and his 1833 home a station on the underground railroad. **William** and **Ellen Craft,** a famous couple who escaped by masquerading as master and slave, stayed here. And in 1853 **Harriet Beecher Stowe,** who had already published *Uncle Tom's Cabin,* visited Hayden and met 13 newly escaped slaves—the first she'd ever met. The Haydens reputedly kept two kegs of gunpowder in the basement, threatening to blow up the house if anyone tried to search it. No one did. ♦ 66 Phillips St

40 Phillips Drug Don't bother to go in now, but if your head starts pounding after the bars close or you wake up at night with a killer cough, remember Phillips—it's open 24 hours a day in a city where so much closes so early. (Prices can be steep, though.) Don't forget the pay phones inside; they're few and far between around the Hill. You can also depend on getting a cab out front. ♦ Daily 24 hours. 155 Charles St. 523.1028 ⚹

41 The King & I ★$ For the past decade or so, Boston's passionate, some say obsessive, affair with Thai cuisine has created so many offspring that it's often hard to tell them apart. This bright, courteous restaurant has always stood out, however, for its entrancing, delicate versions of dishes like Paradise beef. For an after-dinner treat of a different sort, cross Charles Street and enter the passage to the left of the **Charles Street Animal Clinic.** You'll see an arch framing trees, the river, passing cars. Enter here and admire the curved charm of **West Hill Place.** ♦ Thai ♦ M-Th 11:30AM-2:30PM, 5-9:45PM; F 11:30AM-2:30PM, 5-10:45PM; Sa 5-10:45PM; Su 5-9:45PM. 145 Charles St. Reservations recommended for dinner. 227.3320. Also at: 259 Newbury St. 437.9611

42 Period Furniture Hardware Company The 75-year-old shop is aglow with gleaming surfaces to stroke. Many antiquers have abandoned their wearisome Holy Grail quest for such-and-such genuine wall sconce from such-and-such period for the somewhat as satisfying pleasures of these reproductions of hardware from the 18th century onward. If only the price tags weren't the real thing. ♦ M-F 8:30AM-5PM; Sa 10AM-2PM. 123 Charles St. 227.0758

42 Boston Antique Coop I & II These two co-operatives in one building set out a tempting smorgasbord of American, Asian, and European antiques. The place has all the ambience of a garage sale, but it's great fun and local antique dealers snoop about here, too. Downstairs at Coop I, four dealers display sterling, porcelain, paintings, jewelry, bottles, vintage photography, bric-a-brac, and more. Upstairs at Coop II, eight dealers specialize in decorative items, vintage clothing, and textiles. The items change constantly, so check back from time to time. ♦ Coop I M-Sa 11AM-7PM; Su noon-6PM. Coop II daily 10AM-5PM. 119 Charles St. Coop I: 227.9810, Coop II: 227.9811

43 Danish Country Antique Furniture Brightly colored rugs, tableware, crafts, and folk art can be found in, on, and among the handsome blond furniture dating from the mid-18th century onward. So often antique furniture cringes from returning to active service, but owner **James Kilroy's** Danish desks, armoires, tables, chests, and chairs sturdily welcome the prospect. His shop is cheery after the dark and dour environments of many other Hill establishments. ♦ M-W 10AM-6PM; Th 10AM-7PM; F-Sa 10AM-5PM; Su 1-5PM. 138 Charles St. 227.1804

43 Marika's You'll need to navigate carefully through this crowded collection of glassware, furniture, paintings, tapestries, and treasures from all around the world. Owner **Matthew Raisz's** grandmother Marika emigrated from Budapest and founded this shop in 1944. It's prized particularly for its extraordinary jewelry. ♦ Tu-Sa 10AM-5PM. 130 Charles St. 523.4520

44 George Gravert Antiques The pleasant proprietor of this shop has been in the antiques business for more than 30 years, specializing in European furniture and accessories that are clearly chosen by an expert eye. Something timeless and trustworthy about the place will make you want to linger even after you've ogled everything twice. Although he caters mainly to wholesalers, Gravert won't mind at all if you come in and browse. ♦ M-F 10AM-5PM. 122 Charles St. 227.1593 &

44 Helen's Leather Care to prance about in python or buckle on some buffalo? You can even opt for ostrich in this leather emporium, which boasts an exotic collection of handmade boots. The mammoth wooden boot out front tells you you've arrived at New England's biggest Western boot dealer. Helen's also sells shoes, clothing, briefcases, backpacks, and other leather whatnots in many popular brands. ♦ M-Sa 10AM-6PM; Su noon-6PM. 110 Charles St. 742.2077

45 Elements Antique-obsessed Charles Street is not exactly what you'd call trendy, so it's refreshing to see a forward-looking enterprise such as Elements set up shop. Billing itself—

tongue in cheek—as "the ultimate factory store," this producer of avant-garde accessories devotes 80 percent of its space to its own products (from vases to jewelry) and the rest to works by local artisans. The shop is definitely cutting-edge—and fun. ♦ M-F 11AM-7PM; Sa-Su 11AM-6PM. 103A Charles St. 277.3029. Also at: 18-20 Union Park Sq. 457.9990

45 Kiku Sui Gallery The name means "floating chrysanthemum." The largest of its kind in New England, this gallery is one of Charles Street's more exotic residents, with an unusual inventory of reasonably priced Japanese woodblock prints from the past three centuries, ceramics,

Beacon Hill

books, cards, kimonos, flower-arranging materials, and other gifts. You can also get Japanese translated here. The carefully composed window displays reflect owner **David Welker's** fascination with Japanese art forms. ♦ M, W-Su 11AM-6PM. 101 Charles St. 227.4288

45 The Coffee Connection ★$ The coffee is unsurpassable; walk in and let the potent, sultry aroma of the beans engulf you. Sit at one of the tiny windowside tables and nurse your brew or, better still, carry it over to the Public Garden. They also do a brisk mail-order business (call 800/284.5282). ♦ Cafe/Takeout ♦ M-F 7AM-6PM; Sa 8AM-6PM; Su 9AM-5PM. 97 Charles St (at Pinckney St). 227.3812. & Also at: 2 Faneuil Hall Marketplace. 227.3821; Copley Pl. 353.1963; 36 JFK St, Harvard Sq, Cambridge. 492.4881

46 Romano's Bakery & Coffee Shop ★★$ It's short on decor but long on great cheap food, so people keep wending their way back to this cozy downstairs coffee shop. The clutter of newspapers tells you to sit, relax, take your time. The fresh-baked goods, quiches, salads, sandwiches, and soups always hit the spot at lunchtime, and leave you with plenty of money to splurge on dinner. If you're in a dangerous mood, grab a lethal pastry or chocolate something to rev you up for the afternoon. ♦ Cafe/Takeout ♦ Daily 7:30AM-8PM. 89 Charles St. No credit cards. 523.8704

46 The Sevens ★★$ This is the neighborhood's favorite pub. Often crowded, with free-for-all conversations bouncing between the bar and the booths, the gregarious Sevens is a good place to sit back and sip a draft when the world seems a little lonely. Try the pub lunch—a generous, satisfying sandwich and bargain-priced mug of draft beer. The chili, soups, and salads are good, too. ♦ Bar food ♦ Daily 11:30AM-midnight. 77 Charles St. No credit cards. 523.9074

Boston's nickname, "The Hub," comes from an article published by Oliver Wendell Holmes—doctor, author, and father of the famous jurist—in *The Atlantic Monthly* in 1858. Holmes wrote that the "Boston State House is the hub of the solar system." Bostonians have since stretched his grandiose image to include the entire city.

46 The Hungry i ★★$$$$ If you're claustrophobic, think twice before stepping down into this extremely intimate restaurant. Yet for many, this is one of the city's most romantic choices. For Sunday brunch, you can also dine alfresco in a diminutive courtyard. Fish and game star in the brief but inventive menu. ♦ American ♦ M-Sa 6-9:30PM; Su 11AM-2:30PM, 6-9:30PM. 71½ Charles St. Reservations are recommended. 227.3524

47 Eugene Galleries It's easy to lose all track of time in this enthralling emporium of old prints, maps, postcards, photographs, and oddments of every sort—a Victorian dustpan, sheet music, paperweights, fire-and-brimstone sermons, and

Beacon Hill

a *History of the Great Fire of Boston,* to name a few. Specializing in Boston views and maps, Eugene Galleries is the ideal place after touring the city to see how your favorite sights have been commemorated through the centuries. Some 250 other categories are available, too: botanical, medical, legal, women, transportation, and on and on. ♦ M-Sa 10:30AM-5:30PM. 76 Charles St. 227.3062

COURTESY OF JOHN SHARRATT ASSOCIATES

48 Charles Street Meeting House It's a shame they stuck a food shop in the front of this forthright structure (pictured above)—even if it's a popular outpost of the inimitable **Rebecca's** cafe. An octagonal belfry crowns the rectangular central tower, a handsome ensemble by **Asher Benjamin,** the architect who designed **Faneuil Hall** and inherited Bulfinch's unofficial role of architect laureate of Boston. Completed in 1807, the meeting house's first congregation, the **Baptist Society,** found the nearby Charles River convenient for baptisms. Although abolitionists often orated from the pulpit—including **William Lloyd Garrison, Frederick Douglass, Harriet Tubman,** and **Sojourner Truth**—church seating was segregated. **Timothy Gilbert,** a member of the congregation, challenged the tradition and was expelled for inviting several black friends to sit in a white pew. (Gilbert then founded the **Tremont Temple** in 1842, Boston's first integrated place of worship.) The **African Methodist Episcopal Church** met here from 1867 until the 1930s, with the Unitarian Universalists moving in after the Depression. Later, when the **Afro-American Culture Center** was located here, poet **Langston Hughes** gave readings. Renovated in 1982 by **John Sharratt Associates** and put on the **National Register of Historic Places,** shops and private offices have since replaced the community activities that took place here. ♦ 121 Mt. Vernon St (at Charles St)

49 The Church of the Advent The story goes that flamboyant parishioner **Isabella Stewart Gardner,** who founded her signature museum in the Fenway, scrubbed the church steps during Lent as penance. The story also goes that proper Bostonians sniffed and wondered why Isabella wasn't required to scour the entire edifice. This Gothic Revival church (completed in 1888 by **Sturgis and Brigham** and pictured above) distributes its great girth on an awkward site through a chain of conical-roofed chapels, accommodating nearby domestic architecture as a good Hill neighbor should. The interiors are also ingeniously arranged, splendidly embellished. The church boasts one of the finest sets of carillon bells in the United States and a restful garden. ♦ Mass M, W 7:30AM, 6PM; Tu-F 7:30AM; Sa 9AM; Su 8AM, 9AM, 11AM. 30 Brimmer St (at Mt. Vernon St). 523.2377

50 Sunflower Castle Remodeled in 1878 by **Clarence Luce,** this amusing Queen Anne cottage began life in 1840 as a plain-Jane anonymous little building; now it takes its name from the enormous, gaudy sunflower ornament pressed on its brow. Maybe boredom with Beacon Hill's de rigueur palette and mincing detail inspired Luce to paint the stuccoed first floor brilliant yellow and sheath the second story in China-red tile. Whimsy now unleashed, he added exuberantly carved brackets and posts, and a griffin. ♦ 130 Mt. Vernon St (at River St)

Known as "The Way to the Poorhouse" in the 17th century because of the almshouse at the corner of Park Street, Beacon Street began as an undeveloped area on the edge of Boston. Here the free-spirited Reverend Blaxton cultivated the first named variety of American apple—"Blaxton's Yellow Sweeting"—in his beloved orchard near today's Charles Street. Formally laid out in 1708, Beacon Street began to acquire its present sedate and stately character when its brick row houses, most in early Federal style, were built in the first half of the 19th century, following the State House's lead. This bright thoroughfare bordering the Common became known as "the sunny street that holds the sifted few."

| Restaurants/Clubs: Red | Hotels: Blue |
| Shops/ 🌳 Outdoors: Green | Sights/Culture: Black |

51 Another Season ★★★$$$ London-born owner **Odette Bery** proves the English can cook. Her monthly menus are eclectic and international; her food modern, understated, often mercifully free of butter and cream, and served in petite portions. The well-heeled clientele includes many Hill regulars, who don't mind if their knees bump in the cramped dining alcoves because they're fond of the Gay Nineties bistro murals, impressed with the inventive turns beef medallions take here, and enamored of the expressive chocolate or the fruit-based desserts. Insist on the front room. Stroll up to Mount Vernon's summit afterward, and pronounce the evening perfect. ♦ Continental ♦ M, Sa 6-10PM; Tu-F 11:45AM-2PM, 6-10PM. 97 Mt. Vernon St. Reservations are recommended and are required for dinner on Friday and Saturday. 367.0880

52 Charles Street Supply A really good hardware store is an alluring place. Even if you've never gone to war with weeds or handled a 2x4, you'll itch to tackle some project, *any* project, at the sight of all the handy wares spilling onto this overstuffed store's sidewalks. Sure, the prices are high, but then, gregarious owner **Richard Gurnon's** operation dispenses a lot more than tools and how-tos. "We're the friendly store," he says, and it's true. The staff often steers disoriented people in the right direction, and in the neighborhood they're famous for doing "a lot of those little things" that smooth the bumpy course of urban life. If you need a converter, by the way, stop in. ♦ M-F 8AM-6PM; Sa 8:30AM-6PM; Su noon-5PM. 54-56 Charles St. 367.9046

52 Blackstone's of Beacon Hill Owner **Richard Dowd** stocks reproductions for historical societies all across the United States, so this is the place to come for trivets, candlesnuffers, doorknockers, and more of the same in brass and mahogany. Blackstone's also has handmade stained-glass picture frames, and porcelain and enamel renditions of the Public Garden's famous **Swan Boats** designed for the shop by **Limoges** and **Crummles.** ♦ M-F 10AM-6PM; Sa 9AM-6PM; Su 1-6PM. 46 Charles St. 227.4646

52 Paramount Restaurant $ This is a Greek diner squeezed into a Charles Street shoebox. A gathering spot for locals, it offers typical greasy-spoon breakfasts (self-served and very cheap) that one is expected to consume with dispatch during busy hours. You'll know if

you're too slow. Yet *so* many are dedicated to the place, there must be some larger appeal a sensitive soul will perceive. Nothing's small here—try the Greek salad, moussaka, or souvlakia. ♦ Greek/American/Takeout ♦ M-Sa 7AM-10PM; Su 8AM-9PM. 44 Charles St. 523.8832 &

52 Bel Canto ★$ This local chain cooks up tasty *tortas*—thick-crusted (wheat or white) pizzas —perfect for two, so come with an even-numbered party or include a renegade who'll happily tackle a calzone instead. Mix and match toppings to your heart's content, but if you order fresh garlic, advise the waiter that you have no fear of vampires and don't need an

Beacon Hill

entire head thrown on. ♦ Pizza/Takeout ♦ M-Th, Su 11AM-10PM; F-Sa 11AM-11PM. 42 Charles St. 523.5575 &

52 James Billings Antiques & Interiors The one handling the antiques is **James Billings**, who concentrates on 18th-century English and Continental furniture. **Lise Davis,** his wife and partner, is an interior decorator who specializes in the ever-more-popular English countryhouse look. Both belong to the British Antique Dealers Association and have been in business in Essex, England, for 30 years, and in Boston for eight. Their talents blend beautifully in this spacious, opulently appointed shop. It's impossible to pass by without peering within, even if the owners' particular interests aren't your cup of tea. As one glance will inform you, everything comes dear here. ♦ M-Sa 10AM-6PM. 34 Charles St (at Chestnut St). 367.9533

53 Victorian Bouquet One of Boston's most inspired florists, **Susan Bates** uses locally grown flowers and Holland imports, as well as dried and silk varieties. Her bouquets are simply great. There's no access for the handicapped, but the attentive staff willingly provides streetside service. ♦ M-Sa 9AM-6PM. 53A Charles St. 367.6648

53 Ristorante Toscano ★★★$$ Conscientiously patrolled by its ultra-civilized owners, this brisk, friendly Florentine trattoria offers a diverting lineup of daily specials, headlining such luscious stars as rack of lamb, smoked-salmon pasta, and carpaccio. This is one  of the only places you're likely to encounter *bolito misto* (Italian boiled dinner). Start out rifling the bread basket for *focaccia* and *schiacciata,* and end in dignified rapture over tiramisù and espresso. Sophisticated and self-assured, this restaurant is one of Boston's favorites. ♦ Italian ♦ M-Th 11:30AM-2:30PM, 5:30-10PM; F-Sa 11:30AM-2:30PM, 5:30-10:30PM; Su 5:30-10PM. 41 Charles St. Valet parking evenings. Reservations recommended. 723.4090

54 Cedar Lane Way When evening has nearly crept over the Hill, enter this skinny lane from Chestnut Street. Say hello to the cats in the windows of the tiny dwellings, and use sonar to sidestep the residents' trash and potted plants while you look up and admire their gardens spilling over brick retaining walls. The lane turns to cobblestones after crossing Pinckney Street and ends beneath a lantern's intimate glow.

55 The Book Store Just a few strides away from the commotion of Charles Street, this little shop seems to shrink back into the safe embrace of its residential surroundings. A familiar presence on the Hill, as the unassuming name implies, The Book Store has catered to residents for 40

Beacon Hill

years. Soft-spoken owners **Susan Timken** and **Linda Cox** stock many books that no one else seems to have, with wonderful choices in art and children's books. They'll special-order anything for you. ♦ M-F 10AM-6PM; Sa 10AM-5PM. 76 Chestnut St. 742.4531

56 Il Dolce Momento ★$ We'll tell you up front that the service is inexplicably harried and harebrained, and the pastries and cappuccino only so-so in this redbrick storefront caffè. But take a look around, and you'll know right away why you came. Long after the last drop of espresso is a memory, people linger here gazing out at the Charles Street parade. Every table is near a plate-glass window, making this a good place to write a long letter on a winter afternoon. Plus, the *biscotti di Prato*—say "almond cookies," or you'll get a blank look—are great dunkers and the gelati *perfetto,* from the amaretto to the *zuppa inglese.* ♦ Caffè ♦ Daily 8AM-midnight. 30 Charles St (at Chestnut St). No credit cards. 720.0477 ⚬

56 Lauriat's Housed in a handsome former hotel, Lauriat's bookstore offers the Hill's biggest selection. They sell a little bit of everything, with strong sections in cookbooks, gardening, and guides to the Boston area. ♦ M-Sa 9:30AM-10PM; Su noon-6PM. 20 Charles St. 523.0188 ⚬ Also at: 45 Franklin St. 482.2850; Copley Pl. 262.8857

57 O'Tansey's Have you ever seen a barber shop like this one? As one Hill resident put it, "you're absolutely convinced you can get as good a haircut elsewhere for half the price, but there's just something about the atmosphere at Rick's." The brick-and-wood surroundings, comfy leather furniture, and grandfather's clock ticking away in the corner will make you feel right at home in this cozy two-chair shop. Ever-cheerful **Rick O'Tansey** cuts the men, and his associate, **Moya,** cuts the women. Reader, please note: This shop may move to a new location so call ahead to confirm the address. ♦ M-Sa 7:30AM-6:30PM. 21 River St. 227.2335 ⚬

58 Rebecca's ★★★$$ Yes, it's trendy, and you won't want your heart to suspect how much butter the succulent monkfish is swimming in. But silence those qualms and enjoy owner **Rebecca Caras'** consistently good formula of seasonal bounty, which made this cheerful bistro such a success that she's launched little take-out satellites all over the city. Watch the chefs in the open kitchen assemble excellent omelets, salads, and pasta concoctions, or ogle the chorus line of desserts, which always includes pies with sky-high crusts. To avoid the crush, come early for dinner while the loyal clientele are still at their health clubs. While waiting for a table on a late summer's evening, walk down Chestnut Street toward the river and look for No. 101 on your right. Surrounding a charming interior court, these condos look like English mews. And on your way back, watch for No. 90, an architectural oddity on the opposite side of the street. Wheelchair access is available for takeout only. ♦ American/Takeout ♦ Daily 11:30AM-4PM, 5:30-11:30PM. Valet parking evenings. Reservations recommended. 21 Charles St. 742.9747

59 Beacon Hill Thrift Shop Don't be hoity-toity about stopping in here; Boston's resourceful Brahmins would surely look askance at anyone silly enough to snub a bargain. One of Boston's oldest thrift shops, it's pleasingly cramped and cluttered with knickknacks and doodads, plus some truly fabulous finds. Manager **Elizabeth Moore** is always ready to make a deal, ably assisted by a loyal corps of women volunteers from the Hill. All proceeds benefit the New England Baptist Hospital League Nursing Scholarships. ♦ M-Th, Sa 11AM-4PM, during daylight-saving time; M-Th, Sa 10:30AM-3:30PM, rest of year. 15 Charles St. 742.2323

59 De Luca's Market This market has all sorts of gourmet fixings for a sumptuous picnic on the esplanade or supper by a fire. (If it's Oreos you're looking for, you can find them, too.) Expect lines and tight squeezes because everyone on the Hill shops at De Luca's. Of course, such quality commands a high price. There's a little bit of everything here, but if you can't find your favorite treat, they'll order it. In business for 87 years, De Luca's wangled a wine-and-liquor license (a major feat on Beacon Hill) some years back and purveys an extensive selection. ♦ M-Sa 7AM-10:30PM. Closed Christmas Day. 11 Charles St. 523.4343. Also at: 239 Newbury St. 262.5990

60 Hampshire House ★★★$$$ This 1909 town house, borrowing from Greek and Georgian Revival and Federal styles, was built for Brahmins by a Brahmin (**Ogden Codman**), and the silver-spoon spirit still thrives. Try Sunday brunch in the **Library Grill** on the second floor. The polished paneling, leather chairs, and mooseheads create a men's-club milieu, which becomes more and more pleasant, just fine, really, when the splendid eggs Benedict and crisp corned-beef hash arrive. Then it's time for a second impeccable Bloody Mary, while the piano playing gently eases the morning along. Return some evening with your favorite person to gaze at the Public Garden. ♦ American ♦ M-Sa 5:30-10PM; Su 10:30AM-2:30PM, 5:30-10PM. 84 Beacon St. Free parking 5-10PM. Reservations are recommended for dinner. 227.9600 ♿

Within Hampshire House:

Bull & Finch ★$ The bar in the TV sitcom "Cheers" was modeled after this pub, and all the brouhaha has eclipsed a lot of its authentic charm. Still, if you time it right, you can side-step the boisterous throngs of tourists and college students by slipping in at a quiet hour for a beer and one of the great burgers or other pub-style fare. One of Boston's nicest bartenders, **Eddie Doyle,** works here days. Doyle has raised hundreds of thousands of dollars over the years for all kinds of causes. Look for the paper placemats—Doyle's design. ♦ Bar food ♦ Daily 11AM-closing. Dancing F-Sa 10PM-closing. 84 Beacon St. 227.9605 ♿

61 Public Garden The Boston Common belongs to the people and is bedraggled from their free-wheeling use, but the Public Garden belongs to the city (see the map on the following page) and has a much more manicured look. Though you can't lounge as freely on the grass here, the garden is an idyllic, lush retreat that always seems larger than it truly is. Artists love to paint here, and the advertising and film communities stage photo shoots all over. Several out-of-the-way bowers offer haven from urban tumult. And there's no better place for a springtime romance to bloom.

One of the oldest botanical gardens in America, the garden began as desolate, soggy salt-marsh flats located along a great bay of the Charles River estuary. Ropewalks spanned the area (see the description below), and Bostonians clammed and fished when the tides allowed. In April 1775 the British soldiers embarked by boat, near the garden's **Charles Street Gate,** for **Lexington** and **Concord**—the **American Revolution's** debut—catapulting **Paul Revere** and **William Dawes** on their historic horseback dashes to warn the populace and alert the

Minutemen. There's also a remarkable history of outspoken citizen involvement enshrined in the Public Garden. Throughout the early 1800s real-estate developers hankered after its 24 acres, only to be thwarted again and again by vigilant citizens dreaming of a magnificent botanical park. Bostonians finally ratified a bill in 1859 that deemed the garden forever public. That same year, **George Meacham,** a novice local architect, won $100 for his English-inspired vision of a Public Garden dominated by a sinuous pond and ribboned with paths. His grandiloquent scheme was modestly altered in the final form. Today the garden is watched over and beautified by "garden" angels: **The Friends of the Public Garden,** formed in the 1970s.

Within the Public Garden:

Footbridge Enter by taking the ceremonial **Haffenreffer Walk** off Charles Street and step onto the spunky, whimsical footbridge, designed in 1867 by **William G. Preston.** It's an appealing exaggeration of the engineering marvel of its day—the suspension bridge. Repaired and reinforced, the bridge's spiderweb cables are only decorative now. Lean back against the baby bridge and gaze across the garden toward

COURTESY OF THE BOSTONIAN SOCIETY

Ropemaking, one of America's early industries, began in Boston in the 1630s. By the 19th century, ropewalks (long covered buildings where ropes were manufactured) were commonplace fixtures on the town's outskirts. Buildings extended up to a thousand feet long to house the cumbersome hemp-winding process. Inside, the ropemaker walked backward as the hemp fiber unwound from the skein encircling his waist and was simultaneously twisted into yarn. Ropewalks once crisscrossed the Public Garden and the north slope of Beacon Hill, presenting physical barriers that even influenced how neighborhoods developed. And since a coating of hot pitch was often applied to the rope as a preservative, ropewalks were smelly, hazardous firetraps avoided by townspeople out strolling the streets.

Beacon Street, ignoring the ugly Downtown stretch in the distance along Tremont Street. From bridgeside, watch Boston's entire socio-economic spectrum pass by on the walkway.

 Swan Boats and Lagoon One of Boston's most famous sights, the Swan Boats cruise serenely on the four-foot-deep, four-acre lagoon among dozens of chatty ducks waiting for hand-outs. A pair of swans, ceremoniously escorted to the lagoon every spring, sail snootily about. Rowboats, canoes, and a little side-wheeler named the *Dolly Varden* once plied these waters, but the Swan Boats have reigned alone now for more than a century. Their creator, **Robert Paget,** an English immigrant and ship-

Beacon Hill

builder, was inspired by **Richard Wagner's** opera *Lohengrin,* in which the hero crosses a river in a boat drawn by a swan.

Paget's ancestors still own the quaint fleet he launched in 1877. The six existing boats now carry up to 20 passengers per boat instead of the original four, and weigh two tons. The oldest, *Big Bertha,* dates from 1918. Only children are thrilled by this 15-minute figure-eight voyage pedal-powered at two miles per hour—but if you're tired, it's a fine way to rest your feet. In the winter the lagoon becomes a picturesque skating pond (skate rentals are available; call 482.7400). ♦ Nominal fee for Swan Boats. Daily 10AM-5PM, early Apr-mid Sept; daily 10AM-4PM, mid Sept-early Apr. 522.1966

 Plants and Trees Amble amid the colorful legacy of **William Doogue,** the garden's controversial superintendent from 1878 to 1906, who instituted its famous Victorian floral displays, rotated seasonally. Some Bostonians griped about Doogue's extravagant use of showy hothouse plants, including palms, cacti, and yucca; in 1888, some 90,000 plants were laid out in 150 beds. But most people were thrilled, and Doogue's style has endured, though on a more modest scale. Nearly 600 trees of more than a hundred varieties grow in the garden, most labeled with their Latin and common names, a practice inspired by the 19th-century passion for learning. The garden's weeping willows offer splendid shade for reading. Pick a tree to revisit over the years.

Statues Sure, some of the garden's sculpture is mediocre, but all in all it's an oddly appealing lot. The most striking statue is Charlestown native **Thomas Ball's** gallant *George Washington* on horseback (erected in 1869), facing Commonwealth Avenue (near the Arlington Street Gate). Anecdotes tell how Ball was obsessed with accurately depicting the triumphant patriot's steed; he frequented local stables and employed a famous local charger, **Black Prince,** as his model. To George's right (facing Commonwealth Avenue) is the granite and red-and-white-marble *Ether Fountain,* the garden's oldest monument, donated in 1867 to honor the first use of anesthesia, 21 years before, at Massachusetts General Hospital in Boston.

Some others to seek out: Facing Boylston Street are abolitionist senator *Charles Sumner* (sculpted by **Thomas Ball**); antislavery spokesman *Wendell Phillips* (**Daniel Chester French** did the statue in 1914; **Henry Bacon** designed the base); and Polish independence leader *Tadeusz Kosciuszko* (sculpted in 1927 by **Theo Alice Ruggles Kitson**). By the Charles Street Gate is philanthropist *Edward Everett Hale* (completed in 1912 by **Bela Lyon Pratt**), patriot **Nathan Hale's** nephew. Flamboyant Unitarian preacher and transcendentalist *William Ellery Channing* (sculpted in 1903 by **Herbert Adams**) faces Arlington Street. Channing's writing influenced many young authors of his day, including **Ralph Waldo Emerson.** Three fountain statues, all by women, portray images of childhood. Near Arlington Street is sculptor **Mary E. Moore's** *Small Child* (erected in 1929); and near Charles Street are *Triton Babies* (by **Anna Coleman Ladd**) and *Bagheera* (erected in 1986) by **Lilian Swann Saarinen,** wife of architect **Eero Saarinen,** which illustrates the scene from **Rudyard Kipling's** *Jungle Book* in which the black panther Bagheera tries to trap an owl.

Ducklings The newest and best-beloved garden statues (unveiled in 1987) are Boston artist **Nancy Schön's** larger-than-life bronzes of Mrs. Mallard and her eight ducklings, the heroes of **Robert McCloskey's** children's tale *Make Way for Ducklings* (published in 1941). As the story tells, after stopping all traffic on Beacon Street, the canard clan marches off to rendezvous at the lagoon with Mr. Mallard. It's easy to spot the ducks along the path between the lagoon and the gateway at Charles and Beacon streets; you'll always see children sitting on them, embracing and patting them or waddling nearby—quacking. In 1989 news that one of the ducklings had been stolen even made the *New York Times.* A pair of Boston bartenders—**Eddie Doyle** of the nearby **Bull & Finch,** aka "Cheers" bar, and **Tommy Leonard** of Kenmore Square's **Eliot Lounge** together started the "Bring Back Mack" fundraising campaign. Now **Mack** is back with his pack.

Public Garden

Charles Street

Beacon Street

Make Way for Ducklings Statue

Boat Dock

Footbridge

Boylston Street

George Washington Statue

Arlington Street

David R. Godine
Publisher

First, everyone should read **Walter Muir Whitehill's** *Boston: A Topographical History.*

For entertainment, always check out **Jordan Hall** at the **New England Conservatory of Music,** for faculty and student concerts are frequently scheduled here (no admission).

Spend at least a day walking around **Cambridge** and visiting its many museums (Fogg, Busch-Reisinger, Semitic, Houghton Library, Sackler, Carpenter, etc.).

Walk through the **North End;** it's intact, safe, and as close to Little Italy as you'll find in New England.

Ride the subway; it's cheap and will get you everywhere quickly. If you value your sanity, do not (repeat DO NOT) even think about driving in the city.

Eat at least one dinner or lunch at **Locke-Ober;** it's pricier than **Durgin-Park,** but far more civilized. Also consider tea at the **Ritz-Carlton Hotel,** a great bargain and very relaxing.

Remember: Boston is a small city. Everything is accessible by foot and the city is best seen that way. And the **American Institute of Architects (AIA)** has excellent walking tours.

Finally, attend a Sunday morning service at **King's Chapel** or **Trinity Church** in Copley Square.

Try to understand that for the New World, this is an *old* city. Its charms are often hidden within its history, but its history is beguiling.

Kate Mattes
Owner, Kate's Mystery Books

Some of the most unusual shopping—bar none—in the Greater Boston area occurs along Massachusetts Avenue between my bookstore and Harvard Square. Some of the best are: **Irish Imports, Ltd.** (for quality hearthcrafts and woolen outerwear); **Red Dog** (vintage clothing); **Susanna** (unusual women's clothing and jewelry); **The Chocolate Box** (confectioners); and **Saturday's Child** (children's clothing).

A sandwich at **Marcella's** is thick and nourishing; share one for starters. My favorite shop is **Joie de Vivre,** whose charming gift items range in price from $1 to $200.

Christopher's, right across from the Porter Square subway station, is a great place to catch up with a friend over the world's best nachos or Cobb salad. Farther up Massachusetts Avenue, the **Porterhouse Cafe** features good ribs and the best barbecue seafood in town (note: the largest seating is four-person booths). A little farther up is my store, **Kate's Mystery Books.** Two blocks away (at the Davis Square subway stop on the Red Line) is **Red Bones,** where everything is slowly cooked over a hickory fire. I especially recommend the corn pudding, the greens, the catfish fingers, and the pecan pie. This is also a good place for kids because they won't be heard over the restaurant's music and clatter.

Boston is great for live music. For major acts, phone Ticketmaster as soon as you know you're coming to see who's in town. I like casual, but civilized places and my two favorite clubs for jazz and blues are **Johnny D's** in Davis Square (phone to make reservations for a reasonably priced meal and stay to see the show for a cover charge) and the **Regattabar,** in the **Charles Hotel.**

There is no better place for bookstores (more than 20 at last count) than Harvard Square. It's also great for music lovers: **HMV** for classical, jazz, and special orders; **Tower** has great stock and a knowledgeable staff; and **Second Coming** sells used and bootlegged tapes and records.

Beacon Hill

Another "must" is the weekly film noir double bill at the **Brattle Theatre,** followed by a quick bite, just downstairs, at the **Casablanca.** Try the Middle Eastern pizza with ground lamb and spices, one of the best buys in town.

The **Harvest Restaurant,** for haute cuisine.

Step into **Harvard Yard** and catch a piece of serenity inside the ivy walls. **Widener Library** and **Memorial Chapel** will put you in touch with past lives at Harvard. If you're lucky, the mimosa tree in front of **Weld Hall** will be in bloom.

I love to walk on the cobblestones of **Beacon Hill** admiring the Greek Revival architecture and the gardens spied through finely filigreed iron. It's also great to drive through at night—especially in something high like a Jeep—and look in the warmly lit windows for a glimpse of the magnificence dwelling behind the black shutters.

Clara Wainwright
Artist/Founder of the Great Boston Kite Festival

Chinatown—with its Chinese and Vietnamese restaurants—where stir-fried octopus, beefsteak soup, baby octopus, and quail eggs are available on a 24-hour basis. Also take advantage of the great fabric stores here.

Bnu Restaurant in the Theater District with its hip, funky interior, great food, and an understanding of the size of the human stomach. The owner, **Linda Crinitti,** is alone worth the trip, but the seasonal menus are wonderful, particularly the pastas.

JP Licks ice-cream parlor on Centre Street in Jamaica Plain, whose owner, **Vince Petric,** understands that even in Jamaica Plain there is a demand for Kahlua and pumpkin ice cream.

Jamaica Pond is stocked with trout and at any time of day there are people fishing, boating, and parading babies and dogs.

Culture Shock on Newbury Street has great, stylish clothing from London and Boston designers at affordable prices. Just down the street, heading Downtown, is **Nomad,** a fabulous marketplace of ethnic clothing and jewelry. Both shops are for people tired of wearing designer advertising on their bodies. Be sure to check out the **Ken Born** and Mexican T-shirts at Nomad.

Government Center/ Faneuil Hall

This part of town is not so much a neighborhood as it is a collection of interesting sights sprinkled among impersonal office towers and heavily trafficked, characterless streets. More or less bounded by **Cambridge Street** to the west, the tangle of highways at the edge of the **Charles River** to the north, **Court** and **State streets** to the south, and the **Central Artery** to the east, the main attractions are **Faneuil Hall Marketplace**, with its blend of history and contemporary consumer delights; **Blackstone Block**, a tiny remnant of "Old Boston"; and the **Boston Garden** sports arena, home of the **Celtics** basketball team and the **Bruins** ice-hockey team.

Established communities that once existed here were swept away during the '60s, when the city tried to rejuvenate itself through drastic and painful urban renewal, forcing thousands of city residents to move. Architect **I.M. Pei's** master urban-design plan imposed monumental order on 56 acres: 22 streets were replaced with six; slots for big, bold new buildings were carefully plotted; and a vast plaza was created and crowned with an iconoclastic city hall symbolizing "New Boston."

The name **West End**, nearly forgotten now, at one time referred to the 48 acres stretching from the base of **Beacon Hill** to **North Station**. The West End's fashionable days had ended in the 19th century, and by the 20th century many considered the area a slum. Yet more than 10,000 people—Russians, Greeks, Albanians, Irish, Italians, Poles, Jews, Lithuanians—inhabited brick row houses on the lively, intimate streets. Older Bostonians recall when Government Center was the raucous and irrepressible **Scollay Square**, where Boston's racier nightlife crowd caroused in saloons, burlesque shows, shooting galleries, adult theaters, pawnshops, tattoo parlors, and cheap hotels. Many still regret that this historic, freewheeling square was obliterated to make way for businesses and federal, state, and city offices—attracting somewhat more reputable, but much less colorful, residents.

Incredibly altered and dislocated from its past, this area now seems oddly situated. Abutting the history-drenched Waterfront, North End, and Beacon Hill, Government Center is more a passageway to other destinations than a place to linger. Only vestiges of the past remain, like **Old West Church, Harrison Gray Otis'** first house, the **Bulfinch Pavilion** and **Ether Dome** at **Massachusetts General Hospital (MGH)**, and the famous **Steaming Kettle** landmark. Most of the contemporary architecture has a '60s look, often alienating and aloof. The newest buildings still can't decide what they're doing here. The old, authentic languages, layers, color, and complexity are gone. Some say the West End's demise was necessary to let a new city image live; while it's true that much of what's gone doesn't merit mourning, it's also true that most of the new is nothing to brag about.

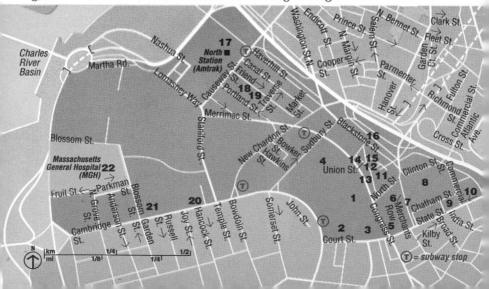

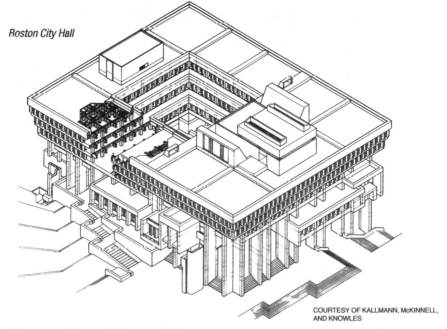

Boston City Hall

COURTESY OF KALLMANN, McKINNELL, AND KNOWLES

The best starting point for touring this neighborhood is the Government Center T stop (Green and Blue Lines) at City Hall Plaza, but the Haymarket (Green and Orange Lines) and Bowdoin (Blue Line) subway stops are also convenient. North Station (Green and Orange Lines) is the stop for Boston Garden; the Charles Street stop (Red Line) takes you nearest to Massachusetts General Hospital and Massachusetts Eye and Ear. (Note: the Haymarket bus and subway stop is behind the Government Center Garage, about a block's distance down New Congress Street from the outdoor Haymarket.)

1 Boston City Hall Dramatically towering over a windswept brick plain, **Kallmann, McKinnell, and Knowles'** massive structure (pictured above) looks precisely like what it is—a factory where Boston governmental operations crank along. **Gerhard Kallmann** and **Michael McKinnell,** also architects for the **Hynes Auditorium** in Back Bay and the **Boston Five Cents Savings Bank** on School Street, won a national competition for this project, the eye-catching centerpiece of New Boston.

Like most old warehouses, the 1968 building's exterior frankly communicates the functions and hierarchies of what's happening inside: its sprawling, open lower levels house departments that directly serve the public, while more aloof bureaucracy is relegated to the upper floors, with the publicly accountable mayor and city council offices suspended between. Civic activities such as summertime concerts and year-round political events spill onto **City Hall Plaza.** Although its interior is somewhat dim and neglected looking, City Hall remains an edifice of heroic intentions, its massing and shadows always eloquent. ♦ City Hall Plaza. 635.4000 &

2 Sears Crescent Building A holdover from old **Scollay Square,** this gracefully curving 1816 building—renovated in 1969 by **Don Stull Associates**—moderates **City Hall's** aggressive stance and softens nine-acre **City Hall Plaza's** impersonality. The Crescent Building recalls the days when Boston streets sprouted every which way and the city didn't care that the shortest distance between two points is a line. Built by **David Sears,** whose Beacon Hill mansion is now the **Somerset Club,** this block was once Boston's publishing center, where **Emerson, Hawthorne,** and other literary types gathered.

Cozying up to the Crescent is the little **Sears Block** building (completed in 1848), where Boston's homey landmark, the gilded **Steaming Kettle,** puffs round the clock. The city's oldest animated trade sign, the kettle was cast in 1873 by coppersmiths **Hicks and Badger,** and commissioned by the **Oriental Tea Company.** Fed steam by a pipe from the company's boiler room, the kettle was an instant curiosity. Its big day came when Oriental Tea held a contest to guess its mascot's capacity. Weeks of fervent speculation ended on 1 January 1875, when more than 10,000 people gathered to watch **William F. Reed,** City Sealer of Weights and Measures, decree the official measure of 227 gallons, two quarts, one pint, and three gills—now engraved on the kettle's side. Eight winners shared the prize: a chest of premium tea. Reporting on the event, the *Boston Sunday Times* referred to the famous **Boston Tea Party** and bragged, "The tea-kettle excitement has run nearly as high as the tea excitement of old, and is almost a historical incident in the career of our noble city." Once Scollay Square was razed, the kettle was relocated in 1967 to the Sears Block. Here it graces the popular, unassuming **Steaming Kettle Coffee Shop.** ♦ One City Hall Plaza

---

Restaurants/Clubs: Red
Shops/ ♣ Outdoors: Green
Hotels: Blue
Sights/Culture: Black

Within the Sears Crescent Building:
Warburton's $ Liberally dotting the town, this chain bakes respectable morning muffins, as well as savories, scones, Danishes, brownies, soups, and sandwiches. City government folk come here often, just as state employees frequent the Warburton's by the State House. ♦ Takeout ♦ M-F 6:30AM-5:30PM. No credit cards. 523.7338. Also at: 22A Beacon St. 720.1094; 1 Federal St. 451.0825; 27 Brattle St, Harvard Sq, Cambridge. 876.1609

Government Center/Faneuil Hall

3 Ames Building Fourteen stories high, the proud and distinctive Ames Building—now on the **National Register of Historic Places**—was once the tallest office building on the Eastern seaboard. Abounding with arches, modulating from the weighty ones at the base to the delicate chain under the cornice, the vigorous building was designed in 1889 by **H.H. Richardson's** successor firm, **Shepley, Rutan & Coolidge.** Although the great architect had died a few years earlier, his influence clearly was not forgotten, especially in the Romanesque architectural details and lacy carvings.

One of Boston's first skyscrapers, the sturdy Ames is supported by nine-foot-thick masonry walls—the second-tallest such structure in the world—not the light-steel frame that became popular soon afterward. The building only briefly dominated the city's skyline. No matter that it has been dwarfed by 20th-century behemoths—the Ames exerts enduring presence. ♦ 1 Court St (between Cambridge and Congress Sts)

4 John F. Kennedy Federal Office Building Indifferent and impersonal in appearance, this one-million-square-foot building designed in 1967 by **The Architects Collaborative (Walter Gropius'** firm) and **Samuel Glaser Associates** is a perfectly appropriate home for the **Internal Revenue Service,** the **Federal Bureau of Investigation,** and many of the other federal agencies one doesn't want to tangle with. A **Robert Motherwell** mural marks the spot where the 26-story tower unites with its long, low-rise mate. ♦ City Hall Plaza (between Cambridge and Sudbury Sts)

On the site of 16 North Street, in what is now known as Government Center, resided William Dawes, who rode to Lexington on the evening of 18 April 1775 to warn John Hancock and Samuel Adams that the British were coming. Meanwhile, Paul Revere was en route to Charlestown to warn patriots there, after watching for the designated signal at the Old North Church in Boston's North End.

5 Bay Tower Room ★★$$$
It's a private club by day, but come evening this restaurant offers stunning views, festive atmosphere, and costly but good food selected "to celebrate the seasons." Located on the 33rd floor of the **Sheraton World Headquarters Building** (pictured at right), the dramatic dining room is an assemblage of alcoves and tiers where every table claims a view: miniaturized Faneuil Hall Marketplace crowds, the Custom House Tower, boats crossing Boston Harbor, and planes circling Logan Airport. (Try to arrive before sunset.) The cuisine is sometimes uneven and other times just fine, with successes including lobster ravioli, oysters, châteaubriand, grilled seafood, rack of lamb, roasted venison tenderloin, and an extraordinary fruit shortcake. After dinner, ascend to the postage-stamp-size lounge and dance to music by a small combo. If you're driving, there's free validated parking under the building after 5PM; enter from **Merchant's Row.** ♦ American ♦ M-Th 5:30-10PM; F-Sa 5:30-11PM. 60 State St (at Congress St). No jeans. Jacket required in dining room. Reservations recommended. 723.1666 &

5 Houlihan's $$ One in a national chain of 56, this watering hole has predictable, passable food—stick to appetizers and simpler fare—and is usually packed, especially with the big business-lunch crowd and major after-work singles scene. The decor is a clutter of English and Irish memorabilia, and there's a sports bar. A DJ entertains nightly, Monday through Friday from 5PM to 2AM and Saturday and Sunday from 4PM to 2AM, attracting people in their late 20s and 30s. (A reservation does not reserve a particular table; it puts your name at the top of the waiting list when you arrive.) ♦ American ♦ M-Sa 11:30AM-2AM; Su 11AM-2AM. 60 State St (at Congress St). No jeans or sneakers in the lounge after 7PM. Reservations recommended. 367.6377 &

5 Walking Distance Locator A marvelous machine that's perfect for Boston (the walker's city), this computerized information terminal prints out free maps of nearby places. Pick the category of information you're interested in, such as General Retail, Food and Beverage, Transportation and Lodging, Cultural and Entertainment; then push a button to select the subcategory to be included in your map printout, such as department stores, cafes, movie theaters, or gas stations. Out comes an easy-to-read map with numbers corresponding to a list of establishments below. It couldn't be simpler. Special features include "What's on Sale Today," and "City Happenings." Other locators, with many more to come, include: **Boylston Street** in front of the **Prudential Tower,** next to **Hynes Auditorium** in Back Bay; **Boston Five**

Cents Savings Plaza, between School and Washington streets; and the **Bank of Boston,** between Congress and Franklin streets.

♦ 60 State St (at Congress St)

5 Dock Square The open area between **Congress Street** and **Faneuil Hall** earned its name in colonial times when it was young Boston's landing place. The **Town Dock** was eventually built out into **Town Cove** and later filled in to create more land, an important threshold to the New World. Newcomers, visitors, and goods passed constantly across the square to and from the boats docked near its edge. On the way to Faneuil Hall, look for **Anne Whitney's** 1880 bronze of *Samuel Adams*.

6 Faneuil Hall From the heights of the steps behind **City Hall,** look for the most familiar and beloved of Boston's many curious objects of affection: spinning in harbor-sent breezes and glinting in the sun atop Faneuil Hall (pictured below) is master tinsmith **Deacon Shem Drowne's** gold-plated grasshopper, a weathervane modeled in 1742 after a similar one topping **London's Royal Exchange.** Grasshoppers symbolize good luck; and in a city where many a fine old building has been lost to fire or progress, this critter has certainly done right by Faneuil Hall. In 1740, when wealthy French Huguenot and English merchant **Peter Faneuil** offered to erect a market building for the town at his own expense, citizens voted on his proposal. It barely passed, 367 to 360, a lukewarm welcome for a landmark that has been a historic center of Boston life ever since.

Painter **John Smibert** designed the original structure. Built in 1742, it housed open market stalls, a meeting hall, and offices. All were gutted by fire in 1761, but an identical building was soon rebuilt. Peddlers and politicians have always peacefully coexisted here, inspiring local poet **Francis W. Hatch** to write: "Here orators in ages past have mounted their attack/ Undaunted by proximity of sausage on the rack." As the Revolution approached, the impassioned oratory of patriots such as **Samuel Adams** and **James Otis** fired up the populace, drawing huge crowds and earning Faneuil Hall the nickname "Cradle of Liberty." At a 1772 town meeting here, Adams proposed that Boston establish the **Committee of Correspondence** and invite the other colonies to join, thus establishing the clandestine information

Government Center/Faneuil Hall

network that promoted united action against British repression. The hall's nickname was further cemented when Boston's famous anti-slavery orator **Wendell Phillips** presented his first address here in 1837. **William Lloyd Garrison** and Massachusetts senator **Charles Sumner** joined the battle for the abolitionist cause from the same rostrum.

In 1806, when the crowds just couldn't squeeze in anymore, **Charles Bulfinch** handsomely remodeled and enlarged the cramped hall, preserving its stalwart simplicity but doubling its width, adding a floor, and creating a marvelous second-floor galleried assembly room that citizen's groups use to this day. Among the room's dozens of portraits of famous Americans, look for **George P.A. Healy's** *Liberty and Union, Now and Forever* depicting Massachusetts **Senator Daniel Webster** on the floor of the US Senate defending the Union in 1830 against a southern senator's contention that states could veto federal laws; and **Gilbert Stuart's** well-known portrait of **George Washington** taking Dorchester Heights from the Redcoats. On the third floor are the headquarters and museum of the **Ancient and Honorable**

Faneuil Hall

There's only one Faneuil Hall—the brick building with the grasshopper on top—but the entire marketplace is collectively called Faneuil Hall, too, and sometimes it's known as Quincy Market. Officially, Faneuil Hall Marketplace includes Faneuil Hall, Quincy Market (with its Rotunda, Colonnade, and North and South Canopies), and the North Market and South Market buildings.

Pronunciations of "Faneuil" abound, with little agreement about which is correct. Is it *Fan'l, Fannel, Fan-you-ill, Fan-yul,* or *Fan-ee-yul?* Who knows, but the first two are by far the most common.

Restaurants/Clubs: Red **Hotels:** Blue
Shops/ ♠ **Outdoors:** Green **Sights/Culture:** Black

Artillery Company of Massachusetts, a ceremonial organization with a proud past as the oldest military organization in the western hemisphere, chartered in 1638 by Massachusetts' first governor, **John Winthrop.** The company displays its vast collection of arms, uniforms, documents, and memorabilia.

Back at ground level, get a foretaste of **Quincy Market** across the way by making a quick tour of the souvenir shops and food counters that have replaced the more down-to-earth provender purveyed in Faneuil Hall of old. Times have changed, but the adaptable hall thrives on. Its political pulse also beats strong; during presidential-election years, contenders in the state's primary debate here. ♦ M-Sa 10AM-9PM; Su noon-7PM. Faneuil Hall Square (between Congress St and Merchants Row). 523.3886 ♦

Government Center/Faneuil Hall

6 Bostix Stop by this outdoor kiosk to purchase half-price tickets on the day of performance, or full-price advance tickets, to many of Boston's arts and entertainment events. This in-person, cash-only service sells tickets for visiting Broadway shows and dozens of local theater, dance, and music companies, plus comedy clubs, sports events, jazz concerts, campgrounds, night clubs, dinner theaters, tourist attractions, and summer festivals. ♦ Tu-Sa 11AM-6PM; Su 11AM-4PM. Faneuil Hall Marketplace (on the south side of Faneuil Hall). Recorded information 723.5181 ♦

7 The Limited and Express Compagnie Internationale Representative of New Boston's sometimes cavalier attitude toward the city's history, this building by **Graham Gund Associates** strives to relate to the other marketplace structures. But as hard as it tries, it's a new kid on the block with too much style and not enough substance. For a shopping foray that's sure to overwhelm, step inside The Limited's superstore: floor upon floor of moderately priced fashions and accessories primarily for women—but some for men and children, too—including Express' international assortment of pricier "Euro" looks. There's a whole floor of lingerie. Teenagers and college students go absolutely crazy over this place. ♦ M-Sa 10AM-9PM; Su noon-6PM. One Faneuil Hall Sq. 742.6837 ♦

7 Bertucci's $ Another spacious outpost of the very popular local pizza and pasta chain, this Bertucci's hops in tune with nearby Faneuil Hall Marketplace. Count on them for tasty fresh pizzas, calzones, and salads. Look for the fun mural, depicting pizza-making, above the bar. ♦ Pizza/Takeout ♦ M-Th 11AM-11PM; F-Sa 11AM-midnight; Su noon-11PM. 22 Merchant's Row. 227.7889 ♦

The number "1" has never been worn by a Boston Celtic; it was retired in honor of Walter Brown, the team's founder.

Restaurants/Clubs: Red   **Hotels:** Blue
Shops/ ☂ Outdoors: Green   **Sights/Culture:** Black

7 Clarke's $$ On one side, there's a big neighborly saloon where crowds flock to watch sports events on TV, eye prospective dates, or wind down after work; on the other, a comfortable, no-frills restaurant and bar where you can order straightforward New England dishes like scrod. Try the big sandwiches and burgers with a side of great fries. A shuttle will take you from here to **Boston Garden** events. Co-owner **Dave DeBusschere,** formerly of the **New York Knicks,** sometimes drops by to watch the **Celtics** play. ♦ American ♦ M-F 11:30AM-2AM; Sa-Su noon-2AM. 21 Merchant's Row (at State St). Reservations recommended for large parties. 227.7800 ♦

8 Faneuil Hall Marketplace Beyond **Faneuil Hall** stands a long, low trio of buildings (pictured on the opposite page) bursting with international and specialty food stalls, restaurants, cafes, boutiques, bars, and an army of pushcarts peddling wares to tempt the impulsive buyer. The extravaganza ranges from junk food to gourmet, kitsch to haute couture. The whole ensemble attracts more than 14 million visitors a year, inviting comparisons to Disney World. But touristy and slick as it is, the marketplace possesses the authentic patina of history. It has lived a long, useful life. Many people are turned off by the throngs and buy-buy-buy mood of this shop-and-snack mecca, but it definitely deserves a visit—if only to glance over the worthy old buildings and enjoy the outdoor spectacle of pedestrians and street performers. An information desk is located under the South Canopy. It isn't easy to spot among the pushcarts, and the staff is often indifferent, but pick up the extremely helpful printed directory.

The marketplace's 535-foot-long granite centerpiece, a **National Historic Landmark,** is named for **Josiah Quincy,** the Boston mayor who revitalized the decrepit Waterfront by ordering major landfills, six new streets, and the construction of a market house to supplement overcrowded Faneuil Hall. Architect **Alexander Parris** crowned the 1826 Greek Revival central building with a copper dome and planted majestic Doric colonnades at either end. The building projected a noble face seaward, for it was right at the harbor's edge in those days. Two granite-faced brick warehouses, today called **North** and **South Markets,** later rose on either side according to Parris' plans. For a century and a half the ensemble was the dignified venue for meat and produce distribution and storage.

By the 1970s, however, the marketplace was decaying, in danger of demolition. **Ben** and **Jane Thompson** of **Benjamin Thompson & Associates** convinced the city and developers that the complex could become Boston's gathering place again, if recycled to suit contemporary urban life. Thompson's firm restored as much of the complex as possible in 1978, adding innovations such as glass canopies flanking the central building and festive signage. On the South Market side, the cobbled pedestrian way (don't try to wear high heels) is more spacious, with plenty of benches. Even in chilly weather,

Faneuil Hall Marketplace

you'll see lots of people enjoying the show while savoring baklava, barbecue, chowder, fudge, gourmet brownies, pizzas, salads, sausage-on-a-stick, raw oysters, Indian pudding, french fries, ice cream—the whole gastronomic gamut. Under the canopy on the north side of **Quincy Market,** a popular piano bar draws a large after-work crowd from the Financial District and nearby offices, inspiring many an impromptu sing-along. When Boston winter finally gives up, sidewalk cafes dot the pedestrian streets. An outdoor flower market near the north side of Faneuil Hall blankets the cobblestones with greenery, bringing colors and smells of each season to this corner of the city: autumn pumpkins, Christmas trees and poinsettias, and summer bouquets.

All in all, breathing life back into the old buildings was done gently, and the scheme has proven a fantastic success, a model for renewal projects across the country. Boston lost its waterside meat-and-potatoes-style market to colorful abundance of another sort. Come early in the morning and enjoy a quiet breakfast in Quincy Market's central rotunda, or brave the Saturday afternoon crowds when the place is full of competing aromas and voices. You'll notice people often gather round the cobblestoned square between Faneuil Hall and Quincy Market's **West Portico,** the prime spot for musicians, jugglers, and other entertainers.
♦ General marketplace M-Sa 10AM-9PM; Su noon-6PM. Information 523.3886

Supposedly the oldest chartered military organization in the world, the Ancient and Honorable Artillery Company of Massachusetts was formed in 1638 (although the name wasn't official until 1738) by Governor John Winthrop to defend the Massachusetts Bay Colony in case of riots or Indian attacks. The 700-or-so members of the "Ancient and Honorables" have met on the top floor of Faneuil Hall since 1748, but there hasn't been much for them to do except dress up in full regalia, put on parades, attend the annual spring commission ceremony with the governor, and go on a fall tour of duty to a foreign land.

Even when the Revolutionary War came to pass the group didn't play an important role and it hasn't served as a body in any war since. Yet every important Massachusetts public ceremony now includes the Ancient and Honorables, whom the infamous Boston mayor James Michael Curley once declared "Invincible in peace. Invisible in war."

Numerous members have distinguished themselves individually; some have even been awarded the Congressional Medal of Honor. Four Ancient and Honorables have served as US President: James Monroe, Chester Alan Arthur, Calvin Coolidge, and John F. Kennedy.

Look for the bronze statue of longtime Boston Celtics coach and manager Red Auerbach on the South Market side of Faneuil Hall Marketplace. The basketball team's famous leader is seated on a bench there, ready to light the customary cigar that signifies a victory at hand.

Within Quincy Market:

BOSTON & MAINE FISH COMPANY

Boston & Maine Fish Company Live lobster up to a whopping 25 pounds and other super-fresh seafood are packed for travel or shipped anywhere in the US from this retail market. The prices are high, but sometimes worth it to satisfy a hankering for fruits of the Atlantic. You can get all the fixings for an

authentic New England clambake, minus the seaside pit: lobsters, steamer clams, chowder, and utensils. Or, if you just want some steamers to take home for supper, they'll steam them for you here while you wait. ♦ M-Sa 8AM-9PM; Su 8AM-6PM. Colonnade. 723.3474; 800/626.7866 ♿

The Salty Dog Seafood Bar and Grille $$ Get some of the best oysters in town, good chowder and fried clams, and other fresh and basic undisguised seafood in this noisy little seafood hut of a place. There's no pastry cart here, and they don't take reservations, but you can dine alfresco from April to November. A lot of regulars stay away during the summer to avoid the inevitable throngs. ♦ Seafood/American ♦ M-Sa 11AM-1AM; Su 10AM-1AM. Lower level. 742.2094

Boston Chipyard The award-winning mouthfuls of the best chocolate chippers in town are always fresh, whether the plain traditional favorite or mixed with ingredients like peanut butter, extra chocolate, nuts, oatmeal, or raisins. A California mom came more than 14 years ago and opened the shop with her own recipe, loved by her son and his friends. Come for a late-night fix of milk and cookies. You can mail order, too. ♦ Cookies ♦ Daily 9AM-midnight. North Canopy. 742.9537 ♿

Within North Market:

Marketplace Cafe ★$$ Dine outdoors in the summer and in a greenhouse setting in the winter on a variety of appetizers, salads, sandwiches, and simple entrées. Light, bright, and casual, the bistro is especially festive and welcoming on warm evenings. ♦ American ♦ M-Th 11AM-11:30PM; F 11AM-1AM; Sa 10AM-1AM; Su 10AM-11:30PM. 227.9660 ♿

The Boston Beach Club Attracting a younger crowd, the BBC books live bands and plays up its seaside theme with surfboard tables, a fish tank, tropical drinks, Hawaiian leis, and assorted games and toys. T-shirts, hats, records, trips, and other freebies are handed out on promotion nights. Drinks only are served. ♦ Daily 6PM-2AM. 227.9660 ♿

The Marketplace Grill and Oar Bar
★★★$$ A cut above the ordinary Faneuil Hall choices, this spacious brick-walled room—sparsely decorated with a pair of impossibly long and skinny sculls hung overhead—overlooks the marketplace hubbub and serves exemplary American cuisine at a very reasonable tariff. Chef **Jamie Mohn** presents artfully composed plates, such as a meal-unto-itself goat-cheese salad, and his improvised pastas of the day—al dente fettuccine, say, topped with grilled salmon, sun-dried tomatoes, and cool slivers of avocado—are nothing less than inspired. It's worth withstanding the allure of the market's clamoring food stands to have a studied, civilized meal in this second-story hideaway, a real find. ♦ American ♦ M-Th 11AM-3:30PM, 4-10PM; F-Sa 11AM-3:30PM, 5-11PM. Reservations are recommended. 227.2972 ♿

Durgin-Park ★★$$ Come here for true Yankee cooking and a taste of Boston's bygone days. Don't listen to detractors who say Durgin-Park is overrated; give it a try and enjoy a fast-paced, filling meal. Founded in 1827 (the same year their Boston logo—pictured above—was drawn), this cranky-creaky but well-loved institution dates from the marketplace's old days, when produce held the fort instead of today's gourmet melee. Notice the ancient plank floors and tin ceilings. Waitresses legendary for their brisk gotta-job-to-do manner serve raw clams and oysters, phone-book-size prime rib, starchless fish chowder, Boston scrod (with baked beans, of course), chops, steaks, fresh seafood, chicken potpie, and more solid old favorites. Save room for Durgin's scrumptious fresh strawberry shortcake, made on the premises, and rich Indian pudding. Everybody dines family style at tables set for 16 and decked out in red-checkered cloths. Visitors from around the world follow the well-worn path here, where 500,000 people are served annually. Durgin-Park stuck it out during the market's '70s transformation; now the venerable restaurant is one of the most genuine features of the place. Ask about validated parking. ♦ Yankee ♦ M-Th 11:30AM-10PM; F-Sa 11:30AM-10:30PM; Su 11:30AM-9PM. Street level. No credit cards. 227.2038

To former West Enders, the famous line "You can't go home again" is tragically apt. Forced out of their neighborhood after the city declared it a slum and replaced affordable housing with luxury apartments and offices, their plight became a casebook example of the terrible consequences of '60s-style urban renewal. Herbert Gans' famous 1962 study, *The Urban Villagers,* spotlights the West End's fate.

Downstairs at Durgin-Park:

The Oyster Bar at Durgin-Park ★★$ Serving appetizers and sandwiches only, this is a great alternative to the noisy place upstairs if you want a light repast and a little calm. Try the soothing clam chowder and briny steamers. There are no tables; just the bar and bar-style counters. Dessert is not on the menu, but just ask and someone will transport it from upstairs. ♦ American ♦ M-Th 11:30AM-10:30PM; F-Sa 11:30AM-11:30PM; Su 11:30AM-10PM. 227.2038

Tales with Tails Family owned and operated, this shop specializes in a huggable menagerie of stuffed animals and toys that debuted in books: **Paddington, Babar, Celeste,** and **Arthur, Curious George, Raggedy Ann** and **Andy, Beatrix Potter** and **Sesame Street** characters, and more. You can get the storybooks, too. Makers include **Gund, Dakin,** and **Applause.** ♦ M-Sa 10AM-9PM; Su noon-6PM. Second level. 227.8772

Zuma's Tex-Mex Cafe ★$$ Subdued, this basement cafe is not—the very first sight that greets you is a sandpit artfully sporting an O'Keeffe-style cattle skull. The small, packed space is abustle with sizzling fajitas and quesadillas about to be zapped with "Inner Beauty" sauce, and abuzz with neon accents and scattered video monitors broadcasting surfer tapes. Owner **Steve Immel's** mission— to serve "foods of the sun"—extends to Italian pasta and Japanese teriyaki, and is typified in a line of fresh-fruit "neon" margaritas. ♦ Tex-Mex/International ♦ M-F 11:30AM-10PM; Sa-Su 11:30AM-11PM. 367.9114 &

Within South Market:

Serendipity 3 $$ Tourists, families, and a younger crowd flock here. This good-humored food boutique makes no bones about its eccentricities, from the whimsical decor to an enormous illustrated menu you'll want to color with crayons. Be basic with a burger or omelet, or venture into blue-corn nachos with goat cheese, scrod Rockefeller, Ftatateeta's Toast, an Eiffel Tower sandwich, or the famous frozen hot

chocolate. Complimentary hors d'oeuvres are served weekdays during the 4PM to 8PM "Attitude Adjustment" hours, live jazz plays Friday night and at Sunday brunch, and a magician performs Thursday night. In warmer weather, tables migrate outdoors. By the way, if you see something you like here, be it a T-shirt, statuette, or lighting fixture, it's probably for sale. ♦ American ♦ M-Th 11:30AM-11:30PM; F 11:30AM-12:30AM; Sa 10:30AM-midnight; Su 9AM-11PM. Street level. Reservations recommended Friday and Saturday nights, Sunday brunch. 523.2339 &

Siam Malee Come here for a feast of fabrics —iridescent, shimmering, gorgeously colored silks, cottons, and linens, all imported from Thailand—metamorphosed into butterflylike day and evening fashions. Almost all are for

Government Center/Faneuil Hall

women, although there's a vivid array of men's ties. The styling is simple but clever, with unusual detailing. Glittery and festive jewelry, beaded bags, jackets, and belts can be found here, too. ♦ M-Sa 10AM-9PM; Su noon-6PM. Street level. 227.7027 &

Alan Lawrence The two friendly young owners put their first names as well as their heads together to create this chic and cozy high-end men's boutique with its emphasis on customer service and "Euro-classic" looks in exceptional textures, colors, and fabrics. Men of all ages come in for custom-made suits and shirts, casualwear, and accessories, some designed by the owners and produced internationally. There's a tailor on the premises. Custom consultations are offered by appointment only. ♦ M-Sa 10AM-9PM; Su noon-6PM. Street level. 227.1144

Whippoorwill A standout among the independent stores that have found a home in the market, this subterranean craft shop tends to specialize in the whimsical. Mixed in among the kaleidoscopes, chimes, woven clothes, and other staples are oddities such as **Josh** and **Michael Cohen's** heart-bedecked ceramic condom boxes— "the perfect gift for the safety-conscious '90s." Whippoorwill is a good place to look for such one-of-a-kind tokens of affection. ♦ M-Sa 10AM-9PM; Su noon-7PM. 523.5149

Le Baggerie This snug shop features unusual, individually selected bags of every sort: briefcases, duffels, purses, portfolios, totes, and hand-beaded evening bags. Things to put in the bags are sold, too, like calendars, wallets, and coin purses. A specialty is the **Laurel Burch** line of bags, jewelry, T-shirts, mugs, and hand-painted and silk-screened sweatshirts. ♦ M-Sa 10AM-9PM; Su noon-6PM. Street level. 367.0578

The parades of pushcart vendors under and just beyond Quincy Market's canopies are known collectively as the Bull Market, named for the bull weathervane above the gold dome.

Folklorica One of the renovated market's older tenants, this shop has established a fine reputation with its captivating mix of antique and contemporary designer jewelry from Victorian to New York funk. For a wide range of prices, you can pick up a lovely necklace of Murano Venetian glass beads, a marcasite brooch, a Bakelite bracelet, or gold estate pieces. The owner/buyer will search for

Government Center/Faneuil Hall

special requests. Pearl stringing and custom design are offered. ◆ M-Sa 10AM-9PM; Su noon-6PM. Second level. 367.1201 ♿

9 The Black Rose ★$ Its name is translated from *Roisin Dubh,* a Gaelic allegorical name for Ireland that symbolizes Irish Catholic repression by the British. Famous Irish faces and mementos line the walls, and Irish music accompanies bargain-priced meals like meat loaf, lamb stew, fish-and-chips, Yankee pot roast, and boiled lobster. (Don't look for gourmet here.) This big, hospitable bar offers numerous Irish beers and stout on tap and live Irish music every day; ask for times. It's a great place to meet after work, sing along with folk music, watch the **Celtics** game on the big-screen TV, and slowly sip Irish coffee. ◆ American/Irish ◆ M-Sa 11:30AM-2AM; Su noon-2AM. 160 State St. 742.2286

10 Marketplace Center This gauche gate-crashing building—erected in 1985 by the **WZMH Group**—tries to look as if belongs on this important historic site, even mimicking its venerable neighbors somewhat in materials and style. While it could have been worse, the building is awkward, especially its graceless atrium gateway with makeup-mirror-style fixtures. Although the opening preserves the pedestrian walk-to-the-sea leading to **Boston Harbor** at **Christopher Columbus Park,** the too-tall, too-wide building is a barrier where none existed before. It adds to the marketplace's stockpile of shops, including many chain stores like **Brookstone, Banana Republic, Mrs. Fields' Cookies, Williams-Sonoma, The Sharper Image, The Gap,** and more. ◆ 200 State St

Within Marketplace Center:

Pavo Real Discover beautifully hued and patterned sweaters here that can't be found elsewhere. The shop imports most of its luxurious alpaca wool and pima cotton. The custom-designed handknit sweaters for men and women from Peru and Bolivia sport hefty mark-ups. Delightful jewelry, hats, gloves, scarves, wallets, and pocketbooks, some quite whimsical in design, make nice gifts. ◆ M-Sa 10AM-7PM, Su noon-6PM, Jan-Mar; M-Sa 10AM-9PM, Su noon-6PM, Apr-Dec. Street level. 439.0013 ♿

Doubleday Book Shop Spacious and bright, with a friendly staff, this link in the Doubleday chain carries books for the general public, with strong sections in fiction, cooking, and local information. It's convenient, too, since bookstores in this neighborhood are scarce. Pick up some reading to accompany a take-out lunch from Quincy Market. ◆ M-Sa 10AM-9PM; Su noon-6PM. Street level. 439.0196. Also at: 99 Park Plaza. 482.8453 ♿

Peacock Papers Almost always crowded and busy, this gift and novelty shop carries the full Peacock Papers line, plus a trendy, amusing, and irreverent selection of cards, wrapping paper, office supplies, T-shirts, pencils stamped with mottos, and just-for-fun gizmos and games. ◆ M-Sa 10AM-7PM, Su noon-6PM, Jan-Mar; M-Sa 10AM-9PM, Su noon-6PM, Apr-Dec. Street level. 439.4818 ♿

Chocolate Dipper Through the window, watch thick streams of fragrant, gooey chocolate blending away while the staff readies luscious fresh fruit and truffles for dipping. Try strawberries, raspberries in season, banana, pineapple, cherries, grapes, and orange slices and rinds enrobed in dark, milk, or white chocolate. The extra-rich truffles come in more than half a dozen flavors, and a wide variety of other chocolates are also made on the premises. ◆ M-Sa 10AM-7PM, Su noon-6PM, Jan-Mar; M-Sa 10AM-9PM, Su noon-6PM, Apr-Dec. Street level. 439.0190 ♿

The first large-scale use of granite and glass in post-and-beam construction occurred when Quincy Market was built. Another innovation is the cast-iron columns marching the length of the markethouse.

Restaurants/Clubs: Red   **Hotels:** Blue
Shops/ 🌳 Outdoors: Green   **Sights/Culture:** Black

11 The Bostonian Hotel $$$$ Intimate and gracious, the Bostonian has been one of the most pleasant places to stay in Boston since opening in 1982. Much of the hotel's charm comes from its residential scale and the way it blends with the historic **Blackstone Block:** incorporated into the hotel complex are an 1890 warehouse that was built by **Peabody and Stearns** (architects for the **Custom House Tower**) and an 1824 building. Many of the 152 rooms have French doors opening onto private balconies that overlook Faneuil Hall Marketplace; rooms in the 19th-century Harkness wing have an imprint of history. Ten honeymoon suites have Jacuzzis and working fireplaces, and two of the rooms have canopy beds. The lobby is appealingly low-key, with historic displays on permanent loan from the **Bostonian Society.** The airy **Atrium** cocktail lounge is a comfortable place to snack on appetizers and listen to live jazz (no jeans or sneakers allowed). Amenities include babysitting and complimentary overnight shoe shines. Request nonsmokers' or wheelchair-accessible accommodations. Rooms equipped for the deaf are likewise available. ◆ Faneuil Hall Marketplace. 523.3600, 800/343.0922; fax 523.2454 ⬥

Within The Bostonian Hotel:

Seasons ★★★★$$$$ The swank, glass-enclosed dining room atop the Bostonian offers generous cityscapes and marvelous views of Quincy Market's gold dome, the famous Faneuil Hall weathervane, and the Custom House Tower's glowing clock. Newcomers to Boston are sure to be dazzled. Seasons is famous as a training ground for Boston's top chefs (**Lydia Shire, Jasper White, Gordon Hamersley,** et al.), and the new anointee, **Tony Ambrose,** has proven his mettle at such top spots as the Charles Hotel's **Rareties** and Le Meridien's **Julien.** An avatar in the new wave of "healthy gourmet" cuisine, Ambrose uses flavor-infused oils and vinegars in lieu of heavy sauces, and the results scintillate. As befits its name, the Seasons' menu changes quarterly, featuring New England and international treats like duckling with ginger and scallions, roasted rack of lamb and pumpkin couscous, baked swordfish with olive compote, and wild mushroom tartlette. Service is gracious. The award-winning all-American wine list is impressive, and the staff ably recommends. The billowy ceiling balloon shades add a romantic touch, and piano music filters up from the **Atrium** lounge. Politicos and businesspeople come for power breakfasts. Seasons is a private club at lunchtime. ◆ American ◆ M-F 7-10:30AM, 11:30AM-2PM, 6-10PM; Sa-Su 7-10:30AM, 6-10PM. Valet parking. No jeans or sneakers at dinner. Reservations recommended. 523.4119 ⬥

12 Union Oyster House ★★$$$ Dine in one of the few spots in Boston where time simply refuses to move forward. Boston's oldest restaurant (founded circa 1715) and the oldest in continuous operation in the United States, Union Oyster House has served its specialty at this spot since 1826. Look in the window and watch oyster-shucking at the bar. This is truly a one-of-a-kind place, best on a cold winter's day when you can follow chilly oysters with steaming chowder or oyster stew and fresh seafood entrées of every kind. The first-floor booths are the original ones, with a plaque adorning the booth where **JFK** liked to dine.

The block's oldest and best-known building is actually a compatible pair of plain-brick row houses. In 1742 **Hopestill Capen** ran a fancy dress-goods business and lived with his family

Government Center/Faneuil Hall

here. Before landfill pushed **Boston Harbor** far away, ships used to dock directly out back to deliver goods. From 1771 to 1775, on the second floor, printer **Isaiah Thomas** published *The Massachusetts Spy,* a newspaper so openly supportive of American independence that the printer was forced to flee to Worcester, MA, where he resumed publication. The exiled **Duc de Chartres,** France's future **King Louis Phillippe,** lived on the second floor in 1796, paying his way by teaching French to Bostonians until family funds arrived.

When **Atwood** and **Bacon** opened their oyster and clam bar, they installed the current half-circle mahogany bar that supposedly became **Daniel Webster's** favorite haunt. Webster reputedly downed each half-dozen oysters with a tumbler of brandy and water, and rarely consumed fewer than six platefuls. ◆ Seafood/American ◆ M-Th, Su 11AM-9:30PM; F-Sa 11AM-10PM. 41 Union St. Reservations recommended. 227.2750 ⬥ (first floor only)

13 Statues of Mayor Curley Follow North Street to an amiable little park tucked between Union and Congress streets, which features two 1980 statues by **Lloyd Lillie** of Boston's controversial but beloved **Mayor James Michael Curley** (1874-1958). In one, Curley is seated on a bench in a very approachable pose; many a photo has been taken of Curley "chatting" with whomever plops down next to him. The other statue portrays an upright Curley as the man-of-action and orator. Four times mayor, four times congressman, and former Massachusetts governor, Curley was born in Boston's South End. Truly a self-made man, this flamboyant politician gave Bostonians plenty to admire, gossip about, and remember him by. Curley smoothly ran Boston's infamous and powerful Irish political machine, inspiring poet **Francis W. Hatch** to quip, "Vote often and early for Curley." **Edwin O'Connor** had Curley in mind when he wrote *The Last Hurrah.* But Curley was also known as the "Mayor of the Poor," and his civic contributions included establishing **Boston City Hospital.**

13 Marshall House ★★$$ When the **Union Oyster House** is too crowded or too much for your wallet—often the case—come here. You may have a wait, but it won't be as long. This place is less than a decade old, yet manages to look as if it's been here a hundred years, with plenty of brass and wood. Eat informally at the bar or bar tables, or in the snug rear dining room. Start off with the raw bar—oysters, steamers, cherrystones, littlenecks—and proceed with fresh seafood entrées prepared in the open kitchen in the middle of the restaurant. There are two lobster specials every day, a wide choice of beers, and big burgers and sandwiches. You can't make a reservation, so leave your name and take a stroll around **Faneuil Hall Marketplace;** you won't be bored. Until recently, the city's oldest hard-

Government Center/Faneuil Hall

ware store stood next door, but times sadly change and now a **McDonald's** franchise has moved in, hungry for tourist trade. ♦ Seafood/American ♦ M-Sa 11:30AM-11PM; Su noon-11PM. 15 Union St. 523.9396 Ꮪ

14 Bell in Hand Tavern Operating since 1795, though not always at this site, this is the oldest tavern in the US. On a cold afternoon, duck in here for a giant draft beer and an appetizer, burger, or sandwich. (Kitchen hours vary, so food isn't always available.) With its moniker illustrated by the curious old sign on its plain facade, the Bell in Hand is much like an English pub. It was named by original proprietor **Jim Wilson,** Boston's town crier until 1794, who rang a bell as he progressed through town announcing the news. **Benjamin Franklin's** childhood home once stood on this site. ♦ M-F 11:30AM-closing; Sa-Su noon-closing. 45 Union St. 227.2098 Ꮪ

15 Ebenezer Hancock House The **Blackstone Block's** second oldest building (circa 1760), this three-story redbrick house was probably built by **John Hancock's** uncle **Thomas,** from whom John later inherited it. Here John's younger brother **Ebenezer** lived and maintained his office as deputy paymaster of the Continental Army. His biggest duty came in 1778, when **Admiral D'Estaing's** fleet conducted two million silver coins from **King Louis XVI** of France to pay local troops, salvaging their morale. Restored, the house is now lawyers' offices and not open to the public. ♦ 10 Marshall St

In *Cityscapes of Boston,* a compendium of before-and-after photographs of the city, *Boston Globe* architectural critic Robert Campbell shows no mercy when it comes to the shortcomings of Government Center: "The new West End is the product of well-meaning but idiotic control freaks, playing in their offices with zoning maps instead of walking out into the world to observe how cities really work… Its only virtue is that it has served for three decades, and will serve for many more, as a helpful textbook of mistakes to be avoided."

15 Blackstone Block A charming snippet of Old Boston, this tiny block is laced with winding lanes and alleys whose names—**Salt Lane, Marsh Lane,** and **Creek Square**—echo an era when water still flowed here. The neighborhood's history dates to colonial times; its architecture spans the 18th, 19th, and 20th centuries. People, chickens, geese, hogs, garbage, and carts laden with goods from nearby ships once commingled on the block's dirt streets. This area was on the narrow neck—frequently under water—that led from the **Shawmut Peninsula** to the **North End.** Meat markets flourished here throughout the city's history, and still do along **Blackstone Street,** named for Boston's first settler **William Blaxton** (his name was spelled both ways).

Benjamin Franklin lived in this neighborhood as a boy, the youngest of the 10 children who survived out of 17, on the second floor of his father **Joseph's** chandlery and soap-boiling shop at the corner of **Union** and **Hanover** streets. Walking along diminutive **Marshall Street,** look for the historic **Boston Stone** embedded in the base of an 1835 building's rear wall across from the **Ebenezer Hancock House.** In 1701 a nearby merchant named **Thomas Child,** who specialized in painting shop signs, used this stone to mix pigment. Decades after Child's death, legend claims this fragment of the original stone was recovered from his backyard and inscribed with the date 1737. The stone was eventually set into this wall and long served as a marker for measuring distances from Boston.

16 The Haymarket On Friday and Saturday a fleet of pushcart vendors selling fruits, vegetables, and fish sets up for open-air business along **Blackstone Street,** in front of old establishments like the **Puritan Beef Company** and **Pilgrim Market,** which purvey meats and cheeses supplementing Haymarket offerings. There's a great greasy stand-and-eat pizza place. The narrow sidewalk is clogged with veteran shoppers making their rounds and bewildered novices trying to learn the ropes. Saturdays are busiest. Come for bargains, especially at the end of the day, but be forewarned that the vendors, many of them North Enders, will treat you brusquely if you pick over their merchandise selectively. *They* fill the bags; you just pay, European style. So what if a tomato or two is worse for the wear; it's satisfying to have avoided the supermarkets' boring sterility.

When the Haymarket finally winds down for the day, squashed produce and scattered cartons make passage here challenging, but the place is soon restored for the next day's deluge. This debris has been honored in **Mags Harries'** bronze reliefs of everyday garbage, embedded in asphalt at the intersection of Blackstone and Hanover streets. ♦ F-Sa dawn-dusk. Blackstone St (between North and Hanover Sts)

The toothpick was first used in the United States at the Union Oyster House in Boston.

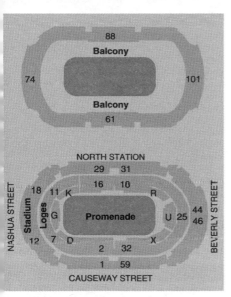

Balcony
88
74 101
Balcony
61

NORTH STATION
29 31
16 10
18 11 K R
Stadium
Loges
G Promenade U 25 44
46
12 7 D X
2 32
1 59
CAUSEWAY STREET

NASHUA STREET

BEVERLY STREET

17 Boston Garden Visit this hulking old barn (see the plan above) while you still can, since it's due for demolition in 1995 to make way for a slick new sports arena. Many will miss its funky Art Deco facade, interestingly juxtaposed with elevated rails that will also come down. Home of the **Celtics** basketball team and the **Bruins** ice-hockey team, Boston's beloved Garden also hosts family events and concerts year-round. Not to be confused with the verdant **Boston Public Garden** near Back Bay, this outdated, dilapidated 1928 structure is much too old for its heavy workload, but manages somehow. On game nights, the place pulses with energy, festooned with championship banners and retired numbers of star players. Notice the famous parquet floor, built during World War II when only short wood was available. If you attend a basketball game, stay past the final score: when the buzzer sounds, even before the last player has left the court, Garden staff whip in and unscrew the bolts holding down 264 five-foot-square panels, storing them within a mere 30 minutes and replacing them with a sea of hockey glass. Then head over to the **Commonwealth Brewing Company** at 138 Portland Street; or just follow die-hard fans to the nearby bars. ♦ 150 Causeway St. Recorded information 227.3200

Behind Boston Garden:

North Station Just like the comfortable current arrangement, the Garden of the future will combine with North Station to make it easy for fans coming in by train from north of the city. Trains operating from here also transport daily flocks of commuters from the North Shore. In the summertime, the station rings with voices as cheerful crowds await the beach train—the route stopping at **Beverly, Manchester, Gloucester, Rockport,** and other towns up the line blessed (or cursed, their residents might say) with spacious public beaches. Located across the street from North Station's main entrance, the MBTA's Green Line carries riders in and out of central Boston.

18 Hilton's Tent City The name is no empty boast. What began as a modest army surplus store in 1947 has ballooned into the biggest and best source of tents, with five floors holding the largest tent display in the country and complete accessories for camping and backpacking. Hilton's also sells men's and women's clothing for skiing, mountaineering, and backpacking. They don't stock running shoes or sneakers, but carry hiking, work, and sporty boots and shoes. Remember the old hardware store in your hometown? This is that kind of funky, dusty place packed with indispensable bargains. And Hilton's guarantees the lowest prices around on all of its stock. ♦ M-F 9AM-9PM; Sa 9AM-6PM; Su noon-6PM. 272 Friend St (at Causeway St). 227.9242 ♿

Government Center/Faneuil Hall

19 101 Merrimac Street Boston's first faux-historic building, a 10-story office complex that looks like a conglomeration of rehabbed warehouses, was, in fact, designed from scratch by **The Architects Collaborative** in 1991. Duck inside to catch New York muralist **Richard Haas'** trompe-l'oeil palm court, a domed winter garden eked out of two dimensions. The ubiquitous **au bon pain** has a small cafe here should you wish to rest and nosh a while. ♦ Between Lancaster and Portland Sts

19 Commonwealth Brewing Company ★$ "Let no man thirst for the lack of real ale" is the motto here. This working brewery and restaurant produces 10 or so kinds of English ale on the premises, including the acclaimed **Boston's Best Burton Bitter,** all dispensed on tap at the appropriate 52 degrees. The cavernous main level glows with copper tables—polished nightly—fixtures, pipes, and huge tanks of beer. In the downstairs tap room, redolent with fermenting yeast, you can watch the brewing process through glass walls. Light meals and snacks are available, but the main attraction is definitely the ale. A lot of people come here before and after **Boston Garden** games, and needless to say, it gets pretty noisy. Live bands play Saturday night. Free brewery tours—but no samples—are offered Saturday at 3:30PM and Sunday at noon (the tours, however, are not wheelchair accessible). ♦ American ♦ M-Th 11:30AM-11:30PM; F-Sa 11:30AM-1AM; Su 11:30AM-9PM. 138 Portland St (at Valenti Way). 523.8383 ♿

20 Old West Church A 1737 wood-framed church stood on this site until the British razed it in 1775, suspicious that Revolutionary sympathizers were using the steeple to signal the Continental troops in Cambridge. The decorous redbrick Federal replacement, a **National Historic Landmark** designed by **Asher Benjamin** in 1806, is kin to **Charles Bulfinch's Massachusetts State House** and **St. Stephen's Church,** and Benjamin's **Charles Street Meeting House**—all flat-surfaced and delicately ornamented with classical motifs. Formerly Unitarian and now Methodist, the church exerts quiet composure along Cambridge Street's physical and architectural chaos. Inquire about concerts featuring the fine **Charles Fisk** pipe organ. ◆ Su service 11AM. 131 Cambridge St (at Staniford St). 227.5088

20 Harrison Gray Otis House (1796) This house was a trial run for Otis and his architect-of-choice, the first in a series of three increasingly lavish residences that **Charles Bulfinch** designed for his friend, who had a taste for flamboyant living and fine architecture. Otis lived here for just four years before moving his family to grander quarters on Mount Vernon Street, followed by another move to Beacon Street. When he lived at house number one, Harry Otis was a prestigious lawyer and freshman member of Congress. He ultimately became Boston's third mayor and a major land

Government Center/Faneuil Hall

speculator who transformed rustic Beacon Hill into a wealthy enclave, again with Bulfinch's help. Set in what was briefly fashionable Bowdoin Square, this Federalist mansion is austerely handsome, much more opulent inside than out. By the end of the 19th century Bowdoin Square's elegance had frayed away, and Otis' former home endured a spotty career as a women's Turkish bath, then a patent medicine shop, and finally a boarding house defaced with storefronts.

In 1916 the **Society for the Preservation of New England Antiquities (SPNEA)** acquired the house—now one of 34 New England properties they run—and meticulously restored its former splendor. SPNEA is headquartered here, including its fabulous architectural and photographic archives, and offers tours of the interior. The house's decor dates from 1790 to 1820 and includes some Otis family belongings. With its next-door neighbor, the **Old West Church,** the Otis house steps back into the early years of the Republic. The two lonely survivors refuse to be overwhelmed by their high-rise surroundings. ◆ Admission. Tu-F noon-5PM; Sa 10AM-5PM. Guided 40-minute tours on the hour, last tour 4PM; groups limited to 15, by reservation only. 141 Cambridge St (at Lynde St). 227.3956

21 Holiday Inn-Government Center $$ Adjacent to **Massachusetts General Hospital,** this 15-story hotel has 300 rooms, with the nicest on the Executive level. There's a seasonal outdoor pool, and nonsmokers' and handicapped-equipped rooms are available. You can easily walk from here to **Government Center** and **Faneuil Hall Marketplace,** or cross **Cambridge Street** and meander over to **Beacon Hill.** Discounted parking is also available. ◆ 5 Blossom St (at Cambridge St). 742.7630, 800/465.4329; fax 742.4192 ᕒ

The historic Green Dragon Tavern once stood on Union Street, the popular patriots' meeting place that Daniel Webster called the "Headquarters of the Revolution." The Boston Tea Party was planned here.

22 Massachusetts General Hospital (MGH) Although a hospital is rarely a voluntary destination, make a trip to MGH to visit the remarkable seed from which sprouted this preeminent institution, consistently distinguished as the nation's best general hospital. To locate the **Bulfinch Pavilion,** a **National Historic Landmark** amid the MGH maze, enter from **North Grove Street** off **Cambridge Street,** or ask directions at the **George R. White Memorial Building** on **Fruit Street,** the main hospital building. (Built in 1939 by **Coolidge, Shepley, Bulfinch, and Abbott,** this late Art Deco city landmark is also worth a look.)

In 1817 Boston's trailblazing architect **Charles Bulfinch** won the commission to create this edifice of Chelmsford granite, quarried by inmates of the state prison. Questions persist about Bulfinch's actual role in the pavilion commission, since it was his last project before he was called to Washington by the president to design the **United States Capitol** rotunda. His assistant, **Alexander Parris**—who later gained fame in his own right, particularly for designing **Quincy Market**—prepared the working drawings and supervised construction, probably influencing the pavilion's final form much more than its name suggests. Delayed by the **War of 1812,** the cornerstone was laid in 1818 and the first patient was admitted in 1821. Today the building is still used for patient care, offices, and research.

Progressive for its day and gracefully proportioned, the Greek Revival building's enduring fame derives from the medical achievements that took place in the amphitheater beneath the skylit dome. It was in this theater, MGH's operating room from 1821 to 1867, now called the **Ether Dome,** that the first public demonstration of the use of ether in a surgical procedure took place. On 16 October 1846, **Dr. John C. Warren,** cofounder of MGH and its first surgeon, operated on a patient suffering from a tumor in his jaw. A dentist named **Thomas Green Morton** administered the ether with his own apparatus, after supposedly almost missing the operation because he was having last-minute adjustments made to the inhaler device. When the operating procedure was finally finished, the patient awoke and said he had felt no pain. Dr. Warren proudly announced to his colleagues, "Gentlemen, this is no humbug." Within a year, ether was in use worldwide to prevent surgical pain.

Not only does the amphitheater house memories of medical success, it's also home to **Padihershef,** a mummy from Thebes, Egypt, who was brought here in 1823—the first mummy in the US. The hospital's original fund raiser, Padihershef is also the only remaining witness to the Ether Dome's finest moments. To visit the Ether Dome, call ahead to be sure it's not in use. There's no charge. ◆ 55 Fruit St 726.2862 ᕒ

Michael and Susan Southworth

Urban Designers, Planners, and Authors of the *A.I.A. Guide to Boston*

The ornamental wrought- and cast-iron fences, balconies, and door and window grilles of Back Bay, Beacon Hill, and the South End.

Arriving at **Rowe's Wharf** by shuttle boat from Logan Airport.

Friday afternoon at **Symphony Hall,** the Stradivarius of concert halls.

Exploring the **Underground Railroad** and the many other significant black history sites in Boston.

Candlelight concerts at the **Isabella Stewart Gardner Museum.**

German sausage, sauerkraut, and beer at **Jake Wirth's.**

The luscious *tarte tatin* at **Maison Robert.**

Chiles rellenos at **Casa Romero,** an intimate Mexican restaurant that transcends tacos and smashed beans.

Bicycling in the **Emerald Necklace,** especially on the **Riverway** under autumn leaves.

The first day the **Swan Boats** paddle the pond in the **Public Garden** each spring.

The *Robert Gould Shaw Memorial,* by Augustus Saint-Gaudens, honoring the first regiment of freed blacks to serve in the Civil War.

The **Boston Early Music Festival** and its cacophony of virginals, clavichords, and sackbuts.

The Italian Renaissance Revival interiors of McKim, Mead & White's **Boston Public Library.**

The **Nichols House** and **Gibson House,** museums that transport us to domestic life in 19th-century Boston.

The **Essex Institute** in Salem, with its collection of important museum houses, furniture, and artifacts of the China Trade.

Saturday morning shopping at the Italian street markets in the **North End.**

A Sunday afternoon walk through the **Back Bay Fens** with its tall rushes, winding waterway, and stone bridge (by H.H. Richardson), followed by visits to the **Museum of Fine Arts** and the **Isabella Stewart Gardner Museum.**

Celebrating **St. Patrick's Day** in any South Boston tavern.

Evacuation Day (17 March), because it's the holiday no other city celebrates.

Trinity Church by **H.H. Richardson,** the best example of Romanesque Revival architecture in the country.

Robert Campbell

Architect and Architectural Critic

Lots of cities surpass Boston's food, architecture, and shopping, but none can top its streets and neighborhoods. Don't miss walking down **Beacon Hill,** along **Mount Vernon Street** to **Louisburg Square,** perhaps on Christmas Eve when the candles are in the windows and the carolers move from house to house.

Also walk through the **Public Garden,** on **Commonwealth Avenue,** along the **Charles River Esplanade,** or past the little shops of **Charles Street.**

Other streets where the city's karma seems to collect: **Union Park Square** in the South End, with sunlight falling through the trees on the bowfronts; **Marlborough Street,** the best proportioned and preserved of the streets of the Back Bay—easily the most successful "planned" residential neighborhood in American history; **Paul Revere Mall** behind Old North Church in the North End, Boston's only European-style "outdoor room"; **Harvard Yard** in November, the essence of austere Puritan New England—and so poignantly contrasted with Harvard Square next door, an explosion of punks and consumers;

Government Center/Faneuil Hall

and **Newbury Street** in the Back Bay, a humanly scaled shopping street, with its stores tucked into three levels of what once were houses.

Two classic examples of an especially American streetscape, shaped by a canopy of trees and a row of congenial mansions, are **Brattle Street** in Cambridge and **Chestnut Street** in Salem.

Art: The Fitz Hugh Lane seascapes at the **Cape Ann Historical Society** in Gloucester—America's greatest painter?—and his *View of Penobscot Bay,* which is in the **Museum of Fine Arts;** the *Robert Gould Shaw Memorial* by Saint-Gaudens in Boston Common; the **Richard Haas mural** on the **Boston Architectural Center;** and **Mount Auburn Cemetery** in Watertown in May, when the landscape is in bloom.

Food: The special pizza at **Bertucci's;** the brownies at **Rosie's Bakery & Dessert Shop** in Inman Square; **Locke-Ober,** an Edwardian survival; the tables outdoors at the **Harvest Restaurant** in Harvard Square; and a frank on a summer evening at **Fenway Park,** one of the last of the intimate ballparks and the home of a team that we know in our Puritan hearts will never win a world championship because of our guilt.

Buildings: McKim, Mead & White's **Boston Public Library,** especially the old grand stair; the **Isabella Stewart Gardner Museum** (especially when there's a Sunday concert); the **Peabody Museum** in Salem, particularly the **South Seas** and **China Trade exhibitions;** the **Harvard Lampoon Castle** on Mount Auburn Street in Cambridge, a rare example of a funny building; and **Rowes Wharf,** approached from across the harbor on the Airport Water Shuttle.

Lovely New England villages such as **Stockbridge, Edgartown, Nantucket,** and so many more, not to mention the exquisite mill village of **Harrisville** up in New Hampshire; the colony of miniature, brightly painted cottages—originally a religious encampment—at **Oak Bluffs** on **Martha's Vineyard;** and a tour of the mills of **Lowell.**

And lastly, of course, the annual influx of college students, tens upon tens of thousands of them, as central to a Boston autumn as new grass is to spring, keeping the old city fueled up and alive.

North End

You'll know you've wandered into the North End when you hear the strains of a plangent tenor solo wafting over the virtually untrafficked streets. North Enders know that if they ever *move* their cars, their precious parking spots will be lost; hence the curbside stasis. The sidewalks, however, are abuzz with impassioned food shoppers and venerated elders who, in summer, haul their lawn chairs down to the sidewalks to create an alfresco living room. Gala window displays brighten up the endless rows of redbrick facades, monotonous except at street level, and alluring aromas from *pasticcerie, trattorie, ristoranti, mercati,* and *caffè* escape into the tangled streets. The happy banter of children, who effortlessly switch between English and Italian depending on whether they're talking to school friends or family, can be heard throughout. And within this insular, fiercely proud Italian enclave winds the red ribbon of the **Freedom Trail**, directing tourists to the **Paul Revere House**, the **Old North Church**, and other vestiges of colonial Boston.

This is the spirited, colorful, bursting-at-the-seams North End. Don't even attempt to come here by car. It's best reached on foot by an ignominious route: from the **Haymarket** subway stop (on the Green or Orange Lines), a short pedestrian tunnel sneaks under the elevated **Fitzgerald Expressway**, commonly called the **Central Artery**. Your path may be gritty and noisy, but you'll be cheered on by sculptor **Mags Harries'** bronze reliefs of typical Haymarket garbage embedded in the pavement below, children's mosaics in the tunnel walls, and outdoor murals that greet you at **Cross Street** once you've reached the North End side of the expressway.

The heart of this vivacious, voluble district is Mediterranean today, but Italians have held sway only since 1920 or so. This is Boston's original neighborhood, where the city's early Puritan residents settled during the 17th century, their eyes on the sea. As piers, wharves, and markets sprang up along the Waterfront, the North End was known as the wealthiest, most populous, and in every way the most important part of town. It has undergone many a sea change since then.

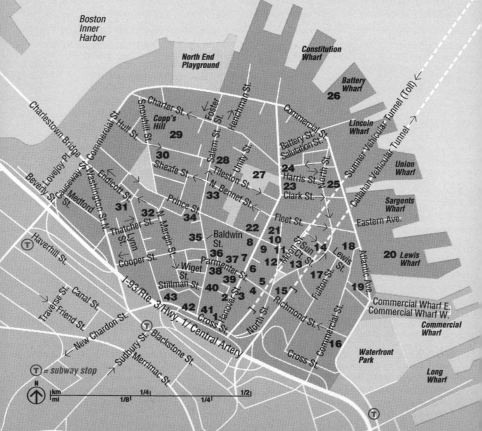

Those glory days ended following the **Revolution**, when the North End's aristocratic Tory population fled to England and elite Bostonians moved to **Beacon Hill** and **Bay Village**. The black community gradually migrated to the Hill as well. In the 19th century waves of immigrants—first Irish, then Eastern European Jews, then Portuguese, then Italians—poured into the North End, which had deteriorated into a slum. Over some 70 years, Italian-Americans have industriously restored the neighborhood. Their traditions have become the North End's bulwark, with a social life focused on the family, the church, caffès, rituals, and festivals.

Most streets follow their jumbled 17th-century pattern, giving you the flavor of colonial history seasoned with Italian culture. When infant Boston still fit onto the **Shawmut Peninsula**, the North End was a second peninsula—almost an island— divided from the first by **Mill Creek**. Today, following the old creek's track, the Central Artery cleaves the North End from Downtown. Work is underway to dismantle and depress the elevated highway, which, loathed at first, has proven to be a blessing in disguise by protecting the North End from gentrification's full force.

Changes are already afoot, so spend some time here while the fascinating cultural layers remain in place. The people you pass on the streets are still the children and grandchildren of *paesani* from villages in **Sicily**, **Abruzzi**, and **Calabria**. On **Hanover Street**, the North End's

main commercial thoroughfare, the caffè jukeboxes play Italian pop music. Parallel and to the left is **Salem Street**, where meat and provisions shops do a brisk business; a block to the right brings you to quaint **North Square** and **North Street**, which followed the shoreline until landfill pushed it blocks away. Notice the loaded laundry lines (you won't see *those* on Beacon Hill), minimal building ornamentation except for a bit of wrought iron here and there, and, aside from some well-used parks and rooftop gardens, scarce room for greenery. Glance up; more than one elderly North Ender is leaning out to check on who's coming, who's going, and who's doing what they shouldn't be doing. This is a close-knit place, after all, where people watch out for one another and strangers get the once-over more than once. Return before noon on a Sunday, when only the restaurants and caffès are open, filled with families in their Sunday best. In the summertime, join the throngs for one of the weekend *feste* in July and August, when North Enders commandeer the streets for morning-till-night processions, dancing, eating, and praying—each weekend dedicated to a different patron saint.

North End Beach and the bridge to Copp's Hill Terrace

Boston's subway service doesn't bring you into the North End, but rather deposits you near its edge. Although making your way into this out-of-the-way neighborhood can be confusing, there are always crowds of tourists headed in that direction. In addition to Haymarket (Green and Orange Lines), the North Station (Green Line) and Aquarium (Blue Line) stops are the most convenient to the North End.

1 Hanover Street The labyrinthine North End's straightest and widest route—which isn't saying much—Hanover Street runs through the heart of the district and boasts the greatest concentration of restaurants, bakeries, caffès,

banks, services, and shops selling everything from saints' figures to Italian-leather goods. Two famous department stores began here: at No. 168 **Eben Jordan** started a dry-goods store that eventually became the **Jordan Marsh Company;** and **Rowland H. Macy** opened a similar operation nearby that grew into the **R.H. Macy Company** of New York City. Block after block, four- and five-story buildings crowd in so closely that the Waterfront's nearness stays a secret until you reach the bend by **Charles Bulfinch's St. Stephen's Church**. Tourists stream along the narrow sidewalks as they follow the **Freedom Trail** to the **Old North Church,** or seek out popular dining spots such as **The European Restaurant** or **The Daily Catch.** But most of the street scene belongs to the people who live here. Even on a sleepy Sunday afternoon, Hanover Street pulses with the vigor of Italian-American culture.

1 Theatre Lobby and Paolo Ristorante
★★$$ This terrific little combination theater/cabaret/restaurant fills a giant gap in Boston's nightlife with aplomb. Nowhere else in the city

North End

can you enjoy an evening of entertainment with such leisurely European style. Owners **Anthony** and **Sally Capodilupo** have created a graceful, satisfying setting for performers and audiences. Paolo offers Tuscan/New England seasonal fare. The 175-seat wraparound square theater and the mauve-and-cream cabaret/caffè, which also serves as the theater's lobby, are intimate and comfortable; the sound and lighting superb; and the cabaret's handsome antique Steinway beautifully reconditioned. Because the theater is young, the program and show times tend to change. Call for information. Discounts are usually available on combination tickets. ♦ Italian/New England ♦ Admission to theater. Restaurant daily 5-10PM. 216 Hanover St. 227.9872

1 The European Restaurant ★$ The North End's "old reliable" since 1917, this restaurant isn't much to look at inside, but its famous clock and neon sign outside are familiar features in a landscape threatened with change. Your finickiest friend will be satisfied with the mammoth menu, and service is usually brisk and friendly. Huge, gloppy portions of Italo-American fare are reasonably priced—no exciting finds, but the extra-large pizza is surely Boston's biggest. Although the lines are long, the elephantine dining rooms mean the wait is generally endurable. The mood here is often boisterous; practically every visit, some table of 20 bursts into "Happy Birthday." Still, once in a while this just seems like the right place to be. Bring the kids—they can bounce off the walls and no one will notice. After your meal, cross Hanover Street to **Mechanic Street,** which ends in a funky cul de sac. Through the wire fence is a great view of the stalwart **Custom House Tower** downtown and its beautiful clock. To the left is

the **Sumner Tunnel** entranceway, with its wonderful pair of Art Deco reliefs: one angel in flight escorts a vintage truck, the other escorts a car. ♦ Italian ♦ M-Th, Su 11AM-12:30AM; F-Sa 11AM-12:45AM. 218 Hanover St (between Cross and Parmenter Sts). Reservations recommended for large parties. 523.5694 ὁ

1 Trio's $ Using recipes from Abruzzi and Sicily, some of which go back 300 years, the Trio family—**Tony, Genevieve,** their son **Louis**—whips up an awesome array of homemade pastas and companion sauces. To name just a few, you can take home gnocchi, tortellini, tortelloni, agnolotti, cavatelli, ravioli, red-pepper linguine, lemon fettuccine—and top them off any which way with ginger-vermouth, gorgonzola, anchovy-nut, white-clam, piquant marinara, or pesto sauces. Everything's made fresh on site; look into the kitchen where the pasta machines are churning out that day's supply. The Trios prepare lasagnas and other entrées for takeout, but there are a handful of stools if you can't wait to dig in. ♦ Italian/Takeout ♦ M-Sa 9AM-6PM; Su 9AM-1PM. 222 Hanover St. No credit cards. 523.9636

2 A&J Distributors Here's where budding vintners or brewers come for supplies. A&J also stocks Italian kitchenware from the practical (six kinds of meat grinders) to the frivolous (the gleaming row of Italian cookie presses). There are plenty of heavy-duty pasta and espresso machines to choose from, plus all those little gizmos for specialized tasks. ♦ Daily 9:30AM-8PM. 236 Hanover St. 523.8490

3 Caffè Paradiso Espresso Bar ★$ Stop by on the night of a *festa* or other celebration when the whole neighborhood seems to be here having a great time. The mainstay of Paradiso's decor is mirrors—they're everywhere, magnifying the caffè's hectic atmosphere. A sunnier setting is much nicer during the day, but this place is—for Boston—a night-owl spot, with the only 2AM liquor license on the street. The lively crowd keeps the jukebox cranking. The *gelati, sorbetti,* and spumoni are homemade. There's a full line of Italian bitter aperitifs, plus an enormous array of designer desserts that you won't see in any of the local bakeries. ♦ Caffè ♦ Daily 7AM-2AM. 255 Hanover St. 742.1768. Also at: One Eliot Pl, Harvard Sq, Cambridge. 868.3240; 3 Water St. 742.8689

Upstairs at the Caffè Paradiso Espresso Bar:

Il Sole $$ A lot of younger locals name this as one of their North End favorites. There are interesting offerings, such as a spicy seafood stew, as well as the usual fish, veal, chicken, and pasta selections. ♦ Italian ♦ M-Sa 11:30AM-11:30PM. Reservations are recommended. 742.1768

3 Modern Pastry Giovanni Picariellos junior and senior are renowned for their diabolically delicious homemade *torrone,* a nougat-and-almond confection drenched in chocolate. This ever-popular, 60-year-old *pasticceria* offers great *sfogliatelli, pizzelle,* and cannoli. ♦ Bakery ♦ M-Th, Su 8AM-9PM; F-Sa 8AM-10PM. 257 Hanover St. No credit cards. 523.3783

4 Villa Francesca $$ Not to be outdone by Felicia's, their high-profile neighbor across the way, these restaurateurs claim their share of star diners, too, including a slew of **Red Sox** baseball players. The food is nothing special—large portions spruced up with lots of lemon and white wine—but an Italian singer Monday through Friday draws a big following and provides the finishing touch to Francesca's overblown, Old World ambience. When you want a little schmaltz with your romance, try this place. And bring a date who has a sense of humor. ♦ Italian ♦ M-Th 5-10:30PM; F-Sa 5-11PM; Su noon-10PM. 150 Richmond St. 367.2948

5 Salumerìa Italiana ★$ The name means Italian deli, which tells you that you won't be rubbing elbows with many North Enders at this grocery store. But most of the neighborhood stores rely heavily on the tourist trade, as proprietor **Erminio Martignetti** will candidly confirm. It's definitely worth a stop to pick up some *prosciutto di Parma,* an import that wasn't available for years. The store also sells a good variety of cheeses, breads, salamis, olive oils, and espresso coffees. Come at lunchtime and Martignetti will make you what celebrity chef **Jasper White** calls "probably the greatest cold-cut sandwich in the world." ♦ Deli ♦ M-Th, Sa 8AM-6PM; F 8AM-7PM. 151 Richmond St. 523.8743

5 Felicia's ★$$ Owner and chef **Felicia Solimine's** place banks on past prestige, and it's undeniably a North End institution. For proof, look at the de rigueur gallery of celebrities' photos on your way upstairs to the dining room. See **Bob**  **Hope? Tom Selleck?** This is a classic overpriced red-sauce-and-chianti-bottle-lamp kind of spot. Still, most North End *ristoranti* overcharge for spiffed-up spaghetti, and Felicia's can be campy and fun if you come with a large group. The chicken *verdiccio* (made with mushrooms, artichokes, and acidic white wine) is worth a try. ♦ Italian ♦ M-Sa 4-10PM; Su 2-9:30PM. 145A Richmond St. 523.9885 ᵴ

6 Galleria Umberto ★★$ Come from the far reaches if necessary, but don't miss out on the best pizza and calzones the North End has to offer, not to mention Italian finger foods such as *panzarotti* (Italian dumplings) and *arrincini* (deep-fried balls of meat filled with rice). They serve only lunch, there's no table service, lines are long, and when the food's gone it's gone. When a new pan of pizza is delivered from the oven, watch the server attack it with a pizza wheel, ferociously "wap-wapping" it into steaming squares overflowing with fragrant cheese and oil. Join the steady stream of North Enders,

including gaggles of school kids in uniform, and rejoice at how inexpensive absolute gluttony can be. ♦ Pizza/Takeout ♦ M-Sa 11AM-2 or 3PM. 289 Hanover St. No credit cards. 227.5709 ᵴ

6 Caffè dello Sport ★$ No question about which sport this sunny caffè's name refers to: fluttering everywhere are pennants for Italian soccer teams. Take a windowside seat and sip an intense espresso or foamy cappuccino while you join in the North End's favorite pastime: people-watching. It gets ever more lively as the day progresses. ♦ Caffè ♦ Daily 6AM-midnight. 307 Hanover St. 523.5063 ᵴ

7 Ristorante Saraceno ★$$ Another family owned and operated restaurant, this one concentrates on Neopolitan recipes. In addition to the usual antipasti and entrée line up, Saraceno features good veal saltimbocca, shrimp and lobster *fra diavolo,* and linguine with seafood. The scrolled menus add a note of pretension to an otherwise straightforward and pleasant place

recommended by many North Enders. Dine in the small upstairs room; downstairs is rather confining with gaudy murals of Capri, the Bay of Naples, and Amalfi. ♦ Italian ♦ M-Sa noon-10:30PM; Su noon-9:30PM. 286 Hanover St. Reservations recommended. 227.5888 ᵴ

8 Caffè Vittoria ★$ This place is almost too much, with its faux marble tables and ornament, *il cortile* that isn't *really* a courtyard, *il grotto* that isn't *really* a grotto, and more-lurid-than-life murals of Venice and the Bay of Sorrento in the back. But a little *braggadocio* isn't all bad, and this 60-year-old caffè—Boston's first—exerts a full-bodied charm all its own. The antique coffee grinders are absolutely real, and so are the black-and-white photos of North Enders on the walls and the operatic espresso makers by the windows. Venture beyond cappuccino; try an *anisetta, grappa,* Italian soda, or maybe a gelato. Come during the day when your caffè companions are older men lingering over newspapers, chatting in Italian, and you'll get a sense of how deeply rooted Italian culture is in this neighborhood. At night it's a totally different place—festive and boisterous. ♦ Caffè ♦ Daily 8AM-midnight. 296 Hanover St. No credit cards. 227.7606 ᵴ

8 Mike's Pastry Every type of caloric Italian treat one could possibly crave—cream cakes, candy, cookies, breads, cannoli, even that most un-Italian of baked goods, the oat-bran muffin—is sold at this perpetually busy bakery. Since Mike's tries to cover all the bases, quality varies, and you should scout out the smaller *pasticcerias* for your favorite sweets. The *biscotti di Prato* are very good and cinnamony here, or go whole hog and try a "lobster tail," a particularly diet-devastating concoction of pastry with cheese, custard, *and* whipped cream. There are some tables and you can get coffee at this popular stopover for Freedom Trail pilgrims. ♦ Bakery ♦ M, W-Th 8AM-9PM; Tu 9AM-6PM; F-Sa 8AM-10PM. 300 Hanover St. 742.3050

9 **Daily Catch** ★★$$ That's the tiny restaurant's official moniker, but the name **Calamari Cafe** and the portrait of a squid lovingly hand-painted on the front window tell the real story. Owners **Paul** and **Maria Freddura** have dedicated their culinary careers to promoting this cephalopod, even manning a traveling squid-tasting show in the '70s when their favorite's popularity sunk to its lowest. A happy ending—calamari has become a big star and can be devoured here in many delicious ways. Since the Fredduras understand that squid is not for everyone, the menu's supporting cast includes Sicilian-style seafood options. Linguine with white or red clam sauce is another hit. The half-dozen-or-so tables flank the open kitchen, so enjoy the show as the young chefs deftly, flamboyantly toss your meal together. Then be prepared, because once the sizzling skillets are plunked down before you, you'll nearly reel from the intense garlic that sneaks into practically every dish. As

North End

long as you stay among good friends all evening, it's worth it. The drawbacks: there's no bathroom, but it doesn't take much resourcefulness to find neighboring facilities; and there's always a line, so come in good weather when you feel gregarious, or eat early. This original Daily Catch has spawned many offspring.
♦ Italian ♦ Daily 11AM-10:30PM. 323 Hanover St. No credit cards. 523.8567 ♿ Also at: 261 Northern Ave, Waterfront. 338.3093; 219 Elm St, Davis Sq, Somerville. 623.0375; 1 Kendall Sq, Cambridge. 225.2300

10 **Ristorante Carlo Marino** ★★$$ The gay green awning announces **Anna Marino's** place, named for her late father. When you've had your fill of silk flowers, travel posters of *Italia,* and the reds and golds splashed about too many North End dining rooms, Anna's crisp, forest-green-and-white-enamel decor is downright refreshing. And her flowers are real. Seating's snug but doesn't detract from the pleasant spirit. The affable owner is committed to tasty classical renditions of enduring Northern Italian peasant dishes, such as *melanzane ripiene* and *cotoletta parmigiana.* ♦ Italian ♦ Tu-Sa 5-10:30PM; Su 4-9PM. 8 Prince St (between Hanover St and North Sq). 523.9109 ♿

11 **North Square** Idiosyncratic interpretations of the civic "square" abound in Boston. This one is, in fact, a cobbled triangle. Nearly overwhelmed by the massive chain along its perimeter—a heavy-handed, almost ludicrous nod to a nautical past—the square is still winsome, made more so by its circular garden. The first part of the North End to be settled, a stone's throw from the Waterfront, the square soon boasted a diverse community of artisans, merchants, seafarers, and traders. The **Second Church of Boston**, nicknamed "Old North," the seat of the powerful, preaching **Mathers** family, was located where **Moon Street** enters the square until torn down by the British in 1776. By late colonial times this had become a very prestigious neighborhood.

Boston's two most lavish mansions overlooked the square, called **Clark Square** then. Today, 17th- to 20th-century structures commune here. Just off the square is Boston's most charmingly named intersection: the celestial meeting of Sun Court and Moon streets. Just around the corner is 4 Garden Court Street, home for eight years to **John F. "Honey Fitz" Fitzgerald**, ward boss, congressman, Boston mayor, and one of the city's most famous citizens. His daughter **Rose, President John F. Kennedy's** mother, was born here in 1890, in what she described as "a modest flat in an eight-family dwelling." While in residence at No. 4, Honey Fitz began his political ascent with his election to Congress in 1894, soon acquiring the nickname the "Napoléon of the North End." After leaving Garden Court, Honey Fitz took his family to No. 8 Unity Street, also in the North End. Throughout his career, Honey Fitz spoke so often of the "dear old North End" that North Enders were dubbed the "Dearos," a name that was adopted by the Irish political and social organization he led.

Honey Fitz was born nearby on Ferry Street in 1863. (Both the Fitzgeralds and the Kennedys emigrated to Boston in the mid-1800s to escape the Irish potato famine. Honey Fitz's father became a grocer on North Street and on Hanover Street.) US **Senator Ted Kennedy** has reminisced about how he and brothers **John** and **Robert** used to play a game to see who could cross Hanover Street first "in a hop, a skip, and a jump."

12 **Pierce-Hichborn House** This stalwart structure to the left of **Paul Revere's** house was home to Paul's cousin, a boatbuilder by the name of **Nathaniel Hichborn.** Another prized colonial urban relic, the house was built circa 1710 by a glazier named **Moses Pierce.** Overstimulated modern eyes might not notice, but this English Renaissance brick structure stylistically leaps far ahead of the Revere's Tudor in a very brief timespan. Even the central stair is innovative—simple and straight instead of windy and cramped like that of the Revere House. The pleasing three-story residence reflects a pioneering effort to apply formal English architectural principles to early Boston's unruly fabric. When the house left Hichborn's family in 1864, it, too, fell on hard times, becoming a tenement until restored in 1950. Four rooms are open to the public for guided tours given twice daily, the only times to see the interior. Enter at the Revere House gate. ♦ Admission. Tours daily 12:30PM, 2:30PM. Closed Monday Jan-Mar; major holidays. 19 North Sq. 523.1676

Around the corner:

Bakers Alley Walk down this alley to a pretty residential piazza ingeniously tucked in among the backsides of apartment buildings. The lucky residents have a number of handsome specimens of that scarce North End commodity: trees.

On 18 January 1950, Tony Pino and 10 partners-in-crime pulled off their famous heist of more than $1.75 million in cash from the Brinks Garage, located at the intersection of Prince and Commercial streets.

12 Mariners' House Dedicated to the service of seamen, this respectable Federalist edifice—erected in 1838 and converted into a seamen's boardinghouse in the 1870s—is a remnant of Boston's great seafaring days, now long gone, which fueled the city's rapid growth and the residents' fabulous fortunes. From the cupola atop its roof, mariner residents reputedly kept watch on the sea, much nearer then than today. Peer in the windows at the exceedingly nautical decor. Bonafide seamen still board here. ♦ 11 North Sq

12 Paul Revere House Here is where America's most famous messenger hung his hat. A descendant of Huguenots named Revoire, **Paul Revere** was an exceptionally versatile gold- and silversmith, as well as a copper engraver and a maker of cannons, church bells, and false teeth—reputedly including a pair for **George Washington**.

Busloads of tourists stream in nonstop, but it doesn't take long to see the humble rooms in Revere's tiny, two-story wooden clapboard abode (pictured below). It's worth inching along because this house and the **Pierce-Hichborn** residence next door are remarkable rare survivors of colonial Boston. Built in 1680 (nearly a hundred years before the "Son of Liberty's" midnight ride), rebuilt in the mid-18th century, and restored by **Joseph Chandler** in 1908, this **National Historic Landmark** has reverted to what it looked like originally, before Paul added an extra story to accommodate his big family. Revere and his second wife, **Rachel** (who gave birth to eight of his 16 children), owned the house from 1770 to 1800 and lived here for a decade until the war-ruined economy forced them to move in with relatives. From here Revere hurried off to his patriotic exploits, including participating in the **Boston Tea Party.** By the mid-19th century the impoverished, blighted North End was abandoned to poor immigrants by middle-class and wealthy Bostonians. The Revere House slipped into decrepitude and became a sordid tenement

with shabby storefronts. The wrecking ball loomed at the start of this century, but a great-grandson of Revere's formed a preservation group that rescued the house.

From across North Square look toward the medieval overhanging upper floor and leaded casements. These throwbacks to late 16th-century Elizabethan urban architecture are reminders that architectural styles were exported to the colonies from England and adapted with Yankee ingenuity long after they were out of fashion in Europe. Built after the devastating Boston fire of 1676, the fashionable town house violated the building code because it was made of wood, not brick. Today 90 percent of its frame and one door are genuine, its skin and insides reproductions. See how artfully the house tucks into its tiny site—every inch of space was built in the colonial North End, with rabbitwarren clusters of small houses linked by a maze of alleyways. The dark, low-ceilinged, heavy-beamed rooms

North End

with their oversize fireplaces bear few traces of the Revere family, but recall colonial domestic arrangements. The pretty period gardens in back are equally interesting when you study them with the help of the posted key and a pamphlet sold at the ticket kiosk. The multipurpose plantings—with old-time names like Johnny-jump-up, Bee-balm, Dutchman's-pipe, and Lady's-mantle—remind visitors that gardens were once commonplace sources of ornament, pharmaceuticals, food, and domestic aids. ♦ Admission. Daily 9:30AM-5:15PM, 15 Apr-Oct; daily 9:30AM-4:15PM, Nov-14 Apr. Closed Monday Jan-Mar; major holidays. 19 North Sq (at Bakers Alley). 523.1676

Across the street:

Rachel Revere Park The park was dedicated to Paul's wife by the **Massachusetts Charitable Mechanics Association,** a philanthropic group that was founded in 1795 with Revere as its first president.

13 Sacred Heart Church **Walt Whitman** described this former bethel (a place of worship for seamen) as "a quaint ship-cabin-looking church." The church opened in 1833, and for 38 years seamen flocked to hear the legendary Methodist preacher **Father Edward Taylor,** once a sailor himself. "I set my bethel in North Square," said Taylor, "because I learned to set my net where the fish ran." Whitman came to the services, calling Father Taylor the only "essentially perfect orator." **Ralph Waldo Emerson** anointed Taylor "the Shakespeare of the sailor and the poor" and often spoke from his close friend's pulpit. On one of his Boston visits, **Charles Dickens** made a special trip to hear the preacher, accompanied by **Longfellow** and **Charles Sumner,** abolitionist and US senator. In 1871 the bethel was sold and enlarged as a Catholic church. ♦ Daily 7AM-7PM. Mass M 7AM, 9AM, noon, 7PM; Tu-F 7AM, 9AM, 7PM; Sa 8AM, 9AM, 5PM; Su 9AM, 10:30AM, noon, 5PM. 12 North Sq. 523.1225

Paul Revere House

Ottavio's

14 Ottavio's ★★$$ Owner and chef **Sammy DiPasquale** freely acknowledges that his clientele doesn't include a lot of North Enders because "who cooks better than their own mother." His mama's specials include soups, the usual array of pasta dishes, and rich ricotta pies. He also serves rabbit and baby lamb dishes, authentic North End fare you can't get in *ristoranti* catering to tourists. A number of dishes are prepared tableside. It's no accident that the plates and glasses are eight-sided; Ottavio's is named for Sammy's grandfather, who was the eighth child in his family. This is not a hustle-and-bustle place, so relax and linger over your cappuccino and homemade cannoli. ◆ Italian ◆ M-W, Su 4-10PM; Th-Sa 4-11PM. 257 North St. Reservations required Friday through Sunday. 723.6060 &

North End

15 V. Cirace & Son **Jeff** and **Lisa Cirace** are the third generation and the second brother-sister act to run this 86-year-old Italian wine establishment. Cirace & Son has been voted the best shop of its kind in the US by Italy's Wine and Food Institute. About half of the store's 1,500-plus wines are Italian, and there's an extensive collection of cognacs, cordials, and venerable vintages. The Ciraces also carry cheeses, pâtés, and other gourmet items. This is not a self-service place; the friendly staff will assemble gorgeous gift baskets if you desire. The "V" in the name, by the way, is for Vincenza, the owners' grandmother. ◆ M-Th 9AM-7:30PM; F-Sa 9AM-10PM. 173 North St. 227.3193

16 Bibelots Housed in the **Mercantile Wharf Building,** an enormous 1857 granite warehouse renovated by **John Sharratt Associates** in 1976, **Renée Koller** and **David Bastian's** gift store is great fun because practically every item is one-of-a-kind and at least slightly eccentric. Most are handmade, imported from Mexico, Guatemala, Africa, England, all over. There are amusing interpretations of teapots, napkin rings, salt-and-pepper shakers; jewelry shaped like flora, fauna, and creatures that can't be categorized; plus more practical items such as dinnerware that resembles a stylish version of Fiestaware. A small gallery downstairs exhibits local artists' work. ◆ M, W, F 11AM-7PM; Th 11AM-8PM; Sa-Su noon-6PM. 75 Commercial St. 523.7336

17 McLauthlin Building New England's first cast-iron building, its soft brownish-mauve facade adorned with lacy rows of arched windows crowned by fanlights, was built circa 1850 and renovated in 1979 by **Moritz Bergmeyer.** The **McLauthlin Elevator Company** once resided here; now condos do. ◆ 120 Fulton St (between Richmond and Lewis Sts)

18 Jasper's ★★★★$$$$ Offer to take a Bostonian out for an extravagant, sumptuous dinner—no matter the expense—and this will be one of your friend's first choices. Owner and chef **Jasper White** is lauded nationally for his culinary wizardry, which, Pygmalionlike, transforms even the heartiest ethnic food into an elegant, refined dish (not *too* refined, however). White clearly thinks food is just wonderful and that it should always taste that way. No Yankee stick-in-the-mode, his nouvelle New England cuisine globetrots. Some of White's inventions are his famous grilled lobster sausage; garlicky pork and clams, Portuguese *Alentejo* style; Maine rock crab cakes; and grilled duck salad with papaya and spiced pecans. Soups and desserts are special here. The dining rooms are spacious, muted, unremarkable—a perfect unobtrusive setting for any evening drama you'd like to supply. Service is highly professional, although some critics say Jasper's has off nights, especially when he's not around. But throw caution to the winds—innumerable Bostonians have gone before you and been delighted. There's piano music on weekends. ◆ Contemporary New England ◆ Tu-Sa 6PM-closing. 240 Commercial St (at Atlantic Ave). Valet parking. Reservations recommended. 523.1126 &

19 Michael's Waterfront and Wine Library $$$ Its windows crowded with wine bottles and books, this restaurant announces up front the two features that keep it from being just another fern bar. The books, some of which are quite old, are donated by libraries and individuals, and patrons may borrow them. The sports-oriented bar, which offers a large selection of international wines by the glass, is frequented by a nonbookish crowd that occasionally includes rock musicians, entertainers, and TV people. As for the food, it's basic New England cuisine and seafood, featuring a great rack of lamb. Shuttle service is available to **Boston Garden** events, the **Theater District,** and local hotels. ◆ American ◆ M-Th 5:30-10:30PM; F-Sa 5:30-11PM; Su 4:30-9PM. 85 Atlantic Ave. Valet parking available 4:30PM-closing. Reservations recommended. 367.6425

The Prince Spaghetti Company used to be located at 45-69 Atlantic Avenue. For years, it ran a television ad campaign with the famous line, "In the Italian North End of Boston, Wednesday is Prince Spaghetti Day." Many Americans can still picture the commercial's star, a boy named Anthony, rushing home through the North End's streets as his mother calls him to a steaming plate of spaghetti at the crowded family table.

Restaurants/Clubs: Red   **Hotels:** Blue
Shops/ ◆ Outdoors: Green   **Sights/Culture:** Black

20 Lewis Wharf In the mid-19th century Boston's legendary clipper-ship trade centered on this wharf, originally named for **Thomas Lewis,** native of Lynn, MA, a canny merchant who acquired much of Boston's Waterfront property after the American Revolution. Ships carried tea to Europe and foodstuffs to be sold at exorbitant rates to prospectors during California's Gold Rush (eggs went for $10/dozen; flour for $44/pound). The warehouse was built of Quincy granite between 1836 and 1840, attributed to **Richard Bond,** and renovated in the late '60s by **Carl Koch and Associates,** at which time the graceful gabled roof was replaced with an unwieldy mansard one. The building now houses residential and commercial units. To the right stretches an attractive harborside park. The **Boston Croquet Club** rents a portion and sets up their wickets—a genteel sight that brings home how long gone the city's seafaring era really is. One story claims that **Edgar Allan Poe's** tale *The Fall of the House of Usher* was inspired by tragic events that took place on the wharf's site in the 18th century. Two lovers, a sailor and another man's wife, were trapped by the angry husband in their rendezvous, a hidden tunnel underneath the Usher house. When the structure was torn down in 1800, two skeletons locked in embrace were discovered behind a gate at the foot of the tunnel steps.

Set back at the **Boston Harbor** end of Lewis Wharf—where old, fallen-in wharf structures look ready for a harbor burial—is the popularly acclaimed **Boston Sailing Center,** which offers a variety of sailing and racing lesson packages, as well as captained harbor cruises aboard 23- to 30-foot-long sailboats. Boats also embark on day sails among the **Boston Harbor Islands** and on overnight trips to **Provincetown, Martha's Vineyard, Newport,** and **Block Island.** The sailing center acts as broker to arrange more extensive charters. ◆ Fees. Daily 9AM-sunset, May-1 Nov. 54 Lewis Wharf. 227.4198

21 Giacomo's ★★$$ The open kitchen is close, but not too close, which means you're enveloped in tantalizing, spicy-sauce aromas, but don't leave this cozy bistro drenched in the smell of garlic and smoke. The grill's the thing here—meaty swordfish and tuna steaks arrive succulent and smoky from the charcoal flame,

and grilled chicken and sausage are a fine duo. Try linguine with *frutte di mare,* a house specialty. Not content with the standard choice of white or red sauce, they've created "Giacomo" sauce—a feisty combination of the two. The unfinished brick walls and refinished wood floors—signs of unwanted gentrification throughout the North End—are OK in owner **Jack Taglieri's** unpretentious place. A handsome tin-stamped ceiling, oils on wood of Rome and Venice, and black-and-white caffè curtains add warmth and character. ◆ Italian ◆ M-Th 5:30-10PM; F-Sa 5-10:30PM. 355 Hanover St. 523.9026

22 St. Leonard's Church Peace Garden With flowers and statuary that are spotlit at night, this is more like a garden center than a garden. But when an open gate leads to an open space in a crowded neighborhood like the North End, people can't resist wandering in. And this is a cheery spot, especially when decked out with

lights at Christmastime. Planted at the close of the Vietnam War and maintained by the **Franciscan Fathers,** the garden endows the church (designed by **William Holmes** in 1891, and pictured below) with some distinction. Two shrubs were brought over from the altar on the **Boston Common** where **Pope John Paul II** celebrated Mass. St. Leonard's was the first Italian church erected in New England. ◆ Daily 9AM-1PM. Hanover St (at Prince St). 523.2110

St. Leonard's Church

Lobster Logistics

Indulging in your first lobster? Or anxious to perfect the cracking of this crafty crustacean? There's hardly a better place to learn than in Boston, where these critters are often caught and served the same day. Getting the meat out of the bright-red crustacean takes practice, patience, and a little perseverance. This guide to the art of lobster-eating should teach you the basics, but it's best to take an experienced lobster-cracking friend along for encouragement and coaching. And, despite how funny you may look, wear a bib—you're going to get more than a little messy.

1 Twist off the claws.

5 Insert a fork where the flippers broke off and push the meat out.

2 Crack each claw with a nutcracker.

6 Unhinge the back from the body. This contains the tomalley (or liver), which some folks are known to consume....

3 Separate the tailpiece from the body by arching the back until it cracks.

7 Open the remaining part of the body by cracking it sideways (the meat in this section is particularly good).

4 Bend back the flippers and break them off of the tailpiece.

8 The small claws are excellent eating—just suck the meat out as illustrated here.

ILLUSTRATIONS BY CHARLES SHIELDS

---

23 St. Stephen's Church Located at Hanover Street's bend, on its sunny side, is **Charles Bulfinch's** sole remaining church. In 1804 he transformed a commonplace meeting house called the **New North** into an elaborate, harmonious architectural composition, for which the congregational society in residence paid $26,570. **Paul Revere** cast the bell that was hung in the church's belfry in 1805. Although Bulfinch was usually drawn to English architecture, Italian Renaissance campaniles also inspired him in this work—an architectural foreshadowing of the North End's future ethnic profile. The dramatic tower crowds to the front of the wide-hipped facade, a bold counterpoint to the subtle Federal architectural gestures inside. Notice how the windows and column styles metamorphose as they move toward the gracefully curving ceiling. Most of the woodwork is original, including the pine columns. The 1830 organ was restored by **Charles Fisk** of Gloucester, MA, a famous American organ conservator. In 1862 the **Catholic Diocese of Boston** bought the church to serve the North End's enormous influx of Irish immigrants, renamed it St. Stephen's, added a spire, raised the entire building six feet, and moved it back 16 feet to install a chapel underneath. **Rose Kennedy, JFK's** mother, was christened here. In 1965 **Cardinal Richard Cushing** launched a successful campaign to renovate and restore the church to Bulfinch's design (**Chester F. Wright** carried out the restoration), respectfully returning the edifice—now on the **National Register of Historic Places**—to its original prominence. ◆ Daily 8AM-4:30PM. Mass Sa 5:15PM; Su 8:30AM, 11AM. 401 Hanover St (at Clark St). 523.1230

Reverend Samuel Mather's home (since demolished) on Moon Street formerly belonged to a sea captain who is remembered in history as the man put in the stocks on Boston Common in 1673 for "lewd and unseemly conduct." The captain's crime: kissing his wife on their doorstep after returning from a two-year voyage—unspeakable behavior, indeed, in Puritan times.

24 Ristorante Lucia $$ The food is pretty good, featuring dishes from Abruzzi. One pasta dish reproduces the Italian flag with a white-cream, red-tomato, and green-pesto sauce. The walls are covered with takeoffs on Italian master-pieces. Upstairs is Lucia's best feature: the opulent pink-marble barroom, whose ceiling is painted with replicas of scenes from the Sistine Chapel. Note the tasteful touch the indiscreet **Michelangelo** omitted: undergarments resem-bling diapers and swaddling clothes. ♦ Italian ♦ M-Th 4-11PM; F 11AM-11PM; Sa-Su 1-11PM. 415 Hanover St (at Charter St). Valet parking evenings. 367.2353 &

25 Davide ★$$$ The interior is bordello-esque, right down to the overstuffed red-velvet ban-quettes and the overheated color scheme. This is no place for a namby-pamby evening—bring a group that can live up to the molodra-matic setting. The menu changes seasonally (uncommon in the North End). Try the duck served in a port sauce flavored with figs, ri-sotto with seafood, or pan-fried bass with lemon-caper butter. ♦ Italian ♦ M-F 11AM-3PM, 5-11PM; Sa-Su 5-11PM. 326 Commer-cial St. Valet parking. Jacket recommended. Reservations required. 227.5745

26 Bay State Lobster Company The East Coast's largest retail and wholesale seafood operation, this 70-year-old busi-ness' biggest draw is the live lobsters you can buy on the spot for tonight's dinner or have shipped by UPS to anywhere in the Continental US. Perhaps you'd like some addi-tional companions on your flight home? Bay State also sells fish of all kinds, shellfish and all the trimmings, as well as the company's own clam and fish chowders and lobster pies. Any of these items can also be packed for traveling. As you might guess, it's often a madhouse here. ♦ M-W 9AM-5:30PM; Th 8AM-5:30PM; F-Sa 7AM-6PM; Su 8AM-1PM; Christmas Eve 5AM-5PM (the biggest sales day of the year). 379 Commercial St. 523.7960

27 Paul Revere Mall (The Prado) Laid out in 1933 by **Arthur Shurcliff,** this tree-shaded park could have been plucked from Italy. It offers residents a comfortable cushion of space in their jam-packed quarter, and sight-seeing pil-grims a pleasant passage from **St. Stephen's** to the **Old North Church** looming up ahead on Salem Street. This modest, slightly scruffy park has more personality than any of Boston's grander spaces. Though it isn't very old, it has a very lived-in look. The mall's brick walls and paving carve out a reposeful realm where all generations of North Enders cheerfully con-verge. A serious game of checkers or cards often goes on among the elders while peram-bulators are wheeled past, kids play, and dogs

race about. The bronze equestrian statue of **Paul Revere** (designed by **Cyrus E. Dallin** in 1885 and erected in 1940) towers near the Hanover Street edge, giving the young park a historical stamp. Hardworking, pragmatic arti-san that he was, not to mention unremarkable in physique, Paul Revere wouldn't recognize himself in this dashing figure. On some of the side walls, plaques commemorate North End-ers' contributions to their city.

The mall ends at **Unity Street;** cross and enter the gate leading into the courtyard behind the **Old North Church.** On the way, look for the **Clough House** (built in 1715) at 21 Unity Street. **Ebenezer Clough** lived here, one of the **Sons of Liberty,** a **Boston Tea Party Indian,** and a mas-ter mason who laid the bricks for the church. The courtyard itself occupies the former site of 19 Unity Street, which **Benjamin Franklin** bought for his two widowed sisters. ♦ Between Hanover and Salem Sts

28 Old North Church (Christ Church) Called the "Old North Church" by nearly everyone, this is the oldest church building in Boston (pictured on the following page) and the second Anglican parish founded in the city. Architect **William Price,** a local draftsman and print dealer, emu-lated **Christopher Wren** quite nicely in this 1723 brick edifice, now a **National Historic Land-mark.** Coping with a tiny site in cramped quar-ters, Price gave the church needed stature and eminence by boldly attaching a 197-foot-high three-tiered steeple—one of New England's earliest.

What points to the sky today, however, is the 1955 replica of the original steeple, which was toppled in 1806 and again in 1954. The weath-ervane on top was made by colonial craftsman **Deacon Shem Drowne.** The eight bells that ring from the belfry were cast in 1744 by **Abel Rud-hall** of Gloucester, England, and range in weight from 620 to 1,545 pounds. Their inscription re-calls long-extinguished aspirations: "We are the first ring of bells cast for the British Empire in North America, Anno 1744." The oldest and sweetest-sounding church bells in America, they have tolled the death of every US President since **George Washington** died in 1799. When he was 15, **Paul Revere** and six friends formed a guild to ring the bells.

Years later, Revere starred in the celebrated drama that has enveloped this landmark build-ing with enduring legend, though a lot of the facts are cloudy. On the night of 18 April 1775 Revere rode on horseback to warn the **Minute-men** at **Lexington** and **Concord** of the approach-ing British troops. And as Revere arranged be-fore departing, or so the story goes, **Robert Newman,** Christ Church's sexton, hung signal lanterns in the belfry to alert the populace that the British were on the march. Although a num-ber of other messengers, including **William Dawes,** rode out into the towns, Paul Revere has eclipsed them all in fame. **Henry Wadsworth**

49

Longfellow can take the real credit for Revere's glory; spellbound by the nearly forgotten tale, he wrote the inaccurate but entertaining poem "Paul Revere's Ride," published in *The Atlantic Monthly* in 1861. Every April, on the eve of **Patriots' Day,** descendants of Revere or Newman hang lanterns in the church belfry to commemorate that spring night. An unresolved controversy, however, concerns whether this is the real Old North Church, or whether the **Second Church of Boston** on North Square—nicknamed "Old North," which was burned by the British—truly held the leading role in the events on the eve of the American Revolution. If this theory is ever proven, it will cause a major rerouting of the **Freedom Trail,** so no one is rushing to verify it. No matter what the truth is, a sad and genuine chapter in Christ Church's past was the divided loyalties of its Episcopalian congregation. Once the Revolution ignited, the church was closed until 1778 because of

the tensions unleashed between Patriot and Tory parishioners.

The church's white interior shimmers with light entering through pristine glass windowpanes. It's too bad there's rarely a chance to enjoy the church's unusual serenity and architectural clarity in solitude. Originally owned by parishioners, with brass plaques indicating which was whose, the tall box pews were designed to hold the warmth of hot bricks and coals during the winter. Look for the Revere family pew—No. 54. Inscriptions abound in the church and on the walls of the **Washington Memorial Garden** in back. Many offer interesting slants on colonial Boston. The clock ticking reassuringly at the rear of the gallery was made by a parishioner in 1726, and it's the oldest still running in an American public building.

The brass chandeliers, also gifts, were first lighted on Christmas Day 1724—with candles, of course. To the right of the apse, a 1790 bust of **George Washington** rests in a niche. When **General Lafayette** returned to Boston in 1824, he noticed this bust and said, "Yes, that is the man I knew, and more like him than any other portrait." Before leaving the church, look for the tablet on the left side of the vestibule, which identifies 12 bricks set into the wall. These were taken from a cell in **Guildhall** in Boston, England, where **William Brewster** and other **Pilgrims** were held after attempting to flee that country in 1607. In 1923 the mayor of Boston, England, sent the bricks on Christ Church's 200th anniversary as a gesture of friendship.

To the left as you exit is a curious museum and gift shop amalgam, housed in a former chapel built in 1917 to serve the North End's tiny community of Italian-speaking Protestants, now vanished. In front of the street entrance, notice the amusing, stout little columns resting on the pair of lions' backs. Inside, look for the "Vinegar Bible," a gift of **King George II** in 1733 and so nicknamed for its famous typo: on one page heading, the "Parable of the Vinegar" appears instead of the "Parable of the Vineyard." Tea retrieved from the boots of a **Boston Tea Party** participant is also on display. There are lots of fun things to buy here, from spice gumdrops and maple sugar candy to copies of Longfellow's poem and Wedgwood china decorated with the church's image.

Behind the church on both sides are charming small gardens nestled among clusters of nearby residences. In early summer the courtyard of the Washington Memorial Garden is awash in the fragrance of roses. Among its many commemorative tablets, one intriguingly states, "Here on 13 Sept. 1757, **John Childs,** who had given public notice of his intention to fly from the steeple of Dr. Cutler's church, performed it to the satisfaction of a great number of spectators." Said Childs did indeed leap from on high strapped to an umbrellalike contraption that carried him safely for several hundred feet.

Old North Church (Christ Church)

Cross Salem Street and look back at the church. Ever since its completion, the Old North has towered over the swath of redbrick that makes up the North End's fabric. The church's colonial neighbors are gone now, but since the newer buildings don't exceed five stories, you can still get a vivid image of the early 18th-century landscape. Unlike the State House, for instance, the Old North has not been overwhelmed by 20th-century urbanism. Historical talks are offered by staff ad hoc. ♦ Daily 9AM-5PM. Services Su 9AM, 11AM, 4PM. Closed Thanksgiving and Christmas. 193 Salem St. 523.6676

29 Copp's Hill Burying Ground Another of Boston's wonderful outdoor pantheons, Copp's Hill not only offers the finest gravestones in Boston, but also some of the best views of the city's most elusive feature—the Waterfront. From this promontory you can see down to the boat-clogged **Boston Harbor** and over to **Charlestown** and its **Naval Yard**, where the venerable warship "Old Ironsides," the USS *Constitution*, is in dry dock. This cemetery was established in 1659 when **King's Chapel Burying Ground** got too crowded. Once an Indian burial ground and lookout point, **Corpse Hill**, as it is also known, has accommodated more than 10,000 burials. In colonial days black Bostonians settled in the North End in what was called the **New Guinea** community, at the base of Copp's Hill. A granite pillar marks where lies **Prince Hall**, black antislavery activist, Revolutionary War soldier, and founder of the **Negro Freemasonry Order**.

Sexton Robert Newman, who flashed the signals from Old North Church—and was imprisoned by the British for doing so—is also buried here. And the formidable dynasty of the Puritan **Mathers**, churchmen and educators—**Increase**, his son **Cotton**, and Cotton's son **Samuel**—reside in a brick vault near the Charter Street gate. (Increase was awarded the first doctor of divinity degree conferred in America.) During the Revolution, British generals directed the shelling of **Bunker Hill** from Copp's Hill and their soldiers used the gravestones for target practice—as you can still discern. Look for **Captain Malcolm's** bullet-riddled marker. His patriotic epitaph particularly incensed the soldiers: "a true son of Liberty/a friend to the Public/an enemy to oppression/and one of the foremost/in opposing the Revenue Acts on America." Copp's Hill legend tells of two tombs that were stolen here: interlopers ejected the remains of the graves' rightful owners, whose names were carved over with those of the thieves for future burial. ♦ Snowhill St (between Charter and Hull Sts)

29 Copp's Hill Terrace After scrutinizing the Puritan view of death, head downhill to this graceful plaza set into the sloping hill, beleaguered by neglect and vandals. It's still a wonderful architectural progression, most frequented by the youngest and oldest neighborhood residents. Near this site on Commercial Street below, the **Great Molasses Flood** occurred on 15 January 1919. A four-story tank containing 2.5 million gallons of molasses burst, releasing a lavalike torrent that destroyed several buildings, killed 24 people, and injured 60. It took a week to clear the streets after the explosion, and a sticky-sweet aroma clung to the neighborhood for decades. Some North Enders claim they can still smell molasses from time to time in the heat of summer. ♦ At Copp's Hill

30 Hull Street Leading up the hill from the Old North and abutting the **Copps Hill Burying Ground**, this is one of the North End's most attractive streets. It was named after Boston's first mintmaster, **John Hull**, who coined the city's famous "pine-tree shillings" and had an estate that encompassed this neighborhood. ♦ Between Salem and Snowhill Sts

30 44 Hull Street Located across from the Hull Street entrance to **Copp's Hill Burying Ground** is a circa-1800 house that is indisputably the narrowest in Boston, one window per floor at the street end, squeezing up for air between its stout companions. An amusing tale claims that

this house was an act of revenge, built solely out of spite to block the light and view of another house behind. In truth, this is a lonely survivor of the breed of modest dwellings called "10 footers," depicted in old prints of colonial Boston-town. This picturesque dwelling is nine feet, six inches wide, to be precise. A floral wrought-iron fence leads to its charming entry. ♦ Between Salem and Snowhill Sts

From early June until the end of August, *feste* take over the North End's streets every weekend. Each celebration is organized by one of the neighborhood's religious societies, most of which honor the patron saint of a village in Italy or Sicily, from whence their original members came. Most kick off with a parade on Friday, when a statue of the saint is transported to a temporary chapel along a route winding through the North End. All weekend long there's music, dancing, and lots of eating—with vendors selling quahogs, calzones, sausage, pizza, fried dough, fried calamari, *zeppoli*, and other wonderful greasy foods. The grand finale is the extravagant procession on Sunday that brings the saint home to the meeting place of the host society. Shouldered by men who may plod along under its weight for eight hours or so, the saint is paraded in a cloud of confetti throughout the gaily decorated neighborhood. Elderly women clutch rosaries, their eyes fixated on the passing saint. Religious offerings are made by pinning money to long ribbons fastened to the figure; the men will raise the statue so that people reaching down from apartment windows can pin on their bills.

The most popular feste are the "Big St. Anthony" and the colorful Feast of the Madonna del Soccorso (nicknamed the "Fisherman's Feast"). This feast's most famous feature is the "flight of the angel," in which a young girl "flies" from a window over North Street to offer a bouquet to the Madonna. The feste have become commercial over time, and many North Enders avoid them now because they draw hordes of outsiders and turn the neighborhood into a circus. Still, these exuberant celebrations are the fullest expression of North End culture you'll ever encounter.

Pick of the Pasta

Oodles of noodles, some of the best in the world, are served in Boston's North End, where the thriving Italian community tends to center around the *ristoranti* and *caffè*. Don't pass up the opportunity to indulge in a pasta feast—one of Boston's more popular treats. This pasta primer should help guide you along the way.

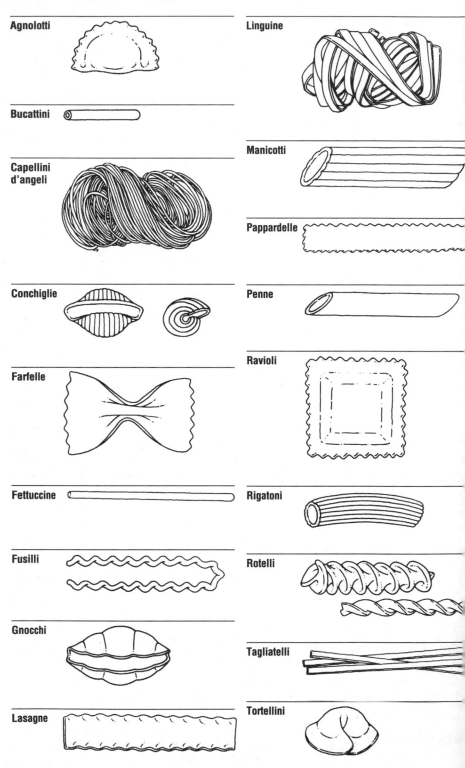

Agnolotti

Bucattini

Capellini d'angeli

Conchiglie

Farfelle

Fettuccine

Fusilli

Gnocchi

Lasagne

Linguine

Manicotti

Pappardelle

Penne

Ravioli

Rigatoni

Rotelli

Tagliatelli

Tortellini

31 Oasis Cafe ★$ If you aren't in the mood for marinara, hop off the Italian express at this casual, comfy little cafe, where the order of every day is American homestyle cookery: meat loaf, barbecue pork, cajun catfish, burgers, corn bread. The Oasis' signature offering is its roast of the day, which can be accompanied by real mashed potatoes if you like. Every day there's an Oasis fritter, too, either fruit or vegetable. Everything's homemade right down to the salad dressings. Be ready for whopping portions. Come hungry and have dessert—Key lime pie maybe. You'll dine to the tune of '30s and '40s jazz in a pink-and-black Art Deco setting. When you leave, find where Endicott Street intersects North Margin Street at odd, appealing **Alfred Wisniski Square.** Looking down Endicott Street toward Downtown from here, you get one of the North End's few unimpeded views. ♦ American/Takeout ♦ Tu-Sa 11:30AM-10PM; Su 11AM-3PM. 176 Endicott St (at Alfred Wisniski Sq). 523.9274

32 Pizzeria Regina ★$$ In Boston, everybody but everybody knows the city's most famous (not best) pizza-pie joint: the North End Regina's. This is brick-oven pizza of the thin-crust, oily variety. Customers from New York and Florida fly home with as many as eight pizzas. It's a little tricky finding the curved corner building Regina's calls home, but any North Ender can point you in the right direction. ♦ Pizza/Takeout ♦ M-Th 11AM-11:30PM; F-Sa 11AM-midnight; Su noon-11PM. 11 ½ Thatcher St (at N. Margin St). No credit cards. 227.0765. Also at: Faneuil Hall Marketplace. 227.8180

33 Salem Street This intimate, bustling street was dominated in the 19th century by the millinery and garment businesses owned by Jews who settled in this area. Now butcher shops, restaurants, markets, and great produce markets, many with no signs and run by proprietors who serve *all* customers—North Enders or not—with the same brusqueness, are tucked into tiny shopfronts. Most of the people you see lugging parcels are returning from this street; here one gets a glimpse of daily North End goings-on. From the south end of the street you get a great view of the trucks and cars creeping along on the elevated **Central Artery**—enjoy your pedestrian freedom. ♦ Between Cross and Charter Sts

At 409 Commercial Street, the USS *Constitution* was built at Constitution Wharf. The ship's keel was laid in 1794 and "Old Ironsides" was launched in 1797.

33 North Bennet Street School Founded in 1881 by **Pauline Agassiz Shaw,** this school originally helped North End immigrants develop job skills. No longer a social-service agency, the school offers classes in furniture-making, carpentry, piano tuning, violin-making and restoration, bookbinding, jewelry-making, watch repair, and other fields. Its graduates are trained in traditional craftsmanship and respected throughout New England. ♦ 39 N. Bennet St (at Salem St). 227.0155

34 Bova Italian Bakery If ever you suffer from insomnia, why not discover what the North End is like at four in the morning, when nary a tourist blocks your way, and get some fresh bread and pastries in the bargain at the Bova family's corner shop—open every hour of every day. For more than 70 years, Bova has been baking all its goods right on the premises—there's nothing fresher. ♦ Bakery ♦ Daily 24 hours. 134 Salem St (at Prince St). 523.5601

North End

34 A. Parziale & Sons Bakery This is a businesslike shop, and its business is to make lots of great bread. The place is bursting with it. The Parziale family sells a thousand loaves a day of French bread alone. But why not stick to the Italian varieties and try a handsome loaf of *Scali, Bostone,* or fragrant, rich raisin bread? The *pizzelles* and anisette toasts are great, too. ♦ Bakery ♦ M-Sa 8AM-6PM; Su 8AM-1:30PM. 80 Prince St (at Salem St). 523.6368

35 Lo Conti's ★$ If you like your Italian fare fresh and light, and are not keen on the heavy trappings of typical bordello-style decor, try this small, bright restaurant with teal-laminate wooden tables and modernist leanings. Some specialties include *gnocchi mascarponi* (potato dumplings tossed in a rich cheese sauce) and *calamari bianco* (fresh squid simmered with white wine). The service here is brisk and no-nonsense; the pricing and portioning quite generous. ♦ Italian ♦ Daily 11:30AM-10PM. 116 Salem St (at Baldwin St). 720.3550 ♿

36 L'Osteria Ristorante ★★$$ **Marge,** one of the waitresses, says she follows co-owner **Nicky DiPietrantonio** wherever he goes because the food is so good. It would be easy to overlook this unassuming spot, but go in for a warm welcome and homestyle Northern Italian fare made from the very freshest ingredients. There's not a lot of elbow room here. ♦ Italian ♦ Tu-Su 11:30AM-11PM. 109 Salem St (at Parmenter St). Reservations recommended. 723.7847 ♿

Enrico Caruso loved the North End. When the Italian tenor came to Boston, he often ate at a restaurant called the Grotta Azura on Hanover Street (the establishment, however, no longer exists). A famous anecdote about Caruso tells how he wasn't able to cash a check at a neighborhood bank because he had no acceptable identification. Caruso launched into *Celeste Aida,* immediately delighting and convincing the skeptical bank manager.

Restaurants/Clubs: Red   **Hotels:** Blue
Shops/ 🌿 Outdoors: Green   **Sights/Culture:** Black

37 Boston Public Library, North End Branch
Come by when the library is open to inspect the remarkable 14-foot-long plaster model-diorama of the **Doge's Palace** in **Venice.** This clever creation was the consuming passion of **Henrietta Macy,** who taught kindergarten in the North End before moving to Europe. After she died in Venice, her handiwork was presented to the library. Painted settings and dolls enacting 16th-century scenes were added by **Louise Stimson** of Concord, MA. As for the 1965 building, architect **Carl Koch's** attention to Italian-American cultural heritage has tempered and transformed the coldness of '60s modernism into an extraordinary neighborhood addition. The library's atrium is cobbled like an Italian piazza, with plants and a small pool. Umbrellalike concrete vaults supported by nine columns form a roof, raised to create a clerestory that illuminates the library interior. The brick exterior is punctuated by colored glass ceramics, add-

North End

ing festive notes to what is an otherwise drab streetscape. ◆ M-W 10AM-1PM, 2-6PM; Th noon-4:30PM, 5:30-8PM; F 9AM-1PM, 2-5PM. 25 Parmenter St (between Salem and Hanover Sts). 227.8135

38 Polcari's Coffee Polcari's has been a fragrant North End fixture since 1932. In addition to his fine selection of coffees, congenial **Ralph Polcari** stocks more than a hundred spices from all over the world, sold by the ounce. Innumerable other specialty items fill every inch of shelf and floor space: chamomile flowers, *ceci* (dried chick peas), Arborio rice, flax seed, carob and vanilla beans, pine nuts, braided garlic, and bunches of fresh oregano. Polcari's wares are the stuff of alchemy in everyday cooking. ◆ M-Sa 8:30AM-6PM. 105 Salem St (at Parmenter St). 227.0786

39 Fratelli Pagliuca's ★$$ There's decidedly nothing fancy about the Pagliuca brothers' very popular place. **Joe, Freddy,** and **Felix** changed the name from *Sabatino's,* but everything else is the same. A goodly number of locals eat here, Monday and Tuesday especially, as do businesspeople who know their way around the North End. This is satisfying, stick-to-the-ribs Northern Italian red-sauce cuisine served in a family atmosphere. Favorites include the chicken-escarole soup, chicken marsala, and sweet roast peppers with provolone and sausage, which come in large portions for reasonable prices. Don't look for the four basic food groups here: pasta and meat, not veggies, get priority. ◆ Italian ◆ M-Th 11AM-10PM; F-Sa 11AM-10:30PM. 14 Parmenter St. Reservations recommended Friday through Sunday. 367.1504

Boston is full of public squares—a street intersection named after someone—but the North End has an especially large supply. Most of them honor Italian public figures, war heroes, and the like, such as Joseph S. Giambarresi Square, Arthur A. Sirignano Square, and Gus P. Napoli Square.

40 Mottola Pastry Shop Armando Mottola has been baking since he was nine years old. In addition to cookies, cannolis, and other traditional pastries, the Mottolas (Armando's brother bakes here, too) turn out a wonderfully rich rum cake—the weight-watcher's nemesis. Another specialty is Armando's black-and-white cake made to look like a volcano—there's surely someone or some occasion it will suit perfectly. ◆ M-Th 8AM-6PM; F-Sa 8AM-7PM; Su 8AM-1PM. 95 Salem St. 227.8365

40 Giorgio's $ "Every pizza weighs a minimum of two pounds," says a sign in the window, a promise that will lure those who like a hefty pie. Judging by the enormous slices, not to mention blimplike calzones (one-pound minimum), Giorgio's keeps its promise. What's really special about this popular pizzeria is the simple sauce, sweet with crushed ripe tomatoes and oil only; the wide selection of fresh toppings; and the owners, **Albert** and **Steven Giorgio** and their mother, **Lillian.** The Giorgios are very friendly, family oriented people—Albert's wristwatch sports a photo of his three sons—who like to get acquainted with their customers. Try to sit by the window overlooking the street. ◆ Pizza/Takeout ◆ Daily 10AM-11PM. 69 Salem St. No credit cards. 523.1373

41 La Piccola Venezia ★★$ Forget decor, forget romance, forget trendy angel-hair pasta concoctions—there's a whole slew of other reasons to frequent this no-frills spot. First, there's the hearty Italian home-cooking that runs the gamut from familiar favorites—lasagna, spaghetti with meat sauce, sausage cacciatore—to hard-to-find, traditional Italian fare like tripe, gnocchi, polenta, *baccala* (salt cod), and *scungilli* (conch). Second, everything's cheap and arrives in hefty portions, so when your wallet's light but your appetite's immense, this place is perfect. Third, it's noisy, it's hectic, it's tacky, it's bursting with people, but La Piccola Venezia is perpetually cheerful. Unlike many touristy North End spots peddling fake ambience and tarted-up cuisine, everything here is exactly what it seems. And finally, look who's dining with you. Among the tourists are a lot of locals, many who've been coming to **John** and **Jimmy's** place for a decade or more. ◆ Italian ◆ Daily 11:30AM-9:45PM. 63 Salem St. No credit cards. 523.9802

41 Dairy Fresh Candies If you like sweets, it's impossible to pass by without stopping in, and once you're inside, it's all over. Those who suffer from chocoholism will tremble at the sight of loose chocolates of every sort, including massive chunks of the plain-and-simple sinful stuff and gorgeous packaged European assortments. The entire confection spectrum is here, including hard candies, old-fashioned nougats, and teeth-breaking brittles. But the amiable **Matara** family, in the retail and wholesale business for more than 30 years, goes way beyond candy: they've got Italian cakes and cookies, dried fruits, nuts, exotic oils and extracts, vinegars, antipasti, pastas, cooking and baking supplies, and more—an extravaganza of delicacies. You can assemble a wonderful gift box here. "Thank you, stay sweet," says the hand-lettered sign by the door. ♦ M-Th 8AM-6PM; F-Sa 8AM-7PM; Su 10AM-5PM. 57 Salem St. 742.2639, 800/336.5536. ♿

42 Maria's Pastry Shop What's a *pasticceria* without a display of marzipan in fruit and animal shapes, lurid with food coloring? Maria's has that popular almondy-sugary confection, and plenty more. Butter, anise, and almond scent the air, and through the kitchen door you can see bakers taking cookies out of the oven. Try Maria's *Savoiardi Napolitani*, lemon-frosted *anginetti*, or intriguing *moscardini ossa di morta* (which really do resemble bones). The *sfogliatelli* are creamy, citrony, and not too sweet. ♦ Bakery ♦ M-Sa 7AM-6:30PM; Su 7AM-1PM. 46 Cross St. 523.1106

43 Purity Cheese Company Four people make all the marvelous ricotta and mozzarella sold fresh daily in this unobtrusive shopfront. It's easy to miss unless you glance in and spot the giant, pungent wheels of Parmesan and tubs of olives. Grating cheeses, pastas, oils, and big serving bowls are available, too. The business began in 1938, and the operation is as unfussy as ever. Cheese, cheese, and more cheese of the highest caliber—that's why people from all over come here. And it smells delicious inside. ♦ Tu-Sa 8AM-5PM. 55 Endicott St (at Cross St). 227.5060 ♿

43 Pat's Pushcart ★$$ The decor here is nothing to speak of, but neither is that of most Italian family kitchens putting out good food for a hungry horde—which is what this place is like. And it, too, is on the noisy side. On the outside, the Pushcart looks like a dive. Inside, it's packed with North Enders and anyone else wily enough to track down this great dining spot. Entrées are basic, tasty, and inexpensive. ♦ Italian ♦ Tu-Sa 5-10:30PM. 61 Endicott St (at Cross St). 523.9616

centerpiece is a magnificent three-story courtyard with seasonal plantings. In the middle of January, leaning out of the balcony into this space is a great refreshment. The little restaurant serves a nice lunch. It's minutes from the **Museum of Fine Arts.**

Try weiner schnitzel, pan-fried potatoes, and spinach at **Locke-Ober;** insist on a table downstairs.

Walk from the **Hatch Shell,** down the esplanade along the **Charles River** to **Cambridge,** and back the other side (or take the Red Line back from **Harvard Square**).

At Harvard visit the **Fogg Art Museum,** the **Houghton Library** (for rare books), and the **Carpenter Center for the Visual Arts** (by Corbusier). Then have lunch at **Bartley's Burger Cottage** on Mass Ave.

In Cambridge, start at the **Harvard Square** T stop and walk down **Brattle Street** through the shops and into the residential area (wonderful colonial and Richardsonian houses) as far as you have time for. Take a different route back.

Avoid the common mistake of calling the North End "Little Italy," the nickname for New York City's Italian district.

Early in the 20th century, a popular Boston schoolchildren's song went:
> "My name is Solomon Levi
> At my store on Salem Street
> That's where you'll find your coats and hats
> And everything that's neat."

The North End consists of one hundred acres, 70 percent of which is used for housing.

Waterfront/Fort Point Channel

Newcomers to Boston who have heard of its great maritime past are often surprised to discover how elusive the Waterfront is. Hills that once overlooked **Boston Harbor** were leveled long ago, and the shoreline, for centuries Boston's lifeline, has been sheared from the city's core by **Atlantic Avenue**, the **Central Artery**, and a shield of modern buildings. With a little perseverance, however, you can cross this man-made divide to see where Boston began. An urban treasure, the Waterfront is vibrant with light and hue and the constant motion of water and air. The history of the neighborhood's heyday is recorded in the street and wharf names, and captured in grand old buildings getting a new lease on life. The harbor itself, long the nation's most polluted, is undergoing a massive cleanup. Eventually, the sprinkling of more than 30 islands here should have the sparkling setting they deserve. From little **Gallops, Grape**, and **Bumpkin** to big **Peddocks** and **Thompson**, the **Boston Harbor Islands** will entice you with picturesque paths, beaches, and views of the city.

In colonial times young Boston looked to the Atlantic Ocean for commerce and prosperity. Throughout the 17th, 18th, and 19th centuries profit-minded Bostonians industriously tinkered with the shoreline, which originally reached to where **Faneuil Hall** and **Government Center** are today, once the **Town Dock** area. Citizens built piers, shipyards, warehouses, and wharves extending ever farther into the sea, until the shoreline resembled a tentacled creature reaching hungrily for its nourishment: trade. The ocean brought profitable European and Chinese trade and established the city's legendary merchant princes.

One of Boston's most glorious moments was the clipper-ship era of the 1850s, when the harbor horizon was alive with masts and sails. Toward the turn of the century, as rails and roads replaced sea routes and manufacturing supplanted maritime trade, fishing, and shipbuilding, Boston's liaison with the sea began to suffer, languishing for decades until the late 1960s, when the city began to reclaim it. Now the Waterfront is being resurrected gradually, its connections to the heart

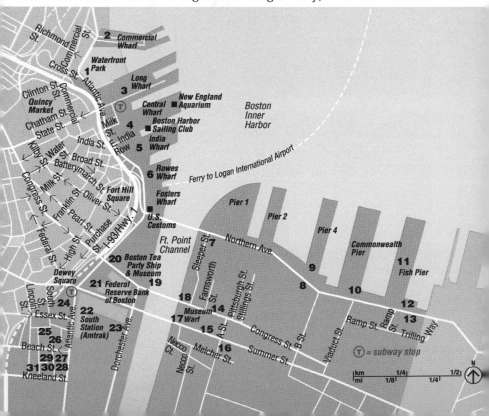

of Boston reforged. The harbor activities that remain have shifted elsewhere, primarily to **Charlestown** and **Fish Pier** in **South Boston**.

Boston is also reinterpreting the Waterfront's role as a place for leisure, luxurious residences and offices, pleasure boats, and waterside restaurants and hotels. Excursion and commuter boats depart from the numerous wharves for the Boston Harbor Islands, **Provincetown** on **Cape Cod, Cape Ann,** and **South Shore** communities. **Harborwalk,** the pedestrian route along the Waterfront, is lengthening; it ultimately will stretch from the **Charlestown Navy Yard,** where "Old Ironsides" is temporarily dry-docked, to **Fort Point Channel,** linking with walks along the **Charles River**—a total of more than 20 miles. For now, however, you can take one great stroll that begins at **Waterfront Park** and **Commercial Wharf,** proceeds past the **New England Aquarium** and around sumptuous **Rowes Wharf,** crosses over the channel via the **Northern Avenue Bridge** into the area where Fish Pier and the **Children's Museum** and **Computer Museum** are located, then doubles back past **South Station,** concluding with a brief meander in the little **Leather District**.

Fort Point Channel and the Leather District aren't part of the historic Waterfront per se, but are natural companions because they, too, reveal facets of Boston's workaday life. Developed during the late 19th century, the Fort Point Channel neighborhood was the center for Boston's fishing, shipping, warehousing, and manufacturing industries; during the same era, the garment and raw leather goods industries thrived in the Leather District. In both atmosphere and architecture, these two neighborhoods, like the Waterfront, are acquiring new vitality as galleries, restaurants, and shops move in, following the trail of artists and other urban pioneers. Walking the entire length of this far-flung neighborhood at one time is an ambitious undertaking, but definitely can be achieved if you're not with children. It's a great Boston experience.

The best way to get to the Waterfront/Fort Point Channel area is to take the subway to the Government Center stop (Green and Blue lines) and cross City Hall Plaza to the right of City Hall, descending the steps behind City Hall to Congress Street, crossing to Faneuil Hall Marketplace, and continuing straight to Christopher Columbus Park—the walk-to-the-sea route. Or, the Aquarium T stop on the Blue Line brings you directly to the Waterfront, to the right of the park. And the South Station stop (Red Line) brings you to the edge of the Leather District and Fort Point Channel.

1 Waterfront Park This friendly park, designed by **Sasaki Associates** in 1976, opened a window to the sea and drew Bostonians back to where their city began. In fact, the park was built to complete the "walk to the sea" that starts at **City Hall Plaza** in **Government Center,** proceeds through **Faneuil Hall Marketplace,** then passes under the **Central Artery** to end by the water. A handsome trellis promenade—short on greenery—crowns the park's center, with huge bollards and an anchor chain marking the seawall. The park offers views of the harbor and wharves, and a sociable scene: From morning until late at night, this versatile oasis hosts sea-gazing, ledge-sitting, suntanning, frisbee-throwing, dog-walking, and romantic rendezvous. Watch planes take off across the harbor at **Logan International Airport** and the steady boat traffic. On a summer afternoon sit and read amid the grove of honey locust trees or in the **Rose Fitzgerald Kennedy Garden,** fragrant with her namesake blooms. **Quincy Market** is just a five-minute walk away; pick up some treats and picnic with the cool ocean breezes rustling by.

2 Commercial Wharf When **Atlantic Avenue** sliced through the Waterfront in 1868, the rugged 1834 building of Quincy granite and Charlestown brick was sadly split in two. Now the western half, renovated by **Anderson, Notter, Feingold** in 1971, is home to **Michael's Waterfront and Wine Library,** and the larger eastern half, renovated by **Halasz and Halasz** in 1969, houses offices and upscale apartments with enviable views. Original architect **Isaiah Rogers** also designed Boston's famed **Tremont Hotel,** long gone, the nation's first luxury overnight digs. If you walk to the wharf's end, you'll see ramshackle buildings, relics of days gone by. Now pleasure boats in the adjacent yacht marina crowd the pier and clamor for attention.

2 Boston Sail Loft $ Strange as it seems in a seaside city, there aren't many restaurants in Boston where you can sit and look out at the water. This is one of the few. Longtime residents fondly recall its predecessor, a run-down, quiet hole-in-the-wall called **The Wharf.** But things change; even if this is now a hopping touristy spot on the happy-hour trail, you get a nice view of **Boston Harbor** along with your oversize portions of decent seafood. ♦ American/Seafood ♦ M-Sa 11:30AM-11PM; Su noon-11PM. No tank tops. 80 Atlantic Ave. & 227.7280. Also at: One Memorial Dr, Cambridge. 255.2222

2 Cherrystone's $$ The food is pretty commercial, but the spacious dining rooms—especially on the first floor—are okay in a casual, country club way. For a change, the nautical theme hasn't been overdone; in fact, the mounted book illustrations of fish are charming. There's lots of surf and some turf. The restaurant's location is its biggest asset—there's plenty of **Boston Harbor** and **Christopher Columbus Park** to see, with the neighboring wharves, the **North End,** or **Faneuil Hall Marketplace** to choose from for a post-prandial stroll. Validated parking is nearby. ♦ Seafood ♦ Daily 11:30AM–10PM. 100 Atlantic Ave (at Commercial Wharf). Reservations recommended. 367.0300 &

3 Long Wharf Boston was already America's busiest port when farsighted **Captain Oliver Noyes** constructed this wharf, the city's oldest—and now a **National Historic Landmark**—in 1710. It originally extended from what is now **State Street** far out into what was then **Town Cove,** creating a dramatic half-mile avenue to the farthest corners of the world. It was the Logan Airport of its day, where even the deepest-drawing ships could conveniently unload

Waterfront/Fort Point Channel

cargo on the pier lined with warehouses. The painter **John Singleton Copley** played here as a child, where his mother ran a tobacco shop. Landfill and road construction demolished most of the wharf by the 1950s, but the restoration of its remaining buildings and the arrival of the **Boston Marriott Long Wharf** have made it a destination once more. Walk to the spacious granite plaza at the wharf's end for fresh air and lovely views.

On Long Wharf:

Boston Marriott Long Wharf $$$$ It's certainly pleasant to stay here at the city's edge in rooms surveying the lively Waterfront, with **Christopher Columbus Park** next door, the **New England Aquarium** one wharf over, and the **North End** *ristoranti* and **Faneuil Hall Marketplace** mere minutes away. Many of the 400 rooms have good views—make sure yours does—and two luxury suites have outside decks. The **Concierge Level** offers premium services; general amenities include a business center, an indoor swimming pool, other exercise facilities, and a game room. This 1982 hotel, designed by **Cossutta and Associates,** has a couple of counts against it as a Waterfront neighbor, however: it rudely crowds what should have remained a generous link in the **Harborwalk,** and the architects' attempt to mimic Waterfront warehouses and the lines of a ship has resulted in an awkward, aggressively bulky building. The Marriott's red-garbed porters are a striking sight. Be sure to see the 19th-century fresco depicting **Boston Harbor** that is mounted in the lobby upstairs. Relax by a window in the ordinary lounge named **Rachael's;** there is also the formal **Harbor Terrace** restaurant and a more casual cafe. ♦ 296 State St (at Atlantic Ave). 227.0800, 800/228.9290; fax 227.2867 &

The Chart House $$ The **Gardner Building,** a simple and solid circa 1763 brick warehouse—the Waterfront's oldest, renovated in 1973 by **Anderson, Notter, Feingold**—was recycled for this chain restaurant. Inside, rustic bricks and beams recall the building's former life. Steak, prime rib, and seafood are the ticket, with children's plates available. Lots of stories circulate about the building's history—some possibly true—claiming it was called **Hancock's Counting House** because **John Hancock** had an office here, and that tea was stored here prior to the **Boston Tea Party.** When closed for the night, the sealed shutters outside convey a snug, sleepytime look. The free valet parking is a great boon in a neighborhood born long before the days of autos. ♦ Seafood/American ♦ M-F 5-11PM; Sa 4:30-11PM; Su 3-10PM. 60 Long Wharf. 227.1576

Custom House Block Before his writing career finally freed him from ordinary pursuits, **Nathaniel Hawthorne** spent two years (1838-40) recording cargoes in the cramped predecessor to this building, demolished in 1847. The "new" structure, designed by **Isaiah Rogers** and restored as a **National Historic Landmark** by **Anderson, Notter, Feingold** in 1973, never did serve as a Custom House (that activity moved to the future site of the **Custom House Tower**), but nonetheless bears the signature eagle and a misleading sign on its imposing granite facade. The building, always held privately, now accommodates offices and apartments.

4 Central Wharf In the early 19th century Boston was rebounding economically from the American Revolution and becoming a booming seaport once more. The brilliantly daring developer **Uriah Cotting** formed the **Broad Street Association** of businessmen to modernize the dilapidated, disorderly Waterfront. With architect **Charles Bulfinch** designing, the association created broad streets flanked by majestic four-story brick-and-granite warehouses, and built this wharf (completed in 1816) and **India Wharf.** A seamen's chapel was also located here. Only a fragment of Central Wharf remains, with a handful of its structures stranded forlornly on the opposite side of the expressway.

On Central Wharf:

New England Aquarium School kids and plenty of adults hurry eagerly across the expansive plaza, pausing to spot the harbor seals in their year-round outdoor pool (watch for **Rigel** the seal, who barks like a parrot), then moving inside to the aquarium's spectacular attraction: a three-story, 40-foot-diameter tank swirling with fish, sea turtles, and sharks. The dim lighting is provided by the aquarium's illuminated displays and exhibit tanks, creating a murky underwater ambience. Visitors walk up the ramp winding around the central tank, transfixed by the constantly circling parade of flashing fins, spiky teeth, waving tails, and opaque eyes. Watch for the divers who feed the fish five times a day, only after the sharks have otherwise dined. And check out the walls opposite the tank, inset with aquariums. At the tank's

New England Aquarium

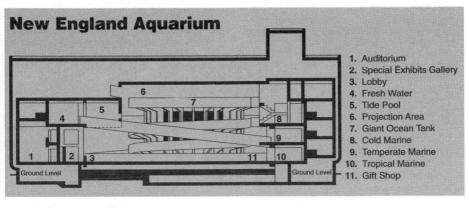

1. Auditorium
2. Special Exhibits Gallery
3. Lobby
4. Fresh Water
5. Tide Pool
6. Projection Area
7. Giant Ocean Tank
8. Cold Marine
9. Temperate Marine
10. Tropical Marine
11. Gift Shop

base, endearing penguins stand at attention or zip about a shallow pool, braying noisily. Next door floats the **Discovery Theater**, where you can see the ever-popular marine mammal shows. On the outdoor plaza, summertime snack stands draw steady business.

Don't miss the kinetic sculpture *Echo of the Waves*, which can move for hours without repeating the same pattern. The work of **Susumu Shingu,** the sculpture dampers to control its movement during high winds. The boxy, concrete aquarium (designed by **Cambridge Seven** in 1969) is now like a sea creature grown too big for its shell; a major expansion is planned. A model in its day, the aquarium (see the map above) is poised for a fabulous renaissance. ♦ Admission. M-Tu 9AM-6PM, W-Th 9AM-8PM (free admission 4-8PM), Sa-Su and holidays 9AM-7PM, 1 July-Labor Day; M-W 9AM-5PM, Th 9AM-8PM, F 9AM-5PM, Sa-Su and holidays 9AM-6PM, day after Labor Day-30 June; noon-5PM, 1 Jan. Central Wharf (between Milk and Atlantic Sts). Recorded information 973.5200 &

New England Aquarium Whale Watching
Since the aquarium considers whales another important exhibit, it takes you 25 miles due east from Boston to visit the extraordinary mammals at **Stellwagen Bank,** a rich feeding ground. During the five- to six-hour voyage (round-trip), aquarium naturalists tell whale tales and describe other marine life. Sometimes whales come up to the boat and let out a blow right into your face and camera. Whales frequenting New England coastal waters include humpbacks, finbacks, and, occasionally, right whales. In 1987 two blue whales, the largest creatures ever to live on earth, were sighted off **Cape Cod.**

Be sure to dress warmly in layers—even in summer—and bring waterproof gear, rubber-soled shoes, and sunscreen. The boat leaves from **Central Wharf** and offers a full-service galley. Children under 36 inches in height aren't permitted on board. Call for times and reservations. ♦ Fee. April-Oct. Reservations by credit card, payment in cash only. Recorded information 973.5277 &

5 India Wharf The other major result of the **Broad Street Association's** 19th-century scheme to revamp the Waterfront, India Wharf (begun in 1805) was once a half-mile stretch of piers, stores, and warehouses designed by **Charles Bulfinch.** The last vestiges of the handsome structures were levelled to make room for the upstart **Harbor Towers.**

Waterfront/Fort Point Channel

On India Wharf:

Harbor Towers Whereas Boston's historic Waterfront buildings stretched like fingers into the harbor, waves lapping among them, these towers aren't so involved in the maritime scene. The standoffish pair (designed by **I.M. Pei** in 1971) is more intrigued by the sky. In their day the 40-story interlopers brought dramatic new style and scale to this part of town. Originally somewhat alienating, the towers have acquired a kind of folk appeal, partly because newer buildings more brazen and far less clever have pushed their way in—such as **International Place** across the street. The Harbor Towers are more exciting to live in than to look at; the residents enjoy stunning views. **David von Schlegell's** *India Wharf Project,* a stark 1972 sculpture composed of four folded planes, stands at the edge of the harborside terrace. The flat surfaces clad in stainless steel also ignore the harbor and reflect what's happening above instead. The human hustle-bustle and colorful disorder this wharf once knew have been replaced by lonely, silent forms. But you won't find it gloomy here, just introspective—like the sea's occasional gray, foggy face.

Boston Harbor Sailing Club Sail in the harbor and among the islands that once witnessed stirring arrivals and departures of Boston's majestic clipper ships. In a city famous for its exclusive clubs, this is not a club per se, but rather a 17-year-old private enterprise offering sailing classes taught by experts. The one-week courses are very popular, attracting novices from all over. Properly certified visitors can rent boats from a fleet of 80 ranging in length from 26 to 39 feet. ♦ Daily 8:30AM-10PM, May-Oct. 72 East India Row. 523.2619

6 Rowes Wharf A resplendent six-story arch lures pedestrians from **Atlantic Avenue** at the water's edge. Many Bostonians consider **Skidmore, Owings, and Merrill's** grand, redbrick complex—luxury condos, offices, shops, a 38-slip marina, and a hotel—the best addition to Boston in years. The 15-story development was built in 1987 on the 1760s Rowes and Fosters wharves. Many don't even realize it's new, because unlike **Harbor Towers,** Rowes Wharf looks backward in time. The ornamental overkill borders on kitsch, but the building is generous, capable of grand gestures. Rowes Wharf has further privatized the Waterfront, yet gives back to Bostonians the heroic arch, an observatory, open space, a splendid **Harborwalk** extension leading past enormous yachts, and best of all, a new entry to the city via the water shuttle that zips between **Logan International Airport** and Rowes. This speedy journey is worth taking for its own sake, sans baggage, to enjoy the most picturesque approach to Boston and see the flipside view through the monumental portal. It's not a cheap thrill, but do it once.

Airport Water Shuttle

The **Airport Water Shuttle** departs from Rowes Wharf and the Logan Airport dock. Dock-to-dock, the trip takes seven minutes, with hotel courtesy buses and **Massport** buses operating on the airport dockside to and from the terminals. Tickets are sold on board. ◆ Fee; elders, children at reduced rates, infants are free. M-F 6AM-8PM, every 15 min; Sa-Su, national holidays noon-8PM, every half-hour. Closed on Thanksgiving, Christmas, Independence days. Shuttle information and 24-hour Massport ground transportation: 800/235.6426

On Rowes Wharf:

Boston Harbor Hotel $$$$ The 230-room hotel's public spaces are tranquil and attractively dressed in warm woods, pearly grays, and subdued burgundies, with companionable textures and tapestry patterns. Cove lighting adds a subtle glow and paintings by Massachusetts artists decorate the first two floors. Pay more for a room where you can gaze out at **Boston Harbor** instead of peering across the elevated expressway at the **Financial District.** In its **Magellan Gallery,** the hotel houses a largely undiscovered treasure: a private collection of early maps and charts depicting New England and Boston. Owned by **The Beacon Companies,** developers of the Rowes Wharf complex, the display includes Virginian **Captain John Smith's** 1614 map of the New England coast, the first ever produced, which later guided the Pilgrims to Plymouth. Another fascinating map (created in 1625 by **Sir William Alexander**) records **The Council of New**

England's scheme to turn the region into an elite association of English estates, which was ultimately overturned by competition from the Massachusetts Bay Colony and support for the Puritan cause.

Pretty **Harborview Lounge** with its comfortable furnishings is a wonderful place to have a drink and watch the light fade to harp or piano music. A Sunday breakfast buffet is accompanied by a live trio, high tea is served Monday through Saturday, a dessert buffet is offered every evening, and a bar dinner menu is available on weekdays. Inquire about live music and dancing on weekends.

Away from the water overlooking empty sidewalks, **Rowes Wharf Bar** is unfortunately placed but blissfully quiet. The hotel's amenities include a posh health club and spa with a pristine three-lane lap pool, 24-hour room service, nonsmokers' and handicapped-equipped rooms, and pet services from counseling to catnip. A year-round airport water shuttle, indoor parking, and marina slips are also available. ◆ 70 Rowes Wharf (at Atlantic Ave). 439.7000, 800/752.7077; fax 330.9450 ৬

Within Boston Harbor Hotel:

Rowes Wharf Restaurant ★★★★$$$$ The views from here are so splendid it would be easy not to care much about what's on your plate. But in fact, the hotel lavishes attention on the roomy restaurant's cuisine. Chef **Daniel Bruce** hails from New York's **"21"** and **Le Cirque,** not to mention Venice and Paris ports-of-call. A blend of regional American and seafood specialties—such as a trio of fish with triplet sauces, bouillabaisse, and crab cakes—are served with finesse amid a sophisticated rendition of the obligatory nautical theme, with fabric-covered walls and lush carpeting to soak up wayward sound. Look for **Dr. Robert Levine's** mahogany, teak, and lemonwood replica of the renowned 1851 clipper ship *The Flying Cloud.* ◆ American ◆ M-F 6:30AM-2PM, 6-10PM; Sa 7-11AM, 6-10PM; Su 7-9:30AM, 10:30AM-2PM. 439.3995 ৬

Rowes Walk Cafe ★★★$$ During spring and summer, weather permitting, enjoy lunch, cocktails, or dinner on the patio outside of the **Harborview Lounge.** The kitchen is outdoors, too, so the menu is simple, but the setting is gorgeous and you don't have to dress up. ◆ Cafe ◆ Daily 11:30AM-10PM, week after Memorial Day-Labor Day. 439.7000 ৬

Fort Point Channel

Most Bostonians have yet to stumble upon this fascinating place, and those who love it hope that won't change too soon. This no-nonsense neighborhood exposes some of the city's practical inner workings. Slender Fort Point Channel is now all that divides the original **Shawmut Peninsula** from **South Boston,** once a far-off neck of land. In the 1870s the **Boston Wharf Company** cut the channel and erected warehouses on the South Boston side to store lumber, sugar, coal, imported fruit, wool, raw pelts, and ice. **Fish Pier** and

Commonwealth Pier were both built on landfill, the second becoming the center of the Boston fishing industry. By the 1890s the area was the major transfer point for raw materials fueling most New England industries, and was bursting with wharves, machine shops, iron foundries, glassworks, wagon factories, soap producers, brickyards, and printing trades. Business boomed through the early 20th century, then slackened as the fishing and wool industries, shipping, and manufacturing declined. The construction of the Central Artery further isolated Fort Point, speeding the area's decline.

Artists rediscovered the neighborhood in the 1970s, creating a SoHo-like atmosphere that early on earned the district the affectionate nickname "NoSo," short for North of South Boston. Now more than 300 artists belong to the Fort Point Arts Community, the largest community of visual artists in New England. Headquartered at 249 A Street, an artists' cooperative, FPAC sponsors several open-studio weekends annually. A few pioneering galleries and museums moved in as well, followed by creative and service industries.

The World Trade Center and the massive Boston Design Center, the latter New England's major showroom facility for the interior-design trade, have comfortably settled in now, too. What port activity remains in Boston is located along Northern Avenue and at Fish Pier, home of the New England Fish Exchange. Megadevelopment of the vacant Fan Pier nearby—an on-again, off-again proposal for a city-in-a-city—would transform the neighborhood. But for now it's great fun to poke around the revival and rubble, still full of the old Waterfront district's industrial flavor and vitality. Look for the Boston Wharf Company's architecturally inventive warehouses on Summer and Congress streets. Trucks and tractor-trailers rule the roads in this part of town. Back across the channel, skyscrapers spread like weeds; here, low-rise buildings and empty lots let light flood in. Unfamiliar vantage points show off the city's skyline.

For such a tiny waterway, the Fort Point Channel bridges offer a remarkable survey of mechanical engineering. Each operates differently: the creaky Northern Avenue Bridge—slated to be replaced by a fixed bridge—is a trussed rolling bridge that swivels 90 degrees on a single axis to clear the channel for ships; the Congress Street Bridge has a giant counterweight to drive a large gear system that lifts up the bridge; and the Summer Street Bridge is engineered to slide sideways out of the way on rails built on piers.

7 **Venus Seafood in the Rough** ★★$ Look for the splashy red-and-yellow banner and the giant flashing arrow, right by the Northern Avenue Bridge. Owners Susan Chused-Still and Maggie McNally serve inexpensive and delicious shack-style seafood cuisine, but with flair and consideration for health-conscious diners—you can even get a green salad here. Fish and seafood of all kinds are fried, boiled, grilled, and steamed. Order a classic New England clambake with all the fixings or one of the nightly grilled fish specials. Out-of-staters—

Maryland and Maine crabs—star in the autumn **Venus Cosmic Clambake**. Dine casually at picnic tables under the giant heated tent, with a wonderful view juxtaposing lobster boats and the city skyline. It's a great place for parties and families. ◆ Seafood ◆ Daily 11:30AM-9PM, mid Apr-Sept. Closed Oct-mid Apr. 88 Sleeper St (at Northern Ave). No credit cards. 426.3388 ⑤

8 **Our Lady of the Good Voyage Chapel** In addition to regular weekend Masses, an annual "Blessing of the Animals" service is held at this humble little chapel. ◆ Mass Sa 7PM; Su 11:30AM, 12:30PM, 7PM, 8PM. 65 Northern Ave. 542.3883

9 **Anthony's Pier 4** ★$$ There are better places to go in Boston for an expensive seafood dinner, but Anthony's is worth a visit once to experience a big-time restaurant formula that keeps 'em coming, and coming, and coming. Owner **Anthony Athanas**, an Albanian immigrant, started out as a shoe-shine boy, built a restaurant, and wound up ruling a fiefdom of five gigantic seafood houses. After an inevitable wait, enjoy towering popovers, raw oysters or

clams, steamed lobster, or simply cooked seafood, and end with Indian pudding or a dessert soufflé. The wine list may be New England's biggest and best.

They milk the colonial-nautical motif for all it's worth, but needn't have gone to the trouble: big views of Boston Harbor steal the show. There are no quiet corners here, where as many as 3,000 meals a day are served. Take a good look at the "Wall of Respect"—make that "Walls"—crammed with photographs of Anthony and the **Pope**, Anthony and **John F. Kennedy**, Anthony and **Frank Sinatra**, Anthony and **Liz Taylor**, Anthony and **Gregory Peck**.... ◆ Seafood/American ◆ M-F 11AM-11PM; Sa noon-11PM; Su 12:30-10:30PM. 140 Northern Ave (at Pier 4). Valet parking. Jacket required and tie preferred for main dining room at dinner; no jeans or sneakers. 423.6363

10 **Commonwealth Pier/World Trade Center** Excursion boats depart from this pier for **Provincetown**, the **Harbor Islands**, and other points. The beflagged World Trade Center accommodates all kinds of enormous functions. Across the street from its lower main entrance, a pedestrian walkway winds to the elevated **Viaduct Street**, a little-known route that offers unusual cityscapes. Behind lies hectic **Fish Pier**; in another direction looms the postmodern **Boston Design Center** and giant **Boston Edison** with its towering stacks; and on the right is Boston's southern flank. Continue straight on Viaduct's sidewalk until you reach Summer Street, then turn right. Look back for the best view of the World Trade Center's monumental pomp and circumstance.

Boston's famous chowder got its name from *chaudière*, the French word for cauldron, in which Canada's early Breton settlers simmered their fish soups.

11 Fish Pier Two long, arcaded rows housing fish-related businesses stretch more than 700 feet out onto the water, with the heroic **New England Fish Exchange** dominating the far end. The century-old building's arch is crowned with a wonderful carved relief of **Neptune's** head, with more fabulous fishy ornamentation above.

No longer the center of New England's—let alone America's—fish industry, Boston's catch keeps shrinking, with more and more fish brought in by trucks, not boats. But the venerable fish auction still starts up every morning around 6:30, presided over by exchange president **Marie Frattollilo.** It's well worth setting the alarm for 5AM to arrive by 6AM and watch the buyers haggle over that day's cod, hake, and pollack, sold right off the boats and rushed to refrigerated trucks.

11 No-Name ★★$$ Once upon a time it had one, but the No-Name sure doesn't need a name now. The hungry hordes all know where to find this big-business restaurant: in the right-hand building of **Fish Pier,** just past the arcade's first curve. The dinnertime line out the door helps

point the way; don't fret at the sight—you may meet some amusing fellow diners. No-Name opened in 1917 and cooked from the crack of dawn onward for fishers and pier workers. Enlarged to accommodate the tourists, businesspeople, and locals who have joined the old crowd, No-Name has kept its hole-in-the-wall look right down to the concrete floor. Hope for a

table in the back overlooking the pier and the boats that brought your dinner. Sitting elbow-to-elbow at boisterous communal tables, fill up on "chowdah" and big portions of impeccably fresh fried seafood, boiled lobster, broiled fish, fish o' the day, and delicious homemade pie. Expect to wait in line; they don't take reservations. ◆ Seafood ◆ M-Sa 11AM-10PM; Su 11AM-9PM. 15 1/2 Fish Pier (at Northern Ave). No credit cards. 338.7539 ♿

12 Jimmy's Harborside Restaurant ★$$ A Waterfront fixture, Jimmy's has been in business since 1924, starting out as a nine-stool joint serving **Fish Pier** workers and fishers. The cavernous seafood house's dated decor shows a refreshing lack of interest in fads. Notice the funky fish mosaics and neon on the facade. Showcased in walls of glass, the views are among the Waterfront's most colorful, with big boats docked close by. The reliably fresh seafood is at its best in simpler preparations. Try the chowder; Jimmy's earned the title "Home of the Chowder King" from the late owner **Jimmy Doulos'** shining moment in the '60s, when he was invited to bring his great fish chowder to Washington, DC, pleasing the palates of **John F. Kennedy** and members of Congress. Jimmy's son is in charge now, but politicians and other celebs still crowd in with the tourists and regulars. While waiting for a table, have a drink at **Jimmy Jr,** the boat-shaped bar. ◆ Seafood/American ◆ M-Sa noon-9:30PM; Su 4-9PM. 242 Northern Ave (at Fish Pier). Valet parking. Jacket preferred; no jeans, sneakers, T-shirts at dinner. Reservations are recommended. 423.1000 ♿

The Young and the Restless: Tips for Traveling with the Tots

With its participatory museums and ubiquitous parks, Boston is a city custom-designed for family sightseeing—provided you don't hard-sell too many of the educational aspects (a temptation to anyone who tends to romanticize such historical events as the midnight ride of Paul Revere and the Boston Tea Party).

Start the minute you hit town. The best way to approach the Hub from the airport is not by land, but by sea—specifically, on the **Airport Water Shuttle** (800/235.6426), which heads straight for the imposing **Boston Harbor Hotel.** Other hotels are only a short ride via cab or subway. But if you want to start right on the sightseeing, and aren't too heavily loaded with luggage, you can check your bags at the **Children's Museum** (426.6500), a short harborside stroll away. Plan to devote a few hours to this rehabbed warehouse packed with lively interactive exhibits. School-age children will enjoy the neighboring **Computer Museum** (426.2800), especially the mammoth "Walk-Through Computer," a discolike cave of flashing floorlights and rainbow-colored spaghetti wiring.

Refreshment awaits outside on the wharf, where a snack stand shaped like a giant **Milk Bottle** serves sandwiches, salads, and ice-cream treats. Also

moored out front is **Lightships** (350.6001), a barge-turned-restaurant that features generous hamburgers. **Venus Seafood in the Rough** (426.3388) offers a survey of coastal delicacies—or perhaps a testing ground for your kids if they've never sampled seafood.

If your children happen to be historically inclined, or at least not totally averse, try them out on a stretch of the **Freedom Trail**—or better yet, sign up for a "Boston by Little Feet" tour (367.2345), which is offered on weekends. If you prefer just a customized sampling of the Freedom Trail, board one of the trolleys that ply the circuit; you can get off at particular stops to prowl around, or just stay put. The guides' patter is entertaining, and best of all, this option is easy on the feet. Other kid-pleasers include the **New England Aquarium** (973.5200); **Faneuil Hall** (stop by for a snack); and the **Public Garden,** where a very tame **Swan Boat** ride (or in winter, a brief spin on ice skates) is a must, plus a visit to the knee-high brass statues commemorating the *Make Way for Ducklings* children's book.

For one last, dizzying look at all you've seen, zoom up the glass-sheathed **Hancock Tower Observatory** (572.6420)—60 floors in 30 seconds flat—to take in the staggering views, as well as a nifty little diorama that re-creates **Paul Revere's** famous ride.

JIMBO'S

13 Jimbo's Fish Shanty ★$ Geared toward the family trade, casual Jimbo's is run by the **Doulos** family, which also owns **Jimmy's Harborside** across the way. Jimbo's has a trains-and-hobos decor, and children are delighted to find three train sets zipping on overhead tracks. You won't find the harbor views, but the low prices for chowder, basic seafood, pizzas, salads, burgers, and other no-frills American food make up for it. Children's plates are available. The restaurant's tiny newsletter-menu advises you to check out the **New England Aquarium** "for a close look at the seafood on the hoof." ♦ Seafood/American ♦ M-Th 11:30AM-9:30PM; F-Sa 11:30AM-10PM; Su noon-8PM. 245 Northern Ave (at Fish Pier). Valet parking at Jimmy's Harborside. 542.5600 ♿

13 Daily Catch ★$$ An offspring of the popular **North End** hole-in-the-wall, this larger place is just as redolent with garlic and serves the same great seafood, although the original has much more personality. Try one of the many variations on the calamari theme; the owners love to turn people on to their favorite seafood. ♦ Seafood ♦ M-Th 11:30AM-10PM; F-Sa 11:30AM-10:30PM; Su noon-10PM. 261 Northern Ave (at Fish Pier). No credit cards. 338.3093. Also at: 323 Hanover St, North End. 523.8567

14 Boston Fire Museum This chunky little 1891 granite-and-brick firehouse is now owned by the **Boston Sparks Association,** which welcomes visitors. ♦ Sa noon-4PM 1 Apr -1 Oct, or by appointment. 344 Congress St (at Farnsworth St). 338.9700 ♿

14 Mobius The name refers to both the **Mobius Performing Group** of 17 artists and to the multimedia gallery and performance space on the fifth floor of a former leather-sole manufacturing building where other artists can also present their work. The founding group works in performance, installation, sound art, new music, film, video, dance, and intermedia. Works-in-progress are presented frequently. Performances change just about every weekend; call for times. ♦ Admission varies. 354 Congress St. 542.7416 ♿ (call ahead to alert the staff)

15 Marco Polo Cafe ★$ Frequented by employees of local architecture offices, this stylishly sparse cafeteria-style lunch spot serves great coffee and Mediterranean fare, ranging from minestrone to moussaka. Most everything's made on the premises, including from-scratch morning muffins. ♦ International/Takeout ♦ M-F 6AM-4PM. 274 Summer St. 695.9039 ♿

16 A Street Deli Express $ While the rest of the city's asleep, get a hearty breakfast with lots of good grease to jumpstart your day. For lunch, the food is cheap, basic, and good: pizza, soup, and salads. Walk up **Melcher Street** to see its gracefully curving warehouses. ♦ American ♦ M-F 5AM-4PM; Sa 6-11AM. 324 A St (at Melcher St). 338.7571 ♿

17 Weylu's ★$$ Enjoy better-than-average Mandarin, Szechuan, and Cantonese food where you'd least expect it—far across the channel from **Chinatown**—with views of Boston's southern skyline. Traditional and innovative dishes mingle on the menu and are courteously served in a large, modern setting. Luncheon specials are offered daily. To the left of Weylu's entrance, stairs descend to a block-long arcaded path that ends at Congress Street. Since Summer Street is elevated and Congress Street isn't, this is a convenient passage between the two, and it also overlooks the **Fort Point Channel.** ♦ Chinese/Takeout ♦ M-Th 11:30AM-10:30PM; F 11:30AM-11:30PM; Sa 12:30-11:30PM; Su 12:30-10:30PM. 254 Summer St. 423.0243

18 The Milk Bottle $ A landmark in its own right, this vintage 1930s highway lunch stand (pictured above) was installed in front of the Children's Museum in 1977, having first been sawed in half and floated down the Charles. Donated to the museum by the **H.P. Hood Company,** the 40-foot-tall wooden bottle would hold 50,000 gallons of milk and 860 gallons of cream if filled. It serves a variety of soups and salads, and, of course, ice cream. ♦ American ♦ Daily 7AM-9PM, summer; daily 7AM-7PM, winter. 300 Congress St (at Museum Wharf). 426.7074 ♿

18 Lightships $ A lengthy, if not especially inventive menu and fabulous views of the Downtown skyline distinguish this congenial restaurant—that and the fact that it's afloat. A rehabbed barge, it serves a family pleasing assortment of sandwiches and seafood, with a nod to traditional Mexican standbys. ♦ International ♦ Daily 11:30AM-1:30AM. 310 Congress St (at Museum Wharf). 350.6001 ♿

18 McDonald's $ Adjacent to **The Children's Museum,** a special entrance also opens directly into the museum. The standard Mc-fare is served, but it's a cut above in decor and has plenty of tables. ♦ Fast food ♦ M-Th 6:30AM-8PM; F 6:30AM-9PM; Sa 7AM-7PM; Su 8AM-6PM. 316 Congress St. No credit cards. 482.1746 ♿

Restaurants/Clubs: Red
Shops/ 🌳 Outdoors: Green

Hotels: Blue
Sights/Culture: Black

The Children's Museum

18 The Children's Museum Kids adore this lively participatory museum located in a former wool warehouse (see the plan below). Whatever your age, a visit here will revive that urge to touch and get into things, even if you restrain yourself and just watch. In ongoing exhibitions for toddlers to teens, kids may blow bubbles and spin tops in the **Science Playground;** scramble on the two-story **Climbing**

Waterfront/Fort Point Channel

Sculpture; learn personal health and well-being in "Mind Your Own Business"; visit "The Kid's Bridge," an exhibition that addresses Boston's multicultural heritage; and investigate what daily life is like in a Japanese silk-merchant's reconstructed home from **Kyoto,** Boston's sister city. One of the museum's newest exhibits is "Teen Tokyo," which is about the international culture of youth in Japan today; it includes a

Japanese subway car, a Karaoke booth, and an animation computer. The **Resource Center** offers educational materials and services to parents and teachers. **RECYCLE** sells industrial raw materials discarded by local factories—sold in bulk, dirt-cheap. **The Children's Museum Shop** is an unbeatable source for unusual gifts, toys, and books. The museum has an active **Outreach Program,** working with local neighborhoods on a variety of cultural events, so this is the place to find out about all sorts of family activities going on around Boston. ◆ Admission; reduced admission F 5-9PM. Tu-Th, Sa-Su 10AM-5PM; F 10AM-9PM. Open Monday during Boston school vacations and holidays. 300 Congress St (at Museum Wharf). Recorded information: 426.8855 &

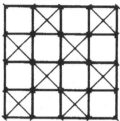

18 The Computer Museum A remarkable repository of technologies past and present, this is the only museum in the world devoted entirely to computers. Forget those graceless terms—nerd, hack, dweeb—computer "companions" are made here, the museum says. Whether you're computer-literate or -leery, more than a hundred interactive exhibitions chronicle computers and their role in society. Walk through a spectacular 50-times-larger-

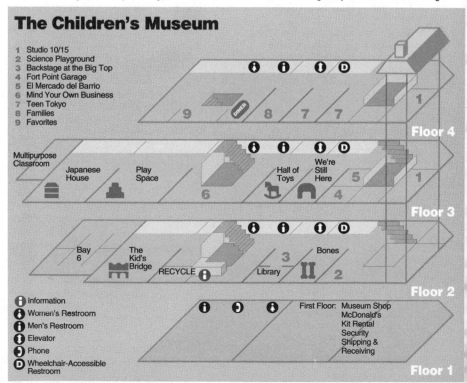

The Children's Museum

1 Studio 10/15
2 Science Playground
3 Backstage at the Big Top
4 Fort Point Garage
5 El Mercado del Barrio
6 Mind Your Own Business
7 Teen Tokyo
8 Families
9 Favorites

Floor 4

9   DINER   8   7   7   1

Multipurpose Classroom   Japanese House   Play Space   6   Hall of Toys   We're Still Here   5   1   4

Floor 3

Bay 6   The Kid's Bridge   RECYCLE   Library   3   Bones   2

Floor 2

First Floor: Museum Shop
McDonald's
Kit Rental
Security
Shipping & Receiving

Floor 1

Ⓘ Information
Ⓦ Women's Restroom
Ⓜ Men's Restroom
Ⓔ Elevator
Ⓟ Phone
Ⓓ Wheelchair-Accessible Restroom

than-life, two-story computer model that demonstrates how a personal computer functions, complete with a 25-foot-long keyboard, a 108-square-foot color monitor, and six-foot-tall floppy disks. **David Macauley,** writer and illustrator of *The Way Things Work* and other delightfully reassuring show-and-tell-style books, illustrated the "Walk-Through Computer" exhibit (pictured below). Hands-on exhibitions let you "paint" pictures, compose melodies, create programs, simulate aircraft flight, design a house or car, even remodel your face.

Visit the amusing **Animation Theater,** and **Smart Machines Gallery** starring more than 25 robots. "People and Computers: Milestones of a Revolution" tracks the development of computers from the punch-card machines of the 1930s to today's microprocessors. "Tools and Toys: The Amazing Personal Computer" explores all the fascinating functions a PC can perform, including animation, video, and virtual reality. Ride the massive glass-enclosed elevator overlooking the **Fort Point Channel.** The techy gift shop even sells chocolate "chips." The museum's Waterfront setting makes sense, since Boston's economy is now as dependent on high tech as it once was on seafaring. ◆ Admission; reduced admission Sa 10AM-noon. M-Th, Sa-Su 10AM-6PM, F 10AM-9PM, summer; Tu-Su 10AM-5PM, winter. 300 Congress St (at Museum Wharf). 426.2800 (for a human voice), 423.6758 (for a computer voice) &

19 Boston Tea Party Ship and Museum The Boston Tea Party took place near here on Griffin's Wharf, long gone (its site is now landfill on Atlantic Avenue between Congress Street and Northern Avenue). On a cold December night in 1773, angry Colonists dressed as Mohawk Indians boarded ships and heave-hoed 340 chests of costly British tea into the harbor to protest the tax imposed on their prized beverage. A *cuppa* was a costly commodity in those days. Moored alongside the **Congress Street Bridge** is the *Beaver II,* a Danish brig resembling one of the three Tea Party ships and

sailed here in 1973. For kids, it's an adventure to climb about the 110-foot-long working vessel, listen to costumed guides, and finally toss a bale of tea defiantly over the side—the fact that it's roped to the ship and hauled back up again doesn't lessen the thrill. On the adjacent pier, the little museum contains exhibitions, films, ship models, and memorabilia, with printed information available in seven languages. Tax-free tea is served at all times. ◆ Admission. Daily 9AM-dusk. Off Congress St Bridge (at Atlantic Ave). 338.1773

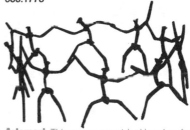

20 Artsmart This roomy, smart-looking shop features personal adornments and quirky home furnishings fashioned by some 120 local artisans.

Waterfront/Fort Point Channel

"It's comfortable, rather than pretentious—we make sure people can touch everything," says co-owner **Drur Ashuah.** Among the "unique objects" you may indeed want to fondle are their velvet hats, hand-painted picture frames, and faux-finished armoires. Be sure to duck next door to visit a sibling enterprise, the **Ashuah-Irving Gallery** (286 Congress Street, 482.3343), a small, raw space whose selections are singularly astute. ◆ Tu-F 10AM-6PM; Sa noon-5PM; Su hours vary, call ahead. 272 Congress St (between Dorchester St and Atlantic Ave). 695.0151

COURTESY OF
THE COMPUTER
MUSEUM

Walk-Through Computer Exhibit

21 Federal Reserve Bank of Boston Whether you think this building (designed by **Hugh Stubbins & Associates** in 1977) resembles an old-fashioned washboard, goal posts, or a radiator, its shimmering aluminum-sheathed form is remarkably visible from many vantage points. The bank's art gallery on the ground floor is an alternative space where nonprofit New England-based artists and arts organizations mount six professional-level exhibitions annually.

A performance series is held in the adjacent auditorium on Thursdays, September through December and March through June; call for program information. Free group tours of the bank's operational departments are offered Monday through Thursday at 9AM and 10:30AM, with a month's notice; public tours are held every Friday at 10:30AM; and individual bank tours are offered by appointment only, generally on Friday. Visitors leave with souvenir packets of shredded money. ◆ Art gallery M-F 10AM-4PM. 600 Atlantic Ave. Recorded gallery information 973.3453. Tours 973.3451 ♿

Waterfront/Fort Point Channel

22 South Station When construction on South Station (designed by **Shepley, Rutan, and Coolidge**) at **Dewey Square** was completed in 1900, it was the world's largest railroad station, holding that title for many years. And by 1913, handling 38 million passengers a year, it was the busiest station in the country—even topping New York's Grand Central Station. In peak year 1907, some 876 trains plied the rails on weekdays. The majestic five-story edifice, its shapely curved facade adorned with a nine-foot-wide clock surmounted by a proud eagle, proclaimed Boston's important place in the world. In its heyday, the station's comforts included a theater that screened newsreels and **Our Lady of the Railways Chapel**. But when airplanes, trucks, and autos eclipsed trains, the station slid into decrepitude. Eventually, most of it was demolished, except for the handsome headhouse, which nearly gave up the ghost in the '60s, too.

Now South Station's aggressive eagle has something worth lording over. Respectful restoration and intelligent planning have made the terminal (on the **National Register of Historic Places**) an exciting destination once more, with pushcart vendors, a food hall, coffee bar, newsstand, bank, and other services to lure pedestrians from nearby streets. Look for the old tin ceilings and beautiful carved details. More than 200 commuter trains and dozens of **Amtrak** runs come and go on the busiest travel days. With a bus station nearby (an $81 million replacement is planned for 1994) and the **Red Line** subway conveniently on site, travelers are linked to the rest of Boston and suburbs. ◆ Between Summer St and Atlantic Ave

23 U.S. Postal Service-South Postal Annex Boston's general mail facility looks like a '20s ocean liner berthed alongside the channel. Always open, this is the mail processing hub for the Boston Division, with more than 1.2 million square feet of space and 12 miles of conveyors. Groups of 10 or more, minimum age 13 or eighth grade, can take a guided tour of the automated and mechanized facility and see how employees sort a daily average of nine million pieces of mail with the help of optical character readers, letter-sorting machines, bar-code sorters, and other sophisticated equipment. Call to arrange a tour at least one week in advance. ◆ Free. Tours Tu-F Jan.-Nov. 25 Dorchester Ave. 654.5081 ♿

Leather District

Like the **Fort Point Channel** area, this tiny appendage to the **Financial District** has a businesslike personality and lots of integrity. You can cover the entire seven-block neighborhood in one half-hour stroll. When Boston's **Great Fire of 1872** swept clean more than 60 acres, it wiped out the city's commercial and wholesale centers, including the dense leather and garment district concentrated here. But slowly, businesses rose from the ashes and built sturdy new warehouses and factories, most along Lincoln and South streets, some Romanesque in style and quite distinguished. Except for a few firms, the leather warehousing industry long ago departed for other countries. In the 1970s artists and urban pioneers began to move in, followed by art galleries, shops and services, and restaurants. The neighborhood's new identity is still in the making. But arty attempts to update and upscale the neighborhood are like dressing up a business suit with a Day-Glo tie.

24 The Essex Grill ★$$ On the first floor of the former **Hotel Essex,** now spiffed up as the **Plymouth Rock Building,** the big dining room looks across at trains idling in the **South Station** yards and fronts a major street, so diners can survey the urban scene. Nicely prepared seafood dominates the menu, including fresh-water varieties. On the same floor is the high-ceilinged, airy **Essex Bar,** a throwback to another era with wonderfully fussy columns and drapes. The old Hotel Essex, built about the same time as South Station, was a popular haunt, and it's easy to imagine the days when both rail-weary and raring-to-go travelers came and went from here, baggage in tow. As you come or go, look for the handsome old clocks in the lobby. A popular take-out place on the premises serves an eclectic menu and delivers locally (call 439.9365 for hours). ◆ Seafood ◆ M-F 11AM-10PM. 695 Atlantic Ave (at Essex St). Reservations recommended for lunch. 439.3599 ♿

Restaurants/Clubs: Red
Shops/ ❧ Outdoors: Green
Hotels: Blue
Sights/Culture: Black

25 **Whit's End** Most Bostonians have yet to discover this captivating shop purveying inexpensive trinkets and toys, though many are familiar with its biggest seller: clever rubber stamps of animals, buildings, cartoons, patterns, names, and hundreds of other designs—practical and outrageous—all manufactured right on the premises. Custom-orders are taken, too.

And if rubber stamps aren't your thing, for peanuts you can get a plastic Hula girl, chocolate cow, lobster-claw-shaped harmonica, blinking Christmas-bulb earrings with matching necklace, itsy-bitsy plastic ants and creepy bigger bugs, plus all sorts of stationery, cards, handmade jewelry, mugs, and wind-up toys—the whole kit and kaboodle of eccentric doodads. ♦ M-F 9AM-6PM; Sa 10AM-5PM. 105A South St (between East and Beach Sts). 426.3458

25 **Bromfield Gallery** Boston's oldest artist-owned cooperative gallery exhibits work ranging from Realist to abstract and conceptual art, displaying prints, paintings, photographs, and other media by a stable of a dozen-or-so artists. Shows change frequently and are individual, group, invitational, and juried. ♦ Tu-Sa 10AM-5:30PM. 107 South St (between East and Beach Sts). 451.3605

25 **John Gilbert Jr. Co.** Established in 1830, this is Boston's oldest spirits shop. It began as a purveyor of fancy groceries and delicacies. (The ancient store ledgers are fascinating for their flowery penmanship alone.) In addition to fine wine and beers, all kinds of liquid treasures are sold. ♦ M-F 9AM-6:30PM; Sa 9AM-5PM. 107 South St. 542.8900

CECIL'S

25 **Cecil's on South Street** ★$ Located in the 1888 **Beebe Building,** friendly Cecil's warms up its exposed bricks-and-beams interior with vivid Caribbean-style posters, fish statues, mobiles, ceiling fans, wooden booths, and background jazz. The Colombian chef orchestrates an interesting rapprochement of Mexican and Latin, Caribbean, Italian, and American dishes at lunch, with a dinnertime focus on excellent Cuban-Latin cuisine. Try *ropa vieja, pollo borracho, pargo al ajillo,* or turkey potpie. ♦ International/Takeout ♦ M-F 7AM-10PM; Sa noon-10PM. Music Saturday night; cover charge. Closed mid June-Labor Day. 129 South St (between East and Beach Sts). Reservations recommended at dinner. 542.5108

n the summer, tourists fill the gap left by vacationing ollege students. The National Park Service reports at in 1991 the Paul Revere House averaged 91 visiters a day in January, ballooning to more than a thousand a day in August, while monthly tallies of people during the USS *Constitution* grew from about 11,000 o 126,000.

26 **Populuxe** Four collectibles dealers contribute to this "20th Century Collective," and the pickings are ultra-kitsch: everything from vintage clothing and accessories to movie star portraits and religious icons. If you'd like to re-create the ambience of decades gone by, this is the place to prowl. ♦ M-Sa 11AM 6PM. 92 South St (between East and Beach Sts). 482.5207

26 **Gallery Per Tutti** Bulgarian-born painter **Gedy Moody** opened this semi-subterranean gallery in 1991 to showcase affordable art in a variety of media (paintings, prints, photographs, and furniture, from $50 to $5,000) and

Waterfront/Fort Point Channel

to foment discussion of art's function. The gallery's 40-or-so artists are also featured in monthly receptions, and on alternate Sunday afternoons, Moody hosts a salon, free and open to all. ♦ Tu-Sa 11AM-6PM; call for additional hours. 112 South St (between East and Beach Sts). 482.2710

26 **Ware on Earth** The showroom for **Pot Specialists, Inc.,** local importers, this shop sells containers and planters from Thailand, Malaysia, Greece, Italy, China, and other countries. Many of the striking vessels are one-of-a-kind or antique, and some are enormous—such as the antique Greek oil drums. Prices start very low and keep climbing. ♦ M-F 11AM-5PM. 104 South St (between East and Beach Sts). 451.5995

27 **Interior Resources** Jonathan Diamond travels extensively to buy objects from throughout the world for residential and corporate interiors. His showroom is an eclectic presentation of contemporary and traditional home furnishings, decorative accessories, and antiques. It's fun to browse through while you're gallery-hopping in the neighborhood. ♦ Tu-F 11AM-6PM; Sa 10AM-5PM; and by appointment. 745 Atlantic Ave (entrance between Beach and South Sts). 542.5797

28 **Howard Yezerski Gallery** A bright, inviting gallery that strives to be a little offbeat and untraditional, it shows contemporary painting, sculpture, and photography by established and emerging artists from the US and Europe. The core group of 20-plus artists and guest exhibitors includes **Natalie Alper, Domingo Barreres,** and **Paul Shakespear.** ♦ Tu-Sa 10AM-5:30PM. 186 South St (between Beach and Kneeland Sts). 426.8085

Sojourns to the Sea: Short Trips to the Boston Harbor Islands

Whether you'd prefer to quietly bask in the summer heat or the silvery winter light, the 30 islands dotting the inner and outer harbors offer wonderful respite from city crowds and new perspectives on Boston's connection to the sea. It's easy to forget these delightful sanctuaries exist, so close but seemingly so far.

Georges Island, the hub of the chain, is dominated by **Fort Warren,** massive 19th-century granite fortifications where Confederate soldiers were imprisoned during the Civil War. (A famous local legend tells of a young southern woman who slipped into Fort Warren to join her imprisoned Confederate husband. Caught in their escape, he was killed and she was executed as a spy. Thereafter, her ghost has appeared from time to time, roaming the fort, dressed in the black mourning gown that has given her the name the "Lady in Black.") Guided tours and programs are offered by state park staff six months of the year. The 30-acre island is the perfect place for a picnic overlooking the distant cityscape, and has restrooms, an information booth, and a first-aid station. Sixteen-acre **Gallops Island** also has picnic grounds, a pier with a large gazebo, shady paths, meadows, and remnants of a World War II maritime radio school. **Lovell Island,** 62 acres large, offers a supervised swimming beach—though you'd probably prefer to do no more than wade a bit until the harbor is cleaned up—a picnic area with hibachis and tables, campsites, and walking trails that take you through meadows, salt marsh, dunes, and woods.

One of the harbor's biggest islands, 188-acre **Peddocks** also has picnic and camping areas and the remains of **Fort Andrews** occupying its **East Head.** Because the **West Head** is a protected salt marsh and wildlife sanctuary, access beyond recreational areas is restricted to organized tours or by permission of park staff. Tranquil **Bumpkin Island** offers trails to an old children's hospital ruins and stone farmhouse, and its rocky beach is popular for fishing. Wild rabbits and raspberry bushes proliferate. Some campsites are available. **Grape Island,** named for the vines that grew here in colonial times, feeds many birds with its wild bayberries, blackberries, and rose hips. Come here for birding, picnicking, camping, and meandering. Rugged **Great Brewster Island's** 23 acres afford splendid views of **Boston Light,** the country's oldest lighthouse, on **Little Brewster,** but can only be reached by private boat. The lighthouse on Little Brewster began blinking in 1716. Destroyed by a 1751 fire, rebuilt, destroyed by the evacuating British in 1776 and rebuilt again, Boston Light is visible 27 miles out to sea. One of only six lighthouses in the country that is still manually operated, the 89-foot-tall lighthouse has been

threatened with automation—forestalled for now with the help of **Senator Edward Kennedy.** The first lightkeeper, **George Worthylake,** drowned with his family when his boat capsized on the way back to Little Brewster in 1718. **Benjamin Franklin** wrote a poem about the tragedy. The names of the present and former keepers are etched on island rocks. Owned by the **Thompson Island Outward Bound Center,** 157-acre **Thompson Island** is open on a limited basis for guided tours, hiking, picnicking, educational programs, and conferences—you must call ahead. The center provides boat transportation to the island.

No fresh water is available on Gallops, Lovells, Bumpkin, Grape, or Great Brewster islands—so be sure to bring your own. Day-use permits are required for large groups; permits are also necessary for camping and for alcohol consumption on some islands. A number of the islands belong to the **Boston Harbor Islands State Park** and are reached by ferries departing from **Long Wharf** or **Rowes Wharf** on the Waterfront. Privately operated, the ferries charge fees and most go to Georges Island, where free water taxis take you to five other islands. The **Department of Environmental Management (DEM)** and the **Metropolitan District Commission (MDC)** work together to manage state-owned islands. For more information or to obtain permits for Georges, Lovell, and Peddocks islands, call the MDC at 727.5290. For Gallops, Bumpkin, Grape, and Great Brewster islands, call the DEM at 740.1605. The Thompson Island Outward Bound Center can be reached at 328.3900. Georges, Bumpkin, and Thompson islands are wheelchair accessible.

Friends of the Boston Harbor Islands, a nonprofit organization dedicated to preserving the islands' resources, sponsors year-round public education programs, history tours, and special boat trips. Call 523.8386 for more information.

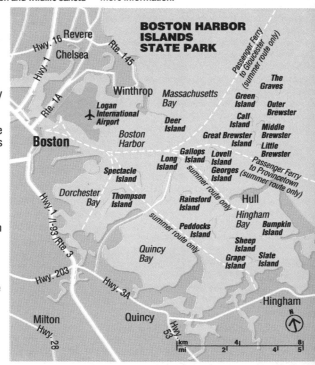

29 Genovese Gallery Annex An outpost of the South End gallery, this pristine space favors big, bold, minimalist art. ♦ Tu-Sa 10AM-5:30PM. 195 South St (between Beach and Kneeland Sts). 426.2062

29 Robert Klein Gallery An important destination for photography collectors, this fifth-floor gallery exhibits, appraises, purchases, and sells stunning international 19th- and 20th-century photographs, many rare. More than 150 photographers are represented, including **William Henry Fox Talbot, Diane Arbus, Ansel Adams, Robert Mapplethorpe, Eugene Atget, Edward Weston, Richard Avedon,** and **Man Ray.** Special offerings have included **Lucien Aigner's** limited-edition *Einstein Portfolio.* ♦ Tu-F 10AM-5:30PM; Sa noon-5PM. 207 South St (between Beach and Kneeland Sts). 482.8188 ઙ

30 The Blue Diner ★$ There's no place like it in Boston. Straddling this corner since 1947, the bluer-than-a-bluebird diner was carefully refurbished to keep its old character but acquire a new sheen. A wonderful hangout—unfortunately, a *lot* of people think so—the diner has its original working Seeburg sound system, with Wall-o-Matic selectors at every booth: two plays per quarter let you listen to a parade of vintage 45s from the likes of **Elvis, Aretha Franklin, Jerry Lee Lewis,** and **Louis Armstrong.** Formerly a workingperson's haunt, the Blue Diner hasn't lost its old clientele, just gained a wider following.

To the requisite rib-sticking diner fare—the daily Blueplate Specials include meat loaf, roast turkey and homemade gravy, and franks and beans—owner **Don Levy** has added imaginative grilled seafood items, Mississippi BBQ, and vegetable fritters. Unlike the average diner, all the food is "real" here—no mixes—right down to the maple syrup and magnificent mashed potatoes. The french fries are from scratch, too. The Blue Diner starts the day early, as any respectable diner should, with hearty breakfasts. Order a cup of coffee to go; it comes in a great Blue Diner-motif paper cup. ♦ Diner/American ♦ M, Su 7AM-midnight; Tu-Sa 24 hours. 178 Kneeland St (at South St). 338.4639

Boston sailor-historian Samuel Eliot Morison wrote: "A summer day with a sea-turn in the wind. The Grand Banks' fog, rolling in wave after wave, is dissolved by he perfumed breath of New England hayfields into a gentle haze, that turns the State House dome to old gold, films brick walls with a soft patina, and sifts blue shadows among the foliage of the Common elms. Out of the mist in Massachusetts Bay comes riding a clipper ship, with the effortless speed of an albatross."

30 Akin Gallery Owner **Ali Righter** was among the first to set up shop in this formerly charmless area, and her pick of mid-level artists, along with the occasional discovery, is still worth searching out. ♦ Tu-F 10:30AM-6PM. 164 Kneeland St (between Lincoln and South Sts). 426.2726 ઙ

30 Loading Zone ★$$ Located in a former warehouse and run by **Don Levy,** who also owns the popular **Blue Diner,** this is a barbecue pit with art gallery aspirations. The food is pretty good, with best bets including the pulled pork (entrée or sandwich), smoked-beef brisket, babyback ribs, Killer Chili, sweet-potato chips, and onion rings. Or come for a down home breakfast complete with grits. But the Zone's real draw is its artful tables: each glass-topped shadow box holds the creation of a local artist, and they range from funny to whimsical to outrageous and arresting. Every few years, the tables are auctioned and a new round commissioned. ♦ Barbecue ♦ M-W 11:30AM-10PM; Th-F 11:30AM-11PM; Sa 5-11PM; Su 1-10PM. 150 Kneeland St (between Lincoln and South Sts). Reservations recommended Thursday through Saturday nights. 695.0087 ઙ

Waterfront/Fort Point Channel

31 F.C. Meichsner Company Founded in 1916, this family owned and operated business is the only East Coast establishment that can actually fix and repair all makes and models of binoculars and telescopes. Meichsner is considered *the* source for binoculars, telescopes and accessories, barometers and ships' clocks, and replicas of old telescopes—the best optics for your money. ♦ M-F 9AM-6PM; Sa 10AM-4PM. 182 Lincoln St (between Beach and Kneeland Sts). 426.7092

Bests

Anita Diamant
Columnist for the *Boston Globe Magazine*

Breakfast at **Charlie's Sandwich Shoppe.**

The **Mapparium** at the **Christian Science Center:** a walk-through, stained-glass globe of the world as it was in 1932.

The **Computer Museum's** "Tools and Toys" exhibit is a place where even "technophobes" can fall in love with machines.

Lunch at any **Bertucci's,** a local pizza chain that provides consistently good food at reasonable prices.

The **Boston Public Library**—once reconstruction is completed on this grand old National Landmark building, this will be *the* place for afternoon tea.

A harbor cruise: The view of the city from a boat is breathtaking at any time of the day.

A ride on the **Swan Boats** in the Public Garden. Never mind that it's hopelessly hokey. Take your cue from the three-year-olds and say hello to the pigeons and the duckies.

Dinner at **Another Season** on Beacon Hill. This restaurant manages to be simultaneously Boston-Brahmin and romantic-cozy.

Financial District/ Downtown

Boston's most on-the-go neighborhood is bounded by the **Boston Common** to the west, the **Central Artery** and **Waterfront** to the east, **Government Center** and **Faneuil Hall Marketplace** to the north, and **Chinatown** and the **Theater District** to the south. The bumper crop of skyscrapers here celebrates the city's economic good health and transforms the skyline. The revitalized **Downtown Crossing** shopping area is cheerfully chaotic with pedestrians, pushcarts, and outdoor performers luring shoppers to the internationally famous **Filene's Basement**—the first off-price store in the United States—and dozens of other stores and boutiques.

History's imprint is here as well: important **Freedom Trail** stops such as the **Old State House, Old South Meeting House,** and **Globe Corner Bookstore** impart a vision of Revolution-era Main Street. The **Custom House Tower, State Street Block,** and surviving wharf buildings designed by **Charles Bulfinch** speak of early wealth from the sea. Come during weekday work hours, when everything is open and in full swing. Walk along the profusion of twisty, tiny colonial lanes that have turned into busy arteries shadowed by architectural giants, creating windy, dark New York City-style canyons. Businesslike street names—State, Court, Broad, Federal, School—reflect the neighborhood's no-nonsense character. Numerous commercial palaces bear carved or fading traces of their original names, paying tribute to past lives.

From the city's earliest days, State Street was Boston's business artery, the most prestigious and spacious in town. Called King Street until the Revolution, State Street stretched 800 feet from the Old State House to **Long Wharf**, the noble

pier that once served as the city's highway to the sea. Where State Street intersects **Washington Street** was the epicenter of Boston's commercial and financial life. Alas, State Street has lost its eminence, but many of its buildings bespeak former glory.

An old Indian trail, Washington Street is now the major Downtown commercial way. Always an important thoroughfare, it was the only road in the 17th and 18th centuries that ran the full length of Boston, linking the Old State House with the town gate at the neck of the **Shawmut Peninsula**. The street was renamed to honor **George Washington's** visit to the city in 1789. Today, it becomes seedy beyond **Temple Place** as it heads south toward the shrinking redlight district, the infamous **Combat Zone** (not a good place to be at night). Chockablock Washington Street is interesting, however, from beginning to end, with great streetscapes down the **Ladder Block** side streets toward the Common. Much of the existing Washington Street area was built after the **Great Fire of 1872**, which leveled 65 acres bounded by Washington, Broad, Milk, and Summer streets; destroyed the heart of major New England industries; and left thousands without jobs. Many buildings still show scars and burns from the conflagration, which stopped just short of a number of Boston's historical treasures. Although the neighborhood was rapidly rebuilt, its residents had fled and commercialism took over. Boston's publishing and newspaper concerns flourished along **Newspaper Row** where Washington Street meets State and Court streets, and insurance, banking, retail, garment, manufacturing, and other industries stuck by their roots. The famous **Omni Parker House** hotel and **Locke-Ober** restaurant also persevered in the face of change, and to this day remain pleasant, if somewhat stodgy, oases of gentility.

Economically, Boston was a Sleeping Beauty from 1895 until around 1965, when its building-boom prince finally arrived. Early skyscrapers are in short supply, but Boston does have its pleasing, peculiar Custom House Tower, Art Deco **Batterymarch Building** and post office, and lithe and lovely **Winthrop Building**. "If it ain't broke, don't fix it" is the Yankee credo, and Bostonians have always had a talent for recycling old structures. The city's fiscally conservative streak even influences new architecture. Unlike Chicago, where buildings shoot up to the sky unimpeded, Boston prefers a modest scale for its towers, so they politely accommodate older neighbors. Developers are subjected to stringent regulations and reviews. Some new buildings are dressed to the nines in decoration, but many are quite plain, even dowdy. It's as if the city is just getting used to its growing cosmopolitan stature and doesn't quite know how to dress the part.

The Financial District/Downtown neighborhood is large, but easily walked from any subway station in the area, including: Park Street (Red and Green Lines), State (Orange Line), Washington/Downtown Crossing (Red and Orange Lines), South Station (Red and Blue Lines), and Government Center (Green and Blue Lines). The Park Street and Washington/Downtown Crossing stops are most convenient to the Downtown shopping area; one block apart, either station can be reached from the other via an underground passage. The Government Center and State stops are near the historical and financial districts, and the South Station stop is just beyond the neighborhood's southeastern edge.

The Vault," formally known as the Coordinating Committee, is a powerful, elite advisory group of influential leaders who represent business interests in setting Boston's public agenda. The group was founded in 1959 by a Lowell and a Coolidge to help revitalize the city's financial state. When the Vault speaks, mayors, legislators, and other public officials listen.

1 Old State House This lovable 1713 brick building (pictured on the following page), nicknamed the "Temple of Liberty," has stubbornly survived centuries of tumult and transformation, witnessing more than its share of dramatic moments in local and American history. The **National Historic Landmark** has been remodeled and restored so often (**Goody, Clancy Associates** performed the latest shoring-up in 1992) that its parts date from many eras. Situated at the head of State Street, Old State originally commanded a clear view to the sea and in the mid-18th century became the political and commercial center of the **Massachusetts Bay Colony**. Its first floor was a merchants' exchange, with the wheels of government turning on the floors above. Even the site occupied an important place in the town's history, for the earliest Boston market square was located here, as were the stocks, pillory, and whipping post used to mete out 17th-century Puritan justice. The building started life as a meeting place used by the British crown's provincial governor, as well as the seat of the government after the Revolution sent the British packing once and for all. The ceremonial balcony at the Congress Street end overlooks the site, marked by a star within a circle of cobblestones, where on 5 March 1770 frightened British soldiers fired on a large, angry mob of Bostonians, killing former slave **Crispus Attucks** and four others in the **Boston Massacre**. From this same balcony, the **Declaration of Independence** was first read to Bostonians on 18 July 1776. The fantastical cavorting lion and unicorn on the elder edifice's gable, emblems of the hated crown, were frowned upon and removed. Every year since, the Declaration has been read from the same spot on the Fourth of July. **John Hancock** was inaugurated at Old State as the first governor under the new state constitution. And when **George Washington** visited Boston in 1789, he surveyed the great parade in his honor from here. But after the new **State House** was built on **Beacon Hill**, the monument became a jack-of-all-trades building, used and abused as a commercial center, newspaper office, and, for a decade, Boston's City Hall.

The outcast's cause was championed just in time in 1881, when a private nonprofit organization called the **Bostonian Society** organized to restore the building and preserve the rich history it had witnessed. Ever since, the society has called Old State home and maintained a marvelous museum featuring changing and permanent exhibitions on the Revolutionary

Financial District/Downtown

era, maritime history, and other important chapters in the city's life. The Old State House's history is chronicled, too. Paintings, portraits, figureheads, ship models, military and domestic artifacts, and other treasures tell the tale of this city quite well. A vial of the original tea from the **Boston Tea Party** is on view, for instance; so is the coroner's report on Crispus Attucks. Look for John Hancock's family Bible and some of his clothing, and for **Fitz Hugh Lane's** painting *View of Boston Harbor*. A lovely spiral

staircase leads to where inaugurations, daily government, and momentous meetings took place. For those who want to dig deeper, the society's splendid library across the street on the third floor of 15 State Street comprises more than 6,000 volumes and a thousand maps and architectural plans, plus rare manuscripts and broadsides.

The library also owns more than 10,000 Boston views in photographs, prints, watercolors, and drawings. Another great resource is librarian **Philip Bergen,** who holds much of Boston's history right in his head. Happily, the Old State House has flourished under the society's care. Unicorn and lion now prance with pride, copies elevated to the original animals' lofty perches. Another testament to the building's resilience: the presence of the State Street subway station that's tucked underneath. ◆ Admission. Daily 9:30AM-5PM. 206 Washington St (at State St)

1 Visitor Center Located across the way from the **Old State House,** the center is operated by the **Boston National Historic Park Service,** which also runs the **Old South Meeting House, Faneuil Hall, Paul Revere House, Old North Church, Bunker Hill Monument, Charlestown Navy Yard,** and **Dorchester Heights.** In addition to offering information about these places, including a brief slide-show presentation, the center's staff of park rangers and volunteers answers questions about Boston and the entire National Park system. Find out about tours, many of which start from here. Pick up free **Freedom Trail** maps and pamphlets about all kinds of places, activities, and events. The center also sells books and souvenirs. And most important, well-kept restrooms, water fountains, and telephones are available here, public conveniences hard to come by in Boston. There are also places to sit and rest weary bones. ◆ Daily 9AM-5PM, Jan-May, Sept-Dec; daily 9AM-6PM, June-Aug. Closed Thanksgiving, Christmas, New Year's Day. 15 State St (between Washington and Devonshire Sts). 242.5642 ق

A bookshop once stood near the Old State House, where the first Bibles printed in America were sold and where Edgar Allan Poe's first volume of verse was published. No copies of Poe's work were sold, a first blow among the many that darkened his view of life.

Old State House

2 Exchange Place Opinions vary wildly about this blending of old and new. Actually, all that remains of the original 1891 **Stock Exchange Building** designed by **Peabody and Stearns** is a 60-foot segment of its worthy granite facade on the State Street side, now engulfed by a glassy tower added in 1984 by the **WZMH Group.** From some vantage points, its dark reflective surfaces shimmer interestingly, but overall the new building is, well, tacky. A handsome restored marble staircase is the atrium's incongruous centerpiece. This was the site of the historic **Bunch of Grapes Tavern,** located at the head of **Long Wharf** during the 19th century. A favorite watering hole for patriot leaders before the Revolution, the tavern reputedly served the best bowl of punch in Boston. ♦ 53 State St (between Congress and Kilby Sts)

3 75 State Street Some love and some hate this unabashedly gilded and gaudy showpiece, erected in 1988 by **Graham Gund Associates,** but it simply refuses to be ignored on the skyline. The lobby looks like an example of tender loving care gone too far, with its plethora of patterns, types of marble, and fancy fixtures—but the vast atrium lets in plenty of pure, unadulterated light. ♦ At Kilby St

4 Cunard Building The boldly inscribed name on this Classical Revival building built in 1901 by **Peabody and Stearns** recalls another bright moment in Boston's past. The building was once the headquarters for the famous **Cunard Steamship Line,** which pioneered transatlantic steamship routes. Boston was proud to beat out New York City as the first American city to enjoy the innovative service. Nautical motifs aplenty—crowned Poseidon heads, anchor-and-dolphin lighting stanchions, a wavelike ornamental band—add an adventurous air to an otherwise sober structure. ♦ 126 State St (between Merchants Row and Chatham St)

5 Board of Trade Building This elaborate, urbane building designed in 1901 by **Winslow and Bradlee** has aged well. Its allegorical figures and vigorous stone carvings hearken to seafaring days gone by, especially the galleons rushing forward into the viewer's space. ♦ 131 State St (between Broad and India Sts)

6 Custom House Tower A preposterous marriage of convenience between a Greek Revival temple dating from one century (**Ammi Young** was the architect in 1847) and a 30-story tower plunked on top during the next (**Peabody and Stearns** added it in 1915) originally appalled many Bostonians. After all, the proud Custom House was once the focal point of the thriving Waterfront.

Situated at the base of State Street, the important colonial route that once led from the **Old State House** and neighboring financial establishments out onto the wharves, the original Custom House was mammoth to begin with, each of its 32 Doric columns a single 42-ton shaft of Quincy granite. As the 20th century progressed and skyscrapers sprouted in other cities, Boston was mired in an economic slump. The federal government forked over the funds for the tower addition, which at 495 feet became the city's first—and, for a long time, only—skyscraper. It took a while, but Bostonians have become very attached to their peculiar landmark, now a familiar friend. No matter how many new structures crowd the skyline, the steadfast tower is the most memorable silhouette, its refurbished clock aglow at night. The little 25th-floor observation balcony is still a great place to scan the harbor and Financial District, and the lobby beneath the original building's rotunda—skylit until the tower leapt on top—deserves a look. Unfortunately, the interior remains off-limits until the building's fate is decided. The city bought the Custom House Tower from the federal government in 1987, and the plan is to open offices and possibly a museum of the City of Boston, but the building remains shut during the funding scramble. ♦ State St (at India St)

7 State Street Block Gridley J. F. Bryant, one of the architects for the **Old City Hall** on School Street, not to mention **Boston City Hospital** in the South End and the **Charles Street Jail** on Cambridge Street, also built a number of large granite warehouses that once extended to the harbor. He designed this massive granite block in 1858. Only one-fifth of its original length, amputated to make way for new roads, it looks proudly stern, as if admonishing: "Don't try to chop off any more of me!" Look for the big granite globe squeezed under the arched cornice facing the **Custom House Tower.** The mansard roofs were added later. ♦ 1 McKinley Sq (at State St)

Financial District/Downtown

There have always been large, active gay and lesbian communities in Boston. For the most current information about gay activities, events, organizations, clubs, services, etc., an excellent source is the Glad Day Bookshop in Back Bay (673 Boylston Street, second floor, 267.3010). They carry all available literature and periodicals, including the *Gayellow Pages* (Northeast Edition), with listings for Boston and Provincetown, and *The Guide,* a monthly about gay travel, entertainment, politics, and sex, which is published in Boston. The bookstore staff is also friendly and knowledgeable about the Boston scene. Other tabloids to look for (often in the South End, Back Bay, or Beacon Hill) are *Bay Windows* and the *Gay Community News.* The Gay Pride March held early each summer is the gay community's most political and festive event of the year, with tens of thousands of marchers and bystanders lining the parade's route through the heart of Boston.

After the Boston Massacre, John Adams and Josiah Quincy bravely undertook the legal defense of the accused soldiers. Although staunch patriots, both men were dedicated to obtaining fair trials for the unfortunate defendants. Seven of the nine were acquitted; two were branded on the hand for manslaughter.

Restaurants/Clubs: Red   **Hotels:** Blue
Shops/ ♠ Outdoors: Green   **Sights/Culture:** Black

7 Tatsukichi ★★$$ Its unremarkable looks are deceiving, since this is one of Boston's superior and authentic Japanese restaurants. Explore the enormous sushi selection. Try teriyaki, sukiyaki, *kushiage* (skewers threaded with meats and vegetables, then batter-fried), or *shabu shabu,* the pot-cooked dinners for two. Twenty percent of the menu is raw fish, and many uncommon entrées will pique an adventurous eater's curiosity. If you'd like privacy for your party, request a tatami room. Tuesday through Saturday nights, friendly **Jim Mullen** runs the bar. ♦ Japanese ♦ M-Th 5-10PM; F-Sa 4-11PM.189 State St (at Surface Artery). Reservations recommended. 720.2468 ♿

7 Dockside $ At one of Boston's most popular sports bars, fans tune in seven TVs and two big screens to watch the games. Dockside has been named one of the country's top 10 sports bars by *Sport* magazine. Better known for its drinks, rah-rah decor, camaraderie, and celebrity customers than for its cuisine, Dockside serves bar food basics like pizzas, BBQ, and burgers. The full menu is available until 11PM, with snacks sold until midnight. One memorable night, **Jack Nicholson** tended bar. Sports stars have been known to drop by, including **Larry Bird, Marvin Hagler,** assorted **Bruins,** and visiting players, so many fans bring auto-

Financial District/Downtown

graph books. ♦ American ♦ Daily 11AM-2AM. 183 State St (at Surface Artery). 723.7050 ♿

8 Central Wharf Buildings On the opposite side of the Central Artery, Central Wharf concludes at the harbor's edge. The humble but handsome row of eight brick buildings between India Street and the elevated expressway are all that remain of the 54 designed by **Charles Bulfinch,** which together extended nearly 1,300 feet to where the **New England Aquarium** now stands. All of these buildings, built in 1817, originally opened onto the water to receive goods from the ships parked out front. ♦ 146-176 Milk St (at India St)

9 Flour and Grain Exchange Building This commercial castle brings a surprising fillip of fantasy to the hard-nosed Financial District. The conical roof of the exchange's curvaceous corner is bedecked with pointy dormers that look like a crown. Architect **H.H. Richardson's** influence is palpable in this 1893 design by his successors, **Shepley, Rutan, and Coolidge,** who also built the impressive **Ames Building** on Court Street. Look for the extraordinary cartouche adorned with an eagle straddling a globe and cornucopias spilling fruit and coins. The exchange was built for the **Chamber of Commerce** and once housed a large trading hall on the third floor. Now architects hold court within. Don't bother to visit the lobby, as

the original was renovated into oblivion. With its lanterns and scattering of trees, the building's triangular plaza is an oasis in this unexpectedly quiet corner of the city. ♦ 177 Milk St (at India St)

10 Mrs. Fields' Cookies Ultrarich, chewy, and chocolaty cookies bring a steady stream of sweet-toothed customers to Mrs. Fields', one of hundreds of shops in the national chain. Choose from the rich repertoire of chocolate-chip varieties, or try oatmeal raisin or cinnamon sugar. The brownies and muffins are equally tempting. ♦ M-F 8AM-7PM; Sa 9AM-7PM; Su 10AM-6PM. 264 Washington St (at Water St). 523.0390 ♿ Also at: 426 Washington St (within Filene's). 357.9727; Copley Pl. 536.6833; Faneuil Hall Marketplace, 200 State St. 951.0855

10 Bakey's ★★$ This upscale delicatessen with full bar serves all sorts of sandwiches for lunch and supper, plus an extensive Continental breakfast. Bakey's amusing logo of a man asleep on an ironing board (see the illustration above) indicates imagination at work. The story is, owner **George Bakey** once found his father in this pose, ensconced on the family ironing board. Bakey's has two very pleasant dining rooms—one called "The Snug," named for the room women retired to when it wasn't considered proper for the sexes to mingle in bars. George has gone all out in his establishment's decor: wooden bars and booths imported from England (be sure to notice the Snug's snug little square bar), antique lighting, Oriental rugs, fresh linen and flowers. Be forewarned—smoking isn't allowed anywhere. Every evening, **LuAnn** plays the piano from 5PM to closing. ♦ American/Deli ♦ M-F 11:30AM-10PM. 45 Broad St (at Water St). 426.1710 ♿

10 Broad Street Indefatigable developer **Uriah Cotting** led his **Broad Street Association** in many ambitious 19th-century urban redevelopment schemes, of which Broad Street itself was but one by-product. Laid out around 1805 according to **Charles Bulfinch's** plans, the street quickly became a handsome commercial avenue to the sea, bordered by many Federal-style Bulfinch buildings. A scattering of these still stand among more recent but distinguished structures such as No. 50 (which was completed in 1863). With its many low-rise buildings, Broad Street is one of the neighborhood's most open, sunny spots. A historical note: **Francis Cabot Lowell,** one of Cotting's partners, developed a power loom in a Broad Street store that ultimately revolutionized American textile manufacture. ♦ At Milk St

10 Sakura-bana ★★$$ Sushi is the house specialty—as you might guess if you notice the poem by the entrance extolling "sushi rapture"—and you can even order "sushi heaven," a sampler of more than two dozen varieties of sushi and sashimi. If you order à la carte, you can be as daring or timid as you wish, staying with salmon, tuna, and mackerel, or exploring exotica like flying fish roe and sea urchin. The daily *bento* (lunch box) specials served with soup, salad, rice, and fruit are also very good choices. For dinner, try seafood *teppan yaki*, broiled with teriyaki sauce and served on a sizzling iron plate. Not only is this trim and tidy restaurant's cuisine outstanding, its prices are reasonable and portions generous. Lots of Financial District workers regularly queue up for lunch. The name, by the way, means "Cherry Blossom." ◆ Japanese ◆ M-F 11:30AM-2:30PM, 5-11PM; Sa 1-11PM; Su 5-10PM (closed first Sunday of the month). 57 Broad St (at Milk St). Reservations recommended for dinner. 542.4311 &

11 Liberty Square Where **Water, Kilby,** and **Batterymarch** streets meet, you'll find another of Boston's quaintly misnamed "squares" squeezed into a busy block. This one is multipurpose: it commemorates angry Bostonians' destruction on 14 August 1765 of the British Stamp Tax office that was located here (a year later, England repealed the Stamp Act). It was formally named in 1793 in a gala ceremony honoring the French Revolution, complete with extravagant feasting and 21-gun salute, and is dominated by **Gyuri Hollosy's** memorial to the Hungarian Revolution of 1956, dedicated in 1986. For those who love old urban pockets lingering in modern cities, Liberty Square is a treat, surrounded by businesslike 19th-century buildings that reveal curious and delightful details if you take time to notice. The old street pattern's turns and angles provide interesting vistas.

11 Appleton Building Coolidge and Shattuck designed this powerful, austere Classical Revival edifice in 1924; **Irving Salsberg** renovated it in 1981. It's named for **Samuel Appleton,** a Boston insurance magnate. The building's most expressive gesture is its generous curve to accommodate converging streets on **Liberty Square,** its best side. (Be sure you're on that side, since the **Milk Street** facade is far less interesting.) All else is measured, pragmatic, restrained—just right for the industry it housed. But the more you study the Appleton, the more inventive it appears, especially its syncopated window patterns and entrance facade friezes depicting a violinmaker, carpenter, glassblower, sculptor, draftsman, and other artisans. Peek into the elliptical lobby with its elegant gilded ceiling. ◆ 110 Milk St (between Oliver and Batterymarch Sts)

12 Sultan's Kitchen $ Located in a remnant of **Charles Bulfinch's** 19th-century **Broad Street** development, this self-service restaurant cooks up fresh and delicious renditions of Middle Eastern and Greek favorites for the lunch crowd: kabobs, grape leaves, Greek salad, baba ghanouj,

egg lemon chicken soup, falafel, tabbouleh. Try the cool, crisp Sultan's Salad or rich *tarama* salad made with fish roe. If too many dishes tempt you, order one of the sampler plates. ◆ Turkish/Takeout ◆ M-F 11AM-5PM; Sa 11AM-3PM. 72 Broad St. 338.7819/8509 (recorded menu) &

13 Country Life ★$ For Boston's most complete vegetarian dining experience, sample Country Life's ample all-you-can-eat lunch, brunch, and dinner buffets. Absolutely no dairy, meat, refined grains, or refined sugar sneak into any of the dishes. Substitutes include soy milk and cheeses made from nuts. The inventive menu changes daily—with a new one printed each month—featuring soups like garbanzo dumpling, lentil, and Russian potato; entrées like lasagna, enchiladas, and vegetable potpie; and always an interesting choice of vegetables. Afterward, treat yourself to one of their desserts. Everything is self-serve and the decor is neat but plain; the emphasis of this restaurant is entirely on hearty, healthy food. ◆ Vegetarian/Takeout ◆ M-Th 11:30AM-3PM; Tu-Th 11:30AM-3PM, 5-8PM; F 11:30AM-2:30PM; Su 10AM-3PM, 5-8PM. 112 Broad St (at Surface Artery). No credit cards. 350.8846/8625 (recorded menu) &

14 Nara ★$$ Lawyers, brokers, bankers, et alia, favor this cozy, private little place located along an alley. One might easily miss Nara altogether, so watch for the Japanese lanterns and red awnings. Sushi-lovers find happiness in the extensive selection, and others can sample tem-

pura, teriyaki or *katsu* entrées, or savory Korean treats like *bool goki*. A family run restaurant, friendly Nara is crowded by day, quieter by night, but always enjoyable. ◆ Japanese/Korean/Takeout ◆ M-F 11:30AM-2:30PM, 4:30-10PM; Sa 5-10PM. 85 Wendell St (at Broad St). Reservations recommended. 338.5935 &

15 Chadwick Lead Works One-upped by the bulky neoclassical **International Place,** a brand-new high rise, this forceful rustic structure, built in 1887, still holds its own on the Financial District fringe. Its architect, **William Preston,** also created the former **New England Museum of Natural History** in Back Bay, now the upscale **Louis, Boston** clothing store. Handsome three-story arches with a graceful ripple of spandrels are topped by a row of little windows and a bold parapet. A gargoyle glares from one corner, and other grotesques and dragonlike lizards cling to the facade. At the back is the square shot tower, inside which molten lead was poured from the top, cooling into shot before reaching the bottom floor. The leadworks was built by its president, **Joseph Houghton Chadwick,** once described as "Lead King of Boston." ◆ 184 High St (between Batterymarch St and Leman Pl)

Commonwealth Avenue and Massachusetts Avenue are most often referred to by their breezy nicknames: "Comm Ave" and "Mass Ave."

16 Batterymarch Building Named for the street it adorns, which was once part of a marching route for military companies from **Boston Common** to now-leveled **Fort Hill**, this heroically optimistic Art Deco assemblage, designed by **Henry Kellogg** in 1928, is wonderful to behold in the midst of a district becoming ever more crowded and shadowed by impersonal modern giants. The three slender towers linked by third-story arcades undergo a truly marvelous transformation as they push through the crowded block to the sky: their dark-brown brick at ground level gradually lightens in color until a glowing buff at the top, as if bleached by sunlight, the one commodity always in short supply in congested downtowns. Under the handsome entrance arches, look for the charming reliefs of boats, trains, planes, stagecoaches, and clipper ships. Unlike the heavy-handed gilding of nearby 75 State Street, this building's discreet touches of gold enhance rather than bedizen its fine form. ♦ 60 Batterymarch St (at Franklin St)

17 Le Meridien $$$ The **Old Federal Reserve Bank**, a Renaissance Revival palazzo designed by **R. Clipston Sturgis** in 1922, has been happily preserved—to the tune of $33 million—as part of this prestigious European hotel located in the heart of the Financial District. It's an easy walk to many popular attractions as well as to the Theater District.

The former bank adjoins **One Post Office Square,** a 41-story tower that was added in 1981 by **Jung/Brannen Associates** and **Pietro**

Financial District/Downtown

Belluschi. French chocolates and a daily weather report appear bedside nightly in each of the Meridien's 326 accommodations. Rooms are contemporary in decor, while the lobby and public spaces feature restored original architectural details. Because a glass mansard roof was plunked on top of the old structure to add additional floors, many rooms feature sloping glass walls with electric drapes, offering great views. Suite 915 is especially popular; so are the loft suites. Fifteen rooms are handicapped-equipped, and three floors are reserved for nonsmokers. There's a posh health club called **Le Club Meridien** on the third floor, featuring a pool, whirlpool, sauna, and exercise equipment; and a full-service business center complete with foreign currency exchange. Amenities include a multilingual staff, valet parking, 24-hour concierge and room services, and express laundry and dry cleaning. Paid parking is offered in the 400-car garage. Because the hotel is owned by Air France, it is often associated with major French cultural events in Boston, such as those hosted by the **French Library** and **Alliance Française**. ♦ 250 Franklin St (between Oliver and Pearl Sts). 451.1900, 800/543.4300; fax 423.2844 ⑤

Within Le Meridien:

Julien ★★★★$$$$ Named for Boston's first French restaurant, which opened on this same site in 1794, Julien draws a predominantly business clientele. Yet the restaurant's lofty refined splendor and haute nouvelle cuisine make it a good choice for a serious evening out. Consulting chef **Marc Haeberlin** of France's three-Michelin-star **Auberge de l'Ill** works with Julien's resident chef **André Chouvin**, combining fresh native ingredients with French creativity in dishes like lobster in phyllo with butternut squash sabayon and stuffed saddle of lamb with rosemary *jus*. Desserts are inspired, and the wine list exceptional. The menu is à la carte, with a "Taste of New England" prix-fixe four-course dinner available, as well as a prix-fixe business lunch.

Julien is located in the high-ceilinged hall that once served as the bank's boardroom. Vast as the dining room is, tables are all generously spaced and diners settle into Queen Anne wingback chairs, promoting privacy and conversation. The **Julien Bar,** resplendent with gilded coffered ceilings and wonderful carved details, provides background piano music. Look for the pair of **N.C. Wyeth** murals portraying **Abraham Lincoln** and **George Washington**. ♦ French ♦ M-F noon-2PM, 6-10PM; Sa 6-10:30PM. Complimentary valet parking for dinner. Jacket and tie required at Julien; no blue jeans allowed at Julien Bar. Reservations recommended. 451.1900 ⑤

Cafe Fleuri ★★$$$ Situated beneath the six-story atrium in **One Post Office Square,** connecting to the hotel, the airy and open cafe features moderately priced brasserie-style cuisine, and is popular for business breakfasts and lunches, and the spectacular, belly-bludgeoning Sunday brunch.

On Friday and Saturday nights, a pianist entertains. Attention all chocoholics: on Saturday afternoons (except in the summer) the cafe puts on a sumptuous all-you-can-eat Chocolate Bar buffet, a truly hedonistic, decadent display of cakes, pies, tortes, fondues, mousses, cookies, brownies, and the like. ♦ Cafe ♦ M-Sa 7-11AM, 11:30AM-2:30PM, 6-10:30PM; Su 7AM-2PM, 6-10:30PM. Valet parking. Reservations recommended. 451.1900

18 State Street Bank & Trust Company Erected in 1966 by an architectural consortium—**Hugh Stubbins & Associates, F.A. Stahl & Associates, LeMessurier Associates**—the bank is directly across the street from the **New England Telephone** building. Take the elevator one flight down and visit the bank's **Concourse Art Gallery**. At least four shows are mounted here each year on art and architecture, often in collaboration with local nonprofit groups like the **Boston Architectural Center** and the **Massachusetts Horticultural Society**. The bank owns a fine maritime folk art collection and 19th-century maps and charts. Works by city youth are shown every summer. ♦ Free. M-F 9AM-5PM. 225 Franklin St (between Pearl and Oliver Sts). 654.3938 &

19 **New England Telephone Headquarters Building** A 1947 design by **Cram & Ferguson**, this step-top Art Deco throwback occupies its place with pride. **Goody, Clancy & Associates** recently renovated the facade in a spiffy homage; check out the spiky beacons, echoed in the phone booths on either side. (Everything has been touched with a Deco wand, from the garden guardrails and trash receptacles, right down to the sidewalk pattern.) Off the main lobby, you can see a re-creation of inventor **Alexander Graham Bell's** garret. **Dean Cornwell's** frenzied and colorful mural, which circles the lobby, is really something—Norman Rockwell-esque eyefuls. Called *Telephone Men and Women at Work*, the 160-foot-long, action-packed painting depicts 197 life-size figures in dramatic groupings. Painted in 1951, it lionizes not only Bell and other telephone pioneers, but also employees on the job and those risking life and limb in the face of disaster to keep those calls coming. Cornwell was an old hand at this sort of thing, creating murals honoring steelworkers, pioneers in medicine, various states' histories, etc.

Bell's laboratory is a painstaking replica of his original studio at **109 Court Street** in old **Scollay Square**, where he electrically transmitted the first speech sounds over a wire on 3 June 1875. (The following March, in a different lab, Bell succeeded in sending not just sounds but intelligible words, when he issued his famous line: "Mr. Watson, come here, I want you.") The studio was saved from demolition, dismantled, and eventually brought here in pieces and rebuilt. On display are models, telephone replicas, drawings, references, and historic artifacts, plus a wonderful diorama of the view of Scollay Square from Bell's window. Pamphlets about Cornwell's creation and Bell's garret are usually available. ♦ Free. M-F 8:30AM-5PM. 185 Franklin St (between Congress and Pearl Sts). 743.4747 & (enter from Franklin St)

20 Post Office Square Another of Boston's many triangular "squares," this is one of the busiest and most visually exciting pockets in the city. Surrounded by worthy buildings, including the Art Deco post office and telephone company headquarters, it opens to wonderful views of the city's densest blocks, where new and old exist cheek by jowl. Topping a 1,400-car garage, this popular new public space, landscaped by Craig Halvorson, harbors 125 species of plants, including seven vines climbing an elegant 143-foot-long trellised colonnade. Harry Ellenzweig designed the sparkling glass quarters of the Milk Street Cafe; sculptor Howard Ben Tre the handsome green-glass fountains. ♦ Surrounded by Congress, Devonshire, Water, and Milk Sts

20 **Angell Memorial Plaza** At the triangle's tip opposite the post office is a pocket park dedicated to **George Thorndike Angell**, founder of the Massachusetts Society for the Prevention of Cruelty to Animals and the American Humane Education Society. A sculpture of a small pond and its inhabitants is located in the middle of a brick circle inset with reliefs of birds, beasts, and bugs—a very sweet assemblage. Look for Angell's wise words: "Our humane societies are now sowing the seeds of a harvest which will one of these days protect not only the birds of the air and beasts of the field but also human beings as well." Looming near the pond is the fountain designed by **Peabody and Stearns** as a watering place for horses in 1912.

20 **John W. McCormack Post Office and Court House** A commanding Art Deco building with plenty of crisp ornament and vertical window ribbons, the post office (designed in 1931 by **Cram & Ferguson** with **James A. Wetmore**) has a nicely weathered gray facade. ♦ Congress St (at Post Office Sq)

21 **Bank of Boston Gallery** Campbell, Aldrich & Nulty designed this ungainly brown tower in 1971 with a big belly; it quickly earned a famous nickname, "The Pregnant Building." The **First National Bank of Boston** operates the marvelous gallery on the 36th floor, which displays the bank's own collection and exhibitions, ranging from fine arts to architecture, design, and furniture. The curator, employed by the bank, often organizes collaborative art shows with Boston-area institutions, museums, and

Financial District/Downtown

schools. Several other retail galleries are located just four blocks away, on **South Street**. ♦ Free. M-F 9-11:30AM, 2-5PM. 100 Federal St (at Franklin St) 434.2200 & (on the Congress St side)

22 **Hole in the Wall** $ One of the district's tiniest tidbits of real estate, this diminutive deli manages to turn out a huge assortment of breakfast and lunch items to go. You'd be hard-pressed to think of a hot or cold sandwich that isn't served here (okay, so there's no peanut butter), not to mention the salads, soups and stews, egg combos, burgers, and snacks. Owner **Benny Yanoff** and his family run the place at top speed. Join the line at the outside counter, or step inside to watch how skillfully counter staff dart past each other in close quarters. It was a passerby's chance remark—"Look at that hole in the wall"—that gave the 12-by-4-foot deli its apt appellation. With brown bag in hand, take a moment to examine **Richard Haas'** trompe l' oeil mural across the street, painted on the back of 31 Milk Street, which portrays a cutaway of the actual facade. Haas also painted the well-known mural on the **Boston Architectural Center** in Back Bay. ♦ Deli/Takeout ♦ M-F 5AM-6PM. 24 Arch St (between Milk and Franklin Sts). 423.4625 & Also at: 125 Summer St. 345.0515

23 Designers' Clothing Should you opt to blend in with the business crowd, this is a good source for men's and women's professional attire (mostly men's). Tailored clothing from designer lines is discounted 30 to 60 percent, and everything is first quality, no irregulars.
♦ Reader, please note: At press time, this store's fate was uncertain. Please call ahead to confirm hours and location. 161 Devonshire St (between Milk and Franklin Sts). 482.3335 &

24 International Trust Company Building **Max Bachman's** allegorical figures *Commerce* and *Industry* adorn the **Arch Street** side, while *Security* and *Fidelity* are ensconced on **Devonshire Street,** adding a fanciful representation of business rectitude modern buildings sorely lack. This edifice, built in 1893 by **William G. Preston,** enlarged in 1906, and now listed on the **National Register of Historic Places,** incorporated the remains of a building partly destroyed by Boston's terrible 1872 fire. ♦ 39-47 Milk St (between Arch and Devonshire Sts)

25 Milk Street Cafe ★$ Downtown shoppers and Financial District denizens love this crowded cafeteria, and many a politician stops in for dairy kosher, vegetarian home-style cooking that includes muffins and bagels, soups, pizzas, pastas, quiches, salads, and sweet treats. Breakfast and lunch only are served. ♦ Cafe/Takeout ♦ M-F 7AM-3PM. 50 Milk St (at Devonshire St). 542.3663 &

26 Winthrop Building Boston's first building with a steel skeleton instead of load-bearing masonry walls, the slim Winthrop slips grace-

Financial District/Downtown

fully into a tapering lot. Conceived in 1893 by one of Boston's more adventurous architects, **Clarence H. Blackall,** the gently curving building flows between Spring and Water streets. Now on the **National Register of Historic Places,** its golden airiness and dressy decoration, especially on the lower levels, delight the eye. Blackall's Chicago training was a fantastic boon to Boston. He designed a number of majestic theaters and other public buildings. Among Boston's other early steel-frame office buildings are this charming pair nearby: **Cass Gilbert's Brazer Building** of 1896 and **Carl Fehmer's Worthington Building** of 1894, standing side by side at 27 and 33 State Street ♦ 276-278 Washington St (between Spring Ln and Water St)

Within the Winthrop Building (around the corner, facing Water Street):

Caffè Paradiso $ Another spin-off of a favorite North End meeting place, the caffè sells quick Italian treats to take away (there are counters, but no tables). In addition to steaming cappuccino, espresso, and Italian beverages, they carry savory calzones, pizzas, quiches, cannoli, and delicious desserts, including a popular hazelnut truffle torte. ♦ Italian/Takeout ♦ M-Sa 6AM-5PM. 3 Water St (at Washington St). No credit cards. 742.8689 & Also at: 255 Hanover St. 742.1768; 1 Elliot Pl, Harvard Sq, Cambridge. 868.3240

26 Bob Smith Sporting Goods Specializing in running, tennis, skiing, fishing, and, of late, blading (in-line skating), this small shop is staffed by "professionals who play and understand the sport they sell." The service is indeed more than perfunctory—it's educational—and the selections are top-of-the-line. In 1989 the shop supplanted a popular lunchroom that dominated the tiny alley since 1877. In 1643 this corner was the site of **Governor Winthrop's** home, conveniently located by **Great Spring,** for which it's named (that source ran dry in the mid-19th century). ♦ M-F 9AM-6PM; Sa 10AM-5PM. 9 Spring Ln (between Washington and School Sts). 426.4440 &

27 Merchants Wine & Spirits This former bank now secures a liquid treasure. One of the city's finest wine and spirits shops, Merchants offers unusual vintages as well as inexpensive drinkable monthly specials. Rare cognacs and superior Burgundies are a specialty; there's also a large California section. Tastings are held regularly in the old bank vault at the back, its walls still lined with safety-deposit boxes. A blooming cheese department sells superb cheeses from small New England farmsteads, plus imports. Merchants publishes a very informative, chatty newsletter. ♦ M-Tu 10AM-6PM; W-F 9AM-6:30PM; Sa 11AM-5PM. 6 Water St (between Washington and Devonshire Sts). 523.7425

28 The Globe Corner Bookstore This prized relic of colonial Boston is quite comfortably ensconced on its corner site. The redbrick, gambrel-roofed house (pictured above), now on the **National Register of Historic Places,** was built circa 1711 for **Thomas Crease,** who opened Boston's first apothecary shop within. In 1828 **Timothy Carter,** a bookseller, took over, installed printing presses, and opened the **Old Corner Bookstore** on the first floor. Thus was inaugurated the building's long career as the locus of Boston's publishing industry and literary life.

Here **Ticknor & Fields** published works by **Harriet Beecher Stowe, Dickens, Tennyson, Browning, Thoreau, Hawthorne, Thackery, Julia Ward Howe,** and **Emerson,** helping to establish a native literature. Gregarious **Jamie Fields** in particular gained respect as counsel, friend, and guardian to writers, and was especially loved as an innovator who believed writers ought to be paid for their pains. Here, too, *The Atlantic Monthly* was founded and rose to cultural eminence. *The Boston Globe's*

Downtown offices once occupied the building, whose preservation the newspaper ensured by opening its namesake bookstore in 1982.

The current shop sells a wealth of works on New England and books by regional authors, plus a fine selection of guidebooks, maps, globes, atlases, and world travel information. You can always find unusual cards, calendars, cookbooks, and marvelous children's books. ♦ M-Sa 9AM-6PM; Su noon-6PM. 1 School St (at Washington St). 523.6658. & Also at: 49 Palmer St (travel and geography only), Harvard Sq, Cambridge. 497.6277

29 Brookstone The brainchild of engineer **Pierre de Beaumont**, a frustrated hobbyist who sought unusual tools that weren't available, Brookstone is a specialty store that stocks more than a thousand well-made, practical, and sometimes pricey tools and gifts. The inventory focuses on unusual, hard-to-find items and includes shop and gardening tools, small electronics, housewares, personal care items, exercise and sports equipment, indoor and outdoor games, office supplies, and travel and automotive accessories. De Beaumont started Brookstone as a mail-order catalog business, then launched the innovative retail system used in the 98 Brookstone stores nationwide. It works this way: each store is like a giant 3D catalog, with information cards accompanying all displayed goods. Customers pick up and examine whatever interests them, fill out order forms and present them at the desk, then wait for purchases to be delivered by conveyor belt. Mail-order catalogs are available, too. ♦ M-Sa 9AM-7PM; Su noon-5PM. 29 School St (between Tremont and Washington Sts). 742.0055 & Also at: Copley Pl. 267.4308; Faneuil Hall Marketplace. 439.4460

30 Kirstein Business Branch A branch of the **Boston Public Library,** designed by **Putnam and Cox** in 1930, Kirstein specializes in non-circulating business and financial references. It's located off the beaten trail on a pedestrian lane connecting School and Court streets. An interesting feature of the building is its Georgian Revival facade, which replicates the central pavilion of daring **Charles Bulfinch's** architecturally innovative (for America) and financially disastrous **Tontine Crescent** residential development, built on Franklin Street in 1794 and demolished in 1858. It was this speculative real-estate scheme's failure that cost Bulfinch his inheritance and turned him from an architect by choice into one by necessity. Several blocks away, part of Franklin Street still follows the footprints of the vanished Tontine's curve. ♦ M-F 9AM-5PM. 20 City Hall Ave (between School St and Pi Alley). 523.0860

30 Pi Alley The printer's term "pi," meaning spilled or jumbled type, is what this alley is probably named after. As the story goes, type would spill from printers' pockets as they went to and from a popular colonial tavern located at the alley's end. A less common account claims the alley is actually **Pie Alley,** paying tribute to the tavern's popular pies. ♦ At City Hall Ave (between Court and School Sts)

31 Hungry Traveller $ Across from the **Kirstein Business Branch,** tucked into a quiet street behind **Old City Hall,** is an ideal cafeteria-style restaurant for early bird eggs and bacon or a quick, cheap sandwich. Five or six hot entrées are prepared daily, plus salads and soups. Hang back until you know what you want, because once the no-nonsense counterhelp spots you, they'll demand your order. A lot of people come here—tourists and on-the-job Bostonians—and the staff likes to keep things moving. ♦ American/Takeout ♦ M-F 5AM-4PM. 29 Court Sq (at Pi Alley). No credit cards. 742.5989 &

32 Rebecca's Cafe ★$ Popping up all over Boston are these popular offspring of the original Rebecca's restaurant on **Beacon Hill.** The made-from-scratch hot entrées, salads, sandwiches, pastas, soups, pastries, and dreamy desserts are winning more and more fans. ♦ Cafe/Takeout ♦ M-F 7AM-8PM; Sa 8AM-3PM. 18 Tremont St (at Court St). No credit cards. 227.0020 & Also at: 112 Newbury St. 267.1122; 65 JFK St, Harvard Sq, Cambridge. 661.8989

33 Old City Hall Replaced by modern **City Hall** at **Government Center,** this empress dowager is an exuberantly ornamental artifact of a more flamboyant era. The days when colorful Boston politicos like **James Michael Curley** held sway are long gone; retired in 1969, the 1865 hall designed by **Gridley J. F. Bryant** and **Arthur Gilman** is no longer in the thick of things. For many visitors, it's a surprise to discover this French Second Empire edifice tucked away from the street. Still graced with ample arched win-

Financial District/Downtown

dows and an imposing pavilion, the **National Historic Landmark** building now accommodates offices and a restaurant; the foyer contains a nice trompe l'oeil reminder of its former finery by muralist **Josh Winer,** and further embellishments are planned. The exterior was painstakingly renovated by **Anderson, Notter Associates** in 1970.

On either side of the entrance stand **Richard S. Greenough's** 1855 statue of **Benjamin Franklin** and **Thomas Ball's** 1879 statue of **Josiah Quincy,** Boston's second mayor, who built **Quincy Market** and served as president of **Harvard College.** Franklin's likeness was the first portrait statue in Boston. Embedded in the sidewalk in front of the hall's cast-iron fence is **Lilli Ann Killen Rosenberg's** appealing 1983 mosaic called *City Carpet,* which commemorates the oldest public school in the US. Erected near this site in 1635, the **Boston Public Latin School** gave School Street its name and contributed influential alumni to American history books, including Franklin, **John Hancock, Charles Bulfinch, Charles Francis Adams,** and **Ralph Waldo Emerson.** The school is now located near the **Fenway.** Rosenberg also created the mosaic located on the wall side of the Green Line's outbound platform in **Park Street Station,** offering a delightful pictorial account of Boston's first subway. ♦ 45 School St (between Tremont and Washington Sts)

Within Old City Hall:

Maison Robert ★★★$$$$ The colorful political wheelings and dealings of **Old City Hall** belong to the past. But at Maison Robert, deals are still made, love affairs launched, marriages proposed, and other momentous occasions celebrated. For 20 years, the superior French restaurant has made a happy home in the old hall. Inside Maison Robert, look for the vaulted brick ceilings and distinguished old doors, vestiges of the original interiors. **Ann** and **Lucien Robert** offer fine classic dishes such as lobster bisque, rabbit sausage, country pâté, Dover sole, rack of lamb, and wondrous *tarte tatin* and crème brûlée. (Lucien has been honored by the French government with the *Chevalier du Merite* award for his contributions to French culture.)

Upstairs is **Bonhomme Richard** ("Poor Richard," in honor of **Benjamin Franklin** and his famous almanac), the beautiful formal dining rooms with butternut woodwork overlooking the **King's Chapel Burying Ground**; downstairs is the less fancy, very inviting **Ben's Cafe** (★★★$$$). It, too, was named for Franklin, and serves somewhat lighter and less expensive dishes. The Roberts' daughter **Andrée** skillfully undertakes the duties of chef. For private parties of 10 to 12 people, ask about dining in the **Vault,** the original City Hall vault. Maison Robert holds wine and champagne tasting dinners (put your name on the mailing list); and on the first Friday of each month hosts "The French Table" prix-fixe dinner, beginning at 7:30PM with an aperitif social hour. As many

Financial District/Downtown

as 80 attend, native speakers and novices alike (reservations are required). The third Friday of every month, a guest chef helps Andrée prepare a Scandinavian dinner with special dishes from countries like Finland and Norway. When spring comes, cafe tables and umbrellas appear on the lovely outdoor terrace, and the garden blooms again, signaling the return of a delightful spot. ♦ French ♦ M-F 11:30AM-2:30PM, 6-9:30PM (cafe), 6-10PM (upstairs); Sa 6-10PM (cafe), 6-10:30PM (upstairs); Su open for private parties and some holidays; inquire. Valet parking (fee). 45 School St (between Tremont and Washington Sts). Jacket and tie required upstairs. Reservations recommended. 227.3370 ♿

34 King's Chapel The original 1688 chapel stirred Bostonians' ire, since it was the city's first place of worship for Anglicanism, the official Church of England that had driven Puritans from their homeland. The plain wooden structure was built at the behest of **Sir Edmund Andros,** the royal governor who took the reins when the **Massachusetts Bay Colony** charter was revoked—just one early link in the long chain of events leading to the Revolution. To avoid interrupting services, the substantial 1754 Georgian chapel of Quincy granite standing today (a **National Historic Landmark**) was actually erected *around* the original building,

which was then dismantled and heaved out the windows of its replacement. If King's Chapel seems squat, it's because the elaborate stone steeple architect **Peter Harrison** envisioned atop its square tower was never built; funds ran out. But in one splendid finishing touch, the facade was embellished with a portico supported by Ionic columns.

The Georgian interior has weathered the centuries well. Its raised pulpit is the oldest still in use in America on the same site. The pew dedicated to early royal governors' use later accommodated **George Washington** on his Boston visits, and other American worthies. Slaves sat in the rear gallery on the cemetery side, and condemned prisoners sat to the right of the entrance for a last sermon before being hanged on the **Common.** After the Revolution, once the British and Loyalists had evacuated Boston, the chapel was converted around 1789 into the first American Unitarian church. Some of the rich presents given to the earlier chapel by **William** and **Mary** of Britain are still in use, but most are now displayed at the **Boston Athenaeum.**

One of the church's other treasures is **Paul Revere's** largest bell, which he called "the sweetest bell we ever made." Come hear the resonant Charles Fisk organ, a replica of the church's 1756 original; every Tuesday free musical recitals begin at 12:15PM; every Wednesday an organ prelude commences at noon, with worship service at 12:15PM. On Thursday free poetry readings in "the King's English" start at 12:15PM. No tours are offered, but guides are on hand to answer questions during the summer months. ♦ Tu-Sa 10AM-4PM, May-Oct; Tu-F 10AM-2PM, Sa 10AM-4PM, Nov-Apr. 58 Tremont St (at School St). 523.1749 ♿

Adjacent to King's Chapel:

 King's Chapel Burying Ground Boston's earliest town cemetery's first resident was **Isaac Johnson,** who owned the land and was buried here, in his garden, in 1630. So many Boston settlers so quickly followed suit that some wag noted, "Brother Johnson's garden is getting to be a poor place for vegetables." A pleasant neighbor today, the church next door was erected on land seized from the burying ground. Burials continued until 1796, although a gravedigger complained in 1739 that King's and two other local graveyards "were so fulled with dead bodies that they were obliged oft times to bury them four deep."

As in other Boston cemeteries, grave markers were moved about to accommodate newcomers, an unsettling practice that caused **Oliver Wendell Holmes** to complain: "The upright stones have been shuffled about like chessmen and nothing short of the Day of Judgment will tell whose dust lies beneath. . . Shame! Shame! Shame!" The burying ground's inhabitants include governors **John Winthrop** and **John Endicott.** On the chapel side, look for the 1704 gravestone of **Elizabeth Pain,** who supposedly bore a minister's child and probably was **Nathaniel Hawthorne's** model for **Hester**

Prynne in *The Scarlet Letter*. Also buried here is Sons of Liberty courier **William Dawes,** who rode through the night just as bravely as **Paul Revere,** but didn't have the posthumous good fortune to be lionized in a **Longfellow** poem. And for a sample of the Puritans' pessimistic stance on the snuffing of life's candle, look for **Joseph Tapping's** marker. Stone rubbings are not allowed. ♦ M-Sa 8:30AM-3:30PM &

35 **Omni Parker House** $$$ Boston's genteel dowager hotel proclaims itself "the choice of legends since 1854," and it's true: US presidents and celebrities of every stripe, from **Joan Crawford** to **Hopalong Cassidy,** have made themselves at home here. The Parker House is the oldest continuously operating hotel in America and represents the success story of Maine native **Harvey D. Parker,** who came to Boston with less than a dollar and became its leading hotelier. Rebuilt numerous times, the current structure dates to 1927. Attracting a business-oriented clientele, the Parker House offers 541 rooms on 14 floors, including handicapped-equipped rooms and nonsmokers' floors. A concierge is in attendance in the lobby, plus there's a computerized concierge system. Paid valet parking is available. Not long ago, this venerable hotel had some hard times and became shabby, but has been lovingly restored and is luxuriant again, the centerpiece lobby clad in original oak woodwork with carved gilt moldings.

Starting around 1855, the famous erudite **Saturday Club** met at the Parker House on the last Saturday of every month, its circle including many of the American literary and intellectual luminaries such as **Hawthorne, Whittier, Emerson,** and **Longfellow;** a spin-off group founded *The Atlantic Monthly* in 1859. During one long Boston visit, the high-spirited, sociable **Charles Dickens** stayed at the hotel and joined the club's congenial gatherings, often fixing gin punch for his pals. The sitting-room mirror before which Dickens practiced his famous Boston readings now hangs on the mezzanine. On a more historical note, just 10 days before assassinating **Abraham Lincoln,** actor **John Wilkes Booth** stayed at the Parker House while visiting his brother **Edwin,** also an actor, who was performing nearby. John spent some time practicing at a nearby shooting gallery. And it was from the hotel's **Press Room** that **JFK** announced his candidacy for US president.

Parker's Bar is known for its classic martini; try one with hors d'oeuvres, which are complimentary from 5PM to 7PM. By the way, the famous secret recipe for the soft Parker House roll was first created here (they bake more than a thousand of the fragrant rolls each day), as was the tasty but very unpielike Boston cream pie. Both are available in the restaurants and to take out. ♦ 60 School St (at Tremont St). 227.8600, 800/843.6664; fax 227.2120 &

Within Omni Parker House:

Parker's Restaurant ★★$$$ With vaulted ceilings and high, wing-backed chairs, the restaurant is tranquil, roomy, and timeless. The good, reliable American cuisine—accompanied by those famous Parker House rolls—is undeservedly overlooked in Boston's frenetic dining scene. A guitarist strums during the award-winning Sunday brunch, and piano music drifts in from **Parker's Bar** Monday through Saturday. ♦ American ♦ M-F 6:30AM-2:15PM, 5:30-10PM; Sa 11:30AM-2:15PM, 5:30-10PM. Valet parking (fee). Jacket preferred at lunch, required at dinner. Reservations are recommended. 227.8600 &

The Last Hurrah! Bar and Grill ★$$ The place looks dated, but that's the point—the walls are plastered with political memorabilia

Financial District/Downtown

nostalgically harking back to when **Old City Hall** down the street was in full swing. And speaking of swing, there's a swing brunch on Sunday. Monday through Friday you can dine as well as drink here, but the food is nothing special. The bar is popular with the **State House** and **City Hall** sets. ♦ American ♦ M-F 11:30AM-11PM; Sa-Su 4:30-11PM. Reservations recommended. 227.8600 &

36 **Boston Five Cents Savings Bank** Adding on to a sedate Renaissance-style bank designed in 1926 by **Parker Thomas & Rice,** architects **Kallmann and McKinnell**—who also designed the new **Boston City Hall**—created a dynamic building that's clearly as hard at work as its occupants. The remarkable 1972 addition has no secrets: its five-story colonnade and enormous beams conduct their structural functions in plain view, and a glass wall exposes all that goes on inside the bank. Big as it is, the building gracefully adapts to a tricky site and has earned its place in one of Boston's most historic quarters. The little park out front offers breathing space from Washington Street crowds, and good views of the nearby **Globe Corner Bookstore** and the **Old South Meeting House.** ♦ 10 School St (at Washington St)

Restaurants/Clubs: Red	**Hotels:** Blue
Shops/ 🌳 Outdoors: Green	**Sights/Culture:** Black

37 Old South Meeting House After the **Old North Church** in the **North End,** this is Boston's oldest church. Built in 1729 by **Joshua Blanchard,** the **National Historic Landmark** (pictured at right) is a traditional New England brick meeting house fronted by a solid square wooden tower that blossoms into a delicate spire. When nearby **Faneuil Hall's** public meeting space grew too cramped, Bostonians congregated here for town meetings peppered with fiery debate to prepare for the coming Revolution and plan events like the **Boston Tea Party** of 1773. That cold December night, which Boston loves to remember, more than 5,000 gathered at Old South to rally against the hated tea tax. Three ships filled with tea to be taxed were anchored at **Griffin's Wharf,** and the royal governor refused Bostonians' demands that the tea be sent back to England. **Samuel Adams** gave the signal igniting the protest that turned Boston Harbor into a teapot. During the British occupation, Redcoats struck back at the patriots by using their revered meeting place for the riding school of **General "Gentleman Johnny" Burgoyne's**

Financial District/Downtown

light cavalry, complete with an officers' bar. By the time the British had evacuated, the church was in a sorry state. The congregation finally moved back in, then decamped in 1875 to the **New Old South Church** in **Copley Square.** Among the Old South Meeting House's early congregation members were **Phillis Wheatley,** a freed slave and one of the first published black poets; **Elizabeth Vergoose,** a.k.a. "Mother Goose"; and patriots **James Otis, Samuel Adams,** and **William Dawes.**

Barely escaping destruction by the Great Fire of 1872, Old South was then nearly demolished to make way for commercial businesses. But Bostonians, including **Julia Ward Howe** and **Ralph Waldo Emerson,** contributed funds to purchase and restore the historic property, which has been maintained as a national monument and museum by the **Old South Association** ever since. Step inside to experience Old South's restful simplicity. Because the British stripped the interior in 1776, only the sounding board and corner stairway are original. The award-winning permanent multimedia exhibition "In Prayer and Protest: Old South Meeting House Remembers," includes walls that talk, tapes of Boston Tea Party debates, a scale model of colonial Boston, profiles of famous churchgoers, and artifacts. The museum

shop sells cards and souvenirs like penny whistles, quill pens, and soldiers' dice made from musket balls. "Middays at the Meeting House," an excellent series of monthly concerts and weekly lectures on American history and culture, runs October through April. Events are free with museum admission. In addition to hosting educational programs and performances, Old South still holds its place in Boston political life as the site for public debates, forums, and announcements of candidacies for office. During July and August, re-creations of 18th-century Boston town meetings are staged every Saturday at 2PM in **Boston Five Cents Savings Plaza** across the street, and bystanders are encouraged to participate. Tours for groups larger than 10 are arranged with two weeks' advance notice. Outside on the corner is one of Boston's largest and prettiest flower stands. ♦ Admission. Daily 10AM-4PM, Nov-Apr; daily 9:30AM-5PM, May-Oct. 310 Washington St (at Milk St). 482.6439 &

Old South Meeting House

Within Old South Meeting House (around the corner, facing Milk Street):

Anything that's a book

Goodspeed's Old South Branch In Old South's basement is an outpost of **Beacon Hill: Goodspeed's Book Shop,** purveyors of antiquarian books since 1898. One step in the door and you'll sniff the unmistakable smell of old books. Goodspeed's sells and buys books on all subjects and does appraisals for institutions, estates, and government agencies, as well as individuals. Pick up a rare tome, or browse among the bargain-book tables. They also carry maps. ♦ M-F 9AM-5PM; Sa 10AM-3PM (closed Saturday, July-Sept). 2 Milk St (at Washington St). 523.5970. Also at: 7 Beacon St. 523.5970

38 Blazing Salads $ This cheap quick-eats place serves all sorts of salads —chicken, tuna, Greek, niçoise, crabmeat, and tabbouleh, to name a few—with lots of pita bread. Or try a tuna melt, chicken Oriental, or steak teriyaki. Breakfast is offered until 11:30AM, and a piano plays from noon on. It's usually crowded here, but the efficient staff keeps traffic humming along. ♦ American/Takeout ♦ M-F 6:30AM-6:30PM; Sa 6:30AM-4PM. 330 Washington St (between Milk and Franklin Sts). No credit cards. 338.9614 &

39 Woolworth's Right in the thick of things is the very large, familiar, granddaddy department store where you can purchase all kinds of inexpensive handy items and oddball gifts. Too bad the old lunch counter is no more, replaced by a **Burger King.** ♦ M-F 9:30AM-6:45PM; Sa 9:30AM-5:45PM; Su noon-5:45PM. 350 Washington St (at Franklin St). 357.5353 & Also at: 633 Massachusetts Ave, Central Sq, Cambridge. 876.7214

40 Bromfield Street This brief little street was once the location of Revolutionary hero **Thomas Cushing's** residence, where the Massachusetts delegates to the first **Continental Congress** assembled, among them **Samuel** and **John Adams** and **Robert Treat Paine.** Today Bromfield is one of Boston's more interesting, lively commercial streets, packed with small establishments specializing in cameras, antiques, collector's coins and stamps, jewelry, watches, and pens, not to mention pawnshops. Some great old buildings reside here, too, such as Nos. 22 and 30 of 1848 and the **Wesleyan Association Building** at No. 36 of 1870, all made of granite.

40 Skylight Jewelers **Edward Spencer,** an old-fashioned artisan with a gift for modern design, has been a Bromfield Street fixture for more than a decade. His studio display cases suggest his range and feature fluid settings for organic shapes (freshwater pearls are a specialty, as

are moonstones—carved into mysterious moon faces). He's happy to accommodate your own design suggestions. ♦ M-Sa 10AM-6PM. 52 Province St (between Bromfield and School Sts). 426.0521 &

40 Sherman's It's an unlikely spot for a department store, but once people discover Sherman's, they come back often for last-minute gifts, travel items, and housewares. In addition to major appliances and office equipment, Sherman's sells cameras, calculators, electronics, luggage, TVs, telephones, small appliances, cookware, jewelry, and miscellany for the manse. They also carry a number of items in other electrical currents, and arrange all shipping—including customs—to foreign destinations. ♦ M-W, F-Sa 9AM-7PM; Th 9AM-7PM; Sa noon-6PM. 11 Bromfield St (between Tremont and Washington Sts). 482.9610

41 Province House Steps From Province Street, mount the weathered steps that once led to the gardens of 17th-century **Province House,** the luxurious official residence of the royal governors of Massachusetts Bay. Renamed **Government House** after the Revolution, the mansion was inhabited until 1796. Here **General Gage** ordered the Redcoats to Lexington and Concord; here, too, **General Howe** ordered his men to flee after **George Washington** and his troops managed to fortify Dorchester Heights, aiming big guns at the British. Years later, **Nathaniel Hawthorne** wrote about Province House, by then a decaying tavern and inn, in *Twice-Told Tales.* Nary

stick nor stone remains of the mansion except these steps. Up on the left, the modest **Cafe Marliave** is dressed up with bits of wrought iron and balconies. ♦ At Bosworth St

41 Cafe Marliave $$ This restaurant has stood on its corner for so long—more than a century—that many Bostonians forget it exists. Then again, a cadre of loyalists keeps coming back. The Italian-American cooking is nothing to swoon over, but it's good and reasonably priced, with plenty of dishes to choose from. The same family has run the place for 60 years or so. The cafe sits high above the street, at the top of the **Province House** steps; dine on the second floor by the windows and become part of the streetscape. ♦ Italian-American ♦ M 11AM-4PM; Tu, Th 11AM-9PM; F-Sa 11AM-10PM. 10 Bosworth St (in the alley off Province St). 423.6340

42 Bromfield Pen Shop Accustomed to cheapo, use-and-abuse disposable pens? Wander into this little shop, gaze upon gleaming rows of new and antique pens, and reconsider your choice of writing instrument. Imagine what that handsome handful of a lovingly restored Bakelite pen might do for your prose! In addition to standard brands such as **Parker** and **Sheaffer,** Bromfield carries **Mont Blanc, Lamy, Pelikan, Yard-O-Led of England, S.T. Dupont, Waterman, Omas of Italy,** delicate glass pens, and plenty of ink varieties. Engraving is free. The best store of its kind in New England, Bromfield Pen attracts customers from all over the country, including author **Jimmy Breslin,** plus a plethora of local politicians, and media, medical, literary, and legal types. Longtime manager **George Salustro** is not only expert at reconditioning or repairing customers' trusty old pens, he's a charmer, too. And he won't shame you if you decide what you *really* need for now is the same never-fail inexpensive pen used by Boston traffic cops. The shop also stocks art supplies. If you have a nice old pen to sell, George might be interested. ♦ M-F 8:30AM-5:30PM; Sa 10AM-5PM. 39 Bromfield St (between Tremont and Washington Sts). 482.9053 &

42 J.J. Teaparty Quality Baseball Cards A city that's passionate about sports in general

Financial District/Downtown

and baseball in particular is the perfect place for this business. The tiny storefront, often crowded with wheeling-and-dealing kids, is owned by **Peter Leventhal,** whose father runs the coin shop with the same name one door away.

Leventhal buys and sells mostly baseball cards, but also some for football, basketball, and hockey. He's got cards from the '50s and '60s, including past and future Hall of Famers. Unusual items crop up, like turn-of-the-century tobacco cards. Collectors can pick up the latest series by **Score, Topps, Fleer,** and others. ♦ M-F 10AM-5PM; Sa 10AM-4PM. 43 Bromfield St (between Tremont and Washington Sts). 482.5705 &

42 J.J. Teaparty Coin Numismatists take note: for more than 30 years, owner **Ed Leventhal** has bought and sold coins at Bromfield Street's premiere coin shop. Both casual collectors and serious investors come by to drop some coins of their own for proof sets, mint sets, and bullion coins like the American Eagle and Canadian Maple Leaf. ♦ M-F 9AM-4:30PM; Sa 9AM-2PM. Closed July-Aug. 51 Bromfield St (between Tremont and Washington Sts). No credit cards. 482.2398 &

43 Tremont Temple The fanciful Venetian stone facade made of 15 delicate shades of terra-cotta that turns into a temple at the top incongruously fronts an office and church complex. It gets more and more curious with the added adornment of several elaborate balconies. The 1895 building, designed by **Clarence H. Blackall,** stands on the site of the famous **Tremont Theater,** where illustrious 19th-century thespians, performers, lecturers, and politicians—including **Abe Lincoln**—enthralled the public. ♦ 88 Tremont St (between School and Bromfield Sts)

44 Bruegger's Bagel Bakery $ Ten varieties of excellent bagels—Boston's best—are baked throughout the day at this family business, and are never more than a few hours old. Bruegger's own factory also produces nine different cream cheeses to spread on top. If you want a more filling meal, try a sandwich-on-a-bagel accompanied by freshly made soup. Its decor is fast-food basic, but the restaurant is neat and clean, with plenty of seating. ♦ Bagels/Takeout ♦ M-Sa 7AM-6PM; Su 8AM-5PM. 32 Bromfield St. No credit cards. 357.5577 & Also at: 636 Beacon St. 262.7939; 83 Mt. Auburn St, Harvard Sq, Cambridge. 661.4664

45 The Food Emporium $ Inside the otherwise undistinguished **Corner Mall** (which features pleasant but predictable chains such as **The Gap** and **The Lodge**) is a food court teaming with international cuisine. Among the 13 fast-food stands are giants such as **McDonald's** and **Sbarro** and tiny local favorites like **Vouros Pastry,** featuring fresh Greek specialties: moussaka, gyros, and spinach pie. Other offerings range from Mexican to Japanese. This bustling arena is a standby for local office workers, and a great place to pick up a multicultural picnic to enjoy on the Boston Common. ♦ International/Takeout ♦ M-F 7:30AM-6:30PM; Sa 8:30AM-6:30PM; Su noon-6PM. 11 Winter Pl (between Tremont and Washington Sts). 451.6117 &

45 Barnes & Noble Discount Bookstore This big general bookstore specializes in reduced-price best-sellers and discounted paperbacks and hardbacks, plus publishers' overstocks. It also sells children's books, magazines, board games, cards, and local maps, and classical and jazz records, tapes, and CDs. ♦ M-F 9:30AM-6:30PM; Sa 9:30AM-6PM; Su noon-5PM. 395 Washington St (between Winter and Bromfield Sts). 426.5502 & Also at: 603 Boylston St, Back Bay. 236.1308

45 Jewelers Building Though stripped of its frilly original copper trim, this Beaux Arts-inspired early "skyscraper" designed by **Winslow and Wetherell** in 1898 still serves the function it was designed for: housing nearly a hundred jewelry dealers, most of whom sell retail as well as wholesale. As *Boston Globe* architectural critic **Robert Campbell** writes in *Cityscapes,* "The gift-wrapped Jewelers promises surprises and delights within." In the lobby, you can't miss a crude but informative bronze bas-relief depicting the history of diamond mining and cutting. ♦ M-F 9:30AM-6PM; Sa 9:30AM-5PM. 379 Washington St (between Winter and

---

Restaurants/Clubs: Red   **Hotels:** Blue
Shops/ ♠ Outdoors: Green   **Sights/Culture:** Black

Bromfield Sts). Check the Yellow Pages of the Boston phone book for individual dealers' listings ⅃

46 Filene's One of 18 stores in New England and New York, Filene's is a full-service department store selling fashions and accessories for men, women, children, and the home. Formal, casual, and career clothing carry designer and major brand labels. The **Gift Gallery** stocks fine crystal, sterling, porcelain, and other specialty merchandise. Founder **William Filene** opened his first retail business in 1851. The present building was designed by **Daniel Burnham & Company** in 1912. Filene's was the first—and probably only—department store to have a zoo on its roof, with a baby elephant flown in from Bangkok, plus lions, monkeys, and other wild animals. Sixty thousand children visited the zoo before it was demolished by the same hurricane that toppled **Old North Church's** steeple in 1954. The distinguished terracotta face of Boston's popular department store is overdue for a good scrubbing, but the Chicago-style building boasts a grand corner clock. ♦ M-Sa 9:30AM-7PM; Su noon-6PM. 426 Washington St (at Summer St). 357.2100 ⅃

Downstairs in Filene's:

FILENE'S BASEMENT

Filene's Basement Far surpassing the fame of its parent store (the companies are now separately owned), America's first off-price store opened in 1908. You can enter its two shopping levels from Filene's proper, or belowground from the **Downtown Crossing** subway station (on the **Red** and **Orange Lines**). There are now 40 Basements in nine states, but the original is unsurpassed. Legends abound about this place and the determined do-or-die shoppers that regularly make it their mission to snag the best buys here. Many a quickie course has been offered locally on how to "do" the Basement and come away flushed with success and laden with uncostly treasures. The simple formula: perseverance, skill, and dumb luck. Every day, trailers replenish the vast supply of overstocks, clearances, samples, and irregulars sold at 20 to 60 percent less than in fine department stores. The inventory includes designer-label and bargain clothing and accessories for men, women, and children, and housewares of all kinds. Retail stock is regularly featured from prestigious stores like **Saks, Brooks Brothers, Bergdorf Goodman,** and **Neiman Marcus.** Strike it lucky and you might come away with a steal of a wedding dress, or a winter coat, business suit, evening attire, luggage, lingerie, diamond ring, goosedown comforter, or fine linen. On the lower level, there's also a designer boutique for women.

The Basement's famous automatic markdown system works this way: After 14 selling days on the floor, merchandise is reduced 25 percent; after 21 days, 50 percent; after 28 days, 75 percent. After 35 days, whatever is unsold goes to charity. If you find something after the 35 days, go to the "charity desk" and write a check

directly to one of the organizations listed on the Basement's charities list. Crowds gather on the legendary "Big Sale" days, when the Basement opens early. Try to flip through a local Sunday paper, since many sales begin Monday. If you watch, you'll see how veterans work the room; you'll also see neat piles and racks of clothing and goods reduced to colorful, chaotic heaps, and glassy-eyed, overstimulated novices escaping to the upper levels in defeat. A women's dressing room was recently added after complaints of sexism (the men's department has long been thus equipped). However, true shopping mavens won't stand for the lines that form and instead take advantage of the Basement's liberal return policy (14 days, with receipt) for home tryouts. Many also still use the time-honored method of slipping stuff on in an out-of-the-way aisle. ♦ M-Sa 9:30AM-7PM, Su noon-6PM. 542.2011 ⅃ (enter from Filene's, use the elevator)

47 Lauriat's Books Part of a chain throughout New England and New York, this bookstore caters to the general public, but it features a large sea-and-sailing section. ♦ M-F 8AM-7PM; Sa 9AM-6PM; Su noon-5PM. 45 Franklin St (at Hawley St). 482.2850 ⅃ (rear entrance). Also at: 20 Charles St. 523.0188

48 The London Harness Company Rest assured you'll find only the finest in very proper gifts for travel, home, office, and personal use, tastefully arrayed amid the shop's gleaming old wooden fixtures. The oldest operating retailer in the country, the shop has done busi-

ness in this general location since the 1700s. **Benjamin Franklin** was among the early shoppers, and traveled with London Harness trunks. Honor momentous occasions—weddings, graduations, christenings—or get yourself something indispensable that will last forever. Perhaps you'd like a wooden box with **Fenway Park** hand-painted on it, or an illuminated globe, or a chess set, or an umbrella that will stand up to Boston's gusty winds. Clocks, candlesticks, luggage, wallets and accessories, scarves, photo albums, jewelry boxes, briefcases, bookends, desk sets, old prints and maps, and more—all the appurtenances for a civilized existence. ♦ M-F 9AM-5:30PM; Sa 10AM-4PM. 60 Franklin St (between Washington and Arch Sts). 542.9234 ⅃ (through rear entrance)

49 One Winthrop Square Ralph Waldo Emerson's nephew, **William Ralph Emerson,** is responsible for several vigorously unconventional Boston structures, including the **House of Odd Windows** (see page 17) on Beacon Hill and the **Boston Art Club** in Back Bay. In this collaborative effort carried out with **Carl Fehmer** in 1873, William Emerson's influence dominates in the eccentric mixing of architectural motifs. Originally a dry-goods emporium and later headquarters for the *Boston Record-American* newspaper, the building has since been adapted to offices. Out front, where trucks once loaded up with newspapers, is an attractive park with **Henry Hudson Kitson's** bronze of **Robert Burns** briskly striding along, walking stick in hand and collie at his side. ♦ Between Devonshire and Otis Sts

Off Winthrop Square:

Winthrop Lane Opening onto the right-hand side of the square (if you're facing **One Winthrop**), this short-and-sweet brick lane would be unremarkable except for the florist and **Boston Coffee Exchange** shops at one end, and an imaginative work of public art called *Boston Bricks: A Celebration of Boston's Past and Present,* created by **Kate Burke** and **Gregg Lefevre** in 1985. The artists have inset dozens of bronze brick reliefs amid the lane's bricks from its start to its finish. Each relief tells a significant, interesting, or entertaining piece of Boston's story. Have fun trying to figure out what's what. Some images and references are quite familiar: the **Custom House Tower,** Boston **Common's** cows, the **Boston Pops,** the city's ethnic groups, the **Underground Railroad,** the **Boston Marathon,** the **Red Sox,** whale watching, rowers on the **Charles River,** swans in the **Public Garden,** and an amusing representation of the notorious Boston driver. Others may keep you puzzling a while. Collectively, the clever bricks present a good likeness of the city. ♦ Enter from Devonshire St

50 Champlain Chocolates Hard to find outside their native Vermont, these treats are surpassingly tasty. Offerings range from truffles and

Financial District/Downtown

Turkish delight to edible gift packs such as a chocolate heart stuffed with nonpareils. There's also a small ice-cream bar on the premises. Be sure to stroll the building lobby, too. **101 Federal** is a new **Kohn Pederson Fox** building appended to the Deco-era **75 Federal** (get a look at the elevators); the result is a handsome hybrid. ♦ M-F 8:30AM-6PM. 101 Federal St (between Franklin and Matthews Sts). 951.4666 &

51 United Shoe Machinery Corporation Building Now renovated, placed on the **National Register of Historic Places,** and renamed "The Landmark," Boston's first Art Deco skyscraper—built in 1929 by **Peter, Thomas, and Rice,** forms a handsome ziggurat crowned by a pyramid of tiles—a majestic architectural physique. At street level, look for the fine cast-metal storefronts set into limestone. Rude new buildings shove against this proud bulwark, which recalls the era when shoes were big business in Boston. ♦ 140-156 Federal St (at High St)

52 Boston Airline Center This is a handy walk-in center—with no phone number—where you can make on-the-spot reservations or pick up tickets for various airlines, including American, Continental, Delta, Northwest, United, TWA, and USAir. ♦ M-F 9AM-5PM. 155 Federal St (at High St) &

Schroeder's

53 Schroeder's ★$$$ A relative upstart opened only 15 years ago, Schroeder's has the look of old money—and a client list and menu to match. All the standbys are here, from the vichyssoise and escargots to lobster thermidor and chateaubriand—plus a quartet of signature schnitzels *à la maison.* Although the decor leans more toward a ladies' club than a men's, Schroeder's clearly aspires to be the new **Locke-Ober,** and judging from the pleased looks on the well-fed, prosperous faces, it's succeeding quite well. ♦ Continental ♦ M-W 11:30AM-3PM; Th-F 11:30AM-9:30PM; Sa 5-10PM. 8 High St (between Summer and Federal Sts). 426.1234 &

54 Bedford Building Red granite, white Vermont marble, and terra-cotta blend well on the Ruskinian Gothic-style facade of this 1876 **Cummings & Sears** creation, renovated in 1983 by the **Bay Bedford Company** and placed on the **National Register of Historic Places.** The proud building lost its original clock, but recently got a new stained-glass one (created by Cambridge artisan **Lynn Hovey**) that's particularly striking at night. ♦ 89-103 Bedford St (at Lincoln St)

55 Church Green Building This fine addition to the city's stock of 19th-century granite mercantile buildings is named for **Church Green,** the triangular intersection of **Summer, Lincoln, High,** and **Bedford** streets, which in turn was named for a lovely church designed by **Charles Bulfinch** that once stood here—just another example of how history haunts many Boston place names. It was built circa 1873 by an unknown architect, although it is widely attributed to **Jonathan Preston.** Behind this structure rises red-roofed 99 Summer Street, a 1987 interloper by **Goody, Clancy & Associates** that tries mightily to fit in. Across the way is the brand-new 125 Summer Street by **Kohn Pederson Fox,** lurking behind an eclectic row of commercial facades now belonging to No. 125. A swath of old streetscape has been nicely preserved, but the huge modern tower bursting from its midst is a little disconcerting in contrast. ♦ 105-113 Summer St (at Bedford St)

56 Proctor Building On sunny days, it's bathed in light and the perch for many pigeons. Every day, the little Jersey-cream-colored Spanish Renaissance-style building, built in 1897 by **Winslow, Wetherell, and Bigelow,** is an orchestra of ornament crowned by a tiaralike cornice. Shells, birds, flowers, garlands, cherubs, urns, and more parade across the curving facade. ♦ 100-106 Bedford St (at Kingston St)

57 Slesinger's Fabric Store When the do-it-yourself urge strikes, dust off the sewing machine and come to **Jack Laven's** emporium of bargain fabrics for bridal, drapery, upholstery, sewing, and craft projects. Search among discontinued decorator fabrics and leftover lots of woolens, cotton, challis, silk, and more. Notions are a steal here. Laven also sells muslin and canvas to artists. Lycra Spandex is popular these days, he says, and the shop is especially busy around Halloween. His father-in-law, a woolen jobber, began the business; Jack himself started out in Boston's garment district more than four decades ago, at age 23. He's usually on the job about 7AM, and lets early bird shoppers in. ♦ M-Sa 9:30AM-6PM. 30 Chauncy St (between Summer and Bedford Sts). 542.1805 &

58 Dakota's ★★$$$ Hailing from Dallas, the clubby-looking restaurant on the second level does big business in Boston, attracting the briefcase crowd at lunchtime and theater clientele in the evening. The menu's focus is on American grill with a Southern accent. Many dishes are good and colorfully presented: try the calamari, venison-sausage quesadillas, onion rings, gulf seafood chowder, tortilla soup, roast chicken, or lamb chops. Desserts are intensely rich, and the freshly made breads pleasantly fragrant. It's fun to sit in the elevated bar area and overlook the fast-paced dining room, although the clientele is rather homogenous. The restaurant is spiffed up with marble, ceiling fans, Roman shades, and club chairs.

Dakota's inhabits a 21-story office tower called **101 Arch,** which incorporated the facade of 34 Summer Street, an 1873 commercial palace. (Be sure to peek around the corner of the lobby to see the old facade, now under glass. Also, if you're arriving by T, look for a vintage wooden escalator—more than 80 years old!—on the outbound [Chauncy Street] side of the Red Line's Downtown Crossing stop. The grooved slats are so slanted, it's a challenge to ascend.) ♦ American ♦ M-F 11:30AM-3PM, 5:30-9PM; Sa 5:30-8:30PM. 101 Arch St (at Summer St). Complimentary valet parking after 5:30PM on Summer St side. Reservations recommended. 737.1777 &

58 Society of Arts and Crafts at 101 Arch A satellite of the nonprofit crafts organization headquartered at 175 Newbury Street in Back Bay (266.1810), this educational outreach gallery on the second level of 101 Arch is the first step toward establishing **The Craft Museum of Boston.** (The hope is that the museum's opening will coincide with the prestigious society's centennial in 1997.)

The Arch Street gallery showcases contemporary works-for-sale in a variety of media by society member artists, plus works on loan from museums and private collections, and rotating exhibitions of crafts by distinguished and emerging artists. The gallery's 1,200-square-foot space is subsidized by **Metropolitan Life Real Estate Investments.** In addition to bringing crafts to the center of the city—a part of town that can always use a little color and creativity—the gallery is a great place to find exceptional, interesting objects like jewelry, glass, ceramics, and small furniture. ♦ M-F 11AM-7PM. 101 Arch St (at Summer St). 345.0033 &

59 Jordan Marsh A stiff competitor to **Filene's** across the way (via a pedestrian mall that's the site of many a summertime concert or impromptu dance performance), Jordan's is also an upscale, comprehensive department store, part of a long-established Northeast chain. You'll find the whole kit and kaboodle here: clothing for men, women, and children, jewelry, shoes, cosmetics, housewares, home furnishings, and so on. Try the bakery's blueberry muffins. "A tradition since 1851," as its slogan says, Jordan's began as a small, high-quality dry-goods establishment founded in Boston by **Eben Dyer Jordan** and partner **Benjamin L. Marsh.** It, too, has a discount basement store, but not in the same big-bargain league as famous Filene's Basement. ♦ M-Sa 9:30AM-7PM; Su noon-6PM. 450 Washington St (at Summer St). 357.3000 &

Financial District/Downtown

60 Locke-Ober ★★★$$$ The winds of change may howl through Boston, but—with one exception—they've barely whispered at this bastion of Brahmin traditions. After trying his hand at numerous occupations, including taxidermy and barbering, **Louis Ober,** a French Alsatian, opened **Ober's Restaurant Parisien** in 1870 in this tiny residential alley. In 1892 **Frank Locke** opened a winebar next door. Ober's successors combined the two restaurants and their founders' names, an ingenious partnership that has flourished to this day. For nearly a hundred years, the **Men's Cafe** downstairs was reserved for gentlemen; escorted ladies were admitted only on New Year's Eve and on the night of the **Harvard-Yale** game.

(Incidentally, if Harvard lost, the nude painting of *Yvonne* in the first-floor barroom was draped in black.) But one fateful day, modern times came knocking, and this hallowed enclave reluctantly began admitting women. Since 1974 both sexes have enjoyed its Victorian splendor, tried-and-true rich Yankee-European cuisine, and perfectly discreet—if not exactly friendly—black-tie, old-world service. Who knows—you may share the dining room with political heavies like the **Kennedy** family, and those ubiquitous Harvard students who come from across the Charles River to toast their graduations.

The famous downstairs is all dark-wood splendor, the hand-carved bar agleam with German silver, but the revamped and gilded upstairs is nice also. Private dining chambers are available for a fee. You'll see plenty of loyalists, mostly male, sitting in their customary places and dining on delicious old favorites like oysters, lobster Savannah, steak tartare, filet mignon, Dover sole, roast-beef hash, rack of lamb, calf's liver, Indian pudding, and baked Alaska. Follow their example and keep to the time-tested selections. After solicitously notifying the regular clientele well in advance that more—gasp!—change was in the works, Locke-Ober recently introduced healthful new dishes to the ancient menu. The cafe's lock-shaped sign, by the way, was inspired by one that adorned Locke's original establishment. Women are discouraged from wearing slacks here—another barrier to breach? ♦ Continental ♦ M-Th 11:30AM-10PM; F 11:30AM-10:30PM; Sa-Su 5:30-10:30PM (hours vary in July and August).

Financial District/Downtown

Winter Pl (at Winter St). Valet parking after 6PM. Jacket and tie required. Reservations recommended. 542.1340

61 Orpheum Theatre Originally called the **Music Hall,** the worldly Orpheum, built in 1852 by **Snell and Gregorson,** has seen a thing or two. It housed the fledgling **New England Conservatory** and witnessed the **Boston Symphony Orchestra**'s debut concert in 1881. The **Handel and Haydn Society** performed here for years. **Tchaikovsky's** first piano concerto had its world premiere, **Ralph Waldo Emerson** and **Booker T. Washington** lectured, and **Oscar Wilde** promoted a **Gilbert and Sullivan** operetta here. Vaudeville shows took a turn, too. In the early 20th century the theater was extensively altered, becoming Boston's first cinema, then later reverted back to a performance space. Today the Orpheum mostly books rock concerts. ♦ Hamilton Pl (enter from Tremont St, between Bromfield and Winter Sts). No credit cards; to charge, call Ticketmaster, 931.2000. Recorded information 482.0650 ♿

62 Fanny Farmer A Boston classic, this shop has been selling chocolates, fudge, and other candy, ice cream, and nuts on this site for more than 50 years. It is part of the huge national chain named for **Fanny Merritt Farmer,** Boston's legendary cookbook author. Among other innovations, Fanny introduced the level measurement system that revolutionized food preparation. The company also owns all rights to Fanny's immensely popular *The Boston Cooking School Cookbook,* which the shop sells. ♦ M-F 10AM-6:30PM; Sa 10AM-6PM; Su noon-5PM. 130 Tremont St (at Winter St). 542.8677 ♿ Also at: 288 Washington St. 542.7045

63 Cathedral Church of St. Paul Most of Boston's old buildings mingle comfortably enough with their modern neighbors, but dignified St. Paul's looks uncomfortable sandwiched between two towering commercial structures—as if wondering what happened to the spacious rural town of its day, the 1820s. Once surrounded by handsome homes, the Episcopalian cathedral, on the **National Register of Historic Places,** is now situated in Boston's workaday district. The church is a simple temple of gray granite, Boston's first example of Greek Revival architecture. The massive sandstone Ionic columns supporting its porch add conviction to a stretch of street that can use it. Architect **Alexander Parris,** the avid practitioner of the Greek Revival style, also designed **Quincy Market.** If the temple's tympanum looks strangely blank, that's because the bas-relief figures intended for it were never carved—another example of a Boston building where ambitious aspirations exceeded funds. Visit the starkly impressive interior, which was revised somewhat by architect **Ralph Adams Cram** in the 1920s. There's a noon service Monday through Friday, but no tours. ♦ M-Sa noon-5PM. 138 Tremont St (between Temple and Winter Sts). 482.5800 ♿ (enter through the side entrance)

64 Santacross Distinctive Shoe Service In business since 1917, this shop will heal your footware woes. All work is done on the premises. Santacross does walk-in repairs, shoe shines, reheeling, and handbag repairs, too. And orthopedic shoes are a specialty here. ♦ M-F 7:30AM-5PM; Sa 11AM-4:30PM. 16 Temple Pl (between Tremont and Washington Sts). 426.6978 ♿ Also at: 35 High St. 737.2010

65 Stoddard's Open since 1800, the country's oldest cutlery shop sells plenty of other invaluable items, too: row upon row of nail nippers—who'd ever think so many kinds existed?—pocket knives, corkscrews, clocks, manicure sets, mirrors, magnifiers, binoculars, brushes, shaving brushes, scissors, lobster shears, fishing rods and lures, and almost anything else that could possibly come in handy. A great source for practical presents, Stoddard's is also one of a handful of places remaining where cutlery is sharpened by hand, the only way to give blades their proper edge. An expert grinder works upstairs, giving scissors and such a new lease on life. ♦ M-Sa 9AM-5:30PM. 50 Temple Pl (between Tremont and Washington Sts). 426.4187 ♿ Also at: Copley Pl. 536.8688

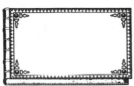

66 Brattle Book Shop Both foreign and domestic bibliophiles find their way to this humble-looking establishment. Not only is the Brattle one of America's few remaining urban-based bookshops of its kind, it's also the successor to the country's oldest operating antiquarian bookshop (founded in 1825). For a good part of this century, the Brattle was run by the late and very literary **George Gloss,** originally a fruit peddler who once exchanged a bunch of grapes for a paperback **Dickens** novel, and who truly earned the nickname "the Pied Piper of book lovers." One time, Gloss drove a covered wagon through the city, tossing free books to passersby. His worthy successor and son **Ken** now runs the place, having worked here since age five.

The three-level shop holds every sort of used and rare book imaginable, with fine selections on Boston and New England, and a wealth of autographs and photo albums. The resilient Brattle has risen from the ashes of two big fires and relocated numerous times; may it long enjoy its present happy home. Many a treasure has passed through these portals, including a well-read copy of *The Great Gatsby,* given by **F. Scott Fitzgerald** to **T.S. Eliot,** which contained Fitzgerald's misspelled inscription and Eliot's annotations. Be sure to peruse the outdoor racks—under the watchful eyes of 18 influential authors (from **Leo Tolstoy** to **Gish Jen**) painted by South End artists **Jeffrey Hull** and **Sarah Hutt.** The Brattle does appraisals, often for free, and the helpful staff are expert book sleuths. ◆ M-Sa 9AM-5:30PM. 9 West St (between Tremont and Washington Sts) 542.0210, 800/447.9595 &

66 15 West Street This three-story town house, described as "Mrs. Peabody's caravansary" by **Nathaniel Hawthorne,** was home to the **Peabody** family from 1840 to 1854. In the rear parlor, Hawthorne married his beloved **Sophia,** the Peabody's youngest daughter, and **Mary Peabody** wed **Horace Mann,** the founder of American public education. In the front parlor, headstrong and brilliant **Elizabeth Peabody** opened Boston's first bookstore selling foreign works. Eldest daughter Elizabeth was a fervent abolitionist, a pioneer for kindergartens in America, and the model for the formidable **Miss Birdseye** in **Henry James'** novel *The Bostonians.* Here, with **Ralph Waldo Emerson,** Elizabeth published *The Dial,* the quarterly journal of the Transcendentalists. And each Wednesday local ladies came to hear journalist **Margaret Fuller's** "Conversations," landmark lectures in the history of American feminism. ◆ Between Tremont and Washington Sts

67 Fajitas & 'Ritas ★$ Unabashedly fun, this ultra-loose joint attracts a surprising number of buttoned-up types. Not content to scribble on the paper tablecloths (crayons are provided), the clientele have spread their doodles and graffiti across every surface; the whole place is a communal work of art in progress. When you fill out your own order forms for assorted fajitas and other Tex-Mex dishes, you can also check off a 'rita (that's margarita) or beer or wine, including sangria by the liter. ◆ Tex-Mex/Takeout ◆ M-W 1-9PM; Th 11AM-10PM; F 11AM-11PM; Sa noon-10PM. 25 West St (between Tremont and Washington Sts). 426.1222 &

68 Opera House Now the home of **Sarah Caldwell's** much-beleaguered **Boston Opera Company** (unable to raise sufficient funds to perform these past few years), the 1928 theater, designed by **Thomas Lamb,** was first named the **B.F. Keith Memorial Theatre** to honor the show-biz wizard who coined the term "vaudeville" and was one of its biggest promoters. Keith introduced the concept of continuous performances of high-quality variety acts suitable for family viewing, to contrast with the lowlife entertainment offered at **Scol-**

Financial District/Downtown

lay Square's notorious **Old Howard** theater. Keith owned a chain of 400 such theaters, after which early movie "picture palaces" were modeled. More recently, this one was called the **Savoy Theatre.** The Spanish Baroque terracotta facade is best seen from **Avenue de Lafayette** across the way. The lobby and auditorium are the worse for wear, but their decadent splendor is impressively dramatic, perfect for opera. It's easy to imagine what a thrill it was to come here during the theater's heyday. Call for information on performances. ◆ 539 Washington St (at Ave de Lafayette). 426.5300 & (enter from Mason St; ushers are trained to assist)

Next to the Opera House:

Paramount Theatre Take note of **Arthur Bowditch's** marvelous sign. A 1932 Art Deco delight, this theater is begging for a fresh start.

"... Which American city can point to so many lovely, queer, and compelling names for its streets as Boston? Beacon, Batterymarch, Pinckney, Tremont, Hereford, Salutation, Merchant's Row, Cornhill, Brick Alley, and Sun Court Street, for example. And who else lives where Winter runs forever into Summer, and Water is always on the verge of turning into Milk?"

Author **David McCord**

Restaurants/Clubs: Red   **Hotels:** Blue
Shops/ ❦ Outdoors: Green   **Sights/Culture:** Black

The first regularly issued American newspaper, *The Boston News-Letter,* was published in 1704.

68 Metropolis $ The three-story dance club's severe black facade and urbane lighting contrast starkly with the faded opulence of the adjacent **Opera House.** The cafe, with swirling bar and booths designed by **Tamarkin Techler Group,** offers nonstellar bistro fare with some Italian specialties. The real action is upstairs, at **The Domain:** a dark, DJ'd disco that spins Top 40, R&B, and "techno." The Metropolis is not quite the tony attraction it was when it opened in 1989 (unfortunately, the depressed area has exerted a depressing influence), but if you're game, it's as good a place as any to get down. ♦ Admission. Cafe M-F 11AM-7PM. Disco Th-Sa 10PM-2AM. 533 Washington St (at Ave de Lafayette). Validated parking at Lafayette Pl. 338.6999 &

69 Boston's Downtown Cafe ★★$ A die-hard crusader in the dwindling **Combat Zone, Dan**

Financial District/Downtown

Holmes ran a charming, albeit cramped cafe at its very heart, grungy LaGrange Street, for five years—right up until the building was condemned. Now he's moved his operation to a sunny, open space on Washington Street, and once again his restaurant is the best the neighborhood has to offer. Great meals are served practically around the clock, all cooked fresh and abundant. Assorted pastas, risotto, and pierogi are among the home-comfort specialties; desserts go all out—bananas Foster, chocolate crepes. The cafe has plans to house a museum of Boston's theater history, with 50 posters dating back half a century. ♦ International/Takeout ♦ Daily 7AM-4AM. 610 Washington St (between Essex St and Hayward Pl). 338.7037 &

70 Baker's Plays The oldest American play publishing company, Baker's was established under the name of the **Herbert Sweet Company** on Washington Street in 1845, relocated after the great Boston fire of 1872, was handed down through several generations, and survives today under the genial custodianship of manager **Jack Welch** and two resident cats "who let us think we run the place." Boston's small but impassioned theater community relies on Baker's for the latest scripts, trade papers, and casting news. ♦ M-F 9AM-5PM. 100 Chauncy St. 482.1280

swissôtel

71 Swissôtel Boston $$$ The Swissôtel's 500 rooms and suites on 16 floors are far more sumptuous and traditional in decor than the hotel's severely impersonal exterior implies. In fact, this hotel is one of the best-kept secrets in Boston, since many don't anticipate finding such stellar accommodations in this part of town. Guest services include a concierge, parking, a multilingual staff, same-day laundry and valet services, an indoor swimming pool and exercise equipment, and a sun terrace. Swiss chocolates appear not only in guest rooms, but in a monstrous bowl at the registration desk.

The 19th floor offers Swiss Butler service, and there are handicapped-equipped rooms plus two nonsmokers' floors. The hotel is the anchor to the adjoining **Lafayette Place** shopping complex. Built in the early '80s, this fortresslike building was badly designed, went bust, and is now undergoing a $26 million makeover. ♦ 1 Ave de Lafayette (between Washington and Chauncy Sts). 451.2600, 800/621.9200; fax 451.0054 &

Within the Swissôtel Boston:

The Lobby Lounge ★$$ A comfortable, low-key space with a two-story atrium, the Lounge fills many guises during the day: at lunch it serves a "business buffet," then there's tea, cocktails, dinner (international nouvelle), and finally, on weekends, a dessert buffet. ♦ International ♦ M-F 11:30AM-2PM, 3-11PM; Sa-Su 3-4:30PM. 451.2600 &

Caffe Suisse ★$$ The setting's a bit bland, except for some contemporary artwork by Swiss émigré artists. The bill of fare is a mix of American and Continental, with a few Swiss specialties (*roesti* potatoes, *spatzli*) thrown in for color. The ambience livens up a bit on Sunday for the jazz brunch buffet. ♦ International ♦ M-Sa 7-11AM, 11:30AM-2PM; Su 11AM-2PM. 451.2600 &

Newspaper Row, Boston's version of London's Fleet Street, once dominated the end of Washington Street near the Old State House. In addition to newspaper publishers, booksellers plied their trade in this neighborhood. For close to a century, *The Boston Globe,* founded in 1872, occupied the site where the 42-story Devonshire Building now stands. The Boston *Journal* was on the north corner of Water Street and the Boston *Traveller* opposite the Old South Meeting House. At the south corner of Milk Street, at 322-328 Washington Street, Gridley J. F. Bryant's Boston Transcript Building still stands, as does Peabody and Stearns' Boston Post Building next door at 17 Milk Street, which coincidentally marks the site of Benjamin Franklin's birthplace. Born in 1706 to Josiah and Abiah Franklin, Benjamin was the youngest of the 10 surviving children in an impressive brood of 17. Benjamin was christened at the Old South Meeting House preceding the current 1729 structure. The extravagant cast-iron facade decoratively registers that fact, by enshrining a Franklin bust.

Seen on Screen

Boston and Cambridge offer plenty of movie houses for first-run films, but listed below are a number of places to go for more unusual and international offerings. Call to find out about current programs, admission prices, and discounts. Also check the "Calendar" section in *The Boston Globe* on Thursday and the *Boston Phoenix* on Friday for special, foreign, and revival films and series, including those shown at local colleges and universities.

Boston Film-Video Foundation Local, national, and international works by independent filmmakers are screened here. ♦ 1126 Boylston Street; 536.1540

Boston Public Library Their free movie series in a comfortable theater attracts the entire spectrum of Bostonians. It's a great place to satiate an urge to see all of **Katharine Hepburn's** or **Cary Grant's** classics or to see **Eugene O'Neill's** plays brought to the screen, or other ever-popular greats. ♦ Rabb Lecture Hall, Copley Square; 536.5400

Brattle Theatre This highly regarded independent repertory movie house in **Cambridge** offers classic Hollywood and foreign films, independent filmmaking, new art films, staged readings, and other performances. Different categories of double features are presented most nights. ♦ 40 Brattle Street, Harvard Square; 876.6837

Ciné Club at the French Library A popular ongoing series of recent and classic French films is screened in a lovely setting. ♦ 53 Marlborough Street; 266.4351

Coolidge Corner Theatre An innovative program of classic and contemporary local, national, and international films is shown in a great old **Brookline** theater that was once rescued from the spectre of gentrification. Animation and cartoon festivals and other special events are held here, too. ♦ 290 Harvard Street, Coolidge Court; 734.2500

Harvard-Epworth Series This **Cambridge** theater shows everything from silent movies with piano accompaniment to more recent art films. ♦ Harvard-Epworth Church, 1555 Massachusetts Avenue; 354.0837

Harvard Film Archive The **Carpenter Center for the Visual Arts** in **Cambridge** features repertory and contemporary international cinema. ♦ 24 Quincy Street; 495.4700

Institute of Contemporary Art Wonderful movies come to the ICA's tiny but very pleasant auditorium. Palestinian and Israeli films and an Argentinian film series have been screened here, too. The schedule is always worth investigating. ♦ 955 Boylston Street; 266.5152

The Museum of Fine Arts The MFA regularly screens interesting alternative films from foreign and ethnic to documentary and avant-garde in **Remis Auditorium.** Japanese or Italian films might be shown, or the **Ingrid Bergman** movies made in Sweden before she became a Hollywood star. Many films are screened here for the first time in this country. ♦ 465 Huntington Avenue; 267.9300, ext. 454

The Wang Center for the Performing Arts The **Classic Film Series** brings old and not-so-old favorites to this former movie palace's fabulous big screen, with live jazz beforehand in the lobby. ♦ 268 Tremont Street; 482.9393

Charles Laquidara
Radio Announcer, WBCN Radio

Fenway Park—Watching a ballgame in the greatest baseball park. The awful food and condiments are bearable. An experience not to be missed—for the whole family.

Davio's, on Newbury Street. Great food, service, and atmosphere; reasonable prices; formal and fine downstairs, and informal and fun upstairs.

Cloud 9 Limousine—A classy, fun way to move through the city in style and security.

Boston Garden—New president, new look, new attitude, old charm.

Watching the students move into Boston in the fall—the hustle, the bustle, the lost looks as the newcomers try to figure out our drivers, our language, our streets.

Jonathan Hyde
Deputy Director, Massachusetts Office of Travel and Tourism

Two sunset views of the city skyline: from the **Logan Airport Water Shuttle** as it heads to its pier at Rowes Wharf; and from the **Longfellow Bridge** (known to locals as the Pepperpot Bridge or the Salt-and-Pepper Bridge) as the setting sun reflects off the mirrored face of the John Hancock Tower.

Shopping at **Haymarket** on a Saturday morning. The open-air stalls offer an abundance of wonderfully

Financial District/Downtown

fresh veggies at bargain prices, and stall holders hawk their wares with the enthusiasm of carnival barkers. Best yet, one of the Haymarket stalls sells raw oysters—a terrific treat.

Sipping a caffe latte at one of **Newbury Street's** innumerable outdoor cafes and indulging in the street's major activity: people-watching. Smart young professionals, proper Bostonians, art and architecture students, punks, and hip young things from the galleries and boutiques—linger long enough and they'll all pass by your table.

Sitting in the serene, white interior of the **Old South Meeting House** and contemplating Boston's rich history—just outside the door is my favorite outdoor flower stall.

Embarking on a bookstore safari in **Harvard Square** (at last count there were about 30). Modern literature, antiquarian books, mysteries, foreign language books, science fiction, religion—they are all here. Some of the bookstores stay open as late as midnight, a perfect place to cap an evening out in the Square with a literary partner.

My favorite museum? That's a tough choice. There's the **Isabella Stewart Gardner Museum** with its flower-filled courtyard (even in the depths of winter). Or the sculpture park at the **DeCordova** in nearby Lincoln. Or the Impressionists at the **Museum of Fine Arts.** And I almost forgot the **Children's Museum** (no, you don't have to have kids with you to get in the museum), the **New England Aquarium....**

Chinatown/Theater District

This checkered neighborhood's story has had many acts, characters, triumphs, and tribulations, the plot now thickening at a quickening pace. For within this geographically awkward and angular fringe of the city converge—and sometimes collide—these principal dramatis personae: the **Theater District,** the **Combat Zone** (Boston's red-light district), and **Chinatown.**

Now clustered near Tremont and Stuart streets, Boston's rialto originally extended much farther—a glittering, glamorous mecca that brought all the big stage names to town. Beginning in the 1920s Boston was a tryout town for Broadway-bound plays. But vaudeville faded, cinema outstripped theater in popularity, the suburbs eclipsed the city, and great playhouses such as the **Wilbur** and the **Majestic** deteriorated. With the subsequent leaking roofs, crumbling walls, and peeling paint and plaster, the shadow of the wrecking ball loomed. But Boston's '80s boom rescued a number of theaters: the Wilbur is repaired, the **Shubert** refurbished, the Majestic resuscitated, and the **Colonial** forges on. Other houses cling to life or remain dark, awaiting a savior, but even in the wake of the "Massachusetts Miracle," there's reason to hope.

The Combat Zone, a sleazy "adult-entertainment" district concentrated on lower **Washington Street,** took root in the '60s and flourished during the '70s as home to the X-rated **Pussycat Cinema, Good Time Charlie's, Glass Slipper, Naked i,** and dozens of other seamy strip joints, peep shows, and porn shops. Development as well as neighborhood pressures are slowly strangling the Zone, which shrunk from 30-plus establishments in 1986 to only a few today. Shady sorts still hang out here, so it's unsafe at night, but the Zone's days are numbered—or so residents hope.

Chinatown's official entry is a massive ceremonial gateway on **Beach Street,** but pedestrians approach this quarter from every which way. Bounded by Kneeland, Washington, and Essex streets and the Central Artery, the four-block-long neighborhood is known for its exotic restaurants, close-knit family life, and colorful storefronts. Cramped it may be, but Chinatown is always full of activity, and exudes a festive ambience with its subtitled signs and banners and pagoda-topped phone booths. Popular events are **Chinese New Year** and the **August Moon**

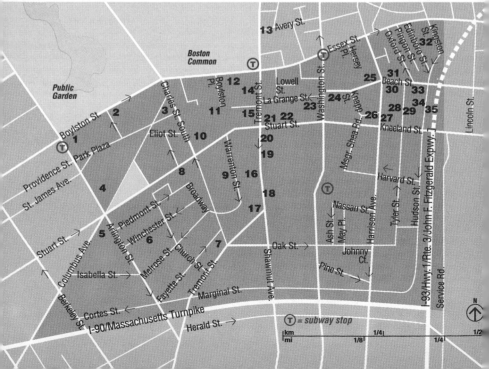

Festival, when local martial-arts groups don dragon costumes and dance through the streets amid exploding firecrackers and crowds of celebrants. Jammed into these dense blocks are about 200 restaurants (many open as late as 4AM), bakeries, gift and curio shops, and markets selling live poultry, fresh fish, and vegetables. The remains of the textile and garment industry, once Chinatown's economic mainstay, are located where Harrison Avenue intersects Kneeland Street. **Tyler Street** is showiest, with some of the most flamboyant storefronts, while **Beach Street** offers the real workaday scene.

A community at a crossroads, Chinatown is struggling to preserve its ethnic character. The first Chinese came to Boston soon after the Revolution. Subsequent China trade brought workers to the seaport, but a permanent community wasn't established until 1875. With the liberalization of immigration laws in the mid-1960s, Chinatown ballooned, but then lost half its land to highway expansion, Downtown encroachment, and the **New England Medical Center (NEMC)**. The population has swelled to more than 7,500, with Vietnamese, Laotians, and Cambodians enriching the ethnic composition. Bursting at the seams, troubled by refuse-strewn streets, and demoralized by the decaying Combat Zone and lack of affordable housing, Chinatown seemed destined to face a grim future, until the **Neighborhood Council** created a plan to control its destiny and reap a fair share of whatever benefits future development may bring.

A dénouement to the neighborhood drama may be the proposed urban mega-development called the **Midtown Cultural District,** a two-square-mile mixed-use community of office towers, department stores, hotels, restaurants, clubs, and cultural space that would encompass **Park Square**, the Theater District, the Combat Zone, and **Downtown Crossing**. It would serve as the catalyst for restoring historic theaters, ensuring Chinatown's prosperity and NEMC's growth, and boosting Downtown nightlife. And one

unsavory character would be eliminated in the process—the troublemaking Zone. Whatever the story's outcome, this neighborhood will remain the source for great performances in the gorgeous old theaters, vibrant comedy club acts, authentic Chinese culture and cuisine, and sophisticated new restaurants perfect for a night on the town.

The subway stations most convenient to this neighborhood are the New England Medical Center and Chinatown stops (both on the Orange Line), and the Arlington and Boylston stops (Green Line). The Park Street stop (Red and Green Lines) is also within easy walking distance.

1 The Heritage on the Garden One of Boston's more accommodating architectural presences is this mixed-use complex of retail and commercial space and luxurious residential condos, designed by **The Architects Collaborative** in 1988. A number of high-powered shops and restaurants are located on the Heritage premises, albeit with confusingly varied street addresses, including **Sonia Rykiel Boutique,** 280 Boylston Street, 426.2033; **Waterford Wedgwood,** 288 Boylston Street, 482.8886; **Escada,** 308 Boylston Street, 437.1200; **Hermès,** 22 Arlington Street, 482.8707; and **Doubleday Bookshop,** 99 Park Plaza, 482.8453. ♦ 300 Boylston Street (at Arlington St) &

Within the Heritage on the Garden:

Biba ★★★★$$$ Boston's wild about Biba, the adventurous inspiration of Boston-born and trained chef **Lydia Shire.** Shire rose to eminence through stints at several renowned local restaurants, then headed for California. Thankfully, she returned and opened this restaurant bubbling over with *joie de vivre.* Daring Shire experiments with international cooking styles and her innovations parade onto the menu. Appetizers and entrées are intermixed so diners may choose any combination suiting their fancy. Marvelous flatbread arrives hot from the Indian tandoori oven in the corner. The menu changes daily, but surprises have included fried boned quail with parsnip chips, calf's brains with crisp-fried capers, green-tea duck with ginger-and-scallion pancakes, maple- and rum-smoked salmon, wood-roasted chicken, and sour-cherry ice cream with chocolate cake and "something crunchy." New York architect **Adam Tihany** designed the restaurant, a quirky ensemble of styles. But the second-floor dining room's best feature is its big views of the Public Garden lagoon. Service at Biba is spotty, but always good-natured. The restaurant gets pretty noisy—don't plan on *sotto voce* confidences. If upstairs is booked, despair not—mix and match a delightful eccentric repast from the bar menu downstairs. The sultry ground-floor bar, decorated with a **Robert Jessup** mural depicting well-fed people, is where many stylish singles find each other. You don't have to look designed, however, to feel comfortable upstairs or down. ◆ Eclectic ◆ M-Th 11:30AM-2:30PM, 5:30-10PM; F-Sa 11:30AM-2:30PM, 5:30-11PM; Su 11:30AM-3PM, 5:30-10PM. 272 Boylston St (at Arlington St). Valet parking except Sunday during the day (fee). Reservations recommended for dining room. 426.7878 ౹

The Spa

The Spa at the Heritage The public can come to this ultrachic and expensive European-style spa/health club/salon for pampering body, skin, and hair care treatments, including six kinds of massage, facials, body wraps, and manicures. You can also take aerobics classes for a fee. But the workout facilities and the three-lane lap pool are limited to members or

Chinatown/Theater District

guests of member hotels. Plenty of special packages with the works are available, some including hotel accommodations and food. **Schwartz/Silver Architects** designed the pristine interior, collaborating with artist **Stephen Knapp.** The same owners operate the equally elite **Le Pli** in Cambridge. ◆ 28 Arlington St (between Boylston St and Park Plaza). Spa 426.6999, salon 482.2424

2 Four Seasons Hotel $$$$ Watch them come and go in the lovely Public Garden from the hotel's rooms and restaurants. Among the celebrities who have stayed in the posh Presidential Suite are **Bruce Springsteen, Glenda Jackson, Christopher Plummer, Luciano Pavarotti,** and **Mick Jagger.** A special Four Seasons asset is its friendly and solicitous staff. The hotel's concern for niceties gives a Boston visit extra sheen: every crib comes with a teddy bear, kids get bedtime milk and cookies and kits with cameras or magic tricks; the concierge distributes duck and squirrel food for those voracious park denizens across the way; and the restaurant packs picnic baskets. For joggers, the hotel offers running shoes and maps with trails starting from its entrance. There are 288 accommodations on eight floors, with handicapped-accessible and nonsmokers' rooms available, and the amenities feature concierge services, around-the-clock room service, same-day laundry and 24-hour valet and pressing services, valet parking, and business services. The health spa has a lap pool, Jacuzzi, sauna, and on-call

trainers. Although it lacks historic charm, the Four Seasons is a serious rival to the celebrated **Ritz-Carlton,** a block away. ◆ 200 Boylston St (at Arlington St). 338.4400, 800/332.3442 (US); 800/268.6282 (Canada); fax 426.9207 ౹

Within the Four Seasons Hotel:

Aujourd'hui ★★★$$$$ An ultra-refined setting for an elegant meal, this restaurant is nicest while light lingers in the Public Garden beyond. Reserve a windowside table. Chef **Michael Kornick's** acclaimed seasonal menu is complemented by the lengthy international wine list. Recent offerings included grilled foie gras with fig relish and blackberry vinegar, rabbit salad with shiitake mushrooms and shoyu vinaigrette, striped bass with caramelized onion soubise, and pan-roasted veal medallions with Calamata olive polenta. Special dishes have reduced calories, sodium, and cholesterol. For a cozier party, reserve one of two private dining rooms. Local designers and shops are featured at lunchtime fashion shows every Wednesday (September through June). Theatergoers pressed for time may opt for the prix-fixe pre-theater menu. ◆ Continental ◆ M-Th 7-11AM, 11:30AM-2:30PM, 6-10:30PM; F 7-11AM, 11:30AM-2:30PM, 5:30-11PM; Sa 7AM-noon, 5:30-11PM; Su 7-10:30AM, 11:30AM-2:30PM; 6-10PM. Valet parking (fee). Jacket and tie requested at dinner. Reservations are recommended. 451.1392 ౹

The Bristol ★★$$ Pick one of the discreetly positioned clusters of chairs and sofas for your conversation, accompanied by lunch, afternoon tea, cocktails, before- and after-theater supper, and dessert. A children's menu is offered. Pianists provide classical music and soft jazz afternoons and evenings. Friday and Saturday evenings, from 9PM to midnight, the Bristol sets out a lush Viennese dessert table. A fireplace warms things during the cold winter months, and tea is served daily from 3PM to 4:30PM. ◆ Continental ◆ M-Th 11:30AM-11:30PM; F-Sa 11AM-12:30AM; Su 2-11:30PM. Reservations recommended for lunch. 338.4400 ౹

Adesso Co-owners **Rick Grossman** and **Françoise Theise** are retail pioneers, dedicated to discovering and introducing the best up-to-the-moment furniture and lighting to America from France, Italy, West Germany, Holland, and Austria. (And some from America, too.) Called "new classics" by the owners, these pieces are smashing in any setting. Often they are architect-designed and available only to the trade in other cities. Adesso ships all over the world and publishes newsletters and catalogs. ◆ M-W, F-Sa 10AM-6PM; Th 10AM-8PM. 451.2212 ౹

3 The Great Emancipator Across the street from the Park Plaza's "flatiron" end, in a motley little green space, stands one statue Boston could well do without. This 1879 hero-worshiping homage to **Abraham Lincoln,** copied from the Washington original and sponsored by legislator **Moses Kimball,** portrays the President anointing a kneeling former slave, with the inscription "A race set free/A country at peace/Lincoln rests from his labors." From today's vantage point, the work appears paternalistic and demeaning. ♦ At Charles St So (between Columbus Ave and Park Plaza)

4 Boston Park Plaza Hotel & Towers $$$ Steps away from the theaters and one block from the **Public Garden,** this 1927 hotel has nearly a thousand rooms, more than 80 of which are in the Plaza Towers atop the main hotel. Decor and room sizes vary considerably At higher rates, the Towers offer more luxurious quarters, concierge, Continental breakfast, and other personalized services. Ask for a room overlooking the Public Garden. The Plaza offers individual voice-mail for every room; a weight room; privileges at the nearby elegant **The Spa at the Heritage,** including pool and sauna for $7; 24-hour room service; nonsmokers' floors; and a pharmacy. You can check out and order breakfast via video. On the premises are major airline-ticket offices, a travel agency, and a ticket agency for sports, theater, and concert events. Within or adjacent to the Park Plaza are restaurants and lounges. **Swans Lobby Lounge,** where **Liberace** began his career, serves tea and pastries and offers a full bar, with piano music after 4PM. *Forever Plaid,* a popular "doo-wop" musical comedy, is performed in the **Terrace Room.** ♦ Shows Tu-W, F 8PM; Th 2PM, 8PM; Sa 7PM, 10PM; Su 3PM, 7:30PM. 64 Arlington St (at Park Plaza). 426.2000, 800/225.2008; fax 426.5545

Within Boston Park Plaza Hotel & Towers:

Legal Sea Foods ★★$$$ "If it's not fresh, it's not Legal." The **Berkowitz** family lives up to their slogan in their fleet of seafood restaurants. This one's the flagship. Observe the long and patient lines—it's hard to believe the Legal empire began as a lowly fish-and-chips joint fewer than 20 years ago. Now an endless menu offers all the fruits of the sea, always superior and flapping-fresh. First, choose your fish, then decide on broiled, grilled, fried, stuffed, sautéed, steamed, pan-blackened, Cajun-style, even spicy Chinese recipes devised for Legal's by visiting chefs from China's Shandong province. The fish chowder could double for wallpaper paste in consistency but wins hordes of fans—including US presidents—as do the smoked salmon and bluefish pâtés. And this is one place where it's always safe to eat raw

clams and oysters—every batch is tested at an in-house laboratory. The extraordinary, extensive wine list lives up to the menu.

But be forewarned: Legal's is not the place for lingering conversation. There are no reservations, so you can easily cool your heels interminably; the loudspeaker incessantly barks out names; the dining rooms are both noisy and jammed; and the policy is to bring food when ready, not necessarily when your companions receive theirs. Still, superb seafood is worth some concession. When you require brain food yet can't endure a mob scene, Legal's smaller cafe/take-out operation next door is the answer. The seating here is more snug, but the cafe offers almost the same menu plus full bar, and operates a little faster. And if the cafe is too full, get your dinner to go. ♦ Seafood ♦ M-Th 11AM-10PM; F-Sa 11AM-11PM; Su noon-10PM. 35 Columbus Ave (at Park Sq). Restaurant 426.4444, Cafe/Takeout 426.5566 & Also at: 100 Huntington Ave, Copley Pl. 266.7775; 5 Cambridge Center, Kendall Sq, Cambridge. 864.3400

Legal Sea Foods Cash Market The gargantuan Legal Sea Foods enterprise has yet another giant offshoot: this one-stop gourmet shop featuring a counter stocking at least a dozen kinds of fresh fish—from the same supplier used by the restaurant. Pick up live lobster packed to travel, whatever fish you wish, fa-

mous Legal chowders, pâtés, cheeses, crackers, salads, soups, sauces, condiments, marinades, coffees and teas, chocolates, etc, etc. Legal's even sells its own cookbook. The liquor department carries 600 wines, cold beer, and a full liquor selection. The Berkowitz family covers all the bases. But don't expect any bargains. ♦ M-Sa 8AM-8PM; Su noon-6PM. 15 Columbus Ave (at Park Plaza). 426.7777 &

Ben & Jerry's Ice Cream This franchise exclusively sells the populist entrepreneurs' popular ice cream, shipped fresh from their Vermont factory. Chocolate Chip Cookie Dough is the current favorite, with all flavors available in sundaes, shakes, cones, ice-cream cakes, and between brownies and cookies. Coffee and muffins baked on the premises are sold in the morning until they run out. The shop is easy to miss; it's in the **Statler Office Building,** just around the corner from Legal Sea Foods. ♦ M-F 7:30AM-11PM; Sa 11AM-11PM; Su noon-11PM. 20 Park Plaza (between Charles St So and Arlington St). No credit cards. 426.0890 &

5 Park Plaza Castle The imposing granite "Castle," as the eye-catching landmark is universally known around Boston, was built in 1897 by **William G. Preston** as an armory for the **First Corps of Cadets,** a private Massachusetts military organization founded in 1741 and commanded at one time by **John Hancock.** The Victorian fortress, now on the **National Register of Historic Places,** was a social center for prominent Bostonians in the late 1800s, and its luxurious, clubby interior was the site for billiards, imbibing fine wine, and the popular **Cadet Theatricals**. The corps now operates a private military museum in **Back Bay**. With its lofty hexagonal tower, turrets, crenellated walls, lancet windows, and drawbridge, the Castle is ready for medieval-style combat, but fulfills much calmer functions as an exhibition and convention center owned by the **Boston Park Plaza Hotel & Towers**. Bostonians flock to the annual **Crafts at the Castle** sale held here in early December and sponsored by **Family Services of Greater Boston**. Among recent major exhibitions was the famous **Names Project** display of quilt panels made by friends and family in memory of AIDS victims. Next door to the Castle is the **Back Bay Racquet Club**—built in 1886 as **Carter's Ink Factory**—which boasts an impressive terracotta-and-brick facade. ♦ 130 Columbus Ave (at Arlington St). For events information, call Boston Park Plaza Hotel & Towers and request the sales office: 426.2000 ௯ (use the Columbus Ave entrance)

6 Bay Village This snippet of 19th-century Boston is difficult to find by car and easy to miss on foot. Take a 15-minute stroll along **Piedmont, Church, Melrose,** and **Fayette** streets for the flavor of this insular nook. The tight cluster of short streets bordered by diminutive brick houses was mostly laid out during the 1820s and 1830s. Many of the artisans, housewrights,

and carpenters who worked on fashionable **Beacon Hill's** prestigious residences concurrently built their own small homes in Bay Village. The neighborhood's residents once encompassed other colorful professions: sailmakers, paperhangers, blacksmiths, harness- and rope-makers, painters, salt merchants, musical instrument makers, and cabinetmakers. **Edgar Allan Poe** was born in a lodging house in the vicinity in 1809; his parents were actors in a stock company playing nearby. Because it's so close to the Theater District, Bay Village gradually acquired a bohemian flavor and spillover nightlife. Just off Fayette Street, look for brief **Bay Street** with its single house, a concluding punctuation mark. ♦ Bordered by Church, Fayette, Arlington, and Stuart Sts

7 Beacon Hill Skate This is where you can rent or purchase roller skates and skateboards to whiz along the esplanade that borders the Charles River, or, in winter, ice skates to skim over the Public Garden lagoon while it's vacated by ducks and Swan Boats for the season. (Skates are available lagoonside, too, through this shop.) ♦ M-Sa 11AM-6PM; Su noon-5PM; closed Christmas, New Year's Day, Thanksgiving. 135 Charles St So (between Warrenton and Tremont Sts). 482.7400

8 57 Park Plaza Hotel/Howard Johnson $$ Smack dab in the middle of this neighborhood, the hotel has 350 rooms on 24 floors, two restaurants and a bar, an indoor heated pool, a sauna, a sundeck, room service, and free on-premises parking with direct access to the hotel. Handicapped-equipped rooms are also available. ♦ 200 Stuart St (at Charles St So). 482.1800, 800/468.3557; fax 451.2750 ௯

9 Nick's Entertainment Center Another fixture on Boston's entertainment scene, Nick's has three parts: the popular **Nick's Comedy Stop,** a club featuring local and national comics; a cabaret theater; and a sports bar called **Playoffs.** Many people opt for the special package that includes dinner and a show. Tickets are also available at **Bostix.** ♦ Admission. Box office: daily 10AM-7PM. Nick's Comedy Stop: M-Th, Su 8:30PM; F-Sa 10:30PM. Cabaret theater: Th-Sa 8PM, Su 7:30PM. Playoffs: Tu-Su 5-10PM. 100 Warrenton St (between Charles St So and Stuart St). No tank tops. Reservations are accepted with credit card payment. 482.0930

9 Charles Playhouse The Theater District's oldest playhouse—built by **Asher Benjamin** in 1843, renovated by **Cambridge Seven** in 1966, and listed on the **National Register of Historic Places**—began life as a church and today is a rental facility for private productions, all managed separately. The show playing on **Stage I** changes sporadically, but on **Stage II,** *Shear Madness* has played for more than a decade, and is likely to go on as long as new visitors come to town. It has already made the *Guinness Book of World Records*. The comedy-whodunit, set in a Boston beauty salon, often stars good local professional actors. An eccentric concert pianist who lives upstairs is bumped off, and everybody has a motive. Boston police officers enlist the audience to find the culprit, with the solution changing nightly and new improvisations, local color, and topical humor added continually. **Stage III** is home for **The Comedy Connection.** ♦ Stage I box office M 10AM-6PM; Tu-Sa 10AM-8PM; Su noon-5PM; shows Tu-F 8PM; Sa 6PM, 9PM; Su 3PM. Stage II box office M 10AM-4PM; Tu-F 10AM-8PM; Sa 10AM-9:30PM; Su noon-7:30PM; shows Tu-F 8PM; Sa 6:30PM, 9:30PM; Su 3PM, 7:30PM. 74-78 Warrenton St (between Charles St So and Stuart St). Cash only at box office. Stage I 426.6912. Stage II 426.5225. Charge-Tix 542.8511

Within Charles Playhouse:

The Comedy Connection Attracting the under-30 crowd, especially college students, this well-established stand-up comedy cabaret books headliner plays Wednesday through Sunday, with new or established talent launching new material scheduled for Monday and Tuesday. Full bar and bar food are served throughout shows. If you charge your tickets in advance, seats will be reserved for you; if you pay cash, you can reserve seats the day of the performance. ♦ Admission. Shows M-Th, Su 8:30PM; F-Sa 8:30PM, 10:30PM. Credit cards are accepted in advance; cash only at door. 391.0022; Charge-Tix 542.8511 ௯

Restaurants/Clubs: Red   **Hotels:** Blue
Shops/ 🌳 Outdoors: Green **Sights/Culture:** Black

STUART STREET PARKING WATER TANKS BOYLSTON PLACE BOYLSTON STREET BOSTON COMMON

COURTESY OF GOODY, CLANCY & ASSOCIATES

10 Massachusetts State Transportation Building

The architectural firm of **Goody, Clancy & Associates** recognized that this enormous office complex (pictured above) for state transportation agencies, occupying an entire city block, was an unprecedented disruption in a traditionally diverse low-rise neighborhood. With the participation of local business, cultural, and neighborhood groups, the architects created a building that exerts itself to relate to the surrounding streetscapes and activities. The redbrick exterior, with asymmetrical terraces, is fairly self-effacing; the real excitement awaits within, where an atrium—with trendily exposed endoskeletal support beams—vaults above a pedestrian mall with shops and restaurants to draw that vitality inward. Noontime music concerts entertain the milling lunchtime throngs, and a small art gallery operated by the **Artists Foundation** adds an avant-garde frisson. ◆ Gallery Tu-F noon-6PM; Sa noon-5PM. 10 Park Plaza

Within the Massachusetts State Transportation Building:

rocco's ★★★$$$ There's no better prelude or finale to an evening at the theater than dinner at rocco's. Or come add a dash of drama to an otherwise uneventful night. Painted murals, enormous arches, flamboyant draperies, and artful props give the restaurant a fantastic stagestruck look perfect for this part of town. **Kevin Schopfer** created the decor, and **Julia Roe Clay** painted the rococo-inspired ceiling frescoes. Dining here is like joining in a perpetually improvised performance, always festive and fun.

Owners **Patrick** and **Jayne Bowe** deserve an ovation for letting collective imaginations run wild—and the extensive use of fabric (which muffles intimate conversations) means you can talk as well as gawk. Dine cafe-style and less expensively on appetizers and wine, or indulge more extravagantly, like the lush, fleshy figures overhead. The *haute* Italian menu spans such delicacies as *cappoletti* with rabbit, and grilled

veal. ◆ Italian ◆ M-Tu 11:30AM-2:30PM, 5:30-9:30PM; W-Th 11:30AM-2:30PM, 5:30-10PM; F 11:30AM-2:30PM, 5:30-11:30PM; Sa noon-3PM, 5:30-11:30PM; Su noon-3PM, 5:30-9:30PM. Reservations recommended. 5 Charles St So (between Boylston and Stuart Sts). 723.6800 ♿

Bnu ★★$$ The cafe's owners have managed to create a charming niche in the vast transportation complex, with frescoes and ornament projecting the pleasing illusion of an Italian piazza. Bnu serves the freshest ingredients prepared simply and deliciously, in dishes like pizzettas with a changing collection of toppings; fettuccine with saffron cream sauce and grilled mussels; veal stew with lemon, cloves, and bay leaves on a bed of polenta; linguine with Parmesan, grilled shrimp, broccoli, pine nuts, roasted red pepper, and garlic; and cannoli with

Chinatown/Theater District

sweet herbed ricotta and roasted almonds. The salads are also noteworthy. By-the-glass beer and wine specials are offered as well. ◆ Northern Italian ◆ M-Th 11:30AM-2PM, 5-9:30PM; F 11:30AM-2PM, 5-11PM; Sa 5-11PM; Su 5-9:30PM. 123 Stuart St (between Charles St So and Tremont St). Reservations recommended. 367.8405 ♿

Joyce Chen ★$$
Run by the son of famous local chef Joyce Chen, this restaurant is both fancier and pricier than most other Chinese restaurants in the neighborhood. This isn't the place to seek exotic new tastes—the tiny, nondescript places

are much better for that—but to enjoy reliable Mandarin and Szechuan dishes in comfort. Popular choices include General Gau's chicken, lobster with ginger and scallions, and Peking duck. On weekdays, there's a fixed-price luncheon buffet. ◆ Chinese/Takeout ◆ M-Th 11:30AM-10PM; F 11:30AM-12:45AM; Sa noon-midnight; Su noon-10PM. 115 Stuart St (at Tremont St). Valet parking (fee). Reservations recommended for five or more. 720.1331, for deliveries call 825.3688 ♿ Also at: 390 Rindge Ave, Fresh Pond, Cambridge. 492.7373

11 Boylston Place Located off **Boylston Street** along **Piano Row,** this pedestrian cul-de-sac reputedly was where football was born in 1860, when a student of **Mr. Dixwell's Private School** organized the first game. The rubber sphere used for a ball is in the **Society for the Preservation of New England Antiquities'** collections. Enter via a fanciful arch replete with theatrical and local allusions, and pass through a phalanx of night spots popular among the young and impecunious, such as **Alley Cat** and **Avenue C.** At the end of Boylston Place, a pedestrian passage leads through the **Transportation Building** to **Stuart Street,** a handy shortcut.

On Boylston Place:

Zanzibar One of the city's most popular dance and party spots is this two-story, tropical paradise-themed playhouse, with soaring palm trees, Caribbean-motif architecture, ceiling fans, and a spacious dance floor. A DJ spins a mix of Top 40 and rock 'n' roll floor-burners for an upscale crowd, generally ranging in age from mid-20s to mid-40s. No one under 21 is admitted. ◆ Cover. W-Su 8PM-2AM. 1 Boylston Pl (off Boylston St, between Charles St So and Tremont St). Valet parking on weekend (fee). Jacket and tie requested. 451.1955 ⑬

Chinatown/Theater District

Sweetwater Cafe $ When you want to be casual and anonymous, try this laid-back, cheap-eats place for big portions of Tex-Mex and bar food like nachos, tostadas, burritos, BBQ beef, and super-hot buffalo wings. There's a bar on the second level, but the downstairs is quieter, with booths. Two jukeboxes crank out tunes, one stocked with old 45s. You can eat outdoors in nice weather. ◆ American ◆ M-W noon-1AM; Th-Sa noon-2AM. 3 Boylston Pl (off Boylston St, between Charles St So and Tremont St). 357.7027

The Tavern Club Since 1887, this exclusive club, only recently open to women, has resided in three quaint brick row houses dating from the early- to mid-19th century. For generations the club has been famed for its private performances of outrageous plays starring club members. ◆ Daily 11:30AM-2:30PM. 4-6 Boylston Pl (off Boylston St, between Charles St So and Tremont St). 338.9682

12 Marais ★★★$$$ Housed in the century-old former home of the **Boston Music Company,** this stylishly retro new restaurant retained the facade, hardwood floors, and mahogany paneling—adding a marble-and-mahogany bar that has been SRO since day one. Founders **Gillian Troy, Kevin Troy,** and **Steven Foster** have a knack for gauging the recreational cravings of their late-30s/early-40s contemporaries: their first venture, **Jillian's Billiards** in the **Fenway,** spawned a national franchise. Marais' surefire formula for success includes a romantic setting (low lights, period posters) divided between the "see and be seen" area of the endless bar and two cozy back rooms with fireplaces. Chef **Jackson Kenworth** trained with **Wolfgang Puck** of **Spago,** and his menu features a delectable list of "premiers" (inventive mix-and-match appetizers, with complementary wines available by the glass and even the shot) and a handful of rather more substantial entrées, such as grilled lobster with creamy bourbon corn sauce. Your best bet is to pile on the internationally influenced premiers: cuisine this skilled and exotic is rare in Boston, so take advantage and sample the fire-roasted dates stuffed with spicy sausage, or charred sweetbreads with maple and bitter greens. Swapping and sharing are encouraged; the energy and camaraderie here are irresistible. ◆ International ◆ Daily 4:30-10:30PM. Bar open until 2AM. 116 Boylston St (between Boylston Pl and Tremont St). 482.7799 ⑬

Within Marais:

Esmé To the back of the restaurant, accessible either via the bar or from adjoining Boylston Place, is an intimate, opulent nightclub where talking and dancing get equal billing. Swathed in burgundy velvet and a Kashmir carpet and featuring conversational alcoves piled high with tapestry pillows, Esmé is the perfect place to give romance a chance. No one under 21 is admitted. ◆ Cover. Th-Sa 10PM-2AM. 482.3399

12 Walker's Riding outfitters since 1932, this stuffed-to-the-ceiling store doesn't play favorites, carrying both English (black velvet helmets and modern Lycra jodhpurs) and Western (cowboy shirts and pointy boots) gear. It's got to be the only place in town to stock scorpion belt buckles. ◆ M-Sa 10AM-6PM. 122 Boylston St (between Boylston Pl and Tremont St). 423.9050 ⑬

12 Boylston Street The slice of Boylston Street facing the **Boston Common** was once known as "Piano Row" for its concentration of piano-making and music-publishing establishments—enterprises in which music-loving Boston led the nation during the 19th and early 20th centuries. The businesses occupied—some still do—several handsome buildings that are physical expressions of the city's traditional high esteem for music: until recently, the **Wurlitzer Company** resided at No. 100 with its elegant, elaborate storefront, designed by **Clarence H. Blackall** and also home to the distinguished **Colonial Theatre**; the **Steinway Piano Company** is located at Beaux Arts-style No. 162, designed by **Winslow and Wetherell** in 1896; and the **E.A. Starck Piano Company Building** at Nos. 154-156 houses **Carl Fischer Music**. While you're on this stretch of Boylston Street, look for the **Little Building**, No. 80, a 1916 commercial edifice designed by Blackall's firm with a Gothic-influenced terracotta facade. Step inside and take a look at Little's arcaded lobby decorated with naif murals of Boston history. Then cross **Tremont Street** to see No. 48, the eye-catching Ruskinian Gothic **Young Men's Christian Union** of 1875, by **Nathaniel J. Bradlee**, listed on the **National Register of Historic Places**. A few steps farther is the **Boylston Building**, an 1887 edifice on the **National Register of Historic Places** and the work of **Carl Fehmer**, architect of numerous important Boston office buildings and homes, including the grandiose **Oliver Ames Mansion** in **Back Bay**. It's now home to the **China Trade Center,** an office/arcade complex organized by the **Bay Group** and the **Chinese Economic Development Group** in 1985 (or 4683, by Chinese reckoning). The **Boston Architectural Team** carved out an appealing atrium, decorated with a mosaic walkway and wall plaque by **Lilli Ann** and **Marvin Rosenberg**, elucidating the Chinese lunar zodiac. Several food shops are on the premises, and at noon the **Winter Company** stages performances on a small stage in the atrium's well.

12 Colonial Theatre The most gloriously grand theater in Boston, the Colonial (built in 1900) is also one of the most handsome in the country. The play may disappoint, but the Colonial, never. Actually, this is a very uncolonial-style structure, a 10-story office building with a theater tucked in. The Colonial brims with classical ornament, ebulliently gilded and mirrored. **H.B. Pennell's** interiors feature glittering chandeliers, lofty arched ceilings, sumptuous frescoes and friezes, allegorical figures—all the ruffles and flourishes imaginable. Yet the 1,658-seat theater is also intimate and comfortable, with excellent sightlines and acoustics. **Clarence H. Blackall's** other local credits include the nearby **Wilbur** and **Metropolitan** (now the **Wang**) theaters, as well as the **Winthrop Building** downtown. Thankfully, Blackall and Pennell's masterpiece has been spared the ups, downs, and indignities of many ravaged Boston theaters, and has been lovingly preserved.

Built expressly for legitimate theater, the Colonial continues to book major productions, often musicals, many on the way to Broadway. In the theater's 90-odd years in business, **Flo Ziegfeld, Irving Berlin, Rodgers and Hammerstein, Bob Fosse,** and **Tommy Tune** have launched shows here; **Ethel Barrymore, Frederic March, Helen Hayes, Katharine Hepburn, Henry Fonda, Fred Astaire, Eddie Cantor, W.C. Fields,** the **Marx Brothers, Will Rogers, Danny Kaye,** and **Barbra Streisand** have all trod the boards. Those lucky enough to find their way deep into the backstage recesses discover a wealth of history and memorabilia from past productions. Half-price fares are offered for handicapped persons and one companion. ♦ Box office M-Sa 10AM-6PM; Su noon-6PM; open until 8PM performance days. 106 Boylston St (at Tremont St). 426.9366 ⓑ

13 The Boston Music Company Open for 107 years, the august music emporium purveys New England's largest selection of sheet music and books on music. One glance inside tells you this shop's an oldie but goodie. Its clientele encompasses music lovers and musicians, professional and amateur, who seek anything from choral pieces to the latest rock 'n' roll hit. Boston Music is proud of its enormous collection of music-related gifts, like its cases of music boxes for $5,000 or so. A musical instrument department sells traditional and electronic instruments. Boston Music is also an educational music publisher, distributing its titles throughout the world. It's owned by **Hammerstein Music and Theatre Corp.**, owned in turn by the estate of the legendary **Oscar Hammerstein.** ♦ M-F 9:30AM-6:30PM; Sa 9:30AM-6PM. 172 Tremont St (at Avery St). 426.5100. Also at: 57 JFK St, Harvard Sq, Cambridge. 497.1567

Chinatown/Theater District

14 Jack's Joke Shop "Yes, We Have Warts!" a shop notice reads. Pick out your latest disguise at owner **Harold Bengin's** wholesale/retail emporium for tricksters. Or make an unforgettable impression with a unique gift from an inventory topping 3,000 different items, including backward-running clocks, instant worms, garlic gum, sneeze powder, and ever-popular gross-outs like severed heads, fake wounds, and worse. Open in Boston since 1922, making it the oldest shop of its type in the US, Jack's is definitely one of the city's more colorful institutions. Halloween is the shop's biggest selling season, naturally, but kids and adults stream in throughout the year for jokes, tricks, magic, novelties, complete costumes, masks, wigs, beards, flags of all countries, and oddities galore. Even New York visitors exclaim over the selection. Bengin and his staff clearly get a kick out of this business. ♦ M-Sa 8:30AM-5:30PM. 197 Tremont St (at Boylston St). No credit cards. 426.9640 ⓑ

The Colonial Theatre's opening day, 20 December 1900, launched an extraordinary blockbuster production of *Ben Hur* in which four hydraulic lifts were used to raise a dozen horses from below the stage for the show's dramatic chariot race. Hitched to Roman chariots, the horses galloped toward the audience on treadmills built into the stage, a thrilling spectacle that won accolades from reviewers. After the show's opening night, *The Boston Globe* enthused: "Nothing So Beautiful, Pictorially and Mechanically, Ever Seen Before on a Boston Stage."

15 Emerson Majestic Theatre Originally famous for its musicals and opera performances, the extravagantly ornate, Beaux Arts-style Majestic, designed by **John Galen Howard** in 1903 was bought by a movie-theater chain in the '50s that slapped tacky fake materials on top of marble and neoclassical friezes. **Emerson College** rescued the theater in 1983, spent several million dollars on renovations, and intends to spend more until the Majestic lives up to its name once again. Today, under Emerson's wing, the 859-seat Majestic is a multipurpose performance center for nonprofit groups, including **Dance Umbrella, Boston Lyric Opera,** the **New England Conservatory,** and **Emerson Stage.** Patrons favor the Emerson Majestic for its sense of excitement and inclusion with performers; performers favor the theater for its rococo high style and fine acoustics—but grumbling is growing over the cramped orchestra pit. This was Boston's first theater with electricity incorporated into the building's design. ♦ Box office daily 10AM-4PM during shows. 219 Tremont St (between Boylston and Stuart Sts). 578.8727 &

Chinatown/Theater District

16 Shubert Theatre Hill, James & Whitaker designed the refined Shubert, with its graceful marquee, in 1910. Now listed on the **National Register of Historic Places,** it's part of the famous chain, but has a fine reputation in its own right among actors and audiences. **Kathleen Turner** heated up the town in **Tennessee Williams'** Cat on a Hot Tin Roof. The illustrious **Sir Laurence Olivier, John Barrymore,** and **John Gielgud** performed here; so did **Sarah Bernhardt, Mae West, Humphrey Bogart, Ingrid Bergman, Cary Grant,** and **Helen Hayes.** It seats 1,680, and greatly discounted tickets are offered to handicapped persons and one companion. ♦ Box office M 10AM-6PM during shows; Tu-Sa 10AM-8:30PM during shows; Su noon-6PM if performance scheduled. 265 Tremont St (at Stuart St). 426.4520 &

TREMONT
H·O·U·S·E

17 The Tremont House $$ Billing itself as "Boston's Affordable Alternative," the Tremont House takes the name of Boston's first grand hotel, long gone, and fills the shoes of the former **Bradford Hotel,** where '50s big bands played. Offering 281 rooms on 15 floors, including handicapped-equipped and nonsmokers' rooms, the renovated hotel now caters to the theater crowd, both performers and spectators. Casts often stay here, and special packages, including tickets, are available. Amenities include room service and valet parking with charge. Sharing the building is the **Stage Deli,** where theater stars and fans alike flock. The hotel's brass Elks Club doorknobs recall when the hotel was built in 1926 as the national headquarters for the **Benevolent and Protective Order of Elks,** which explains why the public spaces are so grand. ♦ 275 Tremont St (at Stuart St). 426.1400, 800/331.9998; fax 482.6730 &

Within The Tremont House:

Stage Deli of New York ★$ Glitzy and frenetic, this New York-style delicatessen is doing its best to satisfy the cravings of deli-starved Boston with provisions trucked in fresh from the Big Apple. Stage is known for its corned beef and pastrami, huge hot entrées, and sky-high Dagwood sandwiches, including more than two dozen named for local and national celebrities. Tackle the Larry Bird Triple Decker, the Raymond Flynn Reuben, or the Chet and Natalie Triple Decker, named for Boston's husband-and-wife TV anchor team. Dive into knackwurst and sauerkraut, stuffed cabbage, potato pancakes, blintzes, apple strudel, and New York-style cheesecake. Somewhat more modest sandwiches are offered for less courageous appetites. Celebrities from whatever shows are in town drop in all the time; their particular deli addictions sometimes make it into a local gossip column. ♦ Deli/Takeout ♦ M-Th 9AM-10:30PM; F 9AM-1AM; Sa 7:30AM-1AM; Su 8AM-10:30PM. 523.3354 &

NYC Jukebox and VHF This is one club with two rooms and two DJs playing two different kinds of music. In one room, Bostonians can shake, rattle, and roll to '50s through '70s dance music; in the other, a younger crowd flocks to watch Top 40 videos on dozens of TV screens. There's a full bar, but no food. No one under 21 is admitted. ♦ Cover. NYC Jukebox Th-Sa 8PM-2AM. VHF F-Sa 10PM-2AM. Casual attire, but no T-shirts, tank tops, or sweats. 542.1123 &

17 Silverado Not since the late, lamented **Hillbilly Ranch** (razed in 1980 to make room for the Transportation Building) have Boston's closet country fans had a place to kick loose. Some mighty fine cowboy boots tread the spacious dance floor here, where two-step ballads alternate with ordinary disco. Subdued types can sip margaritas in the balcony. ♦ Cover. Th-Sa 8PM-2AM. 279 Tremont St (at Stuart St). No T-shirts or sneakers. 227.7699 &

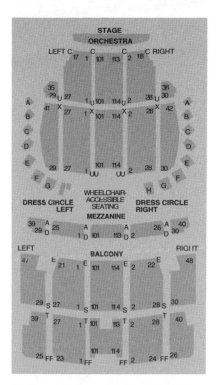

18 The Wang Center for the Performing Arts

It's worth the ticket price to whatever performance you can catch here just to see inside this former motion-picture cathedral. Predating New York City's **Radio City Music Hall,** this mammoth entertainment palace, designed by **Blackall, Clapp and Whittemore,** was considered the "wonder theater of the world" when it opened in the Roaring Twenties, built to pack in huge crowds four times daily for variety revues and first-run movies. An architectural extravaganza, the seven-story, 3,800-seat theater (see plan above) boasts a succession of dramatic lobbies—concluding with the five-story Grand Lobby—bedecked with Italian marble columns, stained glass, bronze detailing, gold leaf, crystal chandeliers, and florid ceiling murals. In the theater's early days, billiards, ping-pong, card parties, and other games in four ornate lobbies occupied the crowds until the next show got started.

First called the **Metropolitan Theater** and later the **Music Hall,** it was expanded by **Jung, Brannen Associates** in 1982, renamed for benefactor **An Wang** in 1983, and renovated by **Notter, Finegold & Alexander** in 1990 to accommodate a variety of performing arts, including opera, ballet, and Broadway musicals. The Wang, on the **National Register of Historic Places,** now has one of the largest stages of any theater in the world. For plays, try to get down-front center seats in the orchestra, where the sight and sound are best.

The Wang's Young at Arts educational outreach program involves Boston children in the visual and performing arts through workshops, performances held in the Wang's lobbies, and an annual art contest. Subsidized tickets are available and many events are free; call to inquire. The theater also brings back a hint of its past history with a classic film series shown on one of the world's largest screens.

The **Boston Ballet** makes its home here, and famous visiting companies such as the **Alvin Ailey American Dance Theater** and the **Bolshoi Ballet Academy** visit frequently. Future restoration work will bring back more of the Wang's former splendor while updating its facilities and theater technology. And the unfortunate statues you see will get new heads. ◆ 270 Tremont St (at Stuart St). General information 482.9393; Ticketmaster 931.2000 ♿

19 Wilbur Theatre

This distinguished Colonial Revival theater has witnessed its share of dramatic debuts, including the pre-Broadway production of **Tennessee Williams'** *A Streetcar Named Desire* starring **Marlon Brando** and **Jessica Tandy.** Another of Boston's **Clarence H. Blackall** treasures, built in 1914 and now on the **National Register of Historic Places,** the Wilbur endured dark days and decay, its nadir a brief stint as a cabaret that flopped. But the lights are on again: the proud theater has rebounded, newly restored.

The 1,200-seat fan-shaped house has been renovated to accommodate Off Broadway-style productions. Some recent smash runs were *Steel Magnolias* and **A.R. Gurney 's** *Love Let-*

ters. Look up at the facade and note the three theatrical masks—grinning, grimacing, agape—above the upper windows. Half-price fares are offered for handicapped persons and one companion. ◆ Box office M-Sa 10AM-6PM; during shows M 10AM-6PM, Tu-Sa 10AM-8PM, Su noon-6PM. 246 Tremont St (at Stuart St). 423.4008 ♿

20 Hub Ticket Agency

Located in a trailer parked on a corner, this agency sells sports and theater tickets, including those for New York events and sometimes for Providence, RI, and Worcester, MA. The friendly staff is often willing to drop tickets off at box offices for pickup before shows. Many local performances are sold out well in advance, so call first. The day of the game or performance is a good time to check on last-minute availability. For those who plan ahead, order by mail; the ZIP code is 02116. ◆ M-F 9AM-5PM; Sa 9AM-noon. 240 Tremont St (at Stuart St). 426.8340

Thomas Brattle—the early Harvard College treasurer for whom Brattle Street was named—ensured himself a spirited send-off by bequeathing "a half crown bill to each of the students of Harvard College that shall come to my funeral."

Arkansas Congressman Wilbur Mills, former chairman of the powerful House Ways and Means Committee, met his political downfall in the shape of stripper Fannie Fox, with whom he cavorted on stage at the racy Pilgrim Theatre in the Combat Zone in December 1974.

21 Zoots On Friday and Saturday nights from 9PM to 1AM, this casual club features live R&B, blues, and rock music. The type of crowd on the dance floor varies with the music, but anyone can come in and feel comfortable. Unlike the other nightclubs nearby, jeans are just fine here. The jukebox plays hits by Guns 'n' Roses, Paula Abdul, and the like, and there's cable TV for sports. Bar food is served. ♦ Daily 3PM-2AM. 228 Tremont St (at Stuart St). 451.5997 ♿

22 Montien ★★$$ A solid favorite with theater-goers, businesspeople, and staff from the nearby medical complex, Montien offers all the classic favorites like *pad Thai, satay,* and cur-ries, plus unusual specials like *kat-thong-tong,* a crisp pastry shell filled with ground chicken, onions, corn, and coriander with a sweet dip-ping sauce. Tamarind duck and fried squid are also superb. The hot-and-spicy set will find their pleasure, as will palates preferring subtler sensations. Service is respectful and prompt, so you'll make that curtain. ♦ Thai/Takeout ♦ M-Sa 11:30AM-11PM; Su 4:30-11PM. 63 Stuart St (at Tremont St). Reservations recom-mended for large parties. 338.5600 ♿

22 Jacob Wirth ★$$ Amid the whirl of Boston's dining fads and fashions, this aged establish-ment—built in 1845 by **Greenleaf C. Sanborn** and now on the **National Register of Historic Places** (see the illustration above)—plods along unwaveringly on its own steady course. Jacob Wirth has been offering up the same hearty traditional German fare—bratwurst, knackwurst, sauerbraten, and sauerkraut, ac-companied by heady, specially brewed dark beer—in the same bowfront row house since its doors opened in 1868. All the furniture and fixtures—globe lighting, brass rails, dark pan-eling—are original. Even the waiters' attire looks vintage. It's easy to step into the past here; in fact, that's the reason to come. The cavernous beer hall is a great place to bring a crowd and sample the long list of lagers. Those

in your party with big appetites might attempt the German boiled dinner: pig's feet, pork roast, ribs, and cabbage. Food service stops after 10PM Monday through Thursday, after 10:30PM Friday and Saturday. Sing along with piano music from 8PM to midnight on Friday. The restaurant provides two free hours of park-ing at the adjacent lot for diners. ♦ German ♦ M-Th 11:30AM-11PM; F-Sa 11:30AM-mid-night; Su noon-8PM. 37 Stuart St (between Tremont and Washington Sts). 338.8586 ♿

23 Hayden Building This overlooked, modest-size 1875 office building isn't one of **H.H. Richardson's** finer works but does display his characteristically vigorous Romanesque Re-vival approach. Unfortunately, the building, which is on the **National Register of Historic Places,** has been put to demoralizing uses and poorly maintained. It patiently awaits better days at the head of **La Grange Street,** once a thriving mercantile stretch with hatters, tailors, shoemakers, and such. From the '60s onward, La Grange was caught in the midst of the Com-bat Zone and its once-reputable appearance has been shamefully besmirched. ♦ 681 Wash-ington St (at La Grange St)

24 East Ocean City ★$ A new contender that opened in 1992, this sparkling restaurant looks like a yuppie haven (marble entrance, snowy tablecloths) but promises—and delivers— Hong Kong-style exotica. Take a good look at the teeming tanks by the door; if you order sea-food, one of these creatures will soon turn up tableside for your pre-cuisine inspection. Steamed and topped with ginger, coriander, and soy sauce, fish doesn't come any fresher. Non-marine specialties include scallion pan-cakes, stir-fried watercress, and assorted "por-ridges"—rice cooked in flavorful stock. ♦ Chi-nese ♦ M-Th, Su 11AM-3AM; F-Sa 11AM-4AM Dim sum Sa-Su 11AM-3AM. 25-29 Beach St (between Washington St and Harrison Ave). 542.2504

25 North End Fabrics Not only do they have the largest selection of fake "fun-furs" around— great for a come-as-you-were-half-a-million-years-ago party—but just about everything else in the way of fabrics you could possibly want: wool challis, velvets and velveteen, Thai silk, drapery and upholstery materials, bridal and theatrical fabrics, handkerchief linen, im-ported lace, odd bolts and remnants, notions— you name it. Professional dressmakers, de-signers, and home sewers all frequent this shop, around now for more than 30 years. ♦ M-Sa 9AM-6PM. 31 Harrison Ave (between Beach and Essex Sts). 542.2763

26 Dong Khanh $ Come to this clean and bright establishment for Vietnamese-style fast food, including more than a dozen great noodle-soup dishes. The *bi cuon* (meat rolls) are very tasty; so are the fish in spicy soup and assorted BBQ meats with vermicelli. Be daring and try a *durian* juice drink, made from the Southeast Asian fruit that looks like a hedgehog and smells like rotting garbage, but has plenty of fans for its flavor. ◆ Vietnamese ◆ Daily 9AM-10PM. 83 Harrison Ave (between Beach and Kneeland Sts). No credit cards. 426.9410

27 Siam Square ★$ A Thai interloper at Chinatown's edge, Siam Square offers its own distinctive palette of tastes. Lemongrass infuses a dish of steamed mussels; a pepper-garlic sauce spices frog's legs; the squid *pik pow* is at once spicy and sweet; and Thai seasonings lend a signature kick to Chinese *chow foon* (fat noodles). ◆ Thai ◆ Daily 11:30AM-midnight. 86 Harrison Ave (between Beach and Kneeland Sts). 338.7704

28 Carl's Pagoda $$ Yes, there is a Carl, and many diners rely on his judgment when it comes to ordering. Carl is like a potentate ruling his personal fiefdom. But even if he's not there, a great meal can be had with tomato soup, Cantonese-style lobster, clams in blackbean sauce, and superb steamed fish. A shrimpy little place it is, but Carl's is one of the few Chinatown restaurants with tablecloths. ◆ Chinese/Takeout ◆ Daily 5PM-midnight. 23 Tyler St (between Beach and Kneeland Sts). Reservations recommended on weekends. No credit cards. 357.9837

29 Golden Palace ★★$ Many Chinatown restaurants are so innocuous looking that they're easy to miss, but not this one—it has the fanciest facade around. The Palace's main attraction is excellent dim sum—perhaps Boston's best—served daily from 9AM to 3PM. There's no menu; when the carts roll up, simply select whatever tidbits strike your fancy in the sea of little plates loaded with dumplings, fried and steamed pastries, and noodle dishes. Try *har gao* (shrimp dumplings), spareribs in black-bean sauce, steamed *bao* (meat-filled buns), *shu mai* (pork dumplings), or more adventurous items like tripe and curried squid. This sprawling place—aglitz with reds, golds, pinks, and painted and carved dragons—is a noisy neighborhood favorite. People come to eat, not unwind, so the service is hurried and the atmosphere minimal. But the dim sum are piping hot, and the regular menu offers loads of superior dishes, including abalone and squab treatments. ◆ Chinese/Takeout ◆ Daily 9AM-11:30PM. 14-20 Tyler St (between Beach and Kneeland Sts). Reservations recommended for 10 or more. 423.4565

29 China Grove ★★$ Run by a young brother and sister, **John** and **Rita Lin,** this bustling little restaurant features highlights from five provinces: Szechuan, Taiwan, Shanghai, Yangchow, and Peking. Old standbys such as Peking ravioli are state-of-the-art; among the more adventurous offerings are sour cabbage and *hog mow* (intestine) soup, jellyfish with sesame oil and a garlicky seaweed salad, shredded eel with yellow leeks, and squid *satay*. Bring an open mind and a ravenous appetite. ◆ Chinese/Takeout ◆ M-Th, Su 11:30AM-10:30PM; F-Sa 11:30AM-12:30AM. 10 Tyler St (between Beach and Kneeland Sts). 542.5857

30 Chau Chow Seafood ★★$ Definitely the Chinatown gem, this very busy, very basic place does great things with all sorts of seafood: crab with ginger and scallions, steamed sea bass and flounder, fried noodles with seafood and vegetables, salted jumbo shrimp in the shell, baby clams in black-bean sauce, seafood *chow foon*. Pork, beef, chicken, and duck dishes abound, and all are excellent. Sample

stir-fried watercress, Swatowese dumplings, or soup with sliced fish and Chinese parsley. Beer is served. Understandably, there's always a long line for dinner. ◆ Chinese/Takeout ◆ 52 Beach St (at Harrison Ave). M-Th 10AM-2AM; F-Sa 10AM-4AM; Su 10AM-1AM. No credit cards. 426.6266

31 Lucky Dragon $ Many of Boston's top chefs, including **Jasper White,** favor this place for dinner in Chinatown. Try *King To* pork ribs, *chow foon* plates, Singapore rice sticks, fried bean cake with shrimp, seafood hot pot, beef with string beans, hot and spicy squid—there's a daunting list of possibilities. Bring your late-night cravings for good Chinese food here. ◆ Chinese ◆ M-F 11:30AM-10:30PM; Sa-Su 11:30AM-3AM. 45 Beach St (at Harrison Ave). Reservations recommended. 542.0772

32 Dynasty ★$$ A big-league kind of restaurant, Dynasty has lots of mirrors and golden columns and offers good Cantonese dishes: panfried spiced shrimp, chicken with cashews, clams in black-bean sauce, and steamed sea bass and gray sole, to name a few. Even better, it stays open nearly round the clock. ◆ Chinese ◆ Daily 8AM-4AM. 33 Edinboro St (at Essex St). 350.7777

Chinatown—originally composed of tents—was born when Chinese workers were imported from the West to break a shoe-industry strike in the 1870s.

32 Moon Villa $ A hangout for hungry night owls, Moon Villa is by no means the romantic place it sounds, but does serve family style Cantonese dishes while the rest of the city snoozes. For dim sum, however, you have to come during the day, on the weekend. The waiters tend to be brusque. ♦ Chinese/Takeout ♦ Daily 11AM-4AM. 15-19 Edinboro St (at Essex St). 423.2061

33 Imperial Tea House ★$ Right at the gateway to Chinatown, this noisy, cavernous restaurant is a good choice for its second-floor dim sum parlor, where a fleet of carts laden with arrays of little treats—pork dumplings, shrimp balls, bean curd, stuffed meat buns, braised chicken's feet, and so forth—whiz past the packed tables. Just point to your selection and it's whisked onto your table. Always mobbed, the tearoom attracts a fascinating mixed clientele. There's usually a short wait. Downstairs, order traditional Cantonese dishes from the regular menu. ♦ Chinese/Takeout ♦ M-Th, Su 8:30AM-2AM; F-Sa 8:30AM-4AM. 70-72 Beach St (at Edinboro St). Reservations

Chinatown/Theater District

recommended for large parties at dinner. No credit cards. 426.8439

34 Ho Yuen Ting ★$ People flock to this no-frills restaurant not for ambience or decor, but for delectable Cantonese seafood specials like lobster with ginger, salted and spiced squid, shrimp with spicy sauce, or stir-fried sole and vegetables served in a crunchy edible bowl made of batter-fried shredded potatoes. Also recommended: pork-and-watercress soup and fish-stomach soup with mushrooms or sweet corn. This is a good place to explore the unknown. The restaurant's located below street level, so be on the lookout or you'll pass right by. ♦ Chinese/Takeout ♦ M-Th 11:30AM-9:30PM; F-Sa 11:30AM-10:30PM; Su noon-9:30PM. 13A Hudson St (between Beach and Kneeland Sts). No credit cards. 426.2316

35 New House of Toy $ It takes some guesswork—or fluency in Chinese—to decide what to order here, but a lot is very good. The dim sum tea brunch features nearly 60 varieties. Try to get the English version of the special menu on the window, which supplements the regular roster of dishes. Sample the steamed oysters in black-bean sauce, bean curd with shrimp and scallops, scallops in satay, short ribs in spiced sauce, or the sizzling platters. Frogs' legs aficionados will rejoice. ♦ Chinese ♦ Daily 9AM-10PM; dim sum 9:30AM-4PM. 16 Hudson St (between Beach and Kneeland Sts). 426.5587

Casing the Clubs

When a garage band called the **Talking Heads** started out in Boston, the music scene revolved around "college bands," nurtured primarily by the many students in the area. Now, years later, **David Byrne's** world-renowned group has split up, and Boston's nightclubs are as diverse as the bands that play them, with everything from country and western to New Wave on line. The following list will give you a better idea of what the top clubs are all about and where to find them. For more on who's playing where, see the "Calendar" section of *The Boston Globe* on Thursday and the *Boston Phoenix* on Friday.

In Boston:

Axis Music changes nightly and includes progressive, punk, funk, heavy metal, hard rock, live bands, alternative dance tunes, and DJ music. On Sunday, Axis connects with **Avalon** next door for gay night; enter through Avalon. ♦ 13 Lansdowne Street, Kenmore Square/Fenway. 262.2437

The Black Rose Irish music and Irish fare, with plenty of great beers and ales on tap. ♦ 160 State Street, Faneuil Hall Marketplace. 742.2286

Esme Sumptuous and sophisticated, Esme is for high rollers who also like to rock. ♦ 116 Boylston Place, Chinatown/Theater District. 482.3399

Metropolis A tripledecker club with a variety of music, from old soul and funk to international, reggae, progressive rock, and late-breaking dance music. ♦ 533 Washington Street, Downtown. 338.6999

NYC Jukebox and VHF Oldies but goodies in one room decorated with old jukeboxes and a 1957 Plymouth; Top 40 rock videos in the other. ♦ Tremont House, 275 Tremont Street, Theater District. 542.1123

Paradise Rock Club One of Boston's best places to see national and international groups in concert. Progressive rock is the mainstay at the Paradise, but it also books jazz, folk, blues, and country. ♦ 967 Commonwealth Avenue, Kenmore Square. 254.2052

The Plaza Bar An elegant cabaret-style setting where local and national entertainers perform jazz, pop, and blues. ♦ The Copley Plaza Hotel, 138 St. James Avenue, Back Bay. Jacket and tie required. 267.5300

The Rat (Rathskeller) Boston's first New Wave club has a star-studded history of supporting local garage bands who've made it big, including **The Cars, The Police,** the **Talking Heads,** and the **Go Gos.** The club books high-quality local and touring rock bands, up to five a night, three to four nights a week. ♦ 528 Commonwealth Avenue, Kenmore Square. 536.2750

Silverado The music is split nightly to include country and western by a DJ, a country and western band and DJ-spun Top 40 dance music. ♦ Tremont House, 279 Tremont Street, Theater District. No sneakers or T-shirts. 227.7699

Wally's Cafe The little red schoolhouse of jazz features young musicians, often from Berklee, and is also a pleasant neighborhood bar. Founded nearly a half-century ago by owner **Joseph Walcott,** tiny Wally's is family run and a Boston institution. ♦ 427 Massachusetts Avenue, South End. 424.1408

Zanzibar A tropical playpen extremely popular for dancing with a decked-out crowd. ♦ 1 Boylston Place, Theater District. Jacket and tie required. 451.1955

In Cambridge:

Cantab Lounge Lots of dancing, and a lot of fun late Saturday night. Rock, blues, and jazz by local bands. ♦ 738 Massachusetts Avenue, Central Square. 354.2685

Manray An arty alternative bar with industrial rock from national and international bands. Mixed crowd with special college, gay, and lesbian nights. ♦ 21 Brookline Street, Central Square. 864.0400

Nightstage Features only "signed people" (musicians with record contracts). The club books rock, blues, zydeco, jazz, folk, country, international—a wide variety of great bands. A spacious medium-size room built expressly for music, with tables, understated decor, and orderly ambience. ♦ 823 Main Street, Central Square. 497.8200

Passim This unpretentious little coffeehouse owned by **Bob** and **Rae Anne Donlin** encourages local folk and bluegrass groups, and has made lots of loyal friends like **Suzanne Vega**. National and local acoustic performers. No liquor license, but a light menu with coffees, teas, cider. By day, its a gift shop and cafe. ♦ 47 Palmer Street, Harvard Square. 492.7679

The Plough and Stars A neighborly Irish bar with Guinness, Harp, and Bass on tap, good pub-style food, live blues, bluegrass, rock, and reggae music that attracts a cross section of Cantabrigians: artists, plumbers, writers, scholars, carpenters, students. Too small for dancing, barely enough room for the band, but there's usually a good-natured crowd. ♦ 912 Massachusetts Avenue, Central Square. 492.9653

The Regattabar An upscale club that showcases nationally known names in jazz. Dress nicely. ♦ Charles Hotel, 1 Bennett Street, Harvard Square. 876.7777

Ryles You can often get a table in this casual, comfortable, quietish club booking top local and national jazz groups on two floors. ♦ 212 Hampshire Street, Inman Square. 876.9330

T.T. the Bear's Place Several new and established local bands are booked each night in this homey rock 'n' roll club. Sunday features a DJ dance format. The restaurant serves West Indian cuisine. ♦ 10 Brookline Street, Central Square. 492.2327

Western Front A long-lived club offering rasta, reggae, ska, funk, Latin, jazz, and Jamaican music—it often showcases very talented local musicians. Lots of loyal regulars dance up a storm here. The Front has collaborated with **New York City's Knitting Factory** to bring in great progressive jazz acts. ♦ 343 Western Avenue, Central Square. 492.7772

In Other Neighborhoods:

Harper's Ferry This dependable club boasts a horseshoe-shaped bar and big dance floor, and emphasizes blues and R&B and lots of favorite local bands, plus some out-of-towners. They give unknown new bands a first shot on Monday night. Wednesday and Sunday are open-mike nights for blues and R&B. ♦ 158 Brighton Avenue, Allston. 254.9743

Johnny D's Uptown Restaurant and Music Club A laid-back dance club that's very popular with locals. Blues, R&B, zydeco, ska, folk, reggae, and world beat. Local bands and newcomers, too. ♦ 17 Holland Street, Davis Square, Somerville. 776.9667

Tam O'Shanter Universally called "The Tam" and as well known for its homey, tasty dinners and brunches as its music—R&B, rock, and live music every night, plus dancing. ♦ 1648 Beacon Street, Brookline. 277.0982

Bests

Barbara Krakow

Art Dealer

The baseball park in the heart of the city—**Fenway Park**—and the **Red Sox**. And a hot dog an inning.

Boston Film Festival—an opportunity to eat popcorn nonstop for days and to role play as film critic.

A **Swan Boat** ride in the center of the extraordinarily beautiful **Public Garden.**

Advanced fashion for the head, hand, and body: **Frank Xavier, Body Sculpture**, and **Alan Bilzerian,** all on Newbury Street.

Skinner's jewelry auctions at the **Ritz-Carlton Hotel.**

A bike ride or walk from the **Museum of Science** along the Memorial Drive side of the Charles River to the **Larz Anderson Bridge,** and back along the Storrow Drive side of the Charles, passing MIT, Harvard,

Chinatown/Theater District

BU, the Hatch Shell, Beacon Hill, and the college crew teams and sailboats on the river.

Restaurants where the chef and owner are one and the same. The quality of the food is consistently high, the menus change often, and the idiosyncrasies of their patrons are graciously attended to without the blink of an eye. These include: **Allegro** in Waltham, **Biba, East Coast Grill** in Cambridge, **Hamersley's Bistro, Harvard Street Grill** in Brookline, **Icarus, Jasper's,** and **Olives** in Charlestown.

And then those favorites with the owners always on the premises: **On the Park, Michela's** in Cambridge, **St. Cloud,** and **Sol Azteca.**

Boston aristocracy does not, as many believe, hark back to the early Puritan settlers or the *Mayflower* set; instead, Boston's elite descended from 19th-century merchant princes, some of whom had made money in rather unsavory ways. Many of these early, privileged Bostonians justified their wordly gains by founding and funding cultural and charitable organizations. Brahmins came to epitomize high standards of thrifty, moral, and simple living. Oliver Wendell Holmes coined this upperclass set's famous label—"Brahmins"—after the ascetic Hindu caste that performed sacred rituals and set moral standards. Cabot, Coolidge, Forbes, Lawrence, Lodge, Lowell, Saltonstall—their names have been recycled and intermingled through the years, but still convey the best and worst of their all-powerful ancestors who once ruled the city.

Restaurants/Clubs: Red   **Hotels:** Blue
Shops/ 🌳 Outdoors: Green   **Sights/Culture:** Black

Back Bay

Boston's sumptuous centerpiece of illustrious institutions and architecture is also the best place in the city for extravagant shopping sprees and leisurely promenades. Back Bay attracts a stylish international crowd that's as fun to look at as any of **Newbury Street's** artful windows. An animated set, Back Bay is also a comfortable, compact neighborhood of broad, gracious streets bordered by harmonious four- and five-story Victorian town houses. Its residents are well-to-do families, established professionals, footloose young people, and transient students for whom the **Public Garden** is an outdoor living room and the **Charles River Esplanade** a grassy waterside backyard.

In the 19th century Boston's wealthy old guard and brash new moneymakers together planted this garden of beautiful homes and public buildings, creating a cosmopolitan, Parisianlike quarter wrapped in an aura of privilege and prosperity. The lingering mystique has even tricked some Bostonians into believing Back Bay is one of the city's oldest neighborhoods, when it's really one of the youngest. What began as Boston's wasteland was transformed in the late 1800s into its most desirable neighborhood by a spectacular feat of urban design.

In the 1850s Boston boasted a booming population and exuberant commercial growth. Railroads and manufacturing supplanted the sea as the city's primary source of capital. The nouveaux riches were hungry for spectacular domiciles, but the almost waterbound city was already overcrowded on its little peninsula. The problem: where to get land? In 1814 a mile-and-a-half-long dam had been built from the base of **Beacon Hill** to what is now **Kenmore Square** to harness the **Charles River's** tidal flow and power a chain of mills. The scheme failed, and the acres of water trapped by the dam became a stagnant, stinking, unhealthy tidal

flat called Back Bay that Bostonians longed to eradicate. This became the unlikely canvas that developers clamored to fill with daring urban design schemes. To do so, land had to be reclaimed from the sea by a fantastically ambitious landfill program. Inspired by the Parisian boulevard system **Baron Haussmann** had built for **Emperor Louis Napoleon**, architect **Arthur Gilman** proposed Back Bay's orderly layout. Starting at the Charles River, the principal east-west streets are Beacon Street, Marlborough Street, Commonwealth Avenue, Newbury Street, and Boylston Street, all bisected by eight streets (named alphabetically after English peers) from Arlington Street to Hereford Street. Sixteen-foot-long public alleys interlace these blocks and provide access to the rear of buildings, originally designed for service and deliveries. Gilman's rational grid remains a startling departure from Old Boston's labyrinthine tangles.

In 1857 the gigantic landfill wave began its sweep across the marshland block by block, from Arlington Street at the Public Garden's western edge toward the **Fenway**. As soon as a lot was ready, another architectural beauty debuted. By the time the wave subsided in 1890, 450 acres and more than 1,500 new buildings had been added to the 783-acre peninsula. Gone was the loathsome eyesore; in its place was a charming neighborhood of the same name. Completed in just 60 years, Back Bay is an extraordinary repository of Victorian architectural styles, perhaps the most outstanding in America. As an urban design scheme, it was surpassed in its era only by **L'Enfant's** plan for Washington, DC.

The newborn Back Bay instantly became Boston's darling, a magnificent symbol of civic pride and the city's coming of age. No Puritan simplicity or provincialism here—affluent Boston had learned how to stage a good show, from **Copley Square's** lofty cultural aspirations to Commonwealth Avenue's architectural revue of fancy brickwork, stained glass, cut granite, gaggles of gargoyles, ornate ironwork, and other European conceits. In Back Bay's golden hours, the city's leading financiers, authors, industrialists, artists, architects, and legendary Brahmins lived here. But as the city's economy soured late in the 19th century, the ostentatious single-family dwellings were gradually converted to more modest uses. Though Back Bay's shining moments as a residential district faded after the Great Depression, the neighborhood has resiliently adapted to 20th-century incursions of shops, offices, apartments, and condominiums.

The T stops most convenient to Back Bay are Arlington, Copley, Prudential, and Hynes Convention Center/ICA (Green Line). The Back Bay/South End (on the Orange Line and also a railway station) and Symphony stops are handy, too. Access to and from the Massachusetts Turnpike is easy; there's an eastbound exit and a westbound entrance at Copley Place.

1 John Hancock Tower When towering new edifices invade historic neighborhoods, they often try to gain public acceptance with lame gestures—by aping local architectural modes or bribing with street-level shops, skimpy parks, or outdoor art. The John Hancock Tower (pictured at right) makes no such insincere overtures. Designed by **I.M. Pei & Partners** in 1976, it is cool, aloof, and inscrutable, with its own singular style. And that's why more and more Bostonians have grown fond of this skyscraper—New England's tallest—as the years pass. A 62-story glass rhomboid, its shimmering surface acts as **Trinity Church's** full-length mirror while reflecting the constant shifts of New England weather. The tower's crisp form is mesmerizing from all angles, whether you glimpse the broad faces or razor-blade edges.

It's amazing the John Hancock Tower has become so popular, considering its rocky start. When it was first erected, inadequate glass was used in its sheathing and the windowpanes randomly popped out due to wind torquing, raining onto the square below. Sidewalks were cordoned off to protect pedestrians. All 13 acres of the 10,344 glass panels were replaced, and are now continuously monitored for visible signs of potential breakage. Making matters worse, a later engineering inspection revealed that the building was in danger of toppling, which required reinforcing its steel frame and installing a moving weight on the 58th floor to counter wind stress. Once Bostonians could walk by the tower without flinching, they began to notice what a dazzling addition it is to the Boston skyline. The tower has become a gift to the city, beautifully wrapped.

For stunning views that will put all of Back Bay and Boston into perspective, visit the **John Hancock Observatory** on the 60th floor. Binoculars are already zeroed-in on some of the city's most famous sights. The taped narrative by the late architectural historian **Walter Muir Whitehill** is wonderful not only for his vast knowledge, but for his Proper Bostonian accent. There's also a little sound and light show about Boston in 1775—with a 20-foot-tall topographical model of the city when all its hills were in place and Back Bay was its watery old self. ◆ Admission. M-Sa 9AM-11PM, Su 10AM-11PM, May-Oct; daily noon-11PM, Nov-Apr (Observatory open until 11PM, but last tickets sold at 10:15PM). 200 Clarendon St (between St. James Ave and Trinity Pl). 247.1977 &

2 Copley Square Once called "Art Square" for the galleries, art schools, and clubs clustered round, the square's modern name honors **John Singleton Copley**, Boston's great colonial painter. Copley Square began as an unsightly patch created by the disruption of Back Bay's grid by two rail lines. After the **Museum of Fine Arts** opened its doors here, the square

blossomed. (The museum stood where the **Copley Plaza Hotel** does today until the institution moved to its current address in the **Fenway** and its old residence was demolished.) **Trinity Church** and the **Boston Public Library** were spectacular additions, and the presence of numerous ecclesiastical and academic institutions nearby, including the **Massachusetts Institute of Technology**

Trinity Church

and the **Harvard Medical School,** enhanced the square's reputation—in Bostonians' minds—as the "Acropolis of the New World." The square's latest look (created in 1989 by **Dean Abbot**) is pleasant, but fails to satisfy Bostonians' century-old dreams of a magnificent public space.

2 Trinity Church Approach **Copley Square** from any direction, and your eyes will be drawn to this grandiose French-Romanesque-inspired edifice (pictured below). A **National Historic Landmark,** it is one of the great buildings in America. The century and more that has passed since Trinity Church first graced the city has taken nothing from its power to fascinate. Like a wise and tolerant elder, Trinity offers a model of urbane dignity and grandeur that has never been equalled in Boston. The church converses most with the old **Boston Public Library** across the way, another handsome building.

H.H. Richardson was at the summit of his career when he designed Trinity Church in 1877. In the 1860s its leaders decided to move the parish from **Summer Street** (Downtown) to the Copley Square site. In retrospect their decision seems prescient; one of Boston's great conflagrations destroyed the Summer Street building in November 1872. In March of that year, six architects had been invited to submit designs for the new Trinity. Thirty-four years old at the time and a New York City resident, Richardson had already contributed one admired piece to the emerging Back Bay fabric, the **First Baptist Church** (then called **New Bratle Square Church**) under construction on Clarendon Street.

Trinity's cruciform church's fluid massing is an inimitable Richardson tour de force, especially the leaping exterior colonnade. To contend with the awkward triangular site, Richardson designed the great square tower as the central element. Assisting Richardson with the tower was apprentice **Stanford White**—later of **McKim, Mead & White,** the Boston Public Library architects. The church's ageless vitality comes from the tension between Richardson's powerful vision of the whole and his spirited treatment of its parts. Elegant bands of red sandstone hold the coarse granite's brute force in check. Inside and out, the church is richly polychromatic in wood, paint, glass, and stone—another Richardson signature. With the aid of six assistants, most notably young **Augustus Saint-Gaudens, John La Farge** decorated the majestic interiors: look for his

Trinity Church Windows

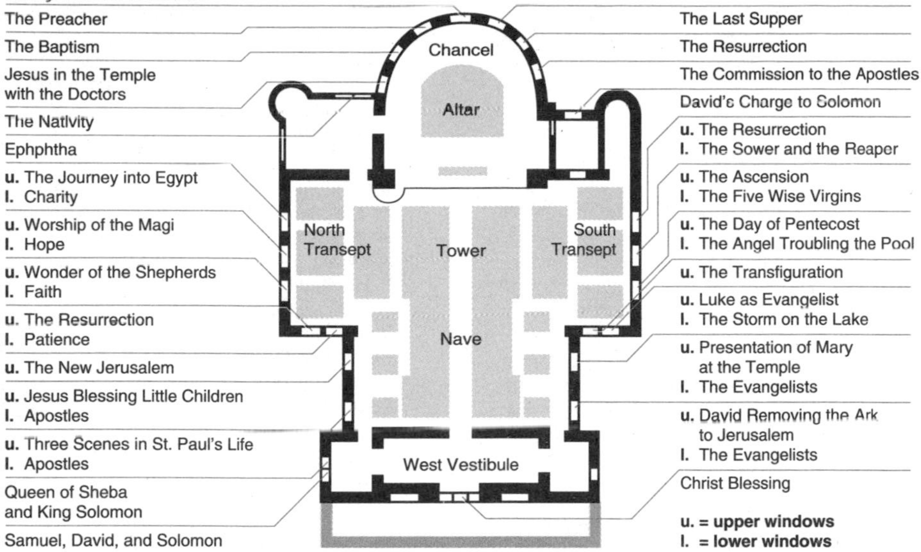
The Preacher
The Baptism
Jesus in the Temple with the Doctors
The Nativity
Ephphtha
u. The Journey into Egypt
l. Charity
u. Worship of the Magi
l. Hope
u. Wonder of the Shepherds
l. Faith
u. The Resurrection
l. Patience
u. The New Jerusalem
u. Jesus Blessing Little Children
l. Apostles
u. Three Scenes in St. Paul's Life
l. Apostles
Queen of Sheba and King Solomon
Samuel, David, and Solomon
Chancel
Altar
North Transept
Tower
South Transept
Nave
West Vestibule
The Last Supper
The Resurrection
The Commission to the Apostles
David's Charge to Solomon
u. The Resurrection
l. The Sower and the Reaper
u. The Ascension
l. The Five Wise Virgins
u. The Day of Pentecost
l. The Angel Troubling the Pool
u. The Transfiguration
u. Luke as Evangelist
l. The Storm on the Lake
u. Presentation of Mary at the Temple
l. The Evangelists
u. David Removing the Ark to Jerusalem
l. The Evangelists
Christ Blessing
u. = upper windows
l. = lower windows

12 oil paintings in the arches beneath the vaulted ceilings below the tower, 103 feet above the nave. La Farge orchestrated production of the stained-glass windows (see the diagram above), among them vividly glowing creations of his own—look for the lancet windows on the west wall in particular—and some jointly executed by **Edward Burne-Jones** and **William Morris and Company.** The interior resembles a gigantic tapestry woven in intricate patterns of opulent gold and medieval tones. Trinity's finest moment comes at Christmastime, when the church is filled with candlelight and carols during a special annual service.

Outside, Saint-Gaudens added a fine flourish: on the church's northeast corner stands his dramatic depiction of **Phillips Brooks,** the Copley Square Trinity's first rector, the Episcopal Bishop of Massachusetts, and author of *O Little Town of Bethlehem.* A somber, shrouded Christ stands behind the orating preacher. It was daring Brooks who convinced his congregation to move to the new frontier of Back Bay. Saint-Gaudens died before his design was sculpted; assistants completed the statue in 1910, and it was set into a marble canopy by McKim, Mead & White. Step into the cloistered colonnade to your left that overlooks a pretty enclosed garden with its much humbler statue of **St. Francis of Assisi.** Free half-hour organ recitals are offered Friday at 12:15PM. And tours are available by arrangement. ♦ Daily 8AM-6PM. 206 Clarendon St (at Copley Sq). 536.0944 ♿

For all Back Bay's French influences, its street names have remained Anglophile.

Building on Back Bay landfill required special engineering considerations. For example, Trinity Church's massive tower weighs 12.5 million pounds and rests on 4,500 wooden piles set in a 90-foot square. Because the pilings have to remain submerged in water to prevent dry rot, the water-table level is periodically checked through a hatch in the subbasement.

3 Copley Plaza Hotel $$$$ The empress dowager of Boston's hotels, the Copley Plaza enshrines the mature, full-flowered Back Bay. It not only draws business and international guests, but also lovers of grand epochs gone by. Designed in 1912 by **Clarence Blackall** and **Henry Hardenbergh** (the latter, architect of the **Plaza Hotel** in New York and the **Willard Hotel** in Washington, DC), this Italian Renaissance Revival structure has endured well. A pair of

gilded lions guard the entrance. Take a walk through the glittering lobby with its mirrored walls and a painted sky hovering over the registration desk—glorious overkill. A few years ago the current owner renovated all 393 rooms into period style. Every June the fabulous ballroom becomes a fantasyland for the debutante cotillion. Corner suites overlook Copley Square and Trinity Church. Nonsmokers' rooms and 15 rooms designed for handicapped people are available. There's also a multilingual staff, room service, and pets are allowed. ♦ 138 St. James Ave (between Trinity Place and Dartmouth St). 267.5300, 800/225.7654; fax 247.6681 ♿

Within Copley Plaza Hotel:

Plaza Dining Room ★★★$$$$ Dine in British Empire magnificence under a barrel-vaulted ceiling, attended by a well-trained battalion of captains, waiters, and busboys. US presidents **John F. Kennedy** and **Jimmy Carter** ate here; so have many movie stars. This unabashedly opulent dining room is gilded, polished, and stately, and under the new and gifted French chef **Gerard Thabius,** the costly European cuisine has finally begun to attain the heights of its setting. The encyclopaedic wine list is one of the city's finest. Piano music streams in from the foyer. ♦ French ♦ Tu-Sa 6-10PM. Valet parking. Jacket and tie required. Reservations required. 267.5300 ♿

Plaza Bar ★★★$$ Collect yourself on posh leather lounges under the Edwardian bar's handsome coffered ceiling, and enjoy jazz piano played from 8PM on. **Alfred Fiandaca** created the staff's attire. Hors d'oeuvres are served from 5PM to 6PM. ◆ M-Sa 5PM-midnight. 267.5300 &

Copley's Restaurant and Bar ★★$$ The hotel offers this atmospheric, clubby place for reasonably priced cuisine with a New England accent. There's a bar lounge at the back. On a cold afternoon, retreat to this wonderful high-ceilinged setting, where enormous draped windows overlook Copley Square. ◆ American ◆ Daily 6:30AM-3PM, 5-10:30PM. 267.5300 &

Tea Court ★$ At the heart of the bustling lobby, yet curiously sedate, this pretty cafe serves light fare throughout the day and one of Boston's tastiest teas. ◆ American ◆ Daily 6:30AM-9:30PM. 267.5300 &

4 Boston Public Library To fully justify its title, the "Athens of America," Boston demanded a splendid public library that would set an example for the nation. After all, America's first free municipal library supported by public taxa-

tion opened in Boston in 1852; today, serving two million people yearly, it's the sixth-largest library in the country. In its every detail, architect **Charles Follen McKim's** coolly serene Italian Renaissance Revival edifice, which was built in 1895 and is on the **National Register of Historic Places,** enshrines and celebrates learning. A "Palace for the People" was what the library's trustees had in mind, and that's precisely what McKim's firm **(McKim, Mead & White)** achieved. The library's decoration and design brought together the most magnificent crew of architects, artisans, painters, and sculptors ever assembled in the US until that time. Materials alone reflect the nothing-but-the-best attitude of its creators; for instance, a palette of more than 25 different types of marble and stone was used. Although years of neglect have diminished much of the beauty, a massive $50 million restoration is underway that will restore the building to its original glory by the end of the century. Meanwhile, parts of the library may be temporarily closed.

Flanking the **Dartmouth Street** entrance are **Bela Pratt's** huge 1911 bronzes of two seated women personifying *Art* and *Science,* their pedestals carved with the names of artists and scientists. Prickly wrought-iron lanterns bloom by the doorways—startlingly Halloweenish. Look at the library parapets carved with the names of

important people in the history of human culture. There are 519 names in all; the carvers mistakenly repeated four. When one local newspaper reported that McKim, Mead & White had amused themselves by working the firm's name into the first letters in three of the panels, enough taxpayers were incensed that the architects had to erase their clever acrostic.

Pass through the bronze portals and enter the main entrance hall. Everywhere you turn there are more inscriptions, dedications, and names of the forgotten great and zealous benefactors. Brass intarsia of the zodiac signs inlay the marble floor; look up at the intricate mosaic ceilings. Climb the grand staircase of tawny Sienna marble past the noble pair of lions to the enormous contemplative Arcadian allegories by **Puvis de Chavannes** (artist of the poetic murals in the **Hôtel de Ville** in Paris), which decorate the second-floor gallery. Adjacent is **Bates Hall,** a cavernous reading room 218 feet long with a barrel-vaulted ceiling 50 feet high. To the right is the former **Delivery Room,** where Bostonians waited for their requested books to arrive, transported from the stacks by a tiny train hidden from view.

In the library's remotest reaches on the third floor resides one of Boston's forgotten treasures: the **Sargent Gallery.** Few people ever find their way up the gloomy stairs to this poorly lit place, yet **John Singer Sargent** considered this gallery the artistic apex of his career. He devoted 30 years to planning the historical murals—their theme is Judaism and Christianity—and designing the entire hall where they were placed. The gallery wasn't quite complete when he died in 1916. The somber murals are tragically faded, but deserve attention. Also on the third floor is the **Wiggin Gallery,** which mounts frequent exhibitions of local artists, and the **Cheverus Room,** housing library treasures such as the **Joan of Arc Collection.**

The most satisfying way to end any trip to "the BPL"—the library's nickname—is to visit its peaceful central courtyard with reading in hand. (If you don't qualify as a borrower, bring your own.) Follow the example of other Bostonians and pull a chair between the sturdy stone columns of the cloister, modeled after the **Palazzo della Cancelleria's** in Rome. The landscaping is simple—just a few trees, a reflecting pool and fountain, and some plantings. Even on a rainy day this is a restful place to read. One-hour tours depart from the lobby at the Dartmouth entrance. ◆ Free. Tours M 2:30PM; Tu-W 6:30PM; Th-Sa 11AM. Dartmouth St (at Copley Sq). 536.5400 &

4 Boston Public Library Addition When the Boston Public Library outgrew **McKim, Mead & White's** palatial structure, this annex was added in 1972. In materials and monumentality, **Philip Johnson's** addition echoes the original BPL, yet is a cold, stark place. The interior connection between the new and old buildings is circuitous—you reach the old from the new by turning left just beyond the entry turnstiles and following a corridor past **Louise Stimson's** appealing dioramas to an innocuous door that leads to McKim's building. Nevertheless, Bostonians use the BPL addition like mad; here the stacks are open, so there's immediate access to the books. Exhibitions are held regularly in the lofty central space. In the basement is a comfortable theater, where a free film series offers weekly screenings and regular readings are held. Many homeless people frequent the library; it's one of the city's few places truly hospitable to all Bostonians.

The **Access Center** on the **Concourse Level** is dedicated to serving handicapped patrons, offering special equipment and materials. Given the local restroom shortage, don't forget that there are large restrooms in the basement here, as well as telephones. ◆ M-Th 9AM-9PM; F-Sa 9AM-5PM. 666 Boylston St (between Dartmouth and Exeter Sts). 536.5400 ໄ.

5 Westin Hotel, Copley Place $$$ One of Boston's many major chain hotels, the Westin has 804 rooms and suites on 36 floors, with good views to be had above the 11th floor and two specialty suites on the 36th floor. Some floors are designed for handicapped persons and nonsmokers.

The hotel calls itself "The Gateway to Copley Place," which sure isn't Oz, but does offer shops aplenty for the shop-until-you-drop crowd. Hotel amenities include 24-hour room service, a bilingual concierge, valet parking, a health club with an indoor pool, a car-rental desk, and several restaurants. Small pets are allowed. ◆ 10 Huntington Ave (at Dartmouth St). 262.9600, 800/228.3000; fax 424.7483 ໄ.

Within the Westin Hotel, Copley Place:

Turner Fisheries ★$$$ This softly lit, spacious restaurant is also *quiet.* You can enjoy conversation along with absolutely fresh, simply prepared seafood. The clam chowder has been elevated to the citywide annual **Chowderfest's** Hall of Fame. For a quick, light meal, there's an oyster bar, or sit in the lounge and order the smoked-bluefish appetizer. ◆ Seafood ◆ Daily 11AM-1AM. Reservations recommended. 424.7425 ໄ.

6 House of Siam ★$ Though tucked in an inconvenient block across Huntington Avenue from the Westin Hotel, this little pink haven is worth seeking out as an inexpensive respite from Back Bay's complacent costliness. The duck and other standard dishes are excellent; try chicken or beef typhoon sautéed with bamboo shoots, minced hot chile, garlic, and basil. ◆ Thai/Takeout ◆ M-F 11:30AM-3PM, 5-10PM; Sa noon-3PM, 5-10:30PM; Su 5-10PM. 21 Huntington Ave. 267.1755 ໄ.

7 Copley Place The largest private development in Boston's history, Copley Place covers 9.5 acres of land and air rights above the **Massachusetts Turnpike,** includes 3.7 million square feet of space, and is the size of 2,500 average American homes, 822 football fields, or more than two John Hancock Towers. It includes two hotels, more than a hundred upscale shops and restaurants, an 11-screen cinema, four 7-story office buildings, 1,400 parking places, and 104 residences. Walkways and pedestrian bridges lead from the complex to the hotels and to the **Prudential Center** complex. In Copley Place's central atrium, a thousand gallons of water per minute cascade over **Dimitri Hadzi's** 60-foot-high water sculpture made of more than 80 tons of travertine and granite.

Needless to say, the genesis of this giant created a furor that hasn't entirely abated. Plunked down at one corner of **Copley Square,** Copley Place, unfortunately, has become a formidable barrier to the neighboring **South End.** But as bland, anonymous, and prefab-looking as the exterior is, many people say Copley Place could have been much worse. Inside, it's marble, marble everywhere, and hardly a bench to sit on. You're meant to come with laden pockets, ready to empty them in shops identical to those in many other cities, with a few exceptions (notably the **Artful Hand Gallery** of crafts). By and large, stick to Newbury Street unless the weather is bad, because although prices are exorbitant there, too, it's much more genuinely

Boston. ◆ Mall M-F 10AM-7PM; Sa 10AM-6PM; Su noon-5PM. 100 Huntington Ave (at Dartmouth St). 375.4400 (information desk) ໄ.

8 Boston Marriott Copley Place $$$ This massive 38-story complex rode into town in the early '80s with the **Copley Place** megadevelopment. With that next door, there's plenty of shopping and movies only minutes away. The highest-up of the 1,147 rooms and suites offer nice views. All are furnished in Queen Anne-style, with cable TV and individual climate control. Many rooms are designed for handicapped accessibility; four floors are for nonsmokers. Two levels of executive rooms cost more and include breakfast, a private lounge, and special concierge service. A waterfall gushes in the four-story atrium. The hotel is also connected to the **Prudential Center** and **Hynes Convention Center** by an enclosed footbridge. Other features include 24-hour room service, valet parking, valet service, a travel agency, an indoor swimming pool, health facilities, barber and beauty shops, meeting facilities and business services, an exhibit hall, and Boston's largest ballroom. The hotel is directly above the **Massachusetts Turnpike.** ◆ 110 Huntington Ave (at Exeter St). 236.5800, 800/228.9290; fax 236.5885 ໄ.

Restaurants/Clubs: Red   **Hotels:** Blue
Shops/ ◆ Outdoors: Green   **Sights/Culture:** Black

9 Copley Square Hotel $$
One of Boston's oldest, this modestly sized 1891 hotel is a Back Bay bargain and attracts an international clientele. It has a pleasantly low-key, informal European style—nothing fancy. All 150 rooms and suites—

varying a lot in size—feature individual climate control, closet floor safes, and windows you can open. For a small fee, use the nearby **Westin Hotel's** health facilities. A coffee shop and lounge, rooms for nonsmokers, inexpensive adjacent parking, and an airport limo are all available. ♦ 47 Huntington Ave (at Exeter St). 536.9000, 800/225.7062; fax 267.3547 &

Within the Copley Square Hotel:

The Cafe Budapest ★★$$$ Serenaded by violin and piano, propose marriage, celebrate an anniversary, or toast true love in the intimate, Old European bar with alcoves for two. For more than 25 years Cafe Budapest has been the most romantic restaurant in Boston—but be *sure* to request the tiny blue or pink dining room. Contrary to common opinion, lovers usually have perfectly good appetites—may even need extra fuel—and Budapest's Central European cooking is certainly rich, hearty comfort food, albeit elegant. Perennial favorites are the iced tart-cherry soup, *Wiener schnitzel à la Holstein,* veal *gulyas,* and sauerbraten. The homemade pastries include extraordinary strudels, of course, and Hungarian wines are

Back Bay

served. The pianist and strolling violinist perform Tuesday through Saturday. ♦ Hungarian ♦ M-Th noon-10:30PM; F-Sa noon-midnight; Su 1-11PM (dinner served all day). Jacket and tie required. Reservations recommended. 266.1979 &

10 Boylston Street Unlike human-scale Newbury Street with its continual retail diversions or Commonwealth Avenue with its architectural ones, Boylston Street seems like a long walk from one end to the other. But the street has been revamped over the last decade and now offers new shops and restaurants among its imposing historic, cultural, and religious institutions. Once an unkempt stretch bordering Boston's rail yards, Boylston is becoming fashionable.

10 The Lenox Hotel $$ When the Lenox opened in 1900 it stood alone in the midst of railroad tracks. That year the *Boston Sunday Post* said the Lenox would "scrape the sky and dally with the gods." In its heyday, **Enrico Caruso** stayed here. Later, like its city, the Lenox hit hard times. But fully refurbished today, this small hotel's 220 soundproof rooms line spacious corridors and feature rocking chairs and settees, walk-in closets, and your choice of Oriental, two types of colonial, or French Provincial decor. The "Green Colonial" and the "Corner Oriental" rooms, which have working fireplaces, are a few of the favorites. Some

rooms are for nonsmokers. Long popular with guests traveling on a budget, prices are moving up as the **Saunders** family spruces up the vintage hotel. But a genuine personal touch is still present. Amenities include valet service, valet pay parking, and baby-sitting. Pets can stay. **The Lenox Pub & Grill** on the premises serves hearty, casual pub fare downstairs and grilled entrées upstairs. ♦ 710 Boylston St (at Exeter St). 536.5300, 800 225.7676; fax 267.1237 &

Within The Lenox Hotel:

Diamond Jim's Piano Bar All night long, it's one great big friendly, spontaneous sing-along at Diamond Jim's, where locals and visitors feel free to come in and pitch their pipes when they are in the mood and have the courage. Regulars are dubbed the **Lenox Singers.** On the second Wednesday of every month, there's a sing-off judged by local celebrities. **Tom Selleck, Guy Lombardo, Tony Bennett,** and assorted **Metropolitan Opera** stars have shown up here. No food is served—that would only vex the vocal chords. ♦ M-F 5PM-1:30AM; Sa 5:30PM-1:30AM. 536.5300 &

11 J.C. Hillary's ★$$ It's a little nondescript, but J.C. Hillary's is well established and nicer looking than the other Back Bay restaurants of its ilk. You'll find respectable burgers and bar food, seafood and pasta at reasonable prices, and a bar. ♦ American/Takeout ♦ M 11:30AM-11PM; Tu-Th 11:30AM-midnight; F 11:30AM-12:30AM; Sa 9AM-12:30AM; Su 9AM-11PM. 793 Boylston St (at Fairfield St). Valet parking evenings. Reservations recommended on weekends. 536.6300

11 The Famous Atlantic Fish Company ★$$
Long on selections and better priced than many seafood houses in Boston, this is a reliable choice for a casual meal. Fried-clam lovers will be particularly content. At lunchtime, they guarantee your meal will arrive within 12 minutes after ordering or it's on the house, so there's always a crowd of time-is-money professionals. ♦ Seafood ♦ M-Th 11:30AM-10:30PM; F-Sa 11:30AM-11:30PM; Su 11:30AM-10PM. 777 Boylston Street (between Exeter and Fairfield Sts). 267.4000 &

11 Buddenbrooks Booksmith This shop boasts that it's the only place in the world where you can buy the illustrated first edition of *Paradise Lost* and a mass-market edition at the same time. True or not, old and new mingle nicely here; the ancients get the handsome cases in the antiquarian section at the back, where books of all kinds jumble together in polite mayhem. Finds include first and early illustrated editions of children's books. Creaky wooden floorboards and disorderly displays add to the proper bookstore mood. Buddenbrooks stocks more than 50,000 titles and will special order. Open 364 days a year, they close only for Thanksgiving and donate all Christmas receipts to charity. ◆ M-F 8AM-11:30PM; Sa-Su 9AM-11:30PM. 753 Boylston St (between Exeter and Fairfield Sts). 536.4433 &

11 Boston Chicken ★$ Queue up with the lunchtime crowds for stellar take-out chicken; it's roasted slowly in a brick-fired rotisserie to seal in a secret marinade. The result is well worth the wait. ◆ Fast food ◆ Daily 11AM-11PM. 745 Boylston St (between Exeter and Fairfield Sts). 859.0015

12 Morton's of Chicago ★★$$$$ The restaurant's stock of tender prime-grade dry-aged beef is flown in fresh from Chicago daily. One of a chain of 18 restaurants, Morton's has a fabulous way with steak, especially the 24-ounce porterhouse, their hallmark. Come famished enough to eat a side of beef, a flock of chickens, or a school of fish—even the baked potatoes are behemoths. There are some smaller cuts of meat for smaller eaters, but that's relative here. Crowds of businesspeople mean a lot of power eating is going on. Morton's is located in what Bostonians have nicknamed "The Darth Vader Building," a modern building so awful it's the architectural equivalent of a bad haircut—odd-looking and sticking out in the wrong places. ◆ Steakhouse/American ◆ M-F 11:30AM-2:30PM, 5:30-11PM; Sa 5:30-11PM; Su 5-10PM. 1 Exeter Plaza (at Boylston St). Valet parking. Reservations recommended. 266.5858 &

12 Glad Day Bookshop The only one of its kind in New England, this bookstore stocks a comprehensive selection of gay and lesbian literature, including foreign-language titles. Magazines, cards, calendars, CDs, LPs, cassettes, and videos are also sold. Special orders are welcome. Just outside is a heavily used community bulletin board. Located on the second floor, the bookstore can be reached by the steps or a cramped elevator—too small for many wheelchairs. ◆ M-Th 9:30AM-10PM; F-Sa 9:30AM-11PM; Su 12:30-9PM. 673 Boylston St (between Dartmouth and Exeter Sts). 267.3010 &

13 Geoffrey's Cafe-Bar ★$ Casual and hectic, this bistro features specialty egg dishes, fresh soups, grilled luncheon sandwiches, and rotisserie and pasta entrées. Breakfast on homemade muffins and yogurt in the sunny front alcove. ◆ American ◆ M-Th 7:30AM-11PM; F 7:30AM-midnight; Sa 8AM-midnight; Su 9AM-10PM. 651 Boylston St (between Dartmouth and Exeter Sts). 437.6400

Romantic Retreats

For a city that's briskly businesslike, Boston has hidden charms that deserve slower savoring. While everyone else goes about their appointed rounds, you and your loved one can meander at a private pace, enjoying your own sweet folie à deux.

Many of Boston's better hotels offer specially priced weekend packages, with amenities ranging from champagne and roses to spa privileges and limo service. The sexiest—simply because it's French—is **Le Meridien** (see page 76), with stunning modern decor superimposed on a venerable old bank building. In its ornate but cozy bar, brass torchères cast a golden glow and two splendid **N.C. Wyeth** murals lend a timeless air; the restaurant, **Julien,** offers outstanding French fare, luxurious service, and a degree of intimacy not matched elsewhere, thanks to comfy, encompassing armchairs. The area tends to shut down at night (all the better for focusing on each other) but by day is conducive to a number of interesting walks around **Beacon Hill,** the **North End, Fort Point Channel,** and the **Leather District.**

Traditionalism has its piquancy, too, and if that's more your style, try the **Ritz-Carlton Hotel** (see page 134), a bastion for Boston's old guard. Ask for a room overlooking the **Public Garden,** and with any luck you'll get a Childe Hassam-like landscape suffused with slanting light. The bar is a cosseting world unto itself, but the elegant dining room, alas, lacks culinary verve. Instead, head outside to explore. The restaurant **Biba** (see page 93) is nearby, for see-and-be-seen types who have the foresight to reserve well ahead.

Back Bay

Another popular restaurant, **29 Newbury** (see page 132), attracts a media and fashion crowd, but is coolly subdued; the banquette alcoves are ideal for a tête-à-têtes. Venture out for brunch at **Rebecca's** (see page 22), plus a bit of sailboat-gazing along the **Charles River Esplanade;** browse the **Newbury Street** shops and galleries; or take in a courtyard concert at the **Isabella Stewart Gardner Museum** (see page 137), always an indulgence for the senses.

Cambridge attracts couples intent on reliving—or prolonging—their youths. **The Charles Hotel** (see page 181) draws on the bustle of **Harvard Square,** while keeping just enough distance: It is calm, pampering, and pretty, with patchwork quilts on the pine beds, a super-spa (**Le Pli**), and even a premier jazz club, the **Regattabar.** The restaurant, **Rarities,** is a pared-down but Lucullan showcase for nouvelle cuisine; the atmosphere is properly worshipful, and no one will notice if you're mostly worshiping each other. Two other romantic venues are only a cab ride away: the much-heralded **Michela's** (see page 190), whose Northern Italian menu merits all the raves in the national press, and **Dalí** (see page 200), a little-known but thoroughly charming Spanish hideaway. Street performers in Harvard Square range from balladeers to an oldies-by-request player piano, and the many cafes and bookstores (search out the **Grolier Book Shop** for love sonnets) collaborate to provide pensive pleasures. And don't forget, one of the greatest perks of being in love in this city is to stroll along the Charles, hand in hand.

13 New Old South Church Yes, that's truly its name, and what would you expect in a city that's as full of odd monikers as Boston? The **Old South Church** moved here from its 18th-century meeting house, which still stands on Washington Street. The puddingstone church's Northern Italian Gothic design—executed by **Cummings and Sears** in 1874-75 and now a **National Historic Landmark**—is pleasingly picturesque with its multicolored ornament, tall campanile, and copper-topped Venetian lantern (see the illustration below). On the entry portico's right wall, look for the tombstone remnant set in concrete that records the death of **John Alden,** congregation member and eldest son of **John** and **Priscilla Alden** of the **Plymouth Colony.** With a subway station entrance and newsstand located near its porte cochere, the church is always witness to lively comings and goings. Only the sanctuary and chapel are open to the public. ♦ M-F 9AM-5PM; Su 9AM-2PM. 645 Boylston St (at Dartmouth St). 536.1970

Next to the New Old South Church:

Copley Square News Max has run this newsstand—where you can get periodicals in English, Spanish, French, Italian, and German, as well as flowers—for 64 years. ♦ M-Sa 3AM-6:30PM. 262.1477 (a pay phone; Max will answer)

14 Bromer Booksellers A stop on the treasure-seeking trail of the serious browser and buyer only, and *not* for casual page-thumbers, this impeccable second-floor gallery displays rare books of all periods. Earnest collectors themselves, **Anne** and **David Bromer** sell literary first editions, private press and illustrated books, books in finely crafted bindings, and rare children's books. The couple is internationally recognized as major dealers in miniature books—less than three inches in both dimensions—on all subjects, such as a miniscule *New Testament* written in shorthand and published in 1665, or *Mite,* a late-1800s English compendium of funny nonsense. ♦ M-F 9AM-5PM; Sa 9AM-5PM. 607 Boylston St (at Dartmouth St). 247.2818

New Old South Church

COURTESY OF THE BOSTONIAN SOCIETY OLD STATE HOUSE

15 Back Bay Bistro ★$$ At this Parisianlike neighborhood bistro, you'll feel comfortable whether nibbling on appetizers or feasting on full-course meals. The pâtés and smoked items are homemade and change daily, as does the interesting parade of entrée specials. There's a generous list of wines available by the glass. The salmon-pink dining room is low-key and agreeable. After dinner on a clear night, walk across **Copley Square** to the **Hancock Tower,** and ride up to the observatory to see illuminated Boston compete with the stars. ♦ French/Takeout ♦ M-Th 5:30-10:30PM; F-Sa 5:30-11PM; Su 5-10PM. 565 Boylston St (between Clarendon and Dartmouth Sts). 536.4477 ♿

15 Mr. Leung's ★★$$$ A world apart from the Formica tabletops and slapdash service prevalent in **Chinatown**, this suave, black lacquer-box restaurant theatrically presents upscale Szechuan-Cantonese dishes to a well-heeled clientele. Taking center stage under tiny ceiling spotlights is a smashing rendition of Peking duck for two. You can order the old standbys here, too, *moo shu* pork and all, but they come quite dear. ◆ Szechuan/Cantonese ◆ Daily 6-10PM. 545 Boylston St (between Clarendon and Dartmouth Sts). Valet parking evenings. Jacket required. Reservations required. 236.4040 ♿

16 Cornucopia ★★★$$ After a long, trying sojourn near the **Combat Zone**, owner **Kristine Fayerman-Pratt** and chef **Stuart Cameron** are partaking of the Boylston Street renaissance. Their elegant duplex fronting **Trinity Church** is a tasteful oasis; Cameron takes an eclectic approach to the bounty of each season. ◆ American ◆ Opening in January 1993; call 338.4600 for hours. 553 Boylston St (between Clarendon and Dartmouth Sts) ♿

17 500 Boylston Street Called "a sort of box covered with architectural clothes" by *Boston Globe* architectural critic **Robert Campbell**, this 1988 building by **John Burgee** and **Philip Johnson** is an overblown, outscaled complex that houses fancy shops and offices. Its famous architects must have lost interest during the project—the building is unimaginative kitsch that turns a cold shoulder to its perennially inviting neighbor, **Trinity Church.** The bowling-ball spheres and urns along 500's parapets look ready to topple. Johnson was the architect of the **Boston Public Library Addition,** and Johnson and Burgee designed **International Place** near South Station in the Financial District, another graceless building that dismays many Bostonians. Even though local citizens tried to stop it, 500 went up. Boston's learning a lesson from this one. ◆ At Clarendon St

Within 500 Boylston Street (an entrance is also located on Clarendon Street):

Skipjack's ★$$ This Art Deco-and-neon restaurant with an underwater motif looks like what it is: an upstart rival to Boston's venerable seafood establishments. The favorite seafood emporium of many younger Bostonians, Skipjack's purveys 33 different types of seafood—including many Pacific varieties like Hawaiian mahi-mahi—that are not just broiled or fried, but in adventurous preparations, such as their signature coating of lemon, soy, and spice. This brash contender draws long lines and gets very hectic; if you feel daunted when you arrive, you can opt for a take-out dinner. Or phone in an order—Skipjack's delivers in Boston, Cambridge, and Brookline. Live jazz accompanies the Sunday brunch. ◆ Seafood/Takeout ◆ M-F 11AM-10PM; Sa 11AM-11PM. Valet parking evenings. Takeout 536.4949, restaurant 536.3500 ♿ Also at: 2 Brookline Place, Brookline. 232.8887; Charles Sq, Cambridge. 876.9900

18 Hard Rock Cafe ★$ The crowds of tourists and teens piling up under a fake rock facade inscribed "Massachusetts Institute of Rock" should clue you in: here's Boston's rendition of the famous chain of restaurants where rock 'n' roll is family fare. There's no live music here, as anyone in the know knows—just eardrum-pummeling recordings of old hits and a menu of surprisingly good bar food starring burgers and BBQ. The rock 'n' roll theme plays itself out all over: the bar's shaped like a Fender Stratocaster guitar; stained-glass windows honor **Elvis Presley, Jerry Lee Lewis,** and **Chuck Berry;** and one wall is covered with bricks taken from the demolished **Cavern Club** in **Liverpool, England,** where the **Beatles** got their start. Like all of its other Hard Rock siblings, Boston's Hard Rock overflows with its share of memorabilia: **Roy Orbison's** autographed Gibson, **John Lennon's** original scribblings for *Imagine,* an Elvis necklace, and a cavalcade of objects belonging to other stars. But really, why come here unless you like din with your dinner, or want to person-

ally experience a legendary marketing coup, or have a young friend who's hot on the idea? ◆ American ◆ Daily 11AM-2AM. 131 Clarendon St (at Stuart St). 424.7625 ♿

19 The Lyric Stage The oldest resident professional theater company in Boston now resides in spacious quarters within the **YWCA** and mounts neglected classics such as **George Bernard Shaw's** works. Led by artistic director **Ron Ritchell,** the company is one of the few non-university-sponsored theaters to warrant critical attention. ◆ 140 Clarendon St (between Stuart St and the Massachusetts Turnpike). 437.7172 ♿

20 Club Cafe ★★$$ Attracting a predominantly (though not exclusively) gay clientele, this sophisticated spot is ideal for a light meal. Chef **Julia Brant's** menu ranges from boboli pizza to cold duck salad with jicama and endive. Also on the premises is **Club Cabaret,** an intimate setting for stellar (if sporadic) live musical performances. ◆ International ◆ M-Sa 2PM-2AM; Su 11:30AM-2AM. 209 Columbus St (between Berkeley St and the Massachusetts Turnpike). 536.0966 ♿

20 Blue Wave ★★$$ A lively pocket of California cuisine (read: healthy, eclectic, inventive), this popular spot is a curious blend of hi-tech decor and warm vibes. Manager **Bruce Ployer** likes to showcase favored artists and is constantly shaking up the mix. Chef/owner **Russ Berger** pushes the envelope with such unique dishes as pan-seared tuna that is walnut-crusted and served with a passion fruit and orange juice reduction sauce. ♦ California/Takeout ♦ M-F 11:30AM-11PM; Sa 5-11PM; Su 11AM-11PM. 142 Berkeley St (between Stuart and Columbus Sts). 424.6711 ᕗ

21 **Grill 23 & Bar** ★★$$$$ A sea of white linen, mahogany paneling, banker's lamps, and burnished brass give GRILL 23 a formal demeanor—the ideal setting for a festive but seemly occasion. During the week you'll see many more wheeling-and-dealing Boston professionals than tourists here. Famous for its savoir faire with red meat, especially the perfectly aged and charbroiled 18-ounce New York sirloin, the restaurant turns out splendid seafood and poultry, too. The old-fashioned American practice of topping off hearty fare with equally hearty sweets is bolstered in a dessert list that features good old apple pie and New York cheesecake. Come famished. With few rugs on its wooden floors and an open kitchen, the cavernous dining room gets very noisy.

Grill 23 is located in the renovated **Salada Tea Building**, designed by **Densmore, LeClear, and Robbins** in 1929; on your way out be sure to look for the fantastic bronze doors at the **Stuart Street** entrance. Cast from Englishman **Henry Wilson's** design, they depict exotic scenes from the tea trade and won a silver medal at the 1927 Paris Salon. Elephants and solemn human figures protrude dramatically

in bas-relief from the bronze doors and their carved stone setting. ♦ American ♦ M-Th 4:30-10:30PM; F-Sa 6-11PM; Su 6-10PM. 161 Berkeley St (at Stuart St). Jacket and tie recommended at dinner. Reservations recommended. 542.2255 ᕗ

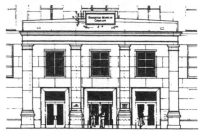

22 **Houghton Mifflin Building** Posh new digs for Boston's venerable publisher (and several other tenants), this 22-story high rise designed by **Robert A.M. Stern** (the entrance is pictured above) turns inward for luxury, unlike its ostentatious neighbor 500 Boylston Street. The outside is all clean, tasteful lines; the interior is creamy marble with a five-story "wintergarden" complete with splashing fountains. This is a secret retreat in the heart of Downtown. ♦ 222 Berkeley St

Within the Houghton Mifflin Building:

Cottonwood Cafe ★★★$$$ Haute Tex-Mex is the most appropriate rubric for this bountiful, robust fare, served in an evocative, pared-down setting that always seems to suggest the desert at sunset, even at high noon. Ask for a booth, and then chow down on their delicious Rocky Mountain lamb (mesquite-grilled, with raspberry chipotle sauce on one-half of the enormous platter, cilantro pesto on the other). The fresh-fruit margaritas here are just heavenly. ♦ Southwestern ♦ Restaurant M-F 11:30AM-2:30PM, 5:30-10PM; Sa-Su 11:30AM-3PM, 5:30-11PM. Cafe M-F 4-10:30PM; Sa-Su 3-11:30PM. Reservations are recommended. 427.2225 ᕗ. Also at: 1815 Massachusetts Avenue, Cambridge. 661.7440

City Sports A popular local outfitter, this rapidly growing chain has chosen to decorate its flagship store, at a prestigious address, with raw beams and exposed ducts, and somehow the stripped-away aesthetic is effective. The high-energy music pumping through doesn't hurt. ♦ M-F 10AM-7PM; Sa 10AM-6PM; Su noon-6PM. 480 Boylston St (between Berkeley and Clarendon Sts). 267.3900 ᕗ

23 **Berkeley Building** Stand on the opposite side of the street to get a full view of this striking Beaux Arts-inspired office building, designed in 1905 by **Codman & Despredelle.** Look for its spectacular cornice and colorful banners waving above. Clad in enameled terra-cotta, the steel frame supports five-story towers of glass edged in sea-foam green. There's only one elegant embellishment of gilt —the facade is dressy enough. Parisian architect Despredelle taught design classes across the street, where the **Massachusetts Institute of Technology School of Architecture** was once located. ♦ 420 Boylston St (at Berkeley St)

24 **Malben's** Years before Bostonians collectively went wild over deluxe and designer foodstuffs, Malben's was stocking its shelves with fancy imported treats. It's not as glossy as Boston's newer gourmet grocers, but it still reels in crowds and takes calls from as far away as New Zealand. Malben's will ship things, too. Browsers come not only to ogle the cornucopia of jams, mustards, cheeses, caviar, cookies, candies, oils, honeys, teas, gourmet gifts, etc., but also to graze at the deli, bakery, and produce counters. Gather all the fixings you need for a fair-weather picnic, including the wicker basket and wine, and head for the **Public Garden** up the street. Come back for a traditional plum pudding at holiday time. ♦ Deli/Bakery ♦ M-F 6AM-6PM; Sa 9AM-6PM. 384 Boylston St (between Arlington and Berkeley Sts). 267.1646 ᕗ

Restaurants/Clubs: Red
Shops/ 🌳 Outdoors: Green
Hotels: Blue
Sights/Culture: Black

Boston was the first city in the country to establish a police department.

The Rattlesnake Bar & Grill

24 The Rattlesnake Bar & Grill ★★$ Oblivious to its high-rent neighbors, **Gordon Wilcox's** down-home joint serves "food of the Americas" (everything from quesadillas to duck confit) and state-of-the-art Sauza Gold margaritas. Out back, there's an "Urban Canyon" patio with an Aztec-motif mural painted by **David Omar White's** class at the MFA. With TVs blaring sports as young singles try to corral one another, brace yourself for bustle and din. ♦ Pan-American ♦ Daily 11:30AM-10PM. 384 Boylston St (between Arlington and Berkeley Sts). 859.8555 &

25 Women's Educational and Industrial Union (WEIU) Floating above this local institution's decorative entry (the building was designed by **Parker, Thomas, and Rice** in 1906, and restored in 1973 by **Shepley, Bulfinch, Richardson & Abbott**) is a gilded swan: WEIU chose this symbol for a logo because the union was launched in 1877, the same year the **Swan Boats** settled in the **Public Garden's** lagoon. A small group of women established WEIU to further employment and educational opportunities and to help the elderly, disabled, and poor. In 1891 **Julia Ward Howe** became the first president of the **Traveler's Information Exchange,** which began as a secret underground organization for women travelers, unaccompanied by men, to share information. Today men participate in all WEIU programs. In 1926 **Amelia Earhart** found a job as a social worker through WEIU's career services program; her application was noted "Has a sky pilot's license???"

The genteel retail shop run by this private social service organization is a favorite with Bostonians, particularly at holiday time. Staffed by WEIU's friendly volunteers, the store is filled with handmade articles of all kinds, books and toys for children, knitting and craft supplies, stationery and wrapping papers, and a wealth of household treasures. Be sure to visit the antique consignment shop on the upper level where great finds often surface. ♦ M-F 10AM-6PM; Sa 10AM-5PM. 356 Boylston St (between Arlington and Berkeley Sts). 536.5651 &

25 Shreve, Crump & Low Since 1800, innumerable Brahmin brides have registered at this renowned institution, and countless marriages have been launched with jewelry, sterling, crystal and china purchased from the city's jeweler of choice. You can also pick up your favorite new baby's little silver cup here, order personalized stationery, or peruse exclusive New England items. Also famous is the antiques department, which displays 18th- and 19th-century English and American furniture and prints; China-trade furniture and porcelain; and English, Irish, and American silver. The service here is assiduous and expert. ♦ M-Sa 9:30AM-5:30PM. 330 Boylston St (at Arlington St). 267.9100

Arlington Street Church, Unitarian Universalist

Back Bay

26 Arlington Street Church, Unitarian Universalist This church's most striking feature is its shapely tower (pictured above), inspired by **St. Martin's-in-the-Fields** in London. The first building erected in Back Bay (completed in 1861), this simple brownstone structure by **Arthur Gilman** was quite conservative in style—as if unsure of its leadership role in storming the mud flats. The outspoken minister **William Ellery Channing** served here for years; his statue just across the way in the **Public Garden** keeps watch still. A staunch abolitionist, Channing invited **Harriet Beecher Stowe** and **William Lloyd Garrison** to address his congregation. During the Vietnam War, the church was active in the peace movement. **Reverend Kim Crawford Harvie** now ministers here; attendance has skyrocketed since her arrival. Inside, look for the numerous Tiffany windows. ♦ Service Su 11AM. 351 Boylston St (at Arlington St). 536.7050

26 The Parish Cafe $ Named for a fictional boîte in Gabriel García Márquez's *Love in the Time of Cholera*, this intentionally funky cafe—owned by **Gordon Wilcox** of **The Rattlesnake Bar & Grill** right across the street—features sandwiches that are homages to the great chefs of Boston: **Lydia Shire, Chris Schlesinger,** et al. ♦ American/Takeout ♦ Daily 11:30AM-1AM. 361 Boylston St (between Arlington and Berkeley Sts). 247.4777 &

27 Harbridge House In 1893 Boston's grande dame and arts patron **Mrs. J. Montgomery Sears** combined 12 Arlington Street, a formidable five-story French-Italian-style mansion built by **Arthur Gilman** in 1860, with 1 Commonwealth Avenue, creating a small palace to house her famous art collection and music room. Pianist **Ignace Paderewski** and violinist **Fritz Kreisler** visited Mrs. Sears here, as did **John Singer Sargent,** who executed a portrait of his patron and her daughter at home. Gilman also designed **Arlington Street Church** down the block. ♦ 12 Arlington St (at Commonwealth Ave)

28 Goethe Institute, German Cultural Center New England's branch of the Munich-based institute inhabits an Italian Renaissance Revival building erected in 1901 by **Ogden Codman** for Boston financier **Eben Howard Gay** to house his formidable Chippendale and Adams furniture collection, parts of which are now in the **Museum of Fine Arts,** where Gay donated the **Chippendale Wing.** The institute's library collection of more than 6,000 volumes and 40 periodicals and newspapers is open to the public, though only cardholders may check out materials. Language programs and film series, exhibitions, and other cultural events are also offered.

Back Bay

♦ Offices M-F 9AM-5PM; Library W, F noon-6PM, Th noon-8PM, first Saturday of every month 10AM-4PM. 170 Beacon St (between Arlington and Berkeley Sts). 262.6050

29 The Gibson House Facades can only reveal so much; here's your best chance to peer into private Back Bay life. Three generations of Gibsons lived in decorous luxury in this Victorian residence, one of Back Bay's earliest. It was built for **Catherine Hammond Gibson** and bequeathed nearly a century later to the **Victorian Society in America** by her grandson **Charles** to be made into a museum enshrining his family's life and times. Not much to look at on the outside, inside is a wonderful six-story repository of perfectly preserved Victoriana. The Gibsons' ghosts would be quite content to wander through their beloved, dim rooms (sunshine was considered common then), still crowded with the ornaments, overstuffed furniture, fixtures, keepsakes, and curios they amassed and passed down to one another. The tour takes you into the kitchen, laundry, and other service areas so you get a full portrait of daily life at the Gibsons'. ♦ Admission. Groups of 12 or more by appointment only. W-Su 2-5PM, May-Oct; Sa-Su 2-5PM, Nov-Apr. Tours 1PM, 2PM, 3PM. Closed all major public holidays and some religious holidays. 137 Beacon St (between Arlington and Berkeley Sts). 267.6338

29 Marlborough Street A peaceful, shady, residential street in the midst of urbane Back Bay, Marlborough Street is humbler than Commonwealth Avenue, but has aged nicely. Many families live in the well-kept town houses adorned with tidy little gardens, and students share the blocks nearer Massachusetts Avenue. Every 14th of July Marlborough is blocked off near the **French Library** for the annual **Bastille Day** celebration, an evening of dining, music, and dancing that Bostonians enjoy with French flair—as if Lafayette never left.

30 The French Library in Boston Ever since the dashing young **Marquis de Lafayette** won over Bostonians' hearts, the city has had a special fondness for all things French. If you're walking on Marlborough Street and overhear a conversation in French—a common occurrence—the speakers could be walking to or from The French Library (pictured above), Boston's center for French language and culture since 1946. The library today holds more than 45,000 books on a great many topics, and hundreds of cassettes, records, and periodicals. A special treat is its collection of *bandes dessinées,* comic books for mature readers, which offer a good workout in idiomatic and colloquial French. You may borrow books only if you're a member. The library offers language lessons and hosts an annual **Bastille Day** celebration, lectures, exhibitions, concerts, children's activities, and many other events. There's a cozy reading room and a theater where French films are regularly screened. Whether to ponder Sartre, flip through a travel guide, get a quick phrase translation, or ask anything at all about *La Belle France,* this is the place to come to. ♦ Tu, F-Sa 10AM-5PM; W-Th 10AM-8PM. 53 Marlborough St (at Berkeley St). 266.4351

31 First and Second Church In 1968 **William Robert Ware** and **Henry Van Brunt's** 1867 First Church burned down, but the conflagration spared some remnants that **Paul Rudolph** ingeniously incorporated into this 1971 hybrid, built under the combined auspices of the First and Second churches. Rudolph is best known for **Yale University's School of Art and Architecture** in New Haven, CT. Even using coarse striated concrete—the brutal material that is his trademark—Rudolph creates poignant connections with the ruined fragments, particularly the square stone tower and rose window. ◆ M-F 9AM-3PM, June-Aug (call first); M-F 9AM-5PM, Sept-May. 66 Marlborough St (at Berkeley St). 267.6730 ఉ

32 First Lutheran Church Entering from Berkeley Street, enjoy a quiet moment in the small landscaped courtyard nestled against this modest brick church, designed by **Pietro Belluschi** in 1959. ◆ 299 Berkeley St (at Marlborough St). 536.8851

33 Commonwealth Avenue This expansive, ruler-straight street was the major clue that the new Back Bay wouldn't resemble Boston's mazelike older districts. Modeled after the grand Parisian boulevards, "Comm Ave"—its undignified, unpunctuated nickname—was the first of its kind in America, setting a chic French example for the rest of Back Bay to follow; in fact, the **French Consulate** is located at No. 3. The boulevard is 240 feet wide, with a 100-foot-long central mall that **Winston Churchill** deemed one of the world's most beautiful. The avenue is shaded with elm trees and planted with statues memorializing both the famous and forgotten. May visitors are lucky, arriving when the magnolias are in bloom. This Victorian promenade was once the place for the fashionable to stroll and be seen. Today a more casual collection of Bostonians ambles along, including plenty of dogwalkers and young matrons wheeling infants. The block after block of handsome buildings were once aristocratic town houses, but now boast luxury condos, apartments, and businesses. Unfortunately, a number of homes bear the indignity of having suburbanite roof decks and unsympathetic stories tacked on, ruining many a graceful roofline. The boulevard's northern, sunny side was the most desirable residential stretch in Back Bay, and many showplaces remain. Comm Ave starts to run out of charm when one nears Mass Ave and Kenmore Square beyond, however, so linger longest closer to the **Public Garden.**

33 Baylies Mansion In the early 1900s textile industrialist **Walter C. Baylies** moved to Boston, married into a wealthy family, and promptly metamorphosed into a full-fledged Brahmin. He tore down an 1861 house to build this showy Italianate mansion (designed by **Thomas and Rice** in 1912), adding a fabulous Louis XIV ballroom for his daughter's debut. A site for glittering society events, the room did its stint of civic service, too: during World War I bandages were rolled here. Cohabiting with the large Baylies entourage was the family's pet squirrel, who reportedly snacked on the costly draperies. Since 1941 this has been the home of the **Boston Center for Adult Education.** Many of the mansion's original ornament and interior finishes remain untouched. ◆ 5 Commonwealth Ave (between Arlington and Berkeley Sts)

The first long-distance telephone call was made from Boston to New York City on 27 March 1884.

34 First Baptist Church Henry Hobson Richardson was just starting to flex his creative muscles when he won the commission for this 1871 puddingstone church (originally called **New Brattle Square Church**) in a competition. Its marvelous campanile springs into the air to create one of Back Bay's most striking silhouettes. The belfry's frieze was modeled in Paris by **Frédéric-Auguste Bartholdi,** sculptor of the **Statue of Liberty** (Bartholdi had a way with drapery), and its scenes depict the sacraments of baptism, communion, marriage, and death. Some of the sculpted faces supposedly belong to famous Bostonians, including **Hawthorne, Emerson,** and **Longfellow.**

Protruding proudly from the corners, the angels' trumpets won them the irreverent nickname, "The Holy Bean Blowers." Come at sunset to admire their profiles etched crisply against a darkening sky. Unfortunately, the original congregation disbanded and funds ran out, so Richardson's lofty plans for the church interior never came to be. ◆ M-F 9AM-4PM. Service Su 11AM. 110 Commonwealth Ave (at Clarendon St). 267.3148

35 Hotel Vendôme You'd think the marsh-bottomed Back Bay would sag under the weight of this magnificent monster, a hybrid of **William G. Preston's** 1871 corner building and **J.F. Ober's** main building, both renovated in 1975 by **Stahl Bennett.** For a hundred years, the Vendôme reigned as Boston's most fashionable hotel, the only one where **Sarah Bernhardt** would deign to lay her weary head. Gen-

eral Ulysses S. Grant, President Grover Cleveland, John Singer Sargent, Oscar Wilde, Mark Twain, and countless other worthies stayed here.

The Vendôme boasted unheard-of luxuries: it was the first public building in the city to have electric lighting, powered in 1822 by a plant **Thomas Edison** had designed; and every room had a private bathroom, fireplace, and steam heat. Inevitably, the Vendôme's heyday passed and it became a run-down white elephant. In the 1970s the hotel's interior decor was obliterated during renovation, and a terrible fire destroyed portions of the roof and building. Now a condominium complex, the hotel has accepted its comedown as gracefully as possible. To the left at **Dartmouth Street** is Preston's original structure, forced to play a supporting role to Ober's enormous addition on the right. The duo's conjoining marble facades ripple with opulent ornamentation. ◆ 160 Commonwealth Ave (at Dartmouth St)

According to a 1701 Boston law that's still alive and kicking, Paul Revere could have been hauled in by the local police for speeding on his midnight ride from Boston to Lexington. The law states: "No person having the care of a horse or other beast of burden shall drive, or ride. . . at a greater rate of speed than seven miles per hour in a public street."

Within the Hotel Vendôme:

Spasso ★★$$ Painted the color of butter, with lively prints and graffiti and a sunken patio on Commonwealth Avenue, this neo-trattoria is jolly and appealing—its very name means "fun." Beyond the unusual pastas and pizzas (e.g., wild mushroom and pine nuts), there are several substantial *secondi*, and an array of *dolci*, too. As the menu advises, "Mangia! Mangia!" ♦ Italian ♦ M-W, Su 11:30AM-10PM; Th-Sa 11:30AM-11PM. 160 Commonwealth Ave (between Dartmouth and Exeter Sts). Valet parking. 536.8656 ♿

36 William Lloyd Garrison Statue In **Olin L. Warner's** posthumous (1885) rendition, Boston's famed abolitionist looks as though he had been intently reading when the artist interrupted and asked him to pose; Garrison suggests a man taut with energy, feigning relaxation, stretching back in his armchair with his books and papers hastily stuffed underneath. His profile is memorable. The fiery inscription

Back Bay

"I am in earnest—I will not equivocate. I will not excuse. I will not retreat a single inch, and I will be heard!" expresses all of Garrison's unquenchable conviction and is from the inaugural manifesto of *The Liberator,* a journal he founded and edited. ♦ Commonwealth Mall (between Dartmouth and Exeter Sts)

37 Ames-Webster House This mansion was built by **Peabody and Stearns** in 1872 for railroad tycoon and US congressman **Frederick L. Ames;** its massive pavilion and porte cochere were added 10 years later by **John Sturgis,** and the whole was renovated in 1969 by **CBT.** The exterior is impressive enough, with wrought-iron gates, a two-story conservatory, a monumental tower, and a commanding chimney. But inside is the extraordinary grand hall bedecked with elaborately carved oak woodwork.

The theatrical staircase ascends toward the skylit stained-glass dome, past murals by French painter **Benjamin Constant.** There's a compact jewel of a ballroom, celery-green-and-gilt and delicately proportioned, particularly its "heavens," the balcony where musicians played. The house is now used for private offices and, unfortunately, it is now inaccessible to the public. ♦ 306 Dartmouth St (at Commonwealth Ave)

38 Admiral Samuel Eliot Morison Statue In **Penelope Jencks'** statue, the sailor and historian is seated on a rock by the sea, binoculars in hand, dressed in oilskins with a jaunty yachting cap on his head. Notice the coppery lichen on his stony perch, and the sand crabs on the beach below. Smaller rocks are inscribed with quotes from Morison's books, such as "Dream dreams then write them/Aye, but live them first." Just across the street is the exclusive **St. Botolph Club,** to which Morison belonged. ♦ Commonwealth Mall (between Exeter and Fairfield Sts)

39 Algonquin Club It would be hard to find a haughtier facade in the city than this one by **McKim, Mead & White,** with its overblown frieze and projecting pair of falcons. The Italian Renaissance Revival palace, built in 1887 for a private club, certainly catches the eye with its self-confident, flamboyant architectural maneuvers. ♦ 217 Commonwealth Ave (between Exeter and Fairfield Sts)

39 First Corps of Cadets Museum This one's for military history buffs. Established in 1726, the **First Corps of Cadets** is one of America's oldest military organizations. Members have served in most US wars and conflicts. The corps began as bodyguards to the royal governors of the Province of Massachusetts Bay. **John Hancock** served as colonel in 1774. The museum holds examples of most arms in existence, dating back to **King George II.** Many weapons and memorabilia were brought back from action by corps members. Also featured are flags, uniforms, drums, and paintings. Free two-hour tours are offered by appointment only. ♦ 227 Commonwealth Ave (between Exeter and Fairfield Sts). 267.1726

40 267 Commonwealth $$ This intimate Victorian hotel is owned—and was restored—by **Bob Vila,** former host of "This Old House," a popular public TV series. An 1880 brownstone that was once a single-family residence, No. 267 is broken up into five one-bedrooms and four studios, with high ceilings, handsome woodwork, marble or handcarved fireplaces, and kitchenettes. The studio rooms actually feel grander since they weren't divided to create sitting rooms. Room No. 7 was the master bedroom and overlooks Commonwealth Avenue and its mall, as does No. 5. The penthouse room is a contemporary addition with modern furnishings. About half the guests are corporate relocations; many are affiliated with hospitals. Opera, ballet, and music stars often stay here. Laundry facilities are in the building; weekly rates are available. Though credit cards aren't accepted, the hotel will bill companies. ♦ Between Fairfield and Gloucester Sts. No credit cards. 267.6776

Restaurants/Clubs: Red
Shops/ 🍂 Outdoors: Green

Hotels: Blue
Sights/Culture: Black

41 Nickerson House Architects **McKim, Mead & White's** last Back Bay residence offers one monumental gesture in the sweep of its bulging granite bowfront. The 1895 building is a model of chilly restraint, but enjoyed a brief fling as the site of two of Boston's most lavish debutante balls, held by **Mrs. Pickman,** wife of the house's second owner, for her daughters. ♦ 303 Commonwealth Ave (between Gloucester and Hereford Sts)

42 Burrage Mansion Not all Bostonians were willing to surrender their highfalutin aspirations to fit Back Bay's decorous mold. Certainly not **Albert Burrage;** his theatrical 1899 limestone mansion simultaneously pays homage to the **Vanderbilts'** Fifth Avenue mansions and **Chenonceaux,** the French château on the Loire. A multitude of strange carved figures peer down from and crawl across the facade's excess of ornament. Burrage once cultivated orchids in the splendid glass-domed greenhouse at the rear. The mansion is now a rather luxurious retirement home. Peek inside to see how enthusiastically the interior competes with the exterior, particularly in the sculpted marble staircase and abundant embellishments. ♦ 314 Commonwealth Ave (at Hereford St)

43 Oliver Ames Mansion The original owner was head of the Ames Shovel Manufacturing Company, president of the Union Pacific Railroad, philanthropist, owner of the Booth Theatre in New York, and a Massachusetts governor. Clearly, a lion like Ames would command Back Bay's biggest mansion. **Henry H. Richardson** prepared a sketch for the house, but it was rejected and **Carl Fehmer** took over in 1882. Look at the frieze panels of putti and floral ornament portraying the activities that occurred in the rooms behind. Now an office building, the Oliver Ames Mansion served as the longtime headquarters of the National Casket Company. ♦ 355 Commonwealth Ave (at Massachusetts Ave)

44 Church Court Condominium In 1978 an up-and-coming young architect named **Graham Gund** caused a furor when he purchased the burnt-out shell of **Mt. Vernon Church** for commercial development, but this elegant amalgam—with a clerestory topped by sculptor **Gene Cauthon's** ethereal bronze angel—set a brave standard for creative reuse. ♦ 492 Marlborough St (near Massachusetts Ave)

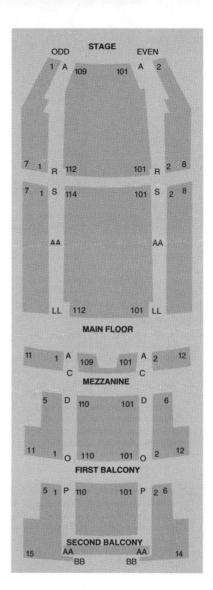

After graduating from Harvard College in 1859, Henry Hobson Richardson, a Louisiana native, launched into architectural studies at the Ecole des Beaux Arts in Paris. Returning to America seven years later, Richardson quickly advanced his individualistic style by creating works that were at once robust and monumental. He began his practice in New York, then moved to Boston after winning the Trinity Church commission. As Trinity's resplendent interior illustrates, Richardson liked to pull out all the stops, enlisting celebrated artists and sculptors to collaborate on the decoration of his houses, churches, schools, libraries, hospitals, bridges, and railroad stations. He even designed furniture like his predecessor—architect Charles Bullfinch—but winning far greater fame.

45 Berklee Performance Center Associated with the highly regarded **Berklee College of Music,** the center (see the plan above) hosts popular performances of all types of contemporary music, especially jazz and folk. Call for performances and times. The box office takes cash only. ♦ Admission. Box office M-Sa 10AM-6PM. 136 Massachusetts Ave (at Boylston St). No credit cards. 266.1400, recorded concert information 266.7455

Fanny Merrit Farmer introduced modern measurements, such as the teaspoon, to American cooking. Her cooking school, founded in 1902, occupied 40 Hereford Street (now the site of condominiums) for years. Farmer's *Boston Cooking-School Cookbook* was a smash hit, and her books still grace kitchens all across America.

In 1972 Boston mayor Kevin White bailed the Rolling Stones out of jail so the band could keep a concert date at Boston Garden.

46 Sheraton Boston Hotel & Towers $$$
Here's where the sports teams stay, with one
staffer solely dedicated to their needs and
wants. The 1,250-room hotel abuts the **Hynes
Convention Center,** which conventioneers can
enter without ever going outdoors. A business
service center handles word processing, copy-
ing, and other office functions. One of the 29-
story twin towers offers four floors that are a
minihotel-within-a-hotel, with quieter rooms,
butler service, and a VIP lounge.

Every December the hotel sponsors the **Bill
Rodgers' Jingle Bell Run**—a fun run to bene-
fit the **Special Olympics**—and about 4,000
people participate, wearing Christmas regalia.
Get a room up high for good views of the
Christian Science International Headquarters'
geometries or the **Charles River.** A number of
floors are dedicated to nonsmokers and handi-
capped persons. Small pets are allowed. Other
amenities: 24-hour room service, an indoor/
outdoor pool, a health club with a Jacuzzi, and
a beauty salon and barber. ♦ 39 Dalton St (at
Boylston St). 236.2000, 800/325.3535; fax
236.1702 ♿

Within the Sheraton Boston Hotel & Towers:

The Mass. Bay Company ★$$ Come here
when you can't tolerate the lines or prices at
Boston's higher-profile seafood houses. Specialties include award-winning clam chowder,
salmon and trout smoked on the premises, and
fish grilled over mesquite charcoal. ♦ Seafood
♦ Daily 5:30-11PM. Reservations are recommended. 236.8787 ♿

Back Bay

47 Back Bay Hilton $$$ A stone's throw from
the **Hynes Convention Center,** this rather non-
descript 25-story Hilton caters assiduously to
the business traveler. All 335 rooms are sound-
proofed, with small bathrooms, bay windows
you can open, and calm decor, and many have
balconies. Amenities include a year-round
swimming pool; access for a daily usage fee to
a Fitcorp® health facility on site; 24-hour room
service and parking garage; meeting and ban-
quet rooms; and nonsmokers' floors. In addi-
tion to a lounge, there's an upscale nightclub.
♦ 40 Dalton St (at Belvidere St). 236.1100,
800/874.0663 ♿

Within Back Bay Hilton:

Boodle's of Boston ★★$$$ A sillier name
for such an earnest grill room would be hard to
find. The English decor is a little ponderous, but
perfectly appropriate to the main business at
hand: expertly grilling massive cuts of meat
over hardwoods such as sassafras and hickory.
Seafood and vegetables take many a pleasant
turn on the grill here, too, and there are oyster
dishes galore. You can dress up the entrées by
choosing from 20 butters, sauces, and condiments. ♦ Steakhouse/American ♦ Daily 7-
10:30AM, 11:30AM-2PM, 5:30-11PM. Reservations recommended for dinner. 266.3537 ♿

**48 Christian Science International Head-
quarters** It's easy to overlook the little acorn
from which this gigantic oak grew: **Franklin J.
Welch's** original 1894 Romanesque Christian
Science Mother Church, which founder **Mary
Baker Eddy** called "our prayer in stone," is now
dwarfed by a behemoth extension (the 1906
addition of **Charles E. Brigham** with **Solon S.
Beman, Brigham Coveney and Bisbee**) soaring to a height of 224 feet. This Renaissance
basilica bears the weight of its towering dome
like giant Atlas holding the world upon his
shoulders. Designed to seat 3,000, the basilica
boasts one of the world's largest working pipe
organs, a 13,595-pipe **Aeolian Skinner** manufactured locally. Located on what was the outer
edge of respectability, in the midst of tenements and crowded residential blocks, the old
and new church clung together until 1973,
when **I.M. Pei's** master plan carved out a great
swath of 22 acres, populating its core with
monumental church administration buildings.

Strategically flanking the mother church like
Secret Service agents are the 28-story **Church
Administration Building;** the fan-shaped **Sunday School;** and the low-slung **Colonnade
Building.** They surround a vast public space
dominated by a 670-foot-long, 100-foot wide
reflecting pool rimmed with red granite, a
pleasant feature with a hidden agenda: to cool
water from the air-conditioning system. The
circular fountain at one end is as dull as an
empty dish when shut off, but, gushing on hot
days, it becomes a hectic playground and con-
tributes a badly needed note of spontaneity to
this austere, over-planned setting. With rows of
manicured trees, flowerbeds, and water, the
plaza is a popular lunchtime spot. But in the
winter the wind can whip through here fiercely,
treating the office tower as a sail.

To one side of the church is the **Christian Science Publishing Society** building, offices for
the well-regarded *Christian Science Monitor,*
founded in 1908. Inside, look up at the two extraordinary glass globe lanterns suspended
from the lobby ceiling; one lights up to tell the
time, the other the date. Follow signs to the
fabulous **Mapparium,** a vividly colored stained-
glass globe 30 feet in diameter, traversed by a
glass bridge. Since glass doesn't absorb sound
you can stand at one end and send whispered
messages echoing eerily across the way to a
partner. Made of more than 600 kiln-fired glass
panels, the Mapparium is illuminated from behind by 300 lights. Designed by the building's
architect, **Chester Lindsay Churchill,** the globe
was completed in 1932 and has not been
altered since. It's outdated, but all the more
interesting for its pre-World War II record of
political boundaries. Free ongoing 10-minute
tours of the Mapparium and free guided tours
of the Mother Church and extension are offered. ♦ Mother Church Tu-Sa 10AM-4PM; Su
11:15AM-2PM; Mapparium Tu-Sa 9:30AM-
4PM. Between Massachusetts Ave and Huntington Ave. 450.2000

49 Horticultural Hall Founded in 1829, the **Massachusetts Horticultural Society** sponsors the nation's oldest annual spring flower show. It is a spectacular event, but has bloomed too large for the exhibition hall (designed in 1901 by **Wheelwright and Haven** and now on the **National Register of Historic Places**); the show had to be uprooted to the impersonal (and remote) **Bayside Exposition Center** in Dorchester. The society launched America's school-gardening movement, which now brings gardening studies into many Boston public schools and spreads the love of growing things via its traveling Plantmobile exhibits. In addition to operating the world's largest independent horticultural library, the society runs a shop selling seeds, books, and prints. You can even call for free advice. The society's decorative building—which it now shares with other organizations, such as *Boston* magazine— makes a striking couple with **Symphony Hall** across the street. ♦ 300 Massachusetts Ave (at Huntington Ave). 536.9280 &

50 Newbury Street This showplace street gets a bit less so toward Mass Ave, although its less fashionable stretch has acquired a youthful panache. With the third-highest rents in the US, coming in behind Beverly Hills' Rodeo Drive and Palm Beach's Worth Avenue, Newbury Street aspires to commercial heights. Partake of the lively Saturday scene. A blend of New York's Columbus and Madison avenues, this is the only street in Boston where you'll feel underdressed just strolling along. Newbury Street pays homage to glamour: in addition to the boutiques and galleries, there are dozens of hair "designers" (several dozen along this stretch), tanning and facial salons, and modeling studios. For those who seek beauty-to-go, there's art, literature, antiques, and costly geegaws galore, plus a thriving cafe society.

50 360 Newbury Street An early 1900s warehouse designed by **Arthur Bowditch** was just recently metamorphosed into a dramatic iconoclast by architect **Frank O. Gehry** with the assistance of **Schwartz/Silver Architects.** No. 360 towers over the Massachusetts Avenue end of Newbury Street. Viewed from the Massachusetts Turnpike and from many Back Bay angles, the building is a challenging, alert, eye-catching presence—and, though critically lauded, not universally beloved. Its brash projecting struts, canopy, and cornice make it appear scaffolded and still in process, as if the building hasn't quite decided what it wants to be yet. Step into the bank-breaking splendor of the lobby on the Newbury Street side, and also check the wall next door for **Morgan Bulkeley's** surrealist mural *Tramount,* depicting—in odd little vignettes—the history of the city.

Within 360 Newbury Street:

Tower Records/Video Calling itself "the largest record store in the known world," this enormous multilevel emporium is one of a chain of 94 stores in the US, England, and Japan, and sells LPs, 45s, CDs, cassettes, cassette and CD singles, and videos. They cover all the music bases, but this isn't the place to come for unconventional, hard-to-find recordings. You can purchase tickets to most concerts in person at the **Ticketmaster** counter. A lot of late-night socializing goes on here here. ♦ M 9AM-12:30AM; Tu-Sa 9AM-midnight; Su 11AM-midnight. 360 Newbury St (at Massachusetts Ave). 247.5900 &

51 The Capital Grille ★★$$$$ Top-grade steak—dry-aged in plain view on the premises—is this upscale restaurant's primary raison d'être; some straightforward seafood is served as well. The decor is modeled after an old-fashioned men's club: lots of dark paneling (lifted from a 16th-century Welsh castle), marble floors, and a long brass bar with private wine lockers. It attracts a prosperous crowd whose business image requires a certain show of conspicuous consumption. ♦ American ♦ M-Th, Su 5-10PM; F-Sa 5-11PM. Lounge 4PM-closing. Valet parking. 359 Newbury St (between Massachusetts Ave and Hereford St). Reservations recommended. 262.8900 &

51 Johnson Paint Company Look for the famous sign with bright multicolored stripes and real gold leaf. For more than 50 years the Johnson family's business has occupied this former carriage house, where horses owned by wealthy Back Bay residents once slept. In addition to selling good old-fashioned paint products—they've carried the same lines of paint since 1936—the store is a fixture in the fine arts community, stocking what the staff refers to as "fancy painting stuff" such as brushes

Back Bay

imported from five countries, easels, tables, pads, powdered pigments, and art books. If you have a tricky wall color to match, try Johnson: renowned city-wide, the color mixer has worked here for more than 30 years and is better than a computer at matching samples. Classes run continually on faux painting, glazing, gilding, and other techniques. You can even buy a T-shirt with the store's gaily colored emblem. ♦ M-F 7:30AM-5:30PM; Sa 8:30AM-1PM. 355 Newbury St (between Hereford St and Massachusetts Ave). 536.4244 &

51 Avenue Victor Hugo Bookshop Just a glance in the window reveals what a treasure trove this used bookstore is. Row upon row of nine-foot-tall bookshelves—be ready for some stretching on tiptoe—are crammed with used books in 250 subject areas, ranging in price from 25¢ paperback romances to $200 limited editions. Put yourself in a nostalgic mood browsing through the used periodicals dating from 1854 to the present. There's some new fiction, comic books, a great card and postcard selection, old maps, and vintage sheet music, too. Prowling the premises is **Feet,** the store's lordly cat— "All used bookstores should have one," says owner **Vincent McCaffrey. ♦** M-F 8AM-9PM; Sa 10AM-8PM; Su noon-8PM. 339 Newbury St (between Hereford St and Massachusetts Ave). 266.7746 &

51 **The Ultimate Bagel Company** This narrow storefront lives up to its boastful name, with the plumpest, tastiest bagels (including a healthful eight-grain wheat germ variety) and assorted cream-cheese spreads (some are yogurt-based and cholesterol-free), plus soups, salads, and sandwiches. The restful decor and tables-for-two make eating inside an appealing option. Check out the rear-wall mural, a faux Florentine garden painted by **Bopäs,** the partnership of decorative painters **Gedas Paskauskas** and **Robert Grady. ♦** American/Takeout ♦ Daily 7AM-7:30PM. 335 Newbury St (between Massachusetts Ave and Hereford St). 247.1010 & Also at: 1310 Massachusetts Ave (at Harvard Sq), Cambridge. 964.8990

52 **Trident Booksellers & Cafe** ★$ Calling itself "Boston's alternative bookstore," Trident sells some fiction but is particularly strong in Jungian psychology, acupuncture, poetry, Eastern religions, and Buddhist, women's, and metaphysical works. Crystals, incense, scented oils, tarot cards, and bonsai trees are also on

Back Bay

sale. The little cafe is a popular neighborhood meeting place for a broad spectrum of Bostonians, who come for its no-fuss, down-to-earth, tasty menu of homemade soups, sandwiches, bagels, croissants, and rib-sticking desserts like carrot cake, plus a variety of coffees and cappuccino. Readings are held every Sunday from 4:30PM to 6PM, and are free (donations requested). ♦ American ♦ M-F 9AM-11PM; Sa 10AM-11PM; Su noon-9PM. 338 Newbury St (between Hereford St and Massachusetts Ave). 267.8688 &

☺ Newbury Comics

52 **Newbury Comics** This oddball store started as a comic-book outpost, then branched into anything music-related. They still sell comics, including some aimed at adult readers, but Newbury's eccentric inventory now encompasses independent label and import music in CDs, cassettes, and records; music and comic T-shirts; music videos; music books; portable "music makers" and accessories; posters; biker-style jewelry; and bizarre novelties. College students flock here for hard-to-find recordings. ♦ M-Sa 10AM-9PM; Su noon-7PM. 332 Newbury St (between Hereford St and Massachusetts Ave). 236.4930 &

52 **John Fleuvog** If your feet want to make a particularly eccentric fashion statement, don a pair of Fleuvog's clunky Munster platforms fit for Frankenstein; or the Bump, a style for L'il Abner; or Doc Marten's incredibly blocky styles. English-made in plenty of leathers and colors, with crests and bows and buckles and tapestry, these shoes are ready for action of some sort. ♦ M-Sa 11AM-7PM; Su 1-6PM. 328 Newbury St (between Hereford St and Massachusetts Ave). 266.1079

52 **The Nostalgia Factory** "The Eye Shall Never Rest" is the credo of this gallery bursting with old collectibles and ephemera. Owners **Rudy** and **Barbara Franchi** scour fairs, flea markets, and England to come up with their ever-changing assortment of rare posters, old postcards and advertisements, political buttons, antique signs, soda-pop art, English royalty souvenirs, and memorabilia of all kinds. A browser's delight, yes, but the gallery also portrays more serious changing attitudes and trends: a fascinating display of magazine advertising from the '20s through the '50s chronicles products once considered safe and now banned or warned against, such as cigarettes, asbestos shingling, and lead paint. ♦ M-Sa 10AM-7PM; Su 11AM-7PM. 324 Newbury St (between Hereford St and Massachusetts Ave). 236.8754

52 **Boston Architectural Center (BAC)** This bulky concrete block of a building (a 1967 exemplar of "Brutalism" by **Ashley, Myer & Associates,** now called **Arrowstreet**) has turned out to be an unexpectedly amiable addition to Back Bay. Don't let the structure's contemporary look fool you; it houses a century-old school of architecture, the BAC, which began life in 1889 as a free atelier run by the **Boston Architectural Club,** where deserving youth were given drawing lessons. The BAC is unique in America today for requiring its students to work full-time as fledgling architects while taking classes at night from an all-volunteer faculty. The inviting, glass-sheathed ground floor is a public space for student work and art and architectural exhibitions.

On the building's exterior west wall, New York artist **Richard Haas** painted one of his best murals in 1977 and it has since become a Back Bay landmark. This six-story architectural trompe l'oeil is a cross-sectional view of a French neoclassical palace in the Beaux Arts style. Look for the mural's teasers: the shadow of a man against a corridor wall; a foot disappearing through a closing door; and a man appearing in a doorway on his way up to the top of the rotunda. ♦ Gallery M-Th 9AM-11PM; F-Sa 9AM-5PM; Su noon-5PM. 320 Newbury St (at Hereford St). 536.3170 &

53 Institute of Contemporary Art (ICA) and Engine and Hose House Number 33 A

19th-century police station and firehouse once shared this building, designed by city architect **Arthur H. Vinal,** but the police eventually moved next door (**Arrowstreet** performed the renovation in 1975) and the ICA moved in after **Graham Gund Associates** handsomely restored its half in 1975. Inside the Romanesque-style shell are multilevel galleries and a 140-seat theater for the ICA's mixed-media exhibitions, films, and performances in the visual arts. Established in 1936, the museum has no permanent collection and is famous for its eclectic, sometimes uneven, but always interesting array of work by known and unknown artists. One-of-a-kind in Boston, the ICA aims to be a research and development laboratory for new ideas. As you head over to the entrance, you'll see firefighters on the job, taking a break from time to time to watch the colorful crowd on the trendy art trail. And the ornate turret tower on the Hereford Street side is still used for drying fire hoses. ◆ Admission, free W-Th 5-9PM. W 5-9PM; Th noon-9PM; F-Su noon-5PM. 955 Boylston St (at Hereford St) 266.5152 ﬂ (limited access, call first)

53 Division Sixteen ★$ Located in a former

police station, this sleek Art Deco restaurant is a popular spot with students and youngish singles seeking same. At night there's inevitably a wait, and the horrendous din and clatter will drown out any conversation unless you insist on a booth in the back. But there is a reason to come here: monster portions of reasonably priced, decently prepared casual food, such as sandwiches, salads, omelets, burgers, nachos, and the like. The shoestring fries are made from scratch. On a weeknight, better still a rainy one, this place goes well with an evening at one of the movie theaters nearby. ◆ American ◆ Daily 11:30AM-2AM. 955 Boylston St (at Hereford St). 353.0870 ﬂ

54 John B. Hynes Veterans Memorial Convention Center Commonly called "the

Hynes," this facility (pictured below) is ordinarily not open to the public. Cross to the opposite side of Boylston Street to study the Hynes' impressive facade and ground-floor loggia, then peek inside at the magnificent main rotunda. Unlike many of Boston's newer buildings, the Hynes is much admired. Rebuilt in 1988 by **Kallmann, McKinnell & Wood Architects,** who also designed Boston's unusual **City Hall,** the convention center is so conciliatory toward its surroundings that it's easy to forget it can handle a convention of 22,000. Bankers, dentists, lumberers, and teachers—even the **Association of Old Crows**—pass through the handsome portals. ◆ 900 Boylston St (at Gloucester St). 954.2000, 424.8585 (recorded information) ﬂ

55 Prudential Center Home of the insurance

giant, "The Pru" is a dowdy complex, unloved by many and the worse for wear. It houses six million square feet of offices, apartments, hotels, and stores in a network of elevated blocky buildings and windy plazas, parts of which appear abandoned to the ravages of time. But when the sprawling 27-acre Prudential Center was plopped down here in the early '60s by **Charles Luckman and Associates** and **Hoyle, Doran, and Berry,** it covered the unsightly **Boston & Albany** rail yards, introduced a new scale to Back Bay, and stirred high hopes for a rejuvenated modern Boston. It's worth a visit to grasp the radical '60s concept of American urban renewal. The Pru is currently undergoing a major overhaul; with luck, the complex will get a brighter image.

Once the city's tallest skyscraper, the inelegant 52-story **Prudential Tower** has been outraced to the heavens by its rival, the sleek **John Hancock Tower.** Still, many Bostonians have grown

fond of the homely Pru Tower. Take an elevator up to the **Skywalk,** the observation deck on the 50th floor, and see what's happening for miles around. Or enjoy the view with a drink at the **Top of the Hub.** (Don't bother with a meal; the restaurant is just further proof that penthouse restaurants don't live up to their aerial heights.) At Christmastime, an enormous tree is illuminated on the plaza in front of the tower, facing Boylston Street. ◆ Admission to Skywalk. M-Sa 10AM-10PM; Su noon-10PM. 800 Boylston St (at Gloucester St). 236.3318 ﬂ

John B. Hynes Veterans Memorial Convention Center

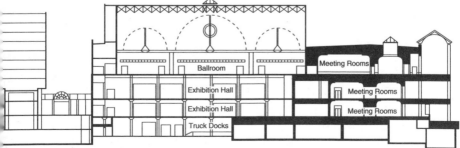

56 The Cactus Club ★$ The American Southwestern motif has gotten so out of hand, it's parody—intense aqua galore, O'Keeffe-esque skulls, a buffalo over the bar—but as the big, high-ceilinged rooms fill up, the design assault recedes. Beneath this garishly cheerful disguise lurks a fern bar. The nouvelle Southwestern cuisine highlights ribs, grilled fish and meats, pastas, barbecue, and the like, far better than you might expect, with welcome accents such as fresh coriander and chipotle peppers. If you have a penchant for swimming in fishbowl-size glasses, you'll like the drinks. This has become a popular hangout for a youngish crowd. The restaurant inhabits the handsome **Tennis and Racquet Club** building (constructed in 1904), which has a splendid gate in its lobby that prevents access to upstairs offices after hours. ♦ Southwestern ♦ M-W, Su 11:30AM-10PM; Th 11:30AM-11PM; F-Sa 11:30AM-midnight. 939 Boylston St (at Hereford St). 236.0200 ♿

57 Steve's Greek & American Cuisine ★$ Lots of locals, students, and conventioneers from the nearby Hynes come to this cheerful restaurant whose owner, **Steve Kourtidis,** says, "It's our pleasure to serve the people." On one side is the take-out operation, on the other the pleasant plant-entwined dining room overlook-

Back Bay

ing Newbury Street. It sometimes gets smoky here from cigarettes. The menu features Greek and Middle Eastern favorites—moussaka, grape leaves, baklava, shish kebabs—and burgers and omelets. ♦ Greek American/Takeout ♦ M-Sa 7:30AM-10PM; Su 10AM-10PM. 62 Hereford St (at Newbury St). No credit cards. 267.1817

58 L'Espalier ★★★★$$$$ This refined and sophisticated establishment started Boston's restaurant revolution in 1978, yanking the city out of its doldrums into a new era of posh cuisine. **Frank McClelland,** acclaimed successor to the original owner, leans a bit more toward contemporary American cuisine using native products these days, but dinner at L'Espalier is as rarefied and highfalutin an event as ever. Set in a stately 1873 town house, the stunning dining rooms will satisfy your whim to experience Back Bay's heyday. The prix-fixe menu might include sautéed yellowfin tuna steaks, squab and fig salad, grilled partridge, or duck breast coupled with foie gras; every dish is tenderly treated and gorgeously presented in modest—

sometimes overly so—portions. The service is exceedingly proper. ♦ French ♦ M-Sa 6-10PM. 30 Gloucester St (between Newbury St and Commonwealth Ave). Valet parking. Jacket and tie recommended. Reservations required Friday through Sunday. 262.3023

58 Casa Romero ★$$$ The prices are steep, though there's compensation in the picturesque dining rooms brightened with hand-painted tiles and Mexican handicrafts. A number of dishes are outstanding: avocado soup, *mole poblano, puerco adobado* (pork with smoked chiles), and *flan al Cognac* are a sampling. Enter from Gloucester Street at the side alley that runs between Commonwealth Avenue and Newbury Street. ♦ Mexican ♦ M-Th, Su 5-10PM; F-Sa 5-11PM. 30 Gloucester St. Reservations recommended. 536.4341

59 Odeon Owner **David Christina** crisscrosses the US picking out one-of-a-kind accessories for men, women, and the home. The boutique's current and vintage selections include reconditioned antique telephones, hand-carved Kenya soapstone, wrought-iron candlesticks, jewelry ranging from rhinestones to avant-garde, amusing housewares, rayon shirts and boxer shorts, and great socks. ♦ M-Sa 11AM-7PM, Su noon-5PM. 285 Newbury St (between Gloucester and Hereford Sts). 536.1515

59 Miyako ★★$$ The former site of several trendy restaurants that lacked staying power, this choice duplex corner spot, with its roomy patio, makes the perfect setting for an elegant Japanese restaurant. The decor is minimalist—gray walls, the odd extravagant floral display—all the better to focus on exquisitely delicate tastes. A sushi bar is tucked into the sub-street level, and the airy second floor features traditional mat seating. ♦ Japanese ♦ M-Th, Su noon-10:30PM; F-Sa noon-11PM. 279 Newbury St (at Gloucester St). 236.0222

60 Culture Shock Twenty-six-year-old **Patrick Petty** is probably the most radical clothing designer working on Newbury Street, and his shop is decidedly the most daring. These are street styles with pedigrees: **Vivienne Westwood, Moschino, BCBG.** The clientele varies from Roxbury kids to suburban matrons, all equally energized by Petty's custom music mix. ♦ M-Th 11AM-8PM; F-Sa 11AM-9PM; Su noon-7PM. 286 Newbury St (between Gloucester and Hereford Sts). 859.7508

60 Cafe Jaffa ★$ An inviting storefront with broad picture windows and bare brick walls, this modest new cafe has been an instant hit with its authentic—and affordable—Middle Eastern fare: hummus, falafel, *schawarma,* and the like. ♦ Middle Eastern/Takeout ♦ M-Th 11AM-10:30PM; F-Sa 11AM-11PM; Su 2-10PM. 48 Gloucester St. 536.0230 &

61 Dad's Beantown Diner ★$ So what if the '50s-era decor (diamond-pattern aluminum paneling, glass bricks, turquoise banquettes, vintage photos) is a re-creation, not the real thing. Families nonetheless love the hearty food— "like Mom's!" boasts the menu—and reasonable prices, at least for this part of town. Meat loaf, pot roast, potpie—you can pile it on and still make room for Jello parfait. ♦ American/Takeout ♦ M-F 11AM-2AM; Sa-Su 10AM-2AM. 911 Boylston St (between Gloucester and Hereford Sts). 296.3237 &

62 Gyuhama ★$$ One of Boston's best sushi bars, Gyuhama is the only place in town serving lobster sashimi—a spectacular presentation that's not for the faint-hearted, since the lobster pieces may still be twitching when served! Less daring choices include delectable sukiyaki. The basement dining room is intimate, though a trifle seedy. There are always many Japanese diners, a testament to the fastidiously fresh and imaginatively prepared food. In fact, Gyuhama lures so many regulars that it can have a cliquey air. Dine early or be prepared for a wait. ♦ Japanese ♦ M-Sa noon-2:30PM, 5:30-10:30PM; Su noon-2:30PM, 5PM-2AM. 827 Boylston St (between Gloucester and Fairfield Sts). 437.0188

63 Fine Time Vintage Watch Gallery The owners are experienced timepiece dealers and specialize exclusively in buying, selling, restoring, and appraising fine vintage wristwatches and antique pocket watches, such as **Patek Philippe, Rolex, Vacheron, Hamilton Watch Company, Cartier,** and **Waltham.** They even carry authentic Mickey Mouse alarm clocks. You won't find any reproductions here—just the splendid real tick-tockers. ♦ Tu-Sa 10:30AM -5PM. 279 Newbury St (at Gloucester St). 536.5858

63 Nomad A one-stop shop for "folk art, jewelry, clothing in a global style," this pleasantly packed shop harbors a panoply of international finds—from Thailand hill-tribe garb to sparkly Frida Kahlo icon earrings. Enjoy the world-beat music while browsing. ♦ Daily 10AM-6PM. 279 Newbury St (between Gloucester and Fairfield Sts). 267.9677

Boston has long endured its prudish reputation. Note, for example, the advice of a 19th-century etiquette pamphlet: "The perfect hostess will see to it that the works of male and female authors be properly separated on her bookshelves. Their proximity, unless they happen to be married, should not be tolerated."

Restaurants/Clubs: Red   Hotels: Blue
Shops/ ✿ Outdoors: Green   Sights/Culture: Black

63 Davio's ★★$$$ This romantic, jewel-box restaurant, a favorite with Back Bay residents, features Northern Italian cuisine with continental finesse. The kitchen makes its own pastas and sausage, and lavishes attention on soups, seafood, venison, and veal. The wine list includes some costly Italian venerables. At the informal cafe upstairs, snack on fashionable pizzas and pastas at lower prices. There's a little terrace out back for fair-weather dining. ♦ Italian ♦ Cafe M-F 11:30AM-3PM, 5-11PM; Sa-Su 11:30AM-11PM. Dining room M-Sa 11.30AM-3PM, 5-11PM; Su 5-11PM. 269 Newbury St (between Fairfield and Gloucester Sts). Valet parking evenings. Reservations recommended in dining room. 262.4810. Also at: The Royal Sonesta, Cambridge. 661.4810

64 Beacon Guest Houses $ Mostly tourists and foreign visitors take advantage of these inexpensive pension-style accommodations. The office screens guests and provides single and double efficiencies (twin beds only) for brief or long-term stays in converted Back Bay town houses. In winter this address is the only building in operation; in summer others open. The rooms have no telephone, TV, or maid or room service, but all have a private bath and kitchenette with some utensils, linens, and towels.

♦ 248 Newbury St (between Fairfield and Gloucester Sts). 262.1771 (M-F 8:30AM-5:30PM). 266.7142 (evenings, weekends, holidays)

64 Ciao bella ★★$$ Convivial singles like to lunch at the bar, looking out at Newbury Street. In the evening the dressy dining room draws a chic clientele. Dabble in the appealing selection of appetizers, like *involtini di melanzani* (stuffed eggplant), then turn to pasta or a simple meat dish like the *coletta di vitello* (veal chop). In nice weather dine alfresco on the patio. ♦ Italian ♦ M-W 11:30AM-3PM, 5:30-11PM; Th-F 11:30AM-3PM, 5:30-11:45PM; Sa 11:30AM-4:30PM, 5:30-11:45PM; Su 11:30AM-3:30PM, 5:30-11PM. 240 Newbury St (at Fairfield St). Valet parking Thursday through Saturday in winter, Tuesday through Saturday rest of year. Reservations recommended Friday through Sunday. 536.2626

64 Frontier Owner **Mimi Packman** has a knack for rounding up resonant retro artifacts, often adapting them to brave new uses. Old upholstery fabrics become charming dresses and jackets, vintage tablecloths, and comfy pillows. The stock is always evolving, but the white picket fence out front is a reliable omen of what you'll find inside. ♦ Tu-Sa 11AM-6PM. 252 Newbury St (between Fairfield and Gloucester Sts). 421.9858

65 Vose Galleries of Boston The fifth generation of Voses now run this art gallery. Established in 1841, it's the oldest continuously run gallery in America. More than 30,000 paintings have passed through Vose Galleries since 1896. The family specializes in 18th-, 19th-, and early 20th-century American painting, and they've sold paintings to nearly every major American museum. They frequently show works by the **Hudson River School, Luminists, American Impressionists**—including **Childe Hassam** and **John Henry Twachtman**—and the **Boston School.** At the turn of the century a Vose agent returned from France with a full-length male nude by **Géricault.** High-minded **Seth Vose** decided to cut off the improper lower portion and sold the torso to the wife of the **Museum of Fine Arts'** president. Fifty years later Vose's descendants came upon the unseemly portion in their basement and gave it to the MFA, where it was joined to the previously donated upper portion, thus making the poor man whole again. ♦ M-F 8AM-5:30PM; Sa 9AM-4PM. 238 Newbury St (between Exeter and Fairfield Sts). 536.6176

66 Eastern Accent Tabletop and desktop items, most imported from Japan, are displayed against a vivid chartreuse backdrop. Lovely glass pens, surrealist cutlery, cast-iron and concrete clocks, artful bowls and teapots, clever jewelry, and textured writing papers reflect the store's motto, "living with design," and the Japanese precept that the functional should be well made. Other straightforward materials in-

Back Bay

clude stainless, celluloid and Bakelite, natural porcelains, silk, and anodized aluminum. ♦ M-F 11AM-6PM; Sa noon-5PM. 237 Newbury St (at Fairfield St). 266.9707

67 Emporio Armani Obviously no longer a fashion backwater, Boston has earned a third Armani outpost (the others are Giorgio Armani at 22 Newbury Street and Armani A/X at Copley Place), this one claiming 24,500 square feet in the rehabbed United Business Services office building. ♦ M-F 10AM-7PM; Sa-Su noon-6PM. 210-214 Newbury St. 262.7300 &

68 Harvard Book Store Cafe ★★$$ Independently operated, the shop and cafe have enjoyed a happy marriage here. The cafe's New American cuisine borrows from international ethnic dishes and has reached new heights under the direction of one of the cafe's managers, **Moncef Meddeb,** the former owner and chef extraordinaire who created the stellar **L'Espalier,** another Back Bay institution. Prices at the cafe are reasonable for Back Bay and the clientele is cosmopolitan. There's something deeply satisfying about dining in the midst of stacks of books; if you're alone, pick one up and linger awhile. Don't settle for a table in the back dining room, with its dull, bookless decor. On a summer day the outdoor cafe is a fine place to relax and watch waves of shoppers flow by.

The bookstore keeps abreast of the latest literary currents, and offers out-of-print and second-hand book searches. It publishes a bimonthly newsletter reporting on new titles and its two author series—one coordinated with the **Boston Public Library** and another at a sister bookstore, sans cafe, in Cambridge (the **Harvard Book Store,** 1256 Massachusetts Avenue, Harvard Square, 661.1515). ♦ American ♦ Shop and cafe M-Th 8AM-11PM; F-Sa 8AM-midnight; Su 11AM-11PM. 190 Newbury St (between Dartmouth and Exeter Sts). Store 536.0095, Cafe 536.0097 &

69 Exeter Street Theatre Building This Victorian gem of granite and brownstone, the 1884 work of **H.W. Hartwell** and **W.C. Richardson,** was built as a temple for the **Working Union of Progressive Spiritualists.** It had a long run as a repertory movie theater, and suffered the indignity of having a greenhouse extension appended to its street level (**Childs, Bertman, Tseckares, Casendino** were responsible for the 1975 renovation that resulted in **Friday's,** a schlocky—albeit popular—singles bar).

Within the Exeter Street Theatre Building:

Waterstone's Booksellers Perhaps the most civilized enclave on Newbury Street, this British shop offers three roomy floors of well-stocked shelves, with a reading area so you can skim before buying. The store's reading series—several events a week—attract stellar talents, and the quarterly newsletter, *Voices,* is at once witty and pithy. A frequent visitor calls the store "literal heaven." ♦ M-Sa 9AM-11PM; Su noon-9PM. 26 Exeter St (at Newbury St). 859.7300

70 Nielsen Gallery Nina Nielsen has run this gallery for more than 25 years, and exhibits contemporary works by **Joan Snyder, Jake Berthot, Harvey Quaytman, Jane Smaldone,** and **Porfirio DiDonna** (his estate) from a roster of roughly 20. Nielsen isn't a trend-chaser; she looks for artists—many young, awaiting their first break—whose work expresses highly personal viewpoints, often spiritual, whom she sticks with and nurtures. She willl also show work by famous 20th-century artists such as **Jackson Pollock** and **David Smith.** Nielsen likes what she likes and has many clients who feel the same. She doesn't shy away from making one of her biggest interests apparent: the continuum of spiritual substance in art. Says Nielsen about purchasing art: "Buy for love after talking to knowledgeable people." ♦ Tu-Sa 10AM-5:30PM. 179 Newbury St (between Dartmouth and Exeter Sts). 266.4835 & (with advance notice)

70 Wenham Cross Antiques Irma and Emily Lampert, mother and daughter, preside over an inviting shop full of folk charm and delightful country antiques: hand-painted furniture, primitive paintings, hooked rugs, quilts, mottoed plates, iron banks and wooden pull toys, and majolica and quimper pottery. The cupboards and tabletops are never, ever bare. ♦ M-Sa 10AM-5PM. 179 Newbury St (between Dartmouth and Exeter Sts). 236.0409

70 Marcoz Something splendid always graces the show windows here. Marcoz occupies two handsomely preserved floors of a Victorian town house, a wonderful setting for decorative merchandise from the 18th to the early 20th century. The hard-to find accent pieces are imported from England or France, or purchased from New England estates. Knowledgeable and friendly, Mr. Marcoz will tell you all about whatever strikes your fancy, be it the 17th-century Madonna and child processional figures, a 19th-century French *boule de petarque* (boccie-style ball), exquisite engravings, ivorine and sterling-silver napkin rings, a desktop inkwell, a pocket watch, furniture, or other singular finds. ♦ M-Sa 10AM-6PM. 177 Newbury St (between Dartmouth and Exeter Sts). 262.0780

70 The Society of Arts and Crafts Stop in here for a special handmade, one-of-a-kind something. The oldest nonprofit craft association in America, operating since 1897, the society promotes established and up-and-coming artisans by putting their wares before the public. All work is selected by jury: jewelry, ceramics, glass, quilts, weaving, wood, collages, leather, clothing and accessories, and furniture—the last is always especially noteworthy. Themed exhibitions are held on the second floor, and a satellite gallery is located in the Financial District (101 Arch Street, 345.0033). ♦ M-Sa 10AM-6PM; Su noon-5PM. 175 Newbury St (between Dartmouth and Exeter Sts). 266.1810

70 Pucker Gallery More than 20 years in the business, this gallery displays local and international contemporary artists' graphics, paintings, sculptures, and porcelains. It also carries modern masters such as **Chagall, Picasso,** and **Hundertwasser.** Israeli art is a gallery specialty, with works shown by **Samuel Bak** and **David Sharir.** ♦ M-Sa 10AM-5:30PM. 171 Newbury St (between Dartmouth and Exeter Sts). 267.9473

70 Monhegan An ideal source for wedding gifts of the pampering, homey kind: cozy wool blankets, throws handwoven in New England, European and domestic custom and handmade linens, cedar chests, even some sweaters. The colors and textures are soft and alluring. You can purchase a gift here that will make a new baby feel very welcome in this world. This store draws a lot of repeat business, as customers keep adding to the comforts of home. ♦ M-F 10AM-6PM; Sa 10AM-5PM. 173 Newbury St (between Dartmouth and Exeter Sts). 247.0666

71 La Ruche The perfect source for whimsical house gifts, La Ruche, owned by **Maria Church** and **Apple Bartlett** (the daughter of legendary designer **Sister Parrish**), is best known for trompe l'oeil and painted furniture and lampshades, as well as Italian and French faience. They also carry flora- and fauna-shaped mugs, teapots, and jars; lovely French ribbon; garden ornaments; unusual glasses; linens; lamps; tapestry pillows; and other decorative wares. Potpourri scents the air here. ♦ M-Sa 10AM-5:30PM. 168 Newbury St (between Dartmouth and Exeter Sts). 536.6366

71 The Copley Society of Boston The oldest art association in America, the nonprofit society was founded in 1879 to promote access to art, particularly new European trends, and to exhibit the work of its members and other artists of the day. Members **John Singer Sargent** and **James McNeill Whistler** showed their work in society galleries. In 1905 the society mounted **Claude Monet's** first American exhibition, a controversial event, and in 1913 **Marcel Duchamp's** *Nude Descending a Staircase* was shown here, creating an enormous furor. Today the society has more than 800 committee-selected members from around the world, though most come from New England. It operates two floors of galleries, with individual artists renting space upstairs and an ongoing members' show downstairs. The society no longer is in the vanguard, having gotten somewhat mired in tradition; its shows are uneven in quality. However, works by noted and rising artists are often on view, so it's worth investigating. ♦ Tu-Su 10:30AM-5:30PM. 158 Newbury St (between Dartmouth and Exeter Sts). 536.5049

72 Boston Art Club This artful 1881 assemblage is the work of **Ralph Waldo Emerson's** clever nephew, **William Ralph Emerson,** also creator of the fascinating **House of Odd Windows** on Beacon Hill. Emerson let loose his entire artillery of architectural forms and ornament on the Queen Anne-style facade: from every angle, there's something peculiar or interesting to see. An alternative high school now occupies the building. ♦ 270 Dartmouth St (at Newbury St)

Back Bay

73 London Lace A bit of fine old lace is a lovely thing indeed. This second-story shop is as snowy and bright as its goods. Owner **Diane Jones** travels to England, Ireland, and Scotland to collect restored antique lace curtains, table and bed linens dating from 1860 to 1920, and reproductions. She also imports new lace made from original Victorian patterns on century-old Scottish looms. ♦ M-Sa 10AM-5:30PM. 167 Newbury St (between Dartmouth and Exeter Sts). 267.3506

73 Kitchen Arts At this wonderful resource for cooks, both expert and far-from, you can pick up any kitchen tool your culinary sleight-of-hand requires. The emphasis here is on performance, not pretty-to-look-at gifts; these wares are ready to go to work immediately—slicing, dicing, decorating, coring, chopping, cracking, grinding, whatever. Kitchen cutlery and knife sharpening are subspecialties. ♦ M-Sa 10AM-6PM; Su noon-5PM. 161 Newbury St (between Dartmouth and Exeter Sts). 266.8701

73 Du Barry $$ Don't expect French cooking worthy of accolades here. Nonetheless, this quiet, old-fashioned restaurant is a Back Bay landmark, family owned and operated since 1936. The owners are French, and their son is responsible for the classical and provincial cuisine. Dine out back on the terrace. Back Bay residents are loyal to this place, and it attracts its share of both students and celebrities. Be sure to peruse **Josh Winer's** amusing faux-facade mural along the side of the building for a roster of nobs local and far-fetched (everyone from **Paul Revere** to **Babe Ruth** puts in an appearance). ◆ French ◆ M-Sa noon-2:30PM, 5:30-10PM; Su 5:30-9:30PM. Closed Sunday from July through September. 159 Newbury St (between Dartmouth and Exeter Sts). Reservations recommended for parties of four or more. 262.2445 ♿

74 Papa Razzi ★★$$ An inviting, busy Italian trattoria complete with a wood-burning pizza oven, Papa Razzi's menu leans toward rustic Northern Italian dishes with California overtones. Chef **Tim Conway's** hearty fare includes an array of splendid crispy-crusted pizzas, polenta with grilled Italian sausages, and bountiful antipasti and pastas. ◆ Italian ◆ Daily 11:30AM-2AM. 271 Dartmouth St (between Newbury and Boylston Sts). 536.9200

75 GBS Geoffrey B. Small is one determined designer. Having launched his business from his mother's suburban attic with some strategic—and costly—full-page ads in *Vogue*, he made the leap to Newbury Street, landing one flight up, where he's now turning out "bespoke" clothing for men and women: custom-made, from the fabric chosen through several computer-aided fittings. For true individualists, it's the only way to go. ◆ By appointment. 129 Newbury St (between Clarendon and Dartmouth Sts). 536.6393 ♿

Back Bay

75 Body Sculpture This gallery of contemporary jewelry and accessories represents a regular group of more than 20 artists who work in media such as metal, polyester resin, acrylics, silicone, stones, precious metals, clay, and silk. Hundreds of white drawers are filled with offbeat jewelry perfect for art-to-wear lovers. Four shows are held each year. ◆ M-Sa 10AM-6PM. 127 Newbury St (between Clarendon and Dartmouth Sts). 262.2200

75 Autrefois Antiques "Yesteryear," says the name: 18th- and 19th-century France is captured here in fine imported hardwood furnishings such as armoires, tables, chairs, chandeliers, and mirrors. Other epochs and origins also slip in, with the biggest shipments of new merchandise arriving in the spring and fall. The expert owners, **Charles** and **Maria Rowe,** will do on-site restoration and adapt old furnishings for modern needs; updating lighting is their specialty. ◆ M-Sa 10AM-5:30PM. 125 Newbury St (between Clarendon and Dartmouth Sts). 424.8823 ♿ Also at: 130 Harvard St, Brookline. 566.0113

76 Serenella Women come to this small, friendly boutique to invest in luxurious, classic, timeless clothes that will serve them well for years. The emphasis is on European designer daytime wear, with some accessories and shoes. Owner **Ines Capelli** does all the buying, and is always on the lookout for styles that are just right for her regular customers. ◆ M-W, F-Sa 10AM-6PM; Th 10AM-7PM. 134 Newbury St (between Clarendon and Dartmouth Sts). 262.5568 ♿

riccardi

76 Riccardi The latest exemplars of European fashion rendezvous at Riccardi. All of the clothing, for men and women, is made in Italy, but designs and influences come from throughout Europe. Even the store's facade looks Italian. Designers include **Ann Demeulemeester** (Belgium), **Comme des Garcons** (Japan), and **Dolce e Gabbana** and **Romeo Gigli** (Italy). The shoes and accessories are multinational, too. An entire department is devoted to sporting wear. The staff is always up-to-date and informative on fashions. This is certainly one of Boston's most worldly shops; they even accept JCB, the Japanese credit card. ◆ M-Sa 11AM-7PM. 128 Newbury St (between Clarendon and Dartmouth Sts). 266.3158

77 Rebecca's Cafe $ Everything is made fresh daily at this gourmet take-out place, a satellite of the original Rebecca's on Beacon Hill. Lines form all day long for homemade muffins and scones, fresh salads, hot entrée specials, and the spectacular desserts and pastries the kickoff Rebecca's made famous. The chocolate-mousse cake and the fresh-fruit tarts are pure pleasure. There are a few tables at the back. ◆ Cafe/Takeout ◆ M-F 7AM-9PM; Sa 8AM-8PM; Su 9AM-6PM. 112 Newbury St (between Clarendon and Dartmouth Sts). No credit cards. 267.1122

78 Bargain Box Many a discarded treasure is discovered at this quality thrift shop run by the **Junior League of Boston, Inc.**, a nonprofit women's organization dedicated to promoting community volunteerism. ◆ M-F 10AM-6PM; Sa 11AM-6PM. 117 Newbury St (between Clarendon and Dartmouth Sts). 536.8580

78 Cuoio Pronounced *coyo,* the name means "leather" in Italian. For women only, this store showcases fashionable leather boots and shoes, lots imported from Italy, and accessories such as jewelry, hats, and fabulous hair ornaments. Many of these smart styles aren't available elsewhere in the city. ◆ M-Sa 10AM-6PM; Su noon-5PM. 115 Newbury St (between Clarendon and Dartmouth Sts). 859.0636 ♿ Also at: 170 Faneuil Hall Marketplace. 742.4486

78 Isabelle Collins of London The British owner concentrates on country furniture and decorative arts from the British Isles and Ireland, with some finds from Scandinavia. Linens, embroideries, majolica, dairy utensils, and kitchenware are sold, too. ◆ M-Sa 10AM-6PM. 115 Newbury St (between Clarendon and Dartmouth Sts). 266.8699 ♿

79 David L. O'Neal Antiquarian Booksellers, Inc. Specializing in antiquarian books for more than 25 years, O'Neal concentrates on fine and rare books from the 15th century to present, including first editions in literature, many with superior bindings or leatherbound in sets. Many works have remarkable printing, typography, and illustrations. Original, historical, and decorative American and European prints from the 16th to the 19th century are also displayed. First-edition **Jane Austen** works; **Nathaniel Bowditch's** wonderful navigation book; **James Fenimore Cooper's** rare, anonymous first novel; **Cotton Mather's** Psalter; **Shelley's** *Prometheus Unbound*—a mere sampling of what many come to covet. Appointments are encouraged. An illustrated catalog is also available. ♦ M-F 9AM-5PM; Sa 10AM-4PM. 234 Clarendon St (between Newbury St and Commonwealth Ave). 266.5790 ♿

79 okw̄ **Irene Kerzner** and **Henry Wong** (the "o" in okw̄, pronounced *oh-koo,* stands for departed partner) are the designers of choice for prominent businesswomen and socialites too distinctive to buy off the rack. okw̄'s creations are impeccably crafted of opulent fabrics, yet they are also compellingly playful. ♦ By appointment. 234 Clarendon St (between Newbury St and Commonwealth Ave). 266.4114 ♿

80 Trinity Church Rectory The massive arched entry bellows the name of the 1879 rectory's masterful architect, **Henry H. Richardson,** who designed its parent **Trinity Church** at Copley Square. The building is now on the **National Register of Historic Places;** look at its surface, vigorously alive with twisting flowers and ornament. A third story was, unfortunately, added by HHR's successor firm after his death. ♦ 233 Clarendon St (at Newbury St)

81 New England Historic Genealogical Society Many an aspirant to the lofty branches of some illustrious Yankee family tree has zeroed in on this private, nonprofit research library, the oldest of its kind in the nation and the first in the world. The mission: to plumb the past, to root out those roots. Housed in a former bank, NEHGS was founded in 1845 and now holds 200,000 volumes and more than a million manuscripts dating to the 17th century. NEHGS is dedicated to the study and preservation of family history, with records and histories for all US states and Canadian provinces, plus Europe. There's no better place to try to entangle one's heritage with that of the **Adams,** the **Cabots,** the **Randolphs,** and other American Olympians. What would caste-conscious Boston do without it? NEHGS has more than 13,000 members with access to its archives. Visitors pay a half- or full-day research fee. ♦ Fee. Tu, F-Sa 9AM-5PM; W-Th 9AM-9PM. 101 Newbury St (between Berkeley and Clarendon Sts). 536.5740

82 John Lewis, Inc. Swinging in the window, wave upon wave of silver strands lure passersby into this serene 1876 brownstone, where veteran Newbury Street proprietors **John** and **Louise Lewis** design jewelry. Working with solid precious metals and natural stones, the couple turns out a glittering array of imaginative designs. Some are simple expressions of rich materials and careful artisanship. Others are more intricate, such as the Lewis' line of Victorian-inspired jewelry with its cherubim, scrolls,

flowers, and bows. ♦ Tu-F 10AM-5:30PM; Sa 10AM-5PM. 97 Newbury St (between Berkeley and Clarendon Sts). 266.6665 ♿

82 Kakas This 134-year-old furrier ("five generations of recognized integrity") gained some unwelcome notoriety when it was learned that erstwhile manager **Charles Stuart** used its safe to store the gun with which he shot his wife. It's still the source of the finest—and costliest—coats in the city. ♦ M-Tu, Th-F 9AM-5:30PM; W 9AM-8PM. 93 Newbury St (between Berkeley and Clarendon Sts). 536.1858 ♿

82 Haley & Steele It's fun to rifle—gingerly, of course—through the flat files crowded with prints of all kinds. The gallery focuses on 18th- and 19th-century prints in scores of categories, including botanical, sporting, architectural, military, New England maritime, birds, historical, and genre. The custom-frame shop specializes in painting conservation and French line matting, and has served local artists since 1899. A print from Haley & Steele will add a handsomely proper accent to any setting. ♦ M-F 10AM-6PM; Sa 10AM-5PM. 91 Newbury St (between Berkeley and Clarendon Sts). 536.6339 ♿

82 Mirabelle ★★$$$ Owner **Stephen Elmont,** founder of the enormously successful catering firm **Creative Gourmets,** envisions his new spot as a neighborhood cafe—geared to the admittedly affluent. Dominated by a mural of western Europe, this bistro aspires to thoughtful conversations and straightforward cuisine: "There will be no food with multiple syllables," Elmont promises. ♦ American ♦ M-F 7AM-11PM; Sa-Su

10AM-11PM. 85 Newbury St (between Berkeley and Clarendon Sts). 859.4848 ♿

82 Martini Carl The **Ventola** family's boutique stocks sophisticated European apparel for men and women ranging from very casual to very dressy, with all the requisite accessories. The designer and private labels emphasize rich fabrics and leathers, superb tailoring, and enduring styles. ♦ M-Tu, Th-Sa 10AM-6PM; W 10AM-7:30PM. 77 Newbury St (between Berkeley and Clarendon Sts). 247.0441 ♿

83 Church of the Covenant R.M. Upjohn designed this 1867 Gothic Revival **Tiffany** treasure-house, with the largest collection of the stained-glass master's work in the world: 43 windows, some 30 feet high, and clerestories, too. Especially noteworthy is the sanctuary lantern with seven angels. It was designed by Tiffany's firm for the Tiffany Chapel exhibited at the **World's Columbian Exposition of 1893** in Chicago, then installed here. Also, look for the **Welte-Tripp** pipe organ, a five-keyboard, manual, 4,500-pipe instrument, which can be heard during the church's fall and spring organ recital series. The church has a long history of giving generously to the community; it also founded the **Back Bay Chorale** and the **Boston Pro Arte Chamber Orchestra,** which perform regularly here and at **Harvard University.** ♦ Tu-Sa 9AM-noon, Jan-Apr, Nov-Dec; Tu-Sa 9AM-5PM, May-Oct. 67 Newbury St (at Berkeley St). 266.7480 ♿

Within the Church of the Covenant:

Gallery NAGA Director **Arthur Dion** mounts interesting exhibitions of contemporary painting, sculpture, photography, and prints by the known and unknown; he likes to bridge the division between fine art and craft, and shows furniture and glass. Exhibitors have included **Henry Schwartz, James Gemmill**, and **Irene Valincius;** and furniture designers such as **Tom Loesser** and **Judy McKie.** The gallery occupies a generous swatch—1,400 square feet—in the Church of the Covenant, whose progressive congregation gives art a boost by making a long-term space commitment to the gallery. ♦ Tu-Sa 10AM-5:30PM, closed mid July-Labor Day. 267.9060

84 Louis, Boston Until the **New England Museum of Natural History** moved to its current site straddling the Charles River and changed its name to the **Boston Museum of Science,** it was jammed into this French Academic structure, designed in 1863 by **William Gibbons Preston.** The museum was one of Back Bay's pioneers. When it vacated, part of the moving-day chaos included lowering a stuffed moose from an upper-story window, a scene captured in a photograph that the museum now prizes. **Bonwit Teller** then resided here for decades until Louis, the city's astronomically priced clothier, took over in 1987 and gave the building a much-needed restoration.

Three floors are dedicated to men's apparel and one to women's—everything's of exceptional quality. The building's splendid isolation makes

Back Bay

it appear even more magnificent than it is. Inside, it's enjoyably spacious for browsing. ♦ M-Tu, F-Sa 10AM-6PM; W-Th 10AM-7PM. 234 Berkeley St (between Newbury and Boylston Sts). 965.6100 ⟁

Within Louis, Boston:

Cafe Louis ★★$$ Louis' cafe deserves a special visit. High-ceilinged and furnished with lacquered bamboo chairs and tapestry banquettes, this pleasant nook echoes the store's sunny palette, but in a warm butterscotch. You can enter at the cafe's main entrance off the parking lot, but why not stroll through the store, past $1,000 sweaters and $200 scarves. The menu marries Italian and French flavors. Indulge in seductive pastries, smoked fish, or French toast ordered by the slice in the morning; antipasto for two or a sandwich handsomely composed and garnished for lunch; or a splendid slice of cake with tea in late afternoon. You can dine outdoors at tables on the cement landing, though the view of the parking lot and the **New England Life Building** across the way isn't exactly breathtaking. A small gourmet shop offers prepared and packaged treats of all kinds to go. The cafe's major flaw: it closes much too early. ♦ Cafe/Takeout ♦ M-F 8AM-5:30PM (dessert and takeout until 6PM); Sa 10AM-6PM. 266.4680 ⟁

85 Alan Bilzerian In Bilzerian's striking display windows, the dramatic clothes need few props—they speak for themselves. A native of Worcester, MA, Bilzerian started out with a college student clientele two decades ago, then began selling to rock stars. Now Bilzerian is the local name in fashion best known outside of Boston. In fact, New Yorkers with the fashion world at their feet still make special trips, and lots of celebrities drop in when in town—**Cher** and **Mick Jagger** among them. The art-to-wear fashions, accessories, and shoes for men and women feature the work of European and Japanese designers: **Yohji Yamamoto, Michele Klien, Issey Miyake, Katharine Hamnett, Rifat Ozbek, Jean Paul Gaultier, Azzedine Alaia,** and **Romeo Gigli,** to name a few. Complementing the other collections, Bilzerian designs for men, and his wife, **Bê,** designs for women. Of course, outlandishly stylish wear commands outlandishly high prices. ♦ M-Th, Sa 10AM-6PM; F 10AM-7PM. 34 Newbury St (between Arlington and Berkeley Sts). 536.1001 ⟁ (The staff will carry wheelchairs up the stairs; once inside, there's an elevator to the second-floor women's department.)

86 J.O.E. Another local success story, **Joseph Abboud** has earned international renown for his ruggedly handsome men's clothes. His clothes are sensual, yet assertively masculine. ♦ M-W, F-Sa 10AM-6PM; Th 10AM-7PM. 37 Newbury St (between Arlington and Berkeley Sts). 266.4200 ⟁

86 Romano's Bakery & Sandwich Shop $ The Back Bay needs all the unpretentious, reliable places it can get, and this little 40-seater is one of the good ones. Casual and cafeteria-style, Romano's has won a dedicated clientele with its fragrant fresh muffins, bagels, Danish pastries, and croissants in the morning—the busiest time—and homemade soups, quiches, sandwiches, and tantalizing desserts later on. You can also get cappuccino and espresso. ♦ Cafe/Takeout ♦ M-F 7AM-6PM; Sa 7:30AM-6PM; Su 9AM-5PM. 33 Newbury St (between Arlington and Berkeley Sts). No credit cards. 266.0770

86 29 Newbury ★★★$$ This perennially trendy bistro, a favorite with modeling, music, and media types, serves inventive cuisine that's considerately priced. Certain dishes sing, such as the wild mushroom ravioli in Madeira cream sauce, and even the burgers are completely *comme il faut.* The semi-subterranean dining room also doubles as an art gallery, and deep-set booths ensure privacy. More sociable types crowd around the bar or, in good weather, spill onto the sidewalk patio. Sunday brunch earns raves. ♦ American ♦ M-Th 11:30AM-5PM, 5:30-11PM; F-Sa 11:30AM-5PM, 5:30PM-midnight;

Su noon-4PM, 5-10:30PM. 29 Newbury St (between Arlington and Berkeley Sts). Reservations recommended. 536.0290

87 Emmanuel Church Its uninspired rural Gothic Revival architecture (an 1862 effort by **Alexander R. Estey,** enlarged by **Frederick R. Allen** in 1899 and pictured above) doesn't do justice to this Episcopal church's lively, creative spirit. Dedicated since the 1970s to "a special ministry through art," the church organizes a variety of music and cultural events. A Bach cantata, performed professionally, accompanies the liturgy every Sunday from September through May, drawing crowds. Jazz celebrations are held here periodically. ♦ 15 Newbury St (between Arlington and Berkeley Sts). 536.3355 ♿ (a portable ramp is available with advance notice)

Within Emmanuel Church:

Leslie Lindsey Memorial Chapel This 1924 Gothic chapel was erected by **Mr. and Mrs. William Lindsey** as a memorial to their daughter, **Leslie,** who with her new husband was bound for a European honeymoon on the ill-fated *Lusitania*. Some time after the boat sank, Leslie's body supposedly washed ashore in Ireland, still wearing her father's wedding gift of diamonds and rubies; they were sold to help pay for her memorial. The chapel is sometimes called the "Lady Chapel" for its marble carvings of female saints. Architects **Allen and Collens** were already nationally renowned for **Riverside Church** in New York when they designed the chapel.

88 Charles Sumner A head-to-toe boutique, Sumner carries great imported and American women's designer apparel—by **Donna Karan, Valentino, Louis Ferraud, Missoni, Akris,** and others—plus shoes, handbags, makeup, hosiery, jewelry, gloves, and hats. In 1991 new owner **Carol Ann Hayes** took over this welcoming place to go for truly wonderful things. The enthusiastic salespeople try hard to work with customers and make them feel at home. ♦ M-Sa 10AM-5:45PM. 16 Newbury St (between Arlington and Berkeley Sts). 536.6225 ♿

---

88 Levinson/Kane Gallery An ambitious up-start founded by art consultants **June Levinson** and **Barbara Kane,** this gallery is keyed into some of the more exciting local talents, such as **Clara Wainwright** (the painter largely responsible for instigating Boston's First Night festivities) and photographer **Elsa Dorfman.** ♦ Tu-Sa 10AM-5:30PM. 14 Newbury St (between Arlington and Berkeley Sts). 247.0545 ♿

88 Alpha Gallery The best free shows in town are often here. A family affair, the gallery is owned by **Alan Fink,** managed by his daughter **Joanna,** and shows work by his wife **Barbara Swan** and son **Aaron Fink**—both of whom merit the attention. Alpha exhibits 20th-century and contemporary American and European painting, sculpture, and prints. Distinguished artists shown here include American painters **Milton Avery, Bernard Chael,** and **Fairfield Porter;** Europeans **Mimmo Paladino** and **Georg Baselitz;** Massachusetts realist **Scott Prior;** and gifted young artists such as **T. Wiley Carr.** Over its 25-year history Alpha Gallery has mounted major exhibitions of work by **John Marin, Max Beckman,** and **Stuart Davis,** and **Picasso's** complete *Vollard Suite*. ♦ Tu-Sa 10AM-5:30PM. 14 Newbury St (between Clarendon and Dartmouth Sts). 536.4465

Back Bay

88 Barbara Krakow Gallery Don't pass by this fifth-floor gallery. That's hard to do anyway because there's an eye-catching marble bench carved with enigmatic messages by **Jenny Holzer** on the sidewalk out front. Krakow Gallery has been in the art-selling business for 30 years and is now at its pinnacle. It is possibly Boston's most important gallery, and Krakow directs its prestige to numerous worthy causes. Many of the most significant contemporary artists are shown here, among them Holzer, **Agnes Martin, Cameron Shaw, Jim Dine, Donald Judd,** and **Michael Mazur.** Despite the superstars on its walls, the gallery is a very hospitable, unpretentious place. Krakow combines sure taste with a willingness to take risks —showing work created by high-school kids, for example. ♦ Tu-Sa 10AM-5:30PM. 10 Newbury St (between Arlington and Berkeley Sts). 262.4490 ♿

89 Skinner, Inc. Founded in 1962, Skinner is the fourth-largest auction gallery in the US, and New England's foremost. Skinner's exhibitions and auctions are free and fascinating fun—even if you come just to observe. A form of live theater, auctions began as a tasteful way to conduct bankruptcy, and evolved into a lively marketplace for collectors of all kinds. The auctioneer's voice and gavel command buyers from all over. Just watching people handle the suspense of bidding is a study in human nature. Skinner holds more than 60 previews and auctions annually in 15 specialty categories, such as American furniture and decorative objects, toys, fine jewelry, musical instruments, and holiday gifts. Unlike museums, the art and objects sold can be examined at close range, with specialists on hand to answer questions. Highlights from select auctions are on view in Skinner's gallery. Auctions are held at the **Ritz-Carlton** and at Skinner's main gallery in **Bolton, MA,** about a 45-minute drive outside Boston. Call to find out what's in store. ◆ M-F 9AM-5PM; Sa only for previews, call for times. 2 Newbury St (at Arlington St), above Burberrys. 236.1700 ♿

89 Cafe de Paris ★$ This is one heck of a fast-food joint, with velvet banquettes, burled paneling, and Deco sconces. The food is a cut above, too: from croissants and omelets to *croque-monsieurs* and true Parisian pastries. Grab a booth, or stock up and cross over to the **Public Garden** for a *dejeuner sur l'herbe*. ◆ French/Takeout ◆ 19 Arlington St (at Newbury St). 427.7121 ♿

90 Domain It's fun to prowl through this mecca of home embellishments, a fantasy habitat for a menagerie of antique, traditional, and designer pieces, none commonplace or conventional. The aim here is to mass-market one-of-a-kind-looking furnishings. A multitude of quirky accessories crowd in with the beds, tables, and sofas. Textures, colors, patterns, and styles veer crazily in all directions. ◆ M-Sa 10AM-6PM; Su noon-5PM (call for later hours in the

Back Bay

summer). 7 Newbury St (at Arlington St). 266.5252 ♿

91 Ritz-Carlton Hotel $$$$ The oldest Ritz-Carlton in the country (built in 1927 by **Strickland and Blodget,** and subtly expanded by **Skidmore, Owings & Merrill** in 1981), the hotel's reputation for luxury, elegance, superlative service, and all the little niceties proper Bostonians love so well has never slipped. The elevator attendants, for example, wear white gloves. The understated edifice perfectly expresses the fastidious courtesies and traditions of its inhabitant. There's nothing flashy or eye-catching about this building, except for its parade of vivid blue awnings, but it has become a timeless, steadfast fixture.

The Ritz's 278 rooms and suites are simply and traditionally appointed in European style. Rooms have safes and locking closets, all windows open, and 41 suites have wood-burning fireplaces. Request a room with a view of the **Public Garden.** Rooms for nonsmokers and handicapped persons are available. You can bring your pet if it's leashed. The Ritz has a small health club and guests have complimentary access to the fancy spa at **The Heritage** a block away. Other amenities are 24-hour room service, valet parking, same-day valet laundry, a multilingual staff, baby-sitting, a concierge, a barber, and a shoe-shine stand. If that's not

enough, the staff "will provide anything legal." ◆ 15 Arlington St (at Newbury St). 536.5700, 800/241.3333; fax 536.1335 ♿

Within the Ritz-Carlton Hotel:

The Ritz Lounge ★★★$$ While a harpist thrums soothingly in the corner of this quiet, lovely drawing room on the second floor, sit in a high-backed chair and nibble tiny sandwich triangles, fruit tarts, and scones with jam, and sip perfectly brewed tea. A lobster buffet is held Friday and Saturday night, and there's dancing Thursday through Saturday after 8:30PM. ◆ Cafe/Tea ◆ Daily 11:30AM-4PM (lunch), 3-5:30PM (tea). Jacket and tie required evenings; no denim or running shoes. 536.5700 ♿

The Ritz Bar ★★★★$$ On a snowy evening, the gorgeous view of the **Public Garden** from this cozy street-level bar is out of a storybook. Inside, there's no entertainment, just plenty of welcome serenity and a crackling fire buring in the hearth. The bar is famous for its perfect martinis; ask for the special martini menu, which featured 13 varieties at last count, including the "James Bond." Boston mystery writer **Robert B. Parker's** fictional sleuth **Spenser** has quaffed many a beer here. Lunch is served, except on Sunday. ◆ M-Sa 11:30AM-1AM; Su noon-midnight. 536.7000 ♿

The Ritz Cafe ★★$$$ With its views of Newbury Street, quiet vanilla decor, and cordial service, this cafe offers respite during a hectic day. When you've had it with the world, come here for a restorative touch of civility. Since you can't see the **Public Garden** from here, the Ritz's prized honorary possession, it's been reproduced in a mural. Weekdays, many of Boston's business heavy-hitters breakfast here. At night the cafe also caters to the after-theater crowd. And children may order from a special menu. ◆ American ◆ Daily 6:30AM-2:30PM, 5:30PM-midnight. Jacket and tie required evenings; no denim. Reservations recommended at lunch. 536.5700 ♿

The Ritz Dining Room ★★$$$$ New hub restaurants open every day—but there will *never* be another Ritz. The second-floor dining room is the hotel's showpiece, with cobalt-blue Venetian crystal chandeliers, gold-filigreed ceiling, regal drapery, and huge picture windows overlooking the **Public Garden.** There's no better place for wedding proposals, anniversaries, and other momentous occasions. Piano music and an occasional harpist add to the spell. Timeless classics such as rack of lamb and châteaubriand for two commune with a few more stylish offerings on the menu. But the chef introduces innovations very carefully; the old-guard patrons would rise up in arms if Boston cream pie and other old-time favorites were seriously challenged. Entrées low in sodium, cholesterol, and calories are available; so is a children's menu. Fashion shows are held here every Saturday, and chamber music accompanies the fabulous Sunday brunch. ◆ French ◆ M-Th noon-2:30PM, 5:30-10PM; F-Sa noon-2:30PM, 5:30-11PM; Su 10:45AM-2:30PM, 6-10PM. Jacket and tie required. Reservations required. 536.5700 ♿

David Breashears
Filmmaker and Himalayan Mountaineer

I like to introduce visiting friends to Boston with a brief two- to three-hour walking tour, given my limited tolerance for this kind of thing. I begin with a view of the city from the **John Hancock Tower** observation deck. This is very important, as Boston's geography can easily befuddle even the most seasoned traveler—local residents, too. While there, take time to view the beautiful illuminated diorama.

Upon leaving the Hancock Tower, visit **Trinity Church** just a few steps away, a masterpiece of 19th-century American Romanesque architecture designed by **Henry Hobson Richardson.** Before entering the church, observe the stunning juxtaposition of architectural styles: the featureless, sky blue Hancock (or slate blue-gray, if the day is overcast) enters the earth without a whisper, while the richly textured Trinity warmly embraces the ground in earth tones.

Cross a block over from Boylston Street to **Newbury Street,** where a multitude of shops and restaurants suit all tastes, with numerous galleries displaying the work of local artists. Walking against traffic, you'll soon arrive at the **Boston Public Garden.** Verdant in summer, the picturesque garden provides a respite from street traffic and sidewalk bustle and a chance to rest your feet. If small children are included in your party, visit the bronze ducklings modeled after the feathered protagonists of **Robert McCloskey's** famed *Make Way for Ducklings* tale (they're near the corner of Beacon and Charles streets).

On **Beacon Hill** across from **Boston Common** sits the **State House;** on the opposite side of Beacon Street is **Augustus Saint-Gaudens'** bas-relief of **Robert Gould Shaw** and the heroic black regiment he commanded. At the back of the State House you'll find **Mount Vernon Street,** erstwhile home of Boston's most prestigious families, abolitionists, industrialists, and philanthropists alike. This area best represents Old Boston. (Visitors from certain areas of London will feel they never left home.)

At the base of Mount Vernon, turn right and walk down **Charles Street,** with its many antique shops. At its end, look for the pedestrian entrance to the **Longfellow Bridge** with its matching sets of "salt and pepper shaker" towers. Stop at the first tower and take in the view of Boston's skyline; once again, the contrast between the old and the new is striking. Beacon Hill appears superimposed against the towering modern structures.

Returning, descend from the bridge to an elevated walkway sloping downward to the esplanade. Proceed upriver past the **Hatch Shell** of Arthur Fiedler and July Fourth renown. With a summer breeze the sailboats should be numerous, tacking back and forth on the **Charles River.** Sit down and enjoy the view of **Cambridge** across the way, then return to Boston proper via another elevated walkway, the unmistakable dusty-pink **Fiedler Footbridge,** which deposits you near the Public Garden. Your walking tour now over, it's time for a meal or an invigorating cup of tea in the **Ritz-Carlton Lounge**—proper dress required. Or, if your party is more casual, seek out one of the outdoor cafes along Newbury Street.

Benjamin Thompson
President, Benjamin Thompson & Associates, Architects

To understand Boston and its architectural styles, walk around this pedestrian-friendly city and look at—besides the well-scaled streets and finely detailed buildings—how the city's site defines and explains both what it is and has been throughout history. Boston is a peninsula pointed at the sea. Today's plan emerges with great clarity from the organic irregularity of its origins. As you walk around the city, it tells you many things.

Start at **Arlington Street** (the logical "A" of an alphabetic **Back Bay** grid) at the edge of the **Public Garden** and **Boston Common.** Sheep once grazed on this rural backside of the original town. Make your way up **Beacon Hill** via **Boylston Street** to the gold-domed **State House** on the ridge, and look east toward the harbor. Fanning out in a bold arc around the base of the hill are the Waterfront piers, where settlement and commerce started, working their way up the hill. (Still on the inner streets of Beacon Hill are lovely brick town houses, quiet streets, and elegant **Louisburg Square**—an 18th-century urban miracle.)

You can make your way to the water by various routes. Down Beacon Hill to **City Hall** and through **South Market Street** to **Waterfront Park** takes you along the scenic "Walk to the Sea," terminating at **Long Wharf** and the adjacent **New England Aquarium.** (Here, **The Chart House** is a good bet for an atmospheric Waterfront dinner.)

Back Bay

In colonial days Long Wharf was Boston's deepwater pier, receiving British goods and unwelcome troops. At **Dock Square,** its watery landing place for small boats, old **Faneuil Hall** was built as the first city market. In 1825, to serve a growing city, **Quincy Market** was built on landfill and **Atlantic Avenue** became the pierhead edge of the harbor, facing east to the great ocean beyond.

Here you have two choices. You can turn south on Atlantic Avenue, reaching **Rowes Wharf** (where a commuter boat will whisk you to **Logan Airport**), then cross the **Northern Avenue Bridge** to **South Boston,** an emerging warehouse district whose first visible attraction is the imaginative **Children's Museum.** Pick up a lobster dinner or a lunch of steamers or oysters at the **Dockside** restaurant at the end of the bridge along the channel (outdoor seating is available when the weather is nice). Or you can travel north on Atlantic Avenue along the piers (which continue to be reclaimed for apartments, offices, restaurants, and people) on a route that runs to the mouth of the **Charles River.** When this gets dull, loop back through the colorful **North End** and reemerge at **Faneuil Hall Marketplace.** Pause for drinks at the **Marketplace Cafe** on **North Market Street** next to the **Flower Market,** and watch the people stroll by. Or try **Marketplace Grill & Oar Bar** upstairs for good French food and great views. Watch the activity in the marketplace from the south windows, or **Haymarket** from the north windows of the dining room.

Kenmore Square/Fenway

This side of Boston befuddles even Bostonians, who regularly scramble references to **Fenway Park** (the famous ballpark), the **Fenway** (a parkway), the **Fens** (part of the park system designed by **Frederick Law Olmsted**), and **Fenway**, the district containing all three. Also part of Fenway is **Kenmore Square**, a student mecca, and **Longwood Medical Area**, a dense complex of world-renowned medical and educational establishments—including **Harvard Medical School**—that's a city unto itself. Unlike Beacon Hill or Back Bay, Fenway lacks a cohesive personality, and its indeterminate boundaries are a constant source of confusion to visitors and residents alike. But it's worth navigating the helter-skelter Fenway to find its main attractions: the **Museum of Fine Arts; Isabella Stewart Gardner Museum; Symphony Hall;** Olmsted's famous **Emerald Necklace;** and, of course, Fenway Park, home of the **Red Sox.**

Fenway was the last Boston neighborhood built on landfill, and only emerged after the noxious and loathsome **Back Bay Fens** was imaginatively rehabilitated by Olmsted. Like the original Back Bay—stagnant tidal flats that metamorphosed into the city's most fashionable neighborhood—the Back Bay Fens was considered an unusable part of town, a stinking, swampy mess that collected sewage and runoff from the **Muddy River** and **Stony Brook** before draining into the

Charles River. The problem worsened after Back Bay was filled in and the Fens' unsanitary state became a concern for the city. A group of commissioners assembled to address the Back Bay Fens drainage problems and to simultaneously develop a park system for Boston, an idea that gained momentum in the 1870s. Co-creator of New York City's Central Park and founder of the landscape-architecture profession in America, Olmsted was called in as consultant and ultimately hired in 1878 to fix the Fens and create the Boston Park System. His ingenious solution involved installing a tidal gate and holding basin, and using mud dredged from the refreshed Fens to create surrounding parkland. Developers quickly recognized the neighborhood's new appeal, and it was "Westward-ho!" once again for overcrowded Boston.

The transformed Fens became the first link in Olmsted's Emerald Necklace, the most important feature in the Boston Park Department's plan for a city-scaled green-space network, the first of its kind in the nation. Instead of a New York-style central park (inappropriate given Boston's topography), Boston wanted a system of open spaces throughout the city, offering breathing room to residents. This plan meshed perfectly with Olmsted's noble esthetic and social ideals for landscape architecture. He envisioned interconnected parks, recreation grounds, boulevards, and parkways that would not only beautify the environment and enhance public health and sanitation, but also direct urban expansion, population density, and the local economy. Boston and Olmsted were ideally matched: city officials appreciated not only his talents and civic-mindedness, but also his interest in solving practical problems through landscape design.

Attracted by Olmsted's lovely park and succeeding Emerald Necklace links, numerous cultural, medical, educational, and social institutions began relocating to the Fenway area. Boston's devastating Downtown fire of 1872 and advances in public transportation also encouraged many to move. During the 1890s and early 1900s the **Massachusetts Historical Society,** Symphony Hall, **Horticultural Hall, New England Conservatory of Music, Simmons College**, Museum of Fine Arts, and Harvard Medical School were built. Another neighborhood pioneer was **Fenway Court,** the fashionable residence where **Isabella Stewart Gardner** installed the magnificent personal museum of art that now bears her name. Since then, other institutions have followed the same trail; **Northeastern University** and **Boston University** now dominate the district. Fenway's resident educational and medical institutions have played the largest role in shaping its contemporary character. Today, the Kenmore Square/Fenway area claims a huge concentration of college students and young adults. It has the lowest median age of all Boston neighborhoods and a transient feel. Originally an extension of prestigious Back Bay, with fine hotels, offices, and shops, Kenmore Square is now largely geared toward its student population, with plenty of fast-food joints and cheap-eats delis, good ethnic restaurants, clubs, record shops, and the like.

To get to the Back Bay side of this neighborhood, take the Green Line to the Symphony or the Hynes Convention Center/ICA subway stop; the Kenmore Square stop (also on the Green Line) puts you in the middle of the club and student scene. After Kenmore, the Green Line branches into three lines (B,C, and D) with different endpoints, so make sure you're on the right one. The B Line to Boston College makes frequent stops aboveground on Commonwealth Avenue (along Boston University's campus), and the C Line to Cleveland Circle does the same on Beacon Street. The D Line (heading for Riverside) stops at Fenway, convenient to Fenway Park, and Longwood, near the Longwood Medical Area. For the Museum of Fine Arts and the Isabella Stewart Gardner Museum, you'll want to take the E Line (branching off at Copley, and headed for Arborway); get off at the Museum stop.

1 Isabella Stewart Gardner Museum On New Year's Day 1903 **Isabella Stewart Gardner** held a glorious gala-to-end-all-galas to unveil her private art collection in its opulent new **Fenway Court** home (pictured on the following page). No one could pass up this event, including those who typically snubbed flamboyant Isabella. Fifty **Boston Symphony** musicians played a Bach chorale, and when the crowd caught sight of the now-famous flowering palace courtyard, a collective gasp was followed by awed silence. Admirers and detractors alike were wowed by Gardner's resplendent array of paintings, sculpture, tapestries, and objets d'art in their dazzling setting. An admiring **Henry Adams** wrote: "As long as such a work can be done, I will not despair of our age....You are a

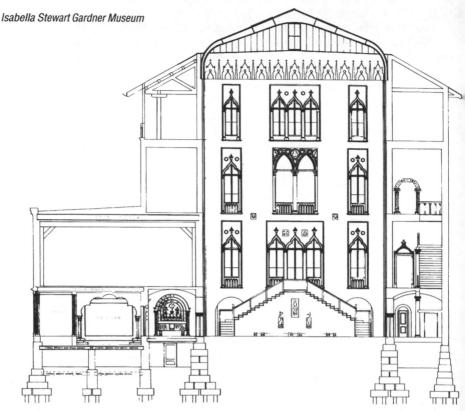

creator and stand alone." Gardner herself described her digs, after 20 years of residence, as "very nice, very comfortable, and rather jolly."

Upon her death in 1924, her will officially turned the mansion into a museum (see the

Kenmore Square/Fenway

plan on the opposite page) and stipulated the demanding terms of its operation: all is to remain *exactly* as it was upon her death, or else all shall be sold and the proceeds given to **Harvard University.** (That accounts for the very hodge-podge manner in which the works of art are displayed—Gardner's preferences at work into perpetuity.) Until recently the museum director lived rent-free in Gardner's own lush apartment; the most liberal reinterpretation of her will to date was to transform these fourth-floor living quarters into office space, a controversial move. More recently, a tiny new gallery (17 by 22 feet) was reclaimed from storage space and deemed a "reasonable deviation" from the will. Museum curators have also initiated an artists-in-residence program (in the carriage house) to perpetuate Gardner's own predilections as patron.

For countless Bostonians and visitors, Gardner's museum has no equal, and many return again and again for another heady dose of her compelling creation. As was true in Gardner's lifetime, the museum's great appeal is in the total impression it creates. In a series of singular stage-set galleries—**the Veronese Room, Gothic Room, Dutch Room, Titian Room**—

look for **Botticelli, Manet, Raphael, Rembrandt, Rubens, Matisse, Sargent, Titian, La Farge,** and **Whistler.** Nearly 2,000 objects are on display, spanning more than 30 centuries, with emphasis on Italian Renaissance and 17th-century Dutch masters. (Be sure to look for the **Blue Room** display of Gardner's correspondence with her distinguished friends.) Objects from different periods and cultures are liberally intermixed in the eclectic manner she favored. But on 18 March 1990, the most devastating day in the museum's history, terrible empty spaces were created on the walls. Thirteen uninsured paintings and artifacts valued at $200 million were stolen by two thieves disguised as policemen in what the *Boston Herald* dubbed "the Heist of the Century." The most famous work, *The Concert,* by Jan Vermeer, cost Gardner $6,000 at an 1892 auction in Paris; it is now priceless. The illustrious art historian **Bernard Berenson,** befriended by Gardner when he was a Harvard College student, sometimes advised her on what to buy, and counseled her to purchase two works by Rembrandt, *The Storm on the Sea of Galilee* (his only known seascape) and *A Lady and Gentleman in Black,* both stolen. In gentler times, Gardner often acted as her own security guard.

With its soft light, cloudy pink walls, picturesque balconies, quiet fountain, and fragrant fresh flowers and plantings supplied by the museum's own greenhouse, the four-story courtyard is one of Boston's most serene and beloved places. It is composed of authentic

Isabella Stewart Gardner Museum

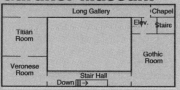

Third Floor

- Long Gallery
- Chapel
- Elev.
- Stairs
- Titian Room
- Gothic Room
- Veronese Room
- Stair Hall
- Down ⟶

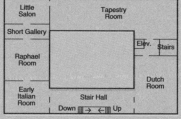

Second Floor

- Little Salon
- Tapestry Room
- Short Gallery
- Elev.
- Stairs
- Raphael Room
- Dutch Room
- Early Italian Room
- Stair Hall
- Down ⟶ ⟵ Up

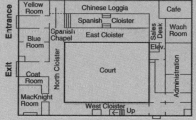

Ground Floor

- Entrance / Exit
- Yellow Room
- Chinese Loggia
- Cafe
- Spanish Cloister
- Spanish Chapel
- East Cloister
- Sales Desk
- Wash Room
- Blue Room
- Elev.
- North Cloister
- Coat Room
- Court
- Administration
- MacKnight Room
- West Cloister — Up

architectural and decorative elements collected by Gardner throughout Europe and Egypt. From September to May, chamber or classical music concerts are held Saturday and Sunday at 1:30PM in the **Tapestry Room** (fee in addition to admission). ♦ Admission, except on Wednesday; members and children under 12 free; reduced admission for senior citizens and students. Tu-Su 11AM-5PM. Free guided tour Friday 2:30PM. Private tours require advance notice. 280 The Fenway. 566.1401; recorded concert information 734.1359 & (limited because of narrow spaces; museum provides wheelchairs that fit everywhere)

Within the Isabella Stewart Gardner Museum:

The Cafe at the Gardner ★$$ The cafe serves excellent lunches that include quiches, salads, sandwiches, and desserts. Weather permitting, dine on the outdoor terrace overlooking the museum gardens. ♦ Cafe ♦ Tu-F 11:30AM-3PM; Sa-Su 11:30AM-4PM &

Socialite and art collector Isabella Stewart Gardner delighted in shocking staid Boston—among other affronts, she wore diamonds mounted on wires like antennae in her hair and walked her two pet lions on Beacon Street. Soirees at her Fenway palazzo featured her favorite refreshments: champagne and doughnuts.

Restaurants/Clubs: Red   Hotels: Blue
Shops/ ● Outdoors: Green   Sights/Culture: Black

The House that Mrs. Jack Built

The larger-than-life **Isabella Stewart Gardner** (1840-1924) was a charismatic, spirited, and independent New Yorker who married into Victorian Boston's high society but never bowed to its conventions. (Her husband, John, was known as Jack to close friends, hence her nickname, "Mrs. Jack.") Though she became a prominent private art collector and flamboyant socialite, many proper Bostonians forever dismissed her as a brash outsider. But Isabella didn't give a hoot—a passionate woman, she loved the spotlight, so much so that she built a showcase mansion, which is now a museum (see page 137), to enshrine her collections and to throw gala parties.

Gardner delighted in upstaging her critics and creating a stir with outrageous behavior, but with a regal awareness of her lofty social stature. Among her many pleasures were art, literature, and music, and she surrounded herself with the most fashionable talents of her time. However, most of her tremendous energy went toward acquiring fabulous art objects. When her posh Back Bay mansion on **Beacon Street** became too small for her treasures, the Gardners started planning for a museum. After John's death in 1898, she built **Fenway Court**, a 15th-century Venetian-style palazzo that proudly towered alone in the unfashionable Fenway. While "Mrs. Jack's Palace" was under construction, Gardner was always on the scene directing and often got into the action—climbing on scaffolds to daub the paint to her liking on the courtyard walls, for instance. She was accompanied by a trumpeter who summoned workers when she wanted to confer with them: one note for the architect, another for the plumber, and so on. Anyone ignoring the summons was fired.

Kenmore Square/Fenway

Gardner held court among her collections, blurring the distinction between residence and museum in an extraordinary, idiosyncratic way. Signs of her presence remain—a table is set for tea as if she were in the next room. Prevented by gender from the prestige and power she was suited for by temperament, Gardner found in her museum the stage, cultural forum, artistic medium, and professional avocation denied her by her times. Look for the plaque she first affixed over the door in 1900, giving her home its official name. Then find the seal designed for her achievement, carved in marble and set into the museum facade's brick wall, which bears her motto, "C'est mon plaisir" (It is my pleasure), and a phoenix, a symbol of immortality. **Henry James** thought she resembled "a figure on a wondrous cinquecento tapestry." **John Singer Sargent's** portrait of Gardner stirred a scandal when it was first unveiled in 1888 at the private, then all-male **St. Botolph Club,** to which her husband belonged. Isabella had posed bare-armed in a clingy décolleté gown, which so shocked proper Bostonians that her husband became infuriated, threatened to horsewhip any gossipers, and forbade the picture to be publicly displayed. But you can see it now through untitillated 20th-century eyes at Isabella's museum, where it finally found its niche in 1924.

The Museum of Fine Arts

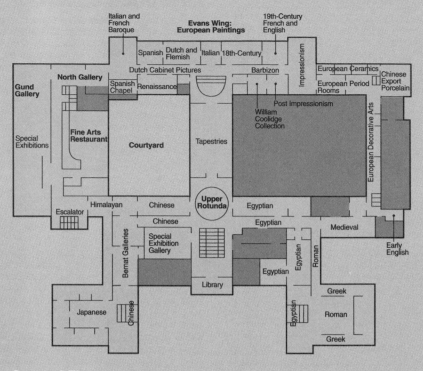

Second Floor

Italian and French Baroque

Evans Wing: European Paintings

19th-Century French and English

Spanish · Dutch and Flemish · Italian · 18th-Century · Impressionism

Dutch Cabinet Pictures

Barbizon

European Ceramics · European Period Rooms · Chinese Export Porcelain

Gund Gallery

North Gallery

Spanish Chapel · Renaissance

Post Impressionism

European Decorative Arts

Special Exhibitions

Fine Arts Restaurant

Courtyard

Tapestries

William Coolidge Collection

Himalayan · Chinese · Upper Rotunda · Egyptian

Escalator

Chinese · Egyptian · Medieval

Bernat Galleries

Special Exhibition Gallery

Egyptian · Roman · Early English

Egyptian

Library

Egyptian · Greek

Japanese · Chinese

Egyptian · Roman

Greek

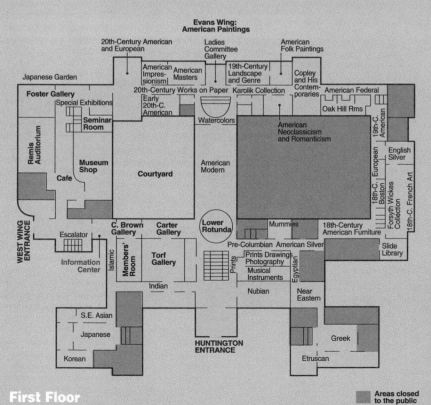

First Floor

Evans Wing: American Paintings

20th-Century American and European

Ladies Committee Gallery

American Folk Paintings

Japanese Garden

American Impressionism · American Masters · 19th-Century Landscape and Genre · Copley and His Contemporaries · American Federal

Foster Gallery

Special Exhibitions

20th-Century Works on Paper · Karolik Collection

Oak Hill Rms

Seminar Room

Early 20th-C. American

Watercolors

American Neoclassicism and Romanticism

19th-C. American

English Silver

Remis Auditorium

Museum Shop

Cafe

Courtyard

American Modern

18th-C. European Boston · Forsyth Wickes Collection · 18th-C. French Art

C. Brown Gallery · Carter Gallery

Lower Rotunda

Mummies

18th-Century American Furniture

WEST WING ENTRANCE

Escalator

Islamic

Members' Room

Torf Gallery

Pre-Columbian · American Silver

Slide Library

Information Center

Prints · Prints Drawings Photography · Musical Instruments

Egyptian

Indian

Nubian

Near Eastern

S.E. Asian

Japanese

HUNTINGTON ENTRANCE

Greek

Korean

Etruscan

■ Areas closed to the public

2 Museum of Fine Arts (MFA) The MFA first exhibited upstairs at the **Boston Athenaeum** on **Beacon Hill,** then moved in 1876 to its own ornate Gothic Revival **Copley Square** quarters, since demolished. In 1909 the museum made the trek out to the newly fashionable Fenway area along with numerous other pioneering public institutions seeking more spacious sites than Boston proper could offer. The MFA now resides in an imposing if dull Classical Revival edifice (designed by **Guy Lowell** in 1909) with a majestic colonnade on the Fenway side and a temple portico on the **Huntington Street** side flanked by two big wings, the newest designed in 1981 by **I.M. Pei & Partners.** Standing in the front courtyard is a statue of a mounted Indian gazing skyward, appealing for aid against the white man's invasion. **Cyrus Edwin Dallin's** *Appeal to the Great White Spirit* won a gold medal at the 1909 Paris Salon and attracted many admirers when erected here in 1913, but looks somewhat odd in this ordered setting today.

The museum's somber starkness ends abruptly indoors, where an embarrassment of riches begins, much of it acquired through the generosity of wealthy Victorian Bostonians committed to creating a truly cosmopolitan cultural repository. The MFA is one of the country's greatest museums and deserves repeated exploration (see the plan at left). Begin with a dose of familiar sights and historic local names and faces in the American collections. The MFA owns more than 60 works by **John Singleton Copley,** including his portrait of **Paul Revere** (whose artistry as a silversmith is on display elsewhere, including his famous Liberty Bowl), and paintings by local boy **Winslow Homer, Gilbert Stuart, Edward Hopper, John Singer Sargent, Fitz Hugh Lane, Mary Cassatt, James McNeill Whistler,** and **Thomas Eakins.** Holdings range from native New England folk art and portraiture to works by the **Hudson River School, American Impressionists, Realists, Ash Can School,** and New York's **Abstract Expressionists.** The **Department of American Decorative Arts and Sculpture** is particularly noteworthy for its pre-Civil War New England products, and includes furniture, silver, pewter, glass, ceramics, sculpture, and folk art. The collection progresses from the rustic functional creations of early colonial times to the elegant pieces popular in the increasingly prosperous colonies. The **Department of Twentieth-Century Art** is a Johnny-come-lately, emphasized only since the '70s, but does include **Jackson Pollock, David Smith, Robert Motherwell, Helen Frankenthaler, Morris Louis, Joan Miró,** and **Georgia O'Keeffe.**

The MFA owns superb works from all major developments in European painting from the 11th to the 20th centuries, with a particularly rich representation of 19th-century French works. Victorian Bostonians loved French painting, eagerly exhibiting the Impressionists who were still awaiting acceptance in their own country. On display in the **Evans Wing** galleries are many of the museum's 38 **Monets** and more than 150 **Millets,** including his best-known painting, *The Sower,* as well as works by **Corot, Délacroix, Courbet, Renoir , Pissarro, Manet, van Gogh, Gauguin,** and **Cézanne.** Other celebrated artists shown in this wing are **van der Weyden, Il Rosso, El Greco, Rubens, Canaletto, Turner,** and **Picasso.** The MFA's extraordinary collection of Asiatic art—the largest under any one museum roof—features one of the greatest Japanese collections in existence, and important objects from China, India, and Southeast Asia. (Before you leave the MFA grounds, be sure to visit **Tenshin-en-Garden of the Heart of Heaven,** on the museum's north side—a contemplative Japanese garden designed by garden master **Kinsaku Nakane.**) The **Egyptian** and **Ancient Near Eastern Art** galleries are a favorite with kids—they have mummies!—and are also treasure troves of jewelry, sculpture, and other objects from throughout Asia's western regions. The MFA's array of Old Kingdom sculpture is equaled only by the **Cairo Museum** because the MFA and **Harvard University** jointly sponsored excavations in Egypt for 40 years. And it is apt that the "Athens of America" boasts a superb representation of ancient Greek, Roman, and Etruscan objects, including bronzes, sculpture dating from the 6th to the 4th centuries BC, and vases painted with fascinating figures and vignettes by some of the greatest early Greek artists.

Another highlight is the **Department of European Decorative Arts,** which features a collection of antique musical instruments that includes lutes, clavichords, harps, and zithers, replicas of which are often played in special MFA concert programs. The **Department of Textiles** displays an international collection of tapestries, batiks, embroideries, silk weavings, cos-

tume materials, and other textiles. The Boston area was the capital of the textile industry in the late 19th century, and the MFA was the first museum in America to elevate textiles to the status of art. Its collection ranks among the world's greatest. Spanning the 15th century to today, the **Department of Prints and Drawings** has particularly outstanding 15th-century Italian engravings and 19th-century lithography, many works by **Dürer, Rembrandt, Goya,** the **Tiepolos,** and the **German Expressionists, Picasso's** complete *Vollard Suite,* the **M. and M. Karolik Collection of American Drawings and Watercolors** from 1800 to 1875, a growing collection of original photographs, and still more.

Special exhibitions are mounted in the modern light-filled West Wing, where you'll find the **Fine Arts Restaurant, Galleria Cafe, Cafeteria,** and **Museum Shop.** Many Bostonians make special trips just to visit the latter for its wonderful selection of books, prints, children's games, cards and stationery, reproductions of silver, jewelry, glass, textiles, and other decorative items aplenty. The MFA's excellent film, concert, and lecture series are held in the West Wing's **Remis Auditorium.** Also in the neighborhood is the **School of the Museum of Fine**

Arts and the **Massachusetts College of Art,** both of which maintain galleries. ◆ Admission (reduced when only the West Wing is open; free Wednesday from 4PM to 9:45PM, except for the Graham Gund Gallery); members and children under six free; reduced admission for students and senior citizens. Entire museum Tu, Th-Su 10AM-5PM; W 10AM-10PM. West Wing only Th-F 5-10PM. Closed most holidays. Free guided tours Tu-F 10:30AM, 1:30PM; W 6:15PM; Sa 11AM, 1:30PM. Free introductory walk in Spanish first Saturday of every month 11:30AM. 465 Huntington Ave (at Museum Rd). Paid parking available on Museum Rd. 267.9300; daily schedules 267.2973; TTY/TDD 267.9703; concerts, lectures, film information 267.9300, ext. 300 ⊛ (handicapped parking near West Wing entrance)

Within the Museum of Fine Arts:

Fine Arts Restaurant ★★$$ The food is unexpectedly good, with special themed menus playing off the current high-profile exhibition. For "Monet in the '90s," a sandwich called the Grainstack and an entrée called Water Lily were among the offerings. This is a popular place for brunch. ◆ American ◆ Tu, Sa 11:30AM-2:30PM; W-F 11:30AM-2:30PM, 5:30-8:30PM ⊛

Galleria Cafe ★$ Refuel for another foray through the galleries over cappuccino or wine and a light meal, fruit, cheese, or dessert at the informal open cafe. ◆ Cafe ◆ Tu, Sa-Su 10AM-4PM; W-F 10AM-9:30PM ⊛

Cafeteria $ If you're on a budget, this is the best option for a quick meal, and there's rarely a wait. ◆ American ◆ Tu, Sa-Su 10AM-4PM; W-F 10AM-8PM. Lower level ⊛

Kenmore Square/Fenway

3 Greater Boston YMCA $ Mainly students and tourists stay in this 50-room YMCA (the first in the US, founded in 1851). There's a 10-day maximum visit, and you must be at least 18 years old with a picture ID and luggage to stay. Two of the three floors are for men, and the other is coed. Single and double rooms are available; all (except for one suite) share baths. Children can stay with a parent. Breakfast is free, as is use of the gym, indoor track, pool, and sauna. There's a cafeteria-style restaurant and laundry facilities on the premises. Smoking is allowed in the rooms only. A modest key deposit is required. Reserve two weeks in advance by mail; walk-ins are accepted daily after 12:30PM. ◆ Office M-F 9AM-7:30PM; Sa 10AM-2PM. 316 Huntington Ave (between Gainsborough St and Opera Pl). 536.7800 ⊛

4 Jordan Hall at the New England Conservatory of Music (NEC) Like **Symphony Hall,** only smaller and more intimate, Jordan Hall—designed in 1903 by **Wheelwright and Haven**—is an acoustically superior concert space, ideal for chamber music. It belongs to the NEC, established in 1867 as the first music college in the country and internationally renowned today for its undergraduate and graduate music

programs. In addition to 400 NEC concerts, most free and held during school months, Jordan accommodates a number of musical groups, including the **Juilliard Quartet, Tokyo String Quartet, Boston Symphony Chamber Players, Cantata Singers, Carlos Montoya,** and the **Boston Chamber Music Society.** The hall was funded by **Eben Jordan,** founder of the **Jordan Marsh** department stores. ◆ Box office M-Sa 10AM-6PM (until 8PM the night of the show); Sa noon-6PM. 30 Gainsborough St (at Huntington Ave). No reservations by telephone or mail. Program information 536.2412, box office 262.1120 ⊛ (call in advance)

5 Boston University Theatre Acclaimed **Huntington Theatre Company (HTC),** the professional company-in-residence, puts on five plays annually at this charming 1925 Greek Revival theater, which seats 850. HTC's focus is both classic and contemporary, ranging from Shakespeare and musicals to new plays. Discounts are offered for senior citizens, students, and groups; subscriptions are also available. ◆ 264 Huntington Ave (at Massachusetts Ave). Ticket information 266.0800 ⊛ (call in advance)

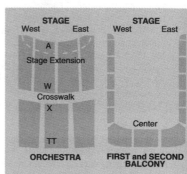

Symphony Hall Floor Plan

6 Symphony Hall Deep-pocketed Brahmin philanthropist and amateur musician **Henry Lee Higginson,** who founded the **Boston Symphony Orchestra (BSO)** in 1881, wanted his creation's new home to be among the world's most magnificent, so he commissioned **McKim, Mead & White** as architects; the building, completed in 1900, is on the **National Register of Historic Places.** The hall's enduring fame stems not from its restrained Italian Renaissance style, however distinguished, but rather from its internationally distinguished acoustics, which have earned Symphony Hall its nickname as a "Stradivarius" among concert halls (see the plan above). Symphony Hall is the first concert hall in the world to be built according to an acoustical formula, the work of **Wallace Sabine,** an assistant professor of physics at **Harvard University** and one of the first to probe the scientific basis of acoustics. The 2,625-seat hall is basically a shoebox-shaped shell built to resonate glorious sound to astound the ears; the eyes matter less (physical comfort, too; the seats are rather hard).

Directed by **Seiji Ozawa,** the BSO remains one of the world's preeminent orchestras. It is in residence at Symphony Hall from October through April; in July and August it performs at **Tanglewood,** an open-air facility in western Massachusetts. The hall is also home to the beloved **Boston Pops,** conducted by Hollywood composer and Oscar-winner **John Williams,** which performs from May to mid-July at Symphony Hall. (The seats are removed from the main floor, replaced by tables and chairs, and food and drink are served.) Williams' predecessor was the late renowned **Arthur Fiedler,** who wielded the baton for more than 50 years. No one should miss the chance to experience the orchestra and hall together, a delight music-loving Boston has always cherished. The **Handel & Haydn Society,** America's oldest continuously active performing arts organization, performs here, too, as do many other local, national, and international groups. The hall also holds a magnificent 5,000-pipe organ. To reserve and charge seats for BSO or Pops performances, call Symphony-Charge at 266.1200; subscriptions are available. Bargain alert: same-day, one-per-customer discounted seats for BSO performances are available on Tuesday, Thursday, and Friday. The line forms near the box office Tuesday and Thursday from 5PM, and from 9AM on Friday. ◆ Box office M-Sa 10AM-6PM; through intermission on concert evenings. 301 Massachusetts Ave (at Huntington Ave). 266.1492 &

7 Thai Cuisine ★$$ After a concert at **Symphony Hall** or a foreign film at the **MFA,** dine on good Thai dishes, fiery or delicate, in this little 30-seater behind the Hall. The owner has opened several other Thai restaurants in Greater Boston, all highly regarded. Go the spicy route with *kang liang* (peppered shrimp soup) or *gai pud gra prao* (chicken, onion, and chiles), or try more subtle tastes like *tom you koong* (soup with shrimp, lemongrass, lime, and chiles), steamed whole fish, Thai seafood combination, or the selection of curries. It's sometimes a little hurried here. ◆ Thai/Takeout ◆ M-Th 11:30AM-3PM, 5-10PM; F-Sa 11:30AM-3PM, 5-10:30PM; Su 5-10PM. 14A Westland St (at Massachusetts Avenue). 262.1485 &

8 Bangkok Cuisine ★$ A favorite with students and people working nearby, Boston's oldest Thai restaurant is still turning out great beef and chicken *sate, duck choo chee* (curry), *pad Thai,* whole fried bass with chile sauce, and Thai bouillabaisse, which features assorted tender seafood served in a puffed pouch. The long, narrow dining room empties and fills quickly, but service is sometimes desultory, so allow extra time if you have a concert or movie ahead. ◆ Thai/Takeout ◆ M-Sa 11:30AM-3PM, 5-10:30PM; Su 5-10:30PM. 177A Massachusetts Ave (at Norway St). 262.5377 &

9 Boston International American Youth Hostel (AYH) $ There's no cheaper lodging available in the city, and it's near the **Museum of Fine Arts.** Offering 150 beds in the winter and 220 in the summer, the hostel accommodates men and women of all ages in dormitory style, with six bunks per room, separated by sex. Every floor has showers and bathrooms, and

the building houses laundry facilities plus two kitchens with utensils. Sleeping bags are not allowed; you can rent a sleep sheet for a modest fee and deposit. The hostel fills up quickly from May until fall. The fee is lower if you're a member of AYH, and you can join on the spot; summer bunks are reserved for members only. Bikes and packs can be stored securely on the premises. No alcohol is allowed, there is no smoking except in one public room, and there's a four-night limit per 30-day period. ◆ Daily 7AM-midnight. 12 Hemenway St (at Haviland St). Reservations recommended; you can reserve by phone if paying with MasterCard or Visa; walk-ins accepted for 25 percent of the beds nightly. 536.9455

9 Looney Tunes This is a good source for serious and dilettante collectors of used and out-of-print jazz, classical, and rock records, some rare. The store also sells movie and Broadway sound tracks, comedy, country, blues, and opera LPs and 45s, plus "cut-outs," CDs, cassettes, and videos. They carry a few new items, too, and also buy and trade. ◆ M-Sa 10AM-9PM; Su noon-9PM. 1106 Boylston St (at Hemenway St). 247.2238 & Also at: 1001 Massachusetts Ave, near Harvard Sq, Cambridge. 876.5624

Kenmore Square/Fenway

9 Counterpoint Cafe ★$ Inexpensive fare is served in a stylish setting. Try the omelets, fresh muffins, and steamed hot chocolate for breakfast, smoked turkey and avocado on homemade mini-baguette, Green Goddess salad, and tasty daily specials for lunch. Counterpoint is an ideal spot for a light pre-concert bite. ◆ Cafe ◆ M-F 7AM-6PM; Sa 9AM-3PM; Su 10AM-2PM. 1124 Boylston St (at Hemenway St). 424.1789

10 The Massachusetts Historical Society The first historical society founded in the New World (done so in 1791), the society is housed in an 1899 **National Historic Landmark** designed by **Edmund March Wheelwright.** It largely operates as a research center for the study of American history and is only surpassed by the **Library of Congress.** The focal point is the library, which contains some 3,200 collections of manuscripts and several hundred thousand books, pamphlets, broadsides, maps, early newspapers, and journals, including **Governor John Winthrop's** and the **Adams** family's papers, **Paul Revere's** accounts of his famous ride, two copies of the Declaration of Independence—one written in **John Adams'**

hand, the other in **Thomas Jefferson's**—and a staggering quantity of other such treasures.

The society's rare-books collection includes most of the important early books printed in America, or about its discovery and settlement. Government, politics, women's history, slavery, the China trade, railroads, science and technology—the breadth of topics addressed is immense. The society also owns prints, engravings, furniture, antique clocks, personal belongings, and several hundred works of art. The first map produced in British North America, an 18th-century Indian archer weathervane by **Deacon Shem Drowne** (maker of **Faneuil Hall's** grasshopper weathervane), a list of Americans killed in the **Battle of Concord,** and Jefferson's architectural plans for **Monticello** are among the items it preserves. Free guided tours are given if requested in advance. All these virtues not withstanding, here's the catch: to use the library, you must pass muster as a "serious" person with a "worthy" pursuit. ♦ Free. M-F 9AM-4:45PM. 1154 Boylston St (at Charlesgate E). 536.1608 ♿

11   The Other Side Cosmic Cafe ★$ The "other side" refers to the extension of Newbury Street (past Massachusetts Avenue) that most people don't even know is here, and "cosmic" alludes, one presumes, to its atmospheric aspirations. Whatever—this "Seattle-style coffeehouse/cafe," with its classical/industrial decor (cast-iron railings, red-velvet drapes) and fresh fare, is just the ticket for the young throngs tipping the balance of trade to the "downscale" end of the street. It's handy, too, for the concert-bound. ♦ Coffeehouse/Cafe ♦ Daily 10AM-midnight. 407 Newbury St (at Massachusetts Ave). 536.9477 ♿

Kenmore Square/Fenway

11   Steve's Ice Cream Popular with just about everybody, Steve's sells super-rich, creamy ice cream in lots of different flavors—some exotic—with all kinds of "mix-ins" mashed into the ice cream order. Sundaes, ice cream sodas, milkshakes, and all that jazz are available. ♦ Ice Cream ♦ Daily 9AM-midnight. 95 Massachusetts Ave (at Newbury St). 247.9401 ♿ Also at: Faneuil Hall Marketplace. 367.0569; 31 Church St, Harvard Sq, Cambridge. 491.0254

11   Oceanic Chinese Restaurant ★$ It would take hundreds of visits to exhaust this versatile restaurant's enormous menu. In addition to unadventurous old favorites like spareribs and spring rolls, Oceanic serves unusual specialty seafood items, including shark's fin and shredded duck soup, whole fried sole, abalone with tender vegetables, clams with black-bean sauce, and various seafoods with ginger and scallions. Treats that don't hail from the sea are crisp roasted duck, spicy Szechuan dishes, and sizzling hot pots. The restaurant is a trifle

fancier than the average Chinatown choice, but it replicates that neighborhood's estimable authentic cuisine—for that's where Oceanic's owners and staff started out. ♦ Chinese/Takeout ♦ Daily 11:30AM-1AM. 91 Massachusetts Ave (between Commonwealth Ave and Newbury St). 353.0791 ♿

12   The Eliot Hotel $$ Located on the edge of Back Bay, this is a convenient place to stay. Just 90 rooms on nine floors, the modest-size 1925 hotel is privately owned and attracts international visitors, conventioneers, and visiting professors. It's one of the city's best buys. The overall ambience is quiet and old-fashioned. There's no restaurant on the premises, but Continental breakfast is served daily in the lobby. Nonsmokers' rooms and pay parking are available. ♦ 370 Commonwealth Ave (at Massachusetts Ave). 267.1607; fax 536.9114

Within The Eliot Hotel:

The Eliot Lounge and Cafe $ The famous sports bar, presided over by gregarious bartender and running guru **Tommy Leonard,** is unofficial headquarters for the **Boston Marathon.** This comfortable, friendly bar attracts all kinds, and students flock in for once-a-week DJ dancing. The cafe serves down-to-earth fare like chili, pizzas, sandwiches, and hamburgers. ♦ American/Takeout ♦ 370 Commonwealth Ave (enter from Massachusetts Ave). Cafe M-F 4-10PM; Sa-Su 11:30AM-10PM. 421.9169. Bar daily 3PM-2AM. 262.1078

13   The B.U. Bookstore You won't have any trouble locating this store, since blinking away atop it is Kenmore Square's famous landmark, the **Citgo Sign. Boston University's** bookstore is one of the largest in New England, with three floors of books to browse among. In addition to textbooks for BU and several other local educational institutions, there's a great selection of current and backlist hardcover and paperback books: best-sellers, cookbooks, children's books, classics, hobbies, gardening, law, women, history, politics—the works. The store sponsors frequent events, including author signings and children's story readings. And beyond books, this six-story department store includes specialty shops selling clothing and accessories, chocolates, stationery, housewares, office supplies, flowers, electronics and cameras, and more. There's even a travel agent. If you're in the square with time to spare before a **Red Sox** game, this is the place to dawdle. ♦ M-Tu 9:30AM-7PM; W-F 9:30AM-9PM; Sa 10AM-6PM; Su noon-5PM. 660 Beacon St (at Commonwealth Ave). 267.8484 ♿

Restaurants/Clubs: Red	Hotels: Blue
Shops/ 🌳 Outdoors: Green	Sights/Culture: Black

Within The B.U. Bookstore:

Cafe Charles ★$ There are plenty of places to grab a quick bite in Kenmore Square, but few are as serene as this pretty cafe tucked far from the madding crowd. Soups, sandwiches on French bread, muffins, cappuccino, and desserts, including an excellent hazelnut torte, are served. Bring a book and relax at a table, or watch the nonstop activity on the streets below from the windowside marble counter. The cafe overlooks the last mile marker for the **Boston Marathon.** A good place for conversation, it attracts BU's students, faculty, president, and local residents, but most Bostonians haven't discovered it. ◆ Cafe/Takeout ◆ M-Sa 9:30AM-6PM; Su noon-5PM. Second floor ♿

Atop The B.U. Bookstore:

Citgo Sign The 60-square-foot, double-sided sign with its two miles of red, white, and blue neon tubing dates from 1965, its pulsating delta controlled by computer. An immediate Pop Art hit, the sign inspired one filmmaker to create a short film called *Go, Go Citgo,* in which the sign did its off-and-on routine to music by the **Monkees** and **Ravi Shankar,** an Indian sitarist. But the sign was turned off during the energy crisis of the '70s, and almost torn down in 1982. However, its fans came to its defense: **Arthur Krim,** a Cambridge resident, college professor, and member of the **Society for Commercial Archaeology** (which works to preserve urban and roadside Americana such as neon signs, diners, and gas stations), helped lead the fight to save **Kenmore Square's** illuminated heartbeat from the scrap heap. Oklahoma-based Citgo agreed to keep the sign plugged in and maintained.

14 Kenmore Club This is really three clubs in one, interconnected so one admission applies to all. **Narcissus** is the largest, a bilevel disco club with glitzy mirrors and lights; and then there's **Alley Pub,** which offers a little more in the way of rock 'n' roll, and **Celebration.** DJ-played Top 40 music is featured throughout, with Latin night on Sunday and heavy metal on Wednesday in Narcissus. Occasionally, special shows with live bands are scheduled. Thursday night is designated college night, although the crowd is young every night. There is a full bar, and light fare is served. Only those 18 and older are admitted. ◆ Cover. Daily 8PM-2AM. 533

Commonwealth Ave (at Beacon St). No sneakers, T-shirts, hats. 536.1950 ♿

15 Nuggets The first store of its kind in the area, Nuggets sells new, used, rare, and out-of-print records, CDs, tapes, and 12" dance singles, as well as related posters, T-shirts, and magazines. You can find jazz, reggae, blues, and more. ◆ M-Sa 10AM-10PM; Su 11AM-6PM. 486 Commonwealth Ave (between Raleigh St and Brookline Ave). 536.0679. Also at: 1354-A Beacon St. 227.8917

15 Cornwall's ★$ Hearty food, games, and magazines up for grabs, and, above all, a great assortment of esoteric brews on tap explain the appeal of this tiny shoebox of a pub, which has fortified BU students for nearly a decade. ◆ English/International ◆ Daily 11:30AM-2AM. 510 Commonwealth Ave (between Raleigh St and Brookline Ave). 262.3749

15 Rathskeller (The Rat)/Hoo Doo BBQ ★$ The Rat is one of the very few clubs in town serving good music and good food. It's not much to look at, to say the least, but the Rat was Boston's first New Wave club. It has boosted many local groups and was the first Boston club to headline the **Cars, Police, Talking Heads,** and **Go Gos.** The club books high-quality local and touring rock bands, up to four a night, three or four nights a week, and they usually go on at 9:30PM. On weekends you can listen for free to bands playing on the balcony. There are four bars serving cheap drinks, plus pinball, video, and a great jukebox.

Chef **James Ryan's** secret sauce slathered on slow-cooked ribs has elevated him to celebrity status and made Hoo Doo BBQ a favorite hangout for anyone with a taste for barbecue.

Kenmore Square/Fenway

A number of musicians (big stars and unknowns) have enjoyed Ryan's ribs, chicken, crisp french fries and onion rings, salads, coleslaw, corn bread, and sweet-potato pie—some struggling performers have even done stints in the kitchen. A generous guy, Ryan cooks for homeless friends as well as the hungry well-to-do. For admittance to the Rathskeller (not the Hoo Doo) you must be 21 or older unless a special all-ages show is scheduled. ◆ American/Barbecue ◆ Cover for club. Daily 11AM-2AM; Hoo Doo BBQ open until 10PM. 528 Commonwealth Ave (at Brookline Ave). No credit cards accepted. 536.2750 ♿ (Hoo Doo BBQ only)

16 Howard Johnson/Kenmore $$ Just beyond Kenmore Square on **Boston University's** campus, this bustling HoJo is convenient to **Fenway Park** and western Boston; it's also near **Back Bay.** Lots of tour groups stay here. An older but well-kept hotel, it has 180 rooms on seven floors—including an executive section with larger rooms and VCRs, and complimentary coffee and newspaper—plus a restaurant, lounge, and indoor swimming pool. Nonsmokers' rooms and free parking are available. ◆ 575 Commonwealth Ave. 267.3100, 800/654.2000; fax 267.3100, ext. 40

17 Photographic Resource Center (PRC) One of the few centers for photography in the country, this nonprofit arts organization leases space from **Boston University** and houses three galleries for exhibitions and a nonlending photography library. PRC's intelligent, award-winning design (by **Leers, Weinzapfel Associates/Alex Krieger Architects** in 1985) evokes the mechanical process of photography, its manipulation of light—particularly in the architects' use of industrial materials and glass. The exhibitions emphasize new and experimental photography from the US and abroad; popular recent shows have included *The Emperor's New Clothes,* an exploration of censorship as it relates to art, pornography, and fashion. Check local papers or call to find out about frequent lectures/slide presentations; **Chuck Close, Mary Ellen Mark, John Baldessari,** and **William Wegman** have all spoken here. Everything is open to the public. PRC publishes a monthly newsletter and the trimesterly journal *VIEWS,* and offers educational programs. Call in advance to arrange a tour. ◆ Admission. Tu-W, F-Su noon-5PM; Th noon-8PM. 602 Commonwealth Ave (at Blandford St); located below street level; enter on the left-hand side. 353.0700 &

18 Mugar Memorial Library of Boston University Few outside the BU community know about this library's marvelous and massive **Department of Special Collections**, dedicated to scholarly research but also open to the public. The Mugar owns and exhibits rare books, manuscripts, and papers pertaining to hundreds of interesting people, famous and not, from the 15th century onward (the 20th-century archives are particularly strong). The

Kenmore Square/Fenway

third-floor **King Exhibit Room** displays documents from the archives of BU alumnus **Dr. Martin Luther King, Jr.**

The library also boasts a huge holding of **Theodore Roosevelt's** and **Robert Frost's** papers and memorabilia. The collections span journalists, politicians, mystery writers, film and stage actors and actresses, and musicians. Browse a while and you'll encounter **Frederick Douglass, Bette Davis, Florence Nightingale, Albert Einstein, Tennessee Williams,** original cartoons of **Little Orphan Annie** and **L'il Abner, Irwin Shaw, Arthur Fiedler, Eric Ambler, Walt Whitman, Michael Halberstam, Rex Harrison, Fred Astaire,** and **Abraham Lincoln.** Call the BU Administration Office to find out about the library tours (353.3710). ◆ Library M-Th 8AM-midnight, F-Sa 8AM-11PM, Su 10AM-midnight, winter; M, Th 8AM-11PM, F-Sa 8AM-5PM, Su 10AM-11PM, summer. Special Collections M-F 9AM-5PM. 771 Commonwealth Ave (at St. Mary's St). 353.3696 &

The alphabetic street-naming of Back Bay (Arlington, Berkeley. . . Hereford) continues in Fenway on the opposite side of Massachusetts Avenue with Ipswich, Jersey, and Kilmarnock streets.

19 Paradise Rock Club This club and adjacent **M-80** are beyond the neighborhood's borders, but shouldn't be overlooked because they are two of Boston's best places to dance and to see national and international groups in concert. Other than for scheduled performances, the Paradise is only open on Saturday night from 10PM to 2AM for dancing to DJ-spun records. New Wave and rock are the mainstays, but the Paradise also books jazz, folk, blues, and country. **The Buzzcocks, Rickie Lee Jones, U2, Tower of Power, The Scorpions,** and **Nick Lowe** have all appeared here. Doors open at 8PM for shows; sometimes two are scheduled per night. Get tickets in advance, since few if any are available for popular groups on the day of the shows. There's a full bar, and minimum age requirements vary by shows. By subway, take the B Line to the Pleasant Street stop. ◆ Admission. Box office M-F noon-6PM; Sa 3-6PM. 967 Commonwealth Ave (between Pleasant and Babcock Sts). Cash only at the door; credit cards accepted at box office and bar. Recorded information 254.2052. Ticketmaster 931.2000

19 M-80 DJs spin dance music at this European-style club. Many international exchange students seek out M-80, which is jammed on some nights. There's a full bar, but no food is served. You must be 21 or older. ◆ Cover. W, F-Sa 11PM-2AM. 969 Commonwealth Ave (between Pleasant and Babcock Sts). No jeans or sneakers. 254.2054

20 Savoy French Bakery Go out of your way to sample the fantastic apple-and-almond, apricot, chocolate, plain, and other croissant varieties baked by Savoy. One owner was trained by a French baker so the goods are classic French. Equally delicious are the decorative fresh-fruit tartlets and minicakes such as hazelnut *frangipane.* They bake all kinds of cookies—try the traditional French *palmier,* nicknamed "elephant's ear"—and breads, including baguettes, *batards,* and *petit pain.* They have truffles, too, and some lunch items. ◆ Bakery ◆ Tu-F 7:30AM-6:30PM; Sa 8AM-6:30PM; Su 8AM-2PM. 1003 Beacon St (at St. Mary's St). No credit cards. 734.0214

21 Sol Azteca ★★$$ Dinner begins with some of the best piquant salsa and chips to be had in Boston, and progresses to marvelous Mexican fare like mole *poblano,* chiles *rellenos,* enchiladas *verdes, camarones al cilantro,* and *puerco en adobo.* With the meal, enjoy excellent sangria or Mexican beer; afterward, try coffee flavored with cinnamon and the great coffee-flavored flan. The rustic dining rooms are gay and festive with hand-painted tile tables and handicrafts. ◆ Mexican ◆ M-Th 5-10:30PM; F-Sa 5-11PM; Su 5-10PM. 914A Beacon St (at Park Dr). Reservations accepted M-Th, Su only 262.0909 &

22 **Stitches/Universal Joint** $$ The well-established comedy club offers local and national headliners, plus an R-rated hypnotist on Tuesday. Dinner and show packages are available; the restaurant joined the act recently and serves rib-sticking down-home fare. There's no dress code, and the clientele is diverse. Park free in the adjacent lot. You must be 18 or older. ♦ American ♦ Club shows Tu-Th, Su 9PM; F-Sa 8:30PM, 10:30PM. Restaurant daily 6PM-2AM. 835 Beacon St (between Miner and Munson Sts). Reservations recommended Saturday. Ticketmaster 931.2000; or charge tickets at the club 424.6995 (after 11AM), or at Universal Joint 859.0087 ♿

23 **Boston Beer Works** ★$$ Yet another on-site brewery complete with gleaming tanks, this one is unusually well situated, a stone's throw from the ballpark. The menu is surprisingly ambitious, with interesting entries such as onion-and-ale soup, barbecued Cajun Andouille sausage, shark shish kebabs, and "beer-basted" burgers. Sunday brunch features a "make your own omelet" option. ♦ American ♦ Daily 11AM-1AM. 61 Brookline Ave (between Lansdowne St and Yawkey Way). 536.2337 ♿

24 **Avalon** This mammoth dance club holds up to 1,500 people for a rotating roster of music. Wednesday is concert night; call for a schedule. Thursday features international music, Friday high-energy dance tunes, Saturday Top 40 and progressive, and Sunday is gay/lesbian night. Avalon packs in a mixed early 20s clientele. You must be at least 21. There's a full bar, but no food is served. Expect a line, but unless it's very late, everyone gets in eventually. There's no dress code Sunday and concert nights; all other nights, no sneakers, jeans, or athletic wear. ♦ Cover, cash only. Th 10:30PM-2AM; F-Sa 9:30PM-2AM; Su 9PM-2AM. 15 Lansdowne St (between Brookline Ave and Ipswich St). 262.2424 ♿

24 **Axis** Music changes nightly and includes progressive, punk, funk, heavy metal, hard rock, live bands, alternative dance tunes, and DJ spins. On some nights you must be at least 21 years old to be admitted, and on others, 19; call to inquire on minimum ages and shows. Creative dress is encouraged; "When in doubt, wear black" is the club's advice. On Sunday, smaller (800 capacity) Axis connects with **Avalon** next door for gay/lesbian night; just enter through Avalon. ♦ Cover. Tu-Su 9PM-2AM. 13 Lansdowne St (between Brookline Ave and Ipswich St). 262.2437 ♿

24 **Venus de Milo** Look for her statue above the entrance, sporting three neon hula hoops. The club strives for a dark Gothic Renaissance decor, its youngish urban crowd dancing to hip-hop, house, and funk music. Wednesday is gay night, Thursday is rave night, Friday features high-energy dance music, and Saturday's theme is Trash Disco. You must be 21 or older except on 19-and-over nights. ♦ Cover, cash only. W-Sa 10PM-2AM. 11 Lansdowne St (between Brookline Ave and Ipswich St). No athletic wear, baseball caps, or workboots allowed. 421.9595 ♿

24 **Bill's Bar** This small (250 people maximum) '50s-homage bar changes personas nightly for a 21-plus crowd. Monday is movie night, featuring offbeat films and music videos; Tuesday brings in a local band; Wednesday means jukebox tunes and no cover; Thursday, with a DJ, is college night; Friday and Saturday are low-key (again, no cover); and Sunday is live reggae. ♦ Hours and cover vary, so call ahead. 5 Lansdowne St (between Brookline Ave and Ipswich St). 421.9678 ♿

24 **Jake Ivory's** Audience participation is prized, what with dueling pianos and regular sing-alongs. "If you don't have a good

time here, it's your own fault," opined the *Boston Globe.* ♦ Cover. W-Sa 8PM-2AM. 1 Lansdowne St (at Ipswich St). 247.1222 ♿

25 **Jillian's Billiard Club** Get behind the eight-ball at one of 50 tournament-quality billiard, pocket billiard, and snooker tables. You'll find darts, shuffleboard, a batting cage, ping pong games, video games, and wide-screen TVs, too. Fees are prorated by the minute. Cafe fare, beer, and wine are served. After 8PM, only those age 18 and over are admitted. ♦ M-Sa 11AM-1:30AM; Su noon-1:30AM. 145 Ipswich St (at Lansdowne St). No hats, tank tops, sweats, cut-offs. 437.0300

The Boston Red Sox, originally called the Pilgrims, were renamed for the color of the players' stockings by owner John Taylor in 1907.

Boston's land area is 46 square miles; the Greater Boston land area is 1,100 square miles. Boston has 790 miles of streets, 47 miles of waterfront, 15 miles of beaches, 349 bridges, 8 historic or preservation districts, and 8 major medical research centers.

Restaurants/Clubs: Red   **Hotels:** Blue
Shops/ ❦ Outdoors: Green   **Sights/Culture:** Black

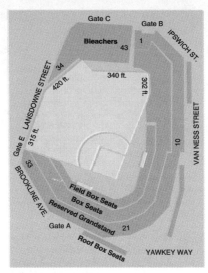

Map labels: Gate C, Gate B, IPSWICH ST., Bleachers, 43, 1, 34, 340 ft., 302 ft., LANSDOWNE STREET, 420 ft., 315 ft., Gate E, VAN NESS STREET, 10, 33, BROOKLINE AVE., Field Box Seats, Box Seats, Reserved Grandstand, Gate A, 21, Roof Box Seats, YAWKEY WAY

26 Fenway Park Fans are thrillingly close to the players at Fenway Park, the country's smallest major-league ballpark, with a 34,000-person capacity (see the plan above). **Carl Yastrzemski, Ted Williams, Dwight Evans,** and **Roger Clemens** have all dominated the diamond. **Babe Ruth** made his debut as a **Red Sox** pitcher at **Fenway Park** on 11 July 1914. He was later traded—not one of the team's smarter moves. The park is a block west of Kenmore Square but easy to find; just join the throngs pouring out of the Kenmore Square and Fenway subway stations before every game, or look up for the lights. Built in 1912 and rebuilt in 1934, Fenway Park is a classic, with plenty of quirks that only enhance its battered charm.

Kenmore Square/Fenway

It still has real green grass, and its idiosyncratic shape is the result of an awkward site, since the surrounding lots weren't for sale when the ballpark was embedded in the city. One of the park's famous landmarks is the notorious "Green Monster," the 37½-foot-high cement wall at left field that has destroyed many a batter's hope for a short, easy homer. And a gustatory institution are the **Fenway Franks.** Even if baseball leaves you unmoved, come for the show—just sitting among Boston's demanding, impassioned, extremely vocal fans is fun.

The ballpark opens one-and-a-half hours before game time. Tickets are available on a first-come, first-served basis to an alcohol-free reserved zone. Ask about special youth, senior citizen, and family discounts available for designated dates. Souvenirs are sold on all sides of the park (look for the amazing **Souvenir Shop** across from the ticket office) and vendors, both legal and illegal, and ticket scalpers do brisk business. Before and after the games, crowds flock to the **Cask 'n Flagon** sports bar (62 Brookline Avenue, 536.4840), among other neighborhood watering holes. ◆ Ticket office: M-F 9AM-5PM. 4 Yawkey Way (between Lans-

downe and Van Ness Sts). To charge tickets, call 267.1700; 267.8661 recorded information ♿ (special section)

27 Buteco Restaurant ★$ Don't be put off by the shabby facade; good food lurks inside. With Latin music pulsing in the background (a live band plays Mondays), a diverse, youngish clientele—lots of regulars—packs the tiny dining room to enjoy plates piled with spicy Brazilian dishes: *mandioca* (fried cassava root with carrot dipping sauce), hearts of palm salad, black-bean soup, *picadinho a carioca* (beef stew with garlic), *vatapá a Baiana* (sole baked in coconut milk and served on shrimp with peanut paste), and *churrasco* (mixed grill). Weekends only, order *feijoada,* the Brazilian national dish, a hearty stew with black beans, pork sausage, beef, collard greens, and orange. There's plenty of noise and camaraderie here. ◆ Brazilian ◆ M-Th noon-10PM; F noon-11PM; Sa 3-11PM; Su 3-10PM. 130 Jersey St (between Queensbury St and Park Dr). Reservations recommended on weekends. 247.9508 ♿ Also at: 57 W. Dedham St. 247.9249

28 Sibel's ★★$$ Hidden on a quiet block off the Fenway, this comfortable cafe serves tasty Caribbean staples such as conch fritters, Jamaican patties, and roti, along with some interesting hybrids (e.g., warm jerk chicken salad) and imports from other cultures. On Friday and Saturday evenings, there's live jazz. ◆ Caribbean/International ◆ M-Th 11:30AM-10PM; F 11:30AM-11PM; Sa 10AM-11PM; Su 10AM-9:30PM. 100 Peterborough St (at Kilmarnock St). 267.7346 ♿

28 Wheatstone Baking Company Through picture windows, watch as bakers whip up the croissants, muffins, sticky buns, coffee cakes, and breads available for sale at the counter. This is primarily a wholesale bakery, with four little cafe tables, but breakfast treats don't come any fresher. ◆ Bakery/Takeout ◆ M-F 7AM-7PM; Sa-Su 7AM-5PM. 86 Peterborough St (between Kilmarnock and Jersey Sts). 247.3566 ♿

28 Sorrento's ★★$$ The decor is pretty dramatic for a neighborhood pizza place: all black-and-white contrast, including the harlequin tile floor. But this is no ordinary pizza, either, not with toppings like imported prosciutto, fried eggplant, fontinella cheese.... A full array of luscious pasta dishes (try the chicken *à la Abruzzi*) share star billing. ◆ Italian/Takeout ◆ Daily 11AM-midnight. 86 Peterborough St (between Kilmarnock and Jersey Sts). 424.7070 ♿

29 Wheelock Family Theatre Boston's only Equity theater company serving younger audiences, Wheelock staunchly upholds a nontraditional casting policy and mounts ambitious, polished productions, ranging from musicals to drama. The theater seats 650. ◆ 180 Riverway (between Park Dr and Longwood Ave). 734.4760 ♿

30 The Best Western Boston $$ Smack dab in the middle of the **Longwood Medical Area,** the economical hotel attracts many guests con-

nected with Longwood in one way or another, but is open to all and is among the city's more affordable options. The **Museum of Fine Arts** and **Isabella Stewart Gardner Museum** are nearby, and it's just 15 minutes to **Back Bay** via the Green Line. Nonsmokers' and wheelchair-accessible rooms are available; and there is a restaurant on the premises as well as room service. The hotel is connected to a galleria of fast-food shops, a health club, and other services.
♦ 342 Longwood Ave (at Brookline Ave). 731.4700; fax 731.6273 ♿

31 The Arnold Arboretum of Harvard University Built on the old **Benjamin Bussey** farm, the arboretum has more than 4,000 woody plants, trees, shrubs, and vines collected on expeditions throughout the world. Olmsted interlaced its acreage with walks and drives offering a pleasant progression through meticulously sited plantings. Arboretum plant-hunters have searched unknown provinces of China and Tibet, and explored Borneo, Japan, and the Americas to bring back rare finds. The arboretum is the focal point of a favorite annual event, **Lilac Sunday.** Azaleas, magnolias, and fruit trees burst forth in full glory, too. Along the **Chinese Path,** some rarer older Asian specimens are planted, including the **Dove Tree** from China, a magical sight in spring when its creamy white bracts flutter like wings. Wind your way up to one of several promontories for splendid views. The **Hunnewell Visitor Center** is closed for renovations until September 1993, but year-round events, workshops, classes, and exhibitions are still available. The shop offers New England's largest selection of books on horticulture and other items. Guided walking tours or bus tours can be arranged for a fee. For further information on Arboretum programs, call 524.1718. ♦ Free (donations welcomed). Daily dawn to dusk. Shop Tu-Su 10AM-4PM. 125 Arborway, Jamaica Plain. Recorded information on what's in bloom 524.1717. Plant questions answered M-Tu 1-3PM, general information 524.1718 ♿ (driving permits for senior citizens and handicapped available for slow-speed touring)

31 Franklin Park Zoo Renovated in 1989 by **Huygens, DiMella, Shaffer and Associates,** the main attraction of this 70-acre zoo (see the zoo map below) is the domed **African Tropical Forest Pavilion,** the largest in North America, with sculpted cliffs and caves, waterfalls, wooden footbridges, and lush African vegetation. The three-acre environmental exhibit is home to gorillas (meet **Vip, Gigi, Kiki, Kubandu,** and **Bobby**), leopards, forest buffalo, bongo antelopes, dwarf crocodiles, three-inch-long scorpions, and exotic birds. One of the stars is 17-year-old **Camille,** a shy 500-pound pygmy hippo, whom you can watch tiptoeing in her lagoon. There are 75 species and 250 specimens in all, with no cages and almost imperceptible barriers between the looked-ons and onlookers. (Before the pavilion opened, local rock climbers clambered over the cliff walls to make sure the gorillas would stay on their side of the moat.) Exhibits educate you on the international crisis of human destruction of African and South American rain forests. When it's cold outdoors, come soak up some warm tropical mist. The exhibit's ecosystem creates periodic rainstorms and rainbows. The zoo also features a **Children's Zoo** with a petting barn, where kids learn about New England farm animals. The **Hooves and Horns** section stars zebras and camels, including **Becky** the dromedary. In **Birds' World,** you can see and touch more than 50 species of birds in a Chinese-pagoda birdhouse and free-flight cage, which dates from the zoo's 1913 opening. Like Franklin Park, the zoo was nearly abandoned from the '60s until recently; now it's enjoying a renaissance. Plans are afoot to add more pavilions and other wondrous attractions.
♦ Admission; discount for senior citizens, uni-

Kenmore Square/Fenway

formed military, children four to 11 (three and under, admitted free). M-F 9AM-5PM; Sa-Su 10AM-6PM. Closed Christmas and New Year's Day. Franklin Park Rd (off Blue Hill Ave). 442.2002 ♿

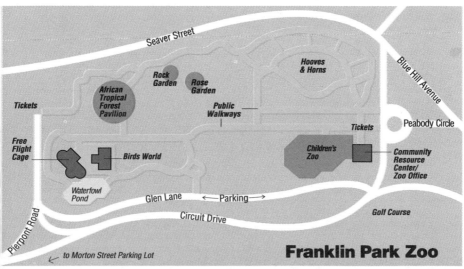

Franklin Park Zoo

The Emerald Necklace

The ponds and parks that are strung together by parkways form Boston's prized Emerald Necklace, which, when charted on a map, look like they're dangling from **Boston Harbor** like a chain around a slender neck. Executed for the **Boston Park Commission** in 1895, **Frederick Law Olmsted's** design for an interconnected park system totaled more than 2,000 acres of open land, its main artery the five-mile-long Emerald Necklace. (When Olmsted found his professional niche at age 35, the notion of creating public parks was still novel; today he is lauded as the creator of landscape architecture as a profession and an art in America.)

The largest continuous green space through an urban center in the country, the Necklace traverses a number of communities and is adorned with five major parks—**Back Bay Fens, Muddy River Improvement, Jamaica Park, Arnold Arboretum**, and **Franklin Park**—which are all connected by parkways. Olmsted's Necklace was further embellished by joining the **Boston Common** and the **Public Garden**. The **Charles River Esplanade** is often considered an additional strand, although it wasn't built until 1931, long after Olmsted's death. Unfortunately, the Necklace has missing links (which the city plans to fix), most importantly the never-realized **Columbia Road** extension by which Olmsted intended to link Franklin Park with **Marine Park** in South Boston. The only way to see the entire Emerald Necklace at one time is to drive its length along the parkways, but the twisting and confusing route will offer frustrating, fleeting glimpses of greenery and water, not at all the restful communion with nature Olmsted had in mind. Instead, pick a fair-weather day and jog, bicycle, walk, or ride a horse through a segment of the park system. The Necklace is dotted with benches, fields to sun in, and shady meadows.

Kenmore Square/Fenway

The Emerald Necklace starts at the **Boston Common (1),** proceeds through the **Public Garden** (2), then continues along **Commonwealth Avenue Mall (3)** to **Charlesgate (4),** the original connection Olmsted forged between the Mall and the **Back Bay Fens (5)** where the **Muddy River** entered the **Charles River Estuary.** But Charlesgate's open wetlands were largely destroyed when elevated overpasses to **Storrow Drive** were built during the '60s. Despite this plundering, the Necklace still joins tenuously with the Back Bay Fens, Olmsted's first contribution. Named after the marshlands of eastern England, the Fens originally embodied its designer's love for idyllic English rural landscapes. Dredging, draining, and landscaping rescued the Fens from its reeking muddy past and made way for tranquil salt-marsh meadows. The damming of the Charles River in 1910 changed the water from salt to fresh, destroying Olmsted's original scheme. Years of neglect have also taken their toll. Yet the park is still a pleasant spot to wander among willows, dogwoods, lindens, and hawthorns. The **Victory Gardens** planted during World War II and the spectacular **Rose Garden** behind the **Museum of Fine Arts,** as well as an athletic field, have settled in to stay. And the puddingstone bridge where **Boylston Street** crosses the river is a poetic charmer, designed in 1880 by Olmsted's friend **H.H. Richardson.** A cautionary note: Don't linger in the Fens after dark, and never stray into the stands of tall reeds.

The **Muddy River Improvement (6)** is the next ornament, although its connection to the Fens via the Riverway was obliterated by construction of the former **Sears Roebuck** building, which will probably be converted into a science/technology complex. A little perseverance returns you to a meandering riverside park with bridle, walking, and running paths; graceful bridges; placid ponds; and lush plantings. The Improvement—unpoetically named for the spruce-up job it accomplished—widens at a section now called **Olmsted Park,** where Leverett, Willow, and Wards ponds are located. And then one arrives at **Jamaica Park (7),** its centerpiece the largest freshwater pond in Boston. Fringed by a tree-shaded promenade lit by gas lanterns, **Jamaica Pond** is popular for sailing, rowing, walking, jogging, and fishing. **Edmund Wheelwright** designed the decorative 1913 boathouse and gazebo where refreshments are sold.

From Jamaica Pond the Jamaicaway leads to the world-renowned **Arnold Arboretum (8),** which belongs to the **Boston Park System** but is administered by **Harvard University. Charles Sprague Sargent,** a landscape gardener and the arboretum's first director for more than half a century, collaborated with Olmsted in 1878 to design this living museum of trees, named for its first big donor, a merchant and amateur horticulturist. Both Olmsted and Sargent envisioned a scientific plein air museum that would also be a delightful, picturesque park.

Linked to the arboretum by the Arborway, the Emerald Necklace's massive pendant is **Franklin Park (9),** named for **Benjamin Franklin.** One of Olmsted's three greatest parks, Franklin Park's design expresses his precept that the natural world offers the ideal antidote to the dehumanizing quality of urban living. Within this 500-acre tract straddling **Dorchester, Jamaica Plain,** and **Roxbury,** Olmsted preserved and enhanced existing natural features. Franklin Park is a great green swath of rolling hills and broad fields and meadows, with hickory, hemlock, locust, oak, tulip trees, and myriad other plantings, and enormous boulders and park ornaments fashioned from Roxbury puddingstone. But because the park is four miles from the heart of Boston and tricky to reach, it never got the popularity it deserved, and languished from the '40s until recently. And like the Fens, changes have been made that spoil the integrity of Olmsted's original plan. But if Franklin Park is not a perfect emerald, it's still a gem, a sanctuary from the city where one can walk, jog, picnic, bird-watch, play golf or baseball, watch the annual September **Kite Festival,** attend festivals such as the August **West Indian Carnival,** visit the zoo, and generally let loose a little. The park's 18-hole golf course has been newly refurbished. No private country-club atmosphere here; city residents come together to play on the par-70 course, the country's second-oldest municipal golf course. Although it will take time for Franklin Park to shake its unfair poor reputation, it is actually one of the city's safer parks. Don't linger after dark or stray into the overgrown areas, but do enjoy an oasis that Bostonians have begun to appreciate anew.

The Necklace breaks after Franklin Park, but should have led via **Columbia Road** through **Upham's Corner** and on to **Marine Park (10).** A lack of funds kept Columbia Road from becoming the spacious green boulevard Olmsted intended. On **City Point** in South

Boston, Olmsted created Marine Park's **Pleasure Bay** by linking the **City Point Battery** to **Castle Island.** The island's prominent feature is a star-shaped Quincy granite fort that was built in 1801 to defend tiny Boston-town. During the Revolution, a subsequent fort served as headquarters for the British troops and gave refuge to local Tories. As the Revolution heated up, the island became the British naval garrison. The British evacuated at last when **General George Washington's** men trained guns on the island from **Dorchester Heights.** Eclipsed long ago by suburban beaches, Marine Park no longer draws crowds, but the sea breezes and harbor views are worth an outing, and this is where you can look at the shiny bellies of the big jets as they descend to **Logan International Airport.** It's best to drive here; there's always plenty of parking.

Now missing from the Emerald Necklace, **Charlesbank** was a pioneering neighborhood park, designed by Olmsted in the 1890s, that bordered the Charles River near **Massachusetts General Hospital.** The park was intended to alleviate the overcrowding suffered by residents of the **West End,** a neighborhood largely wiped out by urban renewal in the '60s. Charlesbank featured

the city's first playgrounds, part of the new playground movement sweeping the country, and America's first sandboxes, called "sand courts." Today Charlesbank is mostly buried under a tangle of roadways.

Boston's **Park Rangers** direct all kinds of activities throughout the Boston Park System: historical strolls and tours, children's learning activities such as "Horse of Course" (about a day in the life of a Park Ranger horse), nature walks through the **Arnold Arboretum,** bird-watching along the **Muddy River,** fishing on **Jamaica Pond,** an architectural exploration of **Commonwealth Avenue,** and more. Some events require reservations; all are free. For information, call the **Boston Parks and Recreation Department** at 635.4505 or the **Boston Park Rangers** at 522.2639.

During the summer, recreational and educational programs are planned for kids throughout the Boston Park System, including golf clinics at Franklin Park, "Sox Talk" with **Red Sox** players, and sailing on **Boston Harbor** and **Jamaica Pond.** Call the **Parks and Recreation Activities Eventline** at 635.4006 for daily updates on what's going on. Boston parks are officially closed from 11:30PM to 6AM.

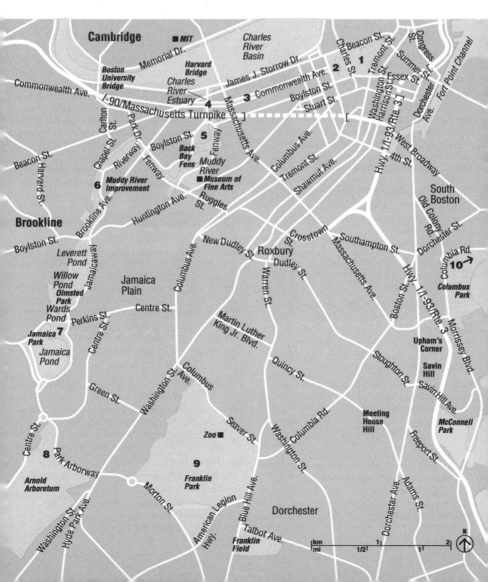

Caroline Knapp

Styles Editor, *The Boston Phoenix*

A burger and Bass draft at the **Miracle of Science,** a bar and grill/neighborhood hangout/essence-of-cool spot near the Massachusetts Institute of Technology (MIT), where the food is great and they use petri dishes as ashtrays.

The **Charles River,** especially on calm days. I'm a rower, and the Charles is one of the finest sculling spots in the country. If you don't row, sit on the banks some sunny morning and watch: rowing is strength and elegance in action and it's one activity that makes Boston stand out as a city.

Martinis at the bar of the **Ritz-Carlton Hotel,** especially if it's snowing outside. Find a window seat overlooking the **Public Garden** (the complimentary bowl of nuts happens to have an exceptionally high number of cashews).

An early morning caffe latte on Hanover Street, in the **North End.** Go on a weekday morning, not over the weekend, when it's too crowded with tourists. Bring the *New York Times* crossword puzzle, and eavesdrop on old Italian men.

The **John Hancock Tower** at twilight is best seen from across the river, in Cambridge, when the tower reflects the sunset and the river reflects the tower and surrounding lights.

Roasted chicken (or just about anything else) at **Hamersley's Bistro,** and a glass of wine at the bar of **Biba** on a Saturday afternoon, before it's crowded. Anything seafood-related at **Jasper's Restaurant.** Dinner with another food-lover at **The Blue Room, Michela's,** or **The East Coast Grill.**

Kenmore Square/Fenway

Michael Webb

Architecture Critic

Louisburg Square on a winter's night, when snow blankets the cars and transports you back to Brahmin Boston in its heyday.

Faneuil Hall Marketplace—Ben Thompson's vision created a great people place, in contrast to the sterility of City Hall Plaza.

If you don't have any kids, borrow one for the afternoon and relive the joys of childhood at the **Children's Museum.**

The **John Hancock Tower** is a high rise whose elegance compensates for the eyesore. The structure is best seen from across the Charles River.

The fifth-floor reading room of the **Boston Athenaeum**—scholarly research in a setting of neoclassic splendor.

Rapid transit—Given the congestion and the homicidal drivers, it's just as well that Boston has America's best subway system.

Cambridge, old and new. Where else could you find Alvar Aalto, Le Corbusier, and James Stirling in such a mellow context?

The **John F. Kennedy Library.** I.M. Pei's building is worth the trip, but it's the images of the president and his slain brother that reach out and grab you.

The emerald perfection of village greens in **Harvard, Lexington, Falmouth,** and **Cohasset.**

Martha's Vineyard out of season, ideally on a cold spring day.

Alan Andres

Trade Paperback Book Editor, Houghton Mifflin Company

Literary Bests:

Most literary room service: **The Charles Hotel,** where guests can have any new book delivered directly to their room.

Literary lunch locales: For publishers—**The Black Goose, Locke-Ober, Cornucopia;** for writers—**Casablanca, The Harvard Book Store Cafe, The Harvest Restaurant.**

Most unusual literary lunch locale: Brown-bag lunch on the top-floor open terrace of the **Boston Athenaeum** overlooking the entire Downtown and the **Granary Burying Ground.**

Best bookstores: **Robin Bledsoe and H.L. Mendelsohn Booksellers** in Cambridge has a truly astounding and superb selection of art and architecture books. It's hard to find but worth the search. And **Much Ado Bookstore** in Marblehead is the kind of friendly secondhand bookstore usually seen only in movies. Much Ado's titles are always interesting and changing, and it's one of the few bookstore/bed-and-breakfasts in the country.

Best statues of an author: **Samuel Eliot Morison,** located at Commonwealth Avenue and Exeter Street, is "dressed" in foul weather gear and surrounded by sea life.

Best statue of fictional characters: Robert McCloskey's very popular *Make Way for Ducklings* in the Public Garden.

The saddest literary addresses (both are in Kenmore Square): The old **Shelton Hotel,** where **Eugene O'Neill** spent his last two years and died after hardly ever leaving his room; and 71 Bay State Road, where a depressed and alcoholic **John Cheever** hit bottom (he once opened his apartment door, while wearing no clothes, to receive a visit from **John Updike**).

Best literary sporting event: The annual baseball-poetry reading outside **Fenway Park** on opening day.

Wittiest bookstore window display: **The Brookline Booksmith** at Coolidge Corner.

Best bookstore reading series: **Waterstones,** where readings and other literary events are held nearly every weeknight in a former spiritualist temple that has also been used as an art-film theater.

Personal Bests:

The **American Repertory Theatre,** which, while often uneven, is well worth the wait when it's good.

Watching visitors exclaim, "Look, it's John Hancock!" as they wander through the tombstones at the **Granary Burying Ground.**

The sculptured cascade of bronzed gloves and other debris on the **Porter Square** subway escalator in Cambridge, one of the wittiest examples of public sculpture in the city.

Klimt's *The Pear Tree* at the **Busch-Reisinger Museum** and Watteau's *La Perspective* at the **Museum of Fine Arts,** two paintings that merit repeated pilgrimages.

For the seriously addicted filmgoer, the **Harvard Film Archive** at the Carpenter Center has eclectic yet entertaining treasures unavailable at even the largest video stores.

The 75-foot-long bar at **Marais.**

A day trip to **Halibut Point State Park** in Rockport; could any granite quarry have had a finer end?

The view of Cambridge from **Summit Park,** one of many tiny parks in Brookline, at the top of the highest hill looking north across the Charles River.

Robert Birnbaum
Publisher, *Stuff Magazine*

Even as a Chicago expatriate who has been in Boston for almost 20 years, I have never quite been able to look at my current longtime residence as home. Nonetheless I have found that this town has a rich reservoir of activities to suit every taste: from the magic of **Fenway Park** (which has very little to do with the Red Sox) to the idyllic **Swan Boat** cruises in the **Public Garden** (not the Celtics' home court), the sanguine calm of **The Ritz Bar,** and the all-American down-home dining of **The Blue Diner** and the **Down-own Cafe.**

Some of my favorites include the bread pudding at **Cornucopia,** the falling chocolate cake at **Olives,** the cocktail *tranquillo* at **East Coast Grill,** the rotisserie chicken at **The Blue Wave,** Michela at **Michela's,** most of the menu and the tequilas at the **Rattlesnake Bar and Grill, Dali** for tapas, and the coffee at **Travis Restaurant** on Newbury Street.

As for stimulation of my nervous system, the **Gund Gallery** at the **Museum of Fine Arts** invariably provides a wonderful feast for the eyes. Strolling through the aisles at the **Avenue Victor Hugo Bookshop** is both therapeutic and informative (say hello to Vince if he's there), and if I feel the need to surrender to my baser consumer needs, a walk through **Louis, Boston** (a national landmark building that once housed the Museum of Natural History) gets me in touch with current designer fashions. And the truly excellent little **Cafe Louis** offers delicious food in a comfortable setting. Down the street on Newbury's first block, **Joseph Abboud** and **Alan Bilzerian** round out the fashion troika of what has come to be known in some circles as the "Street of Dreams."

Nightlife in Boston is just like nightlife everywhere else, except perhaps in Amish communities. The clubs are hot, loud, dark, and smoky arenas for less than the best in human behavior, dancing notwithstanding. **M-80** is hot on Wednesday and Friday, **Avalon** on Thursday night, **Esme** on Wednesday and Thursday, and **Axis** on Tuesday night. Sunday nights are "boys' nights" at almost every club. **Quest** seems to be congenial to humans of most sexual persuasions, even straights. For live music, try **Scullers**

Jazz Club, Ryles, and **Wally's Cafe** for jazz. And look at **Nightstage** for an eclectic menu of music and **Paradise Rock Club** for pop music.

The charm of Boston is particularly evident on a spring or autumnal stroll down its most attractive street, **Newbury Street,** or a walk along the **Charles River.**

Patrick Lyons
Entertainment Impresario, Lyons Group Management

A visit to **Harvard Square,** home to a unique mixture of people who are educated, radical, bohemian, and just plain "out there." Buskers and street musicians there today evoke memories of Bob Dylan in the '60s. Incidentally, it is also the home of Harvard University.

Every other day **Ristorante Toscano** on Charles Street imports fresh mushrooms from Milan. As an appetizer, they are near a religious experience.

Mocha frappes at **Espresso Royal** on Newbury Street.

The Park Square **Baldini's** has the best cheese-and-pepperoni pizza in Boston.

Stroll past **Louisburg Square** on Beacon Hill and capture the essence of Boston Brahmin existence.

Walk along the Charles River, from the Harvard Bridge (opposite MIT) down Memorial Drive for the undisputed best view of Boston day or night.

Take a Sunday afternoon drive north to **Woodmans Lobster in the Rough** in Essex; they invented the fried clam in 1902.

A twilight cruise of **Boston Harbor** with a special stop beneath one of Logan Airport's flight paths. Listening to the 747s scream overhead is a thrill.

See the city nightlife on **Lansdowne Street** (in the shadow of Fenway Park)—rave, R&B, techno, indus-

trial, reggae, world beat, disco, soul, ska, rock, and about every underground fashion statement known to Boston. There are eight nightclubs, and no waiting! (Note: We should know—we operate them.)

Ann Robert
Co-Owner with husband, Lucien Robert, of Maison Robert restaurant

Visiting the rose garden in **Fenway.**

The Sunday afternoon concerts at **King's Chapel.**

A boat ride on **Boston Harbor.**

The Arnold Arboretum, for a walk during any season.

Theater performances at the **Huntington** or the **American Repertory Theatre (ART).**

Window shopping on **Newbury Street.**

Dining with friends at **Maison Robert**—on the outdoor terrace in warm months, upstairs or in the cafe the rest of the year.

Boston Athenaeum, for tea on Wednesday and for concerts.

Beacon Hill garden tours in the spring.

The **Fine Arts Museum**—special and regular exhibits.

South End

This part of Boston is not a destination for sight-seers, but rather for urban explorers who like to stray from the tourist tracks and make their own discoveries. Enticements include block after block of undulating Victorian bowfronts, intimate residential parks, vibrant streetlife, out-of-the-ordinary shops, and unusual restaurants of excellent quality, equal to those of **Back Bay**. Yet the South End is often overlooked, separated from neighboring Back Bay by the **Copley Place** and **Prudential Center** developments.

The South End is one of Boston's most diverse neighborhoods—racially, economically, ethnically, and religiously. Rich variety exists within this square mile. The South End is the largest Victorian row-house district extant in the United States and is listed on the National Register of Historic Places. After a brief flowering as a genteel enclave, the neighborhood became home to Boston's immigrant populations. Today it still exudes port-of-entry flavor: various blocks are predominantly Lebanese, Irish, Yankee, Chinese, West Indian, Black, Greek, or Hispanic. Boston's largest gay population resides here, too. Over the past 20 years young middle-class professionals have moved in, gentrifying patches of this crazy quilt. The neighborhood also has a bohemian side, attracting visual artists, architects, writers, performers, designers, craftspeople, and musicians.

Like Back Bay, the entire South End rests on landfill. The neighborhood was originally marshland bordering **Washington Street,** which was once a narrow neck that linked the peninsula to the mainland. By the mid-19th century upwardly mobile Bostonians wanted fashionable new quarters. From 1850 to 1875 the South End emerged as speculators filled in blocks of land and auctioned them off. Unlike Back Bay, there was no grid or grand plan. And while Back Bay is French-inspired and cosmopolitan in style, the South End follows more traditional English patterns. To attract buyers, developers created London-style residential parks such as **Worcester** and **Union Park squares**, oases loosely linked by common architecture. Although less haphazard in plan than Boston's oldest neighborhoods, the South End still has a transitional, unpredictable feel.

The South End rose and fell from grace in less than a decade, eclipsed by glamorous Back Bay and the allure of streetcar suburbs. By 1900 prosperous Bostonians had abandoned their handsome row houses, which were then divided into multiple units and lodging rooms to accommodate waves of immigrants and working-class families. Industries and businesses sprang up. **Boston City Hospital** was founded in the 1860s, the oldest institution on **Hospital Row**, a dense cluster of university and municipal medical buildings located near the **Roxbury** border. The South End also became the largest lodging-house district in the country, gaining a reputation for dens of vices and unsavory pursuits. Finally declared a federal urban renewal area in 1965, the South End was torn apart by drastic development, which set the stage for pell-mell gentrification in the '70s and '80s.

The neighborhood endures, changeable and fascinating as ever. Residents and community groups take active parts in healing old wounds—the new **Southwest Corridor Park** is but one attractive result. Although the neighborhood fabric has been torn by insensitive institutions and neglect, many buildings and blocks are being recycled and renewed. Visit in the late morning or early afternoon, when the streets are safest and liveliest. Explore **Columbus Avenue** and **Tremont Street** for the greatest concentration of good shops and restaurants. Take a walk through tiny **Rutland Square** or tranquil **Union Park Square**, both hugged by carefully restored residences. Stroll along Chandler, Lawrence, and Appleton streets, lined with appealing, smaller-scale brick houses. From block to block, the architecture changes from down-in-the-dumps to resplendently restored. And with each block you'll sense the presence of different populations, such as the black community to the south, and Middle Easterners and Armenians along **Shawmut Avenue** to the east.

The subway stops most convenient to the South End are the Back Bay/South End and Massachusetts Avenue stations (both on the Orange Line); the Copley, Prudential, and Symphony stops (all on the Green Line) are beyond the neighborhood's borders but mere minutes away on foot. Amtrak also stops at Back Bay/South End, as well as at South Station.

1 Southwest Corridor Park Where an ugly gash once slashed the South End, a ribbon of attractive parkland now curls. In the 1970s more than a hundred acres of housing in the South End and adjoining **Roxbury** and **Jamaica Plain** were demolished to make way for a highway project. Community protests killed that plan, but the blight remained, a sore spot awaiting healing. At last, 52 acres of this area were reclaimed for parkland to reknit divided neighborhoods. More than a decade in the making, the park—landscaped by **Roy B. Mann**—has become a valued part of the city. Twenty-three architectural and engi-neering firms worked with more than 15 community groups to chart the course of the new green trail. The result: 4.7 miles of walkways and bike paths dotted with tot lots, street-hockey rinks, and basketball and tennis courts, and graced with young trees and plantings. An adjunct project, the community-run **Southwest Corridor Farms**, manages 13 acres, providing plots and training to urban gardeners. The lauded fingerlike park is as narrow as 60 feet in spots and as wide as a quarter mile in others, and points all the way to **Franklin Park**, the **Arnold Arboretum**, and **Forest Hills Cemetery**. Starting behind **Copley Place**, stroll as far west as your fancy takes you, and see how intensely used the well-loved park has become by all ages, all races, all economic groups. You can even read your way along, following the chiseled words of 18 local writers located near T stops along the Corridor.

The park is just one piece of the controversial, enormous, $750 million-plus **Southwest Corridor**

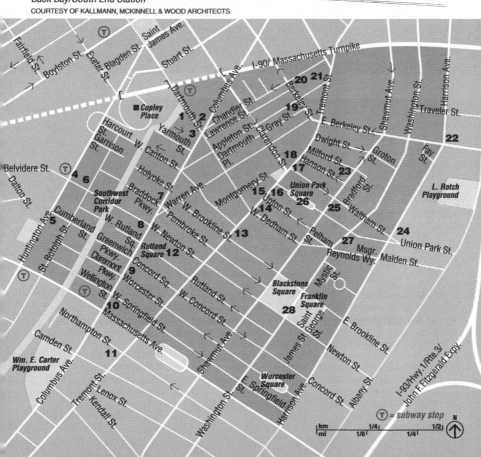

Back Bay/South End Station
COURTESY OF KALLMANN, MCKINNELL & WOOD ARCHITECTS

Project still under way, which also involved relocating and depressing Boston's old elevated **MBTA Orange Line** and constructing nine new rapid transit stations. Two are in the South End: **Back Bay/South End Station** (pictured on the previous page) is a well-crafted structure designed by **Kallmann, McKinnell & Wood Architects,** extending from Dartmouth Street across from the park's beginning to Clarendon Street. In its heroic navelike concourse, vaulted by huge wooden arches and illuminated by clerestory windows, the station recalls the grandeur of Victorian railway stations. The **Massachusetts Avenue Station,** by **Ellenzweig, Moore and Associates,** is a sleek, sinuous brick, glass, and aluminum structure located where the park intersects Massachusetts Avenue. The Southwest Corridor Project is also creating development parcels along this route that are intended to revitalize neglected Boston neighborhoods by providing employment and development opportunities for those communities. ♦ Dartmouth St (between Huntington and Columbus Aves)

2 Mary's ★$$ Another sure-to-be-successful venture of brothers **Harry** and **Evan Anthony** (who own the gay bar **Chaps**), this urban establishment blends postmodern decor—a funky blend of marble and gold-leaf mirrors—with healthful, innovative California cuisine. Wherever this partnership pitches its tent, the nighttime trendsetters tend to follow. ♦ California ♦ Daily 5-11PM; bar open until 2AM. 111 Dartmouth St (at Columbus Ave). Reservations are recommended. No credit cards. 353.0159 &

2 Tim's Tavern $ A great place to get a good pub-style repast, Tim's is very funky, but a bargain. Give it a try for one of the best cheap steaks in town. Although the tavern is always busy, there's hardly ever a wait. ♦ American

South End

♦ M-Sa 11:30AM-midnight. 329 Columbus Ave (at Dartmouth St). 247.7894 &

2 The Claddagh $ This Irish pub offers just the sort of filling, unfussy food you'd expect to find in a neighborhood bar. You're best off with burgers, chicken, stews, and other straightforward items. The walls are adorned with Irish family crests. Quieter on weeknights, the Claddagh becomes boisterous on weekends, often hosting sing-alongs. One room was renovated for live music. The same owners operate **The Black Rose** (160 State Street, Faneuil Hall Marketplace, 742.2286) and **The Purple Shamrock** (1 Union Street, Faneuil Hall

Marketplace, 227.2060)—both of which are extremely popular and are cast from the same mold. ♦ Irish-American/Takeout ♦ Daily 11:30AM-12:30AM. 335 Columbus Ave (at Dartmouth St). 262.9874

3 Moka ★$ A breezy "California-style cafe," this deli-counter establishment with an outdoor patio suggests summer whatever the season, thanks to **Paula Carlton's** surf's-up mural. Breakfast warrants a visit, what with Belgian waffles and homemade granola; actually, the grazing's good right into the evening. ♦ American/Takeout ♦ M-F 7AM-11PM; Sa-Su 8AM-11PM. 130 Dartmouth St (between Huntington and Columbus Aves; behind Copley Pl). 424.7768 &

3 Tent City The construction of affluent **Copley Place** across the way was the catalyst that brought black community activists to this site to protest the South End's gentrification, forcing Boston to alter plans for a parking lot and to build affordable housing instead. The result—designed by **Goody, Clancy & Associates** in 1988—is a gentle addition to the neighborhood. One-quarter of the units in the cheerful patterned-brick complex of apartments and row houses are market-rate, one quarter are for low-income residents, and one-half are for moderate-income residents. The biggest surprise is the name, which preserves the political moment when the activists set up tents here, an early episode in the wave of tent cities that spread across the country as the homelessness crisis worsened. ♦ Dartmouth St (between Huntington and Columbus Aves; behind Copley Pl)

4 The Colonnade Hotel $$ This 280-room hotel's amenities include a restaurant, bar, outdoor rooftop pool, and fitness room, indoor parking, a multilingual staff, 24-hour room service, same-day valet service (for a fee), and foreign currency exchange. Handicapped-equipped and nonsmokers' rooms are available. ♦ 120 Huntington Ave (at W. Newton St). 424.7000, 800/962.3030; fax 424.1717 &

5 The Midtown Hotel $$ A well-kept secret, this two-story, 160-room hotel is older and far less fashionable than the numerous luxury hotels located nearby, and also much less expensive. It's frequented by families, tour groups, and businesspeople. The rooms are spacious and there's free parking, 24-hour laundry service, an outdoor pool with a lifeguard (in season), and a multilingual staff. Children under 18 stay with parents absolutely free. Winter packages are available on request. **Seiyoken** (★$$), a Japanese restaurant, is located on the premises. ♦ 220 Huntington Ave (at Massachusetts Ave). 262.1000, 800/343.1177; fax 262.8739 &

6 St. Botolph Street Stroll down this pleasant stretch of street, which New York City's Ash Can School painter **George Benjamin Luks** portrayed in *Noontime, St. Botolph,* on view in the **Museum of Fine Arts.** Look for the **Musician's Mutual Relief Society Building** at No. 56, an 1886 commercial hall designed by **Cabot and**

Chandler that was renovated and suitably ornamented for the society's use in 1913 (it now houses apartments). Separated by stone lyres beneath the cornice are composers' names. At the **Cumberland Street** intersection is an attractive schoolhouse dating from 1891, converted to condominiums in 1980 by **Graham Gund Associates.**

6 **St. Botolph Street Restaurant** ★$$$ A neighborly restaurant in a rehabbed 19th-century town house, St. Botolph is a good choice for Sunday brunch: a four-course prix-fixe feast featuring muffins, a Bloody Mary or screwdriver, an appetizer, coffee, an entrée, and dessert. The casual street-level cafe—complete with bar and jukebox—offers bistro fare, with a full range of appetizers, grilled pizzas, sandwiches, pastas, risottos, soups, and salads; dinner is served in the upper level, an airy loft. The daring renovation of this turreted building, which seemed clever and cutting-edge in the '70s, is looking rather crude and gauche in retrospect. ♦ American/Takeout ♦ Cafe daily 11:30AM-midnight; main dining room M-Th, Su 5:45-10:30PM, F-Sa 5:45PM-midnight. 99 St. Botolph St (at W. Newton St). Reservations are recommended for dinner. 266.3030

7 **Charlie's Sandwich Shoppe** ★★$ All night, **Christi Manjourides** stays up baking pies and muffins. At 5AM sons **Chris** and **Arthur** arrive and get ready for a day at the grill. Then regulars begin drifting in after 6AM, anticipating a gentle morning start with counter-side conversation over coffee and Charlie's famous breakfast platters such as cranberry pancakes or a Cajun omelet with spicy sausage.

Family run for more than 50 years, this unpretentious luncheonette is a melting pot, attracting anyone with an appetite for hearty breakfasts and lunches. At communal tables, designer suits mingle with blue jeans and work boots, and celebrities mix with folks struggling to get by. Relax among the awards, accolades, and smiling photos taken since opening day in 1927. Stoke up on blueberry French toast, cheeseburgers, Greek salad, turkey hash, frankfurters and beans, fried clams, hot pastrami on a bulky roll, sweet-potato pie, and more. It feels great to hang out here, although there are often hungry people waiting impatiently by the door. Charlie's welcomed famous black musicians such as **Duke Ellington** in the '40s, a period when blacks were barred from most Boston restaurants. ♦ American ♦ M-F 6AM-2:30PM; Sa 7:30AM-1PM. 429 Columbus Ave (between Braddock Pkwy and Holyoke St). No credit cards. 536.7669

8 **Union United Methodist Church** Designed by **A.R. Estey,** the architect of **Emmanuel Church** in Back Bay, this 1877 Gothic Revival creation has the gracious proportions and picturesqueness of a rural parish church. Rather than reaching for the sky, it reaches out to those who approach on foot. ♦ 485 Columbus Ave (at W. Newton St)

9 **Divine Decadence** Taking its name from the movie *Cabaret,* this shop offers a delightfully diverse array of American and European home furnishings and accessories dating from 1900 to yesterday, with occasional earlier pieces. The focus is on unusual investment-quality items that epitomize their era—whether a kicky shoe-shaped '20s chair from a defunct Boston shoe store, a fully functioning '40s jukebox, or an '80s desk with neon. Some collectibles are commonplace items that have become treasures with time, while others are the work of renowned designers like **Charles Eames.** It's always fun to come back, since you never know what owner **Richard Penachio** will chance upon next. The prices range widely, because there are lots of wonderful small items like clocks, tableware, and mirrors. Penachio updates and combines some items into artful new creations. When you leave the store, look up **Claremont Park** for a nice view of the **Christian Science Mother Church's** dome. ♦ Tu-W, F noon-6PM; Th noon-7PM; Sa 11AM-5PM. 542 Columbus Ave (at Claremont Pkwy). 266.1477

South End

9 **Jae's Cafe and Grill** ★$ The healthful Korean fare served in this crowded, bustling storefront has attracted the trendies; there's almost always a line. A full array of sushi and sashimi await, along with soups, satays, and "rice specials" such as *Yuk Hai Bi Bim Bab* (shredded raw beef marinated in seasoned sesame oil). ♦ Korean ♦ M-Sa 11:30AM-3PM, 5-10:30PM; Su noon-10PM. Valet parking. 520 Columbus St (between Worcester St and Concord Sq). 421.9405

9 **Astoria** Proprietor **Twyla Reardon** has an eye for retro finds: a "brand-new" bullet bra from the '50s, perhaps, or a pair of gold lamé go-go boots. Whatever the season or occasion, it's fun to poke around her well-stocked vintage clothing shop. ♦ Tu-Sa noon-7PM; Su 1-5PM. 50-52 Concord Sq (between Columbus Ave and Tremont St). 859.0805

The South End is actually the "New" South End, since the original South End was located in what is now the Financial District/Downtown area.

Restaurants/Clubs: Red   Hotels: Blue
Shops/ ♣ Outdoors: Green   Sights/Culture: Black

10 Harriet Tubman House Named for the "Moses of the South," who was herself a runaway slave and **Underground Railroad** organizer, this iconoclastic complex greets the street with spirit and purposefulness. It's home to the **United South End Settlements,** a social service organization responsible for vital community programs. The architect, **Don Stull Associates,** deserves applause for doing a lot with a little budget. Incidentally, the house stands on the site of one of Boston's famous jazz clubs, **The Hi Hat,** which burned down. ♦ Daily 9AM-6PM. 566 Columbus Ave (at Massachusetts Ave). 536.8610 ♿

COURTESY OF THE BOSTONIAN SOCIETY

11 Piano Craft Guild When new in 1853, the Chickering piano factory (pictured above) was reputedly the second-largest building in the country, dwarfed only by the US Capitol. The surprisingly graceful industrial structure is enlivened by a sprightly octagonal tower, and was renovated in 1972 by **Gelardin/Bruner/Cott** with **Anderson, Notter Associates** for artists' studios and living spaces.

Visit the two-story gallery showing works by residents. This was one of the first and largest mill conversions in the state, an early example

South End

of the creative lengths local artists have gone to in obtaining affordable housing. ♦ F 6-9PM; Sa-Su 2-6PM. 791 Tremont St (between Camden and Northampton Sts). Recorded information 437.9365

12 Rutland Square One of the South End's most intimate oases is this shady, slim, elliptical park bracketed by two rows of three-story bowfronts. A number of facades break from the neighborhood pattern of warm redbrick, and instead are prettily painted and detailed in light colors. Only one block long, the square is a lovely sliver of green. ♦ Rutland Sq (between Tremont St and Columbus Ave)

In the middle of the day on 19 May 1780 it became almost completely dark in most of New England, causing many to fear the Day of Judgment had arrived. That dark day has never been explained, although some hypothesize that the pollution from burning coal fires, or possibly ash and smoke carried over from enormous forest fires in the Great Lakes region, was the cause.

13 Villa Victoria Built in 1976 by **John Sharratt Associates,** this housing complex is a local success story. A largely Puerto Rican community not only participated in every stage of its development, but also collaborated with the architect so that residents' cultural values and traditions would be expressed with dignity. While the complex is by no means beautiful, given limited funds, it has developed its own strong identity.

Located in a former church with a splashy mural adorning the facade, the **Jorge Hernandez Cultural Center** (85 W. Newton Street) is a vibrant creative outlet that hosts events of all kinds: jazz, theater, music, and dance, most featuring Latino performers. ♦ Bounded by Tremont St and Shawmut Ave, and W. Brookline and W. Dedham Sts. Cultural Center information 262.1342

14 Buteco II ★$ This easygoing hole-in-the-wall (its name is Portuguese slang for "joint") serves authentic Brazilian dishes like *mandioca frita* (fried cassava root with carrot sauce), *moqueca de peixe* (fish in spicy coconut sauce), and—weekends only—the popular *feijoada* (black-bean stew with sausage, dried beef, pork, rice, collard greens, and orange). Some traditional Spanish dishes are offered, too. The lively restaurant attracts an appreciative South American clientele. ♦ Brazilian/Spanish ♦ M-Th 11:30AM-10PM; F-Sa 11:30AM-11PM; Su 3-10PM. 57 W. Dedham St (between Tremont St and Shawmut Ave). Reservations for five or more. 247.9249 ♿ Also at: 130 Jersey St, Kenmore Sq. 247.9508

15 Garden of Eden This tiny basement shop has all the fixings for a proper tea, prettily presented. Owners **Kelly Brown** and **Oliver Desnain** have stocked up on top-notch teas, coffees, and jams, arrayed amid dried flowers and garden statuary; also on hand are stellar baked goods, from hearty whole-wheat loaves to rosemary focaccia and several types of fruit tarts. It's the perfect place to grab breakfast-on-the-run, or to linger and stock a larder. ♦ Bakery ♦ Tu-F 7:30AM-7PM; Sa-Su 8AM-6PM. 577 Tremont St (between Dartmouth and W. Canton Sts). 247.8377

15 Botolph's on Tremont ★$$ This chic cafe occupies a carved-out corner of the twin-towered former **St. Cloud Hotel,** built in 1870 by **Nathaniel J. Bradlee.** (The residential hotel's fashionable French flats were forerunners to the apartment houses that soon spread like weeds in American cities.) The menu shares it daring with that of the original St. Botolph's: sausage and fennel egg rolls and duck ravioli are among the more unusual offerings here. Though surrounded by stellar restaurants, this cosmopolitan place is holding its own. ♦ International ♦ Daily 11:30AM-11:30PM. 569 Tremont St (at Dartmouth St). 542.2121 ♿

Back Bay's allure remains so powerful that the dividing line between this neighborhood and the South End is constantly disputed. New residents and businesses often try to push the boundary in order to claim a Back Bay address.

S<u>T</u> CLOUD

15 St. Cloud ★★★$$$ A perennial favorite among the artistic and fashion crowds, this sophisticated spot looks out unabashedly onto the South End street scene, with picture windows on three sides. The interior draws attention, too, with intriguing murals and subdued lighting. The bar attracts an attractive mix; the dining room, upscale bistro-fanciers. Chef **James Murcho's** menu changes seasonally, but is distinguished by well-thought-out combos, such as grilled veal T-bone steak with corn soufflé and red-pepper fondue. Happily, the restaurant stays open later than most in town, and the bar is a lively late-night rendezvous. ◆ American ◆ M-Sa 5:30PM-midnight; Su 11AM-3PM, 5:30PM-midnight. 557 Tremont St (at Clarendon St). Valet parking after 5:30PM and at Sunday brunch (fee). Reservations recommended. 353.0202 &

16 Tremont Ice Cream $ Just the kind of place everyone wants in their own neighborhood, this casual and cheap diner serves homestyle food made on the premises. Sidle up to the six-stool counter or grab a booth. A great choice for breakfast pancakes and French toast, the restaurant also serves clam chowder and makes soups fresh daily, plus basic sandwiches and salads. The ice cream comes from a dairy in Middleton, MA. ◆ American/Takeout ◆ Tu-Sa 6AM-6PM; Su 8AM-6PM. 584 Tremont St (between Clarendon and Dartmouth Sts). No credit cards. 247.8414

16 Hamersley's Bistro ★★★★$$$ Ambitious in cuisine, modest in decor, **Gordon** and **Fiona Hamersley's** restaurant is one of the most appealing in Boston. In the exposed kitchen Gordon and his crew don baseball caps and deftly turn out favorites inspired by French country cooking—golden roast chicken, sirloin with mashed potatoes, bouillabaisse, cassoulet—as well as more adventurous flights of fancy like roasted salmon with oysters, bacon, and hollandaise sauce, or a marvelous grilled mushroom-and-garlic sandwich on country bread. Sunday is a day of rest for Gordon, with a slightly more casual and lower-priced evening menu. In the summer the wine list changes seasonally to suit the food. The cozy dining rooms are filled with an interesting assortment of neighborhood people, suburban visitors, artists, actors, musicians, architects, and the like. Note: Hamersley's is more than likely moving across the street to the **Boston Center for the Arts (BCA),** though the plans were not final at press time. ◆ American/Mediterranean ◆ M-Sa 6-10PM; Su 6-9:30PM. 578 Tremont St (between Clarendon and Dartmouth Sts). Valet parking. Reservations recommended. 267.6068 &

17 Azita Ristorante ★$$$ First, a survival tip: Don't fall for the server's generous offer of "tap water or mineral water." The latter will cost you $2 per minimalist pop, or $7 a liter, and these prices won't be mentioned unless you think to ask. Rather than hustle San Pellegrino, the management would do better to shop around for tenderer veal; the saltimbocca practically bounces. Better stick to the *primi piatti:* the *farfelle* (butterfly pasta) with smoked salmon, vodka, and cream is sublime. The same goes double for the *tiramisù.* But if the management doesn't quit nickel-and-diming, this pretty spot—with its ice-cream pink walls and whitewashed tin ceiling—could go begging. ◆ Italian ◆ M-Th 11:30AM-2:30PM, 5:30-10PM; F-Sa 11:30AM-2:30PM, 5:30-11PM. 560 Tremont St (between Waltham and Hanson Sts). 338.8070

17 Nuts about Beauty It's a sensory treat just to smell the contents of this shop—more than a hundred types of soaps and body-care products from around the world, all cruelty-free.

South End

Customers are encouraged to sample, and needn't be asked twice. ◆ M-Sa 10AM-6PM; Su noon-6PM. 552 Tremont St (between Waltham and Hanson Sts). 482.9411 &

17 Addis Red Sea Ethiopian Restaurant ★★$ Adventurous diners sit around a *mesob* (woven table) and use bits of *injera* (crepelike bread) to snatch up morsels of chicken, lamb, beef, or vegetables. There are two basic preparations to choose from: *wat* dishes are infused with spicy *berbere* sauce; the *alcha* variation tends to be a bit milder. Wash your dinner down with Ethiopian beer or wine. ◆ Ethiopian ◆ M-F 5-11PM; Sa-Su noon-midnight. 544 Tremont St (between Waltham and Hanson Sts). 426.8727

In the Back Bay/South End subway station you'll see a statue of A. Philip Randolph (1889-1979), founding president of the Brotherhood of Sleeping Car Porters. Many of these porters worked at the former Back Bay railway station and settled in the South End (and Roxbury), helping to stabilize the struggling neighborhood and establishing the core of its black community.

C H ☼ N A

17 Chona One glance at the striking windows tells you something interesting is up. A spirited store for men's and women's fashions, Chona emphasizes clothing as entertainment and shopping as a fun experience. The wonderful-looking clothes are colorful, contemporary, and reasonably priced, blending familiar labels with local designers' lines. Chona also stocks accessories galore: belts, jewelry, ties, boxer shorts, and the like. It's impossible not to like a place where the sales help is so friendly and the dressing rooms so inviting. ◆ M-W 11AM-6PM; Th-F 11AM-7PM; Sa 10AM-6PM; Su noon-5PM. 540 Tremont St (at Hanson St). 482.6803

18 Boston Center for the Arts (BCA) Since 1970, the city-subsidized Boston Center for the Arts (BCA) has owned, operated, and organized art and cultural events at a three-acre complex comprising a variety of converted buildings, including the **Cyclorama**—a beautiful, shallow, steel-trussed dome built by **Cummings and Sears** in 1884 to house a novel tourist attraction: a 400-by-50-foot circular mural of the *Battle of Gettysburg* by **Paul Philippoteaux,** now exhibited elsewhere in the US. Subsequently, the building served as a skating rink; a track for bicycle races; a gymnasium and workout ring for boxers, where Boston's famous prizefighter **John L. Sullivan** fought; **Alfred**

South End

Champion's garage, where he invented the spark plug; and a flower market from 1923 to 1968. The Cyclorama now hosts annual art and antiques shows, flea markets, and other large events. The attractive kiosk out front was originally a cupola atop a **Roxbury** building designed by **Gridley J.F. Bryant,** architect of **Old City Hall,** the original **Boston City Hospital** building, and other Boston landmarks. In addition to providing studio space for some 60 artists chosen by the BCA board (one of the more noteworthy current tenants is playwright **David Mamet**), the BCA provides office and performance space for various theater and dance groups. ◆ 539 Tremont St (between Berkeley and Clarendon Sts). 426.5000 &

Within the BCA:

Mills Gallery Run by the BCA, this nonprofit gallery mounts far-ranging group shows by regional contemporary artists working in various media. Some performance pieces and installations are also shown. ◆ W-Su noon-4PM. 549 Tremont St (between Berkeley and Clarendon Sts). 426.8835 & (staff will assist)

18 Boston Ballet Corps of future (and present) ballerinas leapt for joy when work was completed in 1991 on this splendid and spacious dance center—the largest in New England—designed by **Graham Gund.** The foyer itself is like a stage set, with a grand pair of bifurcating staircases. The largest of the studios duplicates the dimensions of the **Wang Center** stage, so that *The Nutcracker*—the most popular rendition in the world—can be rehearsed right at home. Tours are offered Wednesday at 6PM and Saturday at noon. ◆ 19 Clarendon St (at Warren Ave). 695.6950 &

19 Berkeley Residence Club $ Run by the YWCA, this 200-room residence for women combines features of a hotel, dormitory, and old-fashioned rooming house. The clientele is an interesting mix: tourists, students, and working and professional women, some settled in long-term. The rooms are tiny—just the basics—with some doubles available. Each well-kept bathroom is shared by 13 to 16 women. Stay by the night or longer, paying by the week. There's a library, sitting room, laundry room, TV room, and pretty outdoor courtyard. The dining room serves two full meals a day (extra charge) with takeout available. Conveniently located, the residence is affordable and secure. Inquire about the rules, which aren't excessive and protect residents. The second floor has a less restrictive policy on gentlemen callers. To stay here, you must pay an immediate nominal fee for temporary membership. No children or pets are allowed. ◆ 40 Berkeley St (at Appleton St). 482.8850 &

20 The Terrace Townehouse $$ This 1870 bowfront B&B has only four rooms, but they're pips: spacious and luxuriously appointed, with private baths. You'll be coddled by owner **Glori Belknap,** who's up on all the sights and restaurants, and brings fresh-baked breakfast to your room. ◆ 60 Chandler St (between Clarendon and Berkeley Sts). 350.6520

20 Chandler Inn Hotel $ Although a bit drab, it's clean, safe, and a steal. The 56 rooms boast all the basic amenities, including air-conditioning. A "gay-friendly" hotel, the Chandler is in fact friendly to all, especially the budget-conscious traveler. ◆ 26 Chandler St (at Berkeley St). 800.842.3450

21 Icarus ★★$$$ The mood is muted and relaxed; the decor and cuisine, eclectic. A statue of winged Icarus beneath a cool ceiling band of neon surveys the two-tiered dining room, where a diverse clientele enjoys chef/co-owner **Chris Douglass'** seasonal inspirations, such as polenta with wild mushrooms and thyme, lobster in ginger-cream sauce on homemade noodles, grilled tuna with wasabi and sushi, pork loin with mango and jalapeño salsa, caramel-apple tart, and cherry-chocolate-chunk ice cream with icebox cookies. The lengthy wine list is superb ◆ American ◆ M-Th 5:30-10PM; F-Sa 5:30-11PM; Su 11AM-3PM. Closed Sunday in summer. 3 Appleton St (between Berkeley and Tremont Sts). Valet parking Wednesday through Sunday for a fee. Reservations recommended Friday through Sunday. 426.1790

21 Marcella's ★★$ Loftlike in scale, this vast brick-walled cafe—one side harbors a gargantuan grill—serves neo-Italian standbys at prices that are positively charitable. Savvy diners order the steak tips, a platter piled high with protein. Pizzas are outstanding, poufed two inches high with such toppings as chicken pesto plus ripe olives. Two can feast for as little as $25 and end up with a shopping bag of leftovers to lug home. ♦ Italian ♦ M-Th, Su 11AM-11PM; F-Sa 11AM-11:30PM. 1 Appleton St (at Tremont St). 357.9040 &

22 Medieval Manor $$$$ What to say about this inexplicably popular and long-running themed theater/restaurant? Well, simply this: an evening here involves a three-hour, gargantuan, eat-with-your-fingers fixed-price feast of sorts, and bawdy musical comedy starring singing wenches, oafs, strolling minstrels, and a sexist "Lord of the Manor." More than enough said. The whole thing's participatory, which means you can get into the action if you so choose—joined by many others from the typically vocal audience. Students pack the place. Believe it or not, vegetarians can join the orgy, too, with 48 hours' advance notice. Parties of four to eight are recommended, and no party of more than 10 is accepted if all male, all female, or all Harvard. There are more numbers-related rules; call to inquire. The best—possibly only—way to get here is by car: take the Southeast Expressway south to the Albany Street exit; then turn right onto East Berkeley Street. ♦ Admission. Call for show times. 246 E. Berkeley St (at Albany St). Reservations required. 423.4900 &

23 Cedars Restaurant $ All the food is cooked by **Elias Aboujaoude,** an owner who lives in the building. A very informal place, Cedars serves great hummus, tabbouleh, and kibbe. ♦ Lebanese/Takeout ♦ Daily 5PM-midnight. 253 Shawmut Ave (at Milford St). Reservations required for 10 or more. No credit cards. 338.7528 &

Birth control pioneer Margaret Sanger was among the most succinct speakers ever featured at the Ford Hall Forum (a lecture series that began in 1908 and continues to this day). Proscribed by civic authorities from speaking her mind, Sanger appeared in 1929 with her mouth taped shut, and she had historian Arthur Schlesinger, Sr., of Harvard read a short statement, ending: "As a pioneer fighting for a cause, I believe in free speech. As a propagandist, I see immense advantages in being gagged. It silences me, but it makes millions of others talk and think about the cause in which I live."

24 Ars Libri Out of the way and hidden on the third floor in a nondescript converted factory now occupied by architects, designers, and dancers, Ars Libri is renowned internationally for the country's largest comprehensive inventory of rare and out-of-print books and periodicals about the fine arts, including architecture and photography. Here's where one might be likely to encounter all of **Francisco de Goya's** *Los Caprichos;* drawings by **Albrecht Dürer;** a complete set of *Pan,* the stunning journal of the German *Jugendstil;* an extremely rare edition of *La Prose du Transsibérien,* an extended poem illustrated by **Sonia Delaunay,** or any number of other cherishable works. The owners buy and sell out-of-print and rare scholarly works, exhibition catalogs, print portfolios, and books with original graphics dating from the 16th century onward. The shop is quiet, since most business is conducted via subject-oriented catalogs sent to universities, libraries, museums, and individuals. **Machado Silvetti** designed this collector's sanctuary. ♦ M-F 9AM-6PM; Sa 11AM-5PM. 560 Harrison Ave (at Waltham St). No credit cards. 357.5212 &

25 East Meets West To Go $ This is a marvelous bakery for breads, muffins, pastries, and desserts such as the ultrarich chocolate crater cake and chocolate chubby cookies (ignore the name and chomp away). Geared mainly for takeout, the bakery does have a couple of tables and sells some lunch items, coffee, and sodas. Cakes can be made to order, too.

South End

♦ Bakery ♦ M-Sa 7AM-6PM; Su 7AM-2PM. 312 Shawmut Ave (at Union Park). No credit cards. 482.1015 &

25 On the Park ★★$$ A bright, sunny, friendly spot with windows all around, the cafe is a few strides away from the South End's prettiest greenery. It serves homemade breads and satisfying rustic dishes running the gamut from Southeast Asian to Latin American. Sunday brunch, with Bellinis, is a neighborhood event. The ever-changing art on the walls comes from local artists and Newbury Street galleries. Regulars and word-of-mouth keep the cafe's 34 seats filled. ♦ International ♦ M-Th 5:30-10:30PM; F 5:30-11PM; Sa 9AM-3PM, 5:30-11PM; Su 9AM-3PM, 5:30-9PM. Reservations accepted for groups of six or more. 315 Shawmut Ave (at Union Park). 426.0862

In 1951, during his first semester as a doctoral student at Boston University's School of Divinity, the Reverend Martin Luther King, Jr., took a room on St. Botolph Street. He then moved to more spacious quarters on nearby Massachusetts Avenue.

Anatomy of a Town House

Although architectural elements vary from block to block and even from house to house in Boston, here's an illustrated guide to some typical permutations, as well as a lexicon unknown to most town-house dwellers themselves (at least, until they run up against the need for renovations).

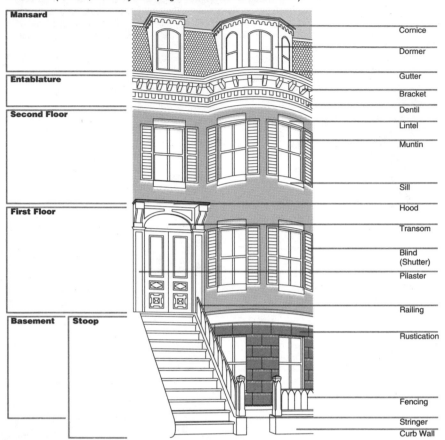

Mansard

Entablature

Second Floor

First Floor

Basement   Stoop

Cornice

Dormer

Gutter

Bracket

Dentil

Lintel

Muntin

Sill

Hood

Transom

Blind (Shutter)

Pilaster

Railing

Rustication

Fencing

Stringer

Curb Wall

South End

26 Union Park Square The first square to be finished in the South End remains one of its most special places. The elliptical park (designed in the 1850s) enclosed by an iron fence is lush and shady, with fountains and flowers. It's bordered by big brick town houses dating from the neighborhood's brief shining moments before Back Bay became *the* place to lay one's welcome mat. The handsome houses and perfect park commune harmoniously in their own little world. Regrettably, gauche modern hands have tacked on unsightly extra stories here and there, marring an otherwise splendid composition. ◆ Between Tremont St and Shawmut Ave

27 Cathedral of the Holy Cross An unexpected sight along a sadly run-down stretch of Washington Street is this heroic Gothic Revival elephant, which was designed in 1875 by **Patrick C. Keeley,** the architect of **St. Patrick's Cathedral** in New York City. New England's largest church, and the largest Catholic church in the country when it was built, the cathedral recalls an era when Irish Roman Catholic im-

migrants were a dominant presence in the South End. (The needs of this burgeoning population had already resulted in a prior Keeley-designed church, the imposing white granite **Church of the Immaculate Conception** at 761 Harrison Avenue at Concord Street, an unusual design worth a look.) The Roxbury puddingstone cathedral accommodates 3,500. It's still the principal church of the **Archdiocese of Boston** but is now used mainly for special occasions, such as when the **Pope** came to call in 1979. The front vestibule's arch contains bricks rescued from a Somerville convent burned during anti-Catholic rioting in 1834. As is true of so many Boston ecclesiastical edifices, the intention was to surmount the two towers with spires, but that never happened. ◆ Washington St (at Union Park St)

The South End's changeable nature means that many shops and restaurants come and go, and those that stay often keep ad hoc hours. The best approach is to call ahead when possible, be prepared for occasional disappointments, and be alert to interesting new finds.

28 Blackstone and Franklin Squares Divided by Washington Street, both squares were built in the 1860s but originated in an 1801 plan to which **Charles Bulfinch,** then chairman of Boston's Board of Selectmen, was a major contributor. Although they have lost a lot to time, the squares' original grandeur remains palpable. Look for the brownstone houses overlooking Blackstone Square on **West Newton Street,** once exemplars of architectural elegance, and project yourself into the neighborhood's genteel past.

At 11 East Newton Street (between St. James and Washington streets) stands the **Franklin Square House** apartments for the elderly. Built as the **St. James Hotel** in 1868, the lumbering French Second Empire building—equipped with two steam-powered elevators—was considered the South End's poshest hotel. At the height of the hotel's brief eminence, **President Ulysses S. Grant** stayed there. ◆ Washington St (Blackstone Sq at W. Newton St; Franklin Sq at E. Newton St)

The Battle Over Busing: A City Divided

On 21 June 1974, **United States District Judge W. Arthur Garrity, Jr.,** ordered the immediate integration of the oldest school system in the country after finding that Boston had maintained separate and unequal systems, relegating black students to inferior schools. The controversial **Boston School Committee** and city officials wouldn't act to redress the illegal segregation, so the federal court intervened. According to racial quotas established by Garrity, students were assigned to schools and bused across the city.

Thus began one of the most painful periods in Boston's history, the city that was a focal point of the Abolitionist movement and proudly proclaimed itself the "Cradle of Liberty" and the "Athens of America." But Boston is a city of close-knit neighborhoods, the boundaries of which often demarcate strong racial and ethnic divisions. The nation watched while the notorious crisis played out in the media. **J. Anthony Lukas'** Pulitzer Prize-winning best-seller *Common Ground* (1985) chronicles the busing saga through the eyes of three very different Boston families—the **Twymons,** the **Divers,** and the **McGoffs**—as they endured the tumultuous, angry days following Garrity's decision. A dense, riveting account of that era, *Common Ground* was shoehorned into a four-hour TV miniseries that aired nationally in 1990.

Nearly two decades after Garrity's order, almost half of the city's students are bused. Reactions among the busing supporters and detractors still run strong. Opinions vary on the results of the court's remedy. Detractors claim it simply condemned all students to a mediocre education; supporters contend there was no other alternative, and that however traumatic busing was, it paved the way for more minority and parent participation in shaping the school system, and for the appointment of the first black school superintendent in Boston's history.

Restaurants/Clubs: Red
Shops/ ♣ Outdoors: Green
Hotels: Blue
Sights/Culture: Black

George Hobica
Travel Editor, *The TAB* newspapers

As someone who was born in Boston and has lived here all my life, you'd think I would have seen and done it all by now. But Boston, like its denizens, takes a while to know well, and I'm constantly discovering new things.

Boston is, above all, a walking city. So walk!

Start by climbing to the observatory at the top of the **John Hancock Tower** to orient yourself.

Wander along Mount Vernon and Chestnut streets on **Beacon Hill,** then cross into the **Public Garden** and down Commonwealth Avenue from Arlington to Gloucester streets, especially in spring when the magnolias are in bloom.

Ride on the subway **Red Line** across the **Longfellow Bridge.**

Ice skate in the **Public Garden** in winter.

Hear the **Boston Symphony Orchestra**—tickets are often available at short notice from the box office, or through hotel concierges.

Dine at **Biba** or **St. Cloud** if you like innovative food and people-watching. If you need to hear yourself think, opt instead for **Seasons Restaurant** at the Bostonian Hotel (not to be confused with Another Season on Beacon Hill or the restaurant at the Four Seasons Hotel). If you want to hear yourself think in the prettiest dining room in Boston, head for the **Plaza Dining Room** at the Copley Plaza Hotel.

For something tasty but cheap, my choice is Indian food at **Tandoor House** in Cambridge, followed by a stroll into Harvard Square for book-browsing at **WordsWorth.**

For the view, have drinks at the **Logan Airport Tower** bar before or after your flight. If I'm meeting friends for drinks, there's only one place I go: the bar at the

Copley Plaza Hotel. Great martinis—big and potent. (And they let me bring **Charlotte,** my Wheaten Terrier, and park her under a table.)

Shop along **Newbury Street,** stopping at **Winston's** for flowers and **Martini Carl** for fashion.

See the **Museum of Fine Arts,** especially the Sargents, Cassatts, and French Impressionists.

Stay at the **Four Seasons** or the **Boston Harbor Hotel** in the luxury category; try the **Eliot Hotel** for something less pricey.

Take the train from North Station to **Concord**—the same line **Henry David Thoreau** decried in *Walden.* If you love that book as much as I do, you'll be moved by a walk around the pond, and a pilgrimage to the original site of Thoreau's house.

If it's beach weather, ride the train to **Singing Beach** in Manchester-by-the-Sea. Bring a box lunch from your hotel or from **Rebecca's** on Newbury Street.

In any weather, walk through the **Arnold Arboretum** in Jamaica Plain. This is best done with a dog—if you don't have one, call me and I'll loan you Charlotte (she's always ready for a w-a-l-k).

Charles River Basin

The basin and its esplanade, laced with paths, playgrounds, lagoons, and lawns, together form a lovely urban water park, the most spectacular section of the **Charles River Reservation.** Of all of Boston's landmarks, the waterway is the most visually striking, with the Boston skyline on one side and Cambridge on the opposite. In this majestic, romantic setting, Bostonians congregate for promenades, outdoor concerts, picnics, jogging, bicycling, games, sailing, sculling, canoeing, and feeding the hungry ducks made famous in **Robert McCloskey's** 1941 children's book *Make Way for Ducklings.* In fall and winter the riverside is still and quiet, and the Cambridge shoreline seems far away. But in spring and summer the two-mile-long esplanade brims with activity from **Beacon Hill** to **Boston University,** and the river sparkles with white sails. As the days heat up, free evening concerts and dance performances draw enormous crowds; the pièce de résistance is the traditional **Fourth of July Boston Pops concert,** which attracts hundreds of thousands—a river of people that eventually overflows the Charles' banks and bridges.

The lazy brown-green Charles casually zigs and zags, coiling left and right, even appearing at times to change its mind and turn back, before traversing an 80-mile course from **Hopkinton** to **Boston Harbor**—a distance of less than 30 miles as the crow flies. In general, the sluggish Charles is not an impressive river, shrinking to a mere stream in some places. But the Charles River Basin is the splendid lakelike section nine miles long that progresses from **Watertown,** past **Harvard University** and the **Massachusetts Institute of Technology (MIT),** and on to the Atlantic Ocean. Here the Charles has been sculpted into a splendid urban waterway—in fact, this river is more man-made than natural.

The river got its name 15 years before the **Puritans** arrived, when explorer **Captain John Smith** sent early maps of New England home to 15-year-old **Charles Stuart,** future **King Charles I,** and asked him to give its prominent features good English names. The river has always been a vital economic asset. Throughout the 18th and 19th centuries, industries fueled by the Charles included gristmills, sawmills, spinning and weaving companies, and manufacturers of paper products, leather, and chocolate. But intense industrialization polluted the river, and its estuary shrank from incessant landfilling. At low tide, the Charles was a malodorous eyesore bordering wealthy **Back Bay,** which is why that district appears to turn its back to the river.

In the early 1900s a long crusade to make the lower Charles healthy and attractive gained momentum. Prominent Boston and Cambridge residents, including landscape architect **Charles Eliot** (a colleague of **Frederick Law Olmsted** and founder of the **Trustees of Reservations,** a nonprofit conservation group) and philanthropists **Henry Lee Higginson** (founder of the **Boston Symphony Orchestra**) and **James J. Storrow,** led the drive to build the Charles River Dam in 1908. This created the freshwater basin, with an embankment extending from Charlesgate West (where the **Back Bay Fens** meets the river) to the old **West End.** In the early '30s **Arthur A. Shurcliff,** landscape architect of colonial **Williamsburg,** greatly embellished the embankment, designing the picturesque esplanade and its lagoons with funding provided by Storrow's widow, **Helen Osborn Storrow.** In 1951 Boston's **Museum of Science** took up residence astride the Charles River Dam on the Boston-Cambridge boundary. In the early '50s, **Storrow Drive,** the frenetic autoway, was built on the original embankment and, ironically, named for James Storrow, the avid supporter of the park it shouldered aside; Storrow Drive's counterpart, on the Cambridge side of the river, is **Memorial Drive.**

On the Boston side of the river, the subway stop handiest to the esplanade is the Charles stop (Red Line). But within easy walking distance (only five or six blocks) are the Arlington, Copley, and Hynes Convention Center/ICA stops (all Green Line); and the Back Bay/South End stop (Orange Line). On the Cambridge side, the Harvard Square, Kendall Square (both Red Line), and Science Park (Green Line) stops are nearest the river.

1 The Publick Theatre Inc.

Boston's oldest resident professional theater company has been staging performances under the stars for more than 20 years, in cooperation with the **Metropolitan District Commission (MDC).** The company has put on classical plays and musicals—including **Shakespeare, Gilbert & Sullivan,** and *Man of La Mancha*—and new shows, too. The company's season runs from late May to early September, with subscriptions available and special discounts for families. Purchase tickets at the on-site outdoor box office after 7PM on performance nights, or charge by phone; tickets are also available at **Bostix** and **Out of Town Ticket Agency.** The theater seats 200. ♦ Shows W-Su 8PM, weather permitting. Christian A. Herter Park, Soldiers Field Rd (across from the WBZ station). Free parking and picnic facilities. 782.5425 ♿

2 Guest Quarters Suite Hotel Boston/Cambridge

$$$ The site is inauspicious, right by the Cambridge/Allston exit on the Massachusetts Turnpike, but the 310 accommodations on 16 floors are all two-room suites, most with good views—request one facing the river. Each suite has two TVs, a wet bar and fridge, a fold-out sofa bed in the living room, and a king-size bed in the bedroom. Some bi-level suites are available on upper floors. Guest Quarters provides complimentary van service to Downtown Boston and Cambridge, an indoor pool, sauna, whirlpool, and exercise room, and reasonably priced on-premises parking. Wheelchair-accessible and nonsmokers' suites are also available. Ask about the hotel's special rates. ♦ 400 Soldiers Field Rd, Brighton (at River St Bridge). 783.0090, 800/424.2900; fax 783.0897 ♿

Within the Guest Quarters Suite Hotel Boston/Cambridge:

Scullers Jazz Club/Scullers Grille ★$$
A new and welcome addition to local nightlife is Scullers Jazz Club, a comfortable listening room that books local and national jazz and cabaret acts, with emphasis on vocalists. Only those 21 and older are admitted; the crowd generally ranges in age from 28 to 45. There's

a full bar, and light fare like pâté and smoked salmon are served. Meanwhile, at Scullers Grille, they prepare great bouillabaisse and other seafood specialties for the dinner crowd. Dine with a river view. ♦ Seafood ♦ Club Tu-W 8-11:30PM; shows Th-Sa 8PM, 10PM. Grille M-F 6:30-11AM, 11:30AM-2PM, 5:30-10PM; Sa 7-11AM; 11:30AM-2PM, 5:30-10PM; Su 7-11AM; 5:30-10PM. Second floor. On-premises parking (fee). No jeans allowed and jackets required in both. Reservations recommended Thursday through Saturday. 783.0811 ♿

3 Howard Johnson Cambridge

$$ Most of the rooms (202 in all) in this modern high rise have lovely views—ask to overlook the river, although the Cambridge skyline is nice, too. This "HoJo" has an indoor pool, free parking, the **Risuteki Japanese Steakhouse** and two other restaurants, and it's about a 15-minute walk along the Charles (best by day) to **Harvard Square.** Nonsmokers' rooms are available, and pets are allowed. ♦ 777 Memorial Dr, Cambridge (between River St and B.U. Bridges). 492.7777, 800/654.2000 ♿

4 Hyatt Regency Cambridge

$$$ A glitzy, glassy ziggurat-shaped structure nicknamed the "Pyramid on the Charles," the hotel has 469 rooms, some with outdoor terraces overlooking the river and Boston. The atrium rises 14 stories, with balconies, trees, fountains, even glass-cage elevators. The skylit health spa has an indoor pool, sauna, whirlpool, exercise room, and sundeck, plus a retractable ceiling and walls. There's also an outdoor basketball court. The hotel has adult's and children's bicycles for rent, so you can take a leisurely riverside journey. The Hyatt offers handicapped-accessible and nonsmokers' rooms; valet and self-parking on premises; a special rate for a second room when traveling with children; a special children's package; and a free shuttle van. The hotel is popular with families and locals seeking a little weekend luxury, and the ubiquitous business and con-

Charles River Basin

vention crowds. ♦ 575 Memorial Dr, Cambridge (between Harvard and B.U. Bridges). 492.1234, 800/233.1234; fax 491.6906 ♿

Within the Hyatt Regency Cambridge:

Spinnaker Italia ★$$ Boston's one and only revolving rooftop lounge and restaurant lets you gaze upon the city's twinkling night skyline, stretching from the **Financial District** and **Beacon Hill** to **Back Bay** and the **Prudential Center.** The room spins like a lazy Lazy Susan. Although the cuisine is not as spectacular as the views, the Northern Italian fare includes tasty pastas, gourmet pizzas, and entrées like *pollo arrosto.* From 4PM to closing daily, the restaurant serves cocktails and light food. ♦ Italian ♦ M-Sa 6-9:30PM; Su 10AM-2PM, 6-9:30PM. On-premises parking is free for two hours. No jeans, sneakers, T-shirts. Reservations recommended. 492.1234 ♿

The **Northeastern University Boathouse,** a deep-orange shingled structure, pays architectural homage to the river's older boathouses, especially Harvard's two from the turn of the century. Designed by **Graham Gund Associates,** the building has playful touches, such as oar-shaped balusters.

Radcliffe College

On Sunday during daylight-saving time, **Memorial Drive** on the **Cambridge** side of the river is closed to traffic from **Western Avenue Bridge** to **Eliot Bridge,** creating what is called **Riverbend Park.**

Fogg Art Museum ■

On the **Cambridge** side of the river near **Harvard University,** it's only a few minutes' stroll up JFK Street to **Harvard Square's** restaurants and shops.

Memorial Dr.

Eliot Bridge

1

JFK St.

Harvard University

Anderson Bridge

Weeks Bridge

Harvard's picturesque **Weld Boathouse,** designed by **Peabody and Stearns,** was built in 1909.

John W. Weeks Bridge is a graceful footbridge and the best place to watch the Head-of-the-Charles regatta in October.

Harvard Stadium ■

In 1911 a special act of Congress closed the Charles River to navigation so the **Anderson Bridge** could be built without a drawbridge. "To a father by a son," a tablet reads; **Larz Anderson,** US ambassador to Belgium, gave the bridge in memory of his father, **Nicholas Longworth Anderson,** also a Harvard graduate. Oddly, locals usually refer to the bridge by the son's name, not the father's.

Harvard University

Western Ave.

Western Ave. Bridge

Hoyt Field

Soldiers Field Rd.

River St.

River St. Bridge

2

3

Harvard University's first permanent boathouse, **Newell Boathouse,** with red-slate walls and delicate finials, dates from 1900 and was designed by **Peabody and Stearns.** The boathouse is dedicated to varsity teams, who often train for the **US Olympic team** or England's famed **Henley Royal Regatta.** Harvard's famous passion for rowing began with the founding of the country's first boat club in the 1840s. The oldest intercollegiate crew meet in the country is the annual **Harvard-Yale competition,** first held in 1854.

Cambridge St.

Above **Watertown,** about eight miles upstream from the Harvard Bridge, the river is rated Class B (okay for swimming and fishing). But below Watertown, the basin is NOT swimmable.

■ *Bath House*

Magazine Beach

Boston Univ Bridge

BOSTON

Ⓣ = *subway stop*

N

km			
mi	1/8	1/4	1/4

1/4 · 1/2

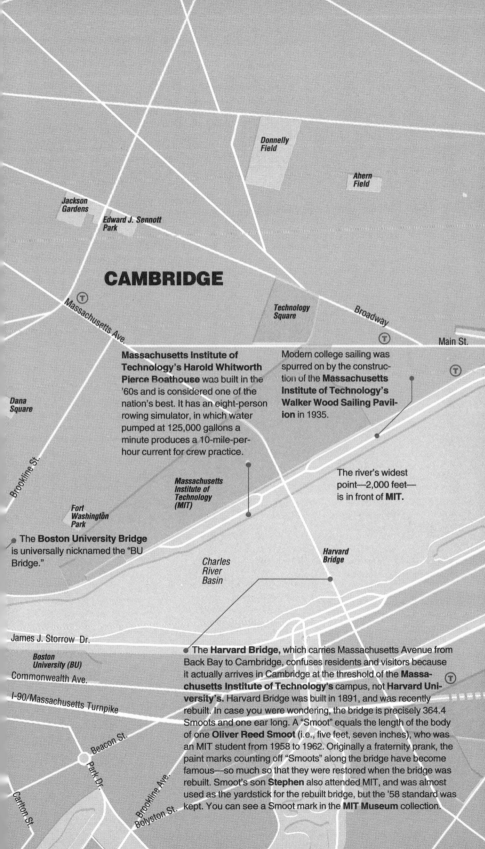

CAMBRIDGE

Massachusetts Institute of Technology's Harold Whitworth Pierce Boathouse was built in the '60s and is considered one of the nation's best. It has an eight-person rowing simulator, in which water pumped at 125,000 gallons a minute produces a 10-mile-per-hour current for crew practice.

Modern college sailing was spurred on by the construction of the **Massachusetts Institute of Technology's Walker Wood Sailing Pavilion** in 1935.

The river's widest point—2,000 feet— is in front of **MIT.**

The **Boston University Bridge** is universally nicknamed the "BU Bridge."

The **Harvard Bridge,** which carries Massachusetts Avenue from Back Bay to Cambridge, confuses residents and visitors because it actually arrives in Cambridge at the threshold of the **Massachusetts Institute of Technology's** campus, not **Harvard University's.** Harvard Bridge was built in 1891, and was recently rebuilt. In case you were wondering, the bridge is precisely 364.4 Smoots and one ear long. A "Smoot" equals the length of the body of one **Oliver Reed Smoot** (i.e., five feet, seven inches), who was an MIT student from 1958 to 1962. Originally a fraternity prank, the paint marks counting off "Smoots" along the bridge have become famous—so much so that they were restored when the bridge was rebuilt. Smoot's son **Stephen** also attended MIT, and was almost used as the yardstick for the rebuilt bridge, but the '58 standard was kept. You can see a Smoot mark in the **MIT Museum** collection.

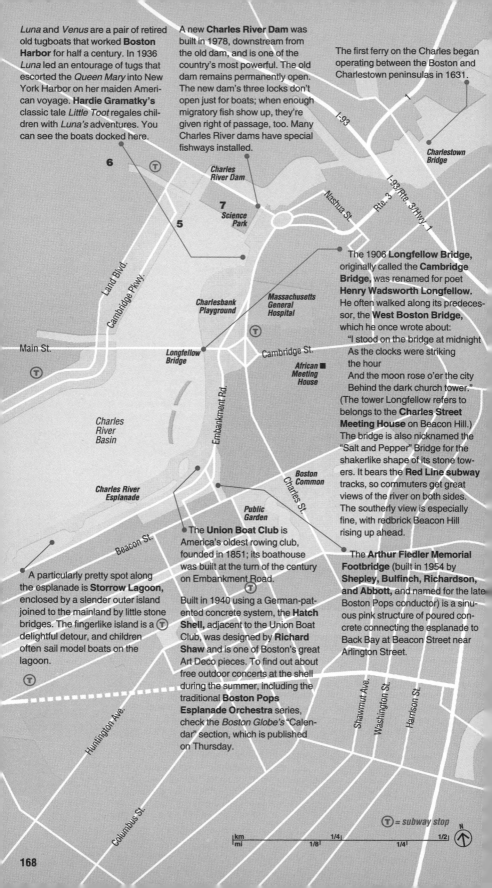

Luna and *Venus* are a pair of retired old tugboats that worked **Boston Harbor** for half a century. In 1936 *Luna* led an entourage of tugs that escorted the *Queen Mary* into New York Harbor on her maiden American voyage. **Hardie Gramatky's** classic tale *Little Toot* regales children with *Luna's* adventures. You can see the boats docked here.

A new **Charles River Dam** was built in 1978, downstream from the old dam, and is one of the country's most powerful. The old dam remains permanently open. The new dam's three locks don't open just for boats; when enough migratory fish show up, they're given right of passage, too. Many Charles River dams have special fishways installed.

The first ferry on the Charles began operating between the Boston and Charlestown peninsulas in 1631.

The 1906 **Longfellow Bridge**, originally called the **Cambridge Bridge**, was renamed for poet **Henry Wadsworth Longfellow**. He often walked along its predecessor, the **West Boston Bridge**, which he once wrote about:

"I stood on the bridge at midnight
As the clocks were striking the hour
And the moon rose o'er the city
Behind the dark church tower."

(The tower Longfellow refers to belongs to the **Charles Street Meeting House** on Beacon Hill.) The bridge is also nicknamed the "Salt and Pepper" Bridge for the shakerlike shape of its stone towers. It bears the **Red Line subway** tracks, so commuters get great views of the river on both sides. The southerly view is especially fine, with redbrick Beacon Hill rising up ahead.

The **Arthur Fiedler Memorial Footbridge** (built in 1954 by **Shepley, Bulfinch, Richardson, and Abbott,** and named for the late Boston Pops conductor) is a sinuous pink structure of poured concrete connecting the esplanade to Back Bay at Beacon Street near Arlington Street.

A particularly pretty spot along the esplanade is **Storrow Lagoon,** enclosed by a slender outer island joined to the mainland by little stone bridges. The fingerlike island is a delightful detour, and children often sail model boats on the lagoon.

The **Union Boat Club** is America's oldest rowing club, founded in 1851; its boathouse was built at the turn of the century on Embankment Road.

Built in 1940 using a German-patented concrete system, the **Hatch Shell,** adjacent to the Union Boat Club, was designed by **Richard Shaw** and is one of Boston's great Art Deco pieces. To find out about free outdoor concerts at the shell during the summer, including the traditional **Boston Pops Esplanade Orchestra** series, check the *Boston Globe's* "Calendar" section, which is published on Thursday.

6

5

7
Science Park

Charles River Dam

I-93

I-93/Rte. 3/Hwy. 1

Rte. 3

Nashua St.

Charlestown Bridge

Land Blvd.

Cambridge Pkwy.

Main St.

Charlesbank Playground

Massachusetts General Hospital

Longfellow Bridge

Cambridge St.

African Meeting House

Embankment Rd.

Charles River Basin

Charles River Esplanade

Public Garden

Boston Common

Charles St.

Beacon St.

Huntington Ave.

Shawmut Ave.

Washington St.

Harrison St.

Columbus St.

(T) = subway stop

N

Charting the Charles

The Charles River has been steadily rebounding from severe abuse and pollution since the late 1970s. The **Massachusetts Audubon Society's Broadmoor Wildlife Sanctuary** is a 600-acre tract along the Charles in **Natick** and **Sherborn**, and this is where you can see the river environment in its most protected natural state (280 Eliot Street off Route 16, South Natick, 508/655.2296.)

Many people run, skate, and bicycle along the banks of the Charles, or you can travel by canoe to the wildlife sanctuary, where many say the waterway is its prettiest. The river's wetlands are home to wood ducks and mallards, great blue herons, great horned owls, wood warblers, ospreys, red-tailed hawks, white-tailed deer, red foxes, river otters, muskrats, minks, snapping turtles, and 30 or so fish species, including carp, northern pike, and large-mouth bass.

Sailing vessels bearing passengers and freight once plied the river, and later tugboats, tankers, and barges, but today recreational craft rule: canoes, rowboats, sailboats, and powerboats. The river is dotted with numerous boathouses and yacht clubs, many dating from the turn of the century, that offer rentals and classes and sponsor competitions.

Sailing Community Boating is a nonprofit organization that offers sailing tours and instruction for everyone at the lowest possible prices. Its fleet includes more than 150 sailboats, plus windsurfers. More than 50 years old, Community Boating is America's oldest and largest public sailing program. In addition to summer and month-long memberships, two- and seven-day visitor memberships are available, as are discounted programs for senior citizens and youths. All kinds of special events and trips are scheduled regularly. ◆ Located behind the Hatch Memorial Shell, 21 Embankment Road (at the Charles Street footbridge). 523.1038; TTY 523.7406 ♿

Canoeing and Rowing More than 60 of the Charles River's 80 miles can be explored by canoe, although a few portages are required. The **Charles River Watershed Association,** a private, nonprofit conservation group founded in 1965, publishes a **Charles River Canoe Guide** and on the last Sunday in April sponsors popular races called **Run of the Charles,** with contestants furiously paddling and portaging canoes around dams. For more information, call 527.2799.

You can rent canoes, kayaks, and rowing shells at the **Charles River Canoe and Kayak Center** at the **Metropolitan District Commission (MDC)** building (2401 Commonwealth Avenue, Newton, 965.5110). The center offers canoeing, kayaking, and rowing classes for all levels. Better still, begin your journey farther up the river and rent your canoe at **Tropicland Marine and Tackle** (100 Bridge Street, Dedham, 329.3777).

Rowing and the Charles have had a long, romantic liaison. A single figure sculling gracefully over the river's surface is a common early morning sight. So, too, are "eights," crew boats with exhorting coxswains, which skim past and then disappear beneath the next bridge. Four colleges, two prep schools, and three distinguished boat clubs maintain handsome boathouses on the river for their crew teams and scullers. The annual **Head-of-the-Charles** regatta,

held on the next to the last Sunday in October, is the world's largest single-day regatta, the oldest head-style racing event in the US, and an amazing spectacle. More than 4,000 male and female athletes from all over the world In almost a thousand boats represent 200-plus colleges, clubs, high schools, and other organizations, or just themselves. The course extends upstream from the **Boston University Bridge** to a half-mile above **Eliot Bridge.** This is not a head-to-head competition; it's computer-timed, with boats departing at 10- to 12-second intervals. For information on the Head-of-the-Charles, call 864.8415.

For group or private rowing instruction, investigate **Community Rowing** at **MDC Daly Ice Rink** (Nonantum Road, Newton, 455.1992). Community Rowing is open to the public from April through October, with very reasonable fees charged on a monthly basis. Community Rowing also organizes adaptive rowers' groups for people with disabilities.

Running, Roller Skating, and Skateboarding
The favorite places to run and bicycle in Boston are the paths on both sides of the Charles. Roller skating and skateboarding are popular here, too; skates and boards can be rented from **Beacon Hill Skate Shop** (135 Charles Street South, Theater District, 482.7400). For more information on bicycling, see "Boston by Bike: Plum Paths for Pedal Pushers" on page 170.

Sweep Rowing: One oar per person

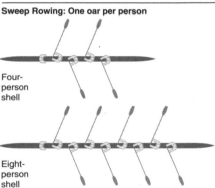

Four-person shell

Eight-person shell

Sculling: Two oars per person

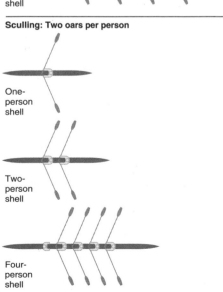

One-person shell

Two-person shell

Four-person shell

Boston By Bike: Plum Paths for Pedal Pushers

Thanks to the many reckless drivers who dominate the city's streets, bicycling in Boston is more akin to navigating the Indianapolis 500 than it is a pleasurable pastime. But hope lingers on the horizon.

Over the past two decades, lobbying groups have made great strides toward making the city more welcoming to two-wheelers—primarily by promoting bike paths. The centerpiece is the **Dr. Paul Dudley White Charles River Bike Path**, a 14-mile loop that's increasingly bucolic the farther out you get. This trail hugs both banks of the Charles from the **Museum of Science** all the way to **Watertown Square**. Shorter in-town stretches include the **Southwest Corridor Linear Park Bike Path** (four miles in reclaimed South End parkland), the wooded **Riverway Bike Path** (from Boston's Park Drive to Brookline's Brookline Avenue), and the scenic **Jamaicaway Bike Bath** (architect **Frederick Law Olmsted's** former bridle path along the **Muddy River**).

New as of 1992 (after 17 years of scheming and wheedling) is the **Minuteman Bike Path**—an 11-mile swath linking the **Alewife Station** in **Cambridge** (the outermost subway stop on the Red Line) to the towns of **Arlington, Lexington,** and **Bedford. Congressman Joseph Kennedy,** himself an avid biker, recently managed to eke out $1.2 million in federal funds to connect the Minuteman with the Dudley. He's also promoting a bill to dedicate three percent of federal-highway funds to the development of bike and pedestrian routes.

Meanwhile, Boston's serious bikers—and they are legion—have grown adept at improvising patchwork itineraries. In many neighborhoods, such as student-packed Cambridge, no one will look askance if you cravenly stick to the sidewalk, as long as you're considerate. All subway lines except the Green Line (which is usually about as

Charles River Basin

roomy as a sardine can) will accommodate bikes during nonpeak hours; call the **Massachusetts Bay Transportation Authority** at 722.3200 for details.

To find out about other trails, including some to **Provincetown** on **Cape Cod,** write or call the **Department of Environmental Management,** Division of Forests and Parks, Salstonstall Building, 100 Cambridge Street, Boston 02202; 727.3180. You can rent wheels at the **Community Bike Shop** in the South End, located at 490 Tremont Street at East Berkeley Street; 542.8623. For general tips on bike trails, rules of the road, and rentals or repairs, call the **Boston Area Bicycle Coalition** at 491.7433. Both the **American Youth Hostels** (730.8294) and the **Appalachian Mountain Club** (5 Joy Street, 523.0636) organize cycling trips, too.

Restaurants/Clubs: Red	**Hotels:** Blue
Shops/ ✿ Outdoors: Green	**Sights/Culture:** Black

5 Royal Sonesta Hotel Boston/Cambridge
$$$ Ask for a room facing the river and look across at the gold dome of the **State House** gleaming above **Beacon Hill.** The hotel has 400 rooms furnished in contemporary style on 10 floors, including nonsmokers' and wheelchair-accessible rooms. From early June until mid-September the Sonesta offers vouchers for a narrated river tour, free to guests. The hotel also provides guests with free ice cream, bicycles, and cameras during the summer. Hotel recreational facilities include an indoor pool under a retractable roof. A courtesy van provides transportation to Harvard and Kendall squares and Boston. The hotel displays an excellent modern art collection with pieces by **Frank Stella, Andy Warhol,** and **Robert Rauschenberg. ♦** 5 Cambridge Pkwy., Cambridge (at the Charles River Dam). 491.3600, 800/766.3782; fax 661.5956

6 The Sports Museum
Housed inside the **Cambridgeside Galleria** mall, this popular spot encapsulates "great moments in New England sports history." Holdings include more than a thousand hours of film and video highlights, star memorabilia, and "action-packed displays." ♦ Admission. M-Sa 9:30AM-10PM; Su noon-6PM. 100 Cambridgeside Pl (off First St). 787.7678 ♿

7 Museum of Science A familiar sight is the museum's funky '50s silhouette above the Charles. Streams of families and fleets of school and tour buses arrive all day long. If you're with kids, you can be sure they'll have a great time. If not, you might wish the crowds would thin and the decibels lower, but you'll still squeeze past many interesting exhibits (see the plan on the opposite page). In the beginning, the museum was the **Boston Society of Natural History,** founded in 1830, then the **New England Museum of Natural History,** residing in an imposing French Academic edifice in **Back Bay.** In 1951 the museum moved to modern quarters on this site straddling the **Charles River Dam** and changed its name to reflect the forward-looking attitude that has made it so innovative. The **Exhibit Hall's** 400-plus exhibits date from 1830 to this minute, covering astronomy, astrophysics, natural history, and much more. All-time favorites are the

Plexiglas Transparent Woman with light-up organs, the chicken hatchery with its active eggs, the world's largest **Van de Graaff** generator spitting 15-foot lightning bolts, a space-capsule replica, and the 20-foot-high model of Tyrannosaurus Rex. Newer exhibits include the *Human Body Discovery Space,* where children (or adults) ride a bike while a bike-riding skeleton mimics. Walk on the moon or fly over Boston at the **Special Effects Stage,** or see how an ocean wave is made.

The museum has three cafeteria-style restaurants, but the one to try is the **Skyline Room Cafeteria** for its captivating views—perhaps Boston's best—of Boston on one side of the Charles, Cambridge on the other, and boats passing through the dam below and cruising upriver. Explore the **Museum Shop,** one of the best around, which has a fantastic inventory of science-related projects, gadgets, toys, jewelry, books, and T-shirts. Under former director **Bradford Washburn,** a world-renowned explorer, mountaineer, and mapmaker, the pioneering museum embraced modern science and the changing nature of museums. It became a flexible participatory place, providing exceptional educational programs to families, schools, and communities. Special events include the **Inventor's Weekend Exhibition,** where students' inventions—such as an automatic baseball-card stacker—are exhibited along with adults' inventions. The museum is located near the **MBTA Science Park** stop on the **Green Line.** ♦ Admission; discounts for elders and children four to 14; children under four free 1-5PM Nov-Apr. (Separate admissions charged for **Charles Hayden Planetarium** and **Mugar Omni Theater,** with combination discount tickets available.) M-Th, Sa-Su 9AM-7PM, F 9AM-9PM, May-early Sept; M-Th, Sa-Su 9AM-5PM, F 9AM-9PM, free W 1-5PM, Nov-Apr. Closed Thanksgiving and Christmas. Science Park (at the Charles River Dam). Paid parking available. 723.2500, TDD 227.3235 ⟁

Within the Museum of Science:

Charles Hayden Planetarium A $2 million Zeiss planetarium projector and state-of-the-art multi-image system create enthralling programs on what's happening in the heavens, such as the seasonal skies over Boston or phenomena like black holes and supernova. You can see special laser shows, too. The Planetarium is not recommended for children under four. ♦ Admission; discounts for senior citizens and children four to 14. Call for show times. 723.2500 ⟁

Mugar Omni Theater In Massachusetts' only OMNIMAX theater, a tilted dome 76 feet in diameter and four stories high wraps around you, and state-of-the-art film technology makes you feel surrounded by the images on the screen. The regularly changing films project you into locales like the tropical rain forest, Antarctica, inside the human body, outer space, or on a roller-coasterlike tour of Boston. The theater is not recommended for children under four. ♦ Admission; discounts for senior citizens and children four to 14. Call in advance for show times; the shows are very popular. 723.2500 ⟁

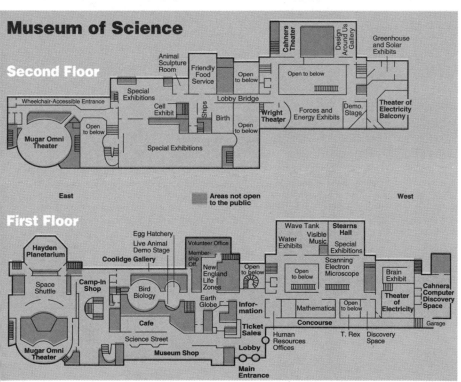

PLAN COURTESY OF THE MUSEUM OF SCIENCE

Cambridge

Across the **Charles River** is Boston's intellectual, self-assured neighbor, Cambridge. Both Boston and Cambridge are crowded with college campuses, but it's Cambridge that exudes a true Ivy-League ambience. Many identify Cambridge with **Harvard University**, which is nearly as old as the city itself; others associate it with the prestigious **Massachusetts Institute of Technology (MIT)**, which moved here from Boston in 1916. The two giant institutions account for more than 26,000 students, hailing from nearly one hundred nations. Harvard alone is the alma mater of six United States presidents. Since World War II, Harvard and MIT, with government and industry support, have made Cambridge a world-renowned research center that focuses on military and aerospace industries, artificial intelligence, and genetic engineering. These partnerships have spurred the growth of related industries in Cambridge and other cities, creating Massachusetts' high-tech economy.

In 1630 **Newtowne** village was founded by the **Massachusetts Bay Colony,** led by **Governor John Winthrop.** Eight years later the settlement was nostalgically renamed Cambridge, after the English university where many Puritans had been educated. That same year, the nation's first college, founded here two years earlier by the colony's Great and General Court, was named **Harvard College** to memorialize **John Harvard,** a young **Charlestown** minister who bequeathed his 400-volume library and half his estate to the fledgling school. And in 1639 the New World's first printing press was established in Cambridge, publishing the first American document, *Oath of a Free Man.* No other settlement in the colony was permitted a press until 1674, so Cambridge became the earliest publishing center of the hemisphere, ensuring prominence as a place of ideas.

It is the engine of academia that drives the 6.25-square-mile city of 93,000 or so "Cantabrigians" (as Cambridge residents are known), half of whom are affiliated in some way with the local universities. But that is by no means the whole story.

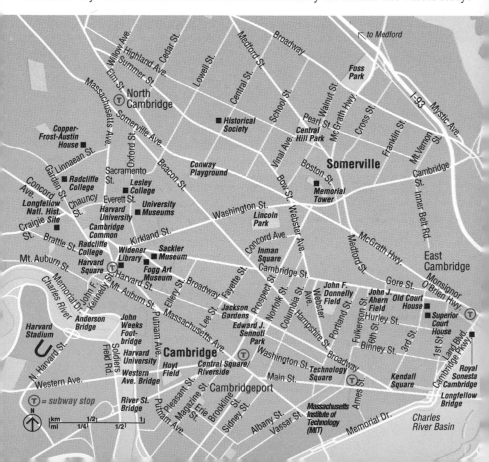

Cambridge has traditionally been a place for progressive politics and lawmaking, where generations of residents have embraced issues such as antislavery, women's rights, the antinuclear movement, environmentalism, opposition to the Vietnam War and the United States' foreign policy in Central America, and many other concerns. Others dismiss Cambridge as an uppity enclave of eggheads and bleeding hearts, so strong is its reputation as a bastion of liberalism. But it's known for cultural diversity as well, for it is full of people from somewhere else. The cafes, bookstores, shops, and restaurants here reflect a multicultural persona—a mélange of Yankee gentry, blue-collar workers, conservatives, liberals, immigrant newcomers, and long-established ethnic groups. They live in **Brattle Street** mansions, crowded tripledeckers, chic condos, and subsidized housing.

In 1846 Cambridge officially became a city when **Old Cambridge** joined with the industrial riverside communities of **East Cambridge** and **Cambridgeport.** Today the city consists of distinctive neighborhoods, loosely defined as Kendall Square, East Cambridge, Inman Square, Central Square, Cambridgeport, Riverside, Mid-Cambridge, North Cambridge, West Cambridge, and the famous **Harvard Square. Massachusetts Avenue** runs the length of Cambridge, leading from the **Harvard Bridge** on the Charles River through MIT's campus to Harvard Square and northward. Travel by the **Red Line** subway to Cambridge's main attractions is fast and easy, whereas street parking requires a permit or a meter and spaces tend to fill up fast.

It would take months to fully comb Cambridge, so most visitors head directly to Harvard Square (commonly referred to as "the Square"), the city's centerpiece and the heart of Old Cambridge. Overdevelopment and the invasion of franchises have eroded some of its quirky charm, but you can still sit in cafes and browse in bookstores, pretending to read while overhearing amazing conversations among an extraordinarily eclectic group. On a warm afternoon sit at the **au bon pain** outdoor cafe and watch all of Cambridge stroll by. In summer the nighttime street life bustles, especially near **Brattle Square** (a tiny square-within-the-Square) where outdoor entertainers hold forth every few yards. The Square boasts a galaxy of bookstores catering to every interest, and many stay open very late. Among the commercial landmarks are the **Harvard Coop, Out of Town News,** the **Tasty, WordsWorth,** and **Charles Square,** a hotel-and-shopping complex. Student-oriented "cheap eats" abound; so do vintage and avant-garde clothing boutiques, and housewares and furnishings stores. Experience the overwhelming aura of **Harvard Yard,** then walk up Brattle Street (formerly **Tory Row**) and visit lovely **Radcliffe Yard.** You'll see plenty of historic edifices and some interesting modern architecture. The Square offers good theater, movies, and music in a variety of settings, plus Harvard's great museums. Along with MIT and other local colleges and institutions, Harvard hosts a long menu of lectures, exhibitions, symposia, and cultural and sports events throughout the academic year.

Take the MBTA Red Line to get to Cambridge: the Kendall Square Station is closest to MIT and it's near East Cambridge. (The Lechmere Station on the Green Line is even more convenient to East Cambridge.) The Central Square Station is a five-minute walk from Inman Square; the Harvard Square Station is convenient to parts of North Cambridge; the Porter Square Station is nearest to North Cambridge.

Big-leaguer of the Ivy League it may be, but Harvard's buildings are regularly stripped of the trailing greenery because of the plants' destructive effects on brick.

Restaurants/Clubs: Red   Hotels: Blue
Shops/ 🌳 Outdoors: Green   **Sights/Culture:** Black

1 Harvard Square Not really a square at all, it's officially located where Massachusetts Avenue heading from Boston turns and widens into a big triangle, on which the landmark **Out of Town News** is located. On one side of this triangle is **Harvard University;** on the other two lie commerce. But to students and Cantabrigians, "the Square" always refers to the much larger area radiating from this central point, with most shops, restaurants, clubs, and services concentrated on Brattle, JFK, and Mount Auburn streets, as well as lots of little side streets like Church, Plympton, Dunster, and that whimsical pair, Bow and Arrow streets. All around the Square, sidewalks are crowded with college students, professors, canvassers,

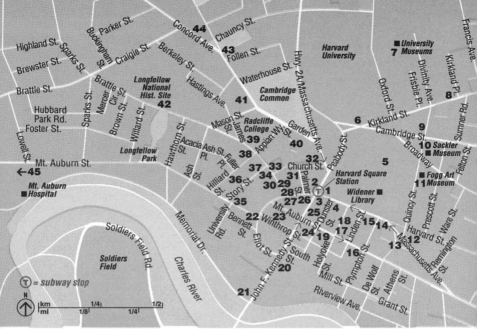

protestors, businesspeople, and entertainers—
in fact, you can safely assume you're heading
beyond the Harvard Square area when the
foot traffic around you starts to dwindle.
♦ Bounded by Peabody St, Harvard St, and
Massachusetts Ave

In Harvard Square:

Cambridge Discovery Information Kiosk
Located near the subway station entrance (the
main entrance is opposite the **Harvard Cooperative Society**) is an information kiosk
where you can get bus and train schedules, maps,
brochures, and a wealth of information on
Cambridge, its universities, and the great self-
guided walking tours to Revolutionary Cambridge, East Cambridge, and more. They sell a
variety of guidebooks, too, highlighting architecture, restaurants, history, Harvard University, the Square, etc. Some of the materials
are free and some are sold for modest fees to
pay the overhead of the nonprofit **Cambridge**

Cambridge

Discovery organization, which operates and
staffs the kiosk.

Cambridge Discovery provides information on
the city to both tourists and residents, offering
guided group tours for a fee (from late June to
Labor Day; inquire at the booth for tour times),
information packages, a newsletter, and school
outreach programs. Many of the volunteers
speak other languages and are ready for your
questions. If you're planning to stay in Cambridge, they have information on local lodging,
too. To get information before your trip, write
to Cambridge Discovery at P.O. Box 1987,
Cambridge, MA, 02238. ♦ M-Sa 9AM-6PM, Su
11AM-5PM, late June-Labor Day; M-Sa 9AM-
5PM, Su 11AM-5PM, Labor Day-late June.
497.1630 &

Out of Town Newspapers Busy from opening to closing, this **National Historic Landmark**
newsstand—universally called "Out of Town
News"—sells newspapers from every major
American city and many large cities worldwide,
plus a huge array of magazines, maps, comic
books, and Harvard T-shirts. Many a rendezvous is kept at the familiar ornate kiosk. If your
craving for newspapers and mags isn't sated
here, try **Nini's Corner** across the way, next to
the **Harvard Coop.** Nini's has lots of souvenirs
and postcards, too.

Also on this traffic island is sculptor **Dimitri
Hadzi's** 21-foot-tall *Omphalos* (Greek for na-
vel), signifying the center of the universe. Generations of Harvard students and Cantabrigians
have considered the Square precisely that.
♦ M-Sa 6AM-midnight; Su 6AM-11:30PM.
No credit cards. 354.7777 & (use the rear
entrance)

Out of Town Ticket Agency Down the main
entry to the **Harvard Square Station,** look for
the mezzanine-level window where you can
purchase tickets to sports events, popular concerts, plays, special events, and anything going
on at **Boston Garden,** from ice-skating shows
to **Bruins** and **Celtics** games. ♦ M-F 9AM-6PM,
Sa 9AM-5:30PM. Cash only. 492.1900; credit
card service at ConcertCharge 497.1118, 800/
442.1854

When Harvard University was young, well-heeled students who paid a higher tuition and gave the university
a silver vessel were honored with the title "Fellow Com-
moners." They sat at the dining hall's high table, where
the ceremonial silver was placed, while poorer students
were stuck "below the salt," an appropriately medieval
designation.

Until 1693 Harvard College was the only college in this
hemisphere.

2 **Harvard Cooperative Society** Universally known as **The Coop** (pronounced like the chicken abode), the society was founded in 1882 by students angered at local merchants' price gouging. Their enterprise sold goods to faculty and students, and gradually blossomed into a full-fledged collegiate department store. The store (pictured above) is owned by its members: Harvard and MIT students, faculty, employees, and alumni.

The Coop is best known for its three floors of books, including best-sellers, paperbacks, non-fiction, remainders, and textbooks; an extensive record collection; New England's largest selection of posters; and anything and everything emblazoned with Harvard colors and *Veritas* seal. The clothing and footwear selection for men and women may not be the height of fashion, but there's a little of everything and frequent sales. The Coop sells housewares, sports equipment, radios and TVs, luggage, computers, typewriters, small electronics, cameras and accessories, lots of stationery products, and just about anything else a student or faculty member might hanker for, including good snacks. Sidewalk sales are often set up in the rear alley, between the original Coop building and its annex. You can also find restrooms here, a relative rarity in the Square. ♦ M-W, F-Sa 9AM-7PM; Th 9AM-8:30PM. 1400 Massachusetts Ave (at Brattle St). 499.2000 &

3 **The Tasty** $ A dozen stools, a counter where doughnuts recline on pedestals under plastic covers, a grill that keeps the place warm winter and summer—that's all there's room for in this closet-size sandwich shop, open since 1916. A remnant of old Harvard Square before terminal trendiness set in, the Tasty serves round the clock. It's the only witness to the Square's brief hushed hours. ♦ Daily 24 hours. 2A JFK St (at Brattle St). No credit cards. 354.9016 &

4 **au bon pain** $ The mass-produced croissants are surprisingly tasty; they also sell muffins, sandwiches, and soups. The real reason to come here is to relax outside on the large terrace in nice weather and watch the incessant tide of humanity flow to and from the Square. Students of human nature won't find a better vantage point or more varied collection of people in Greater Boston. Singers, jugglers,

and promoters of various causes often hold forth alongside the cafe. A local chess master regularly plays against the clock for a small sum at one of the cafe's chess tables, attracting aficionados. ♦ Cafc ♦ M-Th, Su 6:30AM-midnight; F-Sa 6:30AM-1AM. 1360 Massachusetts Ave (between Holyoke and Dunster Sts). No credit cards. 497.9797 &

5 **Harvard University**
The first and foremost of the famed "Ivy League" schools was originally founded to train young men for the ministry. The university's seal (pictured at right) was adopted in 1643; *Veritas* is Latin for "Truth."
Harvard College gradually moved from Puritanism to intellectual independence, and became a private institution in 1865. In the mid-19th century the college became the undergraduate core of a burgeoning modern university, with satellite professional schools.

Today Harvard University's 10 graduate schools are Arts and Sciences, Business Administration, Dental Health, Design, Divinity, Education, Government, Law, Medicine, and Public Health. Harvard and its Cambridge surrounds are so entwined that it's hard to tell where town ends and gown begins. The university has some 400-odd buildings on 380 acres of land in the Cambridge/Boston area. Harvard's current endowment is $5 billion (give or take many millions)—the largest of any university in the world. **Harvard Houses,** where students live after their freshman year, dot the Square toward the river and include lovely Georgian-style brick residences with courtyards. Most memorable are the **River Houses,** best seen from the Charles.

The **Harvard University Information Office** is located on the ground floor of **Holyoke Center,** plainly visible from the street. Maps, pamphlets, self-guided walking tours, and other materials (some free, some sold) on Harvard and area events can be picked up here. Events

Cambridge

tickets are sold here, too. Get a free copy of the *Harvard University Gazette,* which lists activities open to the public. Harvard students also offer free one-hour tours departing from the office that give visitors a good general introduction to the university. ♦ Tours M-F 10AM, 2PM, Sa 2PM, during the academic year; M-Sa 10AM, 11:15AM, 2PM, 3:15PM, Su 1:30PM, 3PM, during the summer. Holyoke Center, 1350 Massachusetts Ave (between Holyoke and Dunster Sts). 495.1573 &

In 1778 and 1779 Massachusetts held the first Constitutional Convention at Cambridge's Fourth Meeting House. The resulting document is the oldest constitution still in use today, and was a model for the Constitution of the United States.

6 Science Center The largest building on Harvard's campus—built by **Sert, Jackson and Associates** in 1973—looks like a giant Polaroid Land camera to some, with a complex and multiterraced exterior. Science buff alert: on the center's lower level you'll find **Harvard's Collection of Historical Scientific Instruments,** a repository for scientific apparatus used for Harvard teaching and research in astronomy, surveying, physics, geology, electricity, navigation, and other subjects since approximately 1765. On view are telescopes, sundials, clocks, vacuum pumps, microscopes, early computing devices, and more, with additional devices donated to the university dating back to 1550. The *Tanner Fountain,* designed by **Peter Walker,** is a jet-misted cluster of rocks that's always alluring to children. On a sunny day, if you stand in the right place, you may see a brightly colored rainbow hovering over the fountain. ◆ Kirkland St (at Oxford St) &

7 Harvard Semitic Museum Founded in 1889, the museum participated in the first United States archaeological expedition to the Near East that year, and the first scientific excavations in the Holy Land, from 1907 to 1912. The museum closed during World War II and reopened in 1982. It now presents special exhibitions drawn from its archaeological and photographic collections, which include 28,000 photographs of 19th-century life in the Near East. ◆ Admission. M-F 11AM-5PM. 6 Divinity Ave (at Kirkland St). 495.3123

7 Museums of Natural History Sharing one roof are four separate **Harvard University** museums dedicated to the study of archaeology, botany, comparative zoology, and minerals. The most famous exhibition is the **Botanical Museum's Blaschka Glass Flowers** collection, handblown by **Leopold** and **Rudolph Blaschka** in Dresden, Germany, using a process that was lost with their deaths. More than 840 plant species are represented, with a few irrevocably lost when shattered by sonic booms. Another odd exhibition is **Rosalba Towne's** 19th-century series of paintings depicting every plant and flower mentioned in the works of **Shakespeare.** Particularly wondrous is the **Mineral-**

ogical and Geological Museums' collection of gemstones, minerals, ores, and meteorites. Look for the giant Mexican crystals.

The **Peabody Museum of Archaeology and Ethnology** is the oldest museum in this hemisphere dedicated to archaeology and ethnology, with treasures from prehistoric and historic cultures from all over the world. Founded in 1866 by **George Peabody,** many items in the museum's displays were brought back from Harvard-sponsored expeditions. The Peabody's largest collections focus on North, Central, and South American Indian cultures. Visit the **Hall of the Maya,** and the **Hall of the North American Indian's** exhibition of some 500 artifacts, which were blessed in 1990 by **Slow Turtle,** chief medicine man of the **Wampanoags.**

The exceptionally comprehensive display includes objects from 10 or so different Indian cultures over five centuries, with a number of items brought back by the **Lewis** and **Clark** expedition, and features magnificent towering totem poles, peace pipes, a Plains Indian ceremonial outfit, warriors' longbows, and a bison skull with a symbol on its forehead representing the four winds.

Tracing the evolution of animals and man, the **Museum of Comparative Zoology** delights kids with its whale skeletons; a 180-million-year-old *Paleosaurus,* the 25,000-year-old Harvard mastodon; the giant sea serpent *Kronosaurus;* **George Washington's** pheasants; the world's oldest egg, 225 million years old; and the largest known fossilized turtle shell. The museum also displays the *Coelacanth,* a fish thought to have been extinct for 70 million years until fishers began to catch some live in 1938. Visit the museums' gift shop, a largely undiscovered treasure trove. The Peabody Museum has a separate gift shop, also excellent. ◆ Admission (one fee for all four museums), reduced for elders, students, and children five to 15; children under five free. M-Sa 9AM-4:30PM; Su 1-4:30PM; free Sa 9-11AM. 24 Oxford St (entrance also on Divinity Ave). Peabody 495.2248, Botanical 495.2326, Mineralogical 495.4758, Zoology 495.2463. Recorded information 495.1910, admission information on all 495.3045 & (inquire at admission desk)

8 Adolphus Busch Hall Named for the famous beer baron, the noble hall with its carved heroes and solemn inscriptions was formerly the **Busch-Reisinger Museum.** It is now occupied by Harvard's **Center for European Studies.** Designed by a German architect and completed in 1917, the medievalesque edifice was built to house Harvard's Germanic collections. It was enormously expensive and is full of lavish detail. Originally lauding German culture, the hall and its purpose have been influenced by the World Wars and changes in international opinion toward Germany. Much of the former museum's 20th-century German art was collected during the rise of **Hitler,** when the works were declared degenerate, banned by the **Nazis,** and shipped to the States.

The Busch-Reisinger's Renaissance, baroque, and modern holdings have been moved to the new **Werner Otto Hall,** behind the Fogg. Busch Hall displays medieval statuary, stained glass, metal, and other works not needing climate control. Overlooking the wonderful courtyard garden are carved stone heads taken from **Wagner's** *Ring of the Nibelungen.* Sunday evening concerts are given on the famous Flentrop organ as part of the Fogg music series; a small fee is charged. Across Kirkland Street from the hall is a Gothic Swedenborgian church, a little jewel. ◆ Courtyard M-F 11AM-3PM; collection 1-5PM second Sunday every month. Kirkland St (at Quincy St). For concert information, call 495.4544

Restaurants/Clubs: Red	Hotels: Blue
Shops/ 🌿 Outdoors: Green	Sights/Culture: Blac[k]

9 Memorial Hall Just north of **Harvard Yard** looms this Ruskinian Gothic giant (pictured above). Alive with colorful ornament, gargoyles, pyramidal roofs, and square tower, the cathedral-like hall has plenty of pomp and circumstance to spare. Designed in 1878 by two Harvardians, **Henry Van Brunt** and **William R. Ware,** the hall was built as a monument to university alumni who died in the Civil War—on the Yankee side, of course. You can see their names inscribed in the transept inside. Some of the stained-glass windows were produced in the studios of **Louis Comfort Tiffany** and **John La Farge.** Innumerable momentous events—depending on one's perspective—have occurred here, from college registration and examinations to major lectures and concerts. ♦ Between Cambridge and Quincy Sts &

Within Memorial Hall:

Sanders Theatre Celebrated painter **Frank Stella** and many other illustrious figures have lectured in the richly carved wooden theater, which seats 1,224. Also appearing here are national performers such as the **Beaux Arts Trio** and local music groups, including the **Pro Arte Chamber Orchestra of Boston, Cantata Singers, Cecilia Society, Cambridge Society for Early Music,** and the festive annual **Christmas Revels.** ♦ Admission charged for most events. Recorded information 495.2420 & (use the Kirkland St entrance)

10 Arthur M. Sackler Museum Across Broadway from the **Fogg,** the Sackler is a relative newcomer to Harvard. Except for its brick stripes, interesting window arrangements, and touches of electric-lime paint, the chunky postmodern building is quite ordinary-looking. It was designed in 1986 by British architect **James Stirling,** who aptly called Harvard's campus "an architectural zoo." The Sackler houses ancient, Asian, and Islamic art, including the world's finest collections of ancient Chinese jades and cave reliefs and Chun-ware ceramics, and an exceptional collection of Japanese woodblock prints.

Special exhibitions are also installed here, and the **Harvard University Art Museum Shop** is on the first floor. The very odd portal and pillar arrangement on the Sackler's upper facade facing Broadway marks where a skyway was to connect the Sackler and Fogg museums, but was quashed by community opposition. ♦ Admission (includes Fogg Art Museum), reduced for senior citizens, students; free for those under 18. Tu-Su 10AM-5PM; free Sa 10AM-noon. Free tours 1PM, with admission. 485 Broadway (at Quincy St). 495.9400 &

10 George Gund Hall Home of the **Graduate School of Design,** the modern concrete building—completed in 1972 by **John Andrews**—is notable for the striking nighttime silhouette created by its stepped-glass roof, beneath which design students visibly toil at their drawing boards late into the night. Within Gund Hall is the **Frances Loeb Library,** which has architecture and urban design collections. On the first floor, look for changing architecture exhibits and a small **Charrette** store. ♦ At Quincy St. 495.4731 &

11 Harvard Yard Verdant and dappled with sun and shade, its great trees sentinels to the education of generations, Harvard Yard (pictured above)—now on the **National Register of Historic Places**—exudes an aura of privilege and prestige, the essence of the institution. But anyone is welcome to relax on its grassy lawns, although when late spring arrives the air becomes thick with lawn fertilizer and noisy with machinery as the university starts sprucing for another commencement. Summer mornings are particularly tranquil here; early fall heralds the return of the students and faculty with their brisk, purposeful traffic to and from classes.

Harvard's oldest buildings date from the early 18th century; its newest were built yesterday. From **Holyoke Center,** cross Massachusetts Avenue and enter the gate, where you'll find the **Benjamin Wadsworth House,** an attractive yellow clapboard house, built in 1726, where Harvard presidents resided until 1849. It briefly served as **General George Washington's** headquarters when he took command of the Continental Army in Cambridge in 1775. Walk

Cambridge

through the Yard (this western side is considered the "Old Yard"); to the left is Early Georgian **Massachusetts Hall,** the oldest university building, dating from 1720, where the president's offices are now. Patriot regiments were once housed here and in several other buildings nearby. Opposite is **Harvard Hall** (built in 1766); between the two halls is **Johnston Gate** (erected in 1889), the Yard's main entrance, which was designed by **McKim, Mead & White.** Standing at attention by the gate is a bit of frippery, a tiny guardhouse designed by **Graham Gund.** Next on the left is **Hollis Hall** (completed in 1763), where **John Quincy Adams, Ralph Waldo Emerson,** and **Henry David Thoreau** roomed. Beyond is **Holden Chapel** (built in 1742), a High Georgian gem, complete with a family coat of arms, once called "a solitary English daisy in a field of Yankee dandelions," but it is tarnished through constant alterations. (The coat of arms originally faced Massachusetts Avenue, but was moved as the college's orientation turned inward on the Yard.) Next is **Stoughton Hall**, designed in 1805 by Harvard graduate **Charles Bulfinch**.

Opposite Johnston Gate on the right stands **University Hall**, designed by Bulfinch in 1815. It was this building that turned the Yard into an academic enclave, instead of the clusters of buildings facing outward. In front stands **Daniel Chester French's** 1884 statue of **John Harvard** (French also sculpted **Abraham Lincoln** in the **Lincoln Memorial** in Washington, DC). The statue is famous for the three lies set forth in its plaque stating "John Harvard, founder 1638." It is the image of an 1880s Harvard student, not of Harvard himself; Harvard was a benefactor, not a founder; and the college was founded in 1636. Nevertheless, the false John is nearly always surrounded by tourists and visitors. Although the light here is generally poor for photos, you'll probably have to swing wide of clusters of people posing. Every now and again, rival schools give the statue a decorative paint job.

Behind University Hall, in the "New Yard," is **Memorial Church** (constructed in 1932) with its soaring needle-sharp spire. By Harvard regulations, the church's wonderful **University Choir** only performs during religious services here. Installed in the church is a glorious organ, a creation of the late **C.B. Fisk** of Gloucester and one of the greatest American instruments built according to baroque principles. Many important international organists have vied to play it. Looming opposite is the massive **Widener Memorial Library**, which is across the grassy **Tercentenary Theatre,** where the university's commencements are held with every ruffle and flourish—even a Latin oration. As you head in that direction you'll pass Romanesque Revival **Sever Hall** on your left, designed by H.H. Richardson in 1880, a **National Historic Landmark** and one of his greatest buildings.

Cambridge

Study its brilliantly animated and decorative brickwork.

Alongside Widener are **Pusey Library,** located underground, where the university's archives and map and theater collections are stored, and **Houghton Library,** home to its rare books and manuscripts, memorabilia and furnishings from **Emily Dickinson's** Amherst home, and the single book remaining from John Harvard's library. Pusey often exhibits selections from its theater collection on the first floor, and Houghton offers public displays of some of its treasures, with emphasis on fine bookmaking. Near **Lamont Library,** which is tucked in the corner, is a **Henry Moore** sculpture called *Four-Piece Reclining Figure.* ♦ Between Massachusetts Ave and Quincy St

Within Harvard Yard:

Harry Elkins Widener Memorial Library

A more triumphal and imposing entrance than Widener's would be hard to find, with its massive Corinthian colonnade and grand exterior staircase. Chilly-gray and austere, Widener (built in 1915) is the patriarch in Harvard's family of nearly one hundred department libraries campuswide. It was named for **Harry Elkins Widener,** who went down with the *Titanic;* a plaque tells the story. The largest university library in the world, Widener's collection of books is only surpassed by the **Library of Congress** and the **New York Public Library.** It has 7.5 million volumes on more than five miles of bookshelves; the entire library system contains more than 12 million volumes, plus manuscripts, microforms, maps, photographs, slides, and other materials. Widener is open to the public, but access to its stacks is limited to the fortunate cardholders with Harvard affiliation or to those with special permission. In the resplendent **Harry Elkins Widener Memorial Room,** bibliophile and collector Harry's books are on display, including a *Gutenberg Bible,* one of only 20 complete copies remaining, and a First Folio of **Shakespeare's** plays dated 1623, the first collected edition. Look for the dioramas depicting Cambridge in 1667, 1775, and 1936; and the **John Singer Sargent** murals in the main stair hall. ♦ M-F 9AM-10PM, Sa 9AM-5PM, Su noon-5PM, when school is in session; M-F 9AM-5PM, during school vacations. 495.4166 ♿

COURTESY OF THE CARPENTER CENTER

11 Carpenter Center for the Visual Arts

Coolly surveying Harvard Yard across the way, the sculptural Carpenter Center (pictured above) is the only structure designed by **Le Corbusier** in North America; it was built in 1963 and is now on the **National Register of Historic Places.** The iconoclastic concrete-and-glass form carries on an interesting dialogue with the sedate **Fogg Art Museum** next door and other conservative architectural neighbors crowding round. Within is Harvard's department of visual and environmental studies. Carpenter orchestrates a rotating program of contemporary exhibitions in its two public galleries, lectures, and the wonderful **Harvard Film Archive** series. The center houses a film archive, photography collection, and studios. ♦ Lobby gallery M-F 9AM-11PM; Sa 9AM-6PM; Su noon-10PM. Sert Gallery Tu-Su 1-6PM. 24 Quincy St (between Massachusetts Ave and Broadway). 495.3251, recorded information on film showings 495.4700 ♿

Cambridge has the highest concentration of book-stores per square mile in the country.

11 Fogg Art Museum Founded in 1891—Harvard's oldest art museum—the Fogg's comprehensive collection represents most major artistic periods in the history of Western art from the Middle Ages to the present. In this 1927 **Coolidge, Shepley, Bulfinch,** and **Abbot** design, art galleries on two levels surround an Italian Renaissance courtyard modeled after a 16th-century canon's house. The Fogg's French Impressionist, British, and Italian holdings are especially strong; look for works by **Whistler, Rossetti, Géricault, Fra Angelico, Rubens, Ingres, Beardsley, Monet, Renoir, Picasso,** and **Pollock.** Visit the **Wertheim Collection** on the second floor.

Also on the second floor is Harvard's first permanent gallery of decorative arts, which rotates displays of treasures from the university's vast collection of furniture, clocks, chests, Wedgwood, silver vessels, and other household goods bequeathed by Harvard alumni and others over the past 300 years. Probably the most famous item is the **President's Chair,** a knobby, uncomfortable-looking triangular-seated chair made in England or Wales in the 16th century and brought to Harvard by **Rev. Edward Holyoke,** president from 1737 to 1769. Since Holyoke (a portrait of whom seated in this chair was painted by **John Singleton Copley**), the President's Chair has supported every Harvard president during commencement ceremonies. The Fogg, by the way, sponsors great concerts in the courtyard during the academic year, from Renaissance Italian composers to **Gershwin.** ◆ Admission (includes **Sackler Museum**), reduced for senior citizens, students; free for children under 18. Tu-Su 10AM-5PM; free Sa 10AM-noon. Free tours 11AM, 2PM, with admission. 32 Quincy St (at Broadway). 495.9400 ♿

12 Inn at Harvard $$ **Graham Gund's** 1992 design earned a "Worst New Architecture" award from *Boston* magazine: "looks like a plywood prop from Universal Studios and feels like an upscale hospital inside." Drop in and decide for yourself. The four-story atrium, with its couches, tables, and shelves of up-to-date books (light meals and bar service are available here) almost achieves the ambience of a "grand residential living room"; it just needs a little breaking in. And they might reconsider the towering replicas of baroque garden statuary, which look plain eccentric. ◆ 1201 Massachusetts Ave (at Harvard St). 491.2222, 800/528.0444 ♿

13 Cafe Pamplona ★$ This is the most European of Cambridge cafes, a place where patrons linger comfortably for hours drinking espresso and writing, reading, or engaging in conversation from the mundane to the supremely esoteric. Tiny Pamplona is in the lower level of a snug red house, with an outdoor terrace where people hang about past midnight in the summer. The eclectic clientele leans toward highbrow. In addition to teas and coffees of all kinds (try the "mokka"), Pamplona serves gazpacho, sandwiches, and specials, as well as flan, parfaits, chocolate mousse, and delightful little pastries. ◆ Spanish/South American/Cafe ◆ M-Sa 11AM-1AM; Su 2PM-1AM. 12 Bow St (at Arrow St). No credit cards. No phone on premises.

14 Harvard Book Store Open since 1932, this Cambridge institution and family business is a general-interest bookstore that emphasizes scholarly works and customer service. The bookstore is particularly strong in philosophy, literary theory and criticism, psychology, black studies, women's studies, classics, and books from university presses. People flock in for its great remainders selection and basement inventory of used paperbacks, hardcovers, and texts. It puts out a monthly newsletter. Owner **Frank Kramer** also operates the extremely popular **Harvard Book Store Cafe** (190 Newbury Street, Back Bay, 536.0095), which has a more general-interest slant and serves good food to hungry book browsers. ◆ M-Sa 9:30AM-11PM; Su noon-8PM. 1256 Massachusetts Ave (at Plympton St). 661.1515 ♿ (street level only)

14 Bartley's Burger Cottage ★$ A fixture in the Square since 1960, the Bartleys (and their son, Bill) have ushered several generations of ravenous college students through their undergraduate years. Bartley's roasted, marinated chicken is, they boast, "a degree above the rest," but the real draw are the big juicy burgers—available in 30 variations, plus a dozen or so topical guises, such as The Madonna ("a naked burger stripped of its roll"). The place is chockablock with tiny tables and decorated with odd remnants of popular culture—e.g., a vintage ad with Reagan hawking cigarettes. For its many fans, it's the next best thing to home. ◆ American ◆ M-Sa 11AM-10PM. 1246 Massachusetts Ave (at Plympton St). 354.6559 ♿

14 The Grolier Poetry Book Shop Inc. This all-poetry bookshop was founded in 1927 as a rare-books store, then converted to its specialty

in 1974 by poetry-loving owner **Louisa Solano,** who bought the shop because she couldn't afford to continue buying book after book. Grolier has 14,000 poetry titles today, including books and cassettes on poetry, first editions, small-press publications, and little magazines. Solano cosponsors a poetry-reading series for nonpublished poets, hosts autograph parties about once a week from September to May, and keeps a mailing list and bulletin board going, as well as a gallery of photographs of poets who are patrons. Her shop is a formal and informal meeting place; lots of visiting poets use the Grolier as an information center and sounding board. ◆ Tu-Sa 10AM-noon, 12:30-6PM. 6 Plympton St (between Massachusetts Ave and Mt. Auburn St). 547.4648, 800/234.7636

15 Briggs & Briggs Established in 1890, distinguished B&B is known for its stock of classical and popular sheet music and books. It also sells musical instrument accessories, stereo equipment, and a variety of classical, jazz, blues, folk, and world music on CDs, records, and tapes. ♦ M-Sa 9AM-6PM. 1270 Massachusetts Ave (at Plympton St). 547.2007 ♿ (they offer assistance)

16 Harvard Lampoon Castle Cambridge's most whimsical building—designed by **Wheelwright and Haven** in 1909—is home to the *Harvard Lampoon* offices, an undergraduate humor magazine that inspired the *National Lampoon* (although there's no affiliation). "Poonies" have long been famous for their pranks, from stealing the Massachusetts State House's Sacred Cod in 1933, to hiring an actress in 1990 to hold a press conference and pretend she was **Marla Maples,** Donald Trump's notorious girlfriend. Pick out the eyes, nose, mouth, and hat on the entrance tower. Atop is a statue of an ibis, frequently absconded by *Harvard Crimson* staffers. **William Randolph Hearst,** a former *Lampoon* business manager, donated the land. ♦ Between Mt. Auburn St and Plympton St

Within Harvard Lampoon Castle:

Starr Book Shop This academic bookstore purveys antiquarian sets and scholarly works in literature, philosophy, classics, history, biography, and general subject areas. They carry current reviewers' copies, too. Graduate and undergraduate students frequent the shop, which is owned and operated by **Peter Starr.** ♦ M-Sa 10AM-8PM; Su noon-6PM. 29 Plympton St (at Mt. Auburn St). 547.6864

17 Pangloss Bookshop Peruse used, out-of-print, and rare scholarly monographs in the humanities and social sciences, as well as literary magazines. Pangloss does book searches and special orders. ♦ M-W, Sa 10AM-7PM; Th-F 10AM-10PM. 65 Mt. Auburn St (between Holyoke and Linden Sts). 354.4003

17 Elsie's Famous Sandwiches $ There was indeed an Elsie, who retired at least a quarter-century ago. Yet she'd probably find the food

Cambridge

here quite familiar, for it never changes; young and old alike troop in for good fat sandwiches like the Turkey Deluxe, the Roast Beef Special, hot pastrami, and 30 or so other sandwiches and subs. You'll find salads, too, with dressings made right here, and bargain breakfasts in the AM. Munch away at a windowside counter, or brown-bag it and walk a few blocks to the river. Harvard alumni recall frequent trips to Elsie's. ♦ Sandwiches/Takeout ♦ M-Sa 7AM-8PM; Su noon-8PM. 71A Mt. Auburn St (at Holyoke St). No credit cards. 354.8781

The original Harvard College was surrounded by cow yards; hence the name Harvard Yard.

Restaurants/Clubs: Red
Shops/ 🌿 Outdoors: Green
Hotels: Blue
Sights/Culture: Black

18 The Hasty Pudding Building This rather ramshackle little theater is home to the undergraduate **Hasty Pudding Theatricals,** a dramatic society established in 1795 and renowned for its annual Hasty Pudding Awards to the Man and Woman of the Year. The celebrity recipients—**Cher, Kevin Costner,** and **Jodie Foster** are past winners—are honored with parades through Cambridge in February, accompanied by male club members in female attire. The guest is then treated to an irreverent performance and comedic roast, and presented with a ceremonial pudding pot. The theater is also used by the **American Repertory Theatre** (see the **Loeb Drama Center** on page 187) for its "New Stages" series; six months out of the year it's home to the **Cambridge Theatre Company,** a new venture stirred up from the ashes of the Poets' Theatre of the '50s. ♦ 10 Holyoke St (between Massachusetts Ave and Mt. Auburn St). Box office 496.8400

Within The Hasty Pudding Building:

Upstairs at the Pudding ★★$$$ On the top floor, beneath high-vaulted ceilings and posters of old Hasty Pudding theatricals, amid forest green, crisp white, and romantic pink, enjoy a convivial repast spilling over with atmosphere, away from the Square's commotion. Upstairs at the Pudding offers ambitious European dishes like grilled quail on gnocchi, clams Florentine, risotto with shrimp, rack of lamb with black-olive butter, venison steak, roast *poussin,* Queen Mother's cake, and Sicilian lemon cream with strawberry sauce. Many entrées are accompanied by a dramatic array of vegetables. The à la carte Sunday brunch is deliciously out of the ordinary. This is definitely not a student stomping ground, except perhaps when Mom and Dad come to town. ♦ Northern Italian/European ♦ M-F noon-2PM, 6-9PM; Sa 6-9PM; Su noon-2PM, 5-8PM. Reservations recommended. 864.1933 ♿

19 Schoenhof's Foreign Books, Inc. Writer **John Updike,** Harvard economist **John Kenneth Galbraith,** and chef **Julia Child** have all shopped here. And soon after arriving in America, many of Boston's foreign residents and students immediately head to the understated shop in the basement of **Harvard's Spee Club** (a student organization). The reason: Schoenhof's is the best foreign bookstore in the country, with more than 35,000 titles—original works, not translations—representing 200 languages (other than English). Founded in 1856 by **Carl Schoenhof** to serve Boston's German community, Schoenhof's today is dedicated to bringing together people and books of all nationalities. The sales staff are fluent in several languages and work together to select books, with an emphasis on history, philosophy, literature, and literary criticism. The biggest selections are French, Spanish, German, Italian, and Russian. Schoenhof's also has a great department of references, records, and tapes for language learning; and children's books, too. The wholesale/retail store runs a worldwide mail-order service and is tenacious at tracking down even the most esoteric special orders—a French book on termites or a $5,000 German edition on **Freud**, for example. ♦ M-W, F-Sa 10AM-6PM; Th 10AM-8PM. 76A Mt. Auburn St (between Dunster and Holyoke Sts). 547.8855

20 Iruña ★★$$ Despite Harvard Square's international population, most of its restaurants have an Americanized style. Not this little cafe tucked down a short alley. Iruña offers a relaxed and simple European ambience and good food that has earned it a devout clientele throughout its quarter-century. The Spanish specialties are moderately priced and good: try the gazpacho, garlic soup, paella, Basque chicken, or potato omelet. Daily specials feature whatever's fresh, maybe Cornish game hen or rabbit. Try the red or white sangria. In warm weather, there's a small outdoor patio for dining, but it's actually more pleasant inside, especially if you dine early. ♦ Spanish ♦ M-F 11:30AM-2PM; 6-10PM; Sa 1:30-10PM. 56 JFK St (between Bennett and Mt. Auburn Sts). Reservations recommended Friday and Saturday. No credit cards. 868.5633

21 John F. Kennedy Memorial Park Often nearly empty of people and very well maintained, the park is a big grassy blanket, wonderful for lounging. There's an interesting variety of trees, many still quite young, since the park was only completed a few years ago. It's behind the **John F. Kennedy School of Government** and **The Charles Hotel,** with the river just across the street. Look for the fountain inscribed with **JFK** quotes. ♦ Between JFK St and Memorial Dr ⑤

22 Harvard Manor House $ In the heart of the Square, the low-key, friendly hotel has 72 rooms on four floors. Lots of visiting parents, professors, and prominent guests of the nearby **John F. Kennedy School of Government** stay here. Despite the name, the hotel is privately owned and run. ♦ 110 Mt. Auburn St (at Eliot St). 864.5200; fax 864.2409 ⑤

22 The Charles Hotel $$$ Harvard University guests, entertainment-industry folk, and business travelers who like to be near the late-night liveliness of the Square stay here, many on a long-term basis. The hotel is also popular with writers and sponsors readings. Part of the **Charles Square** complex, which features shops, condominiums, a health club, and restaurants, the 299-room, 10-story hotel offers many rooms overlooking the **John F. Kennedy Memorial Park** and the **Charles River,** with Shaker-style furniture, telephones and TVs in all bathrooms, and a patchwork down quilt on every bed. The King Charles minisuites have four-poster beds. Eighteenth-century quilts, New England antiques, and works by local artists enliven the hotel's main entry and halls. Handicapped-equipped and nonsmokers' rooms, 24-hour room service, a concierge, a multilingual staff, a complimentary overnight shoe shine, and valet parking and self-parking for a fee are available. Guests have complimentary access to the neighboring **Le Pli Salon's** exercise equipment and pool (868.8087). Through special arrangement with nearby **Barillari Books,** you can order books by room service: on the telephone, key in the special number connecting to the bookstore and a porter will pick up your selection. The hotel and Charles Square jointly sponsor free jazz concerts in the courtyard on Wednesday from 6PM to 8PM (depending on the weather), from late June to September, which attract hundreds. ♦ 1 Bennett St (at Eliot St). 864.1200, 800/882.1818; fax 864.5715 ⑤

Within The Charles Hotel:

Rarities ★★★$$$$ The subtle decor suits the sophisticated American cuisine, with soft piano music from the **Quiet Bar.** Named for a 1672 botanical book, the restaurant displays a collection of its prints. This is not a place to take dinner lightly; the food is too special and the wine list one of the best in town. The ambitious menu changes seasonally, with game and fresh seafood specialties. If you can handle it, the award-winning chocolate pâté dessert—a dense, rich, cakelike brownie served in slices and doused with sauces—will satisfy even the most intense chocolate craving. Sleek and chic it may be, but Rarities isn't too proud to feature a good old banana split, too. And a private dining room can be reserved for up to 16. ♦ American ♦ M-Sa 6-10PM. Jacket and tie required. Reservations are recommended. 864.1200 ⑤

The Quiet Bar At the threshold to **Rarities,** pianists play softly here every night. Cozy and, yes, quiet, this is a nice change and a far cry from the noisy student bars that predominate in the Square. Rarities desserts are served. There's

no dress code, although the clientele generally has a well-heeled look. The bar offers very good wines. ♦ Daily 4PM-1AM. 864.1200 ⑤

Bennett Street Cafe ★$$ Overlooking a sunny courtyard, the cafe is airy and open. The menu ranges from simple offerings to complex regional cuisine with international twists and turns. Doodle away between courses with the crayons provided on the paper table covering. There are three seatings for the popular Sunday buffet brunch: 11AM, 1PM, and 2PM. Come back early on a weekday and enjoy a tasty Continental breakfast before the Square wakes up. ♦ Regional American ♦ M-Th, Su 6:30AM-10PM; F-Sa 6:30AM-11PM. Reservations recommended for six or more, and for Sunday brunch. 864.1200 ⑤

The Regattabar The Charles Hotel pulled it off with panache: it gambled and launched a popular place to listen and dance to local and nationally acclaimed jazz acts. The **George Shearing Duo**, the **Milt Jackson Quartet, Gary Burton, Herbie Hancock, Ahmad Jamal, Pat Metheny, Herbie Mann,** and the **Four Freshmen** have all performed in this comfy venue. Tickets for Friday and Saturday sell out fast, so plan a week in advance. Jazzophiles drive up from New York regularly to hear good jazz for reasonable prices. Hotel guests are admitted free to all Tuesday through Thursday shows and any 11PM show after signing up with the concierge; all customers may purchase one-and-a-half tickets and stay for both shows on one night. ◆ Tu-Sa 8PM-1AM. Shows Tu-W 9PM; Th-Sa 9PM, 11PM. Proper attire required. Tickets sold by Water Music, Inc. 876.7777 &

22 Shops at Charles Square The stark modern complex's numerous shops and restaurants include a new branch of **Skipjack's Seafood Emporium, Giannino Restaurant and Bar,** Le Pli Salon, **Papermint** (extraordinary wrappings and stationery), **Vilunya** (folk art finds), and some national chains such as **Talbot's** and **Laura Ashley.** Originally feared by locals as an unwelcome upscale intruder, this complex has proved very congenial—thanks in part to public events such as courtyard concerts, but mainly because the design is low-key and browser-friendly. The **Charles Square Parking Garage** is open 24 hours. ◆ Shops M-F 10AM-7PM; Sa 10AM-6PM; Su noon-6PM. 1 Bennett St (at Eliot St) &

23 The Spaghetti Club ★★$ The Cambridge cousin of Newbury Street's **Ciao Bella,** this subterranean spot opted for cheap chic: Italian comics and graffiti for the walls, pizzette and risotti for easy-on-the-wallet entrées. ◆ Italian ◆ Daily 5-10PM. Bar M-W, Su 5PM-1AM; Th-Sa 5PM-2AM. 93 Winthrop St (between JFK and Eliot Sts). 576.1210 &

23 Grendel's Den ★$ The food is nothing to flip over, but it's plentiful and cheap (many an impecunious student has subsisted on the refill-

24 Casa Mexico ★★$$ This small basement shrine to fine Mexican cuisine is a real secret treasure. Atmosphere it has in spades, plus some hard-to-find dishes like *mole poblano*. After 25 years in business, this tiny restaurant does everything just right. ◆ Mexican ◆ M-Th noon-2:30PM, 6-10PM; F noon-2:30PM, 6-11PM; Sa noon-2:30PM, 5:30-11PM; Su 6-10PM. 75 Winthrop St (at JFK St). 491.4552

25 The Coffee Connection ★$ Ensconced in **The Garage,** a complex of youth-oriented stores and restaurants, this cafe is the Square's premier rendezvous for potent fresh-roasted coffee, equally full-bodied conversation, and light meals. The food's okay, but the coffee's the thing here, all different kinds served all different ways. Most customers choose the super-strong "melior" brewing method; look around, and you'll likely see at least one frazzled student nursing a giant pot to cope with the course load. There's a coffee bar, but better still, sit at one of the tables on the upper level so you can watch who comes and goes, always an intriguing collection of characters. Weekday mornings and late afternoons are the cafe's quietest hours, but there's usually a line. You can also enter from **Dunster Street,** up a short flight of stairs and to the left. Be forewarned: There are no restrooms on the premises! The retail operation sells 30 different award-winning coffees, excellent teas, and every kind of brewing paraphernalia imaginable. You can order by mail, too. ◆ Cafe ◆ M-Th 7AM-11PM; F 7AM-midnight; Sa 8AM-midnight; Su 9AM-11PM. 36 JFK St (at Mt. Auburn St). 492.4881 &

25 John Harvard's ★★$ What makes this spot so appealing are the eight brews created on the premises and chef **Joseph Kubik's** spirited, out-of-the-ordinary pub fare, which may include grilled sausages with fresh *spaetzle* and buttermilk fried chicken with spiced corn bread. Look for a series of Hogarthian panels conceived by muralists **Josh Winer** and **John Devaney** that depicts a semi-spurious (but hilarious) biography of **John Harvard,** the infamous brewmaster. ◆ American ◆ M-W 11:30AM-1AM; Th-Su 11:30AM-2AM. 33 Dunster St (between Mt. Auburn St and Massachusetts Ave). 868.3585 &

Cambridge

able salad bar). With its high ceilings and wood paneling, this popular spot still has hints of its former grandeur as a Harvard club. ◆ International ◆ M-Th, Su 11AM-11PM; F-Sa 11AM-midnight. Bar daily 4PM-1AM. 89 Winthrop St (between JFK and Eliot Sts). 491.1160 & (staff will assist)

In 1764 the building that was a predecessor to Harvard Hall burned down and the fire destroyed the college's 5,000-volume library, then North America's largest. The entire book collection belonging to the college's benefactor, John Harvard, went up in smoke, except for a single volume borrowed by a student on the night of the fire. According to legend, the following day the student took the precious book to the president, who accepted the book, thanked the student profusely, then expelled the student for taking it without permission.

25 La Flamme A classic eight-seater, this old-fashioned barber shop (ladies welcome) has shorn such heads as **Henry Kissinger's.** Prices are holding steady at a reasonable $9 a clip. ◆ M-Sa 7AM-6PM. 21 Dunster St (between Mt. Auburn St and Massachusetts Ave). 354.8377 & Also at: 49A Brattle St. 876.7986

25 Herrell's Ice Cream Steve Herrell is generally credited with starting the whole gourmet ice cream boom at his out-of-the-way **Somerville** shop back in 1972. He made a few million selling his first name and then started up again with his last. His hand-cranked product, in luscious flavors like moccachino and chocolate pudding, are still among the best, dense and intense, and the "back room" here—a former bank vault painted to resemble an underwater grotto—is the coolest place in the Square on a hot summer evening. ◆ Ice Cream ◆ Daily noon-midnight. 15 Dunster St (between Massachusetts Ave and Mt. Auburn St). 497.2179 & Also at: 155 Brighton Ave. 782.9599; 350 Longwood Ave. 731.9599

25 Catch A Rising Star Part of a national chain, the comedy club books big-name acts with national headliners. Monday and Tuesday are local comedy showcase nights, with nationally known talent featured all other nights. Sandwiches, appetizers, and a full bar are available. (There's no smoking at the tables, only at the bar and open bay area.) It's first-come, first-served for seats, and all shows are for all ages. ◆ Cover. Shows M-Th 8:30PM; F 8:30PM, 10:30PM; Sa 7:30PM, 9:30PM, 11:30PM; Su 8:30PM. 30B JFK St (between Brattle and Mt. Auburn Sts). Reservations recommended, especially on weekends. Recorded information 661.9887, tickets 661.0167

26 Urban Outfitters All the chic-looking students and the general under-30 crowd shop here for the latest in men's and women's urban attire, fashion accessories, housewares, and a whole slew of trendy novelties. You'll find lots of popular name brands and the store's own label. A bargain basement sells vintage clothing, too. You can enter the store from **Brattle Street,** making this a convenient cut-through. ◆ M-Sa 10AM-10PM; Su noon-8PM. 11 JFK St (between Brattle and Mt. Auburn Sts). 864.0070. Also at: 361 Newbury St, Back Bay. 236.0088

27 Brattle Street Called **Tory Row** in the 1770s because its residents were loyal to **King George,** this glorious avenue still retains its share of magnificent summer homes (once country estates, whose spacious lands spilled right to the river's edge). In the summer of 1775 the patriots under **George Washington** appropriated the homes. Today Brattle Street is far more densely inhabited, but its sumptuous properties secure its reputation as one of the country's poshest streets.

H.H. Richardson designed the **Stoughton House** at No. 90 in 1882. No. 159 is the **Hooper-Lee-Nichols House,** parts of which date back to the 1600s, now headquarters of the **Cambridge Historical Society.** The society is open to the public on some afternoons and offers tours of Tory Row and the **Old Burial Ground;** call 497.1630 for information. **John Bartlett,** the Harvard Square bookseller who compiled the famous *Bartlett's Familiar Quotations,* lived at No. 165; the house was erected for him in 1873.

27 WordsWorth A lotta books and a lotta people can be found at the Square's busiest bookshop, where all books but textbooks are discounted. This is a full-service general bookstore with a fully computerized inventory system, developed by the owner and adopted by other bookstores, tracking 60,000 to 100,000 titles in 95 subject areas. WordsWorth publishes a newsletter and sponsors an excellent reading series at the Brattle Theatre (readings are free, but tickets must be obtained in advance). The fine children's section has its own staff, and there's a bountiful selection of greeting cards, calendars, and wrapping papers. ◆ M-Sa 8:30AM-11:15PM; Su 10AM-10:15PM. 30 Brattle St (between Eliot and Mt. Auburn Sts). 354.5201

28 Motto/MDF Side by side are two small shops with different wares, but the same distinctive esthetic. Both are owned and operated by **Jude Silver,** whose own art background influences her emphasis on modern, functional, and sophisticated creations.

Motto sells abstract avant-garde jewelry of striking materials, textures, compositions,

and tones. They can suggest European élan, classical coolness, industrial efficiency, or Southwestern warmth. MDF (**Modern Design Furnishings**) sells personal and home and office accessories, lamps, small furniture, and men's jewelry—all fabricated from nontraditional materials. Brides-to-be can register at MDF, and both of the stores will gladly special-order, pack, and ship all over the country. ◆ Both shops M-W, F–Sa 10AM-6PM; Th 10AM-6PM; Su noon-6PM. 17–19 Brattle St (at Palmer St). Motto 868.8448, MDF 491.2789 & (street level)

The building of bridges—particularly the West Boston Bridge of 1793 and the Craigie Bridge of 1909—turned Cambridge into a more viable city by opening direct routes to Boston.

28 The Learning Store The brainchild of **WGBH,** Boston's public television station, this shop is a lively gallimaufry of media—books, tapes, software products, etc.—arranged under playful rubrics like "Brain Aerobics" (puzzles) and "Socrates' Sandbox" (preschool toys). It's a browser's—and hacker's—heaven. ◆ M-Th 9:30AM-11PM; F-Sa 9:30AM-midnight; Su noon-11PM. 25 Brattle St (at Eliot St). 661.6008 ⑤

29 Jasmine/Sola Moderately expensive women's clothing and accessories, many in unusual rich fabrics and striking styles ranging from casual to dressy, are sold at Jasmine. The jewelry is always fun, much of it produced by independent and emerging jewelry makers. Sola sells women's shoes, ranging widely in price, with some hard-to-find brands. **Sola Men** has a modest selection of great-looking men's clothing and shoes, often European in style. The stunning window displays are the work of **Kristin Lauer's Blue Potato Installations,** whose main source is junkyards. ◆ M-W, Sa 10AM-7PM; Th-F 10AM-8PM; Su noon-6PM. 37 Brattle St (between Eliot and Church Sts). 354.6043 ⑤

BRATTLE THEATRE

30 The Brattle Theatre The year 1990 marked the 100th anniversary of the one-of-a-kind Brattle. Independent movie house extraordinaire, the Brattle is struggling to preserve its identity in the midst of increasingly commercial Harvard Square and an era of movie-chain monopolies. Renovated from top to bottom and retaining its rare rear-screen projection system (originally used on cruise ships), the Brattle is one of the country's oldest remaining repertory movie houses, offering classic Hollywood and foreign movies, independent filmmaking, new art films, staged readings, and music concerts to a faithful following. If it doesn't look much like a movie house, that's because the Brattle opened as **Brattle Hall** in 1890, founded by the **Cambridge Social Union** as a place for literary, musical, and dramatic entertainments.

Cambridge

From 1948 to 1952 the **Brattle Theatre Company** put on nationally acclaimed performances from **Shakespeare** to **Chekhov** with many notable stars, including **Jessica Tandy** and **Hume Cronyn.** It made a policy of hiring actors blacklisted during the US government's political witch hunts of the era, including **Zero Mostel.** The Brattle began running in the red, then was converted to an art cinema in 1953 by Harvard grads **Bryant Haliday** and **Cyrus Harvey, Jr.,** who together founded **Janus Films** and brought the first films of **Fellini, Antonioni, Bergman,** and **Olmi** to America.

A local **Humphrey Bogart** cult was born here in the '50s, when owners **Harvey** and **Haliday** screened neglected "Bogie" movies during

Harvard exam time, drawing college students and other fans in droves. As the revived Bogie mystique spread across the country, a week-long Bogart series became an annual Brattle tradition. In a historic 1955 decision, the **Massachusetts Supreme Judicial Court** broke the state censorship law and ruled for the Brattle that the state commissioner of public safety couldn't ban a movie on Sunday. The movie that caused all of the ruckus was the Swedish film *Miss Julie.*

The Brattle has been operated since 1986 by the **Running Arts** company, which features different categories of double features nearly every night. The general roster: Monday, film noir; Tuesday, author readings sponsored by nearby **WordsWorth** bookstore, independent filmmaking, or other arts activities; Wednesday, theme selections such as a particular director; Thursday, international films; Friday and Saturday, themes such as a particular style or content. Innumerable Cambridge-area movie lovers have assignations at the Brattle every single week, drawn by the attractive lineup and two-shows-for-one-price admission. A free two-month program is available in front of the theater. Since the '60s the movie house has shared its quarters with a variety of retail businesses. Call for screening times. ◆ Admission. Closed Christmas Day. 40 Brattle St (between Eliot and Story Sts). Recorded information 876.6837 ⑤

Within The Brattle Theatre:

Algiers Cafe ★★$ Head upstairs to the domed hideaway to sip minted coffee and feast delicately on *baba gannoush* or tabbouleh. Algiers made out like a bandit in the Brattle Theatre rehab: once a grungy (if atmospheric) underground cafe, now it's airy and gorgeous, with balletic little tables and prize rugs on the walls. Best of all, you're still left in peace to converse or cogitate. ◆ Middle Eastern ◆ M-Th, Su 9AM-midnight; F-Sa 9AM-1AM. 492.1557 ⑤

Casablanca ★★$$ Long the last word in student romance, Casablanca has graduated from mostly bar to full-scale restaurant—keeping its oversize rattan chairs-for-two and **David Omar White's** beloved movie-homage murals (even though it meant moving whole walls). The menu includes Moroccan specialties such as Lamb Tagine (with preserved lemons and dates), but there's also a smattering of pasta, seafood, and good old American burgers. ◆ Moroccan/American ◆ M-W, Su 11:30AM-10PM; Th-Sa 11:30AM-11PM. 876.0999 ⑤

31 The Book Case The crowded window displays reflect this fun little shop's quirky personality. It's a bargain basement of used paperbacks and hardcovers in all subjects, plus a great mishmash of postcards, greeting cards, and doodads of all sorts, including miniatures, novelties, and figurines. ♦ M-Sa 10:30AM-5PM. 42 Church St (between Brattle St and Massachusetts Ave). No credit cards. 876.0832 &

31 The Globe Corner Bookstore An outpost of the Boston original, this shop specializes in books, maps, and guides for New England and world travel, and also carries travel-oriented novelties, games, and accessories. ♦ M-Sa 9AM-9PM; Su noon-6PM. 49 Palmer St (at Church St). 497.6277. Also at: 1 School St, Downtown. 523.6658

31 Passim ★$ One of America's oldest and best-known coffeehouses is **Bob** and **Rae Anne Donlin's** little below-street-level club, where they began featuring folk music around '71. Passim (Latin for "here and there," and pronounced *PASS-im,* although just about everybody says *Pass-FFM*) is the only remaining commercial coffeehouse presenting live music in Boston and Cambridge. The Donlins have always been true-blue friends to local folk and bluegrass groups, and among those they helped boost to fame are **Jackson Browne, Tracy Chapman, Suzanne Vega, Greg Brown, Nanci Griffith, Tom Waits,** and **Patty Larkin.**

The stalwart club has weathered well, and continues to showcase contemporary acoustic music, some traditional, too. Very unpretentious, with no liquor license, Passim seats 50. There's a light menu of soups, sandwiches, quiches, desserts, coffees, teas, and cider. No smoking is permitted (except during the day, in one section). By day, Passim is a combination cafe/gift shop. The admission prices are low; the club deserves lots of support. Call for the performance schedule, which varies. Weekends feature a headliner with opening act, the latter usually new local talent. Seating is first-come, first-served. ♦ Cover. Shows W-Th 8:30PM when scheduled; F-Sa 8PM, 10:30PM; Su 8PM when scheduled. Restaurant Tu-Sa noon-4:45PM. Gift shop Tu-Sa noon-5:30PM. 47 Palmer St (between Church and Brattle Sts). 492.7679

32 First Parish Church and Old Burying Ground The wooden Gothic Revival church, the 1833 creation of **Isaiah Rogers,** was partly funded by Harvard, in return for pews for students' use. Called "God's Acre," the adjacent Old Burying Ground is where numerous Revolutionary War veterans—including two black slaves, **Cato Stedman** and **Neptune Frost,** who fought alongside their masters—and Harvard's first eight presidents are buried. Many of the graves' metal markers were melted down for bullets. ♦ 3 Church St (at Massachusetts Ave)

Within First Parish Church:

Nameless Coffeehouse The country's oldest free, volunteer-run coffeehouse is a neighborly venue where local folk musicians play. **Tracy Chapman** sang here during her days as a Harvard Square street performer. ♦ Free. Shows F-Sa 8PM. Zero Church St (at Massachusetts Ave). Recorded information 864.1630

33 Reading International This inviting store carries all the latest hardcovers and paperbacks, with good fiction, mystery, travel, black, women's, and gay studies sections. There's a general academic slant. The periodicals section is noteworthy, with literary and scholarly journals and foreign newspapers and magazines on subjects from politics to literature, art, and architecture. Bargain books, records, tapes, and cards are sold, too. Owner **Sheldon Cohen** is so active in the local community that he's been dubbed the "Mayor of Harvard Square." ♦ M-Th, Su 7:30AM-11PM; F 7:30AM-midnight; Sa 7:30AM-12:30AM. 47 Brattle St (at Church St). 864.0705 &

33 Colonial Drug The name conjures old-fashioned images, but this tiny drugstore is quite sophisticated, with an award-winning selection of more than 900 fragrances, complete cosmetic and treatment lines, and primarily European and high-quality personal care items of all kinds. Colonial is a local institution, more than 50 years old. Members of the family running the shop call themselves "people with absolutely no common scents." ♦ M-F 8AM-7PM; Sa 8AM-6PM. 49 Brattle St (at Church St). No credit cards. 864.2222 &

34 Charrette Catering to design professionals, the sleek inventory includes top makers' and Charrette's own lines of great-looking fine art and office supplies, portfolios, framing and modeling supplies, drafting instruments, furniture, and desktop-publishing software. The store is a magnet for the local architecture and design community, along with students from the **Harvard University Graduate School of Design.** (There's a small Charrette outlet at the **GSD** for emergencies.) Charrette stocks more than 6,000 products, with 41,000 available at

Cambridge

the warehouse. If you need something the store doesn't have, check out the thick Charrette catalog, and your purchase can sometimes be sent from the warehouse that same day.

In addition, a spin-off enterprise called **Charrette Reprographics** specializes in the latest technologies for design professionals' presentations (located at this shop; at 1033 Massachusetts Avenue, Cambridge, 495.0235; and at 184 South Street, Waterfront, 292.8820). ♦ M-F 8:30AM-7PM; Sa 10AM-6PM; Su noon-5PM. 44 Brattle St (at Church St). 495.0200 & (weekdays only). Also at: 777 Boylston St, Back Bay. 267.2490

Restaurants/Clubs: Red **Hotels:** Blue
Shops/ 🌳 **Outdoors:** Green **Sights/Culture:** Black

34 Design Research Building Ben Thompson built this architectural equivalent of a giant glass showcase in 1969 for **Design Research,** the store he founded to introduce Americans to international modern design products for the home; it now houses **Crate & Barrel.** Thompson's notion had wings and has spread all over the country, though less imaginatively. He certainly knows how to display for interest, as a later project, **Faneuil Hall Marketplace,** attests. ♦ 48 Brattle St (at Story St)

34 Harvest Restaurant ★★★$$$ Restaurants come and go frequently in the Harvard Square area, but the excellent Harvest flourishes. Owners **Jane** and **Ben Thompson** (of **Benjamin Thompson & Associates,** architects of **Faneuil Hall Marketplace** and the **Design Research Building**) have hidden the restaurant from the street in a passageway alongside the **Crate & Barrel** store. Although the decor could use sprucing up, the Harvest has earned its lofty place in the local dining circuit with inventive seasonal entrées. The chef likes to experiment, creating all-original stocks and sauces, and the contemporary American cuisine spotlights wild game and exotic fish specialties; in fact, the Harvest offers an annual international **Wild Game Festival** every February. The pastry chefs bake wonderful breads and desserts on the premises all night. The dining room's evening menu changes to take advantage of fresh native ingredients.

More casual, the adjacent **Ben's Cafe** offers less expensive but delicious regional American dishes. (Both the cafe and main dining room offer the same menu at lunch.) A light bar menu is also served between lunch and dinner and after dinner hours. The Harvest's regular

clientele is a rich Cambridge mix: faculty and international scholars, deans and university presidents, college students and parents, writers, poets, and actors. On a summer night, it's delightful to dine in the courtyard. Evenings, especially Thursdays, the bar is crowded with unattached singles who are seeking more of the same. ♦ American ♦ M-Th 11:30AM-10PM; F 11:30AM-10:30PM; Sa 11AM-10:30PM; Su 11AM-10PM. 44 Brattle St (between Eliot and Story Sts). Reservations recommended for the dining room. 492.1115 ♿ (from Mt. Auburn St)

Nathaniel Eaton was the first headmaster of the new, not-yet-named Harvard College, but was removed from office for severely beating students and feeding them poorly.

34 The Harvest Express $ A separate shop at th same address as Harvest Restaurant, the Express serves delicious food to go, or to eat on the spot at minimal seating. Try the pasta *fagio* soup, pasta salads, sandwiches, calzones, or hot entrées. Express features numerous veggie dishes to please Cambridge's many vegetarians The Harvest is known for its fabulous desserts, so Express always has tons of sweets to choos from, like "expresso" brownies, ginger-oatmea cookies, various cakes, and lots of other square and bars. ♦ Italian/Takeout ♦ M-F 9AM-7PM; S 10AM-6PM. 44 Brattle St (between Eliot and Story Sts). 868.5569 ♿ (from Mt. Auburn St)

34 Brattle House This 1727 frame house, on the **National Register of Historic Places,** belonged to **William Brattle,** a Tory who fled in 1774 and for whom the street is named. From 1840 to 1842 **Margaret Fuller** lived here; she was the feminist editor of *The Dial.* The house is headquarters for the **Cambridge Center for Adult Education,** which sponsors a heady array of courses, as well as a well-attended holiday season crafts fair. ♦ 42 Brattle St (between Eliot ar Story Sts)

35 Barillari Books This very spacious full-range bookstore discounts all hardcovers and paperbacks except text editions, with an extensive fine arts, architecture, and photography department that includes history, monographs, and theory. The cookbook and children's book sections are also good. Pick up the morning paper (they als carry lots of journals and reviews) and sit at the small outdoor patio, where cappuccino, espresso, and imported Italian cookies and chocolates are served. Located off the beaten trail, Barillari is never crowded and you can peruse quite peacefully. Just west of the store is a shortcut to **Brattle Street.** ♦ M-Th 9AM-11PM; F-Sa 9AM-midnight; Su 10AM-10PM. 1 Mifflin Pl on Mt. Auburn St (between Eliot and Story Sts). 864.2400, 800/772.1448 ♿

36 Mandrake Book Store More than 40 years in business, Mandrake specializes in psychotherapy and art, architecture, and design, selected and arranged with fastidious expertise. It's located near **Architects' Corner,** where a number of architects built their own quarters in the early '70s, architectural styles interacting quite amicably. ♦ M-Sa 9AM-5:30PM. Closed Saturday from July to August. 8 Story St (between Brattle and Mt. Auburn Sts). No credit cards. 864.3088 ♿

37 Clothware Mix and match from carefully selected, uncommon women's attire, all made from natural fibers, especially cottons and silks at this small, well-known shop. The designer lines, including a private label made by an origi nal owner, focus on graceful, classic, and fun-to-wear styles. The lingerie selection here is es pecially tempting. Some accessories, including jewelry, leggings and tights, wallets, scarves, hats, handbags, lots and lots of socks, and mo are carried here. The shop has regular sales, b this is not a place for a bargain-hunting excursion. ♦ M-W, F 10AM-6:30PM; Th 10AM-8PM Sa 10AM-6PM; Su 1-6PM. 52 Brattle St (at Story St). 661.6441

37 Blacksmith House Bakery Cafe ★$
"Under a spreading chestnut tree/The village smithy stands/The smith a mighty man is he/ With large and sinewy hands. . ." The smithy in **Henry Wadsworth Longfellow's** famous poem *The Village Blacksmith* lived in this old yellow house dating from 1811, the **Dexter Pratt House.** (A stone nearby commemorates the famous chestnut tree that once was.) For more than 45 years the resident bakery has concocted delicious Viennese-style pastries, tortes like the famous Linzer and Sacher, coffee cakes, croissants, brioches, breads, and cookies. Special offerings, like the *bûche de Noel,* are created for holidays. Buy treats from the bakery, or enjoy them at the cafe's outdoor patio or historic interior, with its quaint rooms and creaky floorboards. The cafe shares the bakery's kitchen and also serves sandwiches, salads, hot entrées, and soups. The house now belongs to the **Cambridge Center for Adult Education,** which offers courses, lectures, seminars, films, and cultural activities. ◆ Bakery/Cafe/Takeout ◆ Bakery M-Sa 8AM-7PM; Su 11AM-3PM. Cafe M-W 8AM-5PM; Th-Sa 8AM-8PM; Su 11AM-3PM. 56 Brattle St (between Story and Hilliard Sts). 354.3036 &

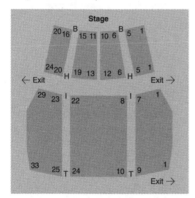

38 Loeb Drama Center/Harvard University
The center—built in 1959 by **Hugh Stubbins**—is home to the prestigious **American Repertory Theatre (ART),** a nonprofit professional company affiliated with Harvard that presents new American plays, neglected works from the past, and unconventional interpretations of classics. The student **Harvard-Radcliffe Dramatic Club** is also based here. The ART has premiered works by **Jules Feiffer, Carlos Fuentes, Philip Glass, Marsha Norman, Milan Kundera, Larry Gelbart,** and **David Mamet.** The "Mainstage" series runs year-round; the company's "New Stage Series" is presented at the **Hasty Pudding Theatre** on Holyoke Street.

The Loeb Center's main stage (see the floor plan above) was the first fully flexible one in the country, easily converting into different stage styles. Frequent free student performances are also held in the experimental theater; information is available at the box office. The theater seats 556 people. ◆ Box office daily 10AM-5PM; 10AM-8PM, when performances scheduled. 64 Brattle St (at Hilliard St). 547.8300 & (hearing aids available on request)

39 Radcliffe Yard Stroll through Radcliffe's pretty green centerpiece and notice the college's first building, **Fay House,** an 1806 Federal mansion. Radcliffe College was founded for women in 1879, named for Harvard's first female benefactor, **Ann Radcliffe.** It was Harvard's sister school until officially united in 1975, when the administrations were merged and equal admission standards adopted for men and women. Radcliffe remains an independent corporation with its own president, but its students share housing, classes, facilities, and degrees.

Radcliffe's buildings include the stately **Agassiz House,** where the **Harvard Gilbert and Sullivan Players** put on operettas. The **Arthur and Elizabeth Schlesinger Library** has the most extensive collection in the country of books, photographs, oral histories, and other materials on women's history, including manuscripts and papers belonging to a number of famous women and organizations. Radcliffe College's **Mary Ingraham Bunting Institute** is a highly regarded postdoctoral program for women scholars, writers, and artists.

40 Christ Church America's first trained architect, **Peter Harrison,** designed this church as well as **King's Chapel** in Boston. The 1760 **Apthorp House,** still standing but surrounded by newer buildings just off Plympton Street, was built for the first rector, **East Apthorp.** Its extravagance so shocked Puritans that they dubbed the house "The Bishop's Palace," sparking a controversy so fierce that Apthorp quickly returned to England. Cambridge's oldest church, the former Tory place of worship served as barracks for Connecticut troops, who melted down the organ pipes for bullets during the Revolution. **George** and **Martha Washington** worshiped here in a special New Year's Eve service in 1775. **Theodore Roosevelt** taught Sunday school here while at Harvard.

Like the Boston chapel, the church's interior is simple and filled with light. Now sadly scruffy and much diminished in size, **Cambridge Common** across from the church was the site of **General Washington's** main camp from 1775 to 1776. At **Dawes Island** in the middle of Gar-

den Street heading toward Harvard Square, look for the bronze horseshoes embedded in the sidewalk, marking **William Dawes'** ride through town on the way to warn the populace in Lexington with the famous cry "The British are coming!" They were given by his descendants as a Bicentennial gift. ◆ Zero Garden St (at Appian Way)

A statue of Charles Sumner, a United States senator and ardent abolitionist, is located between Harvard Yard and Cambridge Common. Anne Whitney of Watertown first designed a statue of Sumner for an anonymous Boston competition in 1875. She won, but when the judges discovered the awardee was female, they gave the commission to a man instead. Finally, in 1903, when Whitney was 80 years old, this bronze version of her original work was unveiled.

41 Sheraton Commander $$ Near **Cambridge Common** and a short walk to the Square, this gracious old reliable has 176 understated but pleasant rooms on six floors. A complimentary *Wall Street Journal* is delivered to each room. Eight "executive king" rooms include a sitting area, a small dining area, a canopied bed, and a whirlpool bath. Hotel amenities include a fitness room, multilingual staff, a concierge, a business center, and complimentary valet parking. Handicapped-equipped and nonsmokers' rooms are available. The **Brandywine** restaurant is on the premises. Prominent political guests stay here. ♦ 16 Garden St (between Berkeley and Mason Sts). 547.4800, 800/ 325.3535; fax 868.8322 &

42 Henry Wadsworth Longfellow House
During the Siege of Boston from 1775 to 1776, **George Washington** moved his headquarters from **Wadsworth House** near Harvard Yard to this stately Georgian residence, built in 1759 by a wealthy Tory, **John Vassall,** who fled just before the Revolution. Longfellow (pictured above) rented a room here in 1837, then was given the house by his wealthy new father-in-law upon marrying heiress **Frances Appleton** in 1843. (She died here tragically years later, burned in a fire in the library.) Longfellow wrote many of his famous poems in this mansion, including *Hiawatha* and *Evangeline.* He lived here for 45 years, with prominent literary friends often gathered round. The house has been restored to the poet's period, with thousands of books from his library, plus many of his possessions. Vestiges of the spreading chestnut tree that inspired him were made into

Cambridge

a carved armchair, on display, presented as a birthday gift from Cambridge schoolchildren. The home stayed in the Longfellow family until 1973, and is now operated by the **National Park Service** as a **National Historic Site.** Call to find out about special events, including children's programs, a celebration of Longfellow's birthday in February, and poetry readings and concerts held on the east lawn in the summer. Half-hour tours are given throughout the day; reserve in advance for groups. A bookstore offers most of the Longfellow books in print, plus books on his life, the literary profession, poetry, and more. Incidentally, the first poem to win national acclaim was Longfellow's *Song of Hiawatha,* published in Boston on 10 November 1855. ♦ Admission; free for those under 16 and over

62. Daily 10AM-4:30PM. Closed Christmas, Thanksgiving, New Year's Day. 105 Brattle St (across from Longfellow Park). 876.4491 & (staff will assist)

43 Longy School of Music Founded in 1915 and housed in the 1889 **Edwin Abbot Mansion** (listed in the **National Register of Historic Places**), this very active and esteemed— music school hosts a wide array of notable concerts of every era and style, in intimate Pickman Hall. Call for listings. ♦ 1 Follen St (at Garden St). 876.0956 &

44 Harvard College Observatory The Observatory is open to the public for **Observatory Nights,** with an hour-long lecture-film program geared toward teenagers and older followed by telescopic observing, weather permitting. For the "Sky Report," a recorded update of astronomical information, call 491.1497. The dome pavilion is the only surviving element of the original building, designed by **Isaiah Rogers** in 1851. It was built after the appearance of "the Great Comet" in 1843 sparked public interest in astronomy. ♦ Free. Third Thursday of each month, 8PM. 60 Garden St (at Madison St, north of Harvard Sq). 495.9059

45 Mount Auburn Cemetery The cemetery is worth seeking out for a sunny afternoon stroll and picnic, and fine bird-watching. Now one of its illustrious residents, **Henry Wadsworth Longfellow** called Mount Auburn the "city of the dead." Founded in 1831, making it the first garden cemetery in America, its 170 acres are verdant with unusual native and rare foreign trees and flowering shrubs. **Oliver Wendell Holmes, Isabella Stewart Gardner, Mary Baker Eddy,** and **Winslow Homer** are also among the more than 70,000 persons buried here. When it was founded, the cemetery introduced a new concept of interment in the US. Before, colonial burial grounds were rustic graveyards where the dead were buried in an erratic fashion. Grave markers were frequently moved about along with bodies, with the dead remains even shuttled from one burial ground to another (Boston's cemeteries offer plenty of evidence of these casual practices). But with the creation of Mount Auburn, the idea of commemorating an individual with a permanent, unencroachable burial place was instituted. A cult of memory took root in America, with personal gravesites becoming a new status symbol. Stop by the office and pick up maps for self-guided walks, either a horticultural tour of more than 3,000 trees, or a walking tour of the cemetery's notable memorials. The **Friends of Mount Auburn** offers special walks, talks, and other activities. ♦ 580 Mt. Auburn St. 547.7105 &

Under MIT's orderly numbering system, a single room number fully identifies any location on campus. In a typical room number, 7-111, for example, the number preceding the hyphen is the building number, the first number after the hyphen is the floor, and the last two numbers are the room numbers. Buildings on the main campus east of the Great Dome (Building 10) have even numbers; those west of the dome have odd.

Kendall Square

The **Red Line** T-stop is the closest to the **Massachusetts Institute of Technology (MIT)**. Located in the **Kendall Square Station** on the Red Line is a three-part kinetic musical sculpture by artist/inventor **Paul Matisse,** grandson of **Henri.** The Kendall Band is a musical trio comprised of three pieces titled *Pythagoras, Kepler,* and *Galileo.* Commuters crank wall handles on either side of the subway tracks and set large teak hammers into motion, which strike 16 tuned tubular chimes and produce melodious bell-like music—that's *Pythagoras.* Pull another handle a number of times, and a triple-headed steel hammer strikes an aluminum ring, producing a low F-sharp note—that's *Kepler. Galileo's* mechanism makes rumbling, windlike music. In unison, the pleasing concert soothes impatient T-riders. The work is part of the MBTA's "Arts on the Line" program, which has commissioned art for 23 Boston-area subway stations.

The Massachusetts Institute of Technology was founded in 1861 on the Boston side of the river by **William Barton Rogers,** a natural scientist. MIT's first president, Rogers envisioned a pragmatic institution fitted to the needs of an increasingly industrialized and mechanized America. The modest technological school, then called **Boston Tech,** moved to its current site in 1916, quite comfortable with its industrial surroundings. MIT has never aspired to Harvard's picturesque Olympian aura, but rather has focused on scientific principles as the basis for advanced research and industrial applications. Appropriately, the school's motto is "Mens et Manus" (Mind and Hand). Often referred to as "the factory," MIT grew rapidly and played a significant role in scientific research with the onset of World War II; in hastily assembled laboratories, Harvard and MIT scientists developed the machinery of modern warfare. In peacetime the same labs have produced instrumentation and guidance devices for NASA and nuclear submarines.

The institute has a very international identity, and MIT graduates have founded local, national, and international high-tech companies in the Greater Boston area. Today coeducational MIT has schools of Engineering, Sciences, Architecture and Planning, Management, Humanities, Health Sciences and Technology, and Social Science.

For general information on MIT or to join one of the free student-guided campus tours, lasting just more than an hour and offered weekdays at 10AM and 2PM, stop by the **Information Center,** open Monday through Friday 9AM to 5PM, Rogers Building, 77 Massachusetts Avenue (near Memorial Drive), 253.4795. Arrange tours in advance if you're with a group.

The numbering system used to identify MIT buildings is but one hint of the institute's practical bent. Take a chance on getting lost for a bit in the domed neoclassical **Rogers Building** at 77 Massachusetts Avenue with its factorylike maze of hallways and numbered office floors. Amble across the 150-acre campus weighted with monumental architecture. Despite MIT's well-deserved image as the temple of high-tech, it gives the arts elbow room, too, and has several excellent museums as well as some superb modern architecture and public art. Admission is free to all but the MIT Museum. Call for times; many of the galleries close during the summer. The **MIT Museum** (open from Tuesday through Sunday) houses photos, paintings, scientific instruments, and artifacts representing themes and ideas related to the institute, and is located at 265 Massachusetts Avenue, 253.4444. The **Albert and Vera List Visual Arts Center's** three galleries present the most challenging art and design in diverse media; the Center is on the first floor of the Weisner Building, 20 Ames Street, 253.4680. If you're an old/young salt or trekking about with kids, visit the little **Hart Nautical Galleries'** display of ships' models and plans representing vessels from all over the world, located in the Rogers Building, 77 Massachusetts Avenue, first floor, 253.5942. If you still have time to spare, walk through "Strobe Alley," a demonstration of high-speed stroboscopic equipment and photographs by the late **Harold E. "Doc" Edgerton,** Class of '27, also at 77 Massachusetts Avenue on the fourth floor.

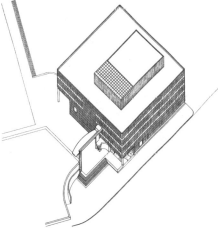

Weisner Building
COURTESY OF PEI, COBB, FREED & PARTNERS

MIT's **East Campus,** on the east side of Massachusetts Avenue, has an impersonal, businesslike look, particularly since new office and research buildings have sprouted around Kendall Square since the early '80s. In the last few years **Main Street** at Kendall Square has gotten a sprucing up, with the arrival of a major hotel and numerous cafes and restaurants serving the MIT population. And MIT has, fortunately, preserved a network of big green spaces, where fine outdoor art can be found. In **Killian Court** behind the Rogers building

Cambridge

is **Henry Moore's** *Three-Piece Reclining Figure* (erected in 1976). (Another Moore work, *Reclining Figure,* is located off Ames Street between **Whitaker College** and **I.M. Pei's Weisner Building, Center for Arts & Media Technology,** pictured above). **Michael Heizer's** sculpture *Guennette* stands opposite.

Looming over Killian Court is the **Great Dome,** MIT's architectural focus. From this grassy expanse, the view to the river and Boston beyond is magnificent. At **McDermott Court,** look for I.M. Pei's **Green Building, Center for Earth Sciences** (constructed in 1964). In front is the giant black-steel sculpture *La Grande Voile* ("The Big Sail"), designed by **Alexander Calder.** Nearby is a 1975 black-steel sculpture by **Louise Nevelson** called *Transparent Horizon.* At the end of Main Street near the **Longfellow Bridge** is a small outdoor plaza adorned with a controversial creation called

Galaxy by sculptor **Joe Davis.** The focal point is a meteoritelike stainless-steel globe encrusted with strange topographic textures and patterns, clouds of steam billowing from below. The mysterious globe is ringed by 12 smaller ones that cast unusual illuminations at night. **Picasso's** *Figure découpée* (completed in 1963) stands in front of the **Hermann Building** at the far east end of campus. A five-mile system of underground passages, the "infinite corridor," connects the East Campus buildings.

The **MIT Press Bookstore** sells scholarly books and journals on engineering, computer science, architecture, philosophy, linguistics, economics, and more, 292 Main Street, 253.5249; and the **MIT Coop,** scion of the Harvard Coop in Harvard Square, is located at 3 Cambridge Center, 499.3200. Boston's punk population—as well as the merely bargain-savvy—outfit themselves at the **Garment District,** where vintage clothing mingles with Doc Martens, 200 Broadway, 876.5230.

For a variety of dining options, visit the **One Kendall Square** development, a handsomely renovated factory complex.

It's home to **The Blue Room,** 494.9034, a jazzy modernist boîte where the floor show consists of chef **Stan Frankenthaler's** boisterous world-beat cooking;

Goemon Japanese Noodle Restaurant, specializing in noodle dishes and tempura, 577.9595; the **Cambridge Brewing Company,** 494.1994, a comfortable pub/restaurant where you can sample the company's own beers and ales; and **The Daily Catch,** 225.2300, featuring seafood of all kinds, which has several popular Boston siblings.

Always crowded and noisy, another chapter of the famous local **Legal Sea Foods** empire serves all kinds

Cambridge

of fresh fish just about any way you could imagine, 5 Cambridge Center, 864.3400. Accommodations can be had at the **Boston Marriott Cambridge** ($$$), 2 Cambridge Center, 494.6600.

MIT's **West Campus,** west of Massachusetts Avenue, has a more residential and relaxed atmosphere. Look for **Kresge Auditorium,** designed in 1955 by **Eero Saarinen,** unmistakable with its curving roof, one-eighth of a sphere resting on three abutments and floating free of the auditorium structure beneath. Also by Saarinen, the exquisite interfaith **MIT Chapel** is illuminated by a skylight that focuses light on the altar and is surrounded by a small moat that casts reflections upward on the interior walls. **Harry Bertoia** designed the sculpture behind the altar. Sought after as a site for weddings, the cylindrical structure is topped by **Theodore Roszak's** aluminum belltower and bell.

Baker House
COURTESY OF THE MIT MUSEUM AND SAMUEL CHAMBERLAIN

Nearby is **Baker House** (pictured above), a 1949 dormitory designed by **Alvar Aalto,** whose serpentine form cleverly maximizes views of the Charles, and **Miracle of Science,** a newfangled bar and grill modeled (loosely) on a chem lab, 321 Massachusetts Avenue, 828.2866.

East Cambridge

This multicultural community, predominantly Italian and Portuguese today, was once a prosperous Yankee enclave. In the 19th century factories turning out glass, furniture, soap, boxes, woven hose, and other goods flourished along the Charles, and the **Quality Row** of fine town houses sprung up. Then, slowly, the riverside industries declined. After suffering through decades as a forgotten backwater, East Cambridge is now undergoing major urban renewal and development. Look for the magnificently restored **Bulfinch Superior Courthouse Building,** original site of the Middlesex County court system, now occupied by the **Cambridge Multicultural Arts Center** (41 Second Street, 577.1400) with its two galleries and theater.

Cambridgeside Galleria
COURTESY OF ARROWSTREET INC. ARCHITECTS

A new addition to the neighborhood is the **Cambridgeside Galleria** (pictured above) on First Street, where you'll find the **Lechmere** department store, a local institution where you can buy anything and everything for the home at bargain prices. **Filene's** and **Sears** are here, too, along with many other shops, services, and the **Sports Museum of New England.** And nearby is pleasant **Lechmere Canal Park** with its lagoon and 50 foot geyser. Bostonians and Cantabrigians alike flock to **Michela's,** loved for innovative new Italian fare—consistently marvelous pastas and sauces made fresh daily by chef **Jody Adams,** 1 Atheneum Street, 225.3366.

Central Square/Riverside

Central Square is a sprawling area located straight down Massachusetts Avenue toward Boston. Central Square has been the section of Cambridge most resistant to gentrification and claims the greatest concentration of international restaurants and interesting clubs. Close to Harvard Square, and relatively upscale, **Cafe Sushi** offers a spectrum of sushi and sashimi, 1105 Massachusetts Avenue, 492.0434. **Dolphin Seafood** is a friendly little family place serving good and reasonably priced seafood, 1105 Massachusetts Avenue, 661.2937. **Roka** serves an extensive array of superior Japanese dishes and sushi, 1001 Massachusetts Avenue, 661.0344. Located off Massachusetts Avenue, **Cremaldi's** is a neighborhood grocery/cafe with European distinction, 31 Putnam Avenue, 354.7969. **Mimi's Oriental Grill** serves spicy Szechuan specialties in an elegant modern setting, 950 Massachusetts Avenue, 354.1665. **Pampas** serves Brazilian *churrasco*-style skewered meats—and more, 928 Massachusetts Avenue, 661.6613. In Central Square proper, **Middle East Restaurant,** a combination restaurant/nightclub, books some interesting eclectic acts, 472 Massachusetts Avenue, 492.9181, 354.8238. **Mary Chung** is a modest-looking place with superb Mandarin and Szechuan specialties, 447 Massachusetts Avenue, 864.1991. Central Square has lots of noteworthy Indian restaurants, the best of which is **India Pavilion,** 17 Central Square, 547.7463. Stellar *patisserie*—cafe fare, too—can be found at **Cezanne,** 424 Massachusetts Avenue, 547.9616.

Heading toward Boston down Main Street, off Massachusetts Avenue, is **Al's Lunch,** a whimsical little storefront luncheonette serving tasty breakfasts and lunches, 901 Main Street, 661.5810. Next door you'll find some of the best ice cream anywhere, at **Toscanini's,** 899 Main Street, 491.5877. For superb regional American cuisine visit **Anago,** 798 Main Street, 876.8444. For homestyle Italian cuisine, try **LaGroceria,** 853 Main Street, 547.9258. A little out of the way, but worth the effort, **Green Street Grill** (sharing space with old-timey **Charlie's Tap**) serves flamboyant dishes with Caribbean influence in a funky setting, 280 Green Street, 876.1655.

Evening entertainment in Central Square centers on music of all kinds, with clubs ranging from neighborhood-casual to somewhat chic. Starting off with the tiniest and rowdiest, stop in **The Plough and Stars,** 912 Massachusetts Avenue, 492.9653, an Irish pub with live Irish blues, country, and bluegrass music. You can hear local bands and dance the night away at the **Cantab Lounge,** 738 Massachusetts Avenue, 354.2685. **T.T. The Bear's Place** is a homey rock 'n' roll club featuring local bands, 10 Brookline Street (off Massachusetts Avenue), 492.0082. An art-bar featuring progressive New Wave and rock dancing, **Man-Ray** is at 21 Brookline Street, 864.0400. Man-Ray connects to **Campus,** a predominantly gay jukebox joint. Out of the way but worth the effort is a long-lived club known for reggae, rasta, and more, and great for dancing, called the **Western Front,** 343 Western Avenue (six blocks off Massachusetts Avenue—don't walk at night), 492.7772. Cambridge's best-looking club, built expressly for music, is **Nightstage,** 823 Main Street, 497.8200, which books a wide variety of great bands. Central Square has quite a few interesting shops, including a great old **Woolworth's.** Other finds are two gold-mine record shops, **Cheapo Records** at 645 Massachusetts Avenue, 354.4455, and **Skippy White's** at 555 Massachusetts Avenue, 491.3345. Cheap lodging is available at the **YMCA** (men only), 820 Massachusetts Avenue, 661.9622. Accommodations are customary Y-style: tiny rooms, shared baths, recreational facilities, some house regulations.

Inman Square

A 20-minute walk south on Cambridge Street from Harvard Square (or the same distance east on Prospect Street from Central Square), Inman Square is a quieter residential district with a surprising array of great restaurants, both ethnic and American, and an outstanding club or two. (It used to have many more, alas.) The square is slowly being gentrified, shedding much of its character as a family neighborhood with a variety of ethnic populations. It's definitely worth making a dinnertime journey here. Although renovated beyond recognition, the **S&S Restaurant Deli** is an Inman Square old-timer, serving traditional and gourmet deli-diner fare, 1334 Cambridge Street, 354.0777.

New Korea is one of Greater Boston's best spots for authentic Korean cuisine, 1281 Cambridge Street, 876.6182. The nationally known and very popular **East Coast Grill** will more than satisfy cravings for gourmet barbecue and great grilled fare, 1271 Cambridge Street, 491.6568. Next door is **Jake & Earl's Dixie BBQ,** owned by East Coast Grill, which purveys simpler, cheaper, but also delicious barbecue and fixings to go, 1273 Cambridge Street, 491.7427. **Chez Vous** features such Caribbean staples as conch and goat; everything's highly spiced, 1263 Cambridge Street, 868.3161. **Cafe China** serves gourmet Chinese/takeout, 1245 Cambridge Street, 868.4300. For spicy cooking, try **Cajun Yankee,** 1193 Cambridge Street, 576.1971. Come with a ravenous group to homey family run **Casa Portugal** to enjoy heaping helpings of excellent Portuguese cuisine, 1200 Cambridge Street, 491.8880. **Daddy O's Bohemian Cafe** affects a beatnik decor but proffers bourgeois '50s comfort food, along with contemporary cuisine, 134 Hampshire Street, 354.8371. For after-dinner music, go to **Ryles,** a casual and comfortable jazz club booking top local and national acts, 212 Hampshire Street, 876.9330; or

Cantares, a Latin American restaurant that also features merengue and salsa dance music and blues jam sessions, 15 Springfield Street (off Cambridge Street), 547.6300. For dessert, visit **Rosie's** for "chocolate orgasms" and other sinfully delicious treats. 243 Hampshire Street, 491.9488.

North Cambridge

First, three pleasant dining prospects are worth a jog westward, toward **Fresh Pond** via Concord Avenue. **The Peacock,** at 5 Craigie Circle, offers marvelous French country cooking, 661.4073. **Chez Nous** demands a special trip for superb French cuisine, 147 Huron Avenue, 864.6670. Come back the next day for brunch at folksy, well-worn **Pentimento,** 344 Huron Avenue, 661.3878.

Now northward on Massachusetts Avenue toward Porter Square: **Chez Jean** offers tasty bistro-style French food, 1 Shepherd Street, 354.8980. Stop in for enchiladas at **Mexican Cuisine**, 1682 Massachusetts Avenue, 661.1634, which shares space with a noisy bar. **Changsho** is magnificently decorated, offering a wide array of Chinese dishes, 1712 Massachusetts Avenue, 547.6565. **Boca Grande** serves some of the tastiest Mexican fare anywhere, 1728 Massachusetts Avenue, 354.7400. **Half Shell**, a "modern diner," offers moderately priced pizzas, 1760A Massachusetts Avenue, 661.6580. **Matsu-Ya** serves good Japanese and Korean dishes, 1790 Massachusetts Avenue, 491.5091. The **Cottonwood Cafe** and its downscaled sidekick, **Snakebites Cantina**, serve neo-Tex-Mex fare, 1815 Massachusetts Avenue (Porter Exchange Building), 354.6555. **Christopher's** is popular with locals for its pubby atmosphere, 1920 Massachusetts Avenue, 876.9180. For Lebanese and Greek cuisine and belly dancers, go to **Averof**, 1924 Massachusetts Avenue, 354.4500. **Tapas** offers reasonably priced tasting portions of an international cuisine, 2067 Massachusetts Avenue, 576.2240. And **Ristorante Marino** features Abruzzo and other Italian dishes in a big, bold atrium, 2465 Massachusetts Avenue, 868.5454.

Massachusetts Avenue toward Porter Square also offers interesting shopping, including international clothing boutiques, shops purveying natural foods and products, and antiques. **Pepperweed** sells contemporary attire from American, Japanese, and European designers, 1684 Massachusetts Avenue, 547.7561. Particularly numerous are vintage clothing and accessories stores, including **Red Dog Antiques**, 1737 Massachusetts Avenue, 354.9676; **Atalanta**, 1766 Massachusetts Avenue, 661.2673; and **Vintage Etc.**, 1796 Massachusetts Avenue, 497.1516. **Joie de Vivre** is a delightful shop selling unusual and artful trinkets and gifts, 1792 Massachusetts Avenue, 864.8188. This stretch of Massachusetts Avenue includes several excellent children's stores, including **The Children's Workshop**, 1963 Massachusetts Avenue at Porter Square, 354.1633. **The Music Emporium**, 2018 Massachusetts Avenue, 661.2099, sells old and antique stringed instruments as well as acoustic and folk-related music and instruments. Keep on going until you get to **Kate's Mystery Books**, 2211 Massachusetts Avenue, 491.2660, an eccentric "Murder-Mystery Central" for all of New England.

For elegant digs, try **A Cambridge House** ($$) bed-and-breakfast inn (pictured above), built in 1892 and listed on the **National Register of Historic Places.** Its 12 rooms are handsomely restored and decorated, and an elaborate breakfast is complimentary. At 2218 Massachusetts Avenue, 491.6300, 800/232.9989; fax 868.2848.

Book Nooks

Boston and Cambridge are internationally renowned meccas for booklovers; after all, both cities have treated the printed word reverentially since their founding days. When the Puritans arrived, books transported from England were among their most prized possessions. Boston's first English settler was **William Blaxton,** a loner whose idea of perfect companionship was communing with his enviable library of 200 or so volumes. Cambridge remains the true booklover's haven for its critical mass of shops clustered in **Harvard Square,** the bookshop capital of the East Coast if not the country. Together Boston and Cambridge bookstores can satisfy any literary interest. Here's a sampling of some of the best.

In Cambridge:

Asian Books Large selection of books on Asia and the Islamic and Arab worlds. ♦ 12 Arrow Street. 354.0005

Robin Bledsoe and H.L. Mendelsohn Out-of-print scholarly works on art history, architecture, archaeology, city planning, graphic design, women artists, landscape architecture, and decorative arts. Also features new, used, and imported books on horses. ♦ 1640 Massachusetts Avenue. 576.3634

Grolier Poetry Book Shop Thousands of poetry titles, plus first editions, literary magazines, and small-press publications. See page 179. ♦ 6 Plympton Street. 547.4648

The Harvard University Cooperative (The Coop) Harvard University's official bookstore, the Coop has a branch at **MIT.** See page 175. ♦ 1400 Massachusetts Avenue. 492.1000

Harvard University Press Display Room Check out the latest Harvard University Press publications for sale, including the Loeb Classical Library. There's a bargain section, too. ♦ 1354 Massachusetts Avenue, Holyoke Center Arcade. 495.2625

Kate's Mystery Books More than 10,000 new and used mysteries amid black cats galore. Also the hangout for the **Cadaver Club,** a loose association of local mystery writers. ♦ 2211 Massachusetts Avenue north of Porter Square. 491.2660

Mandrake Book Store Specializes in the social sciences and art, architecture, and design, and the books are selected and arranged with fastidious expertise. See page 186. ♦ 8 Story Street. 864.3088

The MIT Press Bookstore Scholarly books and journals on engineering, computer science, architecture, philosophy, linguistics, economics, and more. ♦ 292 Main Street, Kendall Square. 253.5249

New Words Bookstore A feminist bookstore with books by and about women, plus records, T-shirts, posters, and postcards. Nonsexist and nonracist books for kids are a specialty. ♦ 186 Hampshire Street, Inman Square. 876.5310

Pangloss Bookshop Used, out-of-print, and rare scholarly books. See page 180. ♦ 65 Mount Auburn Street. 354.4003

Reading International A general bookshop carrying all the latest hardcovers and paperbacks, with a general academic slant and a noteworthy periodical section. See page 185. ♦ 47 Brattle Street. 864.0705

Revolution Books Books and periodicals on revolutionary politics. ♦ 38 JFK Street. 492.5443

Schoenhof's Foreign Books, Inc. America's oldest and largest comprehensive foreign-language bookstore. See page 180. ♦ 76A Mount Auburn Street. 547.8855

Seven Stars New Age books, crystals, and incense. ♦ 58 JFK Street. 547.1317

Starr Book Shop An academic bookstore in the Harvard Lampoon Castle. See page 180. ♦ 29 Plympton Street. 547.6864

WordsWorth The square's busiest bookshop, where all titles but textbooks are discounted. See page 183. ♦ 30 Brattle Street. 354.5201

In Boston:

Ars Libri The country's largest comprehensive inventory of rare and out-of-print books and periodicals about the fine arts. See page 161. ♦ 560 Harrison Avenue, South End. 357.5212

Avenue Victor Hugo Bookshop New and used paperbacks and hardcovers, magazines, and comic books. See page 123. ♦ 339 Newbury Street, Back Bay. 266.7746

Barnes & Noble Giant bookseller of reduced-price books. Also, children's books, magazines, classical and jazz records, tapes, and CDs. For more information about this bookstore, see page 84. ♦ 395 Washington Street, Downtown. 426.5502. Also at: 607 Boylston Street, Back Bay. 236.1308

Boston Cooks Cornucopia of cookbooks in hardcover and paperback, with many privately printed by organizations all over America. ♦ Faneuil Hall Marketplace. 523.0242

Brattle Book Shop The successor to America's oldest operating antiquarian bookshop has three floors with a little bit of everything. See page 89. ♦ 9 West Street, Downtown. 542.0210, 800/447.9595

Bromer Booksellers Rare books of all periods, literary first editions, private press and illustrated books, books in fine bindings, and miniature and children's books. For more information, see page 114. ♦ 607 Boylston Street, second floor, Back Bay. 247.2818

Maury A. Bromsen Associates, Inc. Dr. Bromsen shows his specialties: rare Americana, Latin Americana, autographs and manuscripts, bibliography and reference works, fine arts (19th-century paintings and prints), and exploration and discovery. This store is open by appointment only. ♦ 770 Boylston Street (Prudential Center), Suite 23F, Back Bay. 266.7060

B.U. Bookstore A six-story collegiate department store, as well as New England's largest bookstore. See page 144. ♦ 660 Beacon Street, Kenmore Square. 267.8484

Buddenbrooks Booksmith General bookshop stocking more than 50,000 titles. Good antiquarian section. See page 112. ♦ 753 Boylston Street, Back Bay. 536.4433

ChoreoGraphica A well-established used bookstore specializing in the performing arts, especially dance. Some reviewers' copies, too. It shares space with Sher-Morr Antiques. ♦ 82 Charles Street, Beacon Hill. 227.4780

Glad Day Bookshop New England's only gay and lesbian full literature bookshop. See page 113. ♦ 673 Boylston Street, second floor, Back Bay. 267.3010

The Globe Corner Book Store A wealth of works on New England and books by regional authors; plus a fine selection of guidebooks and world-travel information. See page 78. ♦ 3 School Street, Downtown. 523.6658

Goodspeed's Book Shop Purveyors of antiquarian books, maps, and prints since 1898. Goodspeed's sells and buys books on all subjects and offers appraisals. Everything from rare tomes to bargain books is sold here. See pages 15 and 83. ♦ 7 Beacon Street, Beacon Hill. 523.5970. Also at: Old South Meeting House, 2 Milk Street, Downtown. 523.5970

Harvard Book Store Current and backlist hardcovers and paperbacks. Dine and read in the pleasant cafe. See page 128. ♦ 190 Newbury Street, Back Bay. 536.0095

Priscilla Juvelis, Inc. By appointment, Juvelis purveys *livres d'artiste,* literary first editions, fine bindings, illustrated books, press books, and fine art. ♦ 150 Huntington Avenue, Back Bay. 424.1895

David L. O' Neal Antiquarian Bookseller, Inc. Fine and rare books from the 15th to the 20th century. See page 130. ♦ 234 Clarendon Street, second floor, Back Bay. 266.5790

Pepper & Stern—Rare Books, Inc. Peter L. Stern and James Pepper specialize in first editions of American and English literature, mystery and detective fiction, rare cinema material, signed and inscribed books, autograph letters, and manuscripts. ♦ 355 Boylston Street, second floor, Back Bay. 421.1880

Rizzoli Art and architecture, design, photography, current fiction and nonfiction, and international and classical music. ♦ Copley Place, Back Bay. 437.0700

Spenser's Mystery Bookshop and Marlowe's Used Books New and used mystery books, first editions, and collectible paperbacks. ♦ 314 Newbury Street, Back Bay. 262.0880

Travel Days Bookshop Part of a travel chain owned by Doubleday, with around 5,000 titles, plus maps, videos, globes, atlases, and foreign-language guides. ♦ Copley Place, Back Bay. 247.2291

Cambridge

Trident Booksellers & Cafe In addition to books, crystals, incense, scented oils, tarot cards, and bonsai trees are sold here. The little cafe is a popular neighborhood meeting place. See page 124. ♦ 338 Newbury Street, Back Bay. 267.8688

Waldenbooks Current paperbacks and hardcovers on general subjects are sold in this chain store. ♦ 2 Center Plaza, Beacon Hill. 523.3044

Outside Boston:

New England Mobile Book Fair Well worth a drive, this store is not mobile in the least—it's actually a huge warehouse stocking more than 800,000 books. Everything is discounted by 20 percent, and there's a special mark-down section. Many of the titles are arranged by publisher. ♦ 82 Needham Street, Newton. 527.5817

Mug Shots: Where to Find the Best Home Brews

Beer was the favored colonial beverage. During the 17th century Boston ship crews were issued beer rations of more than a quart per day; Puritan minister **Richard Mather** recommended beer consumption along with fresh air and church-going; and **Harvard College** operated its own brewery in its backyard.

The right to brew was jealously guarded by Puritan leaders, who had the power to giveth and taketh away licenses, and readily did so when a brewer's beer was deemed inferior. The American Revolution interfered with beer production, and in 1789 the state of Massachusetts exempted brewers from taxes for five years to "encourage the manufacture and consumption of strong beer." National and statewide prohibitions during the 19th and early 20th centuries and the growth of beer conglomerates increasingly disrupted Bay State brewing. In fact, there wasn't a single working brewery in the state by the early '80s. But several have opened in the last few years, and these are the best of them:

Boston Beer Company The famous award-winning Samuel Adams Boston Lager is brewed here, plus Boston Lightship Beer, Samuel Adams Double Bock Beer, and others. One-and-a-half-hour tours and tastes at brewmaster **James Koch's** impressive facility are given on Thursday at 2PM and Saturday at noon and 2PM. ♦ 30 Germania Street, Jamaica Plain. 522.9080

Boston Beer Works This brew pub has developed 15 brews to date, including some imaginative fruit selections (watermelon beer?). Of the eight or so varieties on tap at any given time, Boston Red (an amber) and Buckeye Oatmeal Stout are particularly popular. ♦ 61 Brookline Avenue, at Kenmore Square. 536.2337

Cambridge Brewing Company This company features its own Regatta Golden, Cambridge Amber, Charles River Porter, Summertime Wheat Ale, and casual pub fare. ♦ 1 Kendall Square. 494.1994

Commonwealth Brewing Company The brew pub serves a variety of its own creations, including

Cambridge

Golden Ale, Boston's Best Burton Bitter, Classic Stout, Golden Export, and Famous Porter, plus pub cuisine. Ask about free tours. ♦ 138 Portland Street. 522.8383

John Harvard's Brew House The former head brewer for San Francisco's very popular Anchor Steam Brewing Company, **Tim Morse,** is cooking up English-style ales and Germanic lagers in this handsome cellar restaurant. ♦ 33 Dunster Street, Harvard Square. 868.3585

Mass. Bay Brewing Company Sample Harpoon Ale and other brews on hand. Forty-five-minute tours are given Friday and Saturday at 1PM. ♦ 306 Northern Avenue (beyond Jimmy's Harborside). 574.9551

Bests

Corby Kummer

Senior Editor/Food and Wine columnist, *The Atlantic Monthly* magazine

Evidently much goes on in the early morning in Boston, but the only time I've ever seen those terrible hours is waiting for the doors to open at **Filene's Basement** during one of the crucial twice-a-year sales. Coffee from one of the several branches of **au bon pain** inside Filene's is essential to endure this. ("FB," as my more-addicted friends call it, is a necessary stop for any visitor.)

A more civilized morning activity is lining up for the bagels at **Kupel's** on Harvard Street in Brookline. Then go to any branch of the **Coffee Connection** (there's one down the street from Kupel's) for some of the most varied and best brewed coffee in the country (try any Costa Rican, or La Minita Tarrazu).

Afternoons at the **Fogg Art Museum** at Harvard, looking at the Impressionist or early Italian panel paintings, and then walking around the Cambridge bookstores, feeling the winds of the four corners of the earth—a far more cosmopolitan feeling than you get anywhere in Boston.

Late afternoon walks along the **Charles River Esplanade,** watching the sun set over the odd neoclassic marble dome of **Massachusetts Institute of Technology** across the river and feeling glad you don't have to pass a single engineering course there.

Checking the antiques shops of **Charles Street** in Beacon Hill, where you'll find many high-priced shops, and the equally important shops on the hidden parallel **River Street.**

Tea at the **Bristol Lounge** of the **Four Seasons,** where all is grace without pomp; you can look at the flowering trees of the **Public Garden** across the street, and the scones are flaky and warm from the oven.

Dinner at **Hamersley's Bistro,** in the South End, where **Gordon Hamersley** cooks with Mediterranean invention and French frugality, or at **Ristorante Toscano** in Beacon Hill, where **Vinicio Paoli,** a native Florentine, brings the only authentic whiff of *porcini* to Boston, or at **Michela's,** across the Salt-and-Pepper Bridge near Kendall Square, where Northern Italian style meets American invention and the staff makes you glad you came.

Clea Simon

Writer/Author (with Brett Milano) of *Boston Rock Trivia*

Blues and brunch at **Johnny D's Uptown Lounge** in Somerville. The grand bookings at this little bar have brought **Marcia Ball** and **Irma Thomas** to town. And, provided the next morning is a Saturday or a Sunday, their hearty brunch (each dish comes with oatmeal) makes the cure easy. Look for the cinnamon-walnut pancakes.

Afternoon tea at the **Blacksmith House Bakery Cafe** in Harvard Square. Superlative pastries and miniature sandwiches are served on a comfortably bohemian patio—the perfect warm-weather meeting place.

The balcony at **The Rat,** where you can see untried bands and pick-up groups through a haze of smoke. Grungy, loud, cheaper than the headliners downstairs, and very, very Boston rock.

Coffee at **Pamplona** at Harvard Square or **Trident Booksellers and Cafe** on Newbury Street can last all afternoon. Great grounds for serious reading.

The **Middle East** restaurant and club is an unlikely setting for the rock and roll scene; they still have belly dancing some weekends.

The **Garment District,** for used clothes to wear out.

The harbor seal pool outside the **New England Aquarium** is free and can be visited at all hours. Hoover the seal has died, but who knows when one of the sleek, feline beasts will speak again?

The **Fogg Art Museum:** a little gem with free tours and concerts.

The **Brattle Theatre** brought Bogie back. And **Herrell's Ice Cream** is close enough for a double scoop afterward.

Chau Chow for the best seafood dishes in Chinatown, and "cold tea" late into the night.

Lydia Shire
Chef/Owner, Biba Restaurant

Shopping on **Newbury Street.**

Swan Boat rides and feeding the swans in the **Public Garden.**

Cape Cod in August.

A late-night meal at **Moonvilla** in Chinatown.

Driving on **Memorial Drive** from Harvard Square to Boston, and out to **Lincoln** in the fall for pumpkins.

The hot dogs from **John Dewar Meat Company** and pastries at the **Bentonwood cafe,** both in Newton Center.

Patriots games at **Foxboro Stadium.**

Brookline Liquor Mart, for great burgundy.

Mai tais at **Mr. Leung's.**

Sipping cocktails at **Jasper's.**

Diane Carasik Dion
Editor, *'GBH Magazine,* WGBH Boston Public TV Station

In Cambridge:

Cheapo Records in Central Square, where you can find a staggering selection of oldies. You can still get a 45-rpm (yes, vinyl) version of *Tonight, Tonight* by the Mello Kings.

Chez Jean on Shepard Street is the bistro that time forgot: small, charming, family run, and very French.

The Acropolis Restaurant in North Cambridge, for a friendly atmosphere, straightforward Greek fare, and wonderful Mediterranean-style vegetables.

The Coffee Connection in Harvard Square (and several other locations), for "CC Special" beans, the premiere grind.

Boston Chicken at Porter Square (and other locations). Indulge in perfectly roasted birds and *real* mashed potatoes.

The Brattle Theatre at Harvard Square. Even its monthly bulletin is brilliantly done. Of special note, the Brattle's author readings, sponsored by nearby (and also great) **WordsWorth Books.** For lovers of the silver screen, other area rep film houses include: **The West Newton Cinema** (in Newton), **The Somerville Theatre** (at Davis Square in Somerville), **The Coolidge Corner Theatre** (in Brookline), and **The Regent Theatre** (in Arlington).

In Watertown Square:

Hunan Palace. The orange-flavored chicken and *Yu-Hsiang* green beans taste particularly good after a big score at **The Gap Outlet** in Watertown Mall.

In Newton:

Two country-in-the-city seasonal hits: A dip *in* the water at Newton Highlands' own **Crystal Lake,** or an afternoon *on* the water at Auburndale's **Charles River Canoe & Kayak Center,** where beginners are very welcome.

Arthur Dion
Director/Art Dealer, Gallery Naga

After luxuriating in the city's great art galleries (the **Institute of Contemporary Art,** the **Museum of Fine Arts,** the **Isabella Stewart Gardner,** and the **List**), walk around **Newbury Street** and environs.

The King & I has the best Thai cuisine in town—classic *pad thai,* beautiful chicken basil. Ask for Joe.

Davio's, for haute Italian, irresistible homemade sausages, and supernal soups and sauces.

Bob the Chef's is the home of soul food, gracious and real.

The Downtown Cafe is crazy in all the best senses.

The amazing flower beds in the **Public Garden.**

The lights in the trees of the **Public Garden** and the **Boston Common** on a winter night.

Storrow Drive or Memorial Drive day or night, from the **Museum of Science** through Cambridge; it's almost worth renting a car.

Ice skating on the **Swan Boat** pond in the Public Garden (I've never done it, but it looks great).

The **Charles River Esplanade** is just gorgeous, especially if it's the first Sunday in June and you've

just finished the 10K From All Walks of Life, which raised millions of dollars for AIDS care and research.

For the energenic, the adventurous, and the bold:

Fort Hill in Roxbury and **Larz Anderson Park** in Brookline, for great spaces and views.

The **Museum of the National Center of Afro-American Artists**—a gem.

The **Cyclorama** at the Boston Center for the Arts is a huge, odd, wonderful exhibition space.

Spring and fall weekends the largest clusters of Boston's many thousands of artists' studios are open to all. (Check the paper or call a gallery for details.) **Fort Point,** the **South End, Brickbottom,** and **Vernon Street,** to name only the biggest, are all primers to the city's art world.

Other Neighborhoods

Boston's outer neighborhoods are close-knit communities with distinctive personalities. And that makes sense, since most of them developed independently before being absorbed by Boston. Even more than landfilling, annexation increased the city's size. Boston was an overcrowded seaport in 1850, but by 1900 the metropolis had flung itself across a 10-mile radius and engulfed 31 cities and towns. Public transportation—horse-cars, followed by electric trolleys—made it possible for people to live in "street-car suburbs" within easy traveling distance to their workplaces. The expanding middle-class and immigrant families began moving beyond Old Boston, rapidly swelling the commuter ranks, so now these many Boston neighborhoods are largely residential, with a smattering of important historical, recreational, and cultural attractions.

Charlestown

The **North End** and this neighborhood stare at one another across the mouth of the **Charles River.** Now a small satellite that's rather tricky to get to—reached by crossing the **Charlestown Bridge** by car or on foot, departing by boat from **Long Wharf** in the summer, or riding an MBTA bus—Charlestown was actually settled one year before Boston, in 1629. Most of the harborside town was burned by the British during the **Battle of Bunker Hill** in 1775, then rapidly rebuilt as a flourishing port where wealthy captains and ship owners lived in grand mansions on the hillsides. The opening of the **Charlestown Navy Yard** brought jobs and prosperity from the 1800s to the early 1900s, attracting waves of European immigrants while well-to-do families moved out. Charlestown was annexed to Boston in 1874. Maritime activities began shrinking and the Great Depression increased the neighborhood's economic woes. Charlestown deteriorated faster as the Navy Yard dwindled and was finally shut down by the federal government in 1974. But the neighborhood has been rebounding steadily, with the beautifully sited Navy Yard transformed into residential, office, retail, and medical-research space. Many have recognized the charm of Charlestown's narrow colonial streets bordered by neat little residences. A predominantly white, Irish-American enclave since the turn of the century, Charlestown is still a family oriented neighborhood entrenched in tradition. Young professionals have been moving in, however, and enormous change is afoot that will further open up this insular spot.

Ordinarily visible from **Copp's Hill** in the North End, the USS *Constitution*—scheduled to undergo dry-dock repairs until late 1993—is the oldest commissioned ship in the **US Navy,** maintained to this day by Navy personnel. Launched 21 October 1797 in Boston, the ship (pictured above) served in **Thomas Jefferson's** campaign against the Barbary pirates, and won

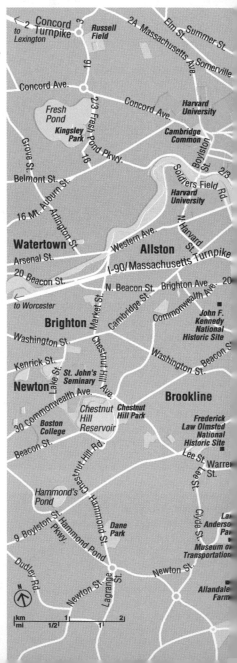

42 battles in the War of 1812, never losing once. Nicknamed "Old Ironsides" for its combat-proven wooden hull, not for any iron plating, the ship (except when under repair) is permanently moored at **Constitution Wharf** in the Charlestown Navy Yard. (It makes one tour, called the "turnaround," of the harbor every Fourth of July, to weather evenly and to remain a commissioned warship.)

Top-to-bottom tours, including the claustrophobic living quarters below deck, have been temporarily suspended, but deck tours are still scheduled, and the **Constitution Museum** will screen a film to compensate. ♦ Admission; discounts for senior citizens and children; special family rate. M-Γ 10AM-4PM, Sa-Su 9AM-5PM, winter; daily 9AM-5PM, spring and fall; daily 9AM-6PM, summer. 426.1812

The enormous Charlestown Navy Yard was founded in 1800 to build warships and evolved over 170 years to meet the Navy's changing requirements. A **National Historic Park,** the distinguished-looking Navy Yard is a physical record of American shipbuilding history. Among its 19th-century workshops, barracks, and other structures: the **Ropewalk**—the last in existence—designed by **Alexander Parris** in 1836 and nearly a quarter-mile long, where all rope for the Navy was made for 135 years; **Dry Dock Number 1,** tied with a Virginia dry dock as the first in the US, and called Constitution Dock because "Old Ironsides" was the first ship to dock here (it's back now for repairs); the ornate **Telephone Exchange Building,** completed in 1852; and the **Commandant's House,** an 1809 Georgian mansion. You can also board the USS *Cassin*

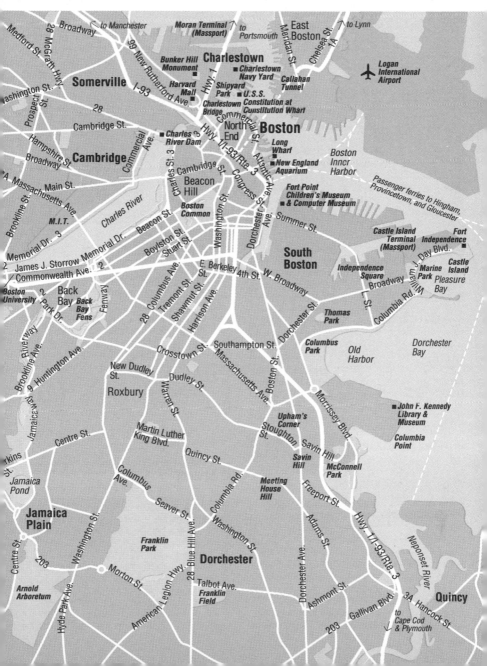

Young, a World War II destroyer of the kind once built here. Originally a pumphouse, **Constitution Museum** displays original documents and other important artifacts from the historic vessel. Before leaving, visit **Shipyard Park** on the waterfront. ♦ Free. Daily 9AM-5PM. 242.5601

Every American schoolchild learns how the Battle of Bunker Hill was really fought on **Breed's Hill,** where **Solomon Willard's Bunker Hill Monument** (pictured below) now points to the sky, visible from many Boston locations. The hill rises from the midst of formal Monument Square and its hand-somely preserved 1840s town houses. Climb the grassy slope to the monument, part of the **Boston National Historic Park.** The **Marquis de Lafayette** laid the cornerstone in 1825, visiting the United States for the first time since his days as a dashing youthful hero. The monument was finally completed in 1843, and **Daniel Webster** orated at the dedication. The 220-foot-tall obelisk of Quincy granite rises from the area where, on 17 June 1775, **Colonel William Prescott** reportedly ordered his citizen's militia not to fire "until you see the whites of their eyes." The Redcoats ultimately seized the hill, but suffered more than 1,300 casualties, a devastating cost that boosted the colonists' morale. Climb the 295 steps to the monument observatory for fine views; back at the bottom, notice the dioramas portraying the battle. **Boston Park Rangers** offer talks in the summer. ♦ Free. Museum daily 9AM-5PM. Monument daily 9AM-4:30PM. Closed Thanksgiving, Christmas, New Year's Day. 242.5641

Leave Monument Square and descend serene **Monument Avenue** to **Main Street.** If you visit the Bunker Hill Monument late in the afternoon and then dawdle, you can plan on enjoying a wonderful dinner at **Olives** (★★★$$), **Olivia** and **Todd English's** European bistro-style restaurant at 10 City Square, 242.1999. Friendly, noisy Olives is known for chef Todd English's creatively rustic dishes like savory tarts, bouillabaisse, spit-roasted chicken, and butternut-squash ravollini; many of the specialties are cooked in a wood-burning brick oven. Reservations are accepted for six or more only, so get your name on the list very early—at least by 5:30PM. That likely means an early dinner, but it's the only way to ensure seating. As a fallback, there's always Olives' new offshoot, **Figs,** a plainer pizza-and-

Other Neighborhoods

pasta place at 67 Main Street, 242.2229. Or bide some time at the circa-1780 **Warren Tavern** nearby, with drinks and plenty of atmosphere, 2 Pleasant Street, 241.8142. Named for the Revolutionary War hero **General Joseph Warren,** who died in the Battle of Bunker Hill, the tavern also serves dinner. You could then continue your sightseeing on Main Street up **Town Hill** to **Harvard Mall** (on the **National Register of Historic Places**); the young minister **John Harvard** and his family lived near here. When Harvard died at 31, he bequeathed half of his fortune and all of his library to the college in **Cambridge** that adopted his name in thanks. At the mall's edge is charming **Harvard Square**—not to be confused with the famous

Cambridge Square—and its modest mid-19th century dwellings. Leaving Charlestown, visit the **Charles River Dam Visitors' Information Center** on the river, 250 Warren Avenue, City Square, 727.0059, for a 12-minute multimedia presentation explaining the Charles River Dam's operations: flood control, fish ladders, and boat locks. You can also take guided tours of the dam, which has one of the mightiest pumping stations in the country.

South Boston

Expanded by landfill since the 18th century, South Boston is now a peninsula of approximately four square miles, with broad beaches and parks. Founded in 1630 as part of **Dorchester,** it was largely undeveloped until annexed to Boston in 1804, with the first bridge to Boston built the next year. Then real-estate speculators arrived, and Yankee gentry built handsome wooden houses along **East Broadway** and around **Thomas Park** on Telegraph Hill. With the building of bridges to Boston, railways, and growth of industry, the arrival of great numbers of Irish Americans at century's end established the tight-knit neighborhood known as "Southie" today. Lithuanians, Poles, and Italians also settled here. The wealthy merchants moved out as immigrants moved in and **Back Bay** became the latest magnet for fashion-seekers. Like **Charlestown** and **East Boston,** South Boston is a white enclave with a family focus and few minority residents. More than half the neighborhood population is of Irish ancestry, and a major local event is the annual St. Patrick's Day parade and festivities. Drive in for great views of the harbor and islands from **Day Boulevard** and **Castle Island** at **Marine Park.** Visit star-shaped **Fort Independence** on the island (actually no longer an island), then walk along **Pleasure Bay,** designed by **Frederick Law Olmsted.** Near the fort is a statue of **Donald McKay,** who designed Boston clipper ships, including the famous *Flying Cloud.* Southie abuts the **Fort Point** artists' community, formerly an industrial and wool-processing area where the **Children's Museum** and the **Computer Museum** are now grand attractions. A popular Irish bar complete with priests is near the Broadway T Station: **Amrhein's** (★$), 80 West Broadway and A streets, 268.6189. Family owned and run, 100-year-old Amrhein's has the oldest beer-pump system in Boston and the oldest hand-carved wooden bar in the country. People come from all over for great meat-and-potatoes meals, fabulous onion rings, and of course, beer.

Dorchester

If it weren't part of Boston, racially, ethnically, and economically diverse Dorchester would be an important Massachusetts city in its own right. Originally, it was even larger and included **South Boston** and **Hyde Park.** Dorchester is an area of intimate neighborhoods, like the close-knit **Polish Triangle,** or **Dudley,** home to Hispanic and Cape Verdean families. **Dorchester Avenue,** nicknamed "Dot Ave," is the community's spine, with lots of ethnic and family owned businesses: Irish pubs and bakeries are alongside Southeast Asian markets alongside West Indian grocers selling curries and spices. In 1630 the Puritans landed at Mattapannock, today called **Columbia Point,** and, fearing Indian attacks, established homesteads near a fort atop **Savin Hill. Upham's Corner** was once known as **Burying Place Corner** because of the cemetery founded there in 1633, the **Dorchester North Burying Ground.** Nearby is Boston's oldest standing house, the 1648 **Blake House;** both burying ground and house are on the **National Register of Historic Places.** Atop **Meeting House Hill** is the **Mather School,** the oldest elementary school in the nation, founded in 1639 as a one-room schoolhouse. From **Dorchester Heights,** now a **National Historic Site** with a monument, patriots commanded a clear view of the Redcoats during the Siege of Boston in 1776. Here **George Washington** and his men set up cannons, heroically hauled through the wilderness for three months by Boston bookseller-turned-general **Henry Knox.** The guns were trained on the British, powerful persuasion that convinced them to flee for good. ♦ Free. Park daily dawn-dusk. Monument open July through August (call for tours at other times). Located in Thomas Park (off Telegraph Street near G Street). 242.5642

Dorchester was an agricultural community well into the 1800s. Gradually, rich Bostonians built country estates and summer residences on its southern hilltops. In the early 1800s commercial villages grew up along the **Neponset River** and the waterfront. With the electric tram's inauguration in 1857, Dorchester became a suburb of Boston, annexed in 1869. Lovely Victorians are sprinkled throughout this neighborhood, but the best-known architectural style in Dorchester is its distinctive three-family houses called "three-deckers," which became the rage in the early 1900s. But after World War II the suburban ideal of single-family homes and shopping malls emerged, and Dorchester suffered from flight and neglect. Though still not a safe place to wander, it's being rediscovered and improving its image. A sign of the neighborhood's vitality is the rejuvenation of the 1918 **Strand Theater** at Upham's Corner, a former movie palace restored as a grand venue for performing arts and community events, 282.8000.

The Boston Globe is headquartered at 135 Morrissey Boulevard, 929.2653. Make an appointment for a free tour explaining how a major metropolitan daily gets printed every day, as *The Globe* has been for 120 years. The hour-long tours are scheduled Tuesday and Thursday, with a 15-minute film included.

The **John F. Kennedy Library and Museum** (a 1979 design of **I.M. Pei & Partners**) couldn't find a home in Cambridge and landed out on Columbia Point—inconvenient for tourists but a dramatic site with glorious unobstructed views of the ocean. The stark, magnificent library is the official repository of JFK's presidential papers and many personal belongings. The library archives contain all of his papers, classified and declassified, all of his speeches on film and video, and also **Robert F. Kennedy's** senatorial papers. The museum displays seven exhibitions on JFK and two on RFK, with tapes and videos. The library also possesses 95 percent of American writer **Ernest Hemingway's** works. Also in the neighborhood is the **Bayside Exposition Center,** where trade shows and events are held. ♦ Admission to JFK Museum; discounts for senior citizens and children under 16; children under six free. Daily 9AM-5PM. Closed Thanksgiving, Christmas, New Year's Day. Columbia Pt. For recorded information call 929.4500. ♿

Jamaica Plain

Originally part of neighboring **Roxbury,** Jamaica Plain ("JP" to Bostonians) was once fertile farmland. In the late 1800s it became a summer resort for wealthy Back Bay and Beacon Hill residents, who drove their carriages along the tree-shaded **Jamaicaway** to pass the season at splendid estates surrounding **Jamaica Pond**—"The Pond." On the other side of town, thousands of factory workers labored in JP's 17 breweries, all of which eventually closed. (**Boston Beer Company,** maker of the multiaward-winning Samuel Adams Lager Beer, recently took up the torch of tradition.) In the 1830s railroads began bringing well-to-do commuters who built Greek Revival, Italianate, and mansard residences; in the 1870s streetcars brought the growing middle class. Today JP is one of Boston's most integrated neighborhoods. Lots of families live in its three square miles.

Centre Street developed early as JP's main artery and retains its small-town character. Along its bumpy, narrow length are good, cheap ethnic restaurants, bodegas, Irish pubs, mom-and-pop stores, and a slowly growing number of upscale establishments. Boston has few vegetarian restaurants, and one of the very good ones is macrobiotic **Five Seasons** (★$) at 669A Centre Street, 524.9016, offering simply prepared, innovative international dishes. Read the paper over coffee and a treat at spacious and spare **Today's Bread** (★$), 701 Centre Street, 522.6458, with its big windows on the street, wonderful croissants—try the poppyseed-and-cheese—muffins, desserts, quiches, salads, and sandwiches.

One of Boston's best Irish bars and a local institution is **Doyle's Cafe** (★★$), 3483 Washington Street, 524.2345, with its famous clock logo. In a cavernous vintage setting full of memorabilia, try fine Irish coffee and Bloody Marys, abundant brunches, basic delicious food, and a variety of beers on tap.

Some of the loveliest sections of **Frederick Law Olmsted's Emerald Necklace** are in or border Jamaica Plain: Jamaica Pond, the **Arnold Arboretum,** and **Franklin Park.** The city's last working farm is likewise in JP: **Allandale Farm,** 259 Allandale Road, 524.1531, open from May to Christmas Day. As spring turns to summer turns to fall, you can buy plants, fruits, vegetables, apples, pumpkins, cider pressed on the premises, and Christmas trees and wreaths. The farm has been operating on the old **Brandegee Estate** for more than 125 years.

Other Neighborhoods

In 1866 Boston had the nation's first state legislature with black representatives.

The *Dictionary of Place Names* suggests that the Jamaica Plain suburb originated with a tribe named the Jamaco or Jameco (Algonquin for "beaver"); in addition, a booklet issued by the City of Boston for the Bicentennial notes that many prominent local families made their fortunes off Jamaican rum. Another apocryphal legend tells of an English woman whose husband told her he was heading for Jamaica; on her way to track him down, she found him, quite by chance, in the Boston suburb.

Brookline

Actually, Brookline isn't part of Boston—although not for lack of Boston's trying. When the cramped city began busily annexing towns to solve its land crunch, independent-minded Brookline refused to be swallowed. It is home to an increasingly diverse ethnic population, and is a somewhat expensive place to live.

Coolidge Corner (pictured above), where Harvard and Beacon streets meet, is a mini-Harvard Square with old-fashioned and new-fashioned establishments. The **Coolidge Corner Theatre,** 290 Harvard Street, 734.2500, was recently saved from the development scourge by movie lovers, and offers interesting, intelligent vintage and contemporary films. A few blocks from the theater is **John F. Kennedy's** birthplace (29 May 1917), 83 Beals Street, now the **John F. Kennedy National Historic Site.** The Kennedys lived here until 1921. ♦ Admission; senior citizens and children under 12 free. Daily 10AM-4:30PM. Closed Thanksgiving, Christmas, New Year's Day. 566.7937

An undiscovered gem in Brookline is the **Frederick Law Olmsted National Historic Site,** the rambling home and office named "Fairsted" by its owner, who was America's first landscape architect and founder of the profession in this country. Olmsted's successor firm practiced here until 1980, and the site archives include valuable plans, photographs, and other documentation of the firm's work. ♦ Free. F-Su 10AM-4:30PM. 99 Warren Street. 566.1689

When you're hungry, try one of the excellent local delis, like **B & D Deli** (★$), 1653 Beacon Street, 232.3727; or kosher **Rubin's** ($), 500 Harvard Street, 731.8787 (on the Allston border). Have a casual, deli-

Other Neighborhoods

cious dinner at the **Tam O'Shanter** (★$$), nicknamed "The Tam," which doubles as a club, 1648 Beacon Street, 277.0982. Also casual, the **Harvard Street Grill** (★★$$$) offers a calmer, more refined setting and elegant American cuisine like lobster terrine and watercress, grilled rack of lamb, and pork loin with pistachios, 398 Harvard Street, 734.9834. Parking, by the way, is limited to two hours during the day and notoriously impossible overnight, when all visitors' cars on the street between 2AM and 6AM are subject to ticketing. While on the subject of cars, the **Museum of Transportation** is also in Brookline and explores the cultural and sociological impact of the automobile on American society; it also has special exhibitions on

other transportation topics, such as German aviation. ♦ Admission; discounts for senior citizens, students, and children. W-Su 10AM-5PM. Carriage House, Larz Anderson Park, 15 Newton St. 522.6140

Allston-Brighton

Polyglot Allston-Brighton is Boston's most integrated district, where Irish, Italians, Greeks, and Russians are joined by growing numbers of Asians, Blacks, and Hispanics. Most Bostonians associate this neighborhood with students from the local universities, large numbers of whom live here. An agricultural community founded in 1635, the neighborhood later was the locale for huge stockyards, slaughterhouses, and meatpacking operations serving the region, then became industrialized. Since World War II there has been dramatic change led by the construction of the **Massachusetts Turnpike,** which further split Allston from Brighton, already divided by railroad tracks. Allston-Brighton has developed in a haphazard way that makes it confusing to navigate, but it has many pleasant streets with nice old homes, apartment buildings, and a cozy feel. The neighborhoods have innumerable ethnic restaurants and markets, pubs, interesting shops, and antique stores. A popular hangout is **Harper's Ferry,** 156 Brighton Avenue, 254.9743, an established blues club; also, **The Sunset Grill and Tap** is known for its international array of beers, 130 Brighton Avenue, 254.1331.

Somerville

Once primarily a working-class suburb, Somerville has grown increasingly popular with students and yuppies crowded—or priced—out of Cambridge. There's a steadily growing restaurant/club scene, whose standouts include: **Dali** (★★★$$), an authentic and lively Spanish restaurant with irresistible *tapas,* 415 Washington Street, 661.3254; **Redbones** (★★$), for real Southern barbecue, 55 Chester St, 628.2200; the **Elephant Walk** (★★$$), a Cambodian-French venue guaranteed to intrigue the most jaded palate, 70 Union Square, 623.9939; **Johnny D's Uptown** for rock, 17 Holland Street, 776.2004; and the **Willow Jazz Club** (self-explanatory), 699 Broadway, 623.9874.

America's first marathon and one of the oldest annual sporting events in the country has been run every year since 1897, except in 1918 because of World War I. The Boston Marathon is run on the third Monday in April, which is Patriots' Day in Massachusetts and a day off from work for many. Early in the morning, walls of enthusiastic fans line both sides of the hilly route, which begins in Hopkinton and ends in front of the John Hancock Tower in Back Bay, home of the race's major corporate sponsor. The famous course's most challenging moment is "Heartbreak Hill" in Newton. Boston's unpredictable weather and wind can be friend or foe to the runners: in 1967 it snowed on the morning of the race, while in 1976 the temperature at the start was 96 degrees. The Boston Athletic Association has organized the race since its inception, when 15 runners started and 10 finished. Women were officially admitted to the race in 1972. In 1990 more than 9,000 runners participated, with $350,000-plus awarded in prize money.

Charlotte Moore

Executive Director, Cambridge Discovery Tourist and Resident Information Services

The **Head-of-the-Charles:** the world's largest regatta, complemented by beautiful New England autumn colors.

Bicycling around the **Charles River Basin.**

Birding in **Mount Auburn Cemetery,** the world's first garden cemetery.

The street musicians in **Harvard Square.**

Brunch at the **Charles Hotel.**

Christmas revels at **Sanders Theatre** at Harvard.

Walking up **Brattle Street** (Tory Row) with a dog.

Picnicking at **JFK Park** in Cambridge.

Jogging in a circle over any two bridges on the Charles.

Espresso and pizza at **Cremaldi's.**

Avant-garde art at the **List Visual Arts Center** at MIT—a stunning gallery.

Book-browsing in Cambridge's bookstores; you need a day for this.

The Wednesday morning antique auction at **Hubley Auctioneers Company.**

Wandering around the 19th-century Federal-style houses in **East Cambridge.**

Taking a riverboat cruise on the Charles—pure visual elegance.

Checking out the jazz scene in Cambridge.

Meeting my best friend at the **"Info Booth"** in Harvard Square.

Susan G. Berk

Uncommon Boston Ltd., Custom Tours and Special Events

The view of Boston from the revolving **Spinnaker Lounge and Restaurant** at the Hyatt Hotel in Cambridge.

Taking the **Airport Water Shuttle** to or from Logan.

Enjoying lunch at the outdoor cafe at **29 Newbury.**

Browsing at the gift boutique at the **Women's Educational and Industrial Union.**

Attending a preview auction at the **Skinner Gallery** on Newbury Street—great jewelry, rugs, paintings.

Sipping a margarita at the **Cottonwood Cafe.**

A game of pool with friends at **Boston Billiards.**

Participating in some of Boston's great walks for AIDS, hunger, or women's health.

The architectural contrasts, from the old brick of Beacon Hill to the glass **John Hancock Tower.**

The energy and vibrancy that comes with the 100,000 new college students each year.

The Mounted Unit of the Boston Police Department first rode city streets in 1883, making it the longest continuous mounted unit in the country.

Gerald Peary

Visiting Professor, Boston University School of Communication; freelance journalist and film critic

Pickup basketball at the **Central Square YMCA** in Cambridge. The noontime games are for scrappy, spirited old-timers, ranging from 25 to 55, and are played out on the Y's patented mini-court.

Zembla Books on Holland Street in Somerville, for used books in extraordinary shape at the best prices in the Boston area. Few Bostonians know about this off-the-track store.

Harvard House of Pizza on Massachusetts Avenue in Cambridge, for the pepperoni-and-mushroom combo of your dreams, baked by a Greek pizza man who resembles a young John Travolta.

For cool, smart, conceptual art and the most adventurous shows in town, the **Akin Gallery** on Kneeland Street. The **Space Gallery,** around the corner on South Street, is great for potent artwork and installations with a political conscience.

The **Dolphin** restaurant on Massachusetts Avenue in Cambridge, where everybody takes their out-of-town parents for cheap, agreeable plates of piled-on fresh seafood.

The perfect corned beef on rye at **Pick-a-Chick** in Brookline. And **Rubin's Kosher Delicatessen** in Brookline for hand-sliced Rumanian pastrami.

Filene's Basement in Boston, the only place around for first-class men's suits (silk and wool) at less than half their regular price.

Am-Vets in Brighton, for used sweaters, T-shirts, and other funky hand-me-downs, and Cambridge's **Garment District,** for post-punk clothes junk. Lace up those bulky black Doc Martin's and you're ready for a "slacker" life on Boston's Kenmore Square.

The **Taqueria** at Davis Square. Buy a burrito as an excuse to pile on the fabulous slew of free salsas: hot, HOT, and HOT!!!!!

Foreign films on the huge, vintage 1933 screen at the **Coolidge Corner Theatre** in Brookline. And the **Brattle Theatre** in Harvard Square for the most inspired double-bills in revival-house America.

Finally, let's spend some money! **Mama Maria's** in the North End has sumptuous Northern Italian food. Ask for chef **Ray Gillespie's** exotic tomato and/or mushroom specials. The **Harvest Restaurant** in Harvard Square features splendid meat and wild-

game dishes in empyrean reduced sauces. Insist on **John Whyte** as your waiter, a charming, gregarious native Irishman with a lovely banter of jokes and blarney.

The best low-price lunch in the USA is the burnt-end barbecue sandwich with a side of coleslaw and a cooling sliver of watermelon at **Jake and Earl's Dixie BBQ** in Inman Square.

For the best view of Boston, cross the **MIT Bridge** into Cambridge, then walk along **Memorial Drive,** peering across the Charles River. There's the Hub in all its splendor, and you can see that Beacon Hill really is a hill.

Day Trips

Boston is a wonderful place to explore, yet when you've had your fill of city life, it's easy to leave town for some stimulating day—or weekend—trips. In just a few hours, public transportation or a car can take you to the rocky beaches of **Cape Ann** or the dunes of **Cape Cod;** the green hills of the **Berkshires;** the beckoning mountains, lakes, and fall colors of **New Hampshire** and **Vermont;** or **Maine's** coastal villages and idyllic islands. And if Boston begins to seem too large an urban center, in only one hour you can escape to **Providence, Rhode Island;** if that's too small for you, in four hours you can be in **New York City.** Many New England spots have seasonal attractions, but don't let the off-season keep you away—it's often their nicest, quietest time. Cape Cod and the islands in winter, for example, have their own compelling moods. A great source for guidebooks on day trips and travel throughout New England—or the world, for that matter—is **The Globe Corner Bookstore,** 3 School Street, 523.6658; and 49 Palmer Street at Harvard Square in Cambridge, 497.6277. Also, get a wealth of free information on what to see and do in Massachusetts by calling or writing the **Massachusetts Office of Travel and Tourism,** 100 Cambridge Street, 13th floor, Boston 02202, 727.3201 or 800/447.6277. The following are destination ideas rather than itineraries; arm yourself with information on hours and prices before you go—or just head out with a good map or two and a spirit of exploration.

North to the North Shore

Head north of Boston for the best clams in the world. While on the quest, there's plenty more to see. The infamous **Saugus Strip** along Route 1, for instance, is an eyesore to some and beloved by others for its Miracle Mile-style roadside signs and attendant establishments, vintage kitsch inspired by America's love affair with the auto. This stretch of Route 1 is home base for several of America's biggest, gaudiest restaurants. A giant cactus sign and herd of life-size cattle heralds **Hilltop Steak House** ("The Hilltop"), home of red-meat-and-potatoes overeating, Route 1 on the southbound side, 233.7700. A Polynesian theme reigns at **Kowloon,** located across from The Hilltop on Route 1 northbound, 233.9719; and for Chinese food in Disneylike ambience, there's gargantuan **Weylu's,** Route 1 northbound, 233.1632. As you ride along, keep an eye out for the **Leaning Tower of Pizza,** a miniature golf course with a towering tyrannosaurus rex, the ship-shaped restaurant, and other quirky sights.

Of a different historical slant is the **Saugus Iron Works National Historic Site,** 244 Central Street, 233.0050 (take the Main Street exit), a reconstruction of the first integrated iron works in North America (created in 1646). The site includes a furnace, a forge, seven water-powered wheels, and a rolling and slitting mill. A

well-kept Saugus secret is the **Breakheart Reservation,** 177 Forest Street, 233.0834, a park with 600 acres of oak, hemlock, pine-covered hills, two freshwater lakes, 10 miles of trails, and lots of birds.

Take Route 1A north from Boston to Route 129 to **Marblehead,** a picture-postcard New England seaside town with early New World flavor and historical attractions, splendid views of the ocean, plus boutiques and good seafood restaurants. It's a perfect place for a leisurely day of walking and poking around. The **Old** Town section predates the American Revolution and boasts Federal-style sea captains' homes and neat cottages. For information, call the **Marblehead Chamber of Commerce** at 631.2868.

Salem, "the witch city," is a short drive from Marblehead on Route 114 to Route 1A. The notorious witchcraft trials of 1692, one of the colony's most troubled chapters, caused 19 people to be hanged before the hysterical Puritan populace regained reason. Pick up self-guided walking tour maps (and any other tourist information you may need) from the **Chamber of Commerce** at Old Town Hall on Front Street, 508/744.0004.

Don't miss the **Salem Maritime National Historic Site,** 174 Derby Street, 508/744.4323, where American maritime history is enshrined in the **Custom House, Derby House/Wharf, Bonded Warehouse, West India Goods Store,** and lighthouse. Explore three centuries of historic Salem at the **Essex Institute Museum Neighborhood,** comprising a library, museum, and seven period houses, 132 Essex Street (museum), 508/744.3390. Less critical to see, but beloved by kids, is the **Salem Witch Museum,** 19½ Washington Square North, 508/744.1692. Visit the inspiration for **Nathaniel Hawthorne's** novel, The House of the Seven Gables, 54 Turner Street, 508/744.0991; and the **Peabody Museum,** 161 Essex Street, 508/745.9500, for its collections of maritime history, ethnology, natural history, and Asian export. If you don't want to direct your own steps, take the **Salem Trolley** tour, 508/744.5463.

Continue north on Route 1A to **Beverly** for an after-noon of Vaudeville-esque **Marco the Magi's Production of Le Grand David and His Own Spectacular Magic Company** at the 750-seat **Cabot Street Theatre**, 286 Cabot Street (for the Sunday show) or at the more intimate 450-seat **Larcom Theatre**, 13 Wallis Street (for the Saturday show), both 508/927.3677. Or catch a Broadway musical (often with Broadway stars) or celebrity concert at the **North Shore Music Theatre**, 162 Dunham Road, 508/922.8500.

En route northeast from Beverly to Gloucester is **Manchester-by-the-Sea,** the first North Shore sum-mer resort, serving Proper Bostonians in the 1840s. The pretty-as-a-picture **Singing Beach** is a favorite for Boston day-trippers. To avoid the parking hassle, rise early and take a morning beach train on the **Rockport Line Commuter Rail** from **North Station** (722.3200). When you've had enough sunning, swimming, and clambering over rocks, it's a short, pleasant walk into town for a bite to eat before the train ride back.

To drive **Cape Ann's** rugged shore, continue north on Route 127 to **Gloucester.** You can also travel here via ferry from the **Rowes Wharf** in Boston on **Mass Bay Lines,** 542.8000. The largest town on the North Shore, Gloucester was settled as a fishing colony in 1623 and is still an important port. Its famous landmark is **Leonard Craske's** statue the *Gloucester Fisherman,* honoring the intrepid fishers who have died at sea. The fishing fleet is blessed annually, with attendant colorful festivities in late June. Whale-watching excursions leave from here.

A favorite pastime is eating fresh lobster. Two local restaurants that are especially good: **Bistro at 2 Main Street,** 508/281.8055, and **White Rainbow,** 508/281.0017. Or spend an illuminating evening at the **Gloucester Stage Company,** housed in a rehabbed fish factory; the plays of patron and resident play-wright **Israel Horovitz** often deal with the local way of life, 267 East Main Street, 508/281.4099.

By day, visit the **Cape Ann Historical Association,** 27 Pleasant Street, 508/283.0455, to see the stunning collection of 19th-century American painter **Fitz Hugh Lane's** luminous views of **Gloucester Harbor** and is-lands. Perched on rocks overlooking the harbor is "Beauport," the **Sleeper-McCann House,** 75 Eastern Point Boulevard, 508/283.0800. Beauport was built in the early 1900s by architect/interior designer **Henry Davis Sleeper,** who greatly influenced contemporary tastes and style-setters, including **Isabella Stewart Gardner.** Within are 18th- and 19th-century decorative arts and furnishings.

The Hilltop Steak House, a kitschy fixture off of Boston's Route 1, claims the highest head count of any restaurant in the country—as many as 30,000 customers a week.

Then move on to the **Hammond Castle Museum,** 80 Hesperus Avenue, 508/283.2080 (recorded information) and 800/283.1643. The medieval-style castle was the humble home of in-ventor **Dr. John Hays Hammond, Jr.,** whose brainstorms included shav-ing cream, the car starter, electrified toy trains, the forerunner of stereo-phonic sound, and the precursor to remote control—more than 437 patented inven-tions. Hammond's resplen-dent digs contain medieval furnishings, paintings, and sculpture. Monthly organ con-certs are played on the 8,600-pipe organ, the largest in a private American home. Tours are given year-round.

A short drive up Cape Ann from Gloucester is tiny **Rockport,** a fishing-community-turned-artists' colony that can be happily meandered in a day. (It's a dry town, by the way.) Parking can be difficult in the center of town unless you arrive as early as the birds, so take the commuter train from **North Station** (722.3200) in Boston if you can—it's a very pretty ride. Rockport's light is particularly beautiful at day's end and in early spring and late fall. The **Toad Hall Book Store,** 51 Main Street, 508/546.7323, is wonderful for old-time friendliness and service and has a large selection on local geography, history, and lore. The more touristy restaurants and shops are densely clustered on **Bearskin Neck** (closed to cars); for more interesting galler-ies and restaurants, walk along Main Street (where, incidentally, *Mermaids* was filmed). Just beyond town is a windswept haven and public park, the 68-acre **Halibut Point State Park and Reservation** (no swim-ming) off Gott Avenue, 508/546.2997. An acclaimed annual event worth coming out for is the **Rockport Chamber Music Festival,** 508/546.7391.

Heading inland on Route 133 from Gloucester is **Essex,** with a staggering concentration of antique shops in a single-mile stretch. Stop for sustenance at super-casual, rambling **Woodman's,** a North Shore favorite, where **Lawrence Woodman** first dipped clams in bat-ter and deep-fried them in 1916, Main Street, 508/768.6451. Come early or late to avoid huge family

crowds, but if you can't, the steamers, lobsters, clams, scallops, chowder, etc., are worth a wait. Nearby **Ipswich,** also prized for its clams and perhaps more so for its beautiful beaches, has more 17th-century houses than any other town in America. On **Ipswich Bay,** the **Crane Memorial Reservation** includes four miles of shoreline and excellent sandy beaches. The old Crane residence—the **Great House**—hosts week-end concerts and art lectures during the summer and has gorgeous Italianate gardens with sea views.

Near the northeastern tip of Massachusetts, via Route 1A North, is **Newburyport,** once a shipbuilding center and birthplace of the **US Coast Guard.** Stroll along the waterfront park, promenade, and through the restored commercial district, an enclave of three-story brick-and-granite buildings. For many, the town has gone overboard gussying itself up for tourists, but it's a nice place to while away a few hours if you're in the mood for shopping, eating, or strolling.

One of Massachusetts' treasures is the **Parker River National and State Wildlife Refuge** on **Plum Island,** 508/465.5753, which offers unsullied beauty, refreshing sea air, and glimpses of wildlife. From Newburyport, head back on Route 1A to Route 113 to **Newbury** and watch carefully for signs to Plum Island and the wildlife refuge. It's headquartered at the old Coast Guard lighthouse at the island's northern end. The 4,662-acre refuge has six miles of sandy beaches, hiking trails, observation towers for spotting more than 300 bird species, saltwater and freshwater marshes, sand dunes, surf fishing, nature-study hikes, cross-country skiing, beach plum and cranberry picking, waterfowl hunting, and clamming. Come early on summer weekends because the refuge closes when its quota of 240 cars is reached, often by 9AM. It then reopens at 3PM, so if you're shut out early, spend the day in Newburyport and try again later. In late summer and autumn the marshland takes on rich, soft coloring and the sunsets are breathtaking. The island really empties out after the summer.

Northwest of Boston is **Lowell,** America's first successful planned industrial complex and now a National and State Historical Park (Visitor Center, 246 Market Street, 508/459.1000). Located at the confluence of the **Concord** and **Merrimack rivers,** Lowell was transformed from a sleepy agricultural village into an industrial powerhouse in 1822 by Boston merchant **Francis Cabot Lowell** and fellow investors. Lowell's **Boston Manufacturing Company** had already successfully developed a textile mass-production system driven by water-powered looms in **Waltham.** Lowell (the town) first played a pioneering role in the American industrial revolution, gradually became a squalid environment after exploiting women mill workers and immigrants, slowly began to improve under labor-reform movements, then floundered as the United States' economy shifted. Now revitalized by high-tech industries, its fascinating past has been preserved. Today you can tour the mill complexes, operating gatehouses, workers' housing, and a five-and-a-half-mile canal system. Self-guided tour maps are available at the visitor center, including one for **Jack Kerouac's** Lowell. Guided interpretive mill and canal tours are offered numerous times daily during the summer; reser-

vations are required. The **Lowell Heritage State Park Waterpower Exhibit** is open daily at 25 Shattuck Street, 508/453.1950. The town is also the birthplace of **James Abbott McNeill Whistler.** The **Whistler House Museum of Art,** 243 Worthen Street, 508/452.7641, displays 19th- and 20th-century American art, including works by Whistler.

Bostonians and visitors alike go beyond Massachusetts' northern border for fall foliage splendor, hiking, cross-country and downhill skiing, rock climbing,

canoeing, shopping at factory outlet stores, tranquility, and natural beauty. To determine which places and recreational activities appeal to you most, contact the **New Hampshire Office of Travel and Tourism,** 603/271.2666; **Vermont Travel and Tourism,** 802/828.3239; or the **Maine Publicity Bureau,** 207/582.9300.

Near Northwest

A few miles northwest of **Cambridge** on Route 2A are **Lexington** and **Concord,** historic towns where the first military encounters of the American Revolution took place, also rich in literary history. Concord grapes were first cultivated here, as were the ideas of **Emerson, Hawthorne, Thoreau,** and **Louisa May Alcott.** The most notable among the many historic sites are the **Lexington Battle Green**—or **Common** (Visitor Center, 1875 Massachusetts Avenue, 862.1450). Here the first skirmish of the Revolutionary War broke out on 19 April 1775 between the Concord-bound British troops and Colonial Minutemen, alerted earlier by messengers on horseback of the Redcoats' approach. (A reenactment of the Battle of Lexington is staged every April.) The second battle of the day was fought in neighboring Concord, where the citizen militia attacked and drove the British soldiers from **North Bridge. Daniel Chester French's** famous *Minuteman* statue now stands guard over the bridge. The **Minute Man National Historical Park** encompasses 750 acres in Concord, Lexington, and Lincoln, commemorating the start of the colonies' War for Independence. The park is a narrow strip running on either side of **Battle Road** (a portion of Route 2A). It begins beyond **Lexington Center** with the **Battle Road Visitor Center** located at one end, off Route 2A on Airport Road in Lexington, 862.7753; and the **North Bridge Visitor Center** on the other end, west of Monument Street on Liberty Street in Concord, 508/369.6993. Though interpretive films and information are on hand, you'll need a bit of imagination to conjure scenes of strife in this bucolic setting. For sophisticated Provençal sustenance, stop in at **Aigo Bistro,** 84 Thoreau Street, 508/371.1333, the latest venture of **Moncef Meddeb,** whose greatest hits to date include L'Espalier and the Harvard Book Store Cafe.

Concord's most precious asset—although sometimes not treated that way—is the **Walden Pond Reservation,** open daily from 5AM to dusk and located along Route 126, 508/369.3254. The quiet pond is 62 glimmering acres nestled in 333 woody ones. The transcendentalist and free-thinking **Henry David Thoreau** lived and wrote alongside the pond from 1845 to 1847 in a 10-by-15-foot hand-hewn cabin. Visitors to the reservation will find woods and pathways descending to smooth water, where sandbars slope to hundred-foot depths. Bostonians delight in this gentle place, so it gets overcrowded and overworked as summer progresses, but slowly recovers during fall and winter—the best time for waterside contemplation.

Architecture enthusiasts inevitably make the trek to the **Gropius House** in **Lincoln,** 68 Baker Bridge Road, 227.3956. Follow Route 2 West to Route 126 South, and watch for Baker Bridge Road. German architect **Walter Gropius** built the house in 1938, the year after he came to America. His iconoclastic modern residence introduced the **Bauhaus** principles of function and simplicity to this country. The house's industrial quallty is derived from its commercial components, a revolutionary architectural approach at the time. Gropius' residence includes furniture designed by him, **Marcel Breuer,** and others, and creates an extraordinary quality of place. The house is part of the **Society for the Preservation of New England Antiquities'** historic homes collection, and SPNEA offers excellent guided tours. Nearby, and also located in Lincoln, is the **DeCordova and Dana Museum and Sculpture Park,** Sandy Pond Road, 259.8355. The castlike museum shows work by mostly New England contemporary artists in its galleries and 35-acre sculpture park. July and August feature outdoor concerts in a shady grove. This is a gorgeous spot for a picnic and stroll any time of year.

Heading back toward Boston, in **Waltham,** take in a dazzling show at the **Rose Art Museum** at Brandeis College, 736.3434; also check what's on stage at the college's **Spingold Theatre,** 736.3400. The best restaurant in this area—it's up there in the Boston pantheon—is the **Tuscan Grill,** 361 Moody Street, 891.5486.

West to the Berkshires

You can take the Massachusetts Turnpike, a.k.a. I-90, west from Boston all the way to New York State, or the more northerly and scenic Route 2, which also traverses the state. A popular destination west of Boston is **Old Sturbridge Village,** on US 20 off I-84, 508/347.5383. The historic museum, encompassing more than 200 acres, re-creates an early 19th-century New England agricultural community. Its vintage displays include a clock gallery, folk art and portraiture, firearms and militia accoutrements, a working farm, blacksmith, shoemaker, potter, and cooper, and gardens of culinary and medicinal herbs. Sturbridge features participatory activities and is perfect for a family outing.

The **Berkshires** refers to the westernmost part of Massachusetts, a verdant region dappled with rivers, lakes, and gentle hills. It's a romantic and serene area with twin legacies: culture and leisure. For information, call or write the **Berkshire Visitor's Bureau,** The Berkshire Common, Pittsfield 01201, 413/443.9186 or 800/237.5747. From March to early April you can see treetapping, watch sap reduce into real maple syrup, and savor the precious end product. Nestled within mountains, the Berkshires offers hiking, camping, biking, fishing, canoeing, fall foliage, skiing—and welcoming country inns to retire to after the day's activities. Head for the town of **Becket,** off Route 2, the summer home of **Jacob's Pillow Dance Festival,** 413/243.0745, the oldest dance festival in the country, where you can see performances by some of the world's most exciting companies. Picnic under the trees before a performance. Stay and dine nearby at the **Federal House,** 102 Main Street (Route 102) in Lee, 413/243.1824. Visit famous **Tanglewood,** summer home to the Boston Symphony Orchestra, Route 183, Lenox, 413/637.1600, summer only (or in Boston call 266.1492). The lush 200-acre estate is a popular destination for a one-day trip from Boston; bring a picnic and dine en plein air. The world-renowned **Tanglewood Music Festival** is held here annually from July through August, and other events include the **Popular Artists Series** (throughout the summer) and **Labor Day Weekend Jazz Festival.**

Not far from **Lee** and **Lenox** in the Berkshires is **Stockbridge,** a perfectly cast New England town known for its **Norman Rockwell Museum** on Main Street, 413/298.3822; and for the landmark **Red Lion Inn,** also on Main Street, 413/298.5545, which has been there since its beginnings as a hostelry in 1773. The well-preserved inn provides rural charm year-round with a lobby fireplace, a cat or two, music from the grand piano, and rockers along the front porch ideal for reading the Sunday paper.

Just beyond Stockbridge is **Chesterwood,** 413/298.3579, the former studio and summer residence of the prolific sculptor **Daniel Chester French,** who created **Abraham Lincoln's** famous image in the **Washington, DC,** memorial and the *Minuteman* statue in Concord, not to mention many works around Boston. Casts, models, tools, drawings, books, and French's personal belongings are displayed here. There's a garden and nature trail, too.

North from here on Route 7/20 is **Williamstown,** home of **Williams College** and the **Sterling and Francine Clark Art Institute,** 225 South Street, 413/458.9545. The institute houses a wonderful collection from the 15th to the 19th centuries of paintings, drawings, prints, and antique silver. The **Williamstown Theatre Festival,** 413/597.3366, is like a summer camp for well-known stars of stage and screen. By day, detour on Route 20 to the **Hancock Shaker Village,** 413/443.0188, a restoration of the Shaker community founded here in 1790. Twenty buildings have been restored, including a remarkable round stone barn. Shakers lived here until 1960.

South to the South Shore

Before opting to leave Boston for more distant destinations, spend an afternoon island-hopping along the lovely local chain of **Boston Harbor Islands** (see "Sojourns to the Sea: The Boston Harbor Islands" on page 68 for more information). Bostonians often lose sight of them, just beyond what was once the city's front door, and yet the islands offer bird-watching, hiking, picnicking, walking, and all sorts of other recreational activities. Enjoy cooling sea breezes on the boat rides to and from the islands, even on the sultriest summer days.

For an unusual architectural tour, from Boston take I-93 South to Route 138 South, heading southwest inland to **North Easton. Oliver Ames,** manufacturer of the common shovel that helped to build America—as well as a railroad tycoon and Massachusetts governor from 1887 to 1890, whose mansion is located at 355 Commonwealth Avenue in Back Bay—chose **Henry**

Hobson Richardson to design numerous public buildings for North Easton, manufacturing home of the Ames shovel.

In the course of nine years, Richardson built a library, train station, civic center, and other buildings in his characteristic Romanesque rugged masonry style, with other major artisans playing important roles. (Richardson's friend and occasional collaborator, **Frederick Law Olmsted,** designed the complementary North Easton Common.) The result: a sampler of late

19th-century civic architecture that vividly portrays Richardson's ideas.

Head for gentle surf on the South Shore. Motor down I-93 South to Route 3A, the winding shore road to **Hingham** with its graceful town center, home of the **Old Ship Meetinghouse,** Main Street, 749.1679. This is the oldest wooden church in continuous use in America, built in 1681, with pulpit, pews, and galleries dating from 1755. Visit a rare pastoral setting made by human design: **World's End Reservation,** a 250-acre part of a harborside estate designed by Frederick Law Olmsted, and one of the **Trustees of Reservations'** beautiful park holdings. It is located at the end of Martin's Lane, 749.8956. Forget about Boston's proximity until you reach the park's edge on the water, where you'll find unusual urban views. Then take a peek at **Boston Light,** the oldest operating lighthouse in America, easily viewed from **Nantasket Beach** on Route 22 in **Hull,** a teeny town at the end

of a peninsula stretching north of Hingham into **Boston Harbor.** Nantasket Beach is a two-mile stretch of beach with a bathhouse, a playground, a promenade, a 1928 carousel, and the **Hull Lifesaving Museum,** 1117 Nantasket Avenue, 925.5433. The beach is also accessible by ferry from **Long Wharf** on Boston's Waterfront, Bay State Cruises, 723.7800. Continue south on Route 3A to **Duxbury** and **Duxbury Beach,** one of the finest barrier beaches on the Eastern Shore and a paradise for birders and walkers year-round.

On the way to Cape Cod, visit **Plimoth Plantation** in Plymouth, Route 3A, Exit 6 off 3 South, 508/746.6544, a "living museum" of 17th-century Plymouth; the famed rock, as well as a replica of the *Mayflower,* are located at the center of town. Also in Plymouth is **Cranberry World,** 255 Water Street, 508/747.2350, with two outdoor working bogs—quite a sight, and you can buy the tart, delicious berry made into all sorts of treats.

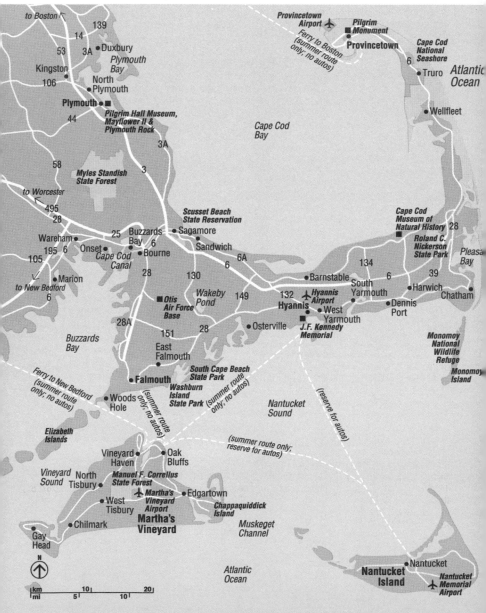

Once a prosperous fishing and whaling center, **Cape Cod** is shaped like a large fishhook curving 75 miles into the Atlantic and gleaming with hundreds of fresh-water ponds and lakes. Bordering **Cape Cod Bay** and the ocean are resort communities with beaches, clam shacks, summer theater, etc., extending all the way to **Provincetown** at the tip, where the **Pilgrims** first landed. Much of the cape has been intensely developed, causing erosion to whittle away some lovely land, but fortunately residents are forcing the pace to slow. One of the state's great treasures is the **Cape Cod National Seashore,** a protected 30-mile-long system of pristine beaches, woodlands, and marshes, culminating in the magnificent Provincetown sand dunes (headquarters: Marconi Station area, South Wellfleet, information 508/349.3785). For more on Cape Cod, including campsites, call or write the **Cape Cod Chamber of Commerce,** Mid-Cape Highway, Hyannis 02601, 508/362.3225. By car take I-93 South to 3 South, and cross the **Sagamore Bridge** onto the Cape to Route 6 East (and get a good look at the imposing **Cape Cod Canal**). Or ride the ferry from Commonwealth Pier on Boston's Waterfront, Bay State Cruises, 723.7800. You can go round-trip in one day to Provincetown, although the best plan is to stay at least one night.

At **Falmouth** (South on Route 28 from 3 South) visit the **Ashumet Holly Reservation and Wildlife Sanctuary,** open year-round, to see a small, unusual sanctuary with many holly varieties, 508/563.6390. Enjoy the Cape Cod natural environment at the **Massachusetts Audubon Society's Wellfleet Bay Wildlife Sanctuary** on the bay side of Route 6 in Wellfleet, 508/349.2615. Both **Wellfleet** and **Truro** are among Cape Cod's loveliest places. But the most special place to be—the timing depends on your tastes—is Provincetown. An artists' and Portuguese fishing community that welcomes everyone, Provincetown's population swells from 3,800 in the off-season to 25,000 people in summer. It's a gay haven that has a sensuous atmosphere and active tourist life from Memorial Day weekend until summer's end, but it has a quiet side also. No matter what time of year, it feels comfortable and safe here; return in winter when "P-town" has shrunk and you'll feel as if you have the town and an ocean to yourself. Endowed with the loveliest National Seashore stretch, the town's outskirts are wonderful for bicycling and jogging. For a sweeping view of the tiny town and its ocean setting, climb the **Pilgrim Monument** (open year-round). The tallest granite structure in the United States, the tower hovers high on the village skyline. Visit the funky, fascinating **Heritage Museum** near its base, open summer only. **Commercial Street** is indeed the Main Street of P-town, where the greatest concentration of restaurants, shops, and lodgings converge. The easiest way to find good accommodations and cuisine, including special off-season listings, is to call or write the very helpful **Provincetown Chamber of Commerce** office in advance, Box 1017, Provincetown 02657. The office is located at 307 Commercial Street, MacMillan Wharf, 508/487.3424.

Martha's Vineyard, an island off Cape Cod southeast of Boston, is another well-loved vacation spot; ferry reservations for cars are often sold out for summer weekends by Christmas. The Vineyard has wonderful beaches, sunsets, sailing, walking, picnicking, and bicycling, but bring the bug spray. Its population balloons from 12,000 to 100,000 in the summer. Down-

island—on the eastern side—are **Vineyard Haven, Oak Bluffs,** and **Edgartown.** The latter is the most popular with tourists and has rich architectural styles from saltbox to Greek Revival. Up-island—on the western side—are **Tisbury, Chilmark,** and **Gay Head,** which is known for its varicolored clay cliffs. The Vineyard, like Cape Cod and Nantucket, is as wonderful or more so out of season. To get there, ride the ferry from Woods Hole, Steamship Authority, 508/540.2022; or from New Bedford, Cape Island Express Lines, 508/997.1688, passengers only. (A historic and still-important seaport, **New Bedford** has an excellent **Whaling Museum,** 508/997.0046, and discount shopping, too.) Seasonal, passengers-only ferries also leave for the Vineyard from Hyannis, 508/775.7185, and Falmouth, 508/548.4800.

For information on Vineyard events, places, and accommodations, call or write the **Martha's Vineyard Chamber of Commerce,** P.O. Box 1698, Vineyard Haven 02568. The office is located on Beach Road, 508/693.0085. Eat fresh and delicious fish at the elegant, expensive **L'Etoile** in Edgartown, 508/627.5187; at the **Beach Plum Inn,** located off North Road en route to Menemsha, 508/645.9454; or at **Oyster Bar** in Oak Bluffs, 508/693.3300. In the latter town, wander among the **Carpenter Gothic Cottages,** a Methodist revival campground of Victorian Gothic cottages from the late 1800s, oddly ornate with filigree trim.

Located 30 miles southeast off the mainland of Cape Cod, **Nantucket** is a historic whaling island known as the "Gray Lady of the Sea" for its gently weathering clapboards, and for the clothes worn by its Quaker settlers. Nowadays, the island is a summer playground for the unflashy, monied crowd (keep an eye out for the famous Nantucket-red pants). When it's sweltering in Boston, the sea breezes keep Nantucket cool and its serene weathered beauty is restorative, with gray-shingled houses and rose-covered cottages, moors of heather, cranberry bogs, and gnarled pines. There's absolutely no need for a car here because you can walk, bicycle, or ride a moped from one end of the island to the other. Arrive via ferry from either Hyannis, Martha's Vineyard, or Woods Hole. You can also fly to **Nantucket Memorial Airport,** 508/325.5300. For tourist information, call or write the **Nantucket Island Chamber of Commerce,** Main Street, Nantucket 02554, 508/228.1700.

Little **Nantucket Town** is the exceedingly picturesque and quaint center of activity. The town is packed with interesting shops and restaurants. The deli-style **Expresso Cafe,** 508/228.6930, is easy on the budget; **21 Federal,** 508/228.2121, and the **Boarding House,** 508/228.9622, aren't, but they're worth every penny. For the ultimate in laid-back (if top-dollar) charm, plan

Day Trips

a visit to the **Wauwinet,** an historic inn surrounded by beaches at the very edge of civilization, 508/228.8768. All of the island's beaches are dazzling and easily accessible; as long as you reserve well ahead, you'll fare well at any of the island's reasonably priced B-and-Bs.

Beyond the commonwealth's southern border, yet within a one- to two-hour ride, are **Providence** and **Newport, Rhode Island.** Providence is the capital of the "Ocean State" and its industrial and commercial center, as well as a major port. The city was founded by **Roger Williams,** who was banished from Boston by the single-minded and often intolerant Puritans. A city guide and map of landmarks is available at the **Greater Providence Convention and Visitor's Bureau,** 30 Exchange Terrace 02903, 401/274.1636. It's worth a special trip to one of **George Germon** and **Johanne Killeen's** renowned restaurants: **Al Forno** or **Lucky's,** both at 577 South Main Street, 401/273.9760. Al Forno offers rustic Italian-style decor and food, the latter mainly grilled over hardwood or roasted in a brick oven; Lucky's tends toward French provincial in decor, but the cuisine is similar to Al Forno, with large portions at moderate prices. For an evening out (the **Trinity Repertory Company,** 401/351.4242, is nationally renowned), try going round-trip by train from **South Station** in Boston.

South of Providence is Newport, which still echoes its origins as a colonial seaport. The town has always been associated with opulence and the sea: yachts, the Navy, competitive sailing, and seaside palaces of the rich. Annual celebrations include the star-studded **Newport Jazz Festival,** the country's oldest. The **Cliff Walk** is Newport's other most popular attraction, a three-and-a-half-mile shoreline path and a **National Historic Walking Trail,** with the Atlantic Ocean on one side and the famous summer mansions on the other.

Bests

Jim Koch

Brewer and Founder, Samuel Adams Boston Lager, Boston Beer Company

Le Meridien's chocolate buffet on Saturday afternoons—all the chocolate dessert you can eat.

Doyles Bar, on Washington Street in Jamaica Plain, offers a full range of beers from the Boston Beer Company, including experimental beers not available anywhere else, on draft.

Harvard Square on a Saturday night—watching the jugglers and listening to the musicians. **Tracy Chapman** started here.

Bike rides along the **Charles River** in summer and fall, from Watertown to the Science Museum along the Boston side then past Harvard and MIT on the Cambridge side.

Browsing for antique prints and books at **Goodspeed's Book Shop** in the Old South Meeting House on Beacon Hill.

Senate President Bulger's **Saint Patrick's Day Breakfast** and politician roast in South Boston (it's broadcast on cable). No one escapes unscathed, and Bulger has a wonderful singing voice.

Day Trips

Fresh oysters at **Union Oyster House;** prime rib and cornbread at **Durgin-Park** and **Bluefish Cafe;** and a three-pound lobster at **Legal Sea Foods.**

A walk in **World's End,** a beautiful park in Hingham—rolling meadows and a great view of Boston.

Saturday morning shopping at **Haymarket,** where bronze sculptures of garbage are cast into the sidewalk and street.

A Saturday afternoon tour of the **Boston Beer Company Brewery.**

Cynthia Hadzi
Exhibitions Coordinator, Harvard University's Carpenter Center for Visual Arts
Dimitri Hadzi
Sculptor/Professor Emeritus, Harvard University

Everything at the **Museum of Fine Arts,** especially the special Japanese wing and garden; weekend afternoon concerts at the **Isabella Stewart Gardner Museum;** the **Institute of Contemporary Art (ICA),** which has a lively exhibit program; the **Fogg, Sackler,** and **Busch museums** at Harvard—fabulous collections; the **Carpenter Center for Visual Arts** (the only **Corbusier** building in the United States), for contemporary exhibits; and the incomparable film program of the **Harvard Film Archive.**

The art galleries along **Newbury Street,** as well as the bookshops, stores, and cafes.

The **American Repertory Theatre** at Harvard and the newly revitalized **Hasty Pudding Theatre.**

Free summertime concerts of the **Harvard Chamber Orchestra** conducted by **Leon Kirchner,** in Harvard's splendid **Sanders Theatre.**

The **Boston Athenaeum,** an utterly Bostonian private library, which occasionally offers exhibits that are open to the public.

The **Charles River**—winding through the city, its activity makes everything seem more human.

The fountain and landscaping at **Post Office Square** (the fountain is by **Howard Ben Tre**), an oasis in the middle of the city.

Boston Public Garden (and not just for Swan Boats or ducklings!).

Trinity Church and the other wonderful Henry H. Richardson buildings scattered around, plus the reflection of Trinity Church in the **Hancock Building** (from here, check the views over the city, too).

The renovated houses around the **South End** and in **Charlestown.**

Magnolias in spring along **Marlborough Street.**

Harvard Square for bookshops, the **Brattle Cinema,** **Casablanca** restaurant, **Harvard Yard,** and flowers from the **Dutch Garden.**

Filene's Basement (sometimes).

Tapas at **Dali;** hamburgers at the **Harvest Restaurant;** pasta at **Michela's;** fish at the **Dolphin;** a cup of espresso in the **North End;** anything at **Hamersley's Bistro.**

Walks around **Walden Pond** in Concord; the **Ralph Waldo Emerson** and **Louisa May Alcott** houses.

The views from **Fruitlands Museum** in the town of Harvard.

And best of all: the feeling of being able to escape to the ocean or mountains when necessary, all in under two hours.

Although Puritans were themselves exiles in pursuit of religious freedom, they were far from tolerant in granting it to others. In 1651 they publicly whipped a Baptist and in 1659 they hung three Quakers. Those not keen on the Puritan code had no choice but to flee to Rhode Island, which the Puritans then derogated as "Rogue's Island."

What's All the Bally-hoo in Beantown?

From Boston's Bunker Hill Day to its famous marathon and wildly colorful Italian *feste,* this is a city that knows how to celebrate its life and times. Here are some of the most popular events that take place year after year. For more information on these activities, call the Greater Boston Convention and Visitors Bureau at 536.4100 or read the *Boston Phoenix* (published on Friday) or the Thursday "Calendar" section of the *Boston Globe.*

January

Chinese New Year (which is sometimes celebrated in February), Children's Museum

Japanese New Year Festival, Children's Museum

February

Black History Month

Chinese New Year (which is sometimes celebrated in January)

Hasty Pudding Awards, Harvard University

Inventor's Weekend, Museum of Science

Kid's Computer Fair, Computer Museum

Massachusetts Camellia Show

New England Boat Show

Uncommon Boston Valentine Chocolate Tour (call 731.5854)

Valentine's Festival

March

Evacuation Day (March 17), when the British army fled in 1776

Flower Show, Bayside Exposition Center

Myopia Polo Matches, South Hamilton

St. Patrick's Day Parade, South Boston

April

American Indian Day, Children's Museum

Artists' Ball, at the Cyclorama in the South End

The Big Apple Circus

Boston Kite Festival, Franklin Park

Boston Marathon (the third Monday in April)

Earth Day

Myopia Polo Matches, South Hamilton

Opening Day at Fenway Park (baseball)

Patriots Day (the third Monday in April), Reenactment of the Battle of Lexington, Paul Revere's and William Dawes' rides, and other events

Swan Boats return to the Public Garden Lagoon

Whale-watching cruises begin

May

All Walks of Life (AIDS march)

Art Newbury Street (open galleries)

Beacon Hill Hidden Garden Tour

Boston Pops season begins, Symphony Hall

Brimfield Outdoor Antiques Show

Lilac Sunday at Arnold Arboretum

Magnolias bloom on Commonwealth Avenue

Myopia Polo Matches, South Hamilton

Walk for Hunger

June

Blessing of the Fleet, Provincetown and Gloucester

Boston Globe Jazz Festival

Bunker Hill Day, Charlestown (June 17)

Dairy Festival, Boston Common

Gay Pride March

Myopia Polo Matches, South Hamilton

Tanglewood Music Festival, Berkshires

July

Bastille Day, Marlborough Street in Back Bay

Boston Harborfest

Boston Pops Esplanade Orchestra Concerts, Charles River Esplanade

Brimfield Outdoor Antiques Show

Chowderfest

Myopia Polo Matches, South Hamilton

North End Italian Feste

US Pro Tennis Championships at Longwood

USS *Constitution* Turnaround (July 4)

August

Myopia Polo Matches, South Hamilton

North End Italian Feste

September

Art Newbury Street (open galleries)

Boston Film Festival

Brimfield Outdoor Antiques Show

King Richard's Fair, South Carver

Myopia Polo Matches, South Hamilton

October

Haunted Happenings, Salem

Head-of-the-Charles Regatta

Myopia Polo Matches, South Hamilton

Uncommon Boston Graveyards and Goodies Tour (call 731.5854)

November

Boston Ballet's *Nutcracker*

Boston Globe Book Festival

December

Boston Ballet's *Nutcracker*

Christmas Tree Lighting, Prudential Center

Day Trips

Crafts at the Castle

First Night (December 31 through January 1)

The first paper money in America was issued in 1690 by the Massachusetts Bay Colony, and was used to pay the soldiers who served on the ill-fated expedition attempting to capture Quebec from the French.

Bostonians *never* call Boston "Beantown," a nickname that lingers nonetheless.

Index

Bold page numbers indicate main references.

Index

218

Restaurants

Only restaurants with star ratings are
listed below. All restaurants are listed
alphabetically in the main (preceding)
index. Always call in advance to ensure
a restaurant has not closed, changed
its hours, or booked its tables for a
private party. The restaurant price
ratings are based on the average cost
of an entrée for one person, excluding
tax or tip.

★★★★ An Extraordinary Experience
  ★★★ Excellent
   ★★ Very good
    ★ Good

$$$$ Big Bucks ($20 and up)
 $$$ Expensive ($15-$20)
  $$ Reasonable ($10-$15)
   $ The Price Is Right (less
      than $10)

Hotels

The hotels listed below are grouped according to their price ratings; they are also listed in the main (preceding) index. The hotel price ratings reflect the base price of a standard room for two people for one night during the peak season.

$$$$ Big Bucks ($250 and up)
$$$ Expensive ($175-$250)
$$ Reasonable ($100-$175)
$ The Price Is Right (less than $100)

Features

Bests

Maps

Index

Credits

Writer/Researcher
Sandy MacDonald

Writers/Researchers (Previous Edition)
Nancy Robins, Julia Collins

ACCESS®PRESS

Editorial Director
Rebecca Poole Forée

Project Editor
Lisa Zuniga

Staff Editors
Margie Lee
Karin Mullen

Contributing Editor
Jean Linsteadt

Assistant Editor
Erika Lenkert

Proofreaders
Suzanne Samuel
Annelise Zamula

Word Processors
Sean M. Hanley
Jerry Stanton
Andréa Zurek

Indexer
Cathryn Farrell

Design Manager
Ann Kook

Senior Designer
Cherylonda Fitzgerald

Designers
Sherrod Blankner
Barbara J. Bahning Chin
Carrē Furukawa
Claudia A. Goulette
Kitti Homme

Senior Map Designer
Kitti Homme

Maps
Julie Bilski
Michael Blum
Patti Keelin
M Kohnke
Laurie Miller

Printing and Otabind
Webcom Limited

Special Thanks
Carol Chirico, Land-
marks Commission
Cullen Curtiss
Leslie Forée
Anne Hayes
Patrick Ng
Daniela Sylvers
Charles Shields
Kimberly Thompson,
Massachusetts Office
of Travel and Tourism
Lisa Winer

Trinity Church